The Wealth of Ideas

The Wealth of Ideas traces the history of economic thought, from its prehistory (the Bible, Classical antiquity) to the present day. In this eloquently written, scientifically rigorous and well-documented book, chapters on William Petty, Adam Smith, David Ricardo, Karl Marx, William Stanley Jevons, Carl Menger, Léon Walras, Alfred Marshall, John Maynard Keynes, Joseph Schumpeter and Piero Sraffa alternate with chapters on other important figures and on debates of the period. Economic thought is seen as developing between two opposite poles: a subjective one, based on the ideas of scarcity and utility, and an objective one based on the notions of physical costs and surplus. Professor Roncaglia focuses on the different views of the economy and society and on their evolution over time and critically evaluates the foundations of the scarcity–utility approach in comparison with the Classical/Keynesian approach.

ALESSANDRO RONCAGLIA is Professor of Economics in the Department of Economic Sciences, University of Rome 'La Sapienza'. He is a member of the Accademia Nazionale dei Lincei and editor of *BNL Quarterly Review* and *Moneta e Credito*. His numerous publications include *Piero Sraffa: His Life, Thought and Cultural Heritage* (2000) and the Italian edition of this book, *La ricchezza delle idee* (2001) which received the 2003 Jérome Adolphe Blanqui Award from the European Society for the History of Economic Thought.

The Wealth of Ideas

A History of Economic Thought

Alessandro Roncaglia

CAMBRIDGE
UNIVERSITY PRESS

CAMBRIDGE UNIVERSITY PRESS
Cambridge, New York, Melbourne, Madrid, Cape Town,
Singapore, São Paulo, Delhi, Tokyo, Mexico City

Cambridge University Press
The Edinburgh Building, Cambridge CB2 8RU, UK

Published in the United States of America by
Cambridge University Press, New York

www.cambridge.org
Information on this title: www.cambridge.org/9780521691871

First published in English by Cambridge
University Press 2005 as The Wealth of Ideas English translation
© Alessandro Roncaglia 2005
First paperback edition 2006
Third printing 2009

A catalogue record for this publication is available from the British Library

Library of Congress Cataloguing in Publication data

ISBN 978-0-521-84337-9 Hardback
ISBN 978-0-521-69187-1 Paperback

Contents

Preface   *page* ix

1 The history of economic thought and its role   1
1. Introduction   1
2. The cumulative view   2
3. The competitive view   5
4. The stages of economic theorising: conceptualisation and
    model-building   11
5. Political economy and the history of economic thought   13
6. Which history of economic thought?   14

2 The prehistory of political economy   18
1. Why we call it prehistory   18
2. Classical antiquity   23
3. Patristic thought   28
4. The Scholastics   31
5. Usury and just price   34
6. Bullionists and mercantilists   41
7. The birth of economic thought in Italy: Antonio Serra   46

3 William Petty and the origins of political economy   53
1. Life and writings   53
2. Political arithmetic and the method of economic science   55
3. National state and economic system   58
4. Commodity and market   63
5. Surplus, distribution, prices   69

4 From body politic to economic tables   76
1. The debates of the time   76
2. John Locke   80
3. The motivations and consequences of human actions   84
4. Bernard de Mandeville   87
5. Richard Cantillon   90
6. François Quesnay and the physiocrats   96
7. The political economy of the Enlightenment: Turgot   103
8. The Italian Enlightenment: the Abbé Galiani   107
9. The Scottish Enlightenment: Francis Hutcheson and David Hume   111

5   Adam Smith   115
    1. Life   115
    2. Method   118
    3. The moral principle of sympathy   121
    4. The wealth of nations   126
    5. Value and prices   134
    6. Natural prices and market prices   139
    7. The origin of the division of labour: Smith and Pownall   145
    8. Economic and political liberalism: Smith's fortune   149

6   Economic science at the time of the French Revolution   155
    1. The perfectibility of human societies, between utopias and reforms   155
    2. Malthus and the population principle   158
    3. 'Say's law'   164
    4. Under-consumption theories: Lauerdale, Malthus, Sismondi   167
    5. The debate on the poor laws   169
    6. The debate on the colonies   172
    7. Bentham's utilitarianism   174

7   David Ricardo   179
    1. Life and works   179
    2. Ricardo's dynamic vision   181
    3. From the corn model to the labour theory of value   186
    4. Absolute value and exchangeable value: the invariable
        standard of value   191
    5. Money and taxation   196
    6. International trade and the theory of comparative costs   201
    7. On machinery: technological change and employment   203

8   The 'Ricardians' and the decline of Ricardianism   207
    1. The forces in the field   207
    2. Robert Torrens   209
    3. Samuel Bailey   215
    4. Thomas De Quincey   218
    5. John Ramsey McCulloch   219
    6. The Ricardian socialists and cooperativism   221
    7. William Nassau Senior and the anti-Ricardian reaction   226
    8. Charles Babbage   230
    9. John Stuart Mill and philosophical radicalism   233
    10. Mill on political economy   238

9   Karl Marx   244
    1. Introduction   244
    2. Life and writings   245
    3. The critique of the division of labour: alienation and
        commodity fetishism   249
    4. The critique of capitalism and exploitation   251
    5. Accumulation and expanded reproduction   256
    6. The laws of movement of capitalism   261
    7. The transformation of labour values into prices of production   263

    8. A critical assessment 268
    9. Marxism after Marx 272

10 The marginalist revolution: the subjective theory of value 278
    1. The 'marginalist revolution': an overview 278
    2. The precursors: equilibrium between scarcity and demand 281
    3. William Stanley Jevons 285
    4. The Jevonian revolution 288
    5. Real cost and opportunity cost 292
    6. Philip Henry Wicksteed and Francis Ysidro Edgeworth 294

11 The Austrian school and its neighbourhood 297
    1. Carl Menger 297
    2. The 'Methodenstreit' 303
    3. Max Weber 306
    4. Eugen von Böhm-Bawerk 308
    5. Knut Wicksell and the Swedish school 312
    6. Friedrich von Hayek 315

12 General economic equilibrium 322
    1. The invisible hand of the market 322
    2. Léon Walras 326
    3. Vilfredo Pareto and the Lausanne school 336
    4. Irving Fisher 340
    5. The debate on existence, uniqueness and stability of equilibrium 342
    6. The search for an axiomatic economics 345

13 Alfred Marshall 350
    1. Life and writings 350
    2. The background 353
    3. The *Principles* 357
    4. Economics becomes a profession 366
    5. Monetary theory: from the old to the new Cambridge school 368
    6. Maffeo Pantaleoni 370
    7. Marshallism in the United States: from John Bates Clark
       to Jacob Viner 372
    8. Thornstein Veblen and institutionalism 374
    9. Welfare economics: Arthur Cecil Pigou 376
   10. Imperfect competition 379
   11. Marshall's heritage in contemporary economic thought 382

14 John Maynard Keynes 384
    1. Life and writings 384
    2. Probability and uncertainty 388
    3. The *Treatise on money* 391
    4. From the *Treatise* to the *General theory* 395
    5. The *General theory* 398
    6. Defence and development 407
    7. The asymmetries of economic policy in an open economy and
       international institutions 409

| | 8. | Michal Kalecki | 411 |
| | 9. | The new Cambridge school | 413 |

15		Joseph Schumpeter	416
	1.	Life	416
	2.	Method	420
	3.	From statics to dynamics: the cycle	422
	4.	The breakdown of capitalism	428
	5.	The path of economic science	431

16		Piero Sraffa	435
	1.	First writings: money and banking	435
	2.	Friendship with Gramsci	438
	3.	Criticism of Marshallian theory	440
	4.	Imperfect competition and the critique of the representative firm	443
	5.	Cambridge: Wittgenstein and Keynes	445
	6.	The critical edition of Ricardo's writings	450
	7.	*Production of commodities by means of commodities*	452
	8.	Critique of the marginalist approach	457
	9.	The Sraffian schools	460

17		The age of fragmentation	468
	1.	Introduction	468
	2.	The microeconomics of general economic equilibrium	471
	3.	The new theories of the firm	474
	4.	Institutions and economic theory	479
	5.	Macroeconomic theory after Keynes	480
	6.	The theory of growth	488
	7.	Quantitative research: the development of econometrics	491
	8.	New analytical techniques: theory of repeated games, theory of stochastic processes, chaos theory	496
	9.	Interdisciplinary problems and the foundations of economic science: new theories of rationality, ethics and new utilitarianism, growth and sustainable development, economic democracy and globalisation	500

18		Where are we going? Some (very tentative) considerations	505
	1.	How many paths has economic thought followed?	505
	2.	The division of labour among economists: can we forge ahead along different paths?	508
	3.	Which of the various paths should we be betting on?	511

		References	515
		Index of names	564
		Subject index	575

Preface

The idea underlying this work is that the history of economic thought is essential for understanding the economy, which constitutes a central aspect of human societies. Confronted with complex, ever-changing realities, the different lines of research developed in the past are rich in suggestions for anyone trying to interpret economic phenomena, even for those tackling questions of immediate relevance. In this latter case, indeed, the history of economic thought not only provides hypotheses for interpretation of the available information, but also teaches caution towards a mechanical use of the models deduced from the (*pro tempore*) mainstream economic theory. Similarly, when confronted with the variety of debates on economic issues, a good understanding of the cultural roots both of the line of reasoning chosen and of its rivals is invaluable for avoiding a dialogue of the deaf.

In fact, the comforting vision offered by the great majority of economics textbooks, that of a general consensus on 'economic truths', is – at least as far as the foundations are concerned – false. In order to understand the variety of approaches within economic debate, it is necessary to reconstruct the different views that have been proposed, developed and criticised over time about the way economic systems function. This is no easy task. The economic debate does not follow a linear path; rather, it resembles a tangled skein.

In attempting to disentangle it, we will focus on the conceptual foundations of the different theories. One of the aspects that distinguishes this work from other histories of economic thought is its recognition that the meaning of a concept, even though it may retain the same name, changes when we move from one theory to another. Changes in analytic structure are connected to changes in conceptual foundations; all too often this fact is overlooked.

In this context, the Schumpeterian distinction between history of analysis and history of thought – the former concerning analytic structures, the latter 'visions of the world' – proves not so much misleading as largely useless. Equally inappropriate is the sharp dichotomy between 'rational reconstructions' and 'historical reconstructions' of the history of economic thought. It is hard to see why reconstructing the logical structure of an economist's ideas should clash with respecting his or her views. Indeed, in the field of the history of thought, as in analogous fields, the criterion of philological exactness is the main element differentiating scientific from non-scientific research.

The limits of the present work hence depend not so much on a priori fidelity to a specific line of interpretation as on the inevitable limitations – of ability, culture and time – of its author. For instance, I have not considered the contributions of Eastern cultural traditions, and very little space – a single chapter – is given to the twenty centuries constituting the prehistory of modern economic science. Of course Western economic theory is deeply rooted in classical thought – both Greek and Roman – and thanks to the mediation of a medieval culture which is richer and more complex than is commonly perceived. Thus, the decision to treat such a long and important period of time in just a few pages is obviously controversial. However, in so wide a field, choices of this kind are unavoidable. Naturally the results presented in the pages that follow are, notwithstanding efforts at systematic exposition, clearly provisional, and comments and criticisms will be helpful for future research.

Our journey begins with a chapter on methodological issues. It is not intended as a survey of, or an introduction to, the epistemological debate. We will only try to show the limits of the 'cumulative view', and the importance of studying the conceptual foundations of different theoretical approaches.

The following three chapters are devoted to pre-Smithian economic thought. Chapter 2 concerns the prehistory of economic science, from classical antiquity to mercantilism. Chapter 3 is devoted to William Petty and his political arithmetic: a crucial episode of our science, with respect both to method and to the formation of a system of concepts for representing economic reality. Focusing upon an individual or a particular group of thinkers, here as in other chapters, will illustrate a phase in the evolution of economic thought and a line of research, looking back and looking on, to precursors and followers.

Between the end of the seventeenth century and the middle of the eighteenth (as we shall see in chapter 4) different lines of research intersect. Although interesting contributions from the strictly analytical point were relatively scarce in this period, we shall note its importance for the closer relations between economic and other social sciences characterising it. The problem of how human societies are organised and what motivations determine human actions – passions and interests, in particular self-interest – as well as the desired or involuntary outcomes of such actions, are in this period at the centre of lively debate at the intersection between economics, politics and moral science.

Already in this first stage two distinct views are apparent: a dichotomy which, together with its limits, will become clearer as our story unfolds. On the one hand, the economy is seen as centred on the counter-position between supply and demand in the market: we may call this the 'arc' view, analogous to the electrical arc, in which the two poles – demand and supply – determine the spark of the exchange, and hence the equilibrium. In this view the notion of equilibrium is central. On the other hand, we have the idea that the economic system develops though successive cycles of production, exchange and consumption: a 'spiral' view, since these cycles are not immutable, but constitute stages in a process of growth and development.

Recapitulation and an original reformulation of such debates is provided by Adam Smith's writings, which we shall consider in chapter 5: the delicate balance between self-interest and the 'ethics of sympathy' is the other side of the division of labour and its results.

The debate on typically Smithian themes of economic and social progress is illustrated in chapter 6. The French Revolution and the Terror constitute the background to the confrontation between supporters of the idea of perfectibility of human societies, and those who consider interference in the mechanisms regulating economy and society useless, if not dangerous.

We thus arrive with chapter 7 at David Ricardo, the first author we can credit with a robust analytical structure, systematically developed on the foundation of Smithian concepts. Ricardo stands out among other protagonists of an extremely rich phase of economic debate, although Torrens, Bailey, De Quincey, McCulloch, James and John Stuart Mill, Babbage and the 'Ricardian socialists' are autonomous personalities with leading roles to play in their own right; they are discussed in chapter 8. In chapter 9 we consider Karl Marx, in particular those aspects of his thought that are directly relevant from the viewpoint of political economy.

The golden age of the classical school runs, more or less, from Smith to Ricardo. The turning point, traditionally located around 1870 and termed the 'marginalist revolution', returns us to the 'arc' view of the counter-position between demand and supply in the market. Although long present in the economic debate, the view now assumes a more mature form thanks both to the robust analytic structure of the subjective theory of value and the greater consistency of the conceptual picture. The central problem of economic science is no longer one of explaining the functioning of a market society based on the division of labour, but one of interpreting the choices of a rational agent in their interactions, through the market, with other individuals who follow similar rules of behaviour.

The main characteristics of this turn and the long path preparatory to it are discussed in chapter 10. In addition, this and the two subsequent chapters illustrate the three main streams into which the marginalist approach is traditionally subdivided: Jevons's English, Menger's Austrian and, finally, Walras's (general equilibrium) French approach. An ecumenical attempt at synthesis between the classical and the marginalist approaches marks Alfred Marshall's work. This attempt, and its limits, are discussed in chapter 13.

Marginalism is strictly connected to a subjective view of value, with a radical transformation of utilitarianism, which originally constituted the foundation for a consequentialist ethic. Jevons's utilitarianism reduces *homo oeconomicus* to a computing machine that maximises a mono-dimensional magnitude: it is on this very thin foundation, as we shall see, that the subjective theory of value builds its analytical castle.

The case of Marshall is quite interesting, since it shows how difficult it is to connect coherently a complex and flexible vision of the world to an analytic structure constrained by the canons of the concept of equilibrium. Something similar happens in the case of the Austrian school, as well as in the thought of Schumpeter, whose theory is illustrated in chapter 15. We can thus understand the contrasting evaluations formulated over time on several leading figures (exalted or despised depending on the point of view from which they are judged), taking account of the richness and depth of their conceptual representation of reality, or the weaknesses and rigidity of their analytic structure.

The problem of the relationship between conceptual foundations and analytic structure takes different forms in John Maynard Keynes and Piero Sraffa, whose contributions are discussed in chapters 14 and 16. Keynes hoped to make his theses acceptable, revolutionary as they were, to scholars trained within the marginalist tradition. However, his conciliatory manner generated glaring distortions of his thought, which became sterilised in the canonical version of the 'neo-classical synthesis'. Sraffa, on the other hand, formulated his analysis in such a way as to render possible its use both in a constructive way, within a classical perspective, and for the purpose of criticism, within the marginalist approach. However, this made it more difficult to reconstruct the method and conceptual foundations of his contribution, again opening the way to a number of misunderstandings.

Finally, mainly on the basis of Keynes's and Sraffa's contributions, and taking into account recent developments illustrated in chapter 17, chapter 18 presents some tentative and provisional reflections on the prospect for economic science.

The by now somewhat remote origin of this work was a course of lectures on *Economic philosophies* given in 1978 at Rutgers University. I had already done research on Torrens, Sraffa and Petty (Roncaglia 1972, 1975, 1977) and I deluded myself that I would be able to write a book of this kind on the basis of my lecture notes in a relatively brief span of time. In the following years I gave courses of lectures in the history of economic thought on various occasions: at the University of Paris X (Nanterre), at the Faculty of Statistics and the doctorate courses in Economic Sciences of the University of Rome (La Sapienza), and at the Institute Sant' Anna of Pisa. I have also taken part in the realisation of an Italian TV series, *The Pin Factory*: twenty-seven instalments on the major protagonists of the history of economic thought. These experiences played an essential part in the endeavour to make my exposition ever clearer and more systematic. The research work benefited over the years from MIUR's (the Italian Ministry for Universities and Research) research grants. It was also greatly helped by remarks and suggestions received at a number of seminars and conferences, and on the papers that I have over time published on issues in the history of economic thought. Many colleagues and friends have been of great help; I wish to recall here the initial stimulus offered by Piero Sraffa and Paolo Sylos Labini, and the useful suggestions of Giacomo Becattini, Marcella Corsi, Franco Donzelli, Geoff Harcourt, Marco Lippi, Cristina Marcuzzo, Nerio Naldi, Cosimo Perrotta, Gino Roncaglia, Mario Tonveronachi, Luisa Valente and Roberto Villetti, who read drafts of some of the chapters. Silvia Brandolin provided precious help with the editing.

The English edition embodies some new material and a number of minor changes, prompted by comments and suggestions of Giuseppe Privitera and other readers of the (by now) two Italian editions and of four anonymous referees. Thanks are also due to Graham Sells (and to Mark Walters for chapters 12, 13 and 17) for help in improving my bastard English style, and to Annie Lovett, Patricia Maurice and Jo North for their kindness and patience while seeing this book through the press. Obviously the responsibility for remaining errors – unavoidable in a work of this kind – is mine. I will be grateful to readers who point such errors out to me (Alessandro.Roncaglia@uniromal.it).

Notice

Bibliographical references will follow the customary system: name of author, date of the work. The latter will be the original date of publication (with the exception of authors of antiquity), while the page reference will be to the edition of the work used here, i.e. the last not in brackets of the editions cited in the bibliography. When this is not an English edition, the translation of the passages quoted is mine. In some cases of posthumous publications, the year in which the work was written is indicated between square brackets. When referring to other parts of this work the number of the chapter and section will follow the sign §, but the chapter number will be omitted when referring to a section within the same chapter.

1   The history of economic thought and its role

> To understand the others: this is the historian's aim. It is not easy to
> have a more difficult task. It is difficult to have a more interesting one.
>
> (Kula 1958, p. 234)

1.   Introduction

The thesis advanced in this chapter is that the history of economic thought
is essential for anyone interested in understanding how economies work.
Thus economists, precisely as producers and users of economic theories, should study and practise the history of economic thought. While
illustrating this thesis, we will examine some questions of method that,
apart from their intrinsic interest, may help in understanding our line of
reasoning in this book.

Our thesis is opposed to the approach now prevailing. Most contemporary economists, especially in Anglo-Saxon countries, are convinced that
looking back may perhaps be of some use in training young economists,
but is not necessary for the progress of research, which rather requires
work on the theoretical frontier.

In the next section we will consider the foundations of this approach,
also known as 'the cumulative view' of the development of economic
thought. We shall see how, even in this apparently hostile context, a crucial
role has been claimed for the history of economic thought.

The cumulative view has been opposed by other ideas on the path pursued by scientific research. In section 3 we take a look at the theses on
the existence of discontinuities (Kuhn's 'scientific revolutions') or competition among different 'scientific research programmes' (Lakatos). As
we shall see, they point to the existence of different views of the world,
and hence of different ways of conceiving and defining the problems to
be subjected to theoretical enquiry.

In section 4 we will recall the distinction, proposed by Schumpeter,
between two different stages in the work process of the economic theorist:

first, the stage of construction of a system of concepts to represent the economy and, second, the stage of construction of models. In section 5, we then go on to see how this distinction points to an important, but generally overlooked, role for the history of economic thought within the very field of economic theory, as a way to investigate the conceptual foundations of different theories.

All this constitutes the background for discussing, in section 6, the kind of history of economic thought which is most relevant for the formation of economic theories. Obviously, this is not to deny that there is intrinsic interest in research into the history of ideas: far from it! Nor will we consider issues such as the autonomy of the history of economic thought or whether, in the division of intellectual work, historians of economic thought should be considered closer to the economists or to the economic historians. The point we wish to make is that economists who refuse to get involved in the study of the history of economic thought and to have some research experience in this field are severely handicapped in their own theoretical work.

2.   The cumulative view

According to the cumulative view, the history of economic thought displays a progressive rise to ever higher levels of understanding of economic reality. The provisional point of arrival of today's economists – contemporary economic theory – incorporates all previous contributions.

The cumulative view is connected to positivism.[1] More specifically, the most widespread version of the cumulative view draws on a simplified version of logical positivism, the so-called 'received view', which found a considerable following as from the 1920s. In a nutshell, the idea was that scientists work by applying the methods of logical analysis to the raw material provided by empirical experience. To evaluate their results, objective criteria for acceptance or rejection can be established. More

---

[1] An illustrious and characteristically radical example of this position is represented by Pantaleoni 1898. According to him, the history of thought must be 'history of economic truths' (ibid., p. 217): 'its only purpose [. . .] is to relate the origins of true doctrines' (ibid., p. 234). In fact Pantaleoni held that a clear-cut criterion for judging the truth or falsehood of economic theories is available: 'There has been a troublesome search for hypotheses that are both clear and in conformity with reality [. . .] Facts and hypotheses have then been used, and what could be deduced from them has been deduced. The theorems have also been checked on empirical reality' (ibid., p. 217). Expressed in these terms, Pantaleoni's criterion mirrors a still rather primitive and simplistic version of positivism; the resolution with which it is stated probably stems at least in part from the harshness of the controversy between the Austrian marginalist school and the German historical school (cf. below, § 11.2).

precisely, *analytic statements*, namely those concerning abstract theoretical reasoning, are either tautological, i.e. logically implied in the assumptions, or self-contradictory, i.e. they contain logical inconsistencies; in the former case, the analytic statement is accepted, in the latter rejected. Similarly, *synthetic statements*, i.e. those concerning the empirical world, are either confirmed or contradicted by evidence, and hence accepted or rejected for 'objective' reasons. All other statements for which no analogous criteria of acceptance or rejection can be found are termed *metaphysical* and are considered external to the field of science.

This view has come in for severe criticism, discussed in the following section.[2] Nevertheless it remains the basis for the cumulative view of economic science, or, in other words, the idea that each successive generation of economists contributes new analytic or synthetic propositions to the common treasure of economic science, which – as a science – is univocally defined as the set of 'true' propositions concerning economic matters. New knowledge is thus added to that already available, and in many cases – whenever some defect is identified in previously accepted statements – substitutes it. Hence, study of a science must be conducted 'on the theoretical frontier', taking into consideration the most up-to-date version and not the theories of the past. Notwithstanding this position, it is granted that the latter may deserve some attention: as Schumpeter (1954, p. 4) says, studying economists of the past is pedagogically helpful, may prompt new ideas and affords useful material on the methods of scientific research in a complex and interesting field such as economics, on the borderline between natural and social sciences.

Similar arguments are proposed by various other historians of economic thought, often in a simplistic way and with rhetorical overtones. However, as Gordon (1965, pp. 121–2) points out, the fact that the history of economic thought may help in learning economic theory is not a sufficient reason to study it. Given the limited time available to human beings, one would also have to show that a course of lectures dedicated to the history of economic thought contributes more to the formation of an economist than an equal amount of time directly dedicated to economic theory. Clearly, if we accept a cumulative view of economic research, this would be rather difficult to maintain. As a consequence, according to Gordon (1965, p. 126), 'economic theory [. . .] finds no necessity for including its history as a part of professional training' (which does not mean that the history of economic thought should be abandoned: 'We study history because it is there').

---

[2] For a survey of this debate, see Caldwell 1982 and, more recently, Hands 2001; for the link between the 'received view' in epistemology and the cumulative view in the history of economic thought, see Cesarano 1983, p. 66.

Interest in the history of economic thought, when justified by its pedagogical usefulness, is reduced whenever the development of economics sees discontinuity in the analytical toolbox. This is how some authors explain the waning interest in the history of economic thought as from the 1940s.[3] However, we may recall that as early as the 1930s economists such as Hicks and Robertson were arguing that there was no reason to waste time reading the classical economists;[4] their attitude is explained not so much by change in the analytical toolbox as by change in the very conception of economics, from the classical (surplus) approach to the marginalist (scarcity) view.

Among adherents of the cumulative view, Viner proposes a subtle defence of the history of economic thought, only apparently modest. Viner points to 'scholarship', defined as 'the pursuit of broad and exact knowledge of the history of the working of the human mind as revealed in written records'. Scholarship, although considered inferior to theoretical activity, contributes to the education of researchers, being 'a commitment to the pursuit of knowledge and understanding': 'once the taste for it has been aroused, it gives a sense of largeness even to one's small quests, and a sense of fullness even to the small answers [. . .] a sense which can never in any other way be attained'.[5]

Education in research, Viner seems to suggest, is a prerequisite for exploitation of the knowledge of analytical tools.[6] Thus, even if the history of economic thought is considered to be of little use in learning modern economic theory, a crucial role is attributed to it in the education of the researcher. The importance of this wider perspective becomes much clearer, however, outside a strictly cumulative view of economic research, as we shall see below.

First, however, it is worth stressing that the cumulative view of the history of economic thought considered in this section is the modern one, which reached a commanding position in the twentieth century parallel with the marginalist approach. A somewhat different kind of cumulative view can be found in the brief digressions on the history of economic thought made by certain leading economists such as Smith and Keynes, who use them to highlight their own theories, contrasting them to those prevailing previously. Thus Smith, in book four of *The wealth of*

---

[3] Cf. Cesarano 1983, p. 69, who also refers to Bronfenbrenner 1966 and Tarascio 1971.
[4] Letter by Robertson to Keynes, 3 February 1935, in Keynes 1973, vol. 13, p. 504; and letter by Hicks, 9 April 1937, in Keynes 1973, vol. 14, p. 81.
[5] Viner 1991, pp. 385 and 390.
[6] Schumpeter (1954, p. 4; italics in the original) says something similar when stating that the history of economic thought 'will prevent a sense of *lacking direction and meaning* from spreading among the students'.

nations, criticises the 'commercial or mercantile system' and the 'agricultural system' (namely the physiocrats). The critique of the mercantilists – an abstract category, devised in order to place under a single label a long series of writers who are often quite different from one another (cf. below, § 2.6) – goes hand in hand with Smith's liberalism, illustrated in other parts of his work; the critique of the physiocrats serves to stress, by contrast, his own distinction between productive and unproductive workers and his tri-partition of society into the classes of workers, capitalists and landowners. Similarly, Marx contrasts his 'scientific socialism' to 'bourgeois' economics (that of Smith and Ricardo) and 'vulgar' economics (that of Say and of Bastiat's 'economic harmonies'); Keynes creates a category – the 'classics' – in which he includes all previous authors who, like his Cambridge colleague Pigou, exclude the possibility of persistent unemployment that is not reabsorbed by the automatic forces of competitive markets. Clearly, we are not confronted here with instances of cumulative views stressing the gradual accumulation of economic knowledge, but rather with historical reconstructions by means of which certain protagonists of economic science stress the leap forward accomplished by their discipline thanks to their own theoretical contribution. Obviously, recalling this fact is not to deny the validity of such historical reconstructions, since in the case of protagonists like Smith or Keynes these reconstructions do identify key steps in the path of economic science.

3.   The competitive view

Over the past few decades a number of economists have referred to Kuhn's (1962) 'scientific revolutions' or Lakatos's (1970, 1978) 'scientific research programmes' in support of the idea that it is impossible to choose among competing theoretical approaches with the 'objective' criteria indicated by logical positivism (logical consistency, correspondence of assumptions to empirical reality).

These criteria had already been the object of debate. Some criticisms specifically concerned the clear-cut distinction between analytic and synthetic statements. Indeed, analytic statements, if interpreted as purely logical propositions, are devoid of any reference to the real world; as a consequence, they are empty from the point of view of the interpretation of real-world phenomena.[7] Synthetic statements in turn necessarily embody a large mass of theoretical elements in the very definition of the

---

[7] In other terms, observations are necessarily 'theory-laden'; cf. Hands 2001, pp. 103 ff. It is on this ground, for instance, that Dobb (1973, ch. 1) develops his critique of the excessively clear-cut distinction, proposed by Schumpeter, between history of economic analysis and history of economic thought, to which we will come back later on (§ 5).

categories used for collecting the empirical data and in the methods by which these data are treated; as a consequence, the choices of acceptance or rejection of any synthetic statement cannot be clear-cut, but are conditioned by a long series of theoretical hypotheses that cannot, however, be subject to separate evaluation.[8] It is precisely the impossibility to have neatly separate evaluations based on univocal objective criteria for analytic and synthetic statements that constitutes a crucial difficulty for the positivistic view discussed in the previous section.

Another important critique of the criterion for acceptance or rejection proposed for synthetic statements – their correspondence or noncorrespondence to the real world – is developed by Popper (1934). No matter how many times a synthetic statement is corroborated by checking it against the real world, says Popper, we cannot exclude the possibility that a contrary case will eventually crop up. Thus, for instance, the statement that 'all swans are white' may be contradicted by the discovery of a single new species of black swans in Australia. The scientist cannot pretend to verify a theory, that is to demonstrate it to be true once and for all. The scientist can only accept a theory provisionally, bearing in mind the possibility that it may be falsified, or, in other words, that it be shown to be false by a new-found empirical event contradicting it. Indeed, in a subsequent book (1969) Popper maintains that the best method for scientific research consists precisely in the formulation of a potentially never-ending series of 'conjectures and refutations'. In other words, the scientist formulates hypotheses and then, rather than looking for empirical confirmation – which in any case could not be definitive – should rather seek out refutations. These, by stimulating and guiding the search for better hypotheses, make a crucial contribution to the advancement of science.[9]

A number of leading figures of positivistic epistemology maintain that it is not applicable to the field of social sciences. The influence of some historians and philosophers of science, such as Kuhn, Lakatos and Feyerabend, contributed then, in the last decades of the twentieth century, to abandonment of the positivistic methodology in the field of economic theory. Let us briefly recall their theories and the competitive view of science that follows from them.

In a few words, according to Kuhn, the development of science is not linear, but can be subdivided into stages, each with its own distinctive

[8] This criticism is known as the 'Duhem–Quine underdetermination thesis' (cf. Quine 1951); according to it, 'no theory is ever tested in isolation', so that 'any scientific theory can be immunized against refuting empirical evidence' (Hands 2001, p. 96).
[9] For debate on the utilisation of Popper's ideas in the field of economic theory, cf. De Marchi 1998.

characteristics. In each period of 'normal science', a specific point of view (paradigm) is commonly accepted as the basis for scientific research. On such a basis, an ever more complex theoretical system is built, capable of explaining an increasing number of phenomena. This process of growth of normal science, however, is accompanied by the accumulation of anomalies, namely of phenomena that are either unexplained or that require for their explanation an increasingly heavy load of ad hoc assumptions. A growing malaise derives from this, which favours a 'scientific revolution', namely the proposal of a new paradigm. This marks the beginning of a new stage of normal science, within which research proceeds without calling into question the underlying paradigm.

Let us stress here that Kuhn does not consider the succession of different paradigms as a logical sequence characterised by a growing amount of knowledge. The different paradigms are considered as not commensurable among themselves; each of them constitutes a different key for interpreting reality, necessarily based on a specific set of simplifying assumptions, many of which also remain implicit. No paradigm can encompass the whole universe in all its details. Strictly speaking, it is incorrect both to say that the earth goes round the sun and that the sun goes round the earth: each of the two hypotheses corresponds to the choice of a fixed point as reference for the study of the universe, or better a part of the universe that is in continuous movement relative to any other possible fixed point. In other words, since both the earth and the sun move in space, those of Copernicus and Ptolemy are but two alternative theoretical approaches which explain in more or less simple terms a greater or smaller number of phenomena.[10] We may also recall in this respect that a heliocentric view had already been proposed by Aristarchus of Samos in the third century BC, nearly five centuries before Ptolemy: thus, paradigms do not necessarily follow each other in a linear sequence, but can reappear as dominant after even long periods of eclipse.

---

[10] Among Kuhn's predecessors in this respect we may recall Adam Smith with his *History of astronomy* (Smith 1795). A connecting link between Smith and Kuhn might be located in Schumpeter, who sets apart the *History of astronomy* as 'the pearl' among Smith's writings (Schumpeter 1954, p. 182), and further on considers the same historical case that was later to be studied by Kuhn: 'The so-called Ptolemaic system of astronomy was not simply "wrong". It accounted satisfactorily for a great mass of observations. And as observations accumulated that did not, at first sight, accord with it, astronomers devised additional hypotheses that brought the recalcitrant facts, or part of them, within the fold of the system' (Schumpeter 1954, p. 318 n.). Kuhn, like most of the protagonists of the epistemological debate, originally developed his ideas as an interpretation of the history of natural sciences, specifically astronomy and physics, and not as a methodological recipe for the social sciences. However, some at least among his ideas can be readily utilised in the field of economic theory. For an attempt in this direction, cf. the essays collected in Latsis 1976.

Kuhn presents his idea of scientific revolutions as a description of the path actually followed by the different sciences rather than as a normative model of behaviour for scientists. In opposition, a normative attitude is adopted by Lakatos (1978).

Lakatos's 'methodology of scientific research programmes' consists in a set of working rules for both critique and construction of theories (negative and positive heuristic), organised around a 'hard core' of hypotheses concerning a specific set of issues and utilised as foundations for the construction of a theoretical system. The hard core remains unchanged even when anomalies arise, thanks to a 'protective belt' of auxiliary hypotheses, and is abandoned only when the scientific research programme based on it is clearly recognised as 'regressive', or in other words when it is clearly recognised that going ahead with it is most likely a waste of time and effort. The acceptance or rejection of a scientific research programme is thus considered by Lakatos a complex process, and not an act of judgement based on a crucial experiment, or in any case on well-defined, univocal, objective criteria.

Thus interpreted, Lakatos's view is not very different from – although admittedly less radical than – that proposed by Feyerabend (1975) with his 'anarchistic theory of knowledge'. Feyerabend stresses the need for the utmost open-mindedness towards the most disparate research approaches; at the same time he is far from accepting without qualification his own motto: 'Anything can go'. Critique of the idea that there exist absolute criteria of truth (or better of acceptance and rejection of theories) may coexist with the idea of the practicability of a rational debate between different, even conflicting, points of view. Obviously, when debating the different viewpoints the advocates of each should be ready to drop the pretence of using as absolute the criteria of judgement based on their own world-view. On the contrary, provisionally adopting the rival viewpoint to criticise it from inside may constitute an element of strength in the debate. We are thus confronted with a procedure for scientific debate analogous to that commonly followed in legal proceedings, where prosecutor and defence each brings the most disparate arguments in support of their positions.

Feyerabend's views were brought into the economic debate by McCloskey (1985, 1994), albeit with some changes. McCloskey speaks of a 'rhetorical method of scientific debate' that rejects neat, monodimensional criteria for the evaluation of theories, and stresses, in contrast, the role of their relative power of persuasion.[11] This does not mean

---

[11] Within the field of the natural sciences, well-conducted experiments as a rule constitute decisive proof of the superiority of one theory over other theories. In the field of the social sciences, however, experiments performed in controlled conditions (that is,

to deny any value to the theoretical debate: far from it, the main message given by this methodology is the need for tolerance in the face of different views of the world and hence of different theoretical approaches. We may also recall that thus interpreted the rhetorical method in economics can be traced back to Adam Smith.[12]

In the case of Kuhn and Lakatos alike, economists have been attracted by the role attributed to the existence of alternative approaches, deduced from the succession of different paradigms or from the coexistence of different scientific research programmes.[13] Obviously Feyerabend's ideas lead in the same direction.

It is here that the history of economic thought comes into play. Those who accept a competitive view of the development of economic thought and participate in a debate between contending approaches are induced to investigate the history of such a debate, looking for the points of strength and weakness which explain the dominance or decline of the different approaches.

In particular, those who support approaches competing with the dominant one may find the history of economic thought very useful.[14] First, analysis of the writings of economists in the past often helps in clarifying the basic characteristics of the approach being proposed and the differences between it and the dominant one.[15]

Second, the history of economic thought helps in evaluating theories based on different approaches, by bringing to light the world-views, the content of the concepts and hypotheses on which they are based. Often this helps in retrieving the notes of caution and the qualifications originally accompanying the analysis, subsequently forgotten in unwarranted generalisation of the field of application of the theory.[16]

Third, recalling illustrious cultural roots sometimes serves a tactical purpose, in order to counter the inertia that constitutes such a strong

---

ceteris paribus) are practically impossible. Hence the greater complexity in this latter field for comparison between different theories.

[12] We refer here not only to the *Lectures on rhetoric and belles lettres* (Smith 1983), but also to the *Glasgow lectures* (the so-called *Lectures on jurisprudence*: Smith 1978). On this subject, cf. Giuliani 1997.

[13] See, for instance, the essays collected in De Marchi and Blaug 1991. For a note of caution, see Steedman 1991, who notes that Lakatos's programmes refer to specific issues rather than to broad views of the world.

[14] Cf. Dobb 1973, Meek 1977 and Bharadwaj 1989 as examples of this interest following the Sraffian revival of the classical approach.

[15] An illustrious example is Sraffa's edition of Ricardo's *Works and correspondence* (Ricardo 1951–5).

[16] An example is the assumption of market clearing. It implies markets that work in a very specific way, either like the 'call bid' markets of old-style continental stock exchanges, or like the 'continuous auction' markets of Anglo-Saxon stock exchanges. Kregel 1992 considers the former in relation to Walrasian general equilibrium theory, and the latter referring to Marshallian theory. Cf. below, chapters 12 and 13.

advantage for the prevailing mainstream. Obviously an appeal to authority does not constitute a good scientific argument; this is also true for the appeal to a majority rule, a proclamation of intellectual laziness so often repeated in defence, for instance, of the persistent use of one-commodity models in theories of employment and growth, or of U-shaped curves in the theory of the firm.

It may be useful to stress here that the competitive view implies neither an equivalence between competing approaches, nor the absence of scientific progress.[17] It simply implies recognition of the existence of different approaches based on different conceptual foundations. Each researcher generally follows the line of research which he or she considers the most promising one.[18] Such a choice, however, is extremely complex, because of the incommensurability of the different conceptual systems. In particular, the claim of the mainstream approach to impose evaluation criteria derived from its own views must be rejected.

What the competitive view specifically rejects is the idea of a mono-dimensional process of scientific advance. There can be progress both within each approach (where indeed it is the general rule, in terms of both greater internal consistency and higher explanatory power) and along the historical sequence of research paradigms or programmes. In the latter case, however, the idea of progress is more imprecise and greater caution is required. An undeniable element of progress is provided by the increasing number of ever more sophisticated analytical tools made available by developments in other fields of research (new mathematical tools, better and more abundant statistical material, higher computing power from new computers). But between successive research paradigms or programmes there are commonly crucial differences in the underlying world-view. Some aspects of reality (cause and effect relationships included) are given greater prominence, others less, so that there are differences in the set of (explicit or implicit)[19] assumptions on which theories are

---

[17] This opinion – the rejection of any idea of scientific progress – is sometimes attributed to Feyerabend's 'anarchistic theory of knowledge' and, within the economic field, to McCloskey's (1985) 'rhetoric'. However, this opinion does not necessarily follow from their main points, the rejection of clear-cut and univocal criteria for assessment of different theories and research programmes, and the proposal of an open – and morally serious – 'conversation' among differently oriented researchers.

[18] That is, if we exclude instances of career-oriented opportunistic choices, which sometimes explain adhesion to the mainstream.

[19] The assumptions will necessarily remain at least in part implicit: a full list of the elements of reality abstracted away in the process of building a theory (that is, elements not taken into account in the theory because they are considered not important for the issue under examination) is impossible. In this sense, axiomatic models rely on a limited number of explicit assumptions but – a fact all too often overlooked – they crucially imply a large, potentially unlimited, number of implicit simplifying assumptions when an attempt is made to relate them to the economic reality which they set out to interpret.

built, and hence in the domain of applicability of the theories. Analytical variables or concepts (such as market, competition, natural price, profit, rent), although indicated by the same name, acquire even widely different meanings when used within different theories. It is here – in the analysis of the conceptual foundations of the different theories, and of the changes in the meaning of the concepts when inserted in different theoretical frameworks – that we come to recognise just how essential the analysis of concepts is to theoretical research work. As we will illustrate in the next section, this in turn implies attributing a crucial role to the history of economic thought in the very activity of theoretical economists.

4.   **The stages of economic theorising: conceptualisation and model-building**

Among those who stress the importance of analysing the conceptual foundations as part of research work, we find one of the most illustrious and, indeed, most wary representatives of the cumulative view in economics. Schumpeter (1954, pp. 41–2) subdivides economic research into three stages. First, we have the 'pre-analytic cognitive act', or 'vision', which consists in locating the problem to be dealt with and suggesting some working hypotheses with which to start analysis, the aim being to establish if not a tentative solution then at least the way the problem should be tackled. Second, we have the stage devoted 'to verbalize the vision or to conceptualize it in such a way that its elements take their places, with names attached to them that facilitate recognition and manipulation, in a more or less orderly schema or picture': what we can call the stage of conceptualisation, to which Schumpeter attributes great importance. The abstract system of concepts thus obtained isolates the elements of reality that are considered relevant to the issue under consideration. Finally, the third stage concerns the construction of 'scientific models'. Let us also recall that the logical sequence of the different stages does not necessarily correspond to their actual sequence in the economist's research activity.

As we saw in the preceding section, the debate between contending approaches concerns above all the choice of the conceptual system to be used in representing economic reality. The history of economic thought plays a decisive role in this respect. Since it is impossible to provide an exhaustive definition of the content of a concept,[20] the best way to analyse

---

[20] Georgescu-Roegen 1985, p. 300, speaks in this context of a 'penumbra' that surrounds '*dialectical* concepts whose distinctive characteristic is to overlap with their opposites'. Sraffa's critiques of Wittgenstein's analytical positivism in the *Tractatus logico-philosophicus* are relevant here; on this, cf. below, § 16.5.

it is to study its evolution over time, examining the different shades of meaning it acquires in different authors and in some cases in the different writings of the same author. This is in fact the common experience of all studies in the humanities, from philosophy to politics.

Furthermore, by utilising the history of economic thought for analysis of a concept (and of a conceptual system) we can investigate two aspects which are decisive for any line of research in economics: first, whether it is possible – and, if so, how far it is necessary – to adapt the content of concepts to the continuous changes in the reality to be explained; second, how the mechanism of interaction between the conceptualisation stage and the stage of model-building operates.

The first point – the interaction between economic history and economic theory – is a well-known issue. The second point is rarely considered, but is crucial. In fact, the difficulties which arise in the stage of model-building and the analytical solutions to those difficulties often imply modifications in the conceptual foundations of the theories;[21] in other instances, such modifications reflect the evolution of the real world to be analysed.[22]

The systems of concepts underlying any theory thus change continuously, which makes it impossible to conceive the evaluation of economic theories on a mono-dimensional scale. As a consequence, there can be no univocal measure of the explanatory power of the different theories. Theoretical advances may constitute scientific progress under certain aspects but not under others. Most importantly, the steps forward continuously made in the direction of a higher logical consistency and a growing use of more advanced analytical techniques do not necessarily imply a higher explanatory power: they may call for further restrictions to the meaning of the variables under consideration, excluding crucial aspects of reality from the field of applicability of the theory.[23] When we are confronted with this problem, the history of economic thought, by concentrating attention on the shifts in the meaning of the concepts used in the

---

[21] An example is provided by the changes in the heuristic power of general equilibrium theories when we move from Walras's original formulation to the axiomatic construction of Arrow and Debreu (cf. below, chapter 12). This example shows, among other things, that the need to analyse the conceptual foundations of theories and their changes over time is not limited to an evolutionary view of the economy, which focuses on institutional changes and path-dependence, although obviously the interaction between theory and history is stronger within this latter approach.

[22] An example (illustrated in Roncaglia 1988) is provided by the evolution in the classification of economic activity in sectors from Petty to Smith, via Cantillon and Quesnay.

[23] For instance, as we shall see in chapter 10, the marginalist theory of consumer equilibrium certainly represents a step forward as far as logical consistency and the use of sophisticated techniques of analysis are concerned, but this is accompanied by the shrinking of the economic agent to a sentient machine.

theory, can help in evaluating the multifaceted path followed by economic research.

5.   Political economy and the history of economic thought

Political economy (or economics) is an investigation of society with two main characteristics. First, it is a scientific investigation, which follows specific methodological rules (although not necessarily unchangeable or univocal). Second, it considers society in a particular, but fundamental, aspect: the mechanisms of survival and development of a society based on the division of labour. In such a society each worker is employed in a specific activity, collaborating in the production of a specific commodity, and has to obtain from other economic agents, in exchange for (part of) the product, the commodities required as means of production and subsistence. These mechanisms consist of institutions, habits, norms, knowledge and preferences, which constitute constraints and behavioural rules. Economists investigate the results, both individual and collective, of specific sets of constraints and behavioural rules.

As an investigation of society, political economy is a social science, with a crucial historical dimension. As a science, it implies adhesion to the methodological criteria prevailing in economists' working environments (which among other things determine, in turn, the criteria of professional selection); economists may thus be induced to adopt methodological rules derived from the natural sciences, as is undoubtedly the case in the present stage. Hence we have an irresolvable tension, given the impoverishment which would result for political economy, on the one hand, from abandoning the scientific rules of logical consistency and, on the other hand, from disregarding its characteristics as a social science.

The history of economic thought[24] plays a central role in favouring a positive resolution of the above-mentioned tension. On the one hand, it brings to the fore the essential role of the historical dimension in economic enquiries. On the other hand, it attributes a central role to the criterion of logical precision, side by side with the criterion of empirical relevance, in selecting and evaluating the theories on which to focus attention and in locating a connecting line of development.

---

[24] Or history of economic analysis: the distinction between the two appears somewhat arbitrary, when we consider the stage of conceptualisation as an essential part of the theoretical work. Schumpeter himself, after drawing a clear-cut distinction between history of thought and history of analysis, shows in his book (Schumpeter 1954) only a vague respect for that boundary. His declaration of principle in this respect is perhaps to be interpreted more as a justification for the many simplifying choices unavoidable even for such an erudite scholar.

A fairly clear answer thus emerges to the question we started from. The history of economic thought is useful not only and not simply on the didactic level, or to provide a 'sense of direction' to economic research, or material for epistemologists. It is an essential ingredient both of the theoretical debate between contending approaches, since it helps to clarify the differences and modifications in their representations of the world, and of the theoretical work within each approach, since it contributes to developing the conceptual foundations and clarifying the changes intervening in them in response to theoretical difficulties and evolving realities.

The history of thought thus also constitutes an education in democracy, in the sense indicated by Kula (1958), in his compelling considerations on the role of history quoted at the beginning of this chapter. In contrast to the scientific absolutism widespread in mainstream economic teaching, the history of thought offers an education in the exchange of ideas, which it also favours thanks to the effort it involves in understanding the ideas of others, the perception it fosters of the complexities of the world-views underlying different theories and determining their potentialities and their limits, and the links it reveals with other fields of human knowledge and action.

6.   Which history of economic thought?

Obviously, the role attributed above to the history of economic thought has implications for the way the discipline should be studied and taught. Here we will limit ourselves to a few brief remarks.

First, the history of economic thought as discussed above belongs more to the broad field of economic science than to the history of culture or of ideas.

Second, there is a basic difference between historians of economic thought taking a cumulative view and those adopting the competitive view. The former see the development of economic science as progressive improvement in internal consistency and the field of applicability of the theory; they thus tend to focus attention on the way each author tackles problems that previous authors had left open. Often this favours reconstructions of the history of economic thought in which references to the historical context appear largely irrelevant, and which furthermore generally disregard links between economic, philosophical or politico-social thought – links considered vital before the intellectual division of labour crystallised into small academic hunting reserves.[25]

---

[25] Winch 1962 raises this kind of criticism against mainstream historiography.

The opposite risk – that of considering the vicissitudes of economic thought over time as the exclusive result of the evolution of the productive and social base – is extremely rare. A more concrete risk is that of 'history based on anecdotes', when attention is focused on the simple opinions of the authors under consideration, disregarding the reasoning which led to, or was developed to support such opinions, and thus sidestepping the difficulties intrinsic to a historical reconstruction of similarities, differences and logical links between different theories.

In order to avoid these risks, we should recognise the existence of a two-way link between historical evolution and theoretical investigations. On the one hand, the material world has an important influence on the work of any social scientist, even if not to the point of determining univocally the path followed by theoretical investigations. On the other hand, the theoretical debate may at times exert a crucial influence both on economic policy choices and – more indirectly – on the beliefs and opinions, and hence also the behaviour, of economic agents, although this influence is considerably constrained and conditioned by the material world.

The history of economic thought has an important role in bringing to light these two-way links. This means that there is room both for historical researches 'internal' to the process of development of economic theory, and for 'outward-oriented' studies, connecting economists' investigations with developments in other social sciences and historical evolution. Inevitably, internal and outward-oriented researches will often proceed separately; what matters is that each researcher, whichever his or her chosen emphasis, keeps an eye on developments in the wider area of historical research encompassing different specialisations.[26]

---

[26] The distinction between internal and outward-oriented researches in the history of economic thought is similar to Rorty's (1984) notions of 'rational reconstructions' and 'historical reconstructions'. While distinguishing these two kinds of enquiries into the history of ideas, Rorty considers them as complementary. The epistemologists' passion for neat methodological categories, which are certainly useful in assessing what a researcher is doing, should not lead us into hair-splitting division of intellectual labour, especially when the aspects considered with the different procedures of analysis are so obviously interconnected, as happens in our field. Even what is considered the best rational reconstruction of the history of economic thought, Blaug 1962, stresses the need for caution in adopting this dichotomy; thus, after stating his standpoint in the very first lines of his book ('Criticism implies standards of judgement, and my standards are those of modern economic theory', ibid., p. 1) and providing a clear definition of the two notions (' "Historical reconstructions" attempt to give an account of the ideas of past thinkers in terms that these thinkers, or their disciples, would have recognized as a faithful description of what they had set out to do. "Rational reconstructions", on the other hand, treat the great thinkers of the past as if they are contemporaries with whom we are exchanging views; we analyse their theories in our terms', ibid., p. 7), Blaug not only adds that 'both historical reconstruction and rational reconstruction are each perfectly legitimate ways of writing the history of economic thought', but also that 'what is separate in principle

Another problem, particularly serious for advocates of the competitive view, is the risk of concentrating attention more or less exclusively on those aspects of economic analysis (that is, value theory) which are of greater help in identifying the basic characteristics of the different approaches, but which often hide the general views of the individual authors on the process of economic development. The very meaning of the term 'value' changes from one theoretical approach to another and, over time, within each of them. In any case, it is a term that designates the central core of economic relations from the point of view of the specific system of abstractions adopted.

Let us consider, for instance, the specific meaning which the notion of value has within the classical and Sraffian approach, which will be illustrated in more detail later. 'Value' does not mean the measure of the importance a commodity has for a human being (which is the meaning that the term 'value' assumes within the marginalist approach, when it is related to scarcity and utility); nor does it refer to a 'natural moral law' (as in the medieval debate on the just price); nor does it embody an optimality characteristic (as the result of constrained maximisation of some target function). The value of commodities reflects the relations interconnecting the different sectors and social classes within the economy; furthermore, the content attributed to the term suggests implicit reference to a specific mode of production, namely capitalism. In fact, the analysis developed by the classical economists and Sraffa refers to a specific set of hypotheses ('law of one price'; division into the social classes of workers, capitalists and landowners; uniform rate of profits) that reflect the basic characteristics of a capitalistic economy.

It is true that 'the relationship between prices and distribution for a given technology relates to what may be called the "skeleton" of an economic system. Historically, this problem has been at the centre of the study of economic theory and logically it forms the "core" of the developments of other problems of analysis, even when some of these theories are developed without any direct, formal links to it' (Roncaglia 1975, pp. 127–8). However, it is also true that the possibility – and opportunity – to build separate theories for the analysis of different issues, and especially the importance of the stage of the formation of a system of concepts in economic science, require that the history of economic thought not be confined to illustrating a sequence of theories of value.

---

is almost impossible to keep separate in practice' (ibid., p. 8). Let us remark in this context that reference to 'the standards of modern economic theory' implies a univocal, universally agreed, definition of modern economic theory: as we shall see in chapter 17, this is far from being the case.

In a sense, the theory of value adopted by an economist points directly to his or her representation of the world. By using the debate between rival theories of value as the connecting thread, and observing the shifts that the theory of value (erroneously considered by some reconstructions as an unchanging monolith) undergoes within each approach, we may also grasp the differences and the changes in the conceptual representation of society. At the same time, on the other side of the continuum constituting the field of work of the economist, we may see how around a theory of value, and in strict connection to it, specific theories are developed to interpret specific – but not necessarily less important – aspects of economic reality, from theories of employment and money to theories of international relations.

Let us try to illustrate with an example the different meanings of the two expressions, 'central role in our historical reconstruction' and 'crucial importance within our world-view'. The labour theory of value has a central role in the analytic reconstruction of Ricardo's *Principles*, but he is above all politically interested in the issue of economic growth and its relationship with income distribution between the main social classes. Another example is the connection between the Walrasian theory of competitive equilibrium and the liberal ideology. In other words, there is some margin of independence between a system of concepts (representation of the working of the economy) and a theory of value, and indeed between the latter and the specific theories concerning the phenomena that, from a policy point of view, constitute central concerns for the economist.

References to history, and in particular to economic history, may be useful in this context to explain both changes in the main policy interests prevailing in the different periods and shifts in the process of abstraction within each school, as well as to evaluate the different systems of abstraction. In this respect it may perhaps be useful to recall that a system of concepts (which is the result of a specific process of abstraction, and which is utilised for simplified representation of a real world whose most essential characteristics are taken to have been captured) can be verified neither through direct comparison with the real world, nor by checking whether forecasts drawn from it actually come about.

'There are more things in heaven and earth, Horatio, than are dreamt of in our philosophy': the history of economic thought, with its own various research strategies, is of great help in keeping economists fully aware of the truth of Hamlet's observation. Not least for this reason, it is a field which every economist should practise.

2   The prehistory of political economy

1.   Why we call it prehistory

The birth of political economy did not take place at any precise time. It was a very complex process evolving over centuries. We must look back at least to the classical Greek period, and from there look ahead to the sixteenth and seventeenth centuries, which can be considered as the culminating stage in the long formative process of our discipline.

Political economy began to be recognised as an autonomous discipline, distinct from other social sciences, very gradually, beginning in the seventeenth century.[1] Only in the nineteenth century, with the creation of the first economics chairs in universities, was the economist recognised as an autonomous professional figure.[2]

Obviously, references to issues now commonly considered as belonging to economics already made their appearance in classical antiquity and the Middle Ages. Authors such as Diodorus Siculus, Xenophon or Plato, for instance, considered the economic aspects of the division of labour, maintaining among other things that it favours a better product quality.

On the whole, however, for a long period – at least up to the seventeenth century – the approach to economic issues was substantially different from present-day practice. Indeed, the very economic mechanisms regulating production and income distribution have since seen

---

[1] In that period the term *political economy* began to be used; the first to use it as a title for a book (the *Traité de l'économie politique*, 1615) was the Frenchman Antoine de Montchrétien (c.1575–1621). He is traditionally considered a second-line mercantilist, to be recalled only for the title of his book. In fact, albeit embedded in a far from systematic discussion of the economic situation of the time, some interesting ideas emerge in this book, such as criticism of Aristotle's thesis of the independence of politics from other aspects of social life, accompanied by the statement that work is the source of wealth, which in turn is crucial for social stability. We return to these themes below.

[2] To be precise, the first chair in political economy was established in Naples in 1754, for Antonio Genovesi; in 1769 Milan followed with Cesare Beccaria. Elsewhere (France, England) things moved more slowly. Alfred Marshall's fight for the institution of a degree course in economics in Cambridge and the professionalisation of economics, between the end of the nineteenth and the beginning of the twentieth century, described in Groenewegen 1995 and Maloney 1985, is briefly recalled below (§ 13.4).

radical transformation. Without going into the subject in depth, suffice it to recall just how much sheer violence, authority and tradition weighed in the economic life of classical antiquity, based on slave labour, as in that of the feudal period, based on serf labour, in comparison with market exchanges. Moreover, given the relatively primitive technology in use in those historical periods, human life was dominated by natural phenomena (such as natural calamities and epidemics), as well as by wars and the arbitrary exercise of political power. Under such conditions a regular life was something to yearn for, to be pursued by sticking to the behavioural rules sanctioned by tradition. If we add to this a largely superstitious religious sensibility, we can understand how repetitive cycles of work and life, day by day, year by year, were systematically preferred to innovation and change. We can also understand why the philosophers of classical antiquity and theologians of the Middle Ages considered it their task not so much to describe and interpret the way the economy works, but rather to provide advice on morally acceptable behaviour in the field of economic relations.

Actually, political economy was born from the conjunction of two major issues. On the one hand we have the moral issue: which rules of conduct should human beings – especially the merchant and the sovereign – respect in the domain of economic activities? On the other hand we have the scientific issue: how does a society based on the division of labour function, where each person or group of persons produces a specific commodity or group of commodities and needs the products of others, both as subsistence and as means of production, to keep the production process going?

Obviously the two questions are connected. For instance, if we are looking for objective grounds for the moral evaluation of human behaviour in the economic domain, the answer to the moral issue depends on the answer to the scientific issue. This link is reinforced by the idea (dominant in the Aristotelian tradition) that 'good' is what 'conforms to nature'. Hence the sway of the former question over the latter, as reflected in the idea, still widespread among classical economists in the first half of the nineteenth century, that the task of the economist consists in identifying the 'natural laws' governing the economy.

These relations between ethics and economic science depend on the way the moral issue was conceived in the historical phase under consideration. At the time, what was commonly adopted was a substantially 'deontological' approach to ethics, moral judgements being based on absolute criteria, independent of circumstances: killing is bad, helping the sick is good. When a utilitarian ethics was later adopted, with moral judgements mainly founded on the factual effects of the act under consideration in the specific circumstances of time and space, ethics came to imply as a necessary prerequisite an understanding of the way society functioned. However, this connection – underlying what has been called 'consequentialist ethics' – gained recognition only in the eighteenth century, in particular with Bentham, as we shall see below (§ 6.7).

For a long time, however, authors writing on economic matters did not distinguish clearly between the two issues: a point illustrated by the ambiguities in the notion of 'natural law' itself. The fact that such ambiguities are still apparent in the work of front-line protagonists of the classical school such as Adam Smith and David Ricardo is an interesting example of the persistence of concepts even when radical changes in the perception of the world have intervened.

Political economy was thus born as a moral science, and as a science of society. At this stage, moreover, distinction between the different aspects now included in the field of economics was in many instances more clear-cut than the dividing line between economics and the other social sciences. Thus, for instance, the distance between the study of economic institutions and that of political institutions was small; much larger was the distance separating the study of institutions from that of the behaviour of the good *paterfamilias* with respect to consumption activities and supervision of the family budget: for instance, discussion on the economic tasks of the *paterfamilias* generally involved reflections on the upbringing of children.

An important factor in the progressive separation between the two fields of research, as we shall see in the next chapter, was a change in perspective prompted by discoveries taking place in the natural sciences: from the discovery of the circulation of blood, announced by Harvey in 1616, up to the shift coming in over a century later with Lavoisier (1743–94) from descriptive chemistry to chemistry based on quantitative relations. Such discoveries favoured gradual recognition of the existence of scientific issues, concerning our understanding of the physical world, to be tackled independently of moral issues, with methods of analysis different from those traditionally applied to the latter. Earlier on Niccolò Machiavelli (1469–1527) had taken a turn in the same direction with his distinction between political science and moral philosophy, between analysis of the behaviour princes must adopt in pursuit of power and moral judgement on such behaviour.

The importance for our purposes of the formative stage of political economy derives from the fact that it left as inheritance to successive stages a set of ideas and concepts, together with a set of – often vague and variegated – meanings for each of them (as we saw above for the notion of natural laws and as we shall see below with respect to the notion of the market).

Around the seventeenth century, however, a change took place in the way economic issues were tackled. In order to understand it, we should consider the radical changes that had intervened in the organisation of economic and social life. In particular, we may take as an example the role of exchanges.[3]

The market, interpreted as exchange of goods against money, was already in existence in Pericles' Athens and Caesar's Rome. However, exchanges then accounted for a relatively limited share of total social production; furthermore, the conditions under which they took place were characterised by extreme irregularity due to climatic influences on crop production, difficulties of transportation, and above all widespread insecurity about property rights arising not only from private criminality but also, and crucially, from the arbitrary intervention of the political authorities, who often exercised a drastic and often unpredictable redistributive function.

As far as the former aspect is concerned – the limited share of exchanges – we may recall, for instance, that in the feudal economy exchanges through the market typically concerned only the surplus product, namely that part of the product which is not necessary as a means of production or of subsistence for the continuance of productive activity. On the other hand, there was already a network of exchanges involving luxury products – spices, lace, precious metals – connecting geographical areas even over great distances; side by side with it, a web of financial relations gradually developed connecting major commercial centres, based mainly on letters of exchange.[4] At this stage, self-production – i.e. production for direct consumption on the part of the producers themselves – characterised small rural communities. In these small communities some degree of productive specialisation and payments in money coexisted with exchanges in kind.

Self-production lost ground to production for the market only as private ownership extended over land and as artisan manufacturing production grew. A different system of social relations and a different technological structure were thus born. With this new system, neither in agriculture nor in manufacturing were the workers now owners of the means of production or the goods they produced which, in any case, were usually different

---

[3] We may also recall here the change in attitude towards mechanical skill, from contempt to acceptance of specialised practical knowledge, as an important component of culture, which took place between 1400 and 1700 and is wonderfully documented in Rossi 1962.

[4] A model of the feudal economy based on these assumptions is analysed in Kula 1962.

from the goods they themselves consumed. Moreover, artisan manufacturing – and later on industrial plants – were increasingly characterised by use of specialised means of production, produced by firms other than those utilising them.

As far as the second aspect is concerned – the irregularity of exchanges – let us recall only one of the most characteristic instances of the absence of uniformity in conditions of exchange: the multiplicity and continuous variability of the standards of measurement for commodities – standards of weight, of length, of volume – only gradually superseded through a course of events beginning, significantly enough, in the eighteenth century.[5]

It is precisely the absence of regularity and uniformity in economic activity that may possibly account for the generic remarks by writers of this period about the conditions of demand and supply as determinants of market prices. In the presence of a marked variability in demand and supply, and in the absence of clear indications on the factors determining them, such generic remarks cannot be considered as adding up to a fully fledged theory of prices, let alone anticipating the marginalist theories that take equilibrium prices to correspond to the point where demand and supply of the given commodity meet. As we shall see more clearly later on, within the marginalist approach demand and supply are defined as (continuous and differentiable) functions – the former decreasing, the latter increasing – of the price of the commodity itself and possibly of other variables such as prices of other commodities and the consumers' income. On the contrary, we would search the earlier, generic remarks on supply and demand in vain for any idea of a well-specified and stable functional relation between demand or supply and other variables such as the price of the given commodity.

Indeed, up to the end of the seventeenth century reflection on economic issues, when not addressing specific technical issues (such as the development of methods of accountancy and the invention of double-entry bookkeeping, commonly attributed to the Italian Luca Pacioli, c.1445–c.1514), essentially formed part of the study of rules for the government of society (we have only to think of Plato's *Republic* or Aristotle's *Politics*, for example). Moreover, political thought focused more on what should be than on what really was: as often noted, separation between ethics and the 'objective' sciences of society had to wait for Machiavelli. This

---

[5] Standards of measurement were, for a long stretch of human history, the object of harsh social conflict regulated by local conventions, generally temporary and fairly flexible. The central authority of the new nation-states succeeded in imposing legal standards of measurement only after great efforts, which came to fruition starting at the end of the eighteenth century. This most interesting story is described in Kula 1970.

is not to say that the writings of the philosophers of classical antiquity or the Middle Ages have nothing to say in relation to political economy; economic ideas and observations were indeed there, but embedded in a context that failed to constitute any systematic analysis of economic issues. We may perhaps speak of a 'conceptual system' as far as political themes are concerned, or for specific economic issues; however, it was not until William Petty (see chapter 3) that there was an explicit and conscious discussion of the notions of price, commodity and market, for instance.

The acceleration in economic debate from the sixteenth century onwards was also connected with a more general technical factor, namely the invention of the printing press with movable type, which led to a rapid and significant reduction in the cost of books.[6]

2.   Classical antiquity

We can find traces of discussion of economic issues going far back in time. The Babylonian code of Hammurabi (around 1740 BC), engraved on a monolith, conserved in the Louvre museum in Paris, provided, among other things, normative prescriptions for economic relations. The first written text of the Old Testament, which contains a wealth of considerations on different aspects of economic life, has been traced back to the twelfth-to-ninth century BC. In India Kautilya's *Arthasastra*, dealing entirely with the functioning of the state in its economic aspects, belongs to the fourth century BC, and is full of references to previous texts. In China, the *Guanzi* brought together writings dating from the fifth century BC and the first century AD, dealing among other things with economic issues.[7]

Among the many themes dealt with in the Bible, the most important from our viewpoint concerns the role of labour in human life. This is a complex issue, which we will have occasion to come back to more than once. In Genesis work was seen both as expiation for original sin and,

---

[6] Gutenberg's Bible dates from 1445; within thirty years the new technique had spread all over Europe (cf. Cipolla 1976, pp. 148–9). The increase in the number of printed works was very rapid; it is likely that an increasing share of these publications concerned economic issues. Spiegel (1971, p. 94) uses as an indicator the catalogue of the Kress Library at Harvard University: around 200 printed works (pamphlets and books) for the sixteenth century, 2,000 for the seventeenth, 5,000 for the period 1700–76. Such an indicator probably implies a slight overestimate of the effective growth rate, due to the lower rate of survival of the more ancient works, but the picture it provides is clear-cut and substantially valid.

[7] Cf. Kautilya 1967 (and Dasgupta 1993 on the history of Indian economic thought) and Rickett 1985–98 for the commented text of the *Guanzi*.

with a decisively positive connotation, as an element intrinsic to the very nature of man and the means for his fulfilment as part of a divine project. God Himself 'works', and on the seventh day rests.[8] When God creates man, He assigns him a task even in the earthly paradise.[9] With original sin, however, work assumes a negative aspect: 'cursed is the ground for thy sake; in sorrow shalt thou eat of it all the days of thy life. [. . .] In the sweat of thy face shalt thou eat bread.'[10] Work, however, represents not only a hard necessity for survival: it is also an essential aspect of good behaviour, conforming to divine law.[11]

The simultaneous presence of 'compulsory labour' and 'labour as self-fulfilment' constitutes a most important contribution of the biblical tradition to modern culture, and we may note that in this respect the biblical tradition proved stronger than Greek culture,[12] which appears rather a typical expression of the dominant classes in a slave society:[13] work (as distinct from the activity of organising and supervising productive activities) was viewed with annoyance, if not indeed contempt. As Finley (1973, p. 81) remarks, 'neither in Greek nor in Latin was there a word with which to express the general notion of "labour" or the concept of labour as a social function'.

In general, Greek culture followed 'an administrative, not a market approach, to economic phenomena' (Lowry 1987a, p. 12). Economic issues were dealt with either in the framework of discussion concerning sound management of the houschold (in the broad sense of a family

---

[8] 'And on the seventh day God ended his work which he had made; and he rested on the seventh day from all his work which he had made' (Genesis 2:2).

[9] 'And the Lord God took the man, and put him into the garden of Eden, to dress it and to keep it' (Genesis 2:15).

[10] Genesis 3:17–19.

[11] 'Six days shalt thou labour, and do all thy work' (Exodus 20:9; cf. also Deuteronomy, 5:13). A strong work ethic inspired Paul's Epistles in particular. The idea of work as the source of dignity and a positive value in human life, as the road to self-fulfilment of man in the world, resurfaced repeatedly in the course of the centuries, in particular among utopian thinkers and currents of the sixteenth and seventeenth centuries. Some such currents, in particular those connected to the Protestant reform, set as their objective liberation of the worker from the subjugation to the masters (and not the liberation of man from the 'serfdom of labour', which is truly utopian!): cf. Spini 1992. Among the authors of 'utopian' writings, let us recall Thomas More (1478–1535; *Utopia* appears in Latin in 1516), Tommaso Campanella (1568–1639; the *Città del sole* is dated 1602, but was published, in Latin, only in 1623), and Francis Bacon (1561–1626; the *New Atlantis* is dated 1626).

[12] As we shall see more clearly below, the two elements, simultaneously present in many economists of the classical period, were counterposed in Marx: 'compulsory labour' is typical of the pre-communist social formations, while within communism working activity becomes exclusively the free fulfilment of the human person. With the marginalist approach, apart from an important exception represented by Marshall, the negative characterisation of work decidedly prevailed.

[13] While the Bible was the expression of a subjected people.

group, slaves included) or in discussion of the political institutions. In the first field – household economics – we find the *Oeconomicon* by Xenophon (c.430–c.355 BC), or the *Oeconomica* that an old tradition attributed to Aristotle and that was probably written between the third century BC and the first century AD. The very term 'economy' derives from *oikos*, house, and *nomos*, norm or law, thus designating the field of household management. In the second field, that of economic-political discussion, we find the *Republic* by Plato (c.427–c.347 BC), for example, or the *Politics* by Aristotle (384–322 BC). However, the distinction cannot be considered clear-cut: in Greek culture we find no contrast between the viewpoint of the family administrator and the viewpoint of government of the *polis*. Xenophon and Plato explicitly stated this fact; among other things, the ability to manage one's own business is considered a good guarantee when it comes to attribution of a public appointment, even a military one.[14] Efficient management of the means of production (including, in particular, the supervision of slave labour) was considered a decisive element for obtaining a good quality of product, while the possibility of technical improvements was on the whole overlooked.

It is in this context that we find, in the *Oeconomica* attributed to Aristotle, the oft-quoted advice: 'no one, indeed, takes the same care of another's property as of his own; so that, as far as it is possible, each man ought to attend to his affairs in person. We may command also a pair of sayings, one attributed to a Persian [. . . who] on being asked what best conditions a horse, replied "His master's eye".'[15]

This reference to the 'master' brings us to the notion of property (or, perhaps better, of possession or dominance, in order to avoid the full identification with the notion of private property current in contemporary society). This notion did not constitute a problem in itself – it was to become so some centuries later, in the times of the Patristic Fathers, as we shall see in the following section – but simply an aspect of the more general problem of political and social organisation. In this respect we find significant differences between the various authors, and in particular between Plato, who favoured collective ownership of the means of production and a collectivistic organisation of consumption activities, and Aristotle, who invoked a realistic view of human nature:

---

[14] Cf. Xenophon [c.390 BC] 1923, p. 189: 'The management of private concerns differs only in point of number from that of public affairs. In other respects they are much alike.' Cf. Lowry 1987a, pp. 12–14.

[15] (Pseudo) Aristotle 1935, p. 341: *Oeconomica*, I. 6.3. This passage was paraphrased by Adam Smith in the *Theory of moral sentiments* (cf. below, § 5.8), but in the new context it was to assume a different meaning: not the advice of the good *paterfamilias* to take personal care of one's own businesses, but the crucial justification for the choice of the liberal field.

'Property that is common to the greatest number of owners receives the least attention; men care most for their private possessions, and for what they own in common less, or only so far as it falls to their own individual share.'[16]

On the other hand, there was a general convergence of ideas on the origins of social stratification, to be found in the differences in the innate abilities of different persons and the consequent subdivision of tasks. Such was, of course, the case of the division between peasants, soldiers and philosophers in Plato's *Republic*. He located the origin of the state in the division of labour between specific roles such as peasant, mason, textile worker; in turn, the division of labour originated from the fact that 'our several natures are not all alike but different. One man is naturally fitted for one task, and another for another.'[17]

Aristotle followed Plato in considering intrinsic to human nature the foundations of social stratification. This held first of all for the basic difference in the roles of man, woman and slave: 'Thus the female and the slave are by nature distinct (for nature makes [. . .] one thing for one purpose [. . .])', Aristotle peremptorily asserted in the *Politics*.[18] Up to this point, however, a distinction of roles within society rather than a distinction of working tasks was being discussed. In Aristotle's opinion, this second aspect concerned the slaves and not the masters:

---

[16] Aristotle 1977, p. 77: *Politics*, II.3, 1261b. We should recall, however, that these statements were accompanied by openings to forms of utilisation of goods in common, which may be stimulated by the public authorities: 'It is clear therefore that it is better for possessions to be privately owned, but to make them common property in use; and to train the citizens to this is the special task of the legislator' (ibid., p. 89: *Politics*, II.5, 1263a).

[17] Plato 1930, pp. 151–3: *Republic*, II.11. On the division of labour Xenophon had something to say. (Xenophon was, like Plato, a disciple of Socrates, who was represented in the *Memorabilia*: Xenophon 1923, and hence belonged to the generation that preceded that of Aristotle, who was a disciple of Plato). Among other things, Xenophon connected the division of labour to the size of the market in a famous passage frequently quoted:

For in small towns the same workman makes chairs and builds houses, and even so he is thankful if he can only find employment to support him. And it is, of course, impossible for a man of many trades to be proficient in all of them. In large cities, on the other hand, inasmuch as many people have demands to make upon each branch of industry, one trade alone, and very often even less than a whole trade, is enough to support a man; one man for instance, makes shoes for men, and another for women; and there are places even where one man earns a living by only stitching shoes, another by cutting them out, another by sewing the uppers together, while there is another who performs none of these operations but only assembles the parts. It follows, therefore, as a matter of course, that he who devotes himself to a very highly specialised line of work is found to do it in the best possible manner. (Xenophon 1914, p. 333: *Cyropaedia*, VIII.2.5).

[18] Aristotle 1977, p. 5: *Politics*, I.2, 1252b. Immediately before this, Aristotle stated: 'for one that can foresee with his mind is naturally ruler and naturally master, and one that can do these things with his body is subject and naturally a slave' (ibid.).

The term 'master' therefore denotes the possession not of a certain branch of knowledge but of a certain character, and similarly also the terms 'slave' and 'freeman'. [. . .] The slave's sciences then are all the various branches of domestic work; the master's science is the science of employing slaves.[19]

Plato and Aristotle thus characterised social and political stratification as a fact of nature, stemming from intrinsic differences existing between the members of society: a thesis with authoritarian connotations that was long to hold sway,[20] but a far cry from the thesis Adam Smith would later advance on the issue (cf. below, § 5.7). From our viewpoint, however, many other aspects of their thought are interesting and would be taken up in subsequent economic debate, albeit occasionally distorted to accentuate their modernity. Below, in § 4, we will recall Aristotle's ideas on money and usury; here, we may briefly mention Plato's reference in the *Laws* to the role of pleasure and pain as a guide to human action,[21] or Aristotle's distinction between value in use and value in exchange.[22] Not quite so easy to interpret is Aristotle's analysis of exchange as set out in

---

[19] Ibid., pp. 30–1: *Politics*, I.7, 1255b.

[20] For instance Thomas Aquinas – and behind him the Scholastic tradition – spoke of an equitable distribution of talents between men on the side of Providence and accepted as just a distribution of incomes and wealth based on the inequalities of rank, merit, capabilities, craft and condition of each individual (De Roover, 1971, pp. 43–4; cf. ibid. for references to Thomas's writings).

[21] Plato (1926, pp. 67–9: *Laws*, I.644) said that 'each of us [. . .] possesses within himself two antagonistic and foolish counsellors, whom we call by the name of pleasure and pain'. However, contrary to what Spiegel (1971, p. 20) appears to believe, this was not a sensistic view in which the confrontation between pleasure and pain quantitatively evaluated mechanically determines human choices: it is 'calculation' (reasoning) that evolves into 'law', 'when it has become the public decree of the State', and which governs, for the wise man, the positive and negative impulses of passions.

[22] 'With every article of property there is a double way of using it; both uses are related to the article itself, but not related to it in the same manner – one is peculiar to the thing and the other is not peculiar to it – take for example a shoe – there is its wear as a shoe and there is its use as an article of exchange' (Aristotle 1977, pp. 39–41: *Politics*, I.9, 1257a). As we can see, in Aristotle the distinction between what was subsequently to be called value in use and value in exchange had an ethical connotation: the 'proper' use, consumption, was counterposed to the 'improper' use, exchange; this mirrored a certain contempt for mercantile activity, typical of the dominant classes in a society based on slave labour. In fact, the passage just quoted is part of an illustration of the 'natural' and 'unnatural' modes of acquiring wealth (pasturage, agriculture, hunting, fishing and even piracy are natural; usury is condemned as most unnatural, but in general all profits from commerce – buying and selling goods in exchange for money – are considered unnatural). According to Lowry (2003, pp. 15 and 22; cf. also the bibliography quoted there), 'Aristotle clearly formulated the concept of diminishing marginal utility' and 'identified the uses of money as a medium of exchange, a unit of measure, and a store of value for future purchases'. Both Meikle's (see following note) and Lowry's appear as examples of 'rational reconstructions' (cf. above, ch. 1, note 26), interpreting authors of the past from the standpoint of present-day (or largely subsequent) theories.

the *Nicomachean ethics* as part of his theory of ethics, which was variously taken up in Scholastic analyses of the just price.[23]

3.   Patristic thought

For reasons of space we shall not discuss here the texts of the Epicureans (and Epicurus himself) or the Stoics, even if their influence is clearly recognisable in the writings of protagonists of the history of economic thought (such as Mandeville and Smith in the eighteenth century, in particular). For the same reason we have to exclude Latin literature (with authors as important as Cicero and Seneca), although it is directly relevant to many aspects concerning law, like property rights. Here we shall only mention the distinction between 'natural rights' and 'rights of the people' that surfaces in the reflections of the early Church Fathers.

Let us, then, briefly look at Patristic thought, represented by the most influential Christian thinkers, in the period from the first century AD up to the eleventh century. During the twelfth and thirteenth centuries, in fact, a new cultural model gradually took over, which found expression mainly in the intellectual life of the 'schools' – hence the term 'Scholastic' – and was characterised by systematic recourse to certain philosophers of antiquity (mainly Boethius during the twelfth century and Aristotle during the thirteenth century).[24]

Once again, the Patristic phase is interesting not from the viewpoint of construction of a system, a fully worked out and well-organised treatment of economic phenomena, but for the influence it exercised on subsequent developments in some areas (in particular the notion of private property and of the relationship between private initiative and social systems).[25]

We should first of all recall that originally the Christian religion was a minority sect, oppressed with persecution, spreading mainly among the

[23] Book V of the *Nichomachean ethics* (Aristotle 1926, pp. 252–323) considered commutative and distributive justice. Here Aristotle explained among other things why from barter men shifted to the exchange of goods against money. Goods are distributed among men according to their 'nature', hence according to the role that each of them is called to play in society; in the exchange between different products we need to respect adequate proportions (but it is far from clear how these proportions should be determined). For opposite evaluations of Aristotle's contribution to economics, cf. the negative one by Finley 1970 and the positive Marxian re-evaluation by Meikle 1995.

[24] Let us recall for instance the diffusion of the Latin translation of the *Nichomachean ethics* made by Robert Grosseteste, bishop of Lincoln, and his assistants, completed around 1246: it is from here that some textbooks date the beginning of the Scholastic period, even if the interest in the philosophers of classical antiquity, and hence the stimulus to translate them, was an effect of the vitality of the 'schools' rather than a cause of their birth.

[25] For a treatment of this period cf. Viner 1978 and the literature there quoted. Cf. also Spiegel 1971, pp. 41–6.

lower strata of society. In this initial stage the search for margins of survival naturally led to a show of indifference towards politics: an acceptance of the existing social structure and economic system following Christ's teaching to 'render unto Caesar the things which be Caesar's'.[26] Things changed after Constantine's policy shift and the advent of the Christian faith as a state religion. However, even after this policy shift attention still focused on 'life after death' and strictly religious aspects, while 'the Fathers accepted the social and political institutions of their time as facts, substantially as unchangeable facts' (Viner 1978, p. 13).

This obviously does not mean that the Church Fathers never considered practical issues: while addressing them always within the framework of moral doctrine, in various ways they contributed to forming a climate of opinion that would exert profound influence in following centuries. Here we will take a brief look at the Fathers' attitude towards private property, alms, slavery and commerce. When considering these issues, we should bear in mind a distinction crucial to thinking in the period, namely the distinction between ideals valid for a small minority of believers and moral precepts applicable to the whole community of believers.

Thus, on the question of private property an opinion widely held among the Church Fathers was to see it as a creation of civil, not divine, law, and that the moral ideal is constituted by some form of common property. John Chrysostom (c.347–407) maintained that God had assigned earthly goods as common property to all men; the same opinion was held by Ambrose (c.340–397), who saw the origin of private property in an act of usurpation, and by Jerome (c.347–c.420), who argued that a rich man is either an unjust person or heir to an unjust person. Augustine of Hippo (354–430) considered private property as a source of wars and social injustice. However, the advice to completely despoil oneself of all property – as many centuries later Saint Francis of Assisi would in fact do – was considered a 'counsel of perfection', not a precept applicable to all. The general norm concerning private property, as indeed all the other aspects of social life, consisted in respecting existing laws.[27] As a

---

[26] Matthew 22:21. Viner 1978, p. 9, speaks of 'otherworldliness' of the Patristic in this stage.

[27] Two exceptions, recalled – also in their limits – by Viner 1978, pp. 17–20, are Lactantius and Theodoretus of Cyr. The former was a harsh critic of collectivism (but the main objective of his attacks was the communality of wives), the latter a defender of social inequalities, including those between master and slave. On the other side we have the different heretical streams – Manichaeans, Donatists, Pelagians, Compocratians and others – who considered the salvation of the rich impossible and held poverty as a precept, at least for priests. Once again see Viner 1978, pp. 38–45, for a balanced summary and further references.

matter of fact, the role attributed to laws on private property after the Fall, hence taking into account the limits of human nature, was that of setting limits to human greed and reducing conflict and social unrest to a minimum. Duns Scotus (c.1265–1308) went so far as to maintain that after the Fall private property had become consonant with natural law.[28]

Frequently repeated exhortations to respect the moral duty of almsgiving followed the same logic. The ideal of perfection was that the Christian should not accept being richer than other men, hence he should give to the poor all in excess of strict subsistence requirements; in practice, however, alms were assigned only the task of relieving from the hardest indigence – a burden the rich could easily bear, and certainly not such as to modify the existing social stratification.

Slavery was recognised as a fact, part of the existing social system, and as such not condemned. The Fathers who discussed it – Augustine and Lactantius, for example – limited themselves to recalling that before God all men are equal, regardless of their place in society, and a slave may be more worthy of Paradise than a rich man. This did, however, represent a step forward from Plato and Aristotle: slavery was no longer considered a natural institution; in so far as it concerned the right to property, it fell within the field of human, rather than divine, laws.

It is easier at this point to understand the attitude of the Fathers towards economic activity, and commerce in particular. The attitude towards labour – positive on the whole, and in any case based on its recognition as a social duty, also useful for keeping men away from sin – looked back to Saint Paul's position (see above, § 2). The quest for luxury or wealth was condemned, especially as it diverted from the pursuit of eternal salvation, which was an absolute priority. Commerce was considered with diffidence, as a likely source of moral risks, but was not the object of direct condemnation: what was important was that it be conducted in an honest way, within a Christian life.[29]

In the Middle Ages the Church became one of the largest landowners in the world; in 1208, Pope Innocent III condemned the Waldenses for their thesis that private property is an obstacle to eternal salvation (cf. Viner 1978, p. 108). Subsequently, in the sixteenth century, the exponents of the so-called Salamanca school (from Francisco de Vitoria, 1492–1546, to Tomás de Mercado, c.1500–75) vigorously asserted the usefulness of private property (cf. Chafuen 1986). Cf. also Wood 2002, pp. 17–67, who illustrates the change of attitude towards property, poverty and wealth which intervened between Augustine's times and the fifteenth century.

[28] Cf. Pribram 1983, p. 11.

[29] Finally, some reference should be made to the anti-population theses of Jerome (cf. Viner 1978, pp. 33–4) and Cyprian, bishop of Carthage (c.200–58: cf. Spiegel 1971, p. 46), in some respects a forerunner of Malthus (cf. below, § 6.2), who opposed the biblical imperative 'Be fruitful, and multiply' (Genesis 1:28) frequently quoted then as in the subsequent debates.

The theses of the Fathers illustrated above became the official doctrine of the Church in the following centuries, through the mediation of Thomas Aquinas (c.1225–74). He argued that private property does not violate natural law and favours socially useful behaviour (a thesis already proposed by Aristotle), while common property constitutes an ideal of perfection suited only to the few (for instance, within monastic orders).[30] Similarly, Thomas considered the pursuit of mercantile profits legitimate in many instances. With Thomas Aquinas we come to the full bloom of Scholasticism.

4.   The Scholastics

As we saw in the previous section, it was the moral issue that dominated debate on economic life in classical antiquity and throughout the Middle Ages. According to one of the major historians of economic thought in that period, Pribram (1983, p. 6), 'medieval economics consisted of a body of definitions and precepts designed to regulate Christian behaviour in the spheres of production, consumption, distribution, and exchange of goods'.

In comparison with political economy as we know it today, both the objective and the method of analysis were different. The primary objective, as we have seen, was to find rules of moral conduct, not to understand the functioning of the economy.[31] The method, in line with the objective, was based on the principle of authority, namely on the deduction of rules of conduct from first principles that amounted to articles of faith. The fundamental task was to verify whether considerations on economic issues accorded with these first principles or with comments on the sacred writings endowed with special authority, such as those of the Fathers.

However, theological debate during the Middle Ages came up with a great many pointers for definition of the conceptual framework that

---

[30] The standing of the Catholic Church subsequently changed. In the encyclical *Quod apostolici muneris*, 1878, and *Rerum novarum*, 1891, Pope Leo XIII proclaimed that the right to property conforms to the laws of nature.

[31] An implication deserving consideration of this fact is the importance of the individual – of his canons of behaviour, of the objective of salvation of the individual soul – in Scholastic writings, in this contrasting with the classical economists (for instance, Ricardo or Marx) who focused on aggregates of individuals, such as social classes. Schumpeter 1954, pp. 86–7, stressed the attention paid by the Scholastic writers to the individual as a crucial aspect for the process of birth of political economy. We should, however, add that in a different context an individualistic spirit already permeated the Roman law (while, on the other hand, the celebrated apologue by Menenius Agrippa, with its comparison between the body politic and the human body, had already become a commonplace for anyone invoking a reduction in social tensions).

constitutes the foundation for any abstract analysis of the economy. In many respects the debate foreshadowed lines of analysis that were to surface again in Smith and various other economists of the classical period.

Such was the case of certain eternal commonplaces, including the view of the social body as an autonomous subject. This indeed was very much the case of the Church, seen as the *corpus mysticum*, as *universitas* of the faithful: a superior reality above the individual Christian or social bodies of secular origin.[32]

From here it was but a short step to the idea that the state is logically superior to the family and the individual. The origins of this idea date back to Plato in some respects and to Aristotle in others: the two Greek philosophers may be considered the founders of the organic doctrine of the state.[33] However, as Pribram (1983, pp. 7–8) stresses, 'The Aristotelian conception of the political community as an integrated whole endowed with real existence was not simply taken over by the Scholastics. They accepted only the Aristotelian proposition that it was a "natural necessity" for man to live in society.' Scholastic writers, hence, adopted a more moderate version of the organic doctrine than Aristotle's original conception: a point worth stressing, also to show the possibility of intermediate positions in the face of the clear-cut dichotomy between methodological individualism and organicism commonly accepted in the twentieth century, especially by dint of the liberal reaction to totalitarian regimes. In some respects, the notion of humans as intrinsically social animals, already present in Aristotle, together with a moderate form of organicism and the attention for the individual typical of Scholastic thought, foreshadowed the position held by exponents of the Scottish Enlightenment, and by Adam Smith in particular, which will be considered below (§ 5.3).

A parallel with the debate between methodological individualism and organicism may be located, within medieval philosophy, in discussion of the so-called problem of universals, and more precisely in the counterposition between 'nominalism' and 'realism' (or, as Popper preferred to

---

[32] The doctrine of the supreme authority of the Church in all temporal and spiritual issues was consecrated by Pope Boniface VIII's bull *Unam Sanctam* (1302).

[33] Popper 1945, vol. 1, insisted on Plato's role, while Russell 1945, especially p. 186, insisted on Aristotle's. Both Popper and Russell stressed the authoritarianism intrinsic to the organic view of society, which was exemplified in modern times by Marxism and nazism. According to the organic view, in fact, in order to understand society it is necessary to take into account collective entities such as 'the proletariat' or 'the nation', and in political action a valence is attributed to these entities superior to that attributable to the individuals composing them. On the contrary, the so-called methodological individualism (which later prevailed in marginalist theory, particularly in the Austrian school: cf. below, ch. 11) maintained that any social phenomenon should be analysed starting only from individual behaviour.

say, 'essentialism').[34] Let us consider this debate in extremely simplified terms.[35]

According to the nominalists, universal terms – those that do not designate individual entities, for instance 'horse' or 'humanity' – are simply names used to designate a set or a class of individual objects: a mere *flatus vocis*, as Roscelin of Compiègne (c.1050–c.1120) apparently put it, while individuals alone were endowed with reality. On the other hand, realists like William of Champeaux associated the universal term with the existence of a property common to a set of objects, and hence with a 'real essence' present in identical form in individuals, distinguishable on the basis of a variety of incidental qualities. A pupil of both Roscelin and William of Champeaux, Pierre Abélard[36] took a position strongly critical of the more extreme versions of both nominalism and realism. According to Abélard, the universal term was born to designate (and communicate) an effective aspect of reality, hence it has a *causa communis* and cannot be considered as a simple *flatus vocis* devoid of objective foundations; at the same time, it is something different from a collective reality or from a well-defined set of individuals: 'to the universal name there corresponds a common and useful image of many things, while to the singular name there corresponds a precise and unique concept which refers to a unique reality.'[37] Abélard therefore, though critical of the realistic view, defended the validity of universal terms: an 'analytical' validity, we might say.

If, following in the wake of Popper, we were to try to translate Abélard's position on the problem of universals in terms of the modern dichotomy between methodological individualism and organicism, we might say that

---

[34] Cf. Popper 1944–5, p. 27. Popper himself (ibid., pp. 26–34) proposed such a connection, siding with nominalism. However, Popper did not point out specific references to individual medieval philosophers; in his brief treatment, moreover, he appeared to completely ignore Abélard's views, presenting the debate between nominalists and realists as a clear-cut opposition.

[35] Cf. Fumagalli and Parodi 1989, particularly pp. 165–85. Here we leave aside authors even as important as the Franciscan Duns Scotus, a realist, and William of Ockham (c.1300–49), a nominalist (or, as some prefer, 'terminalist'). The debate between nominalists and realists was also recalled, in terms closer to Popper's than to those here summarily proposed, by the historian of economic thought Karl Pribram (1877–1973), a leading figure in the Austrian culture of the period between the two World Wars, who may have had some influence on Hayek's and Popper's individualism (cf. Pribram 1983, pp. 20–30; Pribram's role was stressed by Schumpeter 1954, p. 85 n.).

[36] One of the greatest medieval logicians, Pierre Abélard (c.1079–1142), professor at Paris for a number of years and then a monk, is also known for his tragic love entanglement with his pupil, Héloïse, and for the letters they exchanged following their forced separation.

[37] Quoted in Fumagalli and Parodi 1989, p. 171; cf. also ibid.: 'the "common state" [. . .] is not a substance but a way of being'. We thus have a 'process of distinction of the world of names from the world of things' (ibid., p. 172): the term 'rose' would retain a meaning, albeit negative, even in a world in which roses no longer existed.

Abélard would have rejected the extreme versions of both, and would have maintained the legitimacy of an analysis conducted on the basis of aggregate categories, which would avoid dispersing attention on the multiform variety of individual accidents, but without attributing to such categories the nature of essence, of something logically superior to the individuals, and in any case with all the caution due to the fact that the universal term offers a confused image, unlike the precise image we have with the 'singular name'.

Drawing parallels between debates over such great distances of time is obviously of limited value; however, even in the extremely simplified version illustrated here the richness of past debate helps us understand the limitations of the methodological position prevalent today, namely methodological individualism, and of the representation of a clear-cut dichotomy between individualism and organicism. Indeed, the Scholastic writers and Abélard point to an intermediate road between the two extremes, where the importance of the community (or, more generally, of social entities) is recognised because of the social nature of individuals, and where the legitimacy of an analytical use of aggregates (universal terms) is also recognised, without this implying considering them as real entities superior (i.e. politically prior) to individuals. Along this intermediate road we will later find Classical economists such as Adam Smith and John Stuart Mill, or in more recent times John Maynard Keynes.[38]

5.   Usury and just price

After our brief digression into the field of logic and epistemology, let us go back to strictly economic themes. The dominant issues, between the twelfth and the sixteenth centuries, were the just price and usury, always considered from the standpoint of ethics and estranged from interpretation of the functioning of the economic system as a whole.[39] In this section we briefly survey the debate on such themes, focusing attention on the major protagonists, such as Thomas Aquinas at the beginning of the period considered here and Thomas Wilson towards its end.

Thomas Aquinas (c.1225–74) is commonly considered the most important philosopher and theologian of the late Middle Ages. His influence as a teacher in various cities (from Paris to Rome, from Anagni to Naples) was only surpassed by that of his main work, the *Summa*

---

[38] Without attributing too much importance to this, we may note that the young Keynes read and liked Abélard: cf. Skidelsky 1983, p. 113.

[39] Cf. De Roover 1971, pp. 16–19. Wood 2002, p. 1, speaks of 'theological economy': 'medieval economic ideas are heavily imbued with questions of ethics and morality, with the motives rather than the mechanics of economics'.

theologiae, written between 1265 and 1273, which was to remain for centuries a central reference point for Catholic doctrine. Characteristic of this work was an original fusion between the Christian tradition and Aristotle's philosophy.[40]

Aristotle himself considered as unnatural, and hence to be condemned, any wealth stemming from commerce; in particular he condemned commerce in money, i.e. loans with interest.[41] In the Christian tradition we also find decided opposition to interest-bearing loans; in this respect a passage from the Sermon on the Mount is often quoted, when Jesus says 'lend, hoping for nothing again'.[42] Thomas Aquinas adopted a more moderate attitude: condemnation of interest in principle[43] was followed by a detailed casuistry, in which cases of loans at interest to be condemned are distinguished from cases in which it was justified (in particular, cases in which we can speak of a *damnum emergens* for the lender, so as to justify a positive but relatively moderate rate of interest, while justifications based on *lucrum cessans* are rejected, since these would open the way to legitimising a competitive rate of interest – as in fact gradually happened in subsequent centuries).[44]

The road followed by Thomas – casuistry, or analysis of specific cases, with different answers to the question of the legitimacy of the loan at interest according to the circumstances – was adopted in subsequent centuries in a long series of writings that show among other things how little respect was accorded to the prohibition of usury and how much inventiveness was shown by the financial operators of the time in finding new kinds of contracts to circumvent the prohibitions.[45] Given the method adopted, these writings did not lead to generalisations and hence

---

[40] On the personality and economic thought of Thomas, cf. Nuccio 1984–7, vol. 2, pp. 1469–576, and the ample bibliography quoted there.

[41] 'As it is so, usury is most reasonably hated, because its gain comes from money itself and not from that for the sake of which money was invented. For money was brought into existence for the purpose of exchange, but interest increases the amount of the money itself [. . .] consequently this form of the business of getting wealth is of all forms the most contrary to nature' (Aristotle 1977, p. 51: *Politics*, I.10, 1258b).

[42] Luke 6:35; we find analogous expressions in the Gospels of Matthew and Mark. Cf. also Ezekiel 18:8 and 18:13.

[43] In fact interest constitutes payment for the use of a commodity, money, the value in exchange of which is already paid with the pledge to return an equal amount. A more radical but substantially analogous thesis was that interest is the payment for the time that expires between the loan and the return of the money lent: hence, it was condemned because time belongs to God.

[44] Cf. Viner 1978, pp. 88–96.

[45] From this viewpoint, the writings on usury are a crucial source for the economic historian, since they serve as evidence to identify the then current market practices and the development of financial instruments, from the bill and the letter of exchange to insurance agreements and forward contracts, up to composite contracts combining different among the preceding elements.

to theoretical contributions worthy of note. What we may say in general is that these authors, Thomas first and foremost, were well aware of the role of money as means of exchange and standard of measurement, but not as a reserve of value.

Ethical and legal debate often intersected,[46] and the debate on usury thus proved relevant to the practical choice between different financial institutions. Indeed, the importance of this debate was such that some commentators consider it – with the various answers given to the question of the legitimacy of usury – a central element in explaining the rate of transition to capitalism.[47] What is certain is that the condemnation of usury was not accompanied by hostility towards commercial activity in general, as was the case with Aristotle. The Scholastics simply called for correct behaviour: in particular, without fraud or coercion, but also without taking advantage of the counterpart's weaker position in bargaining.

Transition towards the legalisation of interest was slow. Confrontation between 'rigorists' and 'laxists' went on for centuries; the initial dominance of the former very gradually gave way to widespread acceptance of the theses of the latter, especially after the Reformation. An important role was played by the process that Viner (1978, pp. 114–50) calls 'secularisation', namely the abandonment of recourse to Revelation and the shift of emphasis from transcendental to temporal values that took place during the Renaissance.[48]

At the end of the sixteenth century, however, we still find strong opposition to usury. Even as it was substantially being legalised we have, for instance, the severe *A discourse upon usurye* by Thomas Wilson, published in 1572. A modern edition, dated 1925 (reprinted in 1963), contains a long introduction by Tawney. He illustrates the main kinds of

---

[46] As far as canonical law is concerned, the Council of Nicaea (312) only prohibited clergy from involvement in loans at interest; gradually regulations became more severe, extending their field of application to all; then, from the fourteenth century, a move in the opposite direction began, with increasingly shrinking definitions of usury (condemnation of which in principle, however, was confirmed by Pope Benedict XIV in the encyclical *Vix pervenit* in 1745, and which still applies). Pope Leo XIII at the fifth Lateran Council (1515) declared the institution of *montes pietatis* acceptable, where an interest on the loans was charged to cover expenses and the risk of losses, by defining usury as 'a profit that is acquired without labour, cost or risk' (quoted in Wood 2002, p. 204).

[47] Tawney (1926) focused attention on this aspect much more than Weber (1904–5) did in his celebrated study of the role of the Protestant reform for transition from medieval culture to a culture suited to capitalistic development. In contrast, Spiegel (1991, p. 66) maintains that the medieval prohibition of the loan at interest favoured different forms of association between private investors for the sharing of risks, thus stimulating the birth of capitalistic firms.

[48] As Pribram 1983, p. 30, remarked, 'independently of the decisions of secular jurisdiction, religious advice on economic behaviour continued to be heeded in almost all countries until far into the sixteenth century'.

credit transactions utilised at the time (those which concern peasants and small artisans, impoverished nobles, the financing of manufacture, foreign exchange markets, financial institutions forerunning modern banks), the history of the debate and the compromise that had been reached shortly before publication of Wilson's essay, with the Act of 1571. This Act declared all loans for interest at a rate above 10 per cent devoid of legal value, while it did not prohibit loans at lower interest rates – without, however, providing any legal protection for them. This compromise opened the way to the view that not all loans at interest should be considered as usury, but only those which, exploiting the borrower's need, applied 'excessive' interest.[49]

At the doctrinal level, the legitimacy of loans at interest had been affirmed among others by John Calvin (1509–64), although only for commercial loans, while the moral condemnation remained for consumption loans, generally granted to meet situations of need and hence exploiting the bargaining inferiority of the borrower. Spiegel (1971, p. 83) also recalls a French lawman, Charles Dumoulin (his book dates from 1546) who, however, maintained the legitimacy of loans at interest while at the same time arguing the expediency of a maximum limit to the rate of interest set by the public authorities. In the Salamanca school, active in Spain in the sixteenth century and very influential throughout Europe, various authors extended the legitimacy of interest to practically all kinds of contract and all situations.[50] The Belgian Jesuit Lessius (Leonard de Lays, 1554–1623) proposed another justification for interest, the *carentia pecuniae* (scarcity of money in circulation).[51] Reaction to the regulation of loans at interest only arrived with the rise of liberalism – we may mention Turgot (1769), and especially Bentham's *Defence of usury* (1787) – while Adam Smith himself, in *The wealth of nations*, still judged legal limits to the interest rate opportune, maintaining that otherwise 'prodigals and

---

[49] The definition of usury based on imposition of a rate of interest on loans markedly higher than the average recently resurfaced in Italian legislation (Law 108 of 1996), which testifies to the vitality – especially in a Catholic country – of medieval economic ideas, notwithstanding the economists' cogent criticisms. As a matter of fact, usury is today mainly characterised by ways of collection that involve illegal practices and imply a dangerous connection between usurers and petty delinquency (and occasionally organised crime). Prohibition of interest rates markedly above average is obviously ignored by illegal usury, which at the same time exploits the absence of competition from banks in the sector of high risk loans, especially those of modest sums for which collection expenses may be proportionally high, also due to the slowness of civil justice, and for which therefore relatively high interest rates may be actuarially justified by the risk of non-reimbursement of the loan.

[50] Cf. Chafuen 1986, pp. 143–50.

[51] Cf. De Roover 1971, p. 90, who somewhat boldly associates this element with Keynes's liquidity preference (cf. below, § 14.5).

projectors' ready to pay even very high interest rates would crowd 'sober people' out of the loan market.[52] In England, the usury laws were only abolished in 1854.

Let us now turn to the just price, another theme that goes back at least to Aristotle (cf. above, § 2). The division of labour makes exchanges necessary, through which everybody gives and receives: exchange is a *fluxus et refluxus gratiarum*, a giving and receiving of graces, as Albert the Great nicely put it.[53] A problem thus arose, concerning the terms of exchange. Following the tradition of the Roman law doctrine and certain Church Fathers such as Ambrose and Augustine, Thomas identified the just price as the price prevailing in the markets in the absence of fraud or monopolistic practices. This seems to have been the most widespread opinion also among authors coming after Thomas, and in particular among the Romanists, canonists and Thomists; the thesis was opposed by adversaries of Thomism, such as the Scotists and the nominalists.[54] We must, however, stress that reference to the market price had a normative, not a descriptive value, since at the time the competitive market was the exception, while the rule consisted in the possibility of exchange open to few parties.[55] Among other things, let us recall that in the twelfth–thirteenth centuries, at least in Italy, the political authorities (municipalities, corporations) actively intervened, setting compulsory prices, or maximum limits for prices, of many among the main commodities subject to exchange. Moreover, because of the close regulation of productive techniques characterising the arts and crafts corporations, reference to necessary costs of production did not imply competition which eliminates the less efficient

[52] Smith 1776, p. 357. Bentham's reply on this point (1787, 'Letter XIII') was based on identification of the Smithian 'projectors' with entrepreneurs, protagonists with their initiatives of technological change. Here we find, in the opposition to the Smithian view of technical progress as a widespread process, enacted by a wide range of agents, and in the exaltation of the innovative role of the entrepreneur, an anticipation of the Schumpeterian notion of the entrepreneur-innovator (cf. below, § 15.2).

[53] Quoted by Langholm 1998, p. 101. As Duns Scotus (quoted ibid., p. 102) remarked, voluntary exchange is considered advantageous by both sides, buyer and seller, and therefore implies an element of gift. (Langholm's book, probably the best work on medieval economic thought, is also a precious mine of quotations from original sources.)

[54] Cf. De Roover 1971, pp. 25 ff., 52 ff. Thomas's thesis was also taken up by exponents of the 'Salamanca school': cf. Chafuen 1986, pp. 92 ff. Among the opponents of the 'market view', Wood 2002, p. 143, recalls 'Jean Gerson (d. 1428) who [. . .] recommended that all prices [. . .] should be fixed by the state'.

[55] Cf. De Roover 1958. The term 'competition' itself made its appearance only in the seventeenth century, while the term 'monopoly' goes back to Aristotle's *Politics* (1977, p. 57: I.11, 1259a), and 'oligopoly' to Thomas More's *Utopia* (1518, pp. 67–9). Cf. De Roover 1971, p. 16, and Spiegel 1987. Langholm 1998, p. 85, stresses that 'The modern mechanistic conception of the market [. . .] was foreign to the medieval masters. Their frame of reference was a moral universe that obliged any buyer or seller to act for the common good and agree to terms of exchange accordingly.' Cf. also ibid., p. 163.

producers,[56] but to legal costs corresponding to respect for existing regulations.

References to cost of production, and in particular to the quantity of labour necessary to produce a commodity, as an element to be taken into account in determining the just price, do not add up to real anticipation of the classical theory of value.[57] Indeed, while it is true that references to cost of production and particularly to labour costs were numerous, these were decidedly out-numbered by references to utility and rarity, as we shall now see more closely. Moreover, the cost structure was clearly determined by social stratification, which was assumed as a given datum that the 'just price' had to respect: in substance, the Scholastic writers considered as 'just' that price that allowed producers to maintain a standard of living befitting their position in society.[58] In a sense, references to costs of production seemed more relevant to matters of distributive justice than commutative justice.

As already mentioned, prevalent were references to utility in the broad sense of the term.[59] First of all, in the wake of Aristotle and of some Church Fathers such as Augustine, Thomas and others confirmed that the value of goods does not reflect the 'natural' hierarchy (inanimate objects–vegetal world–animal world–human beings), but the ability of goods to satisfy needs (*indigentia*).[60] More precisely, as Peter of Johann

---

[56] In contrast to the oft-repeated observations by Schumpeter (1954, p. 93, referring to Thomas Aquinas, then to Duns Scotus; p. 98, referring to 'the late scholastics').

[57] In contrast to what Tawney (1926, p. 48), among others, believed; he went so far as to state emphatically: 'The true descendant of the doctrines of Aquinas is the labour theory of value. The last of the Schoolmen was Karl Marx.'

[58] This was Thomas Aquinas's view (cf. De Roover 1971, pp. 43–4); we may recall, among others, the similar view held by Heinrich von Langenstein, theology professor at the University of Vienna, who died in 1397. This means assuming as a given datum the social structure of rewards for the different kinds of labour, with even wide differentials that reflect the different social status of different economic activities. This aspect constituted a crucial distinction between appeals to labour costs in just price theories and in classical labour-value theories, which at least as an initial approximation refer to an undifferentiated common labour.

[59] Langholm 1998, pp. 87, 131, insists on the complementariness of two elements, cost and common estimate. However, the two elements may also be considered in opposition: for instance Juan de Medina (1490–1546) criticised Scotus' thesis that the just price should cover production costs, maintaining that the fact that the common estimate of a commodity may be inferior to its cost is part of the risks of commerce (cf. Chafuen 1986, pp. 100–1).

[60] The point is important: it implies the ethical priority of the economic scale of values over the ontological (cf. Viner 1978, p. 83). 'Otherwise, as Buridan remarks, a fly, which is a living being, would have a higher value than all the gold in the world' (De Roover 1971, p. 41). *Indigentia* was recalled among others by Thomas (cf. De Roover 1971, pp. 46–7, for textual references). De Roover (ibid., pp. 47–8) then recalls that Buridan (Jean Buridan, rector of Paris University around the middle of the fourteenth century, d. c.1372) solved the 'paradox of value' for which gold is worth more than water,

Olivi (1247–98: hence an author immediately following Thomas, and preceding Buridan by nearly a century) noted, we must refer to three sources of value: *virtuositas, complacibilitas* and *raritas*, namely ability to satisfy human needs, correspondence to the preferences of the person utilising the good and scarcity.[61]

The problem of the just price should not be confused with that of the legitimate price: following the tradition of Roman law doctrine and of canonical law, any transaction agreed on by the participants free from compulsion was considered as legitimate: *Tantum valet quantum vendi potest* ('A thing is worth as much as it can be sold for': a motto frequently repeated, with small variations, inter alia in Justinian's *Digest*).[62] The legitimacy of an act of sale voluntarily agreed on might be contested only in the case of *laesio enormis* (big damage), or in other words when the price agreed on was so different from the price prevailing in the market as to render wholly anomalous the act of exchange. According to the medieval just price theoreticians who accepted reference to the market price, the motto of the Latin jurists should be modified so as to explicitly connect the just price in the individual act of exchange to the average price: the glossator Accursius (1182–1260) proposed the expression *Tantum valet quantum vendi potest, sed communiter* ('A thing is worth as much as it can be commonly sold for').[63]

As we have seen, reference to the 'common' or market price did not imply recognising competitive mechanisms. The process of transition towards modern theory was long and implied radical changes in the prevailing culture, including the transfer of the economic problem from the field of ethics to that of scientific thinking (cf. below, § 3.2). Some elements of the transition were, however, foreshadowed in the full ripeness of Scholastic thought: such as the idea that justice in the field of economic activity involves keeping faith with the form of the contracts and not with

despite being less useful, referring to the abundance and scarcity of the commodities; according to De Roover, the treatment of value offered by Buridan remained unsurpassed by subsequent authors, Smith and Ricardo included, up to the 'marginalist revolution'.

[61] De Roover 1971, pp. 48–9; De Roover (ibid.) associates *virtuositas* with 'objective utility' and *complacibilitas* with 'subjective utility', and recalls that Bernardine from Siena (1380–1444) and Antoninus archbishop of Florence (1389–1459) repropose Olivi's theses. Buridan, instead, focused attention solely on 'objective utility'. Chafuen (1986, p. 91) and Langholm (1987, p. 124) remark that while the distinction between the two crucial aspects – scarcity and utility – should be attributed to Olivi, the terminology attributed to him is in fact to be found in a manuscript of his, but as a gloss at the margin of the sheet, in Bernardine's handwriting. The remarks by Olivi and the others are then taken up by the scholars of the 'Salamanca school': cf. Chafuen 1986, pp. 91–7. On Bernardine from Siena and Antoninus from Florence cf. Nuccio 1984–7, vol. 3, pp. 2573–684 and 2733–813.

[62] Cf. Langholm 1998, p. 78 and ff.   [63] Quoted in De Roover 1971, p. 53.

their content, once they have been freely agreed on by those concerned; and the progressive depersonalisation of the notion of the market.[64]

6.   Bullionists and mercantilists

In the period of the formation and rise of the nation-states, a new kind of thinking on economic phenomena flanked that of the theologians and philosophers with the 'counsellors of the prince'. Obviously these authors adopted in their writings the viewpoint of the economic power of the prince, as a complement to and necessary prerequisite of his military power. Significantly, a group of authors of this period was designed as *cameralists*, since they approached economic issues as members of the chamber of the counsellors to the sovereign. The notion of national wealth thus took on a central role in economic thinking.

The cameralists constituted an important step in the transition towards the birth of economic science, superseding undifferentiated treatment of the moral and the scientific problem in analysis of economic phenomena. We may distinguish two kinds of interpretations for the economic views prevailing in this period.

On the one hand, the laissez-faire view, from the physiocrats and Adam Smith on,[65] reacted to the viewpoint of the counsellors of the prince, accusing them of holding a basically erroneous notion of wealth: the so-called 'chrysoedonistic view', namely the simplistic identification of wealth with gold and precious metals in general. Hence the term *bullionists*, utilised for authors such as Thomas Gresham and John Hales in sixteenth-century England.[66]

---

[64] The term 'depersonalisation' is proposed by Langholm 1998, p. 99.

[65] The term 'mercantile system' was used by Mirabeau and other physiocrats 'in order to describe an economic policy regime characterised by direct state intervention, [. . .] more commonly known as "Colbertism"' (Magnusson 2003, p. 46). Cf. Smith 1776, pp. 429 ff. Smith's criticisms concerned all aspects of the 'mercantile' (or 'commercial') system: the notions of profit, wealth, foreign trade, the role of money; but in each of these respects Smith appeared to have constructed for himself a scapegoat, at least in part a caricature, in order to put emphasis by contrast on the different aspects of his theoretical building.

[66] Thomas Gresham (1519–79) is universally known for the so-called 'Gresham's law' according to which 'bad money drives out good money': 'bad' money, clipped (that is, from which some particles of gold have been filed away) or of a worse alloy, is used for the payments while 'good' money is treasured, and hence disappears from circulation. As a matter of fact this 'law' was a well-known fact, already recognised in previous writings (for instance by the French theologian Nicholas Oresme, 1320–82, who also anticipated Leibniz's view of the world as a gigantic clock set in motion by God: cf. Spiegel 1971, p. 74). To Gresham we should rather attribute the understanding of the mechanism of the 'gold points', namely of the limits to the oscillations of the rate of exchange between convertible currencies around the central value determined by the ratio between the

On the other hand, beginning with the German historical school and Schumpeter 1914,[67] we see a revaluation of these authors, credited with a less simplistic, and more or less justified view. The preoccupation with monetary issues could be justified by the fact that the stock of metallic money might be considered an index of national wealth in a period when there was virtually no statistical information on a country's yearly production. In addition, abundance of money stimulates trade. The accumulation of real capital was as a rule preceded or accompanied by accumulation of money capital. In any case, 'The scholars' attention focuses on capital movements and on their causes, on policy measures to attract money capital into the state, on good money; they worry about the level of the interest rate in comparison to that of other countries, since relatively high interest rates favour influx of capitals.'[68]

Moreover, this second interpretative current stresses that, apart from verbal homage, the central role attributed to precious metals was soon – at the turn of the sixteenth to seventeenth century – decidedly cut down to size. Still earlier, in 1516, Thomas More's *Utopia* had already stated the case in no uncertain terms against the excessive importance attributed to gold and silver. An example we will be focusing on in the next section concerns the Italian Antonio Serra. As we shall see, in 1613 he published a *Trattato delle cause che fanno abbondare d'oro e d'argento li regni ove non son miniere (Treatise on the causes that make kingdoms rich in gold and silver, where there are no mines)*, the content of which, for anybody who does not stop at the title, makes it clear that Serra identified the welfare of a country with its national product more than with the quantity of precious metals owned by its inhabitants.

On the same lines as Serra – and possibly, at least in some respects, under the influence of his work – we find the influential author Thomas Mun (1571–1641), an Englishman and a managing director of the India Company.[69] In defending the right of the Company to export precious

---

quantities of the precious metal embodied in each of them. (On this path he was followed by Davanzati, to whom we will briefly refer in § 7.) A lively dialogue, probably written in 1549 but published only in 1581 and then reprinted repeatedly, known as *A discourse of the common weal* (Anonymous 1549) is attributed to John Hales (d. 1571) or alternatively to Thomas Smith. With respect to this work, however, the accusation of chrysoedonism appears far from demonstrated, if we avoid isolating individual statements from their context.

[67] For a wider treatment, cf. Schumpeter 1954, pp. 335–76. Positive evaluations of the mercantile literature were more frequent in the 1930s; cf. in particular Heckscher 1931 and, on somewhat different lines, Keynes 1936, ch. 23.

[68] Vaggi 1993, p. 24.

[69] His best-known work (Mun 1664) was published posthumously, edited by his son, and was later included, together with the only known writing he published in his lifetime (Mun 1621), in the collection edited by McCulloch (1856) for the Political Economy Club. On Mun, cf. Forges Davanzati 1994 and the bibliography quoted there.

metals to the East in exchange for local commodities often destined to be re-exported to other European countries, Mun maintained that the export of money allowed the country to increase its wealth. In fact, through international trade, the commodities available to the country are increased, even more than through manufacturing and, at a still lower level, agriculture.

With his writings, Mun was reacting to the influential thesis advanced by Gerard Malynes (1586–1641), according to whom the English depression at the beginning of the 1620s was to be attributed to (merchants' and Jews') speculations on the foreign exchange, which had lowered the value of the English currency. Mun (and Misselden, d.1654) maintained that the fall of the exchange rate was caused by the negative balance of trade.[70] Mun's critique of Malynes's thesis is strikingly similar to Serra's 1613 critique of previous interpretations of the feebleness of the Neapolitan currency, illustrated in the next section.[71]

Mun's writings may be taken as the reference point for the transition from bullionism to mercantilism. In fact, we thus move from a more immediate nexus between wealth and precious metals to a more sophisticated view, characterised by a fully developed theory of the balance of trade, which looked at the balance of the foreign trade of a country as a whole, rather than to bilateral balances computed for each foreign country taken in isolation. This theory, together with the central role of the state in the economy, constitutes one of the main common elements – or so they were seen – which historians of economic thought have referred to in order to include under the same heading – i.e. mercantilism – authors who were often quite heterogeneous and active over a long period of time, stretching from the sixteenth to the eighteenth century, up to the publication of Adam Smith's *Wealth of nations*.[72]

It is however now recognised that the term 'mercantilism' must be applied very gingerly. Historians of economic thought such as Schumpeter (1914, 1954), Heckscher (1931) and Judges (1939) insisted on the fact that we cannot speak of a 'mercantilist school' in a rigorous sense, for

---

[70] 'It is a certain rule in our forraign trade, in those places where our commodities exported are overballanced in value by forraign wares, brought into this Realm, there our mony is undervalued in exchange; and where the contrary of this is performed, there our mony is overvalued' (Mun 1664, p. 208).

[71] It should be added that while Mun focused on the balance of trade, Serra also considered trade in services and capital movements.

[72] For a survey of some interpretations of mercantilism, cf. Wiles 1986; the most in-depth analysis, still compulsory reading, is Heckscher 1931; he interpreted mercantilism as a 'system of power'. A more recent analysis, rich and thorough, is Perrotta 1991; cf. also the essays collected in Magnusson 1993, in particular Perrotta 1993, concerned with Spanish mercantilists, often forgotten in the Anglo-Saxon literature, but historically quite important in the transition from Scholastic to mercantilist thought. Cf. also Magnusson 2003.

two kinds of reasons. First, on the positive side, the economic thinking of the time we are considering is much less simplistic, more differentiated and richer in contributions than the reductive interpretations might lead us to believe. Secondly, on the negative side, the authors of this period fail to attain a coherent system of interpretation of economic reality, not only at the analytical level but also on the plane of definition of concepts. In general, immediate practical interests dominated over theoretical work.

In order to size up the contribution that these authors left as heritage to the subsequent tradition we should first of all recognise its variety; moreover, we should admit that, even if most of them cannot be included in the category of pure laissez-faire exponents, this does not necessarily constitute a crime. On the contrary, it is precisely in the opinions they expressed on the role of the government that we find one of the most interesting aspects of the economic debate of the time.

In particular, we may attribute to the 'mercantile' literature an important role of cultural support to the rise of the nation-states, against the universalism of the Catholic Church and the medieval empire on the one hand, and the localism of the feudal power structure on the other. For the authors of the time, the objective was not so much individual well-being (as it was to be for Adam Smith: cf. below, § 5.4), but rather the politico-military power of the state. The active role attributed to intervention of political authority in the economic field, within this framework, concerned the expediency of stimulating national productive activity in competition with other countries: from discrimination in foreign trade to support for national manufactures through a system of customs duties on exports of raw materials and on imports of manufactures, up to creation of state-owned manufactures (such as the *manufactures royales* in France and the St Gobelin tapestries).[73]

Another salient feature of mercantilism was the 'fear of commodities' – or, in parallel, the 'dearth of money' – which were manifestations of a historical stage of transition between production for self-consumption predominant in the feudal economy, and production for the market, which was to dominate within capitalism. These views did not simply express the opinions of the rising mercantile bourgeoisie, but also showed

---

[73] This set of policies has been labelled Colbertism from the name of Jean Baptiste Colbert (1619–83), the powerful minister of finance of Louis XIV from 1661 up to his death, having for ten years been the main collaborator of Cardinal Mazarino. Together with measures concerning control of prices and productive techniques, Colbert also supported abolition of barriers to French internal trade and fiscal reforms based on direct taxation of consumption, as a tool for taxing the different social classes more equitably than did the then prevalent system of direct taxation (which largely exempted nobility, clergy and the king's favourites); but on this latter front the interests involved were strong, the results obtained by Colbert practically nil.

a notable capacity to interpret the requirements of economic and social development: as Smith later stressed, progress in the division of labour is regulated by gradual enlargement of the markets for the products of the individual firms; in other words, market expansion constituted a prerequisite for the development of the system of capitalistic firms. Furthermore, as a 'system of national power' mercantilism expressed the need for the right political and economic institutions for the rise of the market economy, from a certain and equitable fiscal system to the land registry, and more generally laws supporting the certainty of private property, up to the development of a banking and credit system.[74]

Interpretation of the specific proposals for economic policy and the specific theoretical theses alike can take on a variety of tones, often simply because different authors of the period are being considered. Thus, for instance, if we consider the theory of the 'balance of trade', on the one hand we have the idea that a positive balance of foreign trade is *the cause* – the main if not the sole cause – of national wealth, while on the other hand we have the thesis (to be found, for instance, in Serra's *Treatise*) that an active balance of trade is *an indicator* of the wealth of a country, i.e. of its productive strength and hence of its competitiveness in international markets. This latter view seems, however, to have been prevalent, considering the relationship of cause and effect that many authors of the period (Serra, Montchrétien and Mun being among the first to do so) established between national product and the balance of trade.[75]

Within the debate on foreign trade we also find the thesis of a hierarchy of the various kinds of activity. In fact a number of authors argued the expediency, for the purpose of developing national wealth, of exporting manufactures in exchange for raw materials, or luxury goods in exchange for subsistence goods, or products of skilled labour in exchange for the products of unskilled labour.[76] Furthermore, among the sectors of economic activity foreign trade was given first place, in order of strategic importance, followed by manufactures and then by agriculture.[77] Leaving aside the justifications adduced in support of such theories, we may

[74] We find proposals of this kind in an author like William Petty – cf. below, § 3.3 – who belonged to the mercantile period but who in our interpretation may be considered rather as the first of the classical economists, at least on the analytical plane.

[75] From this point of view Spain was considered a negative paradigm: available gold and silver deriving from mines in the colonies was absorbed, as if by a black hole, by a balance of payments deficit attributed to poor national production. On the relationship between the Spanish economic situation and the economic thought of the time, cf. Perrotta 1993.

[76] Cf. Perrotta 1991 for a series of examples.

[77] This hierarchy was followed by Mun (and then by William Petty), and differed from the one later proposed by the physiocrats: cf. below, § 4.4. It is obvious that, when confronted with the problem of identifying the factors determining national wealth at a given moment in time, once we have identified wealth with national product, any

recall that this historical period was characterised by the development of markets as national and international exchange networks, and by the accumulation of entrepreneurial wealth, above all in the hands of the big merchants at the outset.

Another interpretation only partly justified by the writings of certain mercantilist authors focuses on the notion of the *profit upon alienation*, i.e. profit deriving from sale and hence born of the circulation process, or in other words commerce. According to this thesis, quite simply, profits stem from buying cheap and selling dear. It was a thesis in consonance with the stage of mercantile capitalism, which among other things explained the privileged role attributed to foreign trade. In fact, the gains obtained by one party to the act of exchange correspond to the losses of the other party, so that when buyers and sellers belong to the same country the gains of some exactly offset the losses of the others. Therefore, trade may be the source of gains for the wealth of a country only when we consider exchanges with other countries. However, when it is taken to the extreme – profits stem solely from the act of exchange, with a basic qualitative distinction, not only a distinction of degree, between trade and other economic activities – this thesis proves both erroneous as a representation of the way the economic system works, and misleading as an interpretation of mercantilist authors, or at least a lot of them.[78] Even behind this thesis, however, we can detect crucial signs of the times, which today's economists tend to forget: the importance of military power in international economic relations; the spread of the colonies; and the monopolistic nature of the big trading companies. If we include in foreign trade also the transference of wealth enacted by force, the importance that this sector took on for what Marx called 'original accumulation' becomes clear, and the impression of unequal exchange that the theory of *profit upon alienation* conveys appears fully justified.

7.   The birth of economic thought in Italy: Antonio Serra[79]

The economic vitality of municipal Italy, the financial activity of Florentine bankers and the role of maritime republics – particularly

---

sector is in principle on the same level as any other sector, as Adam Smith stressed in opposition to the physiocrats. However, when confronted with the 'dynamical' problem of the development of the wealth of nations over time, the use of hierarchies between productive sectors may provide interesting pointers; mercantile analyses, in particular, had the distinctive merit from this point of view of preparing the ground for the Smithian distinction between productive and unproductive labour (cf. Perrotta 1988).

[78] As a matter of fact, at the beginning of the eighteenth century the thesis of mutual advantage for countries participating in international trade largely prevailed (cf. Wiles 1987, pp. 157–60, for some examples).

[79] This section utilises material from Roncaglia 1994, which contains a fuller treatment of Serra, his thought and fortune.

Venice – in international trade were accompanied by a flourishing of mercantile tracts and writings that incidentally touched on economic issues. However, there were very few authors of any interest for a history of economics. Among them, let us recall Gaspare Scaruffi from the Emilia region (1515–84; his *Alitinolfo* dates from 1582), and especially the Florentine Bernardo Davanzati (1529–1606), author of a *Notizia dei cambi* (1582) and of *Lezione delle monete* (1588). In the first of these two tracts, Davanzati illustrated the mechanisms of international finance of the time, while in the second he considered money as a social convention and stressed the possibility that its intrinsic value may be inferior, even far inferior, to its exchange value. A quantity theory of money, only vaguely sketched out, associated the exchange value (hence the level of commodity prices) with the quantity of money: a thesis which was not new, having been proposed by various authors particularly in France and Spain, but which, in the absence of a notion of the velocity of circulation, remained devoid of a sufficiently well-defined analytical structure.[80]

A contribution far more relevant to economic science, which we will now consider, emerged from a different environment, characterised by economic decline. This notwithstanding, it is a systematic and very perceptive analysis of the economy, touching on a broad range of economic issues: far superior to later mercantilist literature (including Mun 1621, 1664), and possibly disregarded in English histories of economic thought because of the language barrier. Hence our choice to provide a rather detailed account of his contribution.

On 10 July 1613, a prisoner in the Neapolitan prison of Vicaria, Doctor Antonio Serra from Cosenza, signed the dedication of his book, *Il breve trattato delle cause che possono far abbondare li regni d'oro e d'argento dove non sono miniere con applicazione al Regno di Napoli*. The book offered economic policy advice aimed at improving the conditions of the Neapolitan kingdom, seen to be lagging far behind other parts of Italy in development.

Of Antonio Serra himself we know hardly anything even today – in practice, only what can be gleaned from his book, namely that he was

---

[80] More or less rudimentary formulations of the quantity theory of money were already present in the literature before Davanzati: in Spain, in the famous Salamanca school the Dominican monk Navarro (Martin de Azpilcueta, 1493–1586) in 1556, and subsequently Tomás de Mercado in 1569; in France, Jean Bodin (1530?–96) in 1568. In a report to the Prussian parliament of 1522, which remained unpublished until the nineteenth century, Copernicus had also referred to the relationship between quantity of money and prices. Cf. Spiegel 1971, pp. 86–92, and Chafuen 1986, pp. 67–80. Copernicus' insight was truly notable, since the influx into Europe of gold and silver from the Spanish colonies in America, which drew attention to the relationship between quantity of money and prices, came some decades later: cf. Vilar 1960; Cipolla 1976. These formulations did not constitute a theory in the strict sense of the term, but went well beyond the vague references we find in previous literature, for instance in Pliny the Younger.

from Cosenza and that he was in prison in 1613. The reason for his imprisonment is uncertain; equally uncertain is his profession, unknown the dates of his birth and death.

His work surfaced from oblivion only a century after its publication, thanks to Galiani, who had words of high praise for it in his *Della moneta*.[81] The true artificer of the resurrection of the *Breve trattato* was Baron Pietro Custodi, who declared that he considered Serra 'the first writer of political economy' (Custodi 1803, p. xxvii), and assigned him the first place, violating the chronological order, in his famous collection of *Scrittori classici italiani di economia politica* (Classical Italian writers of political economy, in fifty volumes, 1803–16).

Let us first of all consider the structure and content of the book. After the dedication and the preface, the *Breve trattato* is divided into three parts. The first, and for us the most interesting, discusses 'the causes for which kingdoms may abound with gold and silver', as the title of chapter 1 went: that is, in substance, the causes – even if not the nature – of the economic prosperity of nations in the broadest sense of the term, also through comparison of conditions prevailing in the Kingdom of Naples with those prevailing in other parts of Italy, particularly Venice. The second part is substantially concerned with refuting the proposals advanced a few years earlier by Marco Antonio De Santis (1605a, 1605b) with the aim of reducing the exchange rate to attract money into the kingdom from outside. The third part presented systematic discussion of the different policy measures adopted or proposed 'in order to make money abundant within the Kingdom'.

The economic prosperity of a country, Serra explained, depends on 'own accidents', i.e. original characteristics specific to each country, and 'common accidents', or in other words more or less favourable circumstances that may be reproduced anywhere. Among the former, Serra mentioned 'abundance of materials', i.e. endowment of natural wealth, particularly fertile lands (Serra commonly utilised the term 'robbe', materials, for agricultural products), and 'the site', namely localisation 'with respect of other kingdoms and other parts of the world'. There are four 'common accidents': 'quantity of manufactures, quality of people, large amount of trade and capability of those in power'. In other terms: manufacturing production, moral qualities and professional skills of the population, extent of trade (especially international transit trade), and politico-institutional system, the latter being the most important of the

---

[81] Galiani 1751, pp. 339–40; the passage quoted is in the author's notes to the second edition, dated 1780.

four elements, 'since it may be said to be the efficient cause and the superior agent for all the other accidents' (Serra 1613, p. 21).

Having analysed these elements in the first seven chapters of the first part, Serra noted that, as far as the 'own accidents' were concerned, the Kingdom of Naples was at an advantage (except for the site), particularly in comparison with Venice: if Naples was so much poorer than Venice, this could only depend on 'common accidents'. In showing how this happened, and for what reasons gold and silver flowed out of the Kingdom of Naples, Serra reconstructed with great ingenuity the situation of the country's balance of trade, although without systematic treatment of this notion.

The second part of the *Breve trattato* was the longest of the three, and the least clear in exposition. Half of it (the first five chapters) was dedicated to confutation of De Santis' thesis that 'the high rate of exchange in Naples compared with other places in Italy is the only cause that made the Kingdom poor in money', since it caused letters of exchange to be used for payments from outside the Kingdom, while money was used for payments to outside the Kingdom.[82] Serra denied that the asymmetry could derive from the mechanism of the letters of exchange; the paucity of money in the Kingdom depended on the underlying imbalance in what we would now call the balance of payments. As a matter of fact, if we translate into our terminology what Serra maintained in his chapter 10, the influx of currency corresponding to exports of agricultural products was much more than offset by outflows for interest remittances on public debt and profit remittances on productive activities under the control of 'foreigners', especially Genoese and Florentine merchant-bankers. The remaining chapters of the second part of the *Breve trattato*, from the sixth to the twelfth, lined up the points against De Santis' proposal to fix a low exchange between Naples and other financial centres.[83]

Finally, part three discussed economic policies that could be applied to improve the situation of the Kingdom: administrative regulations on financial and currency markets, some already tried out (such as a ban on exports of money and precious metals, reduction of the exchange rate, use of foreign currency as internal means of payment, overvaluation of foreign currency and/or obligation to consign it to the national mint) and others – our author prudently said – that had only been proposed (increase in the face value of national money, reduction of its gold or silver content). The fifth chapter briefly discussed 'the right proportion between gold and

---

[82] 'The level of the exchange' is the price in national currency of a letter of exchange denominated in foreign currency.
[83] On Serra's contribution to the theory of exchanges, cf. Rosselli 1995.

silver'. Although not in principle opposed to administrative measures, Serra advanced some fairly drastic criticism of such interventions: when not actually counter-productive, they were at any rate ineffective, since – as we have seen – the real problem concerned the passive balance of payments.

In the final chapters, Serra stressed how difficult it was to tackle such basic problems, pointing as the main objective to development of productive activity in the Kingdom.

Thus, Serra considered the unbalance in the currency market to stem from a negative balance of payments, inclusive of so-called invisible items. In turn, this situation was seen to derive from a feeble productive structure and the scant entrepreneurial spirit of the subjects of the Kingdom of Naples: the theme that Serra chose to open his *Breve trattato*. There was, then, a decisive connection between scarcity of money in the Kingdom and its feeble productive structure, and it is precisely this connection that constitutes an answer to imputations that Serra identified wealth with money and precious metals:[84] a thesis which has no textual foundation in his work, where the problem of what constitutes what Adam Smith was later to call 'the wealth of nations' was not tackled directly, and which was in fact contradicted by the primary role attributed to productive activity.

As frequently happens in the historiography of economic thought, the contrasting evaluations of Serra's contribution to the development of economic science depended on the various positions of the participants in the theoretical debate. In this respect we can distinguish two extreme, conflicting theses already present in the historical literature of the nineteenth century. On the one hand we have the extreme laissez-faire approach of Francesco Ferrara, who condemned Serra out of hand together with any other authors who did not in principle reject any kind of public intervention in the economy.[85] On the other hand, we find the nationalism and empirical reformism of authors such as Custodi and Pecchio, and also

---

[84] Cf. Say 1803, p. 30; McCulloch 1845, p. 189; Ferrara 1852, p. xlix. The opposite opinion was held by Einaudi 1938, pp. 132–3, and Schumpeter 1954, pp. 353–4. We should recall that Einaudi was a staunch critic of bullionist views, going so far as to date the birth of economic science precisely at the stage when (with Botero, Petty and Cantillon) identification between precious metals and wealth was rejected (Einaudi 1932, pp. 219–25).

[85] Ferrara had been criticised for not having included Serra and other Italians in the first two volumes of his *Biblioteca dell'economista* (first series), dedicated instead to the physiocrats and Smith. Answering to this criticism in the preface to the third volume of the first series of the *Biblioteca* (dedicated to the 'Italian tracts of the XVIII century': Genovesi, Verri, Beccaria, Filangieri, Ortes), Ferrara 1852, pp. xliii–lvii, expressed a decidedly negative judgement of Serra's qualities as an economist, classifying him as a bullionist ('gold and silver were for him the only and supreme possible wealth', ibid., p. xlix) but saving him (ibid., pp. lv–lvi) as a patriot inspired with civic passion, maintaining that Serra's work actually aimed at insinuating into the reader, through comparison between Naples

List, who maintained the crucial importance of Serra's work as the first manifestation of a new science, precisely because of the reference made to the real economy and the role of industry, in its original sense of spirit of initiative, for the well-being of the nation.[86]

It is, indeed, a mistake to undervalue Serra, classifying him as one among the many mercantilist authors of the time responsible for such errors in representation of the economic system as can no longer be accepted after Adam Smith's critique. As we have seen, in fact, Serra attributed a central role to national productive activity, and thus could hardly be associated with the characterisation of mercantilism that has the wealth of nations stemming (mainly, if not solely) from foreign trade – a characterisation which, moreover, was also faulted by various other authors of the time.[87] However, it is also difficult to accept the opposite interpretative position, which went so far as to consider Serra the founder of economic science. To this end the importance attributed to real phenomena, in particular to manufacturing production, is certainly not sufficient, since in his work we would look in vain for a sufficiently clear exposition of the notion of surplus that constituted in the following two centuries the basis for the development of classical political economy; equally in vain would we look for even the slightest trace of any theory of value and distribution.[88]

It is, however, clear that Serra can have had scant influence if any at all on the initial stages in the development of political economy, given the minimal circulation of his work before it was reprinted in Custodi's series. Serra was not a mercantilist in the disparaging sense attributed to the label by the followers of Adam Smith, who had in fact created it, in book IV of the *Wealth of nations*, as a scapegoat for his animadversions on the feudal obstacles to economic initiative. Serra was an author as immune from sectarian interventionist ideas as he was from extreme laissez-faire views,

and Venice, the idea that the republic was a form of government superior to absolute monarchy, and considering it 'likely that Galiani had intended, by extolling the merits of the economist, to refer to the politician' (ibid., p. lvi). (The legend, widespread in the nineteenth century, of Serra as a patriot, imprisoned because of his political position, has no factual support whatsoever.)

[86] Cf. Custodi 1803; Pecchio 1832, pp. 45–50; List 1841, pp. 265–7, 271.

[87] Cf. Perrotta 1991.

[88] Serra's references to the 'quantity of manufactures [. . .] that exceeds the needs of the country' or to the 'surplus materials' (Serra 1613, p. 11) are insufficient in this respect. Moreover, it is not difficult to find precursors of Serra on specific points that drew praise from the commentators. For instance, Serra was preceded by the anonymous Genoese critic of De Santis (Anonymous 1605) in the importance attributed to invisible items in the balance of payments. Again, he was preceded by authors such as Botero 1589 for the importance attributed to 'man's industry', and by Scaruffi 1582 for the hostility to measures forbidding the export of money and precious metals.

who admitted public intervention in the economy when directed not at containing the interests of individual agents but rather at providing them with the right system to operate in. He was an author who did not identify wealth with money and precious metals, but who, unlike the most schematic among the classical authors of the eighteenth–nineteenth centuries, put his finger – almost intuitively, we might say – on the relationship of interdependence between financial and real aspects of the economy. He was an author not yet constrained by the classical notion of *homo oeconomicus*, who found it natural to connect political, social and economic aspects. Serra was an author of commendable mentality: 'favourable to activism, open to recognise the role of free will, idealistic, in contrast to the fatalistic, mechanical and materialistic [mentality] . . . of the classical economists'.[89] Serra, to sum up, well represented the potentialities of the formative stage of economic science, displaying openness to a variety of possible lines of theoretical development. Re-reading his *Breve trattato* serves to remind us that constructing well-defined conceptual and analytical structures may incur the cost of neglecting certain elements that play an important role in our understanding of reality.

[89] Tagliacozzo 1937, p. xxxiv.

3 William Petty and the origins of political economy[1]

1. Life and writings

Sir William Petty was born on 26 May 1623, the twentieth year of the reign of James I, in the village of Romsey, Hampshire (England), and died 26 December 1687 in London. To say that his life was eventful is an understatement.[2] The son of a clothier, he was a ship-boy on a merchant ship at the age of thirteen, but ten months later he was put ashore on the French coast with a broken leg. He supported himself by giving Latin and English lessons, and soon succeeded in gaining admission to the Jesuit college in Caen where he studied Latin, Greek, French, mathematics and astronomy. After serving in the Royal Navy, when the civil war broke out, he joined other refugees, first in Holland (1643), and then in Paris (1645-6), where he studied medicine and anatomy. When his father died in 1646 he returned to Romsey, but he soon went to London, where he tried unsuccessfully to exploit one of his own inventions, a machine capable of producing duplicate copies of a written text simultaneously, for which he had obtained a patent in 1646. In 1648, after a few months' study, he was awarded the degree of doctor of medicine at Oxford University. Here his career quickly blossomed, favoured by the political unrest of the period that led to the dismissal of the old professors who were considered to be supporters of the king. In 1650 Petty became professor of anatomy. In the following year he moved to the chair of music at Gresham College,

---

[1] In this chapter I use material drawn from my book on Petty (Roncaglia 1977), where the reader can find further details on the subject. Let us recall here that 'political economy' is the term by which economic science was commonly designated, until Marshall shifted to the now dominant term 'economics'; in contemporary economic literature, the term 'political economy' has been revived by those streams of research (such as the Marxists, the post-Keynesians, the Sraffians or neo-Ricardians) which lay stress on the social nature of economic activity.

[2] For Petty's biography see Fitzmaurice 1895; we should take into account that the author, a descendant of Petty, avoided stressing the worst features of his illustrious predecessor, but the information he provided is sufficient for perceiving the different sides of Petty's very complex personality.

53

London.[3] A short time later he left England again (though managing to retain his former appointments and emoluments), this time for Ireland as the chief medical officer of the English army sent there by Cromwell. After the victories over the Irish, Petty was entrusted with the task of conducting a geographical survey of the Irish lands, as the first step for distributing them among the English soldiers, the state domain and the financiers of the military expeditions. This was a most complex task, but Petty succeeded in completing it in only four years, between 1655 and 1658. In the process, he became a very rich man, with large properties in Ireland, and also thanks to the trade in debentures (representing rights to the lands to be distributed) sold by the soldiers.

For the rest of his life, Petty was busy with the administration of his lands, together with unending legal controversies over his Irish titles and taxes, and moved continuously between England and Ireland. In 1660–2 he took part in the founding of the Royal Society for the Improving of Natural Knowledge. In 1667 he married a widow, Elizabeth Waller, with whom he had five children; he had also fathered at least one illegitimate daughter, who later appeared on the scene in London as a dancer.

Only a small part of Petty's manuscripts (contained in many large boxes known as the 'Bowood papers' now deposited at the British Library) was published during his lifetime under his own name.[4] With the exception of the *Treatise of taxes and contributions* (1662), the main writings relating to economic matters were published after his death, when the 1688 revolution rendered the political climate more favourable to his ideas. Thus *Political arithmetick* was published in 1690, *Verbum sapienti* and *Political anatomy of Ireland* in 1691, *Quantulumcumque concerning money* in 1695, though they were written in 1664, 1676, 1672 and 1682, respectively. Among the works published in his lifetime, the *Natural and political observations upon the bills of mortality*, commonly considered as the first ever work of demography, appeared in 1662 under the name of John Graunt (1620–74), one of Petty's best friends, although it is most likely that Petty himself was the author of at least part of the work, probably trying to help Graunt to ensure his admission to the Royal Society.

---

[3] The transition from the chair of anatomy to that of music is less strange than it may appear, if we bear in mind not only the multifaceted nature of the intellectuals of those times, but also the fact that at the time mathematical relations were an essential part in the study both of human anatomy and of the laws of harmony. Thomas Hobbes, for example, studied the geometrical proportions among the various parts of the human body, and Descartes (1596–1650) in the *Compendium musicae* investigated the mathematical ratios that connect consonances, tonalities and dissonances. (The connection between music and mathematics has its roots in classical antiquity: Pythagoras, in the sixth century BC, studied the mathematical proportions expressing intervals in musical scales as numerical ratios: cf. Cammarota 1981, p. 17.)

[4] An extremely accurate bibliography, obviously excluding recent publications, is that edited by Charles Hull and published in the appendix to Petty 1899, pp. 633–60.

A collection of Petty's economic writings, including some unpublished material, appeared in 1899, edited by Charles Hull, under the title *The economic writings of Sir William Petty*. In 1927 and 1928 the Marquis of Lansdowne, a descendant of Petty, edited other previously unpublished material: *The Petty papers*, in two volumes, and *The Petty–Southwell correspondence*. An important manuscript, *A dialogue on political arithmetic*, was published in 1977 in a Japanese review.[5] A perceptive overview of the 'Petty papers' archives, and a comprehensive bibliography of significant secondary literature on Petty, are provided in Aspromourgos (2001).

2.   Political arithmetic and the method of economic science

William Petty is commonly remembered as the founder of political arithmetic.[6] This is not so much a branch of statistics, as an extension to the field of social sciences of the new ideas, and new view of the world, that were taking root in the field of natural science. With political arithmetic, in fact, Petty aimed to introduce the quantitative method into the analysis of social phenomena, so as to allow a more rigorous treatment of them:

[Algebra] came out of Arabia by the Moores into Spaine and from thence hither, and W[illiam] P[etty] hath applyed it to other than purely mathematicall matters, viz.: to policy by the name of *Politicall Arithmitick* by reducing many termes of matter to termes of number, weight, and measure, in order to be handled Mathematically.[7]

This methodological innovation reflected what was happening at the time in the natural sciences. The seventeenth century witnessed the new, quantitative approach to physics taking over from the old view of physics as a description of the sensible qualities of physical objects; in all fields of scientific research, measurement of quantities became the central object of enquiry. This was mirrored in the materialistic-mechanical view of man and the world, supported in particular by Thomas Hobbes (1588–1679), with whom Petty had studied anatomy in Paris in 1645. In Hobbes's view, the method of enquiry – the logic of quantities (*logica sive computatio*) – reflected the very nature of the object of enquiry.

The development of these new methodological criteria was accompanied by a radical critique of traditional culture dominated by Aristotelian thought. Bacon (1561–1626) had preceded Hobbes in this respect, and was one of the few authors whom Petty cited and for whom he expressed

---

[5] More recently, two fragments of algebraic analysis applied to economic issues have been published in Aspromourgos (1999); these fragments confirm the interpretation of Petty's method illustrated in § 2.

[6] Cf. for instance Marx 1905–10, vol. 1, pp. 344–52; Schumpeter 1954, pp. 210–15; Cannan 1932, pp. 14–17.

[7] Petty 1927, vol. 2, p. 15: letter to Southwell of 3 November 1687.

great admiration. In opposition to the syllogistic-deductive method of the Aristotelian tradition and the Renaissance tradition of pure empiricism (technicians and alchemists), Bacon proposed the inductive method, a fusion of empiricism and rationalism:

the men of experiment are like the ant; they only collect and use: the reasoners resemble spiders, who make cobwebs out of their own substance. But the bee takes a middle course; it gathers its material from the flowers of the garden and of the field, but transforms and digests it by a power of its own. Not unlike this is the true business of philosophy; for it neither relies solely or chiefly on the powers of the mind, nor does it take the matter which it gathers from natural history and mechanical experiments and lay it up in the memory whole, as it finds it; but lays it up in the understanding altered and digested.[8]

This was precisely the method followed by Petty, who did not limit himself to describing social phenomena in quantitative terms but also, and crucially, attempted to give a rational explanation to the assembled data. Indeed, he often went so far as to attempt to reconstruct the data required for an investigation on the basis of complicated chains of deductive reasoning of an arithmetic-quantitative nature that permitted the scarce available information to be exploited for a myriad of different purposes and which themselves constitute an excellent applied example of the new logic of quantities.

Furthermore, Petty emphasised his decision to ground his own analysis on *objective* data. This position was also representative of a widely accepted tendency within the new scientific approach, but Petty's explicit affirmations on the subject took on particular importance because his investigations were undertaken in the area of social, rather than natural, sciences.

In this respect, a famous passage from the Preface of his *Political arithmetick* (1690) can be considered as his manifesto.

The Method I take to do this, is not yet very usual; for instead of using only comparative and superlative words, and intellectual Arguments, I have taken the course (as a Specimen of the Political Arithmetick I have long aimed at) to express my self in Terms of *Number, Weight,* or *Measure*; to use only Arguments of Sense, and to consider only such Causes, as have visible Foundations in Nature; leaving those that depend upon the mutable Minds, Opinions, Appetites and Passions of particular Men, to the Consideration of others.[9]

We have here a clear-cut opposition to the logical-deductive method of the Scholastics, which was still dominant, although not all-powerful, in scientific research in the seventeenth century. It is necessary, however, to qualify this point by recalling that for Petty is was not only a matter of *recording* and *describing* reality 'in terms of number, weight, or measure',

---

[8] Bacon 1620, pp. 92–3: Book 1 of the *Aphorisms*, No. 95.   [9] Petty 1690, p. 244.

but rather a matter of expressing reality in such terms in order to *interpret* it by identifying its main characteristics and placing at the basis of his own theory 'only such causes, as have visible foundations in nature', that is, *objective*, rather than *subjective*, causes.

Somewhat hidden in Bacon, but already developed by Hobbes and other scientists, was the tendency to direct research towards identification of precise quantitative relationships between the phenomena under study. The first who had clearly expressed this tendency was Galileo (1564–1642), according to whom 'this great book which is open in front of our eyes – I mean the Universe – [. . .] is written in mathematical characters';[10] knowledge of the world therefore requires the construction of arithmetic or geometric models (Hobbes insisted in particular on the latter in his work).[11] Petty also adopted such a point of view, although in a more qualified form, and even proposed some quantitative relationships, such as those relating the price of commodities (e.g. diamonds) to their main physical characteristics (cf. below, § 4). Furthermore, a view of the world similar to that of Galileo and Hobbes was reflected in the formula 'number, weight, or measure' which Petty repeatedly utilised.[12] Political arithmetic was considered not only as the most appropriate

[10] Galilei 1623, p. 121. This was not a side issue: in the first stages of the theological controversy over Copernicus' and Galileo's thesis, that the earth moves around the sun, the Jesuit, then Cardinal, Roberto Bellarmino (1542–1621) had suggested that there would have been nothing wrong in proposing this as a useful hypothesis, but not as a true statement about reality (cf. Rossi 1997, pp. 118–20). Rejection of Cardinal Bellarmino's position, which at the time could appear as a subtle – typically Jesuit – political compromise but which in fact pointed towards a modern epistemological view, was expressed by Newton with the well-known motto, *hypotheses non fingo* ('I frame no hypothesis').

[11] In the same direction went Descartes (his main work, the *Discours de la méthode*, is dated 1637), founder of analytical geometry – his name has been given to the Cartesian axes – who conceived of the universe as of a mechanism. Younger than Petty were the German philosopher Gottfried Wilhelm von Leibniz (1646–1716) and the Englishman Isaac Newton (1643–1727), inventors of differential calculus.

[12] Such a formula derives from the Bible: 'You ordered all things by measure, number, weight', it is said in the Book of Wisdom, xi:20. The motto by itself is open to various uses; for instance, it was used in a way completely different from Petty's by Pufendorf (1672, p. 731), who represented the theoretical position of the 'natural law' stream of thought. Petty's followers – the 'political arithmeticians' Gregory King (1648–1712) and Charles Davenant (1654–1714) – appear to have interpreted it prevailingly in the limited meaning of description of quantitative phenomena. It is true that there is the so-called 'King's law', connecting increases in the price of corn to decreases in crops compared to the normal level; however – leaving aside the issue of whether such a 'law' should be attributed to King or to Davenant, with Lauerdale (1804) and Tooke (1838–57) favouring the first, and Jevons (1871, pp. 180 ff.) opting for Davenant – we are in any case confronted with a simple presentation of data to which no analytical reasoning was attached. To Petty, political arithmetic meant something more and different: it aimed at discovering the quantitative relations that constitute the very basic structure of social reality – in analogy to what physical laws do according to Galileo – since it identified the elements essential to what had been selected as the object of investigation, and abstracted from the elements that were considered useless or of minor importance: those that, as Ricardo

instrument for the description of reality, but also for representing it, precisely because, according to the materialistic-mechanical conception supported by Galileo and Hobbes, a quantitative structure is embedded in reality itself.

Another essential feature of the new methodological approach adopted by Petty was the sharp separation between science and ethics, necessary for the dominance of man over nature asserted by Bacon in his *Instauratio magna* and enthusiastically adopted by Hobbes: the moral problem could not arise for science in itself, since it is simply a means, but only for the ends that man proposed to attain by means of the utilisation of its results. This position has remained dominant up to the present day, although with recurring crises (consider, for instance, the debate on biotechnologies), and has been of decisive importance for the development of human sciences.[13]

3.   National state and economic system

Money, international trade and the fiscal system were already subjects of everyday debate in Petty's time. What primarily differentiated Petty's treatment of these subjects from that of his contemporaries and predecessors, beyond differences in the positions he supported, was the method that he applied to analyse them: a method that he dubbed 'political arithmetic' and 'political anatomy'. The object of Petty's analysis was the 'body politick', that is, the state, in the combined sense of political system and economic system: common terms nowadays but which Petty never used. Nor, indeed, did either Petty or his contemporaries feel the need to distinguish between the two aspects.

The birth of capitalism is generally connected to the birth of the nation-state. A unified conception of the nation-state, giving particular attention to the problem of the political unification of the city and the countryside, was developed by Machiavelli. From the complex network of social interdependences he singled out, as being of greatest importance, those among citizens of the same state, and between the sovereign and his subjects.

---

was to put it a century and a half later, only 'modify' the analysis but do not change its substance.

With an analogous meaning Petty used the term 'political anatomy', as the study of 'structure, symmetry and proportions' of the 'body politick': once again Petty indicated that his aim was to provide a selective interpretation of the complexities of the real world, focusing attention on what he considered as the essential characteristics of the functioning of the 'body politick'.

[13] Within these latter ones, the crucial point of transition was represented by Niccolò Machiavelli (1469–1527; his main work, *Il principe*, is dated 1513), whose writings, not by accident included in the index of forbidden books, enjoyed a very large circulation in the sixteenth and seventeenth centuries.

Petty adopted a similar view, with his notion of the 'body politick'. This implied a bi-directional choice concerning the level of aggregation. A lower level of aggregation was rejected because relations among citizens of a single state, and between the sovereign and its subjects, are considered as fundamental with respect, for example, to relations between inhabitants of the same village or between a justice of the peace (or any other local government official) and those who are under his jurisdiction. A higher level of aggregation was rejected because the system of international relations among citizens of the various states was considered as being subordinate to the interrelations among the states themselves.

However, the notion of the 'body politick' did not yet correspond to the modern notion of an economic system. Machiavelli was 'only [. . .] able to express his programme and his tendency to relate city and countryside in military terms'.[14] Analogously, in Petty the notion of 'body politick' indicates the fact that the web of relations and exchanges that constitute the life of a productive system are subordinate to a unique political authority. Neither Machiavelli nor Petty perceived the interrelations that exist between city and countryside, or between agriculture and industry, from the point of view of production. They were thus compelled to identify the unifying element in the political superstructure.[15] As we shall see in the next chapter, it was precisely the ability to go beyond this limit, and to discover the technological relations of production that link the various sectors of the economy, which constituted Quesnay's major contribution to the development of economic science.

Machiavelli's and Petty's writings reflected the still-limited development of the productive structure of their period. The mining, manufacturing, agricultural, cattle breeding and fishing activities that Petty had launched on his Irish properties, for instance, were largely vertically integrated, with only very rough bookkeeping distinctions between different stages of the productive processes and different sectors. In addition, changes in political institutions were necessary for the transition from feudalism to capitalism, for example in order to guarantee private property in the means of production and the possibility of buying and selling them. This was especially true for land, both because of the primary importance of agriculture in the economy of the time, and because of the connection between its possession and feudal rights, which imposed obstacles to its unfettered transferability. Let us recall in this respect Petty's insistent

---

[14] Gramsci 1975, p. 1575. Town and countryside correspond by and large to manufactures and agriculture, the two sectors into which initially modern productive activity was classified. Cf. below (§ 4.5) where Cantillon is discussed.

[15] Cf. Roncaglia 1988.

support for the creation of a land registry, and in general for a stan-dardisation of deeds for landed property. The still partial notion of the economic system adopted by Petty, in the wake of the notion of the state proposed by Machiavelli, should be understood as an expression of a par-ticular historical phase, that of the transition from feudalism to industrial capitalism.[16]

The notion of the 'body politick' briefly illustrated here underlay Petty's specific views on subjects such as money, foreign trade and taxes. Petty's writings were not systematic treatises, but immediate interventions in the then current political debates. Often these writings were brief working notes, or memoranda for the king, aimed at demonstrating policy theses, such as the economic strength of England relative to France and hence the possibility for a greater political autonomy of the English king.

As far as money is concerned, we may stress an important differ-ence between Petty's views and those dominant at the time. This dif-ference becomes evident in his substituting the traditional comparison between money and blood[17] with another parallelism: between political and human anatomy:

Money is but the Fat of the Body-politick, whereof too much doth as often hinder its Agility, as too little makes it sick. 'Tis true, that as Fat lubricates the motion of the Muscles, feeds in want of Victuals, fills up uneven Cavities, and beautifies the Body, so doth Money in the State quicken its Action, feeds from abroad in the time of Dearth at Home; evens accounts by reason of its divisibility, and beautifies the whole, altho more especially the particular persons that have it in plenty.[18]

---

[16] For each stage in history, the central object of analysis for the economist may be identified in that level of aggregation that corresponds to the qualitative jump between economic integration and non-integration: the hunting tribe, the agricultural village, the feudal castle with surrounding lands, the principality linking town and countryside, and finally the nation-state. However, definition of the economic system as corresponding to the nation-state is also relative to a specific historical stage, and does not constitute an immutable law of nature: the process of enlargement of the area of integration may not stop at the nation-state, but tend to embrace the whole of the market economies. As a matter of fact, the tendency towards demolition of customs barriers and to the unification of jurisprudence in the field of business is at the heart of increasing worldwide economic integration, both as international division of labour and as unification of the markets (so-called 'globalisation').

[17] As used for instance by Hobbes 1651, p. 300. As we have already recalled in the previous chapter, liberal historians of economic thought, from Smith himself onward, went so far as to attribute to Petty's contemporaries, classified as mercantilists, the identification of wealth with precious metals; to this, they opposed the classical notion of money as a veil, according to which the quantity of money in circulation in an economic system is irrelevant for the explanation of the 'real' variables of the economy, such as income and employment.

[18] Petty 1691b, p. 113. Another interesting definition of money was given by Petty in a brief glossary of economic terms: 'Mony. Is the comon measure of commodityes. A comon bond of every man upon every man. The equivalent of commodityes' (Petty 1927, vol. 1, p. 210).

According to Petty, 'the blood and nutritive juyces of the body politick' are constituted by the 'product of husbandry and manufacture'.[19] This comparison points in the direction of the classical notion of the economic system based on the division of labour as functioning through a circular process of production, exchange, reconstitution of initial inventories of means of production and consumption goods, and new production process. We should recall in this respect that the discovery of the circulation of blood, made by Harvey at the beginning of the seventeenth century,[20] had generated lively interest and that Petty (like Quesnay after him) was a physician.

Petty did not provide an explicit and systematic treatment of the three functions of money – unit of measure, medium of exchange, store of value – but recognised them (which is not particularly striking, since we may say the same for a number of his predecessors and contemporaries), and discussed perceptively aspects of each of them. In particular, together with Locke (cf. below, § 4.2), Petty may be singled out for his notion of the velocity of circulation (though the term is not used), estimated on the basis of the institutional characteristics of the economic system such as the payment periods for wages, rents and taxes and utilised for determining the optimal quantity of money. In order to reduce the quantity of precious metals necessary for monetary circulation (in other terms, in order to increase the velocity of circulation) Petty repeatedly proposed the institution of land banks (followed in this by Nicholas Barbon, 1690).

Connected to his ideas on money are those concerning foreign trade. Petty, agreeing with his contemporaries, considered desirable a surplus in the balance of trade as a means of inducing an influx of precious metals into the country. In fact he maintained the relative superiority of gold, silver and jewels to other goods, due to their durability and to their role as a means of exchange and a store of value. However, he considered the positive balance of trade target as subordinate to that of a high level of internal employment and production. He thus recommended reducing imports through substitution of domestically produced goods, which satisfies both the objective of a positive trade balance and increased domestic employment. At the same time he refused to condemn importation of even luxuries and non-durable consumption goods, if this permits export of domestically produced goods which would otherwise not find a market, thus indicating that a high and increasing level of productive activity was considered the principal objective. To this end he also considered favourably importation of foreign capital and immigration of skilled

---

[19] Petty 1662, p. 28.
[20] William Harvey (1578–1657) announced his discovery in 1616, but published it only twelve years later (*Exercitatio anatomica de motu cordis et sanguinis*, 1628).

foreign labourers, condemning any legislation prohibiting or hindering such movements.[21]

As for taxation, Petty considered a reform of the fiscal system as the first step for ensuring uniformity of conditions within the country and certainty of rules for the economic game: two prerequisites for the development of an economy based on private initiative.

The largest part of the *Treatise of taxes and contributions*, one of Petty's main works, is concerned with the systematic examination of the various types of government income, and he returned to this issue in various places in his other work. He painted a picture of an intricate labyrinth of often self-contradictory regulations. Petty considered such a situation to be one of the major 'impediments of England's Greatness', while at the same time insisting that these obstacles 'are but contingent and removable' (Petty 1690, p. 298), since they derived from the stratification caused by continuous additions to the initial system which, as a result, no longer served its original purpose and had lost its initial coherence. Thus, the burden of taxation was borne almost exclusively, and with varying and unpredictable intensity, by the landowner and depended on 'the casual predominancy of Parties and Factions' (with great anguish for Petty, constantly involved in fighting with the 'Farmers of public revenue' and in general defending his personal interest as a big landowner in Ireland). In addition, the cost of collection, subcontracted to private agents, was very high and brought further elements of injustice and uncertainty into the system (ibid., p. 301). Petty did not propose to rationalise the system by returning it to its original state, conscious of the irreversible changes that over time had intervened in the economy. Thus, for example, in considering public offices (that is, positions assigned to private citizens at the pleasure of the sovereign, to provide public services remunerated not from the public purse but by charges levied directly on users), Petty pointed out that these positions had multiplied, due to society's increasing complexity, and had expanded in size while assuming increasingly a routine character, so that much of the original justification for the high tariffs charged, achieved through the granting of positions of legal monopoly, had been eliminated.

Petty proposed proportional taxation, levied on consumption, since only that constitutes 'actual' riches.[22] The proportionality criterion is 'just', leaving income distribution unaffected by taxation (and in Petty's

---

[21] On these aspects cf. for instance Petty 1662, pp. 59–60; 1690, pp. 271, 309; 1691b, p. 119.

[22] Cf. Petty 1662, pp. 91–2. In this Petty was preceded by Hobbes, and was to be followed by a long series of economists, up to Luigi Einaudi and Nicholas Kaldor in the twentieth century.

opinion the differences in wealth and income are necessary to economic growth). Besides, taxes on consumption encourage parsimony, avoid double taxation ('forasmuch as nothing can be spent but once') and ease the gathering of statistics on the economic conditions of the nation, which are essential for good government. Fiscal regulations must be certain, simple, clear and evident (also in order to avoid controversies and legal proceedings that constitute a social waste), impartial and with low collection costs.

4.   Commodity and market

We saw above (§ 1.4) that the first stage of economic theorising consists in formulation of a set of key concepts, which are then utilised in a second stage of analysis for construction of theoretical systems. Petty's contribution to economic science referred primarily to the first stage. In this section we will consider an aspect of crucial importance, the (obviously interrelated) notions of commodity, market and price, and we will illustrate the form these concepts assumed in Petty's writings.

As for the notions of commodity and market, we may refer to the few pages of a brief essay written in the form of a dialogue, the *Dialogue of diamonds*, that remained unpublished up to 1899, when Hull published it in his edition of Petty's economic writings.[23]

The protagonists of the dialogue are two: Mr A, representing Petty himself, and Mr B, an inexperienced buyer of a diamond. The latter sees the act of exchange as a chance occurrence, a direct encounter producing a relationship of conflict between buyer and seller, rather than a routine episode in an interconnected network of relationships, each contributing to the establishment of stable behavioural regularities.

The problem is a difficult one because the specific individual goods included in the same category of marketable goods – diamonds in our case – differ the one from the other on account of a series of quantitative and qualitative elements, even leaving aside differing circumstances (of time and place) of each individual act of exchange. Thus, in the absence of a norm which might allow the establishment of a unique reference point for the price of diamonds, Mr B considers exchange as a risky act, since it appears impossible for the buyer to avoid being cheated, in what for him is a unique event, by the merchant who has a more extensive knowledge of the market.

In the absence of a web of regular exchanges, that is of a market, the characteristics and circumstances of differentiation mentioned above operate in such a way as to make each act of exchange a unique episode, where the price essentially stems from the greater or lesser bargaining

---

[23] Petty 1899, pp. 624–30.

ability of seller and buyer. The existence of a market, on the contrary, allows transformation of a large part of the elements that distinguish each individual exchange from any other into sufficiently systematic differences in price relative to an ideal type of diamond taken as a reference point. There is thus a relationship between the emergence of a regular market on the one hand and, on the other hand, the possibility of defining as a commodity a certain category of goods, abstracting from the multiplicity of effective exchange acts, a theoretical price representative of them all.

Mr A, the expert, is in fact aware of the existence of precise quantitative relationships between the prices of different types of diamond determined by weight, dimension, colour and defects. After explaining the manner in which each element is quantitatively assessed through determination of grading scales for the qualitative elements, he then goes on to explain how each single element, and then their combinations, affects prices (once the price of a specific kind of diamond assumed as a reference point has been somehow determined: an issue taken up below, in § 5). Thus, for example, 'The general rule concerning weight is this that the price rises in duplicate proportion of the weight.'[24] A similar rule applies to the dimension. The average of the prices obtained on the basis of these two rules determines the 'political price' (a notion to be considered below) as given by both weight and dimension. This will be the price for a diamond without defects and with good colour. Adjustment coefficients will then be applied to determine the price of diamonds exhibiting defects or less valued coloration, scales for such coefficients being provided by the market. Naturally the blind application of these rules to determine diamond prices may lead on occasion to absurd results, whose correction will require the application of adjustments determined by experience as well as by simple common sense.

Petty's writings thus offer a representation of the process of abstraction leading to the concepts of market and commodity from the multiple particular exchanges that occur in the economy. Two qualifications are, however, necessary.

First, a diamond is a commodity whose price is determined more by scarcity with respect to demand than by its cost of production; we have here a market isolated from other markets, at least as far as productive interrelations are concerned.

---

[24] Petty 1899, p. 627. This rule, together with similar ones, was also proposed by Petty in the *Discourse concerning the use of duplicate proportions* (1674), in which he tried to represent in terms of functions the relations between pairs of variables, when there are empirical regularities linking the phenomena being considered, and such phenomena are liable to quantitative expression. This attempt places Petty among the forerunners, if not the founders, of econometrics.

Second, Petty only implicitly specified the analytical consequences of the fact that the market itself is an abstraction. Let us consider this point, and try to integrate the hints offered by the *Dialogue of diamonds*.

As we have just stated, the market is an abstraction, in the sense that each individual act of exchange concerns a specific diamond, exchanged at a specific time and place, at a specific price. The market exists as a concept which is useful, indeed indispensable, to an understanding of the functioning of a mercantile and then capitalistic economic system, precisely because it is possible to abstract from the myriad of individual exchanges a given set of relationships which can be considered as representative of actual experience and which can provide a guide to behaviour.

The same considerations apply to the concept of the commodity. In fact, reality is composed of an infinite number of specific individual objects. We group them into categories, such as diamonds, on the basis of some affinities to which we attribute central importance while ignoring elements of differentiation considered as of secondary importance. In other words, the commodity is not an atom of economic reality, but is itself an abstraction, that already implies a certain level of aggregation.

The most opportune level of aggregation is determined by the extent of the interrelationships between the various acts of exchange. Thus we can speak of different individual diamonds as belonging to a single commodity, with its own specific market, because the links among various individual exchanges of particular diamonds are such as to render acceptable the hypothesis that they are one and the same good, since they permit reduction of all differences of weight, dimension and quality to quantitative price differences. On similar grounds we may speak of the market for apples, or of the fruit market, or of the market for food in general: apples, fruit or food may be considered in turn as a commodity according to the level of aggregation thought to be most adequate, keeping in mind the relationships that come into play within the group of producers and within the group of buyers.[25]

---

[25] A typical example of the possibility of defining a commodity on the basis of the level of abstraction implicit in a particular analytical framework was offered by Petty (1662, p. 89) who identified 'corn' with 'food' in general when he spoke of 'Corn, which we will suppose to contain all necessaries for life, as in the Lords Prayer we suppose the word Bread doth.' This identification was later adopted implicitly by Ricardo in the *Essay on corn* of 1815 (Ricardo 1951–5, vol. 4, pp. 1–42), who was quickly criticised by Malthus (letter to Ricardo dated 12 March 1815, ibid., vol. 6, p. 185). More recently, Petty's hypothesis was explicitly referred to by Marshall (1890, p. 509 n. 2) and by Sraffa (1925, p. 61 n.). The situation is substantially different in the modern theories of intertemporal general economic equilibrium with contingent markets (cf. below, § 17.2), according to which the same physical good constitutes as many different commodities as the possible instants in which the good is made available, multiplied by the 'states

Some abstraction is also necessary in formulating the concept of price so as to deal with the analytical problem of determining relative prices, namely exchange ratios between different commodities. Indeed a 'price' corresponds to a 'commodity'; it represents a multiplicity of values, each relative to an individual act of exchange, when such acts of exchange concern goods sufficiently similar among themselves as to be included under the unique label of the same commodity (as in the case illustrated above of the 'price' of the 'diamond'). Furthermore we have to delimit the set of acts of exchange to which we refer as the basis for our notion of price, relative to the time and space in which they take place.

Petty thus distinguished between current price and *political price*; the latter corresponds to the theoretical price determined on the basis of an analytical scheme which abstracts from a number of elements present in reality but considered as of secondary importance. As we shall see, this distinction corresponds to the distinction between intrinsic causes determining the political price, and extrinsic causes, those variable and contingent causes which combine with the former to determine the current price.

Petty tackled explicitly this problem in a passage of the *Treatise of taxes and contributions* and in the *Dialogue of diamonds*. In the *Treatise* Petty introduced three definitions, which distinguish different concepts of price corresponding to different levels of abstraction in the analysis: natural price, political price and current price. The natural price depends on the state of technological knowledge and on subsistence required for the workers. In addition to this, the political price takes social costs, such as labour input in excess of necessary labour, into account: such costs are considered by Petty as waste, indicative of the fact that actual production is lower than potential production. Finally, the current price is defined

of the world' possible in each instant (so that an umbrella in 227 days' time under rain is a different commodity from the same umbrella available in 184 days' time, or 227 days from now if it does not rain). The axiomatic character of such theories induces theoreticians to think that the meaning of the variables is a problem external to the theory itself. But such a theory requires, as the example shows, that disaggregation be pushed to the maximum extent: up to the 'atom', namely to a notion of commodity not capable of further disaggregation. Thus, bearing in mind the infinity of points in the continuum of space and time, and the infinity of possible 'states of the world' (that add to the myriad of different physical characteristics of a commodity, as in the case of diamonds discussed below), all this implies that the number of commodities grows without limits, so that it seems quite likely that there are more commodities than real acts of exchange. But then, by definition, we are not confronted with a market, that is, with a web of relations between a multiplicity of buyers and sellers: the notion of commodity proposed by such theories is incompatible with the notion of competition. This example, here only sketched, shows the possibility of logical contradictions stemming from the meaning attributed to the variables subject to theoretical analysis.

as the expression of the political price in terms of the commodity used as standard of measure.[26]

Petty's 'natural price' thus has the meaning of a target, or an optimal price. It is in fact the price corresponding to the best technology available, and to the most efficient possible operation of the 'body politick'. For classical economists, from Smith to Marx, the 'natural price' has a different meaning, which corresponds closer to that of Petty's 'political price', since it points to the price which regulates the behaviour of the market and depends on the actual conditions of production prevailing in the economic system (Marx would subsequently refer to these conditions with the expression 'socially necessary labour').[27] It appears that Petty distinguished between these two notions, in a historical period of far from fully developed capitalism, in order to emphasise the higher costs attached to the then still backward level of social organisation. It should also be noted that the current price mentioned in the passage above is itself a theoretical variable, since it is simply the political price expressed in terms of money. On the other hand, it is clear that there are a number of other elements which influence the actual exchange ratios in the marketplace.[28]

---

[26] 'Natural dearness and cheapness depends upon the few or more hands requisite to necessaries of Nature: As Corn is cheaper where one man produces Corn for ten, then where he can do the like but for six; and withall, according as the Climate disposes men to a necessity of spending more or less. But Political Cheapness depends upon the paucity of Supernumerary Interlopers into any Trade over and above all that are necessary, *viz.* Corn will be twice as dear where are two hundred Husbandmen to do the same work which an hundred could perform: the proportion thereof being compounded with the proportion of superfluous expence, (*viz.* if to the cause of dearness abovementioned be added to the double Expence to what is necessary) then the natural price will appear quadrupled; and this quadruple Price is the true Political Price computed upon naturall grounds. And this again proportioned to the common artificiall Standard Silver gives what was sought; that is, the true Price Currant' (Petty 1662, p. 90).

[27] The analogy refers to the technology in use: both Petty's political price, and the natural price of classical economists, are based on what there is, that is, on the prevailing and not on the optimal technology, to which, as already said, Petty's 'natural price' seems to refer. But according to classical economists and Marx there is a mechanism, competition, that eliminates waste and tends to bring the prevailing technology towards the optimal one. Petty instead (understandably, given the epoch in which he lived) attributed such a role mainly to institutional reforms aiming at increasing the efficiency of the system. (There was an element of optimality in the Smithian conception of the natural price as well, because of the reference to conditions of free competition: cf. below, § 5.6, and Roncaglia 1990b.)

[28] 'But forasmuch as almost all Commodities have their Substitutes or Succedanea, and that almost all uses may be answered several wayes; and for that novelty, surprize, example of Superiors, and opinion of unexaminable effects do adde or take away from the price of things, we must adde these contingent Causes to the permanent Causes abovementioned, in the judicious foresight and computation whereof lies the excellency of a Merchant' (Petty 1662, p. 90).

In the *Dialogue of diamonds* Petty returned to the distinction between two groups of factors affecting the price of diamonds: intrinsic factors and extrinsic, or contingent, factors. The former concur in determining the political price (i.e. the theoretical price), while the latter explain the divergence of current price from political price. Extrinsic factors correspond to casual circumstances of specific acts of exchange, so that it is difficult to define them and apply to them precise rules for their reduction to homogeneous, comparable magnitudes. Intrinsic factors, on the other hand, are identifiable with precision, and it is possible to translate them in terms of price differences according to well-defined rules which may be determined by observation of the generality of exchanges that actually occur in the marketplace.

In the *Dialogue of diamonds* Mr A, the market expert, illustrates the point in the following way:

The deerness or cheapness of diamonds depends upon two causes, one intrinsec which lyes within the stone it self and the other extrinsec and contingent, such as are 1. prohibitions to seek for them in the countrys from whence they come. 2. When merchants can lay out their money in India to more profit upon other commoditys and therefore doe not bring them. 3. When they are bought up on feare of warr to be a subsistence for exiled and obnoxious persons. 4. They are deer neer the marriage of some great prince, where great numbers of persons are to put themselves into splendid appearances, for any of theise causes if they be very strong upon any part of the world they operate upon the whole, for if the price of diamonds should considerably rise in Persia, it shal also rise perceivably in England, for the great merchants of jewels all the world over doe know one another, doe correspond and are partners in most of the considerable pieces and doe use great confederacys and intrigues in the buying and selling of them.[29]

Of particular interest is the conclusion of the passage, where Petty described a worldwide market and stressed the fact that contingent events taking place in any one part of the world can have an impact on any other part, because the various local markets for diamonds are integrated in a single, unified world market ('the great merchants of jewels all the world over doe know one another'). On the other hand, it may surprise us to see the prohibitions mentioned above included among the contingent elements, for they are institutional elements, and as such one might expect that they should be included among the elements that determine the political price. Apart from his rather low attention to consistency between his different writings, it is possible that Petty, in his self-attributed role of adviser to the king, considered certain institutional obstacles to the development of exchange, and of the economy as a whole, as susceptible

---

[29] Petty 1899, p. 625.

of elimination. This applied specifically to restrictions on foreign trade. As we have stressed above, the theoretical distinction between natural prices and political prices, like other elements in Petty's analysis, should be interpreted in the light of the practical intentions of the author, who wanted to emphasise the detriment caused by certain institutional elements to the expansion of England's wealth. Leaving this issue aside, we are left with a bi-partition between natural and political prices on the one hand, and current prices on the other, which clearly anticipates the classical distinction between natural and actual, or market, prices.

5.   Surplus, distribution, prices

We have seen how Petty contributed to the formation of a conceptual representation of the working of an economic system. Let us now consider the extent and limits of his contribution with regard to the construction of an analytic system: the issues concerning surplus, prices and distribution, that constituted in the golden period of classical political economy, and still constitute today, the central core of economic theory.

Within relatively advanced analyses, the different aspects of this issue appear as inseparable. In order to measure the surplus, in fact, it is necessary to determine relative prices; this in turn implies hypotheses on distribution of the surplus between different sectors (such as the competitive hypothesis of a uniform rate of profits) and between the main social classes. However, in Petty's analysis the essential nexus – an adequate theory of prices – was missing. This allows us to consider separately his notion of the surplus and his ideas about the measure of value and exchange ratios.

In fact, identification of the concept of the surplus is traditionally considered to be one of Petty's most important contributions, even if for him the surplus took the partial form of rent (and taxes) and, derivatively, that of rent on money capital (interest):

Suppose a man could with his own hands plant a certain scope of Land with Corn, that is, could Digg, or Plough, Harrow, Weed, Reap, Carry home, Thresh, and Winnow so much as the Husbandry of this Land requires; and had withal Seed wherewith to sow the same. I say, that when this man hath subducted his seed out of the proceed of his Harvest, and also, what himself hath both eaten and given to others in exchange for Clothes, and other Natural necessaries; that the remainder of Corn is the natural and true Rent of the Land for that year; and the *medium* of seven years, or rather of so many years as makes up the Cycle, within which Dearths and Plenties make their revolution, doth give the ordinary Rent of the Land in Corn.[30]

[30] Petty 1662, p. 43.

Rent is expressed here in physical terms, as a given amount of corn. This is possible because the product is homogeneous, while heterogeneous means of production are all expressed in terms of the single produced good; this includes labour which is assumed to receive its means of subsistence, also expressed in terms of corn ('what himself hath both eaten and given to others in exchange for Clothes'). The problem of prices does not then exist, for it is implicitly assumed that exchange ratios between produced good and means of production may be considered as given.

In order to overcome this limitation, we may follow another route. Namely, we may consider the sector which produces corn as all-comprehensive, covering all productive activities necessary to ensure replacement of its necessary means of production.[31] Petty made use of such a procedure in order to determine the relative value of commodities, considering as equivalent the surplus quantities of each commodity produced by (vertically integrated) sectors which utilise the same quantity of labour:

> But a further, though collaterall question may be, how much English money this Corn or Rent is worth? I answer, so much as the money, which another single man can save, within the same time, over and above his expence, if he imployed himself wholly to produce and make it; *viz.* Let another man go travel into a Countrey where is Silver, there Dig it, Refine it, bring it to the same place where the other man planted his Corn; Coyne it, &c. the same person, all the while of his working for Silver, gathering also food for his necessary livelihood, and procuring himself covering, &c., I say, the Silver of the one, must be esteemed of equal value with the Corn of the other.[32]

The surplus can also be expressed in terms of the number of persons who can be maintained by a group of labourers who produce enough subsistence for themselves and for the others. Like production of luxury goods and services, unemployment thus appears as a way of employing (or better, of wasting) the surplus:

> if there be 1000. men in a Territory, and if 100. of these can raise necessary food and raiment for the whole 1000. If 200. more make as much commodities, as other Nations will give either their commodities or money for, and if 400. more be employed in the ornaments, pleasure, and magnificence of the whole; if there be 200. Governours, Divines, Lawyers, Physicians, Merchants, and Retailers, making in all 900. the question is, since there is food enough for this supernumerary 100. also, how they should come by it? Whether by begging, or by stealing [...]?[33]

---

[31] We are confronted here, in substance, with a vertically integrated sector, or in other terms what Sraffa 1960, p. 89, was later to call a subsystem.

[32] Petty 1662, p. 43.

[33] Ibid., p. 30. The 'supernumerary 100.' correspond to the difference between the size of the workforce ('1000. men') and the number of workers employed ('in all 900.').

In relation to the question of how to determine the magnitude of the surplus, Petty anticipated the core of Smith's analysis in the *Wealth of nations*, emphasising the number of productive labourers and the level of productivity per worker. These two elements were referred to jointly, for example, in the explanation of the greater wealth of the Dutch. In relation to the first of these two factors, Petty insisted on proposals aiming to provide employment for the greatest possible number of productive labourers, either by engaging unemployed workers or by transferring labour from unproductive to productive activities. He believed that such policies could bring about important increases in income and wealth.

Among the elements determining productivity per worker, Petty recalled those that may be called natural, such as ease of access to the sea, availability of harbours and natural avenues of communication, and original fertility of land. Of much greater importance, however, were technological and organisational factors linked to the social evolution of different peoples. Among such factors Petty singled out land improvements (drainage, irrigation and the like) and investments in infrastructure (roads, navigable canals). He also emphasised the importance of technical progress embodied in new implements of production. Finally, particular importance was given to the division of labour.[34]

Let us now come to the theory of relative prices. A number of different interpretations may be (and have been) proposed in this respect, prompted by the fact that a fully-fledged theory of prices was not the central aim of Petty's writings; for him, the discussion of the functioning of the economy was instrumental to immediate policy interventions, in particular to institutional changes. The first interpretation, put forward by Marx, and adopted by a number of Marxian historians of economic thought, credits Petty with a more or less fully developed and coherent labour theory of value.[35] Indeed, there are a number of passages in Petty's writings which appear to support this interpretation. For example, in *A Treatise of taxes and contributions* we find:

let a hundred men work ten years upon Corn, and the same number of men, the same time, upon Silver; I say, that the neat proceed of the Silver is the price of the whole neat proceed of the Corn, and like parts of the one, the price of like parts of the other.[36]

---

[34] Cf. for instance Petty 1690, pp. 256–7, for the 'natural' factors; ibid., pp. 249–50, 302–3, for the technological and organisational factors; ibid., pp. 260–1, 473, for the division of labour.

[35] Cf. for instance Marx 1905–10, vol. 1, pp. 345–6, 350–1; Meek 1956, pp. 34–6; Pietranera 1963, pp. 31–50; Denis 1965, p. 172; Naldi 1989.

[36] Petty 1662, p. 43. Let us recall also the passage quoted above.

A little later in the same work Petty stated: 'Natural dearness and cheapness depends upon the few or more hands requisite to necessaries of Nature.'[37]

Even more explicit than these passages, however, is Petty's proposal of what appears to be a theory of value based on labour and land:

All things ought to be valued by two natural Denominations, which is Land and Labour; that is, we ought to say, a Ship or garment is worth such a measure of Land, with such another measure of Labour; forasmuch as both Ships and Garments were the creatures of Lands and mens Labours thereupon.[38]

This passage raises an additional problem. Like the quotations given above, it is intended to provide an explanation of exchange relationships. Yet, the reference to 'natural denominations' suggests that it might also be interpreted as a rudimentary statement of a theory of absolute value. The following formula which Petty uses to state his theory of value lends itself to the same interpretation: 'Labour is the Father and active principle of Wealth, as Lands are the Mother.'[39]

This is a traditional saying, and was widely used in writings on economic issues of the period. When we consider the diverse roles of labour and land in the agricultural process of production (the former playing the active, the latter the passive role: an idea which can be traced as far back as the writings of Aristotle), it is easy to see how such an idea might provide the basis for a theory of labour-value grounded in the doctrines of 'natural law'. Within such theories (that, as we saw above in § 2.5, fall within the Scholastic tradition, still strong in the seventeenth century), labour is conceived as a sacrifice made by the producer. The price is then the 'just' reward for such a sacrifice: a price proportional to the quantity of labour contained in the commodity is just, precisely because it is proportional to the sacrifice endured. Theories of labour value of this type became the foundation for views such as the interpretation of the subsistence wage as a just reward for labour, for the 'sweat of thy face', and for developments such as that of Nassau Senior (1790–1864), who was to identify an analogous sacrifice in capitalists' 'abstinence' that finds in profits its just remuneration.[40]

However, such a 'natural law' interpretation of Petty's theory of value would be erroneous. In fact, he considered labour as simply another production cost which is measured by its subsistence, and ignored any possible moral implication of justice or injustice in his treatment of the problem

---

[37] Ibid., p. 90.   [38] Ibid., p. 44.   [39] Ibid., p. 68.
[40] Cf. below, § 7.8. Elements of such an approach surfaced also in Smith (1776, p. 47) when he considered labour as 'toil and trouble', and were re-proposed with Jevons's and, in different form, Marshall's 'real costs' (cf. below, §§ 10.5 and 13.1).

of prices. Furthermore, in Petty's view, land and labour were to be placed on the same footing and the one could be expressed in terms of the other. In fact, 'the most important Consideration in Political Oeconomies' was precisely 'how to make a *Par* and *Equation* between Lands and Labour, so as to express the Value of any thing by either alone'.[41] It is clear from these statements that Petty was not trying to solve the problem of defining a just price within a natural law framework; rather he was seeking to explain the actual exchange relationships which take place in the market: labour and land were not considered as the original sources of wealth, but quite simply as physical costs of production of commodities.

The interpretation of Petty's theory of prices as based on physical costs of production is not contradicted by passages, such as those quoted above, which seem to support a labour embodied theory of value. Indeed, in the same writing the theory of value based on labour and land was explicitly set out, and the problem of the equivalence between labour and land was considered. Those passages should then be interpreted as a simplification with respect to a more complex theory based on labour and land, that may hold under the assumption of proportionality between the quantities of land and the quantities of labour used in the production of the various commodities. Moreover, there are passages in Petty's works in which he went beyond the theory of value based on land and labour, moving further along the path of physical costs of production, up to providing a list of activities necessary to specific processes of production: 'The Price of a Comodity subsists: Of the first naturall materiall. The manufacture to the state of use. Carriage from the place of making to that of use, and vessels. Dutyes to the Soverayne of them that buy and sell.'[42]

Petty mentioned a series of examples of this principle, specifying cost in terms of physical goods. Following this path, indeed, he also provided a correct formulation of the problem of joint production. Consider the first of the fourteen examples that Petty gave: 'For Butter. There is 1. The Cow. 2. Her feeding in winter and somer. 3. The dairy vessells and labor. 4. Carriage. Deducting: 1. Calf 2. Wheyes 3. Coarse cheeses.'[43]

Hence, Petty's analysis essentially concerned not absolute value (that is, the problem of the causes of value), but the problem of relative prices. In analysing such an issue, with the reference to the physical costs of production,[44] Petty gave an objective formulation that, as we will see further

---

[41] Petty 1691a, p. 181; the same problem had already been proposed in the *Treatise of taxes and contributions* (Petty 1662, p. 44).

[42] Petty 1927, vol. 1, p. 190.   [43] Ibid.

[44] Incidentally, physical costs of production cannot be considered as a purely technological notion. Not only does their level (especially in so far as labour is concerned) depend on social factors broadly construed: the very items entering into the cost list depend on

on, was to be taken up by Ricardo among others, and more recently by Sraffa with greater consistency and analytical rigour.

Petty's contribution did not go much beyond the simple formulation of the problem: physical costs of production are the factors that determine political prices. This left the problem far from resolved. Heterogeneous goods such as cow, feed, labour, cannot all be summed together to make up costs of production unless they have been previously expressed in homogeneous units, that is, in terms of quantities of value obtained by multiplying the quantity of each commodity required in the process of production by its relative price. We are thus confronted with a circularity problem: the price of the product cannot be determined unless the prices of the means of production are known, but these are also produced by means of production that may include the first product. Think, for example, of the case of wheat used to produce iron which is itself used in the production of wheat.

Petty appears to have been oblivious to this problem. Yet, it was precisely this difficulty which would account for his attempt to reduce the heterogeneous components of the costs of production to the two primary factors, land and labour, and then to find a relation of equivalence between them so as to express costs in terms of only one of them. But such attempts were not successful, especially the latter, to which Petty attached great importance.

Petty suggested the following method for establishing a relation of equivalence between labour and land:

Suppose two Acres of Pasture-land inclosed, and put thereinto a wean'd Calf, which I suppose in twelve months will become 1 C. heavier in eatable flesh; then 1 C. weight of such flesh, which I suppose fifty days food, and the interest of the value of the calf, is the value or years Rent of the Land. But if a mans labour [. . .] for a year can make the said Land to yield more than sixty days Food of the same, or of any other kind, then that overplus of days food is the Wages of the Man; both being expressed by the number of days of food.[45]

the manner of social organisation. Indeed, we may include in costs only what can be the object of private appropriation (not, for instance, the rain or the sun, that may well be necessary inputs of production and may be scarce).

[45] Petty 1691a, p. 181. In other terms, land alone produces 50, while by adding a labourer the product increases by 10 units (net, we must assume, of production costs, inclusive of the workers' subsistence: 'wages' here means what the land gives in reward of the labour spent on it, not the income of a dependent worker). As a consequence, five labourers are equivalent to two acres of land. This passage has been interpreted (for instance by Routh 1975, p. 40) as an instance of marginal calculus: the 'contribution' of each 'productive factor' is obtained by computing what is produced by given quantities of the two factors (in Petty's example, one of the two quantities is equal to zero), and when the quantity of one of the factors is increased while keeping constant the quantity utilised of the other factor. This interpretation appears rather strained; anyhow, in this case the criticisms

Petty himself saw and tried to solve the most obvious difficulties such as heterogeneity of consumption levels for different individuals and the heterogeneity of consumption goods:

That some Men will eat more than others, is not material, since by a days food we understand 1/100 part of what 100 of all Sorts and Sizes will eat, so as to Live, Labour, and Generate. And that a days food of one sort, may require more labour to produce, than another sort, is also not material, since we understand the easiest-gotten food of the respective Countries of the World.[46]

In fact, the solution Petty suggested recalls the modern notion of efficiency units: land is compared to labour by means of a comparison of their relative net productivities. But this comparison requires the prior knowledge of relative prices, and hence implies circular reasoning. Alternatively, if we measure productivity in physical terms, then the outputs compared should be physically homogeneous (which Petty attempted to ensure by referring to 'daily food'). The latter alternative implies recourse to the wholly unrealistic assumption of a 'one-commodity world', and is therefore as unacceptable as the first solution. What was lacking in Petty's attempts to solve the problem of the determination of relative prices was the perception of the simple fact that the problem is intrinsically related to the operation of the economic system as a whole and not to a single productive sector considered in isolation.

The incompleteness of the conceptual scheme set out by Petty, in particular the absence of a key concept such as that of the rate of profits, seems to have had a decisive role in preventing a correct solution of the problem. This in fact requires construction of an analytical system that takes into account productive interrelations among the different sectors of the economy. But the path that leads to such a system is very long, as we shall see in the following chapters.

recalled below would still hold, concerning the impossibility of adopting this method in the presence of heterogeneous products (that may be reduced to homogeneous products, in terms of utility, only within the framework of a subjective theory of value).

[46] Petty 1691a, p. 181. An analogous criterion to that adopted for establishing a 'par' between land and labour was proposed by Petty for reducing 'art', that is, the qualified labour of the inventor, to simple labour. Cf. Petty 1691a, p. 182. The same line of reasoning is proposed by Petty also to establish 'an Equation [. . .] between drudging Labour, and Favour, Acquaintance, Interest, Friends, Eloquence, Reputation, Power, Authority, & c.' (ibid.).

4   From body politic to economic tables

1.   The debates of the time

In the century stretching between William Petty's writings and Adam Smith's, economic thinking proceeded in many directions. It is impossible here to consider them all with the attention they deserve:[1] some authors and research currents will simply be ignored, others will receive only brief mention, while only a few will be treated in more detail.

It is important to stress just how rich the debate on economic phenomena was during this period, moving forward on various planes, linking up with ethical or philosophical aspects in general or more immediate issues of political choices, and constituting the background from which certain personalities emerged to prominence from the point of view of our account. The contributions of the most important authors would be difficult if not impossible to understand if wholly isolated from the cultural context in which they took shape, and which they helped to enrich. This holds true for the period here considered in a measure that may be difficult to appreciate for those accustomed to the extreme specialisation in research characterising our times. Actually, in the seventeenth and eighteenth centuries the figure of the economist was still far from clearly defined: reflections on economic phenomena were part of general reflections on society and man, and the same authors would in the course of time range over a vast field of issues.

As we have seen, for instance, Petty was an inventor, doctor and professor of anatomy, responsible for a gigantic project for the geographical survey of Ireland, and a landowner actively engaged in the management of his estates. His reflections on economic, institutional and demographic issues were for him at the same time a civic and intellectual pursuit, an exercise of political influence, and an instrument for the defence of his own private interests. John Locke was best known as a philosopher, but he also dealt with strictly economic issues in pursuit of his philosophical

---

[1] A detailed picture of this extraordinarily rich and complex period is provided by Hutchison 1988.

enquiries, as did David Hume a few years later. Locke wrote, among other things, about monetary issues in the course of a debate with, among others, the famous physicist Isaac Newton, who in 1699 was appointed director of the Mint. Bernard de Mandeville was a doctor and philosopher, Richard Cantillon an international banker who also approached systematic thinking on economic matters not professionally but as a pastime, albeit one not unrelated to his main activity. François Quesnay, a physician at the court of King Louis XV, pursued neither professional nor private interests with his writings, but simply joined in the intellectual debate of the time in the hope that his ideas might help to ameliorate social problems. In the intellectual circles of the period both protagonists and simple spectators let their interests range free, faithful to Terentius' motto in the *Heautontimorùmenos*: 'Homo sum: humani nil a me alienum puto' (I am a human being: nothing concerning human beings I consider as foreign to me). Here we isolate the strictly economic contributions from their context, but we must not forget that excisions of the sort would have been considered arbitrary by the protagonists of that time.

Among the research currents which we will mention only briefly there is the statistical-demographical school of 'political-arithmeticians', followers of William Petty including such influential personalities of the time as Gregory King (1648–1712) and Charles Davenant (1656–1714). Although often imprecise and uncertain (Adam Smith asserted: 'I have no great faith in political arithmetick')[2] their activities provided important raw material not only for an understanding of the economy and the society of their time: it might also serve for the policy choices of the sovereign on taxes and contributions or evaluating the relative economic strength of different countries, of great help in the field of foreign policy choices.[3]

From our viewpoint, which departs from that of the economic historian, the writings of the political arithmeticians may provide useful

[2] Smith 1776, p. 534. In substance, the line running from Petty to Smith went through Cantillon and Quesnay rather than through the political arithmeticians, although at the time the latter appeared as Petty's direct heirs. Rather, in some cases (and especially for Davenant) and with a touch of good will, the way in which quantitative data discussed by political arithmeticians were organised may be considered a rudimentary anticipation of modern national accounting. It is hard, however, to attribute to such writings an adequate characterisation of the relations between stocks and flows for the economic system as a whole and for its main components.

[3] King was known at the time mainly through quotations from his writings included in Davenant's works; he was later rediscovered by Marshall, who deduced a demand curve from a relation between percentage decrease in the corn crop and percentage increase in its price (Marshall 1890, p. 106 n.). Subsequently – but not by Marshall – this relation was somewhat pompously christened 'King's law' with (apparently) excessive enthusiasm. For a history of English empiricism in the social sciences, from political arithmetic on, cf. Stone 1997, in particular pp. 49–115 on Davenant and King.

indications, especially about the system of concepts underlying the debates of the time. An example of this (which we return to below) is to be seen in the fact that King and Davenant preferred a territorial classification of information (a geographical partitioning of the economic system) to classification by sectors, while any references to economic sectors were still a long way from the tripartition of agriculture–manufacturing–services which became the rule after Smith.

Another line in economic thinking took a markedly different stance from Petty, insisting on a mixture between analysis and ethics. Here we find the representatives of the 'natural law' doctrine, important for putting ideas of natural rights and natural laws into circulation but, in terms of strictly economic issues, still engaged in 'just price' discussions. Among them was the German jurist Samuel Pufendorf (1632–94), author of a well-known work, *De iure naturae et gentium* (On natural and human rights, 1672), which constituted an important contribution to the foundations of international law.[4] In the field of price theory Pufendorf distinguished between prices determined by laws and regulations ('legal prices'), those determined by a generic common evaluation ('natural prices'), and those determined by the common evaluation of the experts, with a good knowledge of both the commodity and its market ('just price'). In these evaluations both scarcity and cost of production play a role, while usefulness is a prerequisite for a positive price but does not determine it. Thus the optimal situation is the one in which the legal or the natural price corresponds to the just price: Pufendorf's price theory is a normative one. Within the same 'natural law' current we find many other writings on monetary matters that, dealing in particular with determination of the rate of interest, were connected with the Scholastic debates on usury.

The numerous tracts intended to provide merchants with guidance in their activities display a curious analogy to this latter current. In Italy works of this kind had flourished in the fourteenth and fifteenth centuries. In the period we are considering here the most renowned work of this type was *Le parfait négociant* by the Frenchman Jacques Savary (The expert

---

[4] Huigh de Groot (or Hugo Grotius, 1583–1645) had been a precursor of Pufendorf along this road. Pesciarelli (1989, pp. xviii–xix) notes Pufendorf's influence on Hutcheson through the latter's master, Gershom Carmichael (1672–1729), professor at the University of Glasgow and divulger in Scotland of the work and thought of Pufendorf; in turn Hutcheson, Smith's master, transmitted to the latter some elements of Pufendorf's way of thinking: in particular, according to Pesciarelli (ibid., p. xix), 'a view of society represented as an enormous arena of dealers, buyers and sellers'. Locke too – on whose theory of freedom and private property cf. below, § 2 – was an attentive reader of the writings of Pufendorf, his contemporary (they were born in the same year); however, their views on society were decidedly different.

merchant, 1675) which dominated this period in terms of the number of copies sold. In England we may mention – although on the borderline between this current and economic analysis – Malachy Postlethwayt's *Universal dictionary of trade and commerce* (1751–5), composed utilising a large number of plagiarised passages (including an almost complete version of Cantillon's *Essay on the nature of commerce in general*: cf. below, § 5).

Another current that we find frequent examples of in the literature of the period but which, like the previous one, saw lines of research vital in the decades before Petty running dry, was represented by the long series of tracts on trade, which generally dealt with monetary issues in connection with matters of international trade, in the wake of the mercantilist literature discussed above (§ 2.4). This kind of literature captures, generation after generation, the attention of historians of economic thought who consider the ascent of free trade over protectionism the central aspect of economic science. One leading example is the liberal merchant Dudley North (1641–91; his *Discourses upon trade* were published posthumously in 1691). However, the arguments in support of the free trade thesis cannot be said to be remarkably solid. In the absence of a well-developed theory of the functioning of markets (and in the presence, moreover, of far from competitive markets, dominated as they were by large merchant companies like the India Company), we can only consider reference to 'natural laws' that must take their course as begging the question. On the protectionist side, leaving aside simplistic reference to the 'treasury' represented by an active balance of trade, the most common arguments concerned the expediency of protecting infant industries and defending national employment from foreign competition. Another defender of the free trade doctrine was Daniel Defoe (1660–1731), the well-known author of *Robinson Crusoe* (1719), who published a tri-weekly paper, the *Mercator* for some months during the period of heated debate following upon the Treaty of Utrecht of 1713.

In France, the main champion of free trade in the years between the end of the seventeenth and the beginning of the eighteenth century was Pierre le Pesant de Boisguilbert (1646–1714), whose motto – *laissez faire la nature et la liberté* (let nature and freedom do their course) – anticipated expressions by de Gournay and Turgot (cf. below, § 7) to the same effect. Boisguilbert criticised Colbert's statism and policy favouring manufactures, blaming the depressed state of the French economy above all on stagnation in the agricultural sector. In this respect, including support for higher prices for agricultural produce,[5] Boisguilbert was a forerunner

---

[5] According to Boisguilbert, agricultural prices should exceed a minimum level, which he called 'prix de rigueur', corresponding to production costs; but apart from this, and

of the physiocratic doctrines. Among his works is *Le détail de la France* (A description of France, 1695).[6]

In England again, what has been called 'the pre-classical theory of development' (Perrotta 1997), widespread in the period between 1690 and the first decades of the eighteenth century, concerned in particular the thesis that working-class consumption had an influence on productivity and thus on growth. Along with North and earlier than Defoe, this thesis was propounded by, among others, Nicholas Barbon (1637–98), a medical student who became a rich builder thanks to opportunities offered by the devastation of London in the Great Fire of 1666. Author of a *Discourse of trade* (1690), on the theory of value Barbon followed the subjectivist approach based on scarcity and utility.[7] In this latter respect, Barbon was following what appeared to be the prevailing orientation of the time – as we will see in various respects below – apart from some significant exceptions such as William Petty.

2.   John Locke

Among the writers concerned with monetary issues as part of more general reflections on society and human beings, let us now consider the English philosopher John Locke (1632–1704; his main work was the *Essay concerning human understanding* of 1689).[8] He was the author of a renowned tract on *Some considerations on the consequences of the lowering of interest, and raising the value of money* (1692; a preliminary version had been written in 1668). In the eyes of the economist of today, this work has the merit of being one of the first writings of the time (together with Petty's *Quantulumcumque concerning money*, written in 1682 but published only in 1695, and before Cantillon) to show a clear perception of the notion of velocity of circulation of money.

from a rather vague hint to 'prix de proportion', namely to the fact that prices should be in a reasonable proportion to each other, he did not provide an explanation of what determines prices.

[6] Boisguilbert's contribution has been extolled by many historians of economic thought, in particular in France. Suffice it to recall the very title of the collection of his writings (INED, 1966) which identifies in him 'the birth of political economy'. Boisguilbert was attributed, among other things, with the merit of anticipating the idea of general economic interdependence and the multiplier concept. His writings were, however, far less systematic than Cantillon's, Quesnay's or Turgot's.

[7] Hutchison 1988, p. 75, attributed him with an implicit notion of decreasing utility. According to Schumpeter 1954, p. 647, Barbon was the first writer who explicitly identified interest with net income from capital goods.

[8] The original edition was dated 1690, but the *Essay* was already circulating in December of the previous year.

Locke's essay was part of a lively debate that took place in the last decade of the seventeenth century on the relationship between low interest rate and prosperity. Josiah Child (1630–99), governor of the India Company and one of the richest men of his time, in his influential *Brief observations concerning trade and interest of money* (1668; an enlarged edition was published in 1690 as *Discourse about trade*), had maintained that the first element (low interest rates) is the cause of the second (prosperity), and on this ground had asked for legal constraints on interest rates.[9] In criticising this thesis, Locke argued that it is prosperity that favours a moderate level of interest rates, and that any attempt to reduce them by law is doomed to failure; besides, in so far as it may succeed, such an attempt may prove detrimental, slowing down accumulation. North also adopted a similar line of reasoning. We may also mention a work published half a century later, in 1750: *An essay on the governing causes of the rate of interest*, by Joseph Massie, who died in 1794; although presented as a critique of Locke's argument, it actually amounted to a searching and indeed thought-provoking study on the relationship between interest rate and rate of profits, together with the factors influencing them.[10]

Locke also took part in the debate on the need for a new mintage of silver coins which, as a consequence of abundant clipping, had lost on average at least 20 per cent of their value. In this debate we find Josiah Child, Nicholas Barbon, Charles Davenant and Isaac Newton taking an active part, together with various other participants.

Another aspect of Locke's thought worth recalling here concerns his view of private property as a natural right of man. This argument was developed in the *Two treatises of government* (1690), and in particular in book 2, chapter 5 ('Of property'). Based on a sort of a labour theory of value,[11] it opposed the ideas of Hobbes and the natural law writers such as Grotius and Pufendorf, who took private property to have been instituted

---

[9] On Child, cf. Letwin 1959. Among the theses to which Child lent the support of his influence, there was the idea that it is poverty, and not a wage above the subsistence level, that favours the spread of idleness among workers. (The opposite argument had been maintained for instance by Petty 1691a.)

[10] The history of the debate on the relation between interest rate and prosperity between 1650 and 1850 is excellently described by Tucker 1960. Within the more general debate on the nature of money and the functioning of the financial system we may include the writings of John Law (1671–1729), known above all for his adventurous financial enterprises, which culminated in the most gigantic crash in history; on him, see the lively, detailed description by Murphy 1997.

[11] More precisely, on the idea that labour is the source of the right to property, but not on the idea that labour expended for producing the different commodities explains their exchange value. Locke had little to say on the theory of relative prices, and his sparse hints on this topic rather pointed to a subjective theory of value, stressing the role of 'usefulness' in this context. Cf. Hutchison 1988, pp. 68–70.

through an agreement (or 'social contract') marking transition from the state of nature to organised society, and thus to be of a conventional nature.[12]

Locke began his argument by recognising that land and all the lower creatures have been given to all men in common. He argued, however, that

every man has a 'property' in his own 'person'. This nobody has any right to but himself. The 'labour' of his body and the 'work' of his hands, we may say, are properly his. Whatsoever, then, he removes out of the state that Nature hath provided and left it in, he hath mixed his labour with it, and joined to it something that is his own, and thereby makes it his property.[13]

In interpreting these passages we should remember[14] that the meaning Locke attributed to the notions of labour and capital was different from – and wider than – the usual connotation. Labour, in the meaning Locke attributed to the word, included all kinds of productive activity – the entrepreneur's as much as the wage labourer's – and therefore constituted the source of all wealth and the religious duty of every individual. Similarly, Locke defined property as including not only private property in its common meaning, but also man's fundamental rights: 'lives, liberties and estates, which I call by the general name – property'.[15] It is only by using the terms 'labour' and 'property' in their everyday meaning, rather than in the sense explicitly given by Locke in the passage quoted above, that commentators can read his argument as aiming essentially at 'justifying' an economic system based on private ownership of means of production. We should, rather, view his argument as a reaction to 'social contract' theses, particularly Hobbes's, and the conclusions they lead to, favourable to political absolutism. We may then see Locke as a defender of the rights of the individual against government, while denying that this latter should be identified with a Leviathan. This included a defence of

[12] Clear illustration of Locke's arguments is provided by Bedeschi 1990, pp. 50 ff. An innovative aspect of Locke's analysis consisted in the fact that – as Bedeschi (ibid., p. 52) notes – 'in private property he sees no longer something static, but something dynamic, no longer something given once and for all, or established by men by common agreement, but rather something which is the fruit of the effort and economic activity of man. This is a view that well suits the new bourgeois, landowners and mercantile ranks, who knew a rapid ascent in the English society of the seventeenth century.'

[13] Locke 1690, p. 130: II.27. It is worth noting by the way that Locke waxed vehement in extolling labour as a moral duty: a duty he extended even to children of tender age, proposing the whip for those found begging (while for adults, together with hard labour in houses of correction or at sea, he even advocated cutting off their ears). Obviously Locke was not the only one, either then or subsequently, to propose measures of this kind.

[14] Cf. Deane 1989, p. 29.   [15] Locke 1690, p. 180: II.123.

private property, not only of immediate means of subsistence but also of that means of production, namely land, which was fundamental in a still predominantly agricultural economic system. We must remember that Locke looked to the society of his time with a critical eye, characterised as it was by residual feudal elements, and in which political power still played an important role as origin (and not simply guarantee) of property titles, with the arbitrariness that this implied for the distribution of wealth.[16]

The problem of providing a moral justification for private property did not, in fact, usually figure among the issues considered by the economists of the time. For instance, Petty only considered the problem of analysing the functioning of a society founded on private property, as can also be seen when he proposed modifications (such as the institution of the land registry) aiming at avoiding the waste involved with uncertainty about property titles; Smith considered the legal institutions on which private property is based as the result of an evolutionary process which, even if not constantly moving in the direction of progress, has undeniably improved matters, favouring an increasing division of labour and hence increasing productivity and welfare. These are points we shall be returning to in the next chapter.

As for the debate on relations between man and society, we can follow Bobbio (1989, pp. 3–10) in distinguishing two contrasting models: the natural law model and the Aristotelian version,[17] the former based on the dichotomy between state of nature and civil state, the latter seeing the modern government structures as the result of a process which had its starting point in the natural social unit, i.e. the family.

The natural law theory saw the state as 'antithesis to the state of nature', the latter being characterised by the maximum of individual freedom, and hence by a 'struggle of all against all' – a situation that could be overcome not as the result of an inevitable natural process, but as a conquest of reason bringing men to associate according to commonly accepted conventions. Here we have one of the most modern elements of the natural law view: as Bobbio put it (ibid., p. 4), 'consensus is the principle of

[16] Another source of inequality that Locke explicitly considered is the use of money, which permits the accumulation of wealth. Money was considered not an element inherent to human society but an artifice accepted by common consent.

[17] We may see as a side-stream of this debate the abundant literature of the sixteenth and seventeenth centuries on the 'good savage' and the 'bad savage', deriving mainly from geographical discoveries and contact with indigenous inhabitants of the new colonial possessions. An account of this literature is provided by Meek 1976. In the eighteenth century the optimism characterising the period of the Enlightenment favoured the figure of the 'good savage', which became a central theme in the anthropological views of the time.

legitimisation of political society, unlike any other form of natural society and, in particular, family society and owner society'.

By contrast, the Aristotelian model started from the family, considered both as the natural form of association and as a historically concrete form: from it came the state, constituting the natural outlet through a process of continuous development. Like the family from which it derived, the state – the constitutive elements of which were not individuals in isolation, but social nuclei like the family itself – had a natural hierarchical structure; not consensus, but 'the nature of things', was the principle of legitimisation for political society.

As we shall see in more detail below, it is difficult to classify the Scottish Enlightenment – representing the background to Smith's education – within this dichotomy. In a few words, the Scottish Enlightenment sets side by side with an evolutionary theory of society and the state (Smith's 'four stages'), and a 'realistic view of man in society', an individualistic vision and a theory of legitimisation through consent.

However, also in the case of the contract view a form of state authority was considered necessary for keeping society together. What is more, authors considered among the founding fathers of economic liberalism like Mandeville (see below, § 4) and, to a still greater extent, authors of the mercantilist period held that the pursuit of private interests on the part of individuals may lead to collective well-being or progress only if duly guided in the right direction by a capable public authority. The theories of weight and counterweight, applied not only (as in Montesquieu) to the various political institutions that go to make up the modern state but indeed to the interplay of passions and interests, can also be viewed in this light: as we will see in the next chapter, the Smithian fusion of individual interest and 'moral of sympathy' constituted an interesting development along this line of reasoning.

3.   The motivations and consequences of human actions

Over the centuries the world's major social scientists (Machiavelli no less than Mandeville or Smith, Beccaria and Verri as much as Bentham and John Stuart Mill) have tackled analysis of human behaviour and the functioning of society starting from two key questions. The first question is about what impulses drive human actions, while the second addresses the consequences for society of more or less radically egocentric motivations, or in other words motivations not directly aimed at the good functioning of society or collective well-being.

There can be no difficulty in appreciating the importance of the first question as analysis proceeds from 'what should be' to 'what in fact is'.

In the Middle Ages, as we saw above, the idea prevailed that human behaviour should be guided by divine ends and that any action or thought contrary to this idea should be eradicated as not only sinful, but absurd. The definition of 'right' behaviour extended from that correctly practised by the individual to the behaviour that society itself imposed by condemning cases of deviation. Given such grounds, attributing autonomy to 'what it is' meant legitimising behaviours not conforming to the precepts of religious ethics, recognising both their diffusion and, at least in some cases, their expediency.

Machiavelli, as we saw above (§ 3.3), broke sharply away from the medieval view, while the culture of the Protestant reform settled on an intermediate position, viewed by Weber (1904–5) as fundamental for the birth of capitalism, since it recognised legitimacy for actions aiming at individual enrichment. The strong point in the Protestant view lay precisely in the fact that it avoided opposition between individual and collective interests, reconciling recognition of the role of individual interests as a force for constructive action with preservation of a principle of moral judgement, weighing up the different motivations to act and allowing for discrimination between destructive and constructive actions. This was a solution much like the one Smith was to propose with his simultaneous defence of the market and the 'moral of sympathy'.

Naturally, recognising that human beings do not follow the guidance of religious commandments alone did not mean denying any role to them; thus we are dealing with the simultaneous presence of many and various motivations lying behind human behaviour. The debate on such motivations was far more complex than might appear from the way it is all too often presented, in terms of opposition between selfish and altruistic behaviour.

The motives for human action are summed up in two terms, 'passions' and 'interests', each of which in fact encompassed a whole series of specific elements that cannot be reduced to a common denominator. The distinction pointed to the simultaneous presence in human behaviour of instinctual or customary – and in any case a-rational (although not necessarily irrational) – elements with elements that imply reasoned choices but that can certainly not be reduced to a mere matter of maximising wealth or income. We should also bear in mind that in a time of far-reaching uncertainties the room for rational behaviour was certainly not all-embracing, while the role of the passions remained important.[18]

---

[18] We should recall the importance of the 'process of civilisation' discussed by Elias 1939, although Hirschman's 1977 distinction between passions and interests is in fact somewhat different.

In general, however, writers on economic issues tended to be rationalists, both in the sense of reasoning on the possible consequences of different kinds of behaviour, forming value judgements on them by evaluating their consequences, and in the sense of attributing the same behavioural canon to the agents as objects of their analyses.

Let us now turn to the second question, concerning the outcomes of an individual behaviour motivated by individual passions and interests. As we will see more fully in the next section, a somewhat optimistic answer was provided: under certain conditions, and more precisely when a constructive drive is generated from the interrelation between the different passions and interests, individual actions not directly aiming at the public good may still have positive social consequences.

Moreover, the very social connections that developed between participants in a market economy played a civilising role, given a concept of civilisation connoting the ability to preserve some moral control over one's own passions and interests in the choice between alternative lines of behaviour. In the eighteenth century the idea of a civilising role for commerce – the idea of *doux commerce* – dominated over the pessimistic thesis of commerce having a destructive influence on social cohesion.[19]

The idea of *doux commerce* was connected among other things with 'the idea of a perfectible social order [which] arose at about the same time as that of the unintended effects of human actions and decisions'.[20] Montesquieu, Condorcet, Paine and many others discussed the virtues of commerce, followed in this by Hume and Smith. They all shared

the insistent thought that a society where the market assumes a central position [. . .] will produce not only considerable net wealth because of the division of labour and consequent technical progress, but would generate [. . .] a more 'polished' human type – more honest, reliable, orderly, and disciplined, as well as

---

[19] The opposition between *Rival interpretations of market society: civilizing, destructive, or feeble?* is propounded by Hirschman 1982. What Hirschman defines as 'the self-destruction thesis' is exemplified by recalling Schumpeter and Hirsch in the twentieth century, Marx and Engels in the nineteenth century and, in the 1830s, the conservative reaction to Walpole and the Whig government favourable to progress of the market society. In particular, 'Fred Hirsch dealt at length with what he called "the depleting moral legacy" of capitalism. He argues that the market *undermines* the moral values that are its own essential underpinnings, values that are now said to have been inherited from *preceding* socioeconomic regimes, such as the feudal order' (ibid., p. 1466; italics in the original); 'Marx and Engels make much of the way in which capitalism corrodes all traditional values and institutions such as love, family, and patriotism. Everything was passing into commerce, all social bonds were dissolved through money. This perception is by no means original with Marx' (ibid., p. 1467). On Schumpeter cf. below, § 15.4.

[20] Hirschman 1982, p. 1463.

more friendly and helpful, ever ready to find solutions to conflicts and a middle ground for opposed options. Such a type will in turn greatly facilitate the smooth functioning of the market.[21]

In the eighteenth century a basically optimistic interpretation thus prevailed of the path followed by a society based on the division of labour and on the market. Such an optimistic view was intrinsic to the spirit of the time, and in particular to the Enlightenment culture and its faith in the triumph of Reason. However, the idea of a progressive society did not stem, as effect from cause, from hope in the diffusion of individual behaviour guided ever more closely by reason, ever less by the passions. Rather, the causal link worked in the opposite direction, from the economic and social progress achieved by a society driven by the spirit of commerce, and hence by individualistic motivations, to a growing cultural civilisation in which personal interest was not so much superseded as appropriately channelled towards collective progress.

4.   Bernard de Mandeville

Born into a family of doctors, and himself a doctor, the Dutch Bernard de Mandeville (1670–1733) was christened in Rotterdam, attended the Erasmian school and then the University of Leyden, and gained the title of doctor in medicine in 1691. Shortly afterwards he moved to London, where he resided up to his death.[22]

His first publication dates from 1703: an English translation of some fables by La Fontaine, to which he added a couple of his own. In 1705 a small poem of a few pages was published anonymously, *The grumbling hive: or, knaves turn'd honest*. This poem constituted the core of his best-known work: *The fable of the bees: or, private vices, publick benefits*, which appeared under this title and with a comment in prose in 1714, an expanded edition appearing in 1723. For its 'impiety', this publication was criticised by the Grand Jury of Middlesex; Mandeville's defence against these accusations was included in the subsequent editions (1724, 1725, 1728, 1729, 1732). In 1728 a second part to the work was published, to appear in further editions in 1730 and in 1733. Starting with a new edition of 1733, the two parts were published jointly, as two volumes of the same work, and were republished in the 1924 critical edition edited

---

[21] Ibid., pp. 1465–6. The eighteenth-century Enlightenment shared with fifteenth-century humanism an optimistic view of human nature, but substituted the idea of its invariance over time with the idea of its perfectibility.

[22] On Mandeville's life and works, cf. Kaye 1924.

by Kaye.[23] This work was widely circulated and gave rise to heated debate, the author himself taking part in it with the series of enlarged editions.

Educated in a cultural environment which was among the most progressive of the time, in his work the Dutch doctor addressed some themes characteristic of libertine thinking of the seventeenth and eighteenth centuries, tackling what was seen as an irreconcilable clash between the criterion of rigour and the criterion of utility in choices concerning human behaviour. More specifically, Mandeville's polemic was directed against Shaftesbury, an author also criticised – significantly enough – by Smith in his *Theory of moral sentiments*. Shaftesbury advocated the idea of a universal harmony in which Good and Beauty coincided.[24] In Mandeville's opinion, we should recognise that man is commonly driven by passions and interests that are centred on himself and not – or at least not directly – aimed at the good of society. However, the final outcome of a society in which selfish behaviour prevails may be the collective good: 'private vices' may turn into 'public virtues'.

However, it is simplistic and indeed erroneous to sum up Mandeville with the well-known formula 'private vices = public virtues'. Selfish behaviour may, he argued, but would not necessarily lead to collective good. In fact, it all depended on the ability of those in power to play on the simultaneous presence of different passions at the root of human action, never denying them, but channelling them in the right direction. 'Private Vices by the dextrous Management of a skilful Politician may be turned into Publick Benefits.'[25] Thus Mandeville cannot be considered a supporter of 'vice' *tout court* (also considering that it was not understood as anti-social behaviour, but simply as pursuit of individual motivations): he maintained that we should recognise the existence of vice as a matter of fact, for only thus will we be able to reap positive results.

Mandeville contrasted traditional society, typically on a small scale, where everyone could see what everyone else was up to, with mercantile society based on the division of labour and hence necessarily on a broader scale: moreover, since the division of labour favoured technical progress, the larger society grew the richer it would be. In Mandeville's

---

[23] Among the other, less important, writings by Mandeville, we may mention the *Free thoughts on religion* dated 1720, and *A letter to Dion* dated 1732. On the latter, see Viner's introduction (1953), criticising the interpretation – widespread, although with scant philological support – that has Mandeville a *laissez-faire* theoretician.

[24] For this interpretation cf. Scribano 1974. Antony Ashley Cooper, third earl of Shaftesbury (1671–1713), a pupil of Locke, Member of Parliament from 1695 to 1699, who then retired to live in Italy as a consequence of health problems, was the author of three volumes on *Characteristics of men, manners, opinions, times* (1711), in which he maintained that man is endowed with an innate 'moral sense' that allows him to distinguish between right and wrong. Francis Hutcheson, Smith's teacher whom we shall discuss below (§ 9), supported him against Mandeville.

[25] Mandeville 1714, vol. 1, p. 369.

opinion it was the former kind of society that was idealised by moralists like Shaftesbury, taking a misleadingly optimistic view of society. The members of such a society, Mandeville asserted,

shall have no Arts or Sciences, or be quiet longer than their Neighbours will let them; they must be poor, ignorant, and almost wholly destitute of what we call the Comforts of Life, and all the Cardinal Virtues together won't so much as procure a tolerable Coat or a Porridge-Pot among them: For in this State of slothful Ease and stupid Innocence, as you need not fear great Vices, so you must not expect any considerable Virtues. Man never exerts himself but when he is rous'd by his Desires.[26]

It is the large mercantile society, in which the behaviour of men is driven by individualistic motivations, that favours the progress of wealth and with it the very enrichment of human personality, its civic growth.

Obviously, this meant that there had to be pre-established rules of the game: as Viner wrote, 'the discipline imposed by positive law and enforced by government was essential if a prosperous and flourishing society was to be derived from communities of individuals vigorously pursuing their self-regarding interest'.[27] Together with laws, education and the very fact of being accustomed to community life were important, since through them the different passions may be directed towards the collective good.[28] In a sense, the interplay of well-balanced passions constituted a sort of 'invisible hand' that guaranteed the progress of society, even if this was not the immediate objective of individual actions. This invisible hand was not, however, a necessary result of individual actions: it was itself a conscious construction, through which the abilities of those responsible for governing society manifested themselves.[29]

---

[26] Mandeville 1714, vol. 1, pp. 183–4.   [27] Viner 1953, p. 185.

[28] Taking up another theme characteristic of the libertine thought, Mandeville noticed the variability of moral and sexual habits and of religious and political convictions (as were testified by numerous accounts of travels in faraway lands, a literary genre widespread at the time). This implied negation of the idea of a moral conviction innate in men corresponding to dominant opinions (the *consensus gentium*). Hence, the notions of just and unjust are fruits of education and of life in society. On this, cf. Scribano 1974, pp. xx–xxi.

[29] This position is certainly not isolated in the history of economic thought: in its reasonableness, it was propounded again and again by different authors in different epochs. For instance, it came back in the gradualist theses concerning transition from planned economies to the market after the fall of the Berlin Wall in 1989; but already in the sixteenth century it was explicitly proposed by the anonymous author of a fine dialogue, in which it was maintained that men pursue personal interest, but that this should not be to the disadvantage of others, and that ensuring such a result is the true problem of politics: 'Threw it is that thinge which is profitable to eche man by his seule'; 'they maie not purchace them seules proffit by that may be hartfull to others. But how to bringe them that [they] would not doe so, is all the matter' (Anonymous 1549, pp. 51 and 50).

5.   Richard Cantillon

For many economists the publication of Smith's *Wealth of nations* marks the birth-date of economic science, while Marx went back still further, hailing Petty as the father of political economy. Jevons (1881) stopped mid-way; for him the founder of political economy was an international banker, Richard Cantillon. He appears to have been born in Ireland, lived most of his life in Paris, and was murdered in London in 1734.[30] He was the author of an *Essay on the nature of commerce in general*, probably written between 1728 and 1734, and published posthumously in French only in 1755, after having been abundantly plagiarised in English by Postlethwayt,[31] and after a manuscript copy of the essay had remained for sixteen years in the hands of the Marquis of Mirabeau, who seems to have had every intention of using it in the same way.[32] Cantillon's influence on Quesnay and the physiocrats was indeed profound.

The *Essay* has an admirable compactness and follows a rigorous logical scheme; it is composed of three parts, the first concerning the internal organisation of the economic system, the second forming a brief but impressively lucid treatise on money and internal monetary circulation, the third a treatise on foreign trade and exchanges, the author's familiarity with such themes being clearly apparent, particularly with the mechanisms of international finance.[33] The text was followed by a statistical appendix, subsequently lost, which probably contained exercises in political arithmetic on the lines of Petty, as we may surmise from the references to it in the text.

It seems that Cantillon attributed to these arithmetical computations rather less importance than did Petty, considering them approximate tools for describing reality and finding an interpretative key rather than

---

[30] Murphy (1986, pp. 282–98), however, stresses the doubts that surround the story, recalling the suspicion that Cantillon had staged the whole thing to flee abroad without being hunted for.

[31] Malachy Postlethwayt (1707–67), mentioned earlier, is known as the author of a monumental *Universal dictionary of trade and commerce* (1751–5). Cantillon's *Essay* was included in it in near entirety, probably copied from an original English text since lost.

[32] *L'ami des hommes*, which Mirabeau published in 1756 and which had enormous success – more than forty editions in a few years and many translations – was in fact mainly a commentary on Cantillon's book, enriched with abundant doses of rhetoric. Subsequently various other authors including Beccaria drew on Cantillon, often without acknowledging their source.

[33] Cantillon had become rich by speculating first on John Law's scheme (the 'Mississippi bubble'), of which he had foreseen both the initial successes and the inevitable final collapse, subsequently on exchanges in a period of strong capital movements between France, Holland and England, and finally on the Amsterdam and London stock exchanges (the 'South Sea bubble'). Murphy (1986) presents a fascinating account of Cantillon's adventurous life and an introduction to his thought.

revealing underlying quantitative laws.[34] In any case, he took a number of elements from Petty, and in the first place the idea of a 'body politic' able to obtain a surplus produce over and above the requirements of means of production and subsistence. However, while Petty seems to have had the connection between the different parts of the 'body politic' residing mainly in the fact that they are subject to a single state power, Cantillon saw it as stemming from the process of circulation of commodities. Actually, the idea also appeared in Petty when he compared money to the fat of the human body, and commodities to the blood (cf. above, § 3.3). However, it was Cantillon who first explicitly emphasised the link between the processes of circulation of commodities and of production.

The first part of Cantillon's *Essay* is the most interesting, revealing the crucial role he played on the way from Petty to Quesnay and Smith. Obviously, the connections between these authors will be interpreted according to the viewpoint taken on economic science. For instance, according to Jevons, Cantillon was a forerunner of modern theories mainly because of his dichotomy between market value and 'intrinsic value' (which Jevons identified with the opposition of a theory of prices based on supply and demand to one based on production cost).[35] As we see it, on the contrary, Cantillon pursued the path started on by Petty, contributing to the specification of the basic concepts used by subsequent generations of economists in their analytical systems, and by Quesnay in the first place.

Let us focus our attention on two elements of Cantillon's thought: the conceptual categories adopted to subdivide the economy on the basis of localisation, sector and social class, and the theory of value, which we may call a land value theory.

For the first of these two elements, Cantillon associated the division into sectors (agriculture, artisan sector, commerce) with division into social classes (peasants, artisans, merchants and nobility) and the geographical organisation of society (countryside, villages, towns). It will be

---

[34] In a sense, Cantillon resembled Keynes for his awareness of the complexity of real life, requiring simplifications grounded on rational foundations, and for the importance attributed to practical judgement with regard to the possibility that in specific cases the elements disregarded in the theory (that is, in the rational and simplified reconstruction of reality) may prove relevant and lead to results different from those foreseen by the theory itself.

[35] Jevons 1881, p. 345. As a matter of fact, much as Smith was later to do, Cantillon identified market prices with actual prices, influenced by contingent elements summarised in the terms 'supply' and 'demand', which cannot be subjected to theoretical treatment: cf. below, § 5.6. Analogous interpretative conflicts have also arisen over other aspects of Cantillon's work: for instance, his treatment of exchanges has been seen to anticipate both Hume's theory of an automatic re-equilibrating mechanism of the trade balance, and the Keynesian theory that has capital movements dominating in the determination of exchange rates.

noted that Cantillon did not follow the modern division of the economy into sectors (agriculture, industry and services) and social classes (workers, capitalists, landlords), but this does not make his vision of the interconnections between the different viewpoints we may take on an economic system (those of the division into sectors, or social classes, or geographical areas that may be considered as internally homogeneous) any the less relevant. Obviously, this does not mean that drawing direct correspondence between different classifications is the best way to represent the economy.[36] In any case, as we shall see in the next section, the connection between the division of society into classes and into sectors was taken up by Quesnay and the physiocrats. Subsequently, however, at least from Smith onwards, the division into social classes (workers, capitalists, landlords) was to be autonomous from that into sectors, not fully worked out, and from the geographical division, which remained in the background and was often reduced to the town–country dichotomy. The autonomous nature of the different classifications, corresponding to the different viewpoints from which the economic system can be studied, should not, however, make us lose sight of the connections between them. Such classifications are but a tool for analysis, with historically relative validity.

The second element in Cantillon's analysis that we will consider concerns his theory of value. In this respect Cantillon referred directly to Petty's thought (cf. above, § 3.5), of which he (Cantillon 1755, p. 27) took up the main thesis: 'The Price and Intrinsic Value of a Thing in general is the measure of the Land and Labour which enter into its Production.'

However, with regard to the equation between labour and land, the criterion proposed by Petty was criticised as 'fanciful and remote from natural laws': 'he has attached himself not to causes and principles but only to effects, as Mr Locke, Mr Davenant and all the other English authors who have written on this subject have done after him' (ibid., p. 43).

In other words, Cantillon seems to have grasped the limitation of Petty's proposed solution, based on the relative productivity ('the effects') of processes utilising alternatively labour or land, which implied either techniques with a single means of production or a circular reasoning. The solution proposed by Cantillon was in fact more coherent with the

---

[36] A highroad of progress for economic science is constituted by the separation of problems, since only adequate specification of a problem allows for its solution. In the case of Cantillon, as in that of the physiocrats, the problem of the social structure is confused with the problems of subdivision into sectors and of distinction between productive and unproductive labour.

objective approach of the classical theory of prices: labour is reduced to its cost of production. In Cantillon's words (ibid., p. 35), 'the daily labour of the meanest Slave corresponds in value to double the produce of the Land required to maintain him'; in fact, apart from the subsistence of the worker we need compute an equal cost for subsistence of two offspring, so as to ensure substitution of the worker at the end of his productive life, taking into account the mortality conditions of the time.[37]

Thus Cantillon took into consideration a self-sufficient fragment of a vital economic system, in which land is the only non-produced means of production and in which the net product corresponds to the means of subsistence required for maintenance of a worker and two children: the value of a worker corresponds, then, to the quantity of land utilised in such a subsystem.

We should note, however, that land by itself produces nothing; even if all the other means of production are reproduced within the same period, it is not possible to start production without them. The very existence of the product hence depends on the availability of all the means of production in existence at the beginning of the period, workers included; like Petty's theory, Cantillon's also begs the question. However, Cantillon seemed to be searching not so much for determination of exchange ratios (which in fact are assumed as given) as for a solution to the problem of the causes of value. In this respect, the line taken by Cantillon, i.e. reducing labour to its cost of production (which, as we saw above, was hinted at by Petty when he stated that 'the days food of an adult Man, at a Medium, [. . .] is the common measure of Value'),[38] should lead to a pure land theory of value, since land would remain the sole original non-reproducible factor of production creating value.[39] As a matter of fact, Cantillon did not maintain a theory of value of this kind, which would have implied attributing to land alone the capacity to create value, but the direction in which he moved undoubtedly prepared the background for the physiocrats' thought, to be considered in the next section.

Another aspect of Cantillon's thought open to different interpretation lies in the driving role he attributed to upper-class luxury consumption. On the one hand it is considered an element of modernity, analogous to the role of autonomous demand items (particularly investments) in

---

[37] Ibid., pp. 31–7. Because of this approach, Cantillon seemed to anticipate the Marxian treatment of the value of labour power (cf. below, § 9.4), with the difference that Marx reduced the value of labour power to the quantity of labour required to produce the workers' means of subsistence, and Cantillon to the quantity of land.

[38] Petty 1691a, p. 181. Cf. above, § 3.5.

[39] Thus Brewer 1988, 1992, interprets Cantillon's theory, translating it into the terms of a formalised model.

the Keynesian system: as the title of chapter 12 of Part One puts it, 'All Classes and Individuals in a State subsist or are enriched at the Expense of the Proprietors of Land.'[40] On the other hand, however, and perhaps more aptly, it is seen as a residuum of the feudal system, precisely in that it focused attention on consumption by the propertied classes while ignoring the dynamic role assumed by industrial investments within capitalism.[41] In any case, this idea constituted one of the main elements in Cantillon's influence on the physiocratic school.[42]

On the other hand, the physiocrats were not to take up the 'three rents' theory, which would however subsequently reappear in a modified form within the classical tradition. In Cantillon's view, the first rent was the part of the product that the farmer used to meet the costs of production, inclusive of the workers' subsistence; the second rent constituted the farmers' income, corresponding to what we would today call the profit of agricultural entrepreneurs;[43] while the third rent was that going to the landlord for the use of his land. In Cantillon's words: 'The Farmers have generally two thirds of the Produce of the Land, one for their costs and the support of their Assistants, the other for the Profit of their Undertaking [. . .] The Proprietor has usually one third of the produce of his Land.'[44]

The profits of the agricultural entrepreneur (the dominant kind of capitalist, at a time when the agricultural sector dominated the economy and manufactures were characterised by artisan production) were considered jointly with rent proper. Thus profits were not yet related to capital

---

[40] Cantillon 1755, p. 43. Cf. Giacomin 1996.   [41] Cf. Brenner 1978, p. 122.

[42] This is anyhow an idea already present in the literature of the time; for example, in a 'liberal' author such as Boisguilbert: cf. above, § 1. In fact, the issue of luxury consumption was widely debated in the seventeenth and eighteenth centuries, though no longer on the ancient and medieval lines of a moral issue concerning the rightness of the quest for material wealth. Rather, attention was given, in the period now under consideration, to issues such as the role of luxury consumption as a component of demand (with the attending distinction between consumption of home-produced or imported luxuries), hence as a stimulus to production and employment, or (as we will see below, § 9, with regard to Hume) as a positive factor for the 'refinement' of human beings and as a stimulus to industry. These ideas were utilised, in lively debates, in opposition to the repetition of traditional ancient and medieval views but also in opposition to Calvinist and Puritan views.

[43] 'The Farmer is an undertaker who promises to pay to the landowner, for his Farm or Land, a fixed sum of money [. . .] without assurance of the profit he will derive from this enterprise' (Cantillon 1755, pp. 47–9).

[44] Ibid., pp. 43–5. Cf. also ibid., p. 121: 'It is the general opinion in England that a Farmer must make three Rents. (1) The principal and true Rent which he pays to the proprietor, supposed equal in value to the produce of one third of his Farm, a second Rent for his maintenance and that of the Men and Horses he employs to cultivate the Farm, and a third which ought to remain with him to make his undertaking profitable.' Let us recall in this respect that according to Schumpeter 1954, p. 222, it was a great merit of Cantillon to have recognised 'the entrepreneurial function and its central importance'.

advances in order to generate the idea of a uniform rate of return (rate of profits). This aspect, too, may better be understood if we recall the limited strength of competition in the conditions of the time, as can be seen among other things in certain passages in the *Essay* on the relationship between interest rates and real rates of return, where the widespread dispersion of returns in different activities and more generally in different circumstances becomes fully apparent.

An important role was attributed to financial capitalists:

The number of Proprietors of money in a large State is often considerable enough; and though the value of all the money which circulates in the State barely exceeds the ninth or tenth part of the value of the produce drawn from the soil yet, as the proprietors of money lend considerable amounts for which they receive interest [. . .] the sums due to them usually exceed all the money in the State, and they often become so powerful a body that they would in certain cases rival the Proprietors of Lands if these last were not often equally Proprietors of money, and if the owners of large sums of money did not always seek to become Landowners themselves.[45]

Cantillon's ideas on money were much like Petty's: money is necessary for the circulation of commodities, but precious metals do not coincide with wealth; the quantity of money required for the sound functioning of the economy depends on the value of exchanges and the velocity of circulation of money itself. Furthermore, according to Cantillon, the interest rate depends on the ratio between demand for and supply of loanable funds, and is therefore not directly and strictly related to the supply of money.[46] The value of money (and hence, inversely, the general level of prices) depends essentially on its cost of production, as in Petty, and unlike, for instance, the position taken by Locke, who focused on demand and supply. This, however, is something that influences but does not determine the evaluation of money made by the market, which may differ from its 'value'. Notable importance in such an evaluation was held, among other things, by the elements that were considered to influence the velocity of circulation of money: the financial institutions and customs – for instance the existence of clearing agreements – and commercial credit. Moreover, monetary phenomena influenced different goods in different ways. Cantillon appears to have been at his ease examining these relations given that they were connected to his activities as a

---

[45] Cantillon 1755, p. 57. It should be remembered that, as a Catholic, Cantillon was forbidden to acquire land in England, and that in the last years of his life he tried in various ways to be exempted from this rule: for a long period, the institutions of private property have coexisted, in the case of land, with constraints on transferability of property aiming at safeguarding the traditional social structure.

[46] For an illustration of Cantillon's position in the debate of the time on this theme, cf. Tucker 1960, ch. 2.

banker, which, however, he did not illustrate: his *Essay* was undoubtedly an economics treatise, not a treatise on banking and financial technique, though we cannot help noticing how much room monetary issues take up and how little – next to nothing, in fact – do fiscal issues, so important in the debates of the time. Monetary issues, too, both national and international, were dealt with in a logically most rigorous way, so that the discourse appears simple, at some points even obvious. In general, it is clear that even in manuscript form this work had a profound impact on its readers.

6.   François Quesnay and the physiocrats

The physiocrats (or *les économistes*, as they used to call themselves) were a very compact and combative group of French economists grouped around François Quesnay (1694–1774), doctor to Madame de Pompadour at the court of Louis XV. The physiocrats are the first school of economic thought to have equipped themselves with their own press organs in order to advocate definite points of policy. The span of time in which they were dominant was short – little more than a quarter of a century[47] – but their influence on the development of political economy was significantly strong, partly due to the central position Paris occupied in the cultural life of the time. The physiocrats attributed a key role to the development of agriculture, which they considered the only sector capable of producing a surplus. Moreover, as their name suggests (physiocracy originates from the Greek *fùsis* = nature, and *cratèin* = to dominate), they shared with the Cartesian current of French Enlightenment (cf. below, § 7) the idea of a 'natural order', the logic and optimality of which – unchanging over time, since it is intrinsic to the very nature of things – should be evident to any person endowed with the light of reason, and which an enlightened prince should implement as 'positive order', eliminating defects due to the deficiencies of the human legislator.[48] Private property also falls within this natural order, so the defence of property rights was considered one of the main tasks of the 'positive order'. Thus the physiocrats drastically mitigated the absolutism implicit in the traditional view of the enlightened sovereign, although here they seem somewhat more backward than Locke, who antedated

---

[47] According to Higgs (1897, pp. 25 and 58), the birth of the physiocratic school may be dated from the meeting between Quesnay and Mirabeau in July 1757, and its end in 1776–7, when Turgot, then minister of finance, fell in disgrace, and with publication of Smith's *Wealth of nations*.

[48] Quesnay was in particular a follower of the French philosopher Malebranche (1638–1715), in turn a follower of Descartes.

them, or Smith, the author of the *Theory of moral sentiments* (1759), their contemporary.

The importance attributed to agriculture had been evident since Quesnay's first publications of an economic nature: two articles on *Fermiers* (Farmers) and *Grains* (Corn), which appeared in the *Encyclopédie* edited by d'Alembert and Diderot in 1756 and 1757 respectively. However, Quesnay's best-known work is the *Tableau économique* (Economic table), printed in Versailles in 1758. Also worth mentioning here is the article on *Droit naturel* (Natural law), dated 1765.[49]

Among the main followers of Quesnay we may mention Victor Riqueti, Marquis of Mirabeau (1715–89), who achieved celebrity in 1756 with the publication of *L'ami des hommes* (The friend of men) which, as we have already seen, owed much to Cantillon's work, and Pierre Du Pont de Nemours (1739–1817), who edited Quesnay's works (*Physiocratie*, 1767–8) and the journals produced under physiocratic influence (the *Journal de l'agriculture, du commerce et des finances* from 1765 to 1766, then the *Ephémérides du citoyen* from 1768 to 1772), besides collaborating with Turgot up to 1776 and editing his writings in nine large volumes between 1809 and 1811. Also worthy of mention here is Pierre-Paul Mercier de la Rivière (1720–94), author of a treatise entitled *L'ordre naturel et essentiel des sociétés politiques* (The natural and essential order of political societies) dated 1767, which Smith rated the best exposition of the physiocratic doctrines.

Mirabeau and various other physiocrats (but not Quesnay, whose theories are discussed below) saw the capacity of agriculture to generate a surplus as being intrinsic to the fertility of the soil (which produces an ear of wheat from a grain), and hence as a gift of mother nature. This theory on the origin of the surplus may then be used to justify appropriation of the surplus by the nobility – not only the rightful owners of the lands but masters of the serfs living on them to boot.

Quesnay, too, considered agriculture alone capable of yielding a surplus, although his explanation is somewhat different, taking account of the situation prevailing in France at the time: given the prices of agricultural products and manufactures on the world markets, with recourse to the best technologies farmers can obtain a product whose value exceeds production costs, while manufacturers simply recover their costs (including subsistence for manufacturing entrepreneurs). In other words, what Quesnay set out to stress was the potential a reformed agricultural system held for economic development – what he called *grande culture*, as

---

[49] The classical edition (though not exempt from criticism) of Quesnay's economic and philosophical writings is that of INED 1958, vol. 2; vol. 1 contains interpretative essays by various authors and a bibliography.

compared with *petite culture,* the former characterised not only by larger concerns, but also by technologies with higher capital intensity (more specifically, the plough drawn by horses rather than oxen was practically a watchword of the physiocrats).

Thus, in his writings Quesnay stressed the potentialities of an agricultural revolution that had already begun but that, in his opinion, was lagging behind the expansion of capitalism in trade. The stance he took was opposed not so much to the – still very much alive – mercantilist tradition in general, but above all to Colbertism, or in other words Colbert's economic policy of supporting commerce and manufactures by liberalising the importation of raw materials and duties on manufacturing imports (cf. above, § 2.6). This was obviously not going to help the development of agriculture, reducing its profitability while increasing that of manufactures. On the contrary, Quesnay argued, agricultural products should be given a *bon prix,* or in other words a price sufficient not only to cover production costs, but also to favour the financing of investments by ensuring adequate returns.

Neither the *bon prix* nor the *prix fondamental* (which corresponded to mere costs of production, so that differences between the *bon prix* and it corresponded to the profits of the farmer) were prices spontaneously generated by the markets, and Quesnay failed to see any mechanisms that automatically led to either of these two market prices, which depended on supply and demand conditions (while in the case of manufactures prices corresponded to production costs). Implementation of the *bon prix* was thus entrusted, among other things, to a policy favouring the free exportation of agricultural products and consumption habits within the country such as would encourage the *luxe de subsistence* as compared with the *luxe de décoration,* or consumption of agricultural produce – but not of manufactures – in excess of the mere subsistence level.[50] Although the notion

---

[50] The physiocrats thus connected high prices with the idea of a flourishing, developing, economy, in which high prices are the cause (or one of the causes) and economic abundance is the effect. This view was widely held during the whole of the mercantilist period, but far from unanimously, since in many cases high prices were seen as a symptom of dearth. On the contrary, Smith and the classical economists held that moderate prices are connected with a situation of abundance, of which they are essentially the effect. Obviously at the logical level the two theses are not mutually exclusive, since they are based on consideration of different aspects of the process of development, and hence on cause and effect relationships moving in opposite directions. On the one hand, relatively high prices stemming from high demand constitute a stimulus to production, while a low level of prices may signal difficulty in absorption of the products by the market, and may thus constitute a disincentive for producers; on the other hand, increase in productivity accompanying economic development leads, under competitive conditions, to decrease in prices, while high prices signal bottlenecks on the supply side, namely the presence of obstacles to the growth of production. The debate between supporters of the two theses

of a competitive rate of profits was still wanting (it would be outlined by Turgot a few years later, and fully developed by Smith), Quesnay fully recognised the crucial role of capital accumulation for the productive process and above all in allowing improved technologies to be adopted. Quesnay distinguished between *avances foncières* (initial basic investments, required for cultivating a piece of land and increasing its productivity), *avances primitives* (production implements, cattle) and *avances annuelles* (circulating capital: seed, wages and the like). This was therefore, again, an aspect of the economy that drew his attention to agriculture; at the same time, however, he made decided strides in the direction subsequently followed by Turgot, Smith and the whole classical tradition, of considering capital advances as a requirement for the production and accumulation of capital a crucial element for economic development.

Opposing the Colbertian approach to economic policy, Quesnay and the physiocrats developed a theory admirable in its 'spirit of system' and consistency. In particular, Quesnay was the first economist to recognise and represent in an analytical scheme the productive interrelations linking the different sectors that, in an economic system based on the division of labour, stemmed from heterogeneity of means of production in each sector. This problem was tackled, in the *tableau économique*, by focusing on the exchanges required to ensure the continuous functioning of the economic system.

Let us examine in broad outline the functioning of the economic system lying at the foundations of Quesnay's model. Agriculture, as we saw above, was considered the sole productive (i.e. capable of generating a surplus) sector in the economy; in his model, Quesnay assumed that the most advanced technology, the *grande culture*, was generally adopted in agriculture. Other activities, and in the first place manufacturing, were grouped under the 'sterile sector' heading, so-called because these activities merely transformed into processed products a given set of raw materials (including means of subsistence for the workers of the sector); the value of the processed products proved equal to the value of the means of production and subsistence utilised to obtain them, so that there was no surplus, or in other words no creation of new value.

Subdivision of the economic system into sectors thus corresponded to the following subdivision of society into social classes: the productive class composed of those active in agriculture (peasants and farmers), the sterile class composed of artisans (including manufacturing workers and

showed frequent confusion between theoretical discussion concerning different systems of logical relations, evaluation of the greater or lesser applicability to the real world of the underlying relations, and interpretations of specific real-world situations.

merchants), and the aristocratic class, that is, the class of landlords, to which the surplus obtained in the agricultural sector accrued, including the nobility and the clergy.

Quesnay's main contribution to economic theory was his *tableau économique*: a series of graphs which outlined the structure of the economic system, showing the relations (that is, the series of exchanges of commodities against money) that need to take place between the different productive sectors and the different social classes in order to allow for the survival and development of the economy.

Quesnay's economic tables gave rise to considerable interpretative debate.[51] Here we shall illustrate them with a simplified scheme that does not pretend to reproduce precisely all the characteristics of Quesnay's analysis, but shows how it represented the functioning of the economy as a circular process in which, year after year, the phases of production, exchange and consumption follow one upon the other.[52]

Figure 4.1 illustrates the situation at the end of the productive cycle, before the beginning of the exchanges. The aristocratic class (the nobility) has two units of money (let us say, two billion francs), received from the agricultural sector in payment of rents for use of land. The sterile class (the manufacturing sector) has three units of manufactured goods.[53] The productive class has five units of product: three of agricultural food products, and two of raw materials. Let *MG* be the manufactured goods,

---

[51] Cf. Higgs 1897; Tsuru 1942; Meek 1962; Ridolfi 1973; Gilibert 1977; the collection of essays edited by Candela and Palazzi 1979; Vaggi 1987 and the bibliography therein contained.

[52] Specifically, we consider only circulating capital (*avances annuelles*), while Quesnay at least for the productive sector tried to keep into account also *avances foncières* (original investments on land improvements) and *avances primitives* (the stock of capital goods employed by the farmer). The first ones are relevant for the interpretation of landowner's rent as interest on the value of land, but do not give rise to yearly flows of goods; the second ones give rise to commodity flows from the sterile to the productive sector for the reintegration of that part of fixed capital which goes out of use yearly. (Alternatively, we might consider this latter flow as included in the unit of manufactured goods which the productive sector acquires each year from the sterile sector.)

[53] While other data mirror those of Quesnay's *Tableau*, the production of manufactures in our example proves greater by one unit. As we shall see, this additional unit does not enter into circulation: from the point of view of the sterile class as a whole (but not necessarily from the point of view of the single productive unit) this is production for self-consumption, and it is possible that Quesnay had disregarded it precisely for this reason. However, it seems obvious that the sterile class also requires manufactured goods as means of production and subsistence; hence the change to the numerical values utilised by Quesnay (which probably, as Ridolfi 1973 suggests, constituted an implicit evaluation of the main magnitudes of the national accounts of France at that time). Analogously, Quesnay did not consider the use of agricultural products as means of production (e.g. as seed) within the productive sector, while in our scheme we explicitly consider a unit of raw material which is yearly produced and used as means of production within the productive sector, without giving rise to commodity flows between sectors.

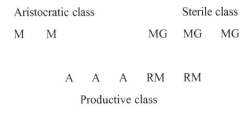

Figure 4.1

RM the raw materials, *IA* the agricultural food products and *IM* money (each symbol represents a unit of commodity or money).

In this situation it is not possible to begin a new productive cycle. The agricultural sector needs manufactured goods as means of subsistence and production (clothing, spades and ploughs), and money with which to pay the rents for the land. The manufacturing workers in turn need food and raw materials, required for subsistence and as means of production. The aristocratic class also needs food and manufactured goods with which to maintain their comfortable lifestyle, but without which they cannot even survive.

The continuous functioning of the economic system thus requires exchanges between the different sectors, or, in Quesnay's representation, between the different social classes. Let a dotted line represent money movements, and a continuous line commodity movements; we may then describe the process of exchange as follows. First (figure 4.2), the nobility utilises money to acquire one unit of manufactured products from the sterile class and one unit of agricultural food products from the productive class. Immediately after this (figure 4.3), the sterile class utilises the money it has received to acquire one unit of agricultural food products from the productive class. In turn, the productive class utilises the money received from the nobility to acquire one unit of manufactured products

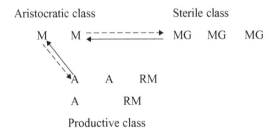

Figure 4.2

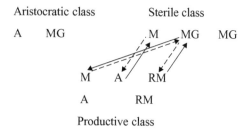

Figure 4.3

from the sterile class. Finally, the sterile class utilises the money thus received to acquire from the productive class one unit of raw materials. The final situation, after the exchanges, is illustrated in figure 4.4.

As we can see, these exchanges set the economy ready to start a new productive cycle. The nobility can enjoy their agricultural and manufactured products. The productive class has the manufactured and agricultural products necessary to their survival, raw materials (such as seed) and manufactured goods required as means of production, and two units of money with which to pay rents. The sterile class has the agricultural and manufactured products required for its survival, and the raw materials required as means of production.

At the end of the productive process, the system comes back to the initial situation. The nobility have consumed their agricultural and manufactured products, and received money from the productive sector as rent for the land. The sterile class have utilised their means of subsistence and of production, three units in all, to produce three units of manufactured products. The productive class have utilised their three units of means of subsistence and of production to produce five units of product (three units of agricultural products and two units of raw materials) on the land rented from the nobility. We are thus dealing with a vital economic system, functioning under conditions of simple reproduction.

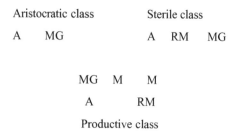

Figure 4.4

As can be seen, the surplus (namely the product left once the means of production and of subsistence for the workers employed in the economy have been reintegrated) corresponds to the consumption of the nobility, who produce nothing and are able to acquire year after year agricultural and manufactured products only because they receive their rents from the productive sector. In Quesnay's scheme, the surplus originates in agriculture: in this sector the use of three units in the productive process (as means of production and of subsistence) yields five units of product.

In the circular process described by Quesnay the different sectors and social classes are interconnected; the distribution of the product among the different social classes takes place simultaneously with the process of exchanges that allow each sector to reintegrate the initial endowments of means of production and of subsistence.

However, Quesnay failed to provide a sufficiently thorough account of the distribution of the surplus among the various sectors and the various social classes. The ideas of his followers in this respect reflected somewhat simplistically the social structure of the time, characterised by a privileged position for the aristocratic class: since all surplus originated within agriculture, it was 'natural' for it to go to the nobility in possession of the land whose productive power guaranteed the very existence of the surplus. As we shall see, this view was criticised by Smith, who saw the surplus as originating not in the agricultural sector but in the economic system as a whole, and to be attributed not to a specific means of production (the land), but rather to the 'active element' in the production process, namely labour (a view that had already been sketched out by Petty, with his reference to labour as the 'father' and land as the 'mother' of all wealth: cf. above, § 3.5).

The physiocratic doctrine did not, however, imply defence of the nobility's incomes: if the rent of the landlords coincided with the surplus, then this alone should obviously bear the entire tax burden. In fact, attempts to bring taxes to bear on other social classes were not only doomed to failure, through the transfer processes, but were also costly for the economic system as a whole given the adjustments they required, in particular for the disincentive to accumulation and technical change entailed by taxes on farmers, viewed by Quesnay and the physiocrats as the active agents for economic development.

7.   The political economy of the Enlightenment: Turgot

As we have seen, the influence of the physiocrats was important, but short-lived. The closed form which they insisted on for their school itself indicates the existence of different opinions in the culture of the time. Along with Cantillon and the physiocrats, the eighteenth century was rich in economists, or perhaps we should say intellectuals who took economic issues into consideration among other things.

The culture of the time, in its general and not strictly economic sense, was dominated by the Enlightenment. The eighteenth century is known as the century of the Enlightenment, or 'the age of reason'. The general characteristic was a faith in both material and civic progress, of society as of man, guided by Reason.[54] In fact, as we saw while considering the idea of the *doux commerce* (above, § 2), human nature itself may progress and improve.[55]

Within these very broad lines, while bearing in mind both the substantially international nature of the culture of the time and the dominant role played by Paris, we may distinguish various currents in the French, Scottish, Italian (Neapolitan, Milanese and Tuscan) and German Enlightenment.

Paris was at the time the centre of European cultural life. A number of leading intellectuals from other countries, such as the Scot David Hume or the Neapolitan Ferdinando Galiani, resided there as staff of their respective embassies; for Adam Smith a visit to France with a period of residence in Paris marked a crucial stage in the development of his ideas.

A deeply rooted characteristic of a great part of the French Enlightenment was represented by the heritage of Descartes[56] – an *esprit de système* and a rationalism raised to the level of an absolute methodology, and ultimately to a cult of the goddess Reason in the season of revolutionary Terror.[57] A clear 'systemic spirit' is evident, for example, in the analytical construction of the physiocratic school and its corollaries for economic policy. However, there were many and various positions: suffice to mention the spirit of openness and tolerance of one protagonist looming large on the scene: Voltaire (1694–1778). An important sign of these manifold trends is to be seen in the economic entries in the monumental *Encyclopédie* edited by Diderot, which saw the collaboration of many of our protagonists, including Quesnay, Turgot, Rousseau and Condillac.

---

[54] For illustration of European society and culture in the eighteenth century, cf. for instance Im Hof 1993; Chaunu 1982.

[55] Cf. Pollard 1968.

[56] René Descartes (1596–1650), French philosopher and mathematician, author of a renowned *Discours de la méthode* (1637) and founder of analytical geometry.

[57] Take, for instance, the influence of Jean-Jacques Rousseau (1712–78; the *Contrat social* is dated 1762) on the ideas prevailing within the French Revolution on the juridical systems. Another example is the Abbé André Morellet (1727–1819), translator into French of the *The wealth of nations*; as Lytton Strachey wrote in his fine portrait of this personage (1931, p. 99), after five years at the Sorbonne Morellet came out of it 'an Abbé and an infidel': which was not a rare occurrence at the time. To 'Cartesian economics' Pribram (1983, pp. 97–114) devotes a chapter of his history, dealing there among other things with the physiocrats. In a sense, we may consider Walras first and Debreu later as heirs of the rationalistic tradition of French Enlightenment: cf. below, ch. 12.

One of the economic commitments of the Enlightenment was a critique of the institution of guilds inherited from the Middle Ages, with their rigid regulation of production techniques, product quality, wages and the working conditions of apprentices. Let us recall for instance the brilliant apologue by Gabriel François Coyer (1707–82), *Chinki, a Cochin-Chinese story that could be useful to other countries*, where the misadventures are told of a serious and laborious worker who is hamstrung in any activity he undertakes by absurd regulations, leading to ruin for him and his family (Coyer 1768).

As we have already seen (§ 1), the Enlightenment distinguished itself from mercantilism in its revaluation of agriculture in comparison with foreign trade and manufactures. Moreover, in the wake of Petty and Cantillon, the best authors dealing with economic issues based their analyses on the notions of surplus and value, and took production, distribution and circulation (exchange) as connected processes. Often they were supporters of high wages for economic reasons, and were driven by a humanitarian spirit to approach the problems stemming from misery and the difficulties of the poor in practical terms (consider, for instance, the debate – which will shortly be considered below, in § 6.1 – on the creation of charitable institutions and hospitals and on public assistance for the sick and orphans). More generally, the writers of this period tended to attribute importance to the connection between economic development and civic progress.

On the other hand, the Enlightenment can be differentiated from the subsequent classical school on account of its – at least partly – pre-capitalistic view, failing to take full account of productive interrelations and competition between sectors while, on the problem of value, tending – especially on the continent, and with important exceptions like the physiocrats – towards subjective theories (in which the price of each commodity was determined by comparison between demand and scarcity).[58]

An eminent representative of French economic culture in this phase was Anne-Robert Jacques Turgot (1727–81), a man of letters, economist and high-ranking functionary, responsible for economic affairs in Limoges from 1761, then minister of finance from 1774 to 1776. His best known work is the *Réflexions sur la formation et la distribution des richesses* (Thoughts on the building up and distribution of wealth, 1766).[59]

---

[58] As far as economic policy is concerned, common elements were the proposal of a single tax on the net income of land, and the hostility to arts and crafts guilds already recalled above.

[59] Among the various editions of Turgot's works, after the first, in nine volumes, edited by Du Pont de Nemours (1809–11) and after the edition in five volumes edited by Schelle (1913–23), which is the most commonly utilised, we may mention the recent paperback edited by Ravix and Romani (1997), with Turgot's major writings and useful bio-bibliographical apparatus.

Turgot belonged to the next generation after Quesnay, and in various respects represented a bridge between the physiocrats and his contemporary, Adam Smith. In many respects Turgot was nearer to the latter than to the physiocrats: while sharing their support for free trade (specifically, freedom of exports of agricultural products), he was clearly not at ease with absolute political power, sharing Smith's belief (stated in the *Theory of moral sentiments*, 1759: cf. below, § 5.3) that each human being is better able than anybody else to rule his or her own life. Turgot's theories are remembered in particular for the role attributed to capital and the capitalist-entrepreneurs in the process of production and for his decidedly liberal views, summed up by the phrase *laissez-nous faire* which he cited in the lengthy obituary dedicated to his friend Vincent de Gournay (1712–59), stressing his fervent economic liberalism.[60] *Laissez-faire* was also the hallmark of a number of policy measures adopted by Turgot in Limoges and then as minister, including notably liberalisation of the corn trade and abolition of the *jurandes*, or craft guilds. His policy measures constituted possibly the last attempt at rationalising state intervention in the French economy before the Revolution, but they clashed with vested interests, arousing antagonism and eventually leading to Turgot's downfall.

Following Montesquieu's idea (in *L'esprit des lois*, 1748) of a connection between the political institutions and the social structure of a country and its productive organisation (or, in stronger terms, the materialist idea that the conditions of economic life influence all other aspects of a society), Turgot developed the so-called 'four stages theory', according to which human history is marked by a sequence of four stages: hunting, cattle-raising, agriculture and commerce. More or less simultaneously with Turgot, whose writing on 'Universal history' was published posthumously,[61] a similar theory was propounded by Adam Smith in his Glasgow lectures, also published posthumously, and then in the *Wealth of nations*.

On a strictly analytical level, Turgot outlined a theory of exchange value based on utility. All evaluations are subjective; buyer and seller accept the exchange because they have different evaluations (*valeurs estimatives*) of the commodity in question, constituting the lower and upper price limits.

---

[60] Cf. Turgot 1759, p. 151. Turgot attributed to Gournay the thesis according to which 'a man knows his own interest better than another man to whom that interest is wholly indifferent' (ibid., p. 131) – an expression recalling an observation by Smith in the *Theory of moral sentiments* (published in the same year as the *Éloge*): 'Every man is [. . .] fitter and abler to take care of himself than of any other person' (Smith 1759, p. 219; cf. below, § 5.3), which may be traced back to the Greek tradition (cf. above, § 2.2).
[61] Cf. Ravix and Romani 1997, pp. 95–121.

The actual price would, according to Turgot, come midway between these two limits, coinciding with the *valeur appréciative* given by the average of the *valeurs estimatives*.[62]

Other aspects of his analysis foreshadowed – or have been considered as precursors of – subsequent theories. For instance, his theory of increasing returns focused on what was to be called the intensive margin, that is, utilisation of an increasing number of doses of capital and labour on a given plot of land; this theory was to be one of the main points of reference in Sraffa's criticisms in an article of 1925 (cf. below, § 16.4), but it was disregarded in the debates giving rise to the differential rent theory in 1815 (below, § 7.2). We may now feel that certain metaphorical references to the interrelations linking elements in the economic field were somewhat overvalued, including the parallel drawn between the various commodity markets and a system of hydraulic connections in equilibrium. This parallel apparently sufficed for many a historian of economic thought to hail Turgot as a forerunner of Walras and the theory of general economic equilibrium.[63] As a matter of fact, Turgot did not get much further than mere metaphors, and these simply expressed the idea, well rooted at the time and already widespread in the previous century, that there is a parallel between the 'social body' and the physical world, and in particular the astronomic system governed by the Newtonian law of gravitation. Furthermore, while Quesnay elaborated upon these ideas in the attempt to build an analytic scheme, Turgot left us with a few somewhat generic observations.

8.   The Italian Enlightenment: the Abbé Galiani

In comparison with the French Enlightenment, the Scottish (which we briefly consider in the next section in relation to Smith's background) and Neapolitan brands, on the fringe of European cultural life centred on Paris, showed greater readiness to recognise the imperfections of human nature and the impossibility of deducing directly from a priori reasoning interpretations of specific economic phenomena or clear-cut recipes for economic policy.

An example of this approach is provided by the *Dialogues sur le commerce des bléds* (Dialogues on the commerce of corn, 1770) by the Abbé

---

[62] This thesis, which Turgot enunciated but did not elaborate and which appeared unjustified within the framework of the modern subjective theory of value, possibly derived from the Scholastic debate on the just price, and in particular from the thesis widespread in the Spanish Scholastic school at the beginning of the sixteenth century, according to which 'there is parity when each participant receives an equal advantage' (Chafuen 1986, p. 106).

[63] Cf. for all Schumpeter 1954, p. 249, who points to a sequence Turgot–Say–Walras.

Ferdinando Galiani (1728–87), who had already written a celebrated treatise, *Della moneta* (On money, 1751), at the tender age of twenty-three.[64] His remarks on the physiocratic doctrines were based on direct criticism of the *esprit de système* and showed the importance of the specific circumstances of each real situation when reasoning on economic policy.[65]

The *Dialogues* were published anonymously in French and met with wide favour in the intellectual circles of Paris. Galiani had recently had to leave Paris after a stay of some years to return to Naples, and was missed in many salons of Europe's cultural capital for his lively style and impudent irony. The 'little Abbé', a great lover of Parisian life and women, then entered upon a copious exchange of correspondence with his friends (in particular Louise d'Épinay), leaving us with an exceptionally rich picture of that world and that crucial phase in the development of European culture.[66] Galiani was moreover the intermediary through which the *Encyclopédie* entourage absorbed the influence of the Neapolitan philosopher Giambattista Vico (1668–1744), held by Schumpeter (1954, pp. 135–7) to be 'one of the greatest thinkers to be found in any age in the field of the social sciences', who developed 'an evolutionary science of mind and society' (in the sense 'that mind and society are two aspects of the same evolutionary process'). Vico thus fed in some historicist antibacteria that to a certain extent counteracted the anti-historicist rationalism of the Cartesian current of the Enlightenment.

Galiani was a champion of theoretical minimalism. 'I am in favour of nothing. I am of the opinion that we should not talk nonsense',[67] he declared, and all his writings consistently show the validity of any idea at the level of theory or economic policy as relative to time and place. In this respect he stands as a major exponent of the sceptical current of the Enlightenment, even more extreme in this than Voltaire.

Galiani can also be considered the most important exponent of the subjective approach in Italy. In his *Della moneta* (1751), he spent a few pages (section 2 of book 1) on the role of scarcity and utility in determining the value of commodities. Here Galiani saw a predecessor in

---

[64] A second edition, published in 1780, includes a new long preface and thirty-five long end-notes, but the main text is substantially unchanged.

[65] 'Nobody ever makes a mistake without a reason. Thus everybody wants to follow reason and experience, but if you follow an idea reasonable in itself and rely on an experience or a true and demonstrated fact, but which does not fit in – is not applicable to the case at hand – you think you are doing well, and you are wrong' (Galiani 1770, p. 55). Or again: 'Nothing in politics can be pushed to the extreme. There is a point, a limit up to which good is greater than evil; if you pass beyond it, evil prevails over good. [. . . This point] only the sage knows how to find. People feel it by instinct. The man in power needs time to find it. The modern economist does not even suspect it' (ibid., p. 233).

[66] Part of it has been translated into Italian, cf. d'Épinay and Galiani 1996.

[67] Galiani 1770, p. 61.

Bernardo Davanzati, in the second half of the sixteenth century, while stressing, however, the latter's inability to solve what was to be known as the 'paradox of water and diamonds', that is, the high value of goods to which normally low utility is attributed, and on the contrary the low value of goods that are considered as not just useful, but necessary. In fact Davanzati was concerned with monetary and currency problems, and only *en passant* with the themes under discussion here; all Galiani (1751, p. 44) could quote with approval was the following passage: 'The rat is a most disgusting animal; but in the siege of Casilino everything was so dear that two hundred florins were paid for a rat; and it was not dear, since the person who sold it died of hunger, while the person who bought it survived.'

As was his wont in his early writing, Galiani developed his reasoning with a wealth of erudite quotations. His thesis was that 'the estimate, or value, *is the idea of a proportion between ownership of one thing and ownership of another in a man's mind*' (ibid., p. 39). The subjective approach to the theory of value, however, was moderated by recognition that 'in the estimate men, as the Schoolmen say, *passive se habent*' (ibid., p. 38), so that the estimate depended on the characteristics of the commodity itself and on the conditions, again external, determining its abundance or scarcity. Indeed, 'Value [. . .] is a reason; and this in turn is composed of two reasons, which I call: utility, and rarity' (ibid., p. 39), where 'I call *utility* the attitude of something to give us happiness' (ibid.), and 'I call *rarity* the proportion between the quantity of a thing and the use which is made of it' (ibid., p. 46). At this point, the conclusion reached by Galiani may sound surprising – but it was far from uncommon among authors considered as forerunners of the subjective theory of value. Indeed, Galiani distinguished two categories of goods: those which are scarce by nature and those which are produced and can be reproduced, for which he adopted the assumption of constant returns; with respect to this latter category he referred again to production costs, in particular to labour requirements:

there are two classes of bodies. In one class, [the quantity available of things] depends on the different abundance with which nature produces them; in the other class, it only depends on the toil and work employed. [. . .] If we refer to the first of these two classes in our computations, we should only keep into account the toil for harvesting, since the quantity of the material only corresponds to it. (ibid., p. 47)

While still in Naples, we should also mention Antonio Genovesi (1713–69), the first holder (since 1754) of a chair in political economy, who stressed in his writing the close link between the economy and the civic issues of institutional organisation and public morals. His major work in the economic field, *Delle lezioni di commercio* (Lectures on commerce, 1765–7), was essentially didactic, aimed at uplifting the human spirit and enhancing the knowledge of the young within the perspective of the Enlightenment. The theses he supported were not new: a theory of economic development through stages, a position favourable to consumption (but not to high wages), a subjective theory of value including some reference to the cost of production side (possibly derived from Galiani, 1751) and discussion of the factors favouring the wealth of nations, not unlike Serra's but less well structured. The great success of Genovesi, praised to the point of being placed on the same plane as Adam Smith, may well be due to his adroit blending of philosophy and political economy, well befitting the spirit of the time.[68]

The intellectuals writing about economic issues in Milan and in Tuscany were more interested in the immediate problems of reforms aiming at favouring economic development, above all in the management of state assets and agriculture. Cesare Beccaria (1738–94), rated by Schumpeter superior to Adam Smith, was the author of a treatise, *Elementi di economia pubblica* (Elements of public economics), published posthumously in 1804 in the series edited by Custodi. But he was best known for his essay *Dei delitti e delle pene* (On crimes and punishments, 1764), a work that probably owed much to his friend Pietro Verri (1728–97). In his condemnation of the all too liberal application of the death penalty Beccaria had recourse to a sort of utilitarianism anticipating Bentham (cf. below, § 6.7). Both Verri and Beccaria adopted a subjective theory of value based on comparison between scarcity and utility; in general, they conceived the market as the point where buyers and sellers met (and this held true also for the rate of interest, determined by demand for and supply of loans). Moreover, both Verri and Beccaria took a wide interest in practical issues, from the fiscal and monetary situation to problems of customs duties, seasonal unemployment, and concession to private agents of monopolies for commodities such as salt and tobacco. On the latter issue, for instance, Verri, in his capacity as a high-ranking functionary in the Austro-Hungarian empire, succeeded in obtaining an important victory with abolition of the concessions in 1770.[69]

---

[68] On Genovesi's thought and fortunes cf. Faucci 2000, pp. 49–57, and the bibliography quoted there. Cf. also the extensive 'Nota introduttiva' by Venturi, the 'Vita di Antonio Genovese' and the selection of texts collected in Venturi 1962: respectively, pp. 3–46, 47–83 and 84–330. To Genovesi's school belonged various protagonists of the Neapolitan reformism of the second half of the eighteenth century, including Gaetano Filangieri (1752–88) and Giuseppe Palmieri (1721–93).

[69] Verri was the author, among other works, of the *Discorsi sull'indole del piacere e del dolore; sulla felicità; e sulla economia politica* (1781). On Verri and Beccaria cf. Biagini 1992; Faucci 2000, pp. 72–91, and the literature quoted there. Schumpeter 1954, p. 178, attributed to Verri, with some excess of enthusiasm, a 'constant-outlay demand

9.   The Scottish Enlightenment: Francis Hutcheson and David Hume

The Enlightenment notion of a 'natural order' was adopted in Scotland purged of Cartesian rationalism and hence transformed into the view of a 'spontaneous order'. Such an order was considered the result of an adaptive evolutionary process, in which a multiplicity of individual choices led to a result – a set of complex, sufficiently well-functioning, social structures – not assumed as the objective of a broad, rational design (thus somewhat distant from the tradition of constructive rationalism that began with Descartes and ultimately led to attribution of a central role to the *deus ex machina* represented by a benevolent and enlightened legislator).

Smith was the most illustrious exponent of this current, but his contribution did not emerge from a vacuum. Before him, and around him, other protagonists offered important contributions in various fields connected to the central theme of the organisation and evolution of human societies, from matters like the origin of language to juridical procedures. Obviously some reference was also made to questions commonly included in the field of political economy.

We may begin with Francis Hutcheson (1694–1746), who taught Smith in Glasgow and wrote, among other things, a *System of moral philosophy* in three volumes, published posthumously in 1755. As we shall see below (§ 6.7), Hutcheson contributed to the utilitarian approach the thesis that the best moral action is that which ensures the maximum of happiness to the greatest number of persons. On price theory, he had little to say: prices depend on the demand for the commodity under consideration and on the difficulty of acquiring it (with simultaneous hints as to its scarcity and to its cost of production: there is an analogy, here, with Pufendorf's ideas illustrated above, in § 1). His major contributions, however, moved in a different direction. Hutcheson considered man as an essentially social animal, to the extent of rejecting any separation between ethics and politics. Benevolence towards others, together with utility, regulates human 'moral' actions; following this behavioural rule people can obtain their own good without this constituting the direct objective of their actions,

---

curve' and 'a clear if undeveloped conception of economic equilibrium based, in the last instance, upon the "calculus of pleasure and pain"'. On the terrain of pragmatic reformism we find various other protagonists of the Lombard Enlightenment and – with the focus on agricultural matters – of the Tuscan Enlightenment. For an ample selection of texts accompanied by rich critical apparatus, cf. Venturi 1968. On the Italian Enlightenment as a whole the main reference text is the painstaking reconstruction offered by Venturi 1969–90.

and thus without any contrast arising between utility and virtue. As we will see in the next chapter, Smith opposed the thesis that benevolence constitutes the guiding principle of human actions. Nevertheless, even if the private good–public good link is inverted, an interesting parallelism remains: according to Smith each person follows his or her own private interest, but in doing so also realises the public good, albeit involuntarily. Furthermore, Hutcheson introduced the concept of 'sympathy' into his analysis of human nature, although without attributing to it the role it was to have in Smith's analysis; also his treatment of economic issues showed, in embryonic form, some of the characteristics that reappear in Smith, such as the choice of the division of labour as the starting point for analysis.

Adam Ferguson (1723–1816) belonged to Smith's generation; his main work, *An essay on the history of civil society* (1767; it went through seven editions before the author's death) argues among other things an evolutionary view of the birth of language. Moreover, Ferguson dealt at length with the division of labour, also stressing its negative aspects. For some of his theses he probably drew, without acknowledgement, on Smith's university lectures; thus Ferguson was credited with first publication (*The wealth of nations* came out ten years later than his book) but at the cost of some tension between himself and Smith.[70] Younger than Smith were John Millar (1735–1801), his pupil, and Dugald Stewart (1753–1828), who was to be Smith's first biographer (Stewart 1811).[71]

A little older than Smith, James Steuart (1713–80) was one of the major protagonists of Scottish politics and culture. In exile for a long time after the defeat of the Jacobite rebellion in the battle of Culloden (1746), hence in direct touch with French and German culture, Steuart was the author of a massive work, *An inquiry into the principles of political oeconomy* published in 1767, nine years before Smith's *Wealth of nations*, which would then overshadow it.[72] However, Steuart is not to be seen as one of the protagonists of the Scottish Enlightenment, but classed rather among the last representatives of mercantilism given the role he attributed to active public intervention in the economy and the protection of manufactures with duties, together with the place he ascribed to demand in

---

[70] Cf. Ross 1995, p. 230.

[71] For an interpretation of the Scottish Enlightenment that assigns a central role to the theory of spontaneous order cf. Hamowy 1987, who also provides an ample bibliography of writings by the major authors of the period.

[72] Considered by Schumpeter 1954, p. 250, as 'the one great pre-Smithian system of economics that England produced', this work was valued negatively by Smith himself, who in a letter of 1772 spoke of it in the following terms: 'Without once mentioning it, I flatter myself, that every false principle in it, will meet with a clear and distinct confutation in mine' (Smith 1977, p. 164).

macroeconomic equilibrium. He dealt at length with population, which in his view tends to grow until checked by food supplies: this appears to foreshadow Malthus, but also echoes Cantillon and others. On value, we find the simple notion that prices depend on supply and demand.[73] There is also the idea that demand for luxuries stimulates production, but demand for foreign luxuries may be damaging; a deficiency of demand for internal products may reduce employment. In fact, Steuart's main policy objective was a high level of employment, while leaving aside technical progress (hence the role of the division of labour and of capital accumulation); he stressed repeatedly the need to preserve 'the balance of work and demand'. Like Galiani, Steuart strongly opposed the idea of 'general rules': 'in every [. . .] part of the science of political oeconomy, there is hardly such a thing as a general rule to be laid down' (Steuart 1767, p. 339).[74]

Twelve years older than Smith, and who became a great friend of his, was the renowned empiricist philosopher David Hume (1711–76), author of the celebrated *Treatise of human nature* (1739–40). A spontaneous order in institutions as different as language and money gradually emerges as an unforeseen consequence of manifold individual actions guided by selfishness tempered with a sentiment of benevolence. As for human actions, it is habit rather than reason that guides them.

Economists are best acquainted with Hume's *Political discourses* (1752). In the first essay of Part Two, 'Of commerce', Hume tried to demonstrate 'the beneficence of economic progress and its complementarity with the increase of happiness and freedom' (Hutchison 1988, p. 202). In the second essay, 'Of refinements in the arts', the role of luxury consumption in providing stimulus to economic activity in commercial societies is stressed. In fact, imports of luxury goods are considered as the element of novelty in stagnant agricultural societies which gives impetus to the generation of surplus produce and the transition to a commercial society. Excessive luxury is of course castigated; but luxury, in so far as it is identified with 'refinement', enhances the mind, favours sociableness and stimulates activity, so that it simultaneously contributes to progress in 'industry, knowledge and humanity' (Hume 1752, p. 271).

---

[73] More specifically, 'the value of things depends upon many circumstances, which however may be reduced to four principal heads: First, The abundance of the things to be valued. Secondly, The demand which mankind make for them. Thirdly, The competition between the demanders; and Fourthly, The extent of the faculties of the demanders' (Steuart 1767, p. 409).

[74] On Steuart see Skinner's introduction to the critical edition of his book, Sen 1957, Hutchison 1988, pp. 335–51. Akhtar 1979 proposes a translation of Steuart's theory of growth into a macroeconomic model, his aim being to revalue it in comparison with the Smithian theory.

In the third and fourth essays, 'Of money' and 'Of interest', Hume maintained, against the mercantilist tradition, that 'the greater or less plenty of money is of no consequence' (ibid., p. 281), and that 'lowness of interest' should not be 'ascribed to plenty of money', but rather to 'an increase of commerce', so that it is connected to 'low profits of merchandize' (ibid., pp. 295 and 302). In the fifth essay, 'Of the balance of trade', Hume illustrated the adjustment mechanism that – under the gold standard – brings the balance of trade of different countries into equilibrium. This mechanism was based on the quantity theory of money: in each country prices increase (decrease) when the quantity of money in circulation increases (decreases). Thus, whenever a country has a favourable balance of trade, and so experiences an influx of gold, the supply of money within it increases, together with internal prices. This reduces the competitiveness of internally produced commodities and hence the country's exports. Exactly the opposite happens for countries with a balance of trade deficit.[75] In this way, Hume criticised the traditional mercantilist tenet according to which in order to increase wealth a country should aim at a positive balance of trade. On the same line, in an additional essay published in 1758, 'Of the jealousy of trade', Hume maintained that progress in any country is beneficial to the other countries, and that trade is beneficial to all.

As far as we are concerned here, however, Hume and Hutcheson, and with them the other protagonists of the Scottish Enlightenment, are important above all for the notion of man and society which they propounded: a notion that, notwithstanding some even important differences between the different authors, displayed a moderate optimism with regard to the automatic, involuntary realisation of sound institutional organisation for society, and a moderately positive evaluation of human nature, while nevertheless recognising its many imperfections.

[75] Obviously this theory, to which Hume did not attribute the importance somewhat inaptly attached to it by so many subsequent scholars, is based on a sizeable set of assumptions: that the quantity theory of money holds, that the ratio between gold base and quantity of money in circulation (including banking money) is sufficiently stable, that the balance of trade is the dominant component of the balance of payments and/or that the other components do not undergo significant variations, that the percentage increase of quantities exported and imported is superior to the percentage decrease (increase) of the level of prices for imported and exported goods. Finally, as is obvious, the gold standard must rule.

5   Adam Smith

1.   Life[1]

Adam Smith was born in the small town of Kirkaldy (population about 1,500 at the time), on the eastern coast of Scotland, in 1723. The precise date of his birth is not known; we only know that it must have been a few weeks after the death of his father, a customs officer, which occurred in January, and before 5 July, the day of his christening. The young Smith had a placid childhood, raised by his mother Margaret with the help of relatives – a moderately well-to-do family of landowners – until 1737, when he moved to Glasgow in order to attend the local university. Among his teachers, his favourite was Francis Hutcheson, whom we met in the previous chapter (§ 4.9).

At the time, fourteen was not an uncommon age to enter university, which was in fact a sort of upper secondary school. The young Adam had already studied some Latin in Kirkaldy, and was immediately admitted to Greek lectures; he also took lessons in logic, which apparently followed the Aristotelian tradition but also included some recent developments (Descartes and Locke), in natural philosophy, in mathematics and physics (Euclid's *Elements* and Newton's *Principia mathematica*) and in moral philosophy (with Francis Hutcheson).

In the Scottish educational system, at all levels, the students paid their teachers course by course. The total salary of the latter hence depended on their students' assessment of their teaching: a system that Smith himself would experience later as a professor, and would consider by far superior to that of the great English universities like Oxford, financed by public funds and private donations, where the professors, receiving a regular salary, had no incentive to put zeal into their profession.

---

[1] After a long gestation, the biography painstakingly compiled by Ross (1995) is now at last available. Smith's first biographer was his pupil Dugald Stewart (1753–1828); on his interpretation (Stewart 1794) we return below, in § 8. Among recent biographical writings, let us mention at least West 1976.

It was in fact at Oxford, at Balliol College, that Smith continued his studies as from 1740, with a scholarship (the Snell scholarship) that guaranteed £40 yearly for eleven years, as preparation for an ecclesiastical career. As mentioned, Smith did not take to the celebrated English university, traditionalist and authoritarian as it was. Learning by rote and reading summaries rather than original works, were the rule. Traditionally sanctioned topics – Aristotle over and again – were imposed on the students, but the workload was far from heavy; compulsory prayers dominated over compulsory lessons, and Smith had plenty of time to spend in the Bodleian Library, following his own interests, 'perhaps in defiance of the Oxford guardians of orthodoxy' (Ross 1995, p. 78). For instance, the young Adam was punished when caught reading the *Treatise of human nature* (1739–40) by David Hume, a supporter of a vague theism and who would later become one of Smith's best friends. It may have been these readings that put Smith off the idea of embracing an ecclesiastical career.[2] Thus, after six difficult years, in 1746 Smith decided to return to Scotland, to Kirkaldy, where he spent two years studying on his own and writing some essays on literary and philosophical subjects.

For three years, from 1748 to 1751, Smith held public lectures in Edinburgh on rhetoric and English literature, with some success in terms of audience and finance (about a hundred people paid a guinea a year each to listen to the young lecturer, while the sponsors, including Lord Kames, paid the expenses). On the strength of the fame obtained with these lectures, in 1751 Smith became a professor at Glasgow University, first holding the chair of logic (but his lessons were essentially on rhetoric, like his Edinburgh lectures) and subsequently the moral philosophy chair.[3] This involved lecturing on natural theology, ethics, jurisprudence and, in the same set of lessons, politics and political economy.

From those years we have the notes on a course of lessons on rhetoric, taken by a student in 1762–3, found in 1958 and published in 1963, and the notes of two courses on 'jurisprudence' (taken in 1762–3 and in 1763–4, discovered respectively in 1958 and 1895 and published in 1978 and 1896). These texts, apart from having considerable interest in themselves – in terms of the study of human nature and the forms of communication, and for analysis of institutions and their development in the course of history – show that the author already, hence before coming

---

[2] In Protestantism, which is declaredly his own religion, Smith 1977, pp. 67–8, appreciates above all 'the pretious right of private judgement for the sake of which our forefathers kicked out the Pope and the Pretender'. When teaching in Glasgow, Smith asked to be exempted from the traditional prayer at the beginning of the lessons, and it is said that his prayers were anyhow inspired by 'natural religion' (Ross 1995, p. 118).

[3] On Smith's experiences as a teacher and on his pupils, cf. Ross 1995, pp. 128–56.

in touch with the French physiocrats, had the main themes that would weave together into *The wealth of nations* clear in his mind.

In the same period Smith wrote and published his first book, *The theory of moral sentiments* (1759), which is discussed below (§ 3). This book met with success, and reached six editions before Smith's death.

Among the readers of the book was Charles Townshend, stepfather to the young Duke of Buccleuch, who invited Smith to act as tutor to the young nobleman, accompanying him on a tour on the continent. The proposal was an attractive one, not only because it meant a life annuity of £300, but also because of the prospect of coming into direct contact with the liveliest centres of cultural life of the time. Smith accepted and, at the beginning of 1764, resigned from his chair at Glasgow. The travels on the continent gave Smith the opportunity to meet Voltaire in Geneva, and in Paris d'Alembert, Quesnay and many others.[4]

Scotland had at the time a fair cultural life, relatively free (especially in comparison with the authoritarianism and conformism that prevailed in the English universities) and rich in solid good sense, especially in the field of the social sciences; but the real centre of intellectual life was France, especially Paris. When Smith arrived there, Quesnay had published a few years earlier his *Tableau économique* (1758), while Turgot had still to publish his *Réflexions*. The culture of the *Encyclopédie* (publication of which began in 1751), based on faith in reason and progress, was also felt in other European countries, but the liveliness of the celebrated Parisian salons was unique. The stay in Paris offered Smith stimuli that he would work upon in the following years.

At the end of his travels on the continent, in fact, thanks to the annuity of the Duke of Buccleuch, Smith was able to dedicate himself fully to the composition of *The wealth of nations*, in the tranquil environment of his native Kirkaldy where he lived with his mother between 1767 and 1773. In 1773 he moved to London to follow the printing of his book which, however, took three more years of work. Finally, on 9 March 1776, the most famous economics book of all time arrived in the bookshops, meeting with a warm reception from the public (the book went through five editions in twelve years). His great friend Hume wrote him an enthusiastic letter about it.

After a long illness, David Hume died in the same year. Smith wrote an account of the last months of his friend's life, stressing his stoic courage: published in 1777, it 'brought upon me ten times more abuse than the very violent attack I had made [in *The wealth of nations*] upon the whole

---

[4] On Smith's travel on the continent and on his activities as a tutor, cf. Ross 1995, pp. 195–219.

commercial system of Great Britain' (as Smith wrote in a letter to Andreas Holt of October 1780).[5]

In 1778, consulted on the American situation, Smith wrote a memorandum in which he argues the case for adopting a uniform system of taxation for Great Britain, Ireland and the American colonies, accompanied by the election of representatives of these latter populations to Parliament (on the basis of the principle commonly summarised in the saying 'no taxation without representation'). Furthermore, Smith foresaw the loss of the American colonies (with the exception of Canada) and the gradual shift of the economic and political centre of gravity from England to America.[6]

In the same year of 1778 Smith was appointed commissioner of customs for Scotland; he thus moved to Edinburgh, accompanied by his mother. There he lived quietly (though deeply saddened, in 1784, by his mother's death), attended scrupulously to his duties and meticulously edited the new editions of his books, until his death on 17 July 1790. Complying with his instructions, the executors of his will destroyed sixteen volumes of manuscripts.

2.   Method

It would be a mistake to ignore Smith's 'minor' writings, including the notes on his lectures taken by students, and to concentrate solely on the *Wealth of nations*, although this is what generations of historians of economic thought have done. As we shall see in the next section, *The theory of moral sentiments* is in particular decisive for our understanding of the notion of 'self-interest' on which Smith relies in his more strictly economic analysis. Even the *Lectures on rhetoric and belles lettres*, although apparently remote from economics in contents, are important, together with the *Essays on philosophical subjects*, for an understanding of some aspects of the method of enquiry adopted by Smith.

---

[5] The loving account of the last months of Hume's life is written in the form of a letter to the publisher William Strahan (1715–85), dated 9 November 1776 (Smith 1977, pp. 217–21), subsequently published, with Smith's consent, in a pamphlet (Hume 1777, pp. 37–62). The final lines of the letter show the high regard that Smith had for Hume: 'Upon the whole, I have always considered him, both in his lifetime and since his death, as approaching as nearly to the idea of a perfectly wise and virtuous man, as perhaps the nature of human frailty will permit.' On the subject cf. Ross 1995, pp. 288–304. The letter to Holt is in Smith 1977, pp. 249–53; the quotation is drawn from p. 251.

[6] Smith was for a long time a friend of Benjamin Franklin (1706–90), one of the protagonists of the independence of the United States, whom he had met in Glasgow in 1759 and with whom he had remained in touch through William Strahan. As his teacher Hutcheson and other intellectuals of the time had already done, Smith furthermore declares himself against the slave trade (cf. Ross 1995, p. 171).

Our point of departure is in fact one of these essays, the *History of astronomy* (the full title of which, significantly, is: *The principles which lead and direct philosophical enquiries; illustrated by the history of astronomy*). Schumpeter (1954, p. 182) singles out this among all Smith's works as the only one really deserving praise; and not solely for love of paradox since, as we shall see (§ 15.2), Schumpeter's 'liberal' methodology appears very similar to the Smithian approach.

Smith's point of departure in the field of epistemology, too, is based on analysis of the motivations for human action. In his view, our attitude towards scientific theories is explained by three 'sentiments': 'Wonder, Surprise, and Admiration'. Wonder is excited by 'what is new and singular', surprise by 'what is unexpected', admiration by 'what is great or beautiful'.[7] 'Nature', Smith says, 'seems to abound with events which appear solitary and incoherent with all that go before them, which therefore disturb the easy movement of the imagination'; the task of philosophy (defined as 'the science of the connecting principles of nature') is 'to introduce order into this chaos of jarring and discordant appearances', 'by representing the invisible chains which bind together all these disjointed objects'.[8] In this way philosophy 'render[s] the theatre of nature a more coherent, and therefore a more magnificent spectacle'.[9]

In accomplishing this task of enquiring into nature, 'philosophical systems' are built (such as the two different cosmological views, Ptolemaic and Copernican) which – Smith stressed – are 'mere inventions of the imagination, to connect together the otherwise disjointed and discordant phaenomena of nature'.[10] In other words, the intellectual ('philosopher') who considers the world and tries to interpret its functioning has an active role, *creating* rather than *discovering* the theories. With this thesis, Smith opposed the Galilean idea (shared by Petty, as we have seen above, § 3.2) according to which the task of the scientist consists in *revealing* (in the literal etymological meaning of taking away the veils which cover them) the 'laws of nature' which constitute the skeleton of the real world: as he says, these are 'mere inventions of the imagination'. All this should come as no surprise: after all, in this respect Smith is simply following in his great friend David Hume's footsteps.

In this way we may also interpret Smith's declared mistrust (cf. above, § 4.1) towards Petty's political arithmetic. It was not, as some commentators have maintained, a matter of doubting the statistical data which political arithmeticians construct with a notable effort of the imagination, in a situation where statistics collection was rudimentary. For Smith, it is

---

[7] Smith 1795, p. 33.   [8] Ibid., p. 45.   [9] Ibid., p. 46.   [10] Ibid., p. 105.

rather a question of denying the idea of a mathematical structure of reality, which Hobbes and then Condillac's sensism had already extended to the human body, and which Petty and the political arithmeticians extended to the 'political body', namely society.[11]

The 'philosophical systems', though 'inventions of the imagination', may help us to get our bearings in the chaos of real events. However, it is clearly not possible to verify the theories by demonstrating their correspondence to supposed natural laws, unless we assume that the laws with which they are compared have a real existence independent of the theories themselves (unless, that is, such laws are inscribed, so to say, in the real world, and not a creation of our thought). Smith does not tackle this issue, which as we have seen above (§ 1.3) Feyerabend and McCloskey propose to solve by referring to 'honest discourse' and 'rhetoric'. It is, however, interesting to note that Smith himself, in the *Lectures on rhetoric* (1983, p. 178), proposes the method of rhetoric, with particular reference to the model of legal proceedings, as the way to select the propositions to be accepted and those to be rejected.[12] This idea should, however, be understood (with a connection, typical of Smith, between ethics and theory of knowledge) in terms of the notion of the impartial spectator. As we shall see in the next section, to this spectator we may assign the role of the arbiter, in this case not of what is just and what unjust, but (provisionally, not absolutely) true and false.

Smith thus adopts a flexible methodology, which leaves room for a good degree of eclecticism. Moreover, abandonment of the idea of a mathematical structure intrinsic to reality corresponds to attributing to men a complex set of motivations – the 'passions' and the 'interests' discussed above, § 4.3 – the balance of which is the object of the *Theory of moral sentiments*. These elements – diffidence towards the idea of 'laws of nature' hard and fast in their objective reality, in the natural as in the human world, and systematic openness to recognising the complexity of the motivations of human action – are characteristic of the Scottish Enlightenment, the cultural environment in which Smith had grown up and to the development of which he contributed with his writings.

---

[11] In many respects, this Smithian view resurfaces in Keynes. Cf. below, § 14.2.

[12] These ideas have a long history. Suffice it to recall the Sophists' opposition to Socrates' (and Plato's) thesis on the existence of Truth, discovery of which must be the aim of philosophical enquiry. The Sophists prescribed, rather, open debate on the elements in favour and against any and every thesis, believing no thesis to be true in an absolute sense.

On the Smithian thesis of rhetoric as an instrument of research, cf. Giuliani 1997. As Giuliani stresses (ibid., p. 205), 'Rhetoric is the method of enquiry into the domain of the opinion and the probable truth.' In this respect, too, we note a significant affinity between Smith's ideas and those of Keynes.

3. The moral principle of sympathy

As we have already seen, the broad context of Smith's work was the debate on the different motivations for human action. In short, his contribution consisted in pointing out the complementarity between pursuing self-interests and attributing a central role to moral rules for the sound functioning of common life in society.

This interpretation of Smith's contribution, which conforms largely to that of the editors of the critical edition of his works,[13] emerges from reading Smith's two main works, *The theory of moral sentiments* and *The wealth of nations*, as complementary rather than contradictory.

The thesis of a contradiction between the two works prevailed for a certain time, constituting what has been labelled *das Adam Smith Problem*. According to this thesis, defence of the free pursuit of self-interest within a market economy proposed by Smith in *The wealth of nations* would correspond to the mature position of the Scottish economist. Smith is taken to have reached it after rejecting the position he initially defended in *The theory of moral sentiments*, according to which sympathetic behaviour among the members of a community is necessary for the very survival of the collective entity.[14]

This thesis appears untenable when we recall that *The theory of moral sentiments* was repeatedly reprinted, on all occasions under the control of the author, who took advantage of the opportunity offered by the reprints to introduce changes into the work, even after the publication of *The wealth of nations*. Smith would have had a schizophrenic personality had he simultaneously submitted to his readers two works contradicting each other! Moreover, in Smith's correspondence there is no hint that he

---

[13] The six volumes of the *Glasgow edition of the works and correspondence of Adam Smith* (edited by D. D. Raphael and A. S. Skinner, Oxford University Press, Oxford 1976–83; paperback facsimile reprint, Liberty Press, Indianapolis, 1981–5) include *The theory of moral sentiments*, edited by A. L. Macfie and D. D. Raphael; *The wealth of nations*, edited by R. H. Campbell and A. S. Skinner; *Essays on philosophical subjects*, edited by W. P. D. Wightman; *Lectures on rhetoric and belles lettres*, edited by J. C. Bryce; *Lectures on jurisprudence*, edited by R. L. Meek, D. D. Raphael and P. G. Stein; and *Correspondence*, edited by E. C. Mossner and I. S. Ross.

The literature on Smith is enormous; here we can mention Macfie 1967; Skinner and Wilson 1975; Wilson and Skinner 1976; Winch 1978; Pack 1991; Skinner and Jones 1992. A radically different interpretation is offered by Hollander 1973b, who maintains the thesis – insistently repeated, but very rarely investigated: Hollander is an important exception, from this point of view – of Smith as a founder of the theory of general economic equilibrium; for a critique of such a thesis cf. below, § 6.

[14] This thesis was developed by a group of German scholars in the second half of the nineteenth century, first of all Karl Knies. For references to this literature, and for a detailed criticism of their thesis, cf. Raphael and Macfie 1976.

himself or any of his correspondents saw even the slightest contradiction between the two works.

The mistake of those arguing a contradiction between the two works, and hence between self-interest and the ethics of sympathy, is a typical example of a reading misled by the theoretical (and cultural, in the broad sense of the term) tendencies prevailing in the period in which the interpreter lives. In our case, the prevalence of a mono-dimensional notion of man[15] led commentators to consider as contradictory the simultaneous presence of two motivations of human actions. We should recall that, as we saw above (§ 4.3), in the eigthteenth century the simultaneous presence of even conflicting passions and interests as the foundation for human action was considered a matter of fact with which to come to terms. In fact, the complementarity suggested by Smith between the moral principle of sympathy and self-interest constitutes both the basis for a richer and more complex notion of the market than those proposed later and a theoretical contribution that remains highly relevant.

Let us now consider the contribution offered by Smith in *The theory of moral sentiments*. It is centred on the proposal of the 'moral principle of sympathy', the importance of which in driving human behaviour had already been maintained by Hume (1739–40).[16]

According to Smith, 'the chief part of human happiness arises from the consciousness of being beloved'; sympathy, namely the ability to share the feelings of others, leads us to judge our actions on the basis of their effects on others in addition to their effects on ourselves. Thus man

must [. . .] humble the arrogance of his self-love, and bring it down to something which other men can go along with. [. . .] In the race for wealth, and honours, and preferments, he may run as hard as he can, and strain every nerve and every muscle, in order to outstrip all his competitors. But if he should justle, or throw down any of them, the indulgence of the spectators is entirely at an end. It is a violation of fair play, which they cannot admit of.

This kind of moral attitude is a prerequisite for the very survival of human societies: 'Society [. . .] cannot subsist among those who are at all times ready to hurt and injure one another.'[17]

---

[15] On this view, connected to Benthamite utilitarianism and to the subsequent affirmation of the subjective theory of value within the framework of marginalism, cf. below, §§ 6.7, 8.9 and 10.4.

[16] However, the meaning attributed to such a principle is somewhat different in the two authors: by the term 'sympathy' Hume 'means the communication of feeling, and Smith means the psychological mechanism that provides an approach to mutuality of feelings' (Ross 1995, p. 183).

[17] Smith 1759, pp. 41, 83, 86.

In other words, Smith's liberal views are based on a two-fold assumption, namely that commonly each person knows better than anybody else her or his own interests, and that among the interests of each there is the desire to be loved by the others and hence respect for the well-being of the others. The first assumption explains the rejection of a centralised management of the economy, even if by an enlightened prince; hence the preference for a market economy over a command economy. The second assumption constitutes, within the Smithian edifice, an essential precondition to ensure that the pursuit of self-interest on the part of a multitude of economic agents in competition among themselves leads to results conducive to the well-being of society; however, in the development of the classical school of political economy itself this assumption – which corresponds to the Smithian principle of 'sympathy' – was submerged by the growing influence of utilitarianism.

Another central element in *The theory of moral sentiments* is the notion of the 'impartial spectator'. According to Smith, individuals evaluate their own actions by taking the viewpoint of an impartial spectator who, endowed with the knowledge of all the elements they know, judges such actions as an average citizen.[18] Juridical institutions, the functioning of which is indispensable to guarantee the security of market exchange, find in this principle of moral behaviour their necessary concrete support. Thus the most famous Smithian statement, according to which 'it is not from the benevolence of the butcher, the brewer, or the baker, that we expect our dinner, but from their regard to their own interest', should not be considered in isolation. In the context it implies the assumption – vital for the functioning of a market economy – of a civilised society, grounded on the general acceptance of the moral principle of sympathy, and endowed with the administrative and juridical institutions necessary to deal with the instances in which the common morality is violated.[19]

[18] Naturally this thesis presupposes the existence of a common cultural basis (in the broad sense) for the individuals belonging to a given social system. In this respect the reference to the nation-economy customary in the tradition of classical political economy implies relatively minor difficulties compared with modern reference to the world-economy.

[19] Smith 1776, pp. 26–7. This passage, or variants of it, also occurs in the *Lectures on jurisprudence* and in the *Early draft of parts of 'The wealth of nations'* (now reprinted in Smith 1978, pp. 562–81). Cf. Smith 1978, pp. 348: LJ-A, vi. 45–6; 493: LJ-B, 219–20; 571–2: *Early draft*, 23. As noted above (§ 4.9), Smith's reference to benevolence is an implicit way of drawing attention to the thesis of his master Hutcheson, who attributed to it an important role as a guide to human action. It may be worth stressing that in a society in which merchants felt no compunction in selling adulterated food (and in which merchants who did so would not be sued by the state justice) production for self-consumption would grow, with regression in the division of labour and hence economic decline, upon which civic decline would inevitably follow.

The distinction between private and public interest becomes opposition, irreconcilable conflict – Smith says in substance – only if the private interest is interpreted in a restrictive way, as selfishness rather than self-interest, the latter implying attention to one's own interests moderated by the recognition (or, better, 'sympathy') for the interests of others.[20]

What Smith attempts, following in the tradition of the Scottish sociological school, is a difficult task of definition of a third way for the theory of man and society, differing both from the Aristotelian tradition and from the natural law philosophers discussed above (§ 4.2). Smith rejects the arbitrary absolutism that the social and political structure of his times inherited from feudalism, and which can be associated with the Aristotelian tradition. However, he equally rejects Hobbes's contractualism, in which a state, though enlightened and benevolent, dominates the life of its subjects. (It is this statism, which the 'mercantile' theories are imbued with, that Smith is opposed to, more indeed than he is to the 'mercantile' identification of wealth with money and the thesis of the preference for an active balance of payments, the latter being Smith's own interpretation of the history of economic thought preceding him, proposed in the fourth book of *The wealth of nations*, although in many respects it appears forced.)

Smith proposes the line of a greater confidence in the self-governing capacity of individuals: 'Every man is, no doubt, by nature, first and principally recommended to his own care; and as he is fitter to take care of himself than of any other person, it is fit and right that it should be so.'[21] However, the free pursuit of personal interest comes up against two limits: one external to the individual (the administration of justice, one

---

[20] In *The theory of moral sentiments* (section 7.2.4) Smith criticises the 'licentious systems', in particular Mandeville's one: 'It is the great fallacy of Dr. Mandeville's book to represent every passion as wholly vicious, which is so in any degree and in any direction. It is thus that he treats every thing as vanity which has any reference, either to what are, or to what ought to be the sentiments of others: and it is by means of this sophistry, that he establishes his favourite conclusion, that private vices are public benefits' (Smith 1759, pp. 312–13).
   An articulate view of self-interest, not reducible to the monomania for the accumulation of wealth (or, in other terms, to a mono-dimensional maximising behaviour), is evident for instance in the following passage: 'What can be added to the happiness of the man who is in health, who is out of debt, and has a clear conscience? To one in this situation, all accessions of fortune may properly be said to be superfluous; and if he is much elevated upon account of them, it must be the effect of the most frivolous levity' (Smith 1759, p. 45).

[21] Smith 1759, p. 82. The passage is repeated with nearly the same wording further on in the text (ibid., p. 219): 'Every man, as the Stoics used to say, is first and principally recommended to his own care; and every man is certainly, in every respect, fitter and abler to take care of himself than of any other person.' As we can see, Smith does not say that every man is fitter than anybody else to take care of himself, but that every

of the fundamental functions that Smith attributes to the state), and one internal to him, 'sympathy' for his fellow human beings. The simultaneous recourse to these two elements shows how Smith, faithful in this to the Aristotelian tradition of hostility to extreme positions, has a positive but not idealised vision of man.[22]

Smith (1759, p. 77) is explicit in this respect:

We are not at present examining upon what principles a perfect being would approve of the punishment of bad actions; but upon what principles so weak and imperfect a creature as man actually and in fact approves of it. [. . .] The very existence of society requires that unmerited and unprovoked malice should be restrained by proper punishments [. . .]. Though man, therefore, be naturally endowed with a desire of the welfare and preservation of society, yet the Author of nature has not entrusted it to his reason to find out that a certain application of punishments is the proper means of attaining this end; but has endowed him with an immediate and instinctive approbation of that very application which is most proper to attain it.

It is precisely from the non-idealised view of man and society that the various examples stem of state intervention that, as we shall see below (§ 8), may be attributed to Smith.[23]

To sum up, in Smith's view various elements concur to guarantee the very survival and development of civilised societies: moral behaviour based on the sentiment of sympathy (hence grounded on a sentiment which is innate in man, not imposed from outside), the driving force of a well-conceived personal interest, a set of juridical rules and customs,

---

man is fitter to take care of himself than he could of anybody else. The difference is not enormous; however, Smith's meticulousness and caution emerge on such occasions, qualifying his liberalism.

John Stuart Mill reproposes this thesis (without quoting Smith) in his famous essay *On liberty* (Mill 1859, p. 76): Each person 'is the person most interested in his own well-being'.

[22] This view of human nature constitutes a central element for the Scottish Enlightenment, but is widespread. For instance, Kant (a year younger than Smith) also adopts a position similar to Smith's (one of his favourite readings, by the way: cf. Ross 1995, pp. 193–4; the German translation of *The theory of moral sentiments* is dated 1770). Let us compare two passages: 'The coarse clay of which the bulk of mankind are formed, cannot be wrought up to such perfection' (Smith 1759, pp. 162–3); 'From a twisted wood, such as that of which man is made, nothing entirely straight can come out. Only the approximation to this idea is imposed on us by nature' (Kant 1784, p. 130). Before both Smith and Kant, the idea of a substantially benevolent human nature is maintained, for instance, by Hutcheson and Shaftesbury, who oppose it to the thesis of a substantially selfish human nature argued in particular by Hobbes and Mandeville.

[23] Viner (1927) recalls such examples in order to criticise the interpretations of Smith 'as a doctrinaire advocate of laisssez-faire' (ibid., p. 112). The article by Viner, one of the most authoritative exponents of the 'first Chicago school', is an *ante litteram* critique of Stigler's saying at the bi-centennial celebrations of *The wealth of nations*: 'Smith is alive and well, and living in Chicago.'

and public institutions designed among other things to guarantee the administration of justice. This is a view that is grounded on solid good sense; at the same time, it is the fruit of refined theoretical elaboration involving the whole field of the social sciences and entailing, step by step, fine-tuned selection among the different cultural traditions and streams of thought contributing to the liveliness of the 'century of Enlightenment'.

4.   The wealth of nations

Smith's contributions, as we have seen, concern many fields: rhetoric, moral philosophy, jurisprudence, political economy. Here we focus attention on the latter field, the one which Smith owes his fame to. However, it is important to stress that, as we saw in the previous section, his reflections on this topic (and thus the book in which they are illustrated, *The wealth of nations*) are part of a wider research on man and society: two elements that, as his master Hutcheson held, actually constitute a single object of study.[24]

An inquiry into the nature and causes of the wealth of nations (Smith, 1776) is subdivided into five books. The first concerns the division of labour (and thus technological progress), the theory of value and income distribution; the second deals with money and accumulation; the third is a brief, thought-provoking excursus in the history of institutions and the economy since the fall of the Roman empire; the fourth critically illustrates the mercantile doctrines and the physiocratic tenets; finally, the fifth concerns public expenses and receipts and, more generally, the role of the state in the economy.

The starting point of Smith's economic reflection is represented by the division of labour. His object is to explain the functioning of an economic system in which each person is engaged in a specific task and each firm produces a specific commodity.

The division of labour is not a new phenomenon, and Smith is not the first to draw attention to it. Schumpeter (1954, p. 56) called it 'this eternal commonplace of economics': authors from classical Greece such as Xenophon and Diodorus Siculus, Plato and Aristotle (cf. above, § 2.2), had already discussed it, as well as authors of the previous century such as William Petty. Smith, however, is the first to bring the division of labour to the centre of analysis applied to explain which are the elements that

---

[24] In *The wealth of nations* and in other writings (especially the *Lectures on jurisprudence*: Smith 1977) Smith adopts a theory of the stages of social development – hunting, stock-raising, agriculture, commerce – analogous to the one proposed, probably independently, by Turgot, under the influence of Montesquieu's *De l'esprit des lois* (1748, in particular book eighteen): cf. Meek 1977, pp. 18–32.

determine the standard of living of a given country and its tendencies to progress or regress.

Smith's thesis may be summarised as follows. First of all, the 'wealth of nations' is identified with what today we call per capita income, or in substance the standard of living of the citizens of the country under consideration.[25] This is an identification we now take for granted, but it was by no means so when Smith introduced it. Indeed, with it was abandoned the tendency of the cameralist and mercantilist writers, counsellors to the prince in the previous decades, to take as the goal the maximisation of the total national income of a country as source of economic power and hence of military and political power (a view that would see Switzerland as less 'wealthy' than India).

Secondly, let us recall that national income (Y) is equal to the quantity of product obtained on average by each worker (or labour productivity, π) multiplied by the number of workers employed in production (L):

$$Y = \pi L.$$

If we divide national income by population (N), we obtain per capita income; as a consequence, per capita income proves equal to labour productivity multiplied by the share of active workers over total population. In other terms: from $Y = \pi L$, dividing by N, we obtain

$$Y/N = \pi L/N.$$

Namely, the standard of living of the population depends on two factors: the share of citizens employed in productive labour and the productivity of their labour.

Here the division of labour comes into play. In fact, according to Smith, labour productivity depends mainly on the stage reached by the division of labour. In turn, this depends on the size of the markets.

---

[25] These are the very first lines of *The wealth of nations* (Smith 1776, p. 10):

> The annual labour of every nation is the fund which originally supplies it with all the necessaries and conveniences of life which it annually consumes, and which consist always, either in the immediate produce of that labour, or in what is purchased with that produce from other nations.
>
> According therefore, as this produce, or what is purchased with it, bears a greater or smaller proportion to the number of those who are to consume it, the nation will be better or worse supplied with all the necessaries and conveniences for which it has occasion.

As a matter of fact, Smith's view is wider: in a civilised society material wealth, liberty, individual dignity and shared rules (laws and moral norms) all matter. A flourishing economy is important both in itself and as a prerequisite for the development of letters and arts, and because of the civilising function attributed to commerce (the *doux commerce* thesis mentioned above, § 4.1).

Let us take a closer look at these two theses. The first one – the positive effect of the division of labour on productivity – is illustrated by Smith (1776, pp. 14–15) with the well-known example of the pin factory, which is taken from the item *Épingle* in the *Encyclopédie* edited by d'Alembert and Diderot.[26] Smith identifies three circumstances that connect productivity to the division of labour: the improvement in the skills of the worker, when he regularly accomplishes a specific task rather than a multiplicity of tasks; the saving of labour time usually lost when shifting from one task to another; and technical progress induced by the possibility of focusing attention on one specific work task.[27]

Let us now consider the second thesis, the connection between growth of the market and development of the division of labour.[28] Let us recall that when a firm expands in order to realise an improved division of labour within itself, it will have to place on the market a product that has increased both because of the increase in the number of workers employed and the increase in their productivity. In Smith's example of the pin factory, a worker who does everything by himself produces around ten pins a day, while a small factory with ten workers produces about 50,000 pins a day. Production as a whole has increased by five thousand times, as a result of a tenfold increase in the number of workers and a five-hundredfold increase in their productivity. Thus the market must also grow by five thousand times, in order to absorb the production of the small factory, compared with the size of the market sufficient for a

[26] The item *Épingle* (written by Alexandre Deleyre, known as the translator of Francis Bacon) is included in the fifth volume (1755) of the *Encyclopédie*, published between 1751 and 1772, and mentioned (with erroneous reference to the needle, 'aiguille') in the programmatic manifesto of the work, d'Alembert and Diderot's *Discours préliminaire* (1751, p. 141). The importance of the division of labour had, however, already been recognised by the Greek writers (cf. above, § 2.2) and, nearer to Smith, by authors such as William Petty, who uses as examples the fabrication of dresses, ships and clocks (Petty, 1690, pp. 260–1 and 1899 [1682], p. 473), and the anonymous author of the *Considerations on the East India trade*, who uses the same examples (Anonymous 1701, pp. 590–2). The example of pins might have appeared suggestive to Smith because of the possibility, for himself and for the readers among his fellow citizens, of a direct comparison with the conditions in which the Scottish seamen produced the nails for their boats, as a subsidiary part of their fishing and smuggling activities (with the result of low productivity and bad quality of the product). The example of the needle was used by a medieval Muslim author, Ghazali (1058–1111): cf. Hosseini 1998, p. 673.

[27] Cf. Smith 1776, pp. 17–20.

[28] The Smithian connection between the size of the market and the division of labour has often been interpreted, in the terms of the traditional marginalist theory of the firm based on the U-shaped cost curves (cf. below, ch. 13), as a thesis concerning increasing returns to scale. Cf. for instance Stigler 1951. In the context of the marginalist theory, however, the returns to scale concern static comparisons among alternatives equally available to the entrepreneur at a given instant of time, while in the Smithian framework the division of labour (more specifically, technological change) and the expansion of the market are processes that take place in time.

single worker producing pins. Clearly, therefore, the size of the market constitutes the main constraint on the development of the division of labour. Hence Smith's economic liberalism: whatever is an obstacle to commerce, also constitutes an obstacle to the development of the division of labour, and so to increases in productivity and the increase in the welfare of the citizens, or in other words to the wealth of nations.

Obviously, in analysing a market economy based on the division of labour we cannot stop at an aggregate notion such as that of the wealth of nations. Indeed, there are three connected but distinct aspects of the division of labour: the microeconomic division of labour, among the different workers within a same plant;[29] the social division, among different jobs and professions; and the macroeconomic division, among firms and sectors producing different commodities or groups of commodities.[30] It is therefore necessary to consider both the social stratification typical of such an economic system, and the relations that set in between the different productive sectors. On these aspects Smith goes well beyond the economic thought preceding him, although he takes a number of elements from it.

The 'political arithmeticians' King and Davenant had illustrated the economic situation of England utilising a partition of the national economy into geographical areas: a choice we can understand for a time when commerce was greatly hindered by the difficulty of transportation. Subsequently, instead, the criterion gained ground of dividing society into social classes and productive sectors. In the wake of Cantillon and Quesnay, Smith considered a society divided into three classes. His tripartition – workers, capitalists and landlords (with the three corresponding kinds of

---

[29] The example of pins obviously concerns the microeconomic division of labour, namely the division of labour within an individual productive unit (or firm). The expansion of the market may therefore consist not only in an increase in the quantity of the product demanded by the buyers as a whole, but also in an increase in the market share of the individual firm through a process of industrial concentration. However, such a process implies a growing efficiency of the market. For instance, the number of firms producing pins in Great Britain may decrease if transport logistics allow the product of any firm to reach distant areas of the country. It is in any case clear that Smith, although not excluding it, does not refer so much to the expansion of the market for the individual firm as to the market for a product as a whole. (It is only within the marginalist theory of the equilibrium of the firm that increasing returns, conceived in statical terms, enter into contradiction with the assumption of competition; on this point cf. below, §§ 13.3 and 16.4; here we limit ourselves to stressing the dynamic, not static, nature, of the Smithian analysis of the division of labour, and the absence in it of the marginalist notion of equilibrium.)

[30] Even if Smith did not explicitly discuss this connection (nor distinguish explicitly these different aspects of the division of labour), it is clear that the macroeconomic division of labour stems from the microeconomic division, through the externalisation of some areas of activity of a firm giving rise to new firms and new branches of activity. Cf. Corsi 1991.

income: wages, profits and rents) – is different from that of his predecessors (agricultural workers and farmers, artisans, nobility and clergy). The latter classification mirrors a society in transition from feudalism to capitalism, while Smith's classification mirrors a capitalist society (though nowadays landlords have lost practically all their importance, while the middle classes have expanded). Thus, in this respect too Smith marks the rise of the conceptual scheme that characterised subsequent economic science.

The notion of the rate of profits, though not new (it had already been utilised by Turgot and others), definitively acquires a central role: the expediency of alternative lines of activity is evaluated by looking at the ratio between profits and the value of capital advances, rather than at the difference between receipts and costs.

Because of the differences in bargaining power between capitalists and workers,[31] we may assume that the latter receive a wage just sufficient to maintain themselves and their families. The incomes of capitalists and landlords, namely profits and rents, may thus be considered equal in their total to the surplus obtained within the economy.

In the process of development, Smith adds, rents increase, while the rate of profits tends to decrease due to the 'competition of capitals'. As a consequence, the interest of landowners accords in this respect with the general interest of society, while the opposite holds true for the capitalists.[32]

---

[31] What are the common wages of labour depends every where upon the contract usually made between those two parties, whose interests are by no means the same. The workmen desire to get as much, the masters to give as little as possible. The former are disposed to combine in order to raise, the latter in order to lower the wages of labour.

It is not, however, difficult to foresee which of the two parties must, upon all ordinary occasions, have the advantage in the dispute, and force the other into a compliance with their terms. The masters, being fewer in number, can combine much more easily; and the law, besides, authorises, or at least does not prohibit their combinations, while it prohibits those of the workmen. We have no acts of parliament against combining to lower the price of work; but many against combining to raise it. In all such disputes the masters can hold out much longer. [. . .] In the long-run the workman may be as necessary to his master as his master is to him; but the necessity is not so immediate. (Smith 1776, pp. 83–4)

It should be noted that Smith maintains the thesis of a downward pressure on the wage towards the subsistence minimum (for the necessary consumption of the worker and his family) with arguments of a historico-institutional kind; changes such as the legalisation of the trade unions and the right to strike modify the situation and make it possible for wages to be raised, even a great deal, above the subsistence level, but do not detract from the validity of Smith's approach to the issue of distribution, seen as a problem of relative bargaining power. The same cannot be said for the 'iron law of wages' based on the Malthusian population principle, which will be discussed below (§ 6.2).

[32] Cf. Smith 1776, pp. 264–7. This does not mean that Smith's attitude is favourable to the landlords: they 'love to reap where they never sowed' (ibid., p. 67), and rent 'is naturally

The surplus – a notion that Smith takes over from Petty, Cantillon and Quesnay – is equal to that part of the product that exceeds what is necessary to reconstitute the initial inventories of means of production and means of subsistence for the workers employed in the productive process. This notion is the core of the classical representation of the functioning of the economy as 'production of commodities by means of commodities'. Period after period, within the economic system firms utilise the initial inventories of means of production (and the workers utilise the initial inventories of means of subsistence) in the course of the productive process, at the end of which they obtain a product which is used first of all to reconstitute the initial inventories so as to be able to repeat the productive cycle; what is left after this, namely the surplus, may be utilised to increase the inventories of means of production and subsistence, increasing the number of workers employed in the productive process and hence the product, or for 'unproductive' consumption (which includes together with luxury consumption also the subsistence consumption of the unemployed or of those whose work does not give concrete results, that is, does not give rise to commodities that can be sold in the market).

Smith attributes notable importance to the process of accumulation, or in other words to the productive utilisation of the surplus. Accumulation consists not only in investment in new means of production but also in the increase in the number of workers employed, and so in the wage advances for such workers, consisting in the use of part of the surplus as means of subsistence for the additional productive workers.

Here the problem arises of the distinction between productive and unproductive workers. In this respect, Smith appears to oscillate between three different definitions. According to the first one, productive labour is that labour that gives rise to physical goods: labour in agriculture and manufacture, that is, but not labour in the services sector. The second definition identifies as productive that labour which recoups the funds employed in production and in addition generates a profit. According to the third definition, that labour is productive the wage for which is drawn from capital, while we are confronted with unproductive labour when the wage is drawn from the income of the master, as is the case for servants.[33]

---

a monopoly price' (ibid., p. 161). But the attitude towards 'those who live by profits' is even harsher; not only is their interest opposed to economic development, it is also 'to narrow the competition' (ibid., p. 267: cf. the passage quoted below, in note 63).

[33] For the three definitions, cf. Smith 1776, respectively pp. 330–1, 332, 332–3. It should be stressed that because of this notion of productive labour, Smith's notion of national income (Y in the equations above) is more restrictive than the current definition of income in modern national accounts. Nearer to Smith's (because of Marx's adoption of a variant of the Smithian concept of productive labour) was the notion of national income adopted until recently in the national accounts of communist countries.

As a matter of fact, these are not necessarily three alternative definitions. The last is useful for illustrative purposes, since it helps the reader to concretely understand Smith's reasoning, but as a theory it would imply a logically vicious circle.[34] The second and the first definition may coincide, if we assume that agriculture and manufacture correspond to the field of action of capitalistic enterprises. With such an assumption, we may credit Smith with an able compromise between the tradition that identifies productive labour with the production of durable goods (along a scale topped by precious metals and foreign trade, the latter being the means to obtain them) and the subsequent view, that will become dominant in Karl Marx's work, according to which the distinction between productive and unproductive labour, as far as the historical stage of capitalism is concerned, corresponds to the distinction between what comes within and what remains outside of the capitalistic area of the economy. In other words, Smith keeps account of the traditional view but at the same time transforms it, throwing a bridge towards the less ambiguous Marxian definition.[35]

As for the theme of productive labour, again on the issue of the origin of the surplus Smith goes beyond the traditional view of a hierarchy of productive sectors. In particular, the physiocratic idea that agriculture alone is capable of generating a surplus came under fire from Smith a few years after publication of the main works of the physiocrats.[36]

[34] Indeed, when a capitalist hires a worker, we may say that the expense for the wage comes from his capital if the worker is a productive worker, while it comes from his income if the worker is unproductive: the distinction depends on what the worker does, not on the fact that his wage comes from one specific banking account rather than another. (Similarly, the purchase of a car on the part of an entrepreneur may today be classified as an investment or a consumption expenditure according to the use that is made of the car.)

[35] The identification of productive labour with that which gives rise to material goods is the object of criticism on the part of Jean-Baptiste Say (1803), who defines services as 'immaterial products'. According to Say, we may define as productive any activity that gives rise to use values, namely to goods and services considered useful by the purchaser: a view that falls into the tradition of the subjective theory of value. (On Say cf. below, § 6.3).
   As far as unproductive labour is concerned, Smith suggests a distinction between useful and useless jobs (for instance, the physician and the buffoon; cf. Smith 1776, p. 331). In essence, we may consider as useful that work which contributes indirectly to the functioning of the economic system, for instance by guaranteeing the observance of property rights; we may include in this field teachers and physicians, who contribute to the survival of the workers and to the development of their abilities.

[36] Smith 1776, pp. 674–9. Here Smith explicitly also considers as productive the labour of the merchants, at the same level as that of agricultural workers, artisans and manufacturers, and in maintaining this thesis he again recalls the elements that characterise the three definitions of productive labour illustrated above. The arguments here used

Let us summarise the points made so far. We have seen that according to Smith the wealth of nations, interpreted as the average per capita income of the citizens of a country (Y/N), depends on two factors: the productivity of the workers employed in the production of commodities (productive workers), π, and the share of productive workers in the total population, L/N.

Let us recall that labour productivity depends on the stage reached by the process of increasing division of labour, which in turn depends on the consumers' income (that is, on Y/N) and on the more or less free trade policies adopted by public authorities, in addition to improvements in transport.

At the same time, the share of productive workers in the total population, L/N, depends on the stage reached by the process of accumulation, namely on the amount of means of production available to give work to new productive workers, on institutional elements and on customs, such as laws on primary public education for all or child labour, or customs concerning women's attitudes towards working in a factory. In turn, such institutional factors and customs are influenced by the political choices of the public authorities.

Using arrows to indicate cause and effect relations, we may represent the complex of relations as in figure 5.1. As we can see from the scheme, the adoption of policies aiming at eliminating the obstacles to free trade and at favouring the expansion of the markets may set in motion a 'virtuous spiral': the expansion of the markets favours an increasing division of labour, and with it an increase in productivity that in turn gives rise to an increase in per capita income and, consequently, a further expansion of the markets. At the same time, these and similar policies favour an increase in per capita income thanks to their action in favour of an increase in the share of productive workers in the total population. These

by Smith, however, mainly refer to the erroneousness of considering unproductive the manufacturing and the mercantile sectors, rather than the fact that in a system of productive interrelations, in which the different sectors depend one upon another for the provisioning of their means of production, it is nonsense to say that the surplus can only spring from the natural power of the land, and so only in the agricultural sector. Indeed, land has no autonomous role in the productive process, and would not yield anything if left uncultivated, if labour (hence means of subsistence) and means of production had not been utilised together with it. Therefore the product cannot be attributed to a single element among the various elements employed in any individual productive process. Thus, since means of production at least in part come from other sectors (because of the division of labour, in agriculture manufacturing products are used, and vice versa), it is not possible to establish whether the surplus springs from one sector or from another, without first explaining how the exchange ratios are determined. Indeed, the surplus is a notion related to the economic system as a whole, not to an individual economic sector.

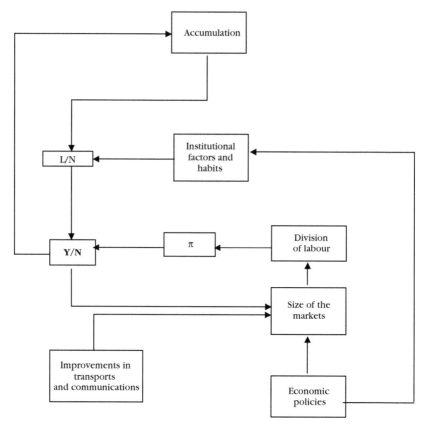

Figure 5.1

dynamic mechanisms, of a cumulative kind, constitute the essence of the Smithian theory of the wealth of nations.

5.   Value and prices

One of the crucial conceptual distinctions for the development of classical political economy is that concerning value in use and value in exchange. This distinction is perfectly clear in Adam Smith:

The word *value* [. . .] has two different meanings, and sometimes expresses the utility of some particular object, and sometimes the power of purchasing other goods which the possession of that object conveys. The one may be called 'value in use'; the other, 'value in exchange'. The things which have the greatest value in use have frequently little or no value in exchange; and, on the contrary, those which have the greatest value in exchange have frequently little or no value in use. Nothing is more useful than water: but it will purchase scarce any thing; scarce any thing can be had in exchange for it. A diamond, on the contrary, has scarce any value in use; but a very great quantity of other goods may frequently be had in exchange for it.[37]

According to Smith and classical economists in general, value in use is a prerequisite of value in exchange: a good which has no use, and which is not desired by anybody, cannot have a positive value in exchange.[38] But once this condition is satisfied, the value in exchange of any commodity is determined on the basis of elements different from value in use: as we shall better see below, value in exchange depends on the conditions of reproduction of the economic system, not on the utility of the commodity under consideration. More precisely, the classical economists do not consider the value in use of a commodity as a measurable quantity. At most, like Smith in the passage quoted above, we may speak of a greater or lesser value in use, but in a rather generic way that certainly does not entitle us to think of a complete ordering of the preferences of economic agents. In any case, Smith himself explicitly rejects the idea that it is possible to explain the value in exchange of two commodities on the basis of their greater or lesser value in use. Nevertheless, a connection between the two notions based on the representation of value in use as a mono-dimensional magnitude (either as a measurable magnitude, as in the cardinal utility approach, or as simply subject to comparison, as in the ordinal utility approach and in the theory of revealed preferences) was to be the basis for the marginalist theory of value.[39]

When they refer to the value of a commodity, the classical economists commonly mean value in exchange. However, the problem of value may assume different features, according to whether: (i) the aim is to go back to the first principle – the 'source' – of value; (ii) the focus is on the practical issue of the standard of value for inter-temporal comparisons or comparisons involving different countries; (iii) the theoretical problem is tackled of determining exchange values.

---

[37] Smith 1776, pp. 44–5. The paradox of water and the diamonds is a commonplace in economic literature. Galiani, for instance, refers to it in order to stress the role of scarcity, alongside that of utility, in the determination of exchange values (cf. above, § 4.8).

[38] For Smith, as for so many other authors before the 'marginalist revolution', utility has an objective sense as the capacity of a good to satisfy some need, not in the sense of subjective evaluation on the part of one or more individuals. Let us recall that these two aspects had already been distinguished – as *virtuositas* and *complacibilitas* – by Bernardine of Siena and Antoninus of Florence at the beginning of the fifteenth century: cf. above, § 2.5

[39] The idea of a connection between value in use and value in exchange was already present both in earlier authors and in Smith's times. Cf. below, § 10.2.

It is understandable that, whatever specific problem came under consideration, the economists should initially have focused on labour. As we have already seen, theories of labour-value were already common among the natural law philosophers; labour reappears, side by side with land, among the elements that constitute the content in value of a commodity in the theories of Petty and Cantillon. As we have seen, however, labour-value theories assume different meanings in the different authors. On the one hand, the natural law philosophers conceive labour-values as an index of the sacrifice made by people in order to obtain the desired commodity. On the other hand, authors like Petty and Cantillon are nearer to a theory of physical production costs; labour-values have for them the meaning of a simple matter of fact, devoid of the metaphysical features that characterise the idea of labour as sacrifice: that is, labour-values are nothing but a simplified way of expressing the relative difficulty of production of the commodity under consideration in relation to that of other commodities.

In Smith both features are simultaneously present; furthermore, the labour-value theory is proposed both as a theory of necessary labour (labour required for the production of the commodity: labour contained, in Marx's terminology) and as a theory of labour commanded. Let us consider this latter first:

Every man is rich or poor according to the degree in which he can afford to enjoy the necessaries, conveniences, and amusements of human life. But after the division of labour has once thoroughly taken place, it is but a very small part of these with which a man's own labour can supply him. The far greater part of them he must derive from the labour of other people, and he must be rich or poor according to the quantity of that labour which he can command, or which he can afford to purchase. The value of any commodity, therefore, to the person who possesses it, and who means not to use or consume it himself, but to exchange it for other commodities, is equal to the quantity of labour which it enables him to purchase or command. Labour, therefore, is the real measure of the exchangeable value of all commodities.[40]

We may note that in the passage quoted above Smith does not intend to point out the factors that determine exchange values, but simply to indicate the standard with which to measure them, and among other things he justifies this choice by referring more generally to the central role of labour in the economy. Labour commanded moreover constitutes a standard particularly suited to comparison between different countries or different times within the same country,[41] and is thus appropriate for

---

[40] Smith 1776, p. 47.

[41] Even today the use of such a standard is frequent: a haircut 'commands' an hour of labour in one country, two hours of labour in another. The choice of the standard is here motivated not by a logical necessity internal to the theory, but by the particular role of the man, and especially the worker, in the economists' eyes. Let us also observe that

a 'dynamic' theory of the wealth of nations such as that proposed by Smith. We may also note that according to Smith labour commanded is an appropriate measure for a society based on the division of labour. In fact, when a society is based on the division of labour, exchange between the products of different sectors is in substance an exchange that connects the workers of the different sectors: behind the act of exchange there is a relationship reciprocally connecting the workers of the different sectors, bringing them together in a single economic system, in a single society, within which each person depends on the labour of the others. On the basis of work time we can thus express in quantitative terms the economic relations that hold together the different producers in a society based on the division of labour.

However, the problem of value remains open, at least in the sense it usually has in economic literature, namely that of identifying the factors which determine the value in exchange of the different commodities. In a society where the workers do not own their means of production (that is, in which they are mostly dependent workers), labour commanded gives the number of hours of labour required to earn a wage equal to the price of the commodity. Thus, for instance, we may say that two hours of labour 'acquire' (or 'command') a kilogram of meat. We may obtain the quantity of labour commanded by a given commodity by dividing its price by the wage rate, although this clearly presupposes knowledge of both price and wage rate.

A solution to the problem of the determination of exchange values, already suggested in the passage quoted above, is provided by the necessary labour theory, according to which the exchange ratios between two commodities are proportional to the quantities of labour necessary to produce them. Smith, however, considers this theory valid only in an 'early and rude society':

In that early and rude state of society which precedes both the accumulation of stock and the appropriation of land, the proportion between the quantities of labour necessary for acquiring different objects seems to be the only circumstance which can afford any rule for exchanging them for one another. [. . .] It is natural that what is usually the produce of two days or two hours labour, should be worth double of what is usually the produce of one day's or one hour's labour.[42]

in Smith's times a theory of index numbers was not available, such as could have supplied an alternative instrument of measurement of the changes in economic magnitudes; moreover, even index numbers provide only approximate solutions to the measurement problem.

[42] Smith 1776, p. 65. We must stress that Smith does not refer to any real primitive society, but to an ideal model of society in which economic agents (hunters and fishers) adopt the 'rational' behaviour typical of a mercantile society, while the primitive character is given by the abstract hypothesis of absence of division into the social classes of workers, capitalists and landlords.

However, Smith says, we can no longer utilise necessary labour to explain exchange values when we refer to a society in which workers are no longer the owners of the capital goods and land which they use in their work. In fact, necessary labour takes no account of the rents and profits that enter into the price of every commodity when capitalists and landlords constitute social classes distinct from the working class.

In such a society, exchange values correspond to the 'natural prices', which Smith defines in the following passage, distinguishing them from 'market prices': 'When the price of any commodity is neither more nor less than what is sufficient to pay the rent of the land, the wages of the labour, and the profits of the stock employed in raising, preparing, and bringing it to market, according to their natural rates, the commodity is then sold for what may be called its natural price.'[43]

In other words, the market price is the price we see looking at the actual acts of exchange; the natural price, instead, is the theoretical price that expresses the conditions of reproduction of the productive process. In a society divided into social classes, the exchange values or 'natural prices' must cover production costs and guarantee, in addition, a return equal to that obtainable in other sectors for the capital invested in the productive activity.

Obviously reference to costs of production is in itself insufficient to build a theory of prices, since it would imply circular logical reasoning: if we need steel in order to produce coal, and coal in order to produce steel, we cannot determine the price of coal if we do not already know it. For this reason some economists, before and after Smith, had recourse to a first principle such as necessary labour (or labour-and-land, as in the case of Petty and Cantillon), which allowed them to explain prices without having to be explained in turn. However, as we have seen, Smith did not agree, since he considered necessary labour as an explanatory principle acceptable only for an 'early and rude society'.

Exchange values remain an open issue in Smith's analysis. An attempt at solving it is seen by some interpreters (for instance by Dobb 1973, pp. 44 ff.) in what has been called the 'adding-up-of-components-theory': namely, the idea that 'the price of every commodity finally resolves itself into some one or other, or all of those three parts', 'rent, labour, and profit'.[44] In other words, the price of a commodity corresponds to wages, profits and rents plus the costs borne for the means of production other than labour and land; such costs are in turn decomposed into wages,

[43] Ibid., p. 72.
[44] Ibid., p. 68. The inclusion of profit in the price may be considered a step forward from Petty, Cantillon and Quesnay: cf. O'Donnell 1990, p. 54.

profits, rents and costs for the means of production; we thus proceed backwards until the costs for the means of production have disappeared or become insignificant. The value of a commodity thus depends on the technology and on the 'natural' rates for wage, rent and profit.

In this theory, however, there seems to be implicit an idea, which was to come under criticism from Ricardo, that an increase in the wage rate causes an increase in the price while leaving unchanged the rate of profits. As a matter of fact such criticism only holds if we assume – as Smith did not, at least not explicitly – that the three distributive variables are independent the one from the other. The adding-up-of-components-theory, however, does not constitute an adequate solution to the problem of exchange values, since the residual of means of production cannot in general be reduced to zero.[45] The theory thus represents rather re-proposal at the level of an individual commodity of a national accounting principle: the value of the national product corresponds to the value of national income, namely to the sum of the incomes of the different social classes. In fact, it is precisely this point which is stressed by Smith (1776, p. 69).

We can say, in conclusion, that Smith does not provide a fully adequate theory of exchange values; what he does provide, with the labour commanded theory, is more simply an indication of how to measure the prices of commodities that appears to be particularly useful for an economy based on the division of labour and in which continuous technological evolution takes place.[46] It is only with Ricardo that the theory of value, in its modern meaning of theory of relative prices, comes to centre stage.

6.   Natural prices and market prices

As we have already seen, the division of labour poses a problem of coordination among the different economic agents. Each firm produces a commodity or group of commodities and, in order to continue producing, it needs to dispose of part at least of what it has produced in exchange for the means of production required for the continuance of its activity. Similarly, the workers obtain a wage that they need to convert into their means of subsistence.

---

[45] Strictly speaking, 'complete reduction' is only possible when no commodity is directly or indirectly required for the production of itself: cf. Sraffa 1960, pp. 34 ff.

[46] Following similar lines, and showing how relevant the problem of measurement in spatial and intertemporal comparisons was to Smithian analysis, was the proposal to take corn as standard of measure: cf. Smith 1776, pp. 55–6. Sylos Labini 1976, illustrating the proposal, remarks that in Smith's opinion the production of corn is characterised by relative costs more or less stable over time, unlike, on the one hand, other agricultural products, characterised by increasing costs, and, on the other hand, manufactures, characterised by decreasing costs.

According to Smith, the market economy as a whole functions in a fairly satisfactory way: for each commodity, the flow of production coming out of the firms producing it more or less corresponds to the flow of the demand coming under normal conditions from the buyers. The market mechanisms guide the economy in such a way as to ensure the material welfare that is an indispensable precondition for a civilised life.

Let us consider the issue in some more detail. The exchanges between the different sectors, necessary for the continuous functioning of the economy, may be coordinated by a central authority with a plan for the repartition of the global product among the different sectors and the different productive units: such is the case in a command or planned economy. In a market economy, on the contrary, exchanges take place freely and the decisions on quantities to be produced, sold and acquired and on exchanges and prices are decentralised. It is the market that links up the productive units operating in the different sectors of the economy, in two distinct ways. First of all, through market exchanges each productive unit obtains from the others what it needs to continue its activity in exchange for its own product. Second, the market links up the productive units through the competition they conduct among themselves; it is from here that the mechanism derives ensuring the required coordination among the myriad of decentralised decisional centres, producers and buyers.

We may distinguish two kinds of competition, both taken into consideration by Smith. The first is competition within the market for each commodity. Each buyer seeks among the many sellers present in the market the one that sells the desired commodity at the lowest possible price; the seller who asks too high a price risks being left with unsold merchandise. Similarly, each seller seeks among the many buyers present in the market the one that is ready to pay the highest price for the commodity on sale; the buyers offering too low a price risk being left empty-handed. Under ideal conditions, when competition among the sellers and among the buyers does not meet with obstacles, the price of each commodity is one and the same for all the buyers and all the sellers. This is the so-called 'law of one price', emerging as a necessary outcome of competition.

There is then a second kind of competition, which Smith calls the 'competition of capitals': namely, the competition among capitalists in search of the employment that offers the highest returns on their capital. When capitalists are free to move their capitals from one sector to another in search of the most fruitful employment (in Smith's 1776, p. 73, terms, 'where there is perfect liberty'), there is free competition: its characteristic is precisely the absence of obstacles to the free movement of capital (or, as it is also put, the absence of barriers to entry into the different sectors of economic activity).[47]

When free competition rules, it is not possible for a sector to offer capitalists a return higher than that obtainable in other sectors for a long stretch of time, since otherwise new capitals would flow into it, with the consequence that production would increase, the market price would diminish, and with it also profits and the rate of return would decrease. In the same way, it is not possible for a sector to offer capitalists a return lower than that obtainable in other sectors, since otherwise there would be an outflow of capitals from that sector, causing a fall in production, with an ensuing rise in the market price and hence in profits and in the sector's rate of return. Therefore, under 'perfect liberty', namely generalised free competition, the return on capital – the rate of profits – tends to be equal in all sectors. In this way the 'competition of capitals' links up in a single capitalistic market the different sectors of the economy. Here we see the central role of this kind of competition, which distinguishes the capitalistic system from a non-capitalistic market economy.[48]

As a result of the assumption of competition, we may identify the conditions which define the theoretical ('natural') price. It is the exchange value which corresponds to reproduction over time of an economy based on the division of labour; therefore, the price must be such as to allow the recovery of production costs and the possibility of earning a 'natural' profit. In Smith's words: 'when the price of any commodity is neither more nor less than what is sufficient to pay the rent of the land, the wages of the labour, and the profits of the stock employed in raising, preparing, and bringing it to market, according to their natural rates, the commodity is then sold for what may be called its natural price' (Smith 1776, p. 72).

This theoretical variable, defined on the basis of analytical conditions, has an empirical counterpart in the so-called market price: 'The actual price at which any commodity is commonly sold is called its market price. It may either be above, or below, or exactly the same with its natural price.' And Smith goes on: 'The market price of every particular commodity is regulated by the proportion between the quantity which is actually

---

[47] For the comparison between this notion of competition and the neoclassical one, cf. Sylos Labini 1976.

[48] This element is lost sight of in the marginalist theories, which consider the capital market a market like all others, and the tendency to a uniform rate of profits as a specific instance of the law of one price. In this way the marginalist theories confuse the notion of competition within each individual market, based on the number of buyers and sellers, with the notion of the free competition of capitals, based on the freedom of entry into the various sectors of the economy.

brought to market, and the demand of those who are willing to pay the natural price of the commodity', namely effectual demand.[49]

The counterposition between natural and market price may be considered not only as the distinction between a theoretical variable and its empirical correlate, but also as a subtle way in which Smith counterposed his own theory of exchange values, based on the analytical conditions defining the natural price, and the subjective theories of value, vaguely referring to scarcity and utility, to supply and demand, prevailing among Scholastic writers or in authors such as Galiani and Turgot. Focusing on the problem of reproduction over time of a society based on the division of labour, Smith, while apparently bringing into his exposition the elements on which the traditional subjective theories of value relied, confined such elements to the role of (irregular, non-systematic) disturbances and by the very definition of natural price ruled them out of his own theory of exchange values.

Attempts at interpreting Smith so as to establish a connection between the objective elements on which the notion of natural price is based, and the subjective elements which are brought into the picture with respect to the market price, focus attention on the adjustment mechanism between market and natural price. This mechanism relies on the two kinds of competition illustrated above: when production of a commodity is in excess of the 'effectual' demand (i.e. the quantity that buyers are prepared to absorb at the natural price), then competition between sellers will push the market price below the natural price: the producers will be unable to obtain the 'natural' profits, and an outflow of capitals from that sector will take place; production will decrease, and the excess supply will thus be absorbed.

It was in connection with this adjustment mechanism that Smith used the famous 'gravitation' analogy:

The natural price, therefore, is, as it were, the central price, to which the prices of all commodities are continually gravitating. [. . .] But though the market price of every particular commodity is in this manner continually gravitating, if one may say so, towards the natural price, yet sometimes particular accidents, sometimes natural causes, and sometimes particular regulations of police, may, in many commodities, keep up the market price, for a long time together, a good deal above the natural price.[50]

---

[49] Ibid., p. 73. Smith already discussed natural and market prices, and their relationship, in the *Lectures on jurisprudence* (Smith 1978, pp. 356–66: vi. 67–97); but these pages can only be considered as a rough first draft of the mature treatment of the issue in book I, chapter 7, of *The wealth of nations*.

[50] Smith 1776, pp. 75 and 77. Again in chapter 7 of book I of *The wealth of nations*, Smith states that the market price may prove higher than the natural price 'for many years

Many authors, especially in recent years, have interpreted the metaphor of gravitation as if it implied a theory of market price based on supply and demand. Specifically, market prices came to be interpreted as short run (Marshallian, market-clearing) equilibrium prices.[51] This idea is in fact totally alien to Smith's thinking, both because the market price, as we have seen, is not a theoretical variable for him, but an empirical correlate, and because the reference to gravitation itself, which seems to imply a precise theoretical structure, that of Newton's theory (in which the behaviour of the body that gravitates around another one is described by precise mathematical laws), is in fact quite vague.[52] This is testified among other things by the fact that in each of the two sentences in which the term 'gravitation' appears, it is accompanied by expressions ('as it were', 'if one may say so') which point to its use as an imprecise metaphor.

The interpretation of the market price as a theoretical variable determined by the confrontation between demand and supply according to general and precise rules makes its appearance only towards the end of the golden period of classical political economy, with John Stuart Mill and Thomas De Quincey, to be developed later by Alfred Marshall in the way that has become familiar through textbooks. In Smith's times, the terms 'demand' and 'supply' did not indicate curves, or more generally stable and well-identified functional relations connecting price and quantity of a commodity,[53] but a set of elements, possibly fortuitous or contingent, that cannot be reduced solely to technological (economies and diseconomies of scale) or psychological factors (consumers' preferences). Rather, reference to the role of demand and supply in the determination of price typically reflects, before Smith, a situation preceding the development of regular markets, with prices, as in village fairs or in sea-port cities, subjected to the influence of non-systematic events.

---

together', 'for centuries', 'for ever', whenever the operation of competition is impeded by customs, regulations, laws and natural monopolies. The 'natural price' thus appears not only as a theoretical variable which expresses the conditions of reproduction of the economic system, but also as a norm corresponding to the full operation of competition.

[51] Cf. for instance Blaug 1962, p. 39.

[52] According to Phyllis Deane 1989, pp. 61 and 68, the reference to Newton corresponds to the representation of the market economy as a self-regulating system. 'The essence of the Newtonian world-view was that it started from two axioms, two articles of faith about the real world in its social as well as its physical aspects: 1) that it was characterized by uniformities and constancies which were sufficiently regular to have the force of laws of nature; and 2) that it was designed and guided by an intelligent creator. [. . .] there was a systematic, god-given harmony in the operations of the universe.' However, such an optimistic and simplistic view of the social world appears alien to the tradition of the Scottish Enlightenment and closer to the French Cartesian tradition.

[53] Demand curves appear in economic literature more than half a century later, with Cournot and Rau: cf. below, §§ 10.2, 11.1.

The modern interpretations of the market price in Smith, as determined by demand and supply, are commonly based on the second part of the definition of the market price quoted above: it 'is regulated by the proportion between the quantity which is actually brought to market, and the demand'. However, in this passage Smith speaks of the market price as 'regulated', not 'determined', by the proportion between demand and supply; nor can the expression 'proportion between the quantity [. . .] brought to market, and the demand' be taken as pointing to a precise mathematical relationship. This passage constitutes neither a definition of the market price, nor a theory to explain its determination. Smith does not then go on to illustrate laws concerning the way demand and supply react to a market price different from the natural price, nor laws on how the market price reacts to disequilibria between demand and supply and to fluctuations in these variables. In particular, there is no hint of the idea, common in modern theory but not at the time of the classical economists, of a market clearing mechanism determining the market price.[54]

What Smith suggests are only a few general rules. First, the market price will be above the natural price when for any reason supply proves lower than the 'effectual' demand, and below it when the opposite holds true. Second, deviation of the market price from the natural price will provoke reactions on the part of buyers and producers alike; with free competition such reactions tend to favour resolution of the disequilibrium situation. From the examples that Smith gives, it is clear that the concrete action of these general rules depends on circumstances, and it is not therefore possible to formulate precise reaction functions for the market prices to the disequilibria between demand and supply, and of these two latter variables to the prices.[55]

Thus, for Smith gravitation is nothing but a metaphor used to evoke the role of competition as a force making for the stabilisation of the market. This is also the role of the 'invisible hand' metaphor, which moreover Smith uses only once in *The wealth of nations*, and in a specific context

---

[54] As we have already seen, market clearing – namely the idea that the market has a position of equilibrium in which demand and supply are exactly equal – is characteristic of financial markets, not of the markets for industrial products; modern theory has had to resort to artificial constructions such as 'reserve prices' in order to extend such a notion to agricultural and manufactured products. Let us also stress that the notion of market clearing should not be confused with the much vaguer idea of market adjustment mechanisms.

[55] Let us add that, as shown by Egidi 1975 and Steedman 1984, these rules should be reformulated, referring them to the sectoral rate of profit compared to the general rate; furthermore, Steedman shows that in the context of multi-sectoral analysis the sign of the deviation of the market price from the natural price is not necessarily the same as that of the deviation of the sectoral profit rate from the general rate, in contrast with Smith's supposition.

(the capitalists' preference for investing in the most profitable sectors of the national industry rather than in foreign countries, although motivated by personal interest, has a positive effect for society since it tends to increase the national income, as 'led by an invisible hand').[56] This is a long way from any theory based on market clearing mechanisms, supply and demand curves and the like. The difference may seem to represent progress at the level of the formal completeness of analysis, but it implies radical changes in the concepts utilised by the classical economists – so radical as to modify the theoretical context in a decidedly restrictive direction. We thus have a net loss as far as the conceptual representation of the economic system is concerned.[57] What, however, is certain is that the notion of the market price as a theoretical variable is totally alien to Smith. Furthermore, the idea of the 'invisible hand of the market' is a distortion of the history of thought; the fact that it has been – and still is – so frequently repeated, especially on the part of general economic equilibrium theorists, only shows their ignorance of the texts and their historical superficiality.

7.   The origin of the division of labour: Smith and Pownall

The issue of the origin of the division of labour is connected to various issues of social philosophy, and constitutes their unifying ground. As we shall now see by examining Smith's views and the criticisms they received

---

[56] Cf. Smith 1776, p. 456. The term 'invisible hand' is used only twice elsewhere by Smith, in different works and contexts (the *History of astronomy*, III.2: Smith, 1795, p. 49; and *The theory of moral sentiments*, IV.1.10: Smith 1759, p. 184) and, moreover, at least on the first of these occasions, in somewhat ironical tones. On the subject cf. Rothschild (1994; 2001, pp. 116–56) and Gilibert (1998). As this latter commentator notes, neither Smith's contemporaries nor the students of his thought up to the middle of the twentieth century gave any attention to the theme of the 'invisible hand'; it began to be propounded only after Arrow and Debreu had developed the axiomatic general economic equilibrium theory and the two 'fundamental theorems' of welfare economics according to which perfect competition ensures an optimal equilibrium and any optimal equilibrium may be interpreted as the outcome of a perfectly competitive market (cf. below, § 12.4). In this way, by attributing to Smith the idea of the market as an invisible hand that leads to optimal equilibria, modern theory has some claim to be seen as crowning the Smithian cultural design. In reality, however, the two views are quite different.

[57] Consider, on the one hand, the complexities of motivations of human action within the Smithian analytical framework in comparison to the mono-dimensional economic agent of modern theory, who only aims at maximising utility and, on the other hand, the disappearance of classical themes such as distributive conflicts and employment problems if it is held that the competitive market ensures optimal equilibria and the distributive variables (wage, rent, rate of profits) are considered, under competition, as equilibrium prices of the 'factors of production'.

from Pownall,[58] the origin of the division of labour may be traced to the human propensity for social life, or to innate differences in abilities. The two theses have profoundly different implications for issues such as the social contract theory, the view of social stratification as a fact of nature and indeed the positive or negative evaluation of labour itself. Before considering these aspects, however, it may be useful to illustrate first Smith's position, and then Pownall's criticisms.

Smith tackles the issue of the origin of the division of labour in chapter 2 of book I of *The wealth of nations*:

This division of labour, from which so many advantages are derived, is not originally the effect of any human wisdom, which foresees and intends that general opulence to which it gives occasion. It is the necessary, though very slow and gradual consequence of a certain propensity in human nature which has in view no such extensive utility; the propensity to truck, barter, and exchange one thing for another.

Whether this propensity be one of those original principles in human nature, of which no further account can be given; or whether, as seems more probable, it be the necessary consequence of the faculties of reason and speech, it belongs not to our present subject to enquire. It is common to all men, and to be found in no other race of animals, which seem to know neither this nor any other species of contracts.[59]

Smith's thesis is, then, that division of labour originates in the tendency of men to enter into relations of reciprocal exchange, or in other words – we might say – into human sociability. To this characteristic Smith also attributes the origin of language; moreover, it distinguishes men from animals.

In Smith's own words (1776, p. 26):

Nobody ever saw a dog make a fair and deliberate exchange of one bone for another with another dog [. . .]. When an animal wants to obtain something either of a man or of another animal, it has no other means of persuasion but to gain the favour of those whose service it requires. [. . .] Man sometimes uses the same arts with his brethren [. . .]. He has not time, however, to do this upon every occasion. In civilized society he stands at all times in need of the cooperation and assistance of great multitudes, while his whole life is scarce sufficient to gain the friendship of a few persons. In almost every other race of animals each individual, when it is grown up to maturity, is intirely independent, and in its natural state has occasion for the assistance of no other living creature. But man has almost

---

[58] Thomas Pownall (1722–1805) had been in 1757–9 governor of Massachusetts; from 1767 to 1780 he was a Member of Parliament.

[59] Smith 1776, p. 25. This is a thesis that constitutes a fixed point in Smith's thought; he had already stated it, in virtually the same terms, in the university lectures and in the first draft of *The wealth of nations* (Smith 1978, p. 347: LJ-A, vi. 44; pp. 492–3: LJ-B, 219; pp. 570–1: *Early draft*, 20–1).

constant occasion for the help of his brethren, and it is in vain for him to expect it from their benevolence only. He will be more likely to prevail if he can interest their self-love in his favour, and shew them that it is for their own advantage to do for him what he requires of them.

This long quotation is useful because it brings to the fore an important logical step that Smith takes perhaps too rapidly, from the propensity to barter as the basis for the division of labour to the role of self-interest for the sound functioning of a system based on the division of labour. This nexus implies that the propensity to barter may be seen as sociability only if we do not confuse the latter concept with the idea of altruism. On the other hand, as we saw in our illustration of *The theory of moral sentiments*, Smith considers the market economy as based on self-interest rather than mere selfishness. It is this specification of the two terms, propensity to barter and self-interest, that allows for their immediate connection.

Let us now return to the propensity to barter, seen as the desire to make contact with our fellow creatures, without, however, having to bear costs for this but, rather, looking for advantages. At first sight this idea might seem not to differ greatly from Pownall's thesis, according to which – as we shall now see – the division of labour originates in the desire to exploit the innate differences of labour abilities of the different individuals.

In fact, Pownall (1776, pp. 338–9) criticised Smith not because of mistakes in his statements, but because he had stopped his analysis too soon, without reaching the first principles:

I think you have stopped short in your analysis before you have arrived at the first natural cause and principle of the division of labour. [. . .] Before a man can have the propensity to barter, he must have acquired somewhat, which he does not want himself, and must feel, that there is something which he does want, that another person has in his way acquired [. . .]. Nature has so formed us, as that the labour of each must take one special direction, in preference to, and to the exclusion of some other equally necessary line of labour [. . .]. Man's wants and desires require to be supplied through many channels; his labour will more than supply him in some one or more; but through the limitation and the defined direction of his capacities he cannot actuate them all. This limitation, however, of his capacities, and the extent of his wants, necessarily creates to each man an accumulation of some articles of supply, and a defect of others, and is the original principle of his nature, which creates, by a reciprocation of wants, the necessity of an intercommunion of mutual supplies; this is the forming cause, not only of the division of labour, but the efficient cause of that community, which is the basis and origin of civil government.

Pownall's position has two presuppositions that appear extraneous to Smith's view of the functioning of the society and the economic system. The first presupposition is that each individual knows what he wants and what the others can offer before coming into contact with them, and in particular before entering into relations of exchange. In modern terms, we might say that Pownall presupposes the knowledge on the part of each economic agent of his own abilities and preferences and of the goods that other economic agents make available, or better of their abilities and preferences; such knowledge should be innate, in order to constitute the origin of the division of labour and of exchanges. The second presupposition of Pownall's thesis is that there are original differences in abilities among the different individuals: such differences, apart from constituting the original spring that determines the division of labour, also constitute a 'natural' presupposition of society's economic stratification.[60]

As far as the first aspect is concerned, the view of the individual as a logical *prius* with respect to society is opposed to the Smithian idea, typical of the whole tradition of the Scottish Enlightenment, of the individual as an intrinsically social being. As for the second aspect, namely the existence of a natural basis for economic and social differentiations, it is explicitly rejected by Smith. In fact, he affirms that he considers the different working abilities as mostly acquired as a consequence of the division of labour:

The difference of natural talents in different men is, in reality, much less than we are aware of; and the very different genius which appears to distinguish men of different professions, when grown up to maturity, is not upon many occasions so much the cause, as the effect of the division of labour. The difference between the most dissimilar characters, between a philosopher and a common street porter, for example, seems to arise not so much from nature, as from habit, custom, and education.[61]

[60] The doctrine of the intrinsic differences of abilities is already present (and dominant) in the Greek tradition and then in the Scholastic period: cf. above, §§ 2.2 and 2.4. Around the middle of the eighteenth century, this doctrine is taken up, in the framework of a subjective theory of value, by Galiani (1751, p. 49): 'By providence men are born to various crafts, but in unequal proportions of rarity, corresponding with wonderous sagacity to human needs.' This passage also indicates a crucial difficulty of the traditional view: if we admit that the distribution of abilities among the individuals is innate, only the 'invisible hand' of Providence can guarantee that the availability of abilities corresponds to the requirements of society, since any social mechanism of adjustment is ruled out by definition. Galiani (ibid., p. 50) is also aware of the implications of the doctrine of the innate differences of abilities for income distribution, conceived as 'just' in so far as it mirrors the innate abilities of the individual: 'It will be seen that wealth does not go to any person otherwise than in payment for the just value of his works.'

[61] Smith 1776, pp. 28–9. On analogous lines we find the Smithian view of the entrepreneur as a normal person, with at most the characteristics of a good *paterfamilias*, quite different from the heroic view of the entrepreneur that would subsequently be proposed by Marshall, and especially by Schumpeter. Actually Smith, with characteristic prudence, does not deny the existence of original individual differences or, as we would say today, differences due to genetic characteristics: what he maintains is the crucial importance of the elements of differentiation acquired through the vicissitudes of life, and in particular through working experience. Thus work acquires an additional dimension, as a formative factor, be it positive or negative.

The contrast between the democratic content of the Smithian thesis and the conservative element in Pownall's thesis thus appears evident: a contrast worth stressing, both because it may help us in understanding the innovative and progressive nature of Smith's social philosophy, and because the contrast between the two views repeatedly manifests itself in the course of time.[62]

8.   Economic and political liberalism: Smith's fortune

To say that Smith was the founder of economic science would be wrong: apart from the problems intrinsic to the notion of an individual founder of political economy, there is the fact that before him authors like Petty, Cantillon, Quesnay and many others had tackled analysis of specific economic issues or, more generally, of how a social system functions in terms of its material aspects. It was indeed on the many writings already existing on such issues that Smith largely relied in his work, drawing on them in many respects. Perhaps, in comparison with previous authors, Smith's distinctive characteristic is that of being an academician, dealing with the object of his analysis under the stimulus of political passion, too, but sufficiently detached from immediate problems and interests and, above all, dedicating great care and an enormous amount of time to the precise definition and accurate presentation of his ideas, with a great capacity to mediate between different views and theses while capturing the positive elements in each of them.

This Smithian subtlety, the refusal of clear-cut theses without qualifications and specifications, renders interpretation of his works difficult and interesting at the same time. In the next few pages we will discuss some examples of the interpretative issues that have attracted particular interest.

The first of these examples concerns Smith's liberalism. We should stress, in this respect, that Smith's was a progressive attitude to the major political themes of his time, such as the conflict over the independence of the American colonies. In pre- and post-revolutionary France *The wealth*

---

[62] The modern marginalist theory of wage differentials may be traced back to Pownall's position (innate differences among the different kinds of personal abilities) or to different capacities of accumulation and investment in 'personal capital', while Smith points rather to the importance of circumstances that determine the work role of each individual, largely connected to the pre-existing social placement, so that social stratification emerges as a mechanism endowed with self-reproducing capacity. Policy interventions in the field of education, such as those suggested by Smith in book V of *The wealth of nations* (cf. below, § 8), thus have not only the function of a remedy to the perverse effects that the division of labour has on human nature, but also the function of a democratic mechanism of fluidification of social stratification.

of nations was viewed with favour by the progressive elements of the time, including Condorcet (1743–94), who published a summary of it in 1791 (while after his death his widow, Madame de Grouchy, prepared a translation of *The theory of moral sentiments*). In England, Smith became a reference point in the years immediately following his death for radical thinkers such as Thomas Paine (1737–1809) and Mary Wollstonecraft (1759–97). Together with Hume, Smith was seen as a dangerous subversive by the conservative intellectuals of the time. The point is that all these thinkers, favourable or averse to Smith's views, saw no difference in his thought between liberalism in the political field and economic liberalism, between the defence of political freedom and the defence of free trade.[63]

The situation went through far-reaching change in the years immediately following. English public opinion showed a sharp negative reaction to the excesses of the French Revolution (the Terror), which initially implied a growing diffidence towards Smithian liberalism. Soon, however, thanks especially to Smith's first biographer, Dugald Stewart (1753–1828), reinterpretation of Smithian thought began with the aim of making it more acceptable, based precisely on the distinction between economic and political liberalism. With this fine-tuned reinterpretation, a politically progressive thesis bringing to the fore the need to fight concentrations of power of any kind was transformed into a conservative thesis – to leave maximum freedom of action to entrepreneurs – which in the stage of industrialisation went so far as to take on reactionary tones, serving to justify a total indifference of the new entrepreneurial class towards the heavy human costs of the new productive technologies and the widespread misery they brought: a far cry from the sensitivity repeatedly shown by the Scottish economist for human sufferings, and from his interest in the

---

[63] The history of these early progressive readings of Smith, and of the subsequent conservative reinterpretation, is illustrated in an interesting article by Emma Rothschild (1992). According to her reconstruction, 'Freedom consists, for Smith, in not being interfered with by others: in any aspect of life, and by any outside forces (churches, parish overseers, corporations, customs inspectors, national governments, masters, proprietors)' (ibid., p. 94). Cf. also Rothschild 2001, pp. 52–71.

In this respect we may also recall an aspect of Smith's liberalism – his diffidence towards entrepreneurs taking on a direct political role – that appears relevant in the present Italian political conjuncture, but that clearly has a more general validity:

The interest of the dealers, however, in any particular branch of trade or manufactures, is always in some respects different from, and even opposite to, that of the publick. [. . .] The proposal of any new law or regulation of commerce which comes from this order, ought always to be listened to with great precaution, and ought never to be adopted till after having been long and carefully examined, not only with the most scrupulous, but with the most suspicious attention. It comes from an order of men, whose interest is never exactly the same with that of the publick, who have generally an interest to deceive and even to oppress the publick, and who accordingly have, upon many occasions, both deceived and oppressed it. (Smith 1776, p. 267)

continuous improvement of living standards for the great mass of the population.[64]

For a better understanding of Smith's liberalism, we may refer to books IV and V of *The wealth of nations*. Most of book IV is devoted to critique of 'the commercial, or mercantile system', taken more as an array of interventions by the nation-state in the economy than as a theoretical system of political economy or, perhaps better, a set of ideas commonly collected under the label of 'mercantilism' (discussed above, § 2.6).[65] Restraint on imports, support for exports, treaties establishing commercial preferences, colonies – all are examined in detail and subjected to specific criticism. A chapter on the physiocratic ('agricultural') system concludes the book, but here too the account consists of criticism of specific instances of active state intervention, and a plea for 'the obvious and simple system of natural liberty' (Smith 1776, p. 687).

'Natural liberty' means political and economic freedom, but within a set of rules supported by public intervention and public institutions. As a general rule (ibid., pp. 687–8):

According to the system of natural liberty, the sovereign has only three duties to attend to [. . .]: first, the duty of protecting the society from the violence and invasion of other independent societies; secondly, [. . .] an exact administration of justice; and, thirdly, the duty of erecting and maintaining certain publick works and certain publick institutions, which it can never be for the interest of any individual, or small number of individuals, to erect and maintain; because the profit could never repay the expence to any individual or small number of individuals, though it may frequently do much more than repay it to a great society.

---

[64] The conservative view of economic liberalism became decidedly dominant as from the beginning of the nineteenth century, and has since continued to take reference from Smith notwithstanding the interpretative twist illustrated above. In the last few decades, for instance, the 'Chicago school' has directly placed itself in a line from Smith, notwithstanding the caution originally expressed by the most cultured of its exponents (cf. Viner, 1927). In Italy we may recall the ultra-liberism of Francesco Ferrara (1810–1900), editor of the first series of the important *Biblioteca dell'economista* (Cugini Pomba Editori-librai, Torino), the second volume of which (1851) offers readers an Italian translation of *The wealth of nations* (on Ferrara cf. Faucci 1995).

[65] Book IV also contains a 'digression concerning banks of deposit' (Smith 1776, pp. 479–88), which, together with chapter 4 of book II (ibid., pp. 350–9), constitutes the main references for Smith's treatment of monetary and financial issues. In very broad outline, Smith considers the interest rate to be determined by supply of and demand for loans, where demand is influenced by the prospective return, namely the prevailing rate of profits; usury laws, setting a maximum limit to the interest rate, are favourable to accumulation. Banks may be induced by 'prodigals and projectors' (ibid., p. 357) to an over-issue of notes; the rule which banks should follow is the so-called 'real bills doctrine', which would dominate the field for more than a century, and which held that the issue of bank notes should be limited to the discount of sound commercial bills. Smith's ideas on money and banking have been the subject of a lively interpretative debate; cf. for instance Laidler 1981; Gherity 1994 reconstructs the development of Smith's thought on the issue.

Book V of *The wealth of nations* goes on to deal with 'the revenue of the sovereign or commonwealth': first the expenses for defence and justice, but also public works – mainly transport infrastructures: navigable canals, roads, bridges – and education, with a long section devoted to the latter, in striking contrast to the half-page devoted to 'the Expence of supporting the Dignity of the Sovereign',[66] and then public revenue. Smith prefers public expenditure to be financed by taxes rather than by public debt; and as for taxes, four principles which would become canonical are clearly set out and illustrated: proportional taxation, certainty, least inconvenience for the taxpayer, and low cost of collection.[67]

In sum, Smith is no dogmatic liberal, but a pragmatic one: strongly critical not only of feudal institutions and of policies characteristic of the absolutist state, but also of capitalistic concentrations of economic power, and diffident towards the inclination of 'the dealers' to establish monopoly.

Another interpretative issue[68] stems from comparison between the first and fifth book of *The wealth of nations*, concerning the apparently contradictory position taken by Smith towards the division of labour. In the first book, the division of labour is extolled as the foundation for increases in productivity, hence for the well-being of the population and for civic progress itself; in the fifth book, in an often quoted passage referred to as the precursor of the Marxian theory of alienation, Smith stresses the negative characteristics of fragmented labour, that can make a brute of man:

---

[66] Specific discussion is devoted to the 'regulated companies for foreign commerce' and to the joint stock companies. Smith (1776, p. 731) recognises that 'some particular branches of commerce, which are carried on with barbarous and uncivilized nations, require extraordinary protection'; but his detailed discussion of the actual affairs of the South Sea Company, the East India Company and similar institutions then develops into a real indictment (ibid., pp. 731–56).

[67] 'I. The subjects of every state ought to contribute towards the support of the government, as nearly as possible, in proportion to their respective abilities; that is, in proportion to the revenue which they respectively enjoy under the protection of the state. [. . .] II. The tax which each individual is bound to pay ought to be certain, and not arbitrary. The time of payment, the manner of payment, the quantity to be paid, ought all to be clear and plain to the contributor, and to every other person. [. . .] III. Every tax ought to be levied at the time, or in the manner, in which it is most likely to be convenient for the contributor to pay it. [. . .] IV. Every tax ought to be so contrived as both to take out and to keep out of the pockets of the people as little as possible, over and above what it brings into the publick treasury of the state' (Smith 1776, pp. 825–6).

[68] On the history of this debate, which dates back to Marx, cf. Rosenberg 1965. The negative implications of the division of labour were widely recognised in the environment of the Scottish Enlightenment, for instance by Ferguson (1767, part 2, chapter 4: 'Of the subordination consequent to the separation of arts and professions').

In the progress of the division of labour, the employment of the far greater part of those who live by labour, that is, of the great body of the people, comes to be confined to a few very simple operations; frequently to one or two. But the understandings of the greater part of men are necessarily formed by their ordinary employments. The man whose whole life is spent in performing a few simple operations, of which the effects too are, perhaps, always the same, or very nearly the same, has no occasion to exert his understanding, or to exercise his invention in finding out expedients for removing difficulties which never occur. He naturally loses, therefore, the habit of such exertion, and generally becomes as stupid and ignorant as it is possible for a human creature to become. The torpor of his mind renders him, not only incapable of relishing or bearing a part in any rational conversation, but of conceiving any generous, noble, or tender sentiment, and consequently of forming any just judgement concerning many even of the ordinary duties of private life. Of the great and extensive interests of his country, he is altogether incapable of judging.[69]

However, the contradiction between the first and the fifth book of *The wealth of nations*, between an optimistic and a pessimistic view of the division of labour, is only apparent. We should not wonder if an author like Smith, so careful in capturing the different sides of any issue, attributed different effects, some of them positive and some negative, to a single cause. It is clear from the context that Smith considered as dominant the positive effects of the division of labour. Indeed, confronted with the concomitant negative effects, he did not hesitate an instant on which road to take, and far from raising doubts on the opportunity of pursuing the continuous deepening of the division of labour, he propounded recourse to elementary education as a counterweight.

There is in this respect an aspect that should be stressed, since it constitutes perhaps the main point of difference between Smith's social philosophy and that of Marx, and on which we may maintain that it was the Scottish philosopher who was right. Both Smith and Marx, as we saw above, are fully conscious of the negative implications of the division of labour, and of the need for work (or 'compulsory labour') that accompanies them. Marx, however, held that the hard need of compulsory labour can be overcome in a communist society, in which it will be possible to reach the full development of the productive forces, that 'makes it possible for me to do one thing today and another tomorrow, to hunt in the morning, to fish in the afternoon, rear cattle in the evening, criticise after dinner, just as I have a mind, without ever becoming hunter, fisherman,

---

[69] Smith 1776, pp. 781–2. Before Smith, we can trace the notion of alienation in the writings of the Swiss Jean-Jacques Rousseau (1712–78), whom Smith was acquainted with through Hume. (Hume and Rousseau, initially good friends, subsequently had a harsh clash: cf. Ross 1995, pp. 210–12). Differently from Smith, Rousseau is a radical critic of the market economy: cf. Colletti 1969b, pp. 195–292.

sheperd, or critic'.[70] The possibility of reaching full freedom from compulsory labour morally justifies, and renders politically acceptable, the costs in blood and tears of the proletarian revolution and of the subsequent dictatorship of the proletariat, as necessary stages (together with capitalistic accumulation) for development of productive forces which constitutes the indispensable premise for reaching the final objective.

Smith, on the contrary, considered overcoming the division of labour clearly impossible. Increases in productivity and growing economic welfare made possible by the deepening of the division of labour are the presupposition for progress in human societies. This is, however, conceived as a continuous process, without there being in sight a 'way out' of the set-up of market economies and an overcoming of their limits and defects, such as compulsory labour and the inequalities of social conditions. This Smithian view may perhaps be likened to the reformist theses present in the contemporary political debate, which oppose both the conservative streams of thought that consider as useless any intervention aimed at countering the situations of social malaise and, on the opposite side, the revolutionary hopes for social regeneration.[71]

A substantive faith in man, though recognised as an essentially imperfect being, and in the possibility of progress in human societies, constituted the common element for Smith and for eighteenth-century Enlightenment culture. But it also and mainly constitutes the positive message that renders the work of the Scottish thinker a central point of reference for pondering over man and society.

[70] Marx and Engels 1845–6, p. 265.
[71] Cf. Roncaglia 1989 on Smith and 1995c on Marx.

6   Economic science at the time of the French Revolution

1.   The perfectibility of human societies, between utopias and reforms

The English 'Glorious Revolution' of 1688 took place with practically no bloodshed and, albeit marking a radical change in the political order, producing no drastic break in continuity for the English institutions. On the contrary, the French Revolution of 1789, and especially the radicalisation it subsequently went through, once again, and in dramatic terms, faces social scientists with two crucial issues. First, can a change in institutions lead to a better society, also – and perhaps above all – as far as material life is concerned, and hence in the functioning of the economy? Second, if the change has a cost in terms of violence and bloodshed, as was apparent in the case of the French Revolution, do the advantages that may be reaped justify these costs?

In the eighteenth century the tradition of the Enlightenment gave a more or less positive answer to the first question: intervention by benevolent sovereigns, guided by reason, may favour social progress, which in any case remains the direction human history tends to move in. The second question, on the other hand, hardly represented a real issue for exponents of the Enlightenment, who by and large accepted as a matter of fact the absolute power of national monarchies and limited their proposals for intervention to the fields of economic issues and social policies.

However, at the time of the French Revolution, other currents of thought had long been present that gave different answers to the basic issues concerning the organisation of society. On the one hand, we have the conservatives, who held that endeavours to foster social progress are futile, and on the other, the revolutionaries, who held that radical change is a necessity, for political institutions also.

The latter often drew strength from Utopian models of ideal societies, frequently characterised by forms of collectivism extending not only to control over means of production, but also and above all to the customs of everyday life. As a literary genre Utopian writings had been circulating

155

since the late sixteenth century;[1] in eighteenth-century France they seem to have chimed in with the rationalistic spirit of the Enlightenment, dedicated to the cult of 'clear and distinct' ideas (to recall an expression used by Descartes). It was a cultural climate that encouraged intellectuals to believe that human intelligence is capable of designing institutional systems surpassing those inherited from history; furthermore, some particularly bold spirits went so far as to assert that when such 'systems' were deemed superior to the old ones, there was the right and indeed the duty to impose their implementation in the face of resistance by diehard rulers or ignorant masses.

The tradition of the Scottish sociological Enlightenment was also favourable to institutional changes: for instance, we may recall Smith's fight against the remnants of feudalism. However, this was not a matter of a priori designs for ideal institutions, but rather indications on possible improvements to the existing institutions. Trust in reason was, moreover, tempered by two elements: the liberal idea, maintained by Smith in *The theory of moral sentiments*, that each is the best judge of his own interests; and a non-idyllic, although basically optimistic, vision of human nature, open to a certain amount of scepticism as to the true abilities and motivations of rulers. In turn, this implied diffidence, if not hostility, towards projects for revolutionary change inspired by theoretical models of ideal societies. This position was substantially shared by the Neapolitan Enlightenment, from Galiani and Genovesi to Palmieri and Filangieri, as also by the Tuscan intellectuals, mainly concerned with agrarian reforms, and a Milanese circle including Verri and Beccaria. France, too, counted a number of active protagonists in political life – Turgot being the most illustrious example – who might be included in the 'reformist' current.[2]

It is in fact in pre-Revolutionary France that we have an interesting example of confrontation between reformist and conservative theses in the clash that saw Necker versus Turgot, and subsequently Condorcet versus Necker.[3]

Turgot, the minister of finance from 1774 to 1776, not only offered theoretical support (cf. above, § 4.7) but also sought to give practical effect to reforms aiming at abolishing feudal constraints (restrictions on free trade in agricultural produce, corporatist regulations on labour and productive processes) and improving social policies for the poor.

[1] Cf. above, ch. 2, note 11.
[2] Even more than the terms 'conservative' and 'revolutionary' used above, the term 'reformist' has in this context a somewhat generic meaning, which only in part corresponds to that which the term has assumed in today's political debate.
[3] For reconstruction of this debate, cf. Rothschild 1995, 2001.

Jacques Necker (1732–1804), a banker, political opponent of Turgot and the last minister of finance before the Revolution, by contrast, described 'the misery of the poor as a fact of nature' and population growth 'as the consequence of "the impetuous attraction that nature has placed between the sexes". It will eventually come to an end, "with sufferings and mortality" when population exceeds subsistence.'[4]

Marie Jean Antoine Nicholas Caritat, Marquis de Condorcet (1743–94) was a philosopher belonging to the circle of the Encyclopaedists, and a mathematician renowned for his studies on probability theory, which influenced the modern theory of social choices.[5] Reacting to theses such as Necker's, he maintained that the problems of contemporary society stemmed not from the forces of nature, but from human institutions: therefore, measures of institutional reform might influence economic and civil progress. Like Smith, Condorcet supported public interventions in favour of universal education; he also advocated schemes for collective insurance against accidents and to guarantee an income to the old. More generally, 'The characteristic presumption of Smith's early friends and followers in France was, rather, that political liberty and social integration of the poor were causes (as well as consequences) of economic development.'[6]

Condorcet was among those progressive intellectuals who played leading roles in the early phases of the French Revolution only to fall prey to the Terror, whose exponents saw moderate reformism as an enemy possibly even worse than conservatism itself. Like the fate of Condorcet, the reformist currents in France were eventually physically suppressed by the followers of Utopian extremism.

As a reaction to the radicalisation of the French Revolution, there was also radicalisation in the opposition to change. We have already seen an example of this (§ 5.8) in the hostility that gathered against Smith's social

---

[4] The quotations are drawn from Rothschild 1995, p. 721. Evidently we have here one of the many precursors of the Malthusian principle of population, which will be discussed in the next section.

[5] Cf. Moulin and Young 1987, McLean and Hewitt 1994.

[6] Rothschild 1995, p. 712. The 'Smithian' thesis was that uncertainty constitutes, in general, a hindrance for economic initiative. Institutions adequate for economic development should create security with respect both to personal rights and to property rights; 'security was a psychological as well as a juridical condition, and one that was founded on social as well as legal reforms' (ibid., p. 713). Security must be widespread: 'A civilised society is one in which even the poor have the right to secure lives' (ibid.). For this reason Smith could maintain that social policies in favour of the lower classes were not only 'just' but also important to favouring economic development: 'No society can surely be flourishing and happy, of which the far greater part of the members are poor and miserable' (Smith 1776, p. 96; quoted in Rothschild 1995, p. 714). Let us recall (cf. above, § 5.8) that Condorcet was the author of a pamphlet that included a summary of *The wealth of nations*. On Condorcet's attitude towards reforms, cf. Rothschild 2001.

philosophy around the end of the eighteenth century, after the favourable reception accorded *The wealth of nations* on publication. We shall see another famous example in the next section with Malthus's pamphlet on population, which took up and developed Necker's views. What we wish to stress here is that the reformist currents, squeezed between the Utopian extremism of revolutionary Terror and the conservative reaction, not only lost ground but, more importantly, survived only with a significant change in its very nature: what originally had been reformism in the broad sense of the term – social and economic at the same time – became restricted to the purely economic aspects. 'Reformist' thought in the comprehensive sense would again play a principal role in the political and cultural debate only half a century later, with the cooperative movement in England and with John Stuart Mill; but once again it was soon to find itself hemmed in, at least in continental Europe, between revolutionary radicalism on the one hand (there was not only Marx, but also the Paris Commune) and conservative reaction on the other.

2.   Malthus and the population principle

In the years immediately following the French Revolution, as we have seen, the sympathetic response that various intellectuals in Great Britain had shown to the storming of the Bastille gave way to conservative reaction against the Terror. Among the few who retained a position favourable to the Revolution, together with Thomas Paine,[7] we find William Godwin (1756–1836). Author of a widely read *Enquiry concerning political justice* (1793) and partner of the radical feminist Mary Wollstonecraft, Godwin is commonly known as a votary of anarchism; he advocated small-scale production and social decentralisation, together with a drastic redistribution of income in favour of the neediest strata of the population. Like Condorcet, Godwin was a strenuous upholder of the perfectibility of human beings: an end to be pursued by abolishing or modifying those institutions, both political and social, that obstructed economic development and the development of human reason alike. His influence on the 'Ricardian socialists', the cooperative movement and the Owenites was important; among those who threw themselves behind him immediately

---

[7] An Englishman, Thomas Paine (1737–1809) moved to America in 1774, and there published an essay, *Common sense* (1776), which constituted one of the immediate intellectual foundations of the Declaration of Independence of the United States; emigrating to France, in 1792–5 he became a member of the Convention, opposing Robespierre. In the *Rights of man* (1791) he supported, among other things, a progressive fiscal system to finance subsidies to poor families and old-age pensions, and extension of the right to vote to all adult males.

after the publication of his book we also find Daniel Malthus (1730–1800).

Daniel's son, Thomas Robert Malthus (1766–1834) took an entirely different view.[8] A student at Cambridge's Jesus College between 1784 and 1788, on graduating he was appointed a minister of the Anglican Church. He married in 1804 and had three children. In 1805 he became professor of history and political economy at the East India College; his teaching was based on Smith's *Wealth of nations*.

We shall be seeing quite a lot more of Malthus in the following pages, in particular in connection with his discussions with Ricardo. His most famous work is the *Essay on population* (1798), which constituted the conservative answer to the views held by the English radicals and heralded by Godwin. The first edition had the air of a lively, provocative political pamphlet; in subsequent editions[9] it gradually swelled into a heavy, erudite volume, stuffed with empirical references and qualifications to the central thesis, but somewhat indigestible. The *Essay* had a wide readership and a strong influence, stimulating lively, prolonged debate.[10]

Malthus's thesis is often summed up in a famous formula: agricultural production tends to grow in arithmetical proportion, while population tends to grow in geometrical proportion and, more precisely, to double every twenty-five years.[11] Actually, the point – illustrated by Malthus in various numerical examples – was not essential to his argument. The 'principle of population' consisted, quite simply, in the idea that population growth is necessarily limited by the availability of means of subsistence. As soon as these become available in excess of the strictly necessary, the population tends to grow more rapidly than agricultural production. The consequent disequilibrium has negative effects on the

---

[8] The *Essay on population* was born of a discussion between father and son. Daniel Malthus was the friend Thomas referred to when writing in the preface to the first edition: 'The following Essay owes its origin to a conversation with a friend, on the subject of Mr. Godwin's Essay', and it is to him that he referred when criticising those who believe in 'the perfectibility of man and of society' (quoted by Meek 1953, p. 4). The relationship between a conservative father and a revolutionary son, so frequent in our times, was inverted here, a conservative son opposing a progressive father. For a biography of Malthus, cf. James 1979; for an introduction to his thought, cf. Winch 1987.

[9] 1803, 1806, 1807, 1817, 1826; cf. the 1989 critical edition, edited by Patricia James.

[10] Some of the immediate reactions of the time are reprinted in Pyle 1994.

[11] Schumpeter (1954, p. 579) dryly – and correctly – points out that 'there is of course no point whatever in trying to formulate independent "laws" for the behaviour of two interdependent quantities' (a remark that also applies to the simplest formulation of the 'law of supply and demand', as Sraffa showed in his 1925 article with respect to Marshallian partial equilibrium analysis: cf. below, § 16.3). Let us also remark here that Malthus's thesis concerns the dynamics of agricultural production: as such, it cannot be deduced from the assumption of different land fertilities on which the theory of differential rent is based (cf. below, § 7.2).

living conditions of the poorest classes, until the population comes back in equilibrium with the availability of food.[12]

More precisely, population growth outrunning the availability of resources generates increase in food prices, and hence reduction in real wages. As the process unfolds, the reduced per capita availability of food spells deterioration in the living standards of the workers, thus forcing down the growth rate of the population as the mortality rate rises or the birth rate falls, both effects being determined by ever more widespread poverty and hardship.

Alongside this automatic mechanism of an economic nature, Malthus pointed out two other possible routes based on active intervention on the part of men and women to preserve equilibrium between population and means of subsistence: the path of 'virtue', namely chastity in celibacy and continence within marriage, or the path of 'vice', namely contraception. The latter element was to receive particular attention from the so-called neo-Malthusians (like Francis Place, 1771–1854; his *Illustrations and proofs of the principle of population* is dated 1822), but had already been addressed approvingly before Malthus by authors such as Bentham and Condorcet.[13]

Malthus's thesis was not new.[14] We have already seen how it emerged in France, shortly before the Revolution, in the debate between Turgot and Necker, but as early as the sixteenth century an Italian, Giovanni Botero (1544–1617), contrasting *virtus generativa* with *virtus nutritiva*, had stressed the tension between the potential of population growth and the difficulties in increasing production of means of subsistence to keep up with it (*Delle cause della grandezza delle città* (About the causes of the greatness of cities, 1588), was also translated into English in 1606). Just a few years before Malthus's pamphlet came out, another Italian, Gianmaria Ortes (1713–90), had published *Riflessioni sulla popolazione*

---

[12] The Malthusian thesis of a conflict between population growth and availability of food resources was explicitly recognised by Charles Darwin (1809–82) as a source of inspiration for his revolutionary theory of evolution based on natural selection, set out in Darwin 1859: cf. Darwin 1958, p. 144.

[13] On Condorcet, cf. below, note 17. Bentham referred to contraception as a tool useful in reducing the fiscal burden deriving from the poor laws in the manuscript of the *Manual of political economy* (Bentham 1793–5, pp. 272–3). Following Bentham, James Mill made cautious reference to the issue under the heading of 'Colonies' (1818) in the *Encyclopaedia Britannica*. His son, John Stuart, when still seventeen years old, was caught by the police in 1823 distributing contraception propaganda prepared by Place. (Some decades later, similar work in favour of contraception was undertaken by the Swedish economist Knut Wicksell: cf. below, § 11.5.)

[14] We can go back as early as the bishop of Carthage, Cyprian (c.200–58), who contradicted the optimism intrinsic in the Bible saying 'grow and multiply', considering overpopulation a source of poverty even in his times, and proposing chastity as a remedy: cf. above, ch. 2, note 29.

in 1790 (Thoughts on population), which was included a few years later in the series of writings of Italian economists edited by Custodi. Among other things, Ortes stressed the potentiality of population to grow in geometrical progression.[15]

Neither Botero nor Ortes nor Cantillon was quoted by Malthus, although he did make reference to Necker and various other writers, including Robert Wallace (1697–1771). In the case of Wallace, however, Malthus limited reference to a secondary work, with not so much as a mention of the fundamental *Various prospects of mankind, nature and providence* (1761), to which Godwin explicitly referred, criticising its pessimism, and from which, some commentators argue, Malthus may have derived his main theses.[16]

Be that as it may, Malthus's pamphlet played a specific role, and correspondingly had a stronger impact than the previous literature on the subject, focusing attention not simply on the relation between growth of population and growth of the means of subsistence, but also and above all on the implications this relationship held for the strategic choice on whether or not to pursue objectives of change – even radical change – in the political institutions.[17]

A number of economists of the time, including David Ricardo, referred to the Malthusian principle of population in support of a theory of wages frequently brought up in debate on policy, the so-called iron law of wages, according to which the wage rate tends to oscillate around the subsistence level. The latter was not interpreted in merely biological terms, but in the social sense, as that level which allowed workers not only to

[15] At the beginning of the eighteenth century Cantillon, too, (1755, p. 81) had stressed the potentialities of population growth, which rapidly adapts to the available means of subsistence: 'If the Proprietors of Land help to support the Families, a single generation suffices to push the increase of Population as far as the produce of the Land will supply means of subsistence.' As we have already seen (§ 4.5), Cantillon's work as a source for Mirabeau (1756). Schumpeter (1954, p. 252) went so far as to state, perhaps with some exaggeration, that 'the cradle of the genuinely anti-populationist doctrine was France'. On some English precursors of Malthus and on the German author Sussmilch, cf. Bonar 1931.

[16] Cf. the critical edition, edited by P. James, of Malthus (1798, vol. 2, pp. 351–2). Ibid. (pp. 253–357) there is an 'Alphabetical list of authorities quoted or cited by Malthus in his *Essay on the principle of population*'. Most of the references were, however, added in the editions following the first, and concerned authors contemporary with Malthus who took part in the debate following the original publication of Malthus's pamphlet.

[17] In the *Esquisse d'un tableau historique des progrès de l'esprit humain*, published posthumously in 1794, Condorcet had advanced similar arguments on the dangers of excessively rapid population growth; however, his conclusions on the prospects for human societies were optimistic, in sharp contrast to Malthus's. Condorcet stressed the existence of a simple remedy, contraception, which could reconcile improvements in the standard of life with moderate population growth. The so-called neo-Malthusians, including Place and – later – Wicksell, rediscovered Condorcet's ideas, predating Malthus's work.

survive – within the economic system considered, hence excluding emigration – but also to form a family and raise children.[18]

To sum up the argument briefly, let us assume that the wage of the great mass of workers is above mere subsistence level. The population begins to grow, and agricultural production is unable to keep up; food prices consequently rise, and the real wage declines, returning to the subsistence minimum. If, on the contrary, we start from a wage rate lower than the subsistence level, then the population decreases (due to a rising mortality rate and falling birth rate, but also due to increasing emigration); hence the demand for wage goods diminishes, their prices fall, and the real wage increases.

The thesis that the wage tends to remain at subsistence level had already been propounded before Malthus with arguments other than the population principle. For instance, as we saw above (§ 5.4), Smith attributed a downward pressure on the wage rate to the different bargaining power of workers and capitalists.

As we have already seen, Smith's thesis appears more solid than the one based on the population principle. Suffice it to recall that, if the increase in population due to a wage rate above subsistence level is associated with an increase in the birth rate or decrease in the rate of infant mortality, then the downward pressure on wages can only be felt on the labour market after a lag of fourteen–sixteen years, or in other words after the time has elapsed necessary for a newborn baby to join the labour force.[19] Moreover, the 'iron law of wages', based on the Malthusian population principle, presupposed the absence of technological progress in the primary sector; in actual fact, as historical experience has shown, a decreasing share of population has succeeded in producing food more than sufficient for a continuously growing population.[20]

The aim of Malthus's *Essay*, however, was not to provide a theory of income distribution but rather to assert the uselessness of any attempt at improving the situation of the great mass of the workers.[21] Even if

---

[18] On the definitions of subsistence wage in Malthus, Ricardo and Torrens, cf. Roncaglia 1974.

[19] This point was brought up by Malthus himself in the first edition of his *Principles* (Malthus 1820, p. 242 of the first edition, in Ricardo 1951–5, vol. 2, p. 225).

[20] In the second half of the nineteenth century, in particular, the second agricultural revolution, based on the use of chemical fertilisers, spelt a great leap forward in productivity per worker and per acre of cultivated land. The famines of the nineteenth century were essentially due to problems of misallocation of resources, certainly not to absolute scarcity of food at the world level.

[21] Malthus's thesis, in the first edition of his *Essay*, was that the population principle is 'conclusive against the perfectibility of the mass of mankind' (quoted by Meek 1953, p. 4). We should, however, avoid painting Malthus as an ultra-reactionary (as Marx and Engels did): indeed, reproposing some ideas advanced by Smith, in his *Essay* Malthus advocated free elementary education for all, and free medical care for the poor.

we assume these attempts to be successful in the short run, Malthus said, improvement in the standard of living is nevertheless immediately followed by a faster rate of population increase, which brings wages and the standard of living of the great mass of the workers back to simple subsistence level. Hopes for improvement should not rely on institutional changes or social policies in favour of the poor: such hopes can only rely on 'preventive checks' on population growth which, Malthus went on to argue, the workers will only exercise with the goad of the spectre of poverty hanging over them. Therefore, measures aiming to eliminate poverty are counter-productive. Moreover, the fear of poverty also acts as a stimulus to industriousness.

On this latter point Malthus's thesis (and Necker's, and indeed other conservative economists') was in total contrast with the ideas of Smith, Condorcet, Godwin and the whole of the reformist tradition. As Rothschild notes, according to the latter tradition it is the hope to improve one's conditions, and not the fear of poverty, that constitutes 'a universal inducement to industry'; Smith, in particular, declared in *The wealth of nations* that 'fear is in almost all cases a wretched instrument of government'; Condorcet maintained that 'fear is the origin of almost all human stupidities, and above all of political stupidities'.[22]

Godwin too, in his essay *On population* (1820) containing his answer to Malthus, maintained that 'preventive checks' on population increase are prompted by improvement in the standards of living of the workers, not the spectre of poverty.[23] Similarly, the cooperativist William Thompson (cf. below, § 8.6) upheld that operation of the law of population could be radically modified with the economic independence of women and a higher standard of living, such as could be made possible – he held – with change in the organisation of the social institutions.

However, it was Malthus's theses that eventually dominated the field of classical political economy. It was these that, with their pessimism regarding the prospects of progress for the working classes and society as a whole, led the public opinion of the time to identify political economy as the 'dismal science':[24] a bleak construction of abstract theories that led to defeatism cloaked in scientific rigour since, confronted with the human

[22] Cf. Rothschild 1995, p. 731, our source for the quotations of Smith (1776, p. 798) and Condorcet.

[23] Also Malthus's successor to the chair of the East India College, Richard Jones (1790–1855), a critic of the deductive method who was considered a precursor of the 'historical school' (cf. below, § 11.2), maintained that the facts did not accord with Malthus's thesis. Given the scarcity of statistics at the time and their poor qualitative level, however, treatment of the issue had to be based mainly on general impressions.

[24] The expression, which immediately became famous, was due to Thomas Carlyle (1795–1881), in an essay of 1849, *The nigger question* (in Carlyle 1888–9, vol. 7, p. 84: quoted by Milgate 1987, p. 371). Carlyle's blow, however, originated in a different context, the pro-slavery movement of mid-nineteenth century led by Carlyle himself together with

will to improve conditions, it asserts the impossibility of lasting progress. In a sense, political economy would represent the pessimism of science as opposed to the optimism of the will; however, it was a pessimism that, when confronted with the facts, proved substantially misleading, since it underrated the potentialities opening up with technological progress. The romantic climate that began to take over in the first half of the nineteenth century was thus able to stimulate a negative reaction against the cold abstract logic and pessimism of economic science, in so far as it was perceived to be based on unreal assumptions. Thus the whole of classical political economy, and in particular Ricardo and his followers, met with growing diffidence on the part of public opinion despite the fact that the Malthusian population principle was not an essential component of their analytic structure. Actually, this characterisation of political economy as the 'dismal science' contributed to widening the gulf between the 'scientific laws' of the economists, on the one hand, and the study of social issues on the other, and hence in paving the way to the marginalist revolution.[25]

3.   'Say's law'

A few years after Malthus's *Essay on population* came the proclamation of what has come to be known as 'Say's law', enunciated by the French economist Jean-Baptiste Say (1767–1832). In its simplest formulation, it said that 'supply creates its own demand'.

There have been different interpretations of this 'law'. Originally it was propounded in criticism of certain aspects of the physiocratic doctrine utilised by various economists of the time who were opposed to the central role Smith attributed to savings and accumulation as the foundation for growth of the 'wealth of nations' and who tried to refute his criticism with respect to 'unproductive' consumption.

As we have already seen (§§ 4.5 and 4.6), Cantillon and the physiocrats had the landlords and nobility playing an active role in setting the circulation process into motion: at the end of the productive process they are in possession of the money and utilise it to acquire commodities from

John Ruskin (1819–1900), the passionate critic of industrial capitalism widely read also among socialists in the decades around 1900.

[25] The role of political economy in bringing to light the limits of what can be achieved with public intervention has been an object of debate for centuries, although the approaches have changed in the course of time, a good example being the heated controversy of the last few decades over the growth of the public debt and on the 'free lunches' that appeared to be suggested by Keynesian policies aiming at increasing the level of income (cf. below, chapter 14). Perhaps stronger analogies with the debate on the principle of population are offered by the ongoing debate on the welfare state.

the 'sterile' and the 'productive' classes. However, if the landlords and nobility decide not to spend part of their income, and if for any reason their demand fails, the possibility arises of a situation of 'general over-production' or want of market outlets. Given the active role that it plays in the circulation process, the spending of the landlords and nobility regulates the rate of exchanges and production.[26]

It was in answer to views such as these that Say set out his 'law' in his *Traité d'économie politique* of 1803, a successful publication also utilised as a university textbook in the United States and in Britain (as well as France, where Say became the first professor of political economy in 1815), and which contained among other things a theory of value based on utility, and on the balance between supply and demand.[27] 'Say's law' was then taken up, with subtle but often significant differences, by many economists of the classical school: first of all by James Mill[28] in *Commerce defended* in 1807, to be followed in 1808 by Torrens in *The economists refuted*,[29] and then by McCulloch, Ricardo and John Stuart Mill. In fact, 'Say's law', in a rather strong version (as an *ex ante* identity between aggregate demand and supply), became a distinctive characteristic commonly attributed to the 'Ricardian school'.

---

[26] Notwithstanding this general orientation of their reasoning, we can find in the physiocrats some passages which appear to foreshadow Say's motto. A couple of such passages are quoted by Blaug (1962, p. 29); however, they seem to point in the direction of a system of national accounting identities rather than in the direction of equilibrium relations brought about by market forces.

[27] Another thesis for which this book is known is the identification of productive labour with labour generating utility. In opposition to Smith, this meant that labour that provides services is also productive, and not only labour that produces commodities. Obviously this was connected to Say's theory of value, according to which the value of a commodity expresses its utility (while its price expresses its value, thus defined). Above all, however, Say's book is important for the notion of economic equilibrium it propounded; it is for this reason that, as Schumpeter said (1954, p. 492), 'Say's work is the most important of the links in the chain that leads from Cantillon and Turgot to Walras'; we will return to this aspect later (§§ 10.2 and 12.1). Once again according to Schumpeter (ibid., p. 555, italics in the original), Say 'was the first to assign to the entrepreneur – per se and as distinct from the capitalist – a definite position in the schema of the economic process [. . .] to *combine* the factors of production into a producing organism'; furthermore (ibid., p. 560), he 'established the triad schema and the practice of dealing, both in the theory of production and in the theory of distribution, with the "services" of the three factors [labour, capital and land (or better, 'natural agents')] on the same footing'.

[28] James Mill (1773–1836), father of John Stuart, a scholar and a friend of Bentham's, among the leading exponents of philosophical radicalism (cf. below, § 10.3); he was also a friend to Ricardo and offered him support in the writing of the *Principles*. For some years he was a top executive of the East India Company; he also wrote a manual of political economy showing a Ricardian bent (*Elements of political economy*, 1821).

[29] Significantly, the physiocrats were known as *les économistes*. In particular, Mill and Torrens reacted to the essay by William Spence (1783–1860), *Britain independent of commerce* (1807). On Torrens cf. below, § 8.2.

In its original version, however, 'Say's law' was less clear-cut, the main aim being to reassert two theses already present in Smith. The first one was the possibility of technological progress giving rise to long period development of production, with marked improvement in the living standards of the population accompanied by a parallel growth in demand; the second was the idea that growth is favoured by savings (and by investments, which savings automatically turn into) more than by unproductive consumption.[30] In upholding these two theses, which were the true objects of the current debate, Say (and subsequently James Mill) also developed other arguments: in particular the thesis that money per se is not in demand, but only as a means to acquire goods, with the consequence that aggregate supply would necessarily equal aggregate demand, and that no general over-production crisis would be possible. The latter thesis was later christened 'Say's identity' by historians of economic thought, in order to distinguish it from a less strong thesis, the so-called 'Say's equality', according to which short period disequilibria between overall supply and demand for goods may exist, but 'there exist reliable equilibrating forces that must soon bring the two together'.[31]

---

[30] Cf., for instance, the often quoted passage: 'What is annually saved is as regularly consumed [in acquiring additional capital] as what is annually spent, and nearly in the same time too' (Smith 1776, pp. 337–8).

[31] Baumol 1977, p. 146. Baumol distinguishes different theses ('Say's First [Second, Third . . .] Proposition'), for each of which it is possible to find some reference in Say's writings:

1. 'A community's purchasing *power* (effective demand) is limited by and is equal to its output, because production provides *the means* by which output can be purchased' (ibid., p. 147; italics in the original).
2. 'Expenditure increases when output rises' (ibid., p. 147).
3. 'A given investment expenditure is a far more effective stimulant to the wealth of an economy than an equal amount of consumption' (ibid., p. 149).
4. 'Over the centuries the community will always find demands for increased outputs, even for increases that are enormous' (ibid., p. 152).
5. 'Production of goods rather than the supply of money is the primary determinant of demand. Money facilitates commerce but does not determine the amounts of goods that are exchanged' (ibid., p. 154).
6. 'Any glut in the market for a good must involve relative underproduction of some other commodity, or commodities, and the mobility of capital out of the area with excess supply and into industries whose products are insufficient to meet demand will tend rapidly to eliminate the overproduction' (ibid., p. 154).

It may be seen that, while the less restrictive versions of 'Say's law' had already been taken up by Smith in support of the importance attributed to savings for accumulation and development, the stronger versions of the law were utilised in the Ricardian school to criticise the Smithian theory of the 'competition of capitals', according to which accumulation of capital would imply a gradual reduction of the profit rate, as a consequence of the progressive exhaustion of the most profitable employments of capital and the need to shift to ever less profitable uses. In the strong version 'Say's law' actually maintains that production by itself creates *ex novo* market outlets which guarantee the new employments of capital the same returns as the preceding uses. On 'Say's law' cf. also Sowell 1972.

It was only against the most radical versions of 'Say's law' that authors such as Sismondi, Malthus and Lauerdale levelled their criticism. What these authors actually argued was not the existence of long period tendencies to stagnation, but more simply the possibility of general overproduction crises. Much the same line was, moreover, followed by various other 'Ricardian' economists, like Robert Torrens and, notably, John Stuart Mill, in the second of the *Essays on some unsettled questions of political economy* (1844). This line was later adopted by Marx and especially by Keynes, who presented his theories as directly opposed to 'Say's law', interpreting it in the 'strong' sense that it had acquired, much more than in the writings of classical economists, within the marginalist tradition.

4.   Under-consumption theories: Lauerdale, Malthus, Sismondi

In the first two decades of the nineteenth century, after Malthus had published the first edition of his *Essay on population* and Say the first edition of his *Traité*, and before the Ricardian orthodoxy based, among other things, on 'Say's law' had asserted itself, a number of authors entered the arena upholding the possibility of general over-production crises.

Declaredly hostile to the Smithian assumption of an automatic transformation of savings into accumulation and to Smith's views on the passive role of demand was a Scottish nobleman, James Maitland, eighth Earl of Lauerdale (1759–1839). In his *Inquiry into the nature and origins of public wealth* (1804; 2nd edn., 1819), Lauerdale criticised not only the Smithian distinction between productive and unproductive labour, but also the central role attributed to progress in the division of labour in the process of economic development. Moreover, Lauerdale propounded a theory of value based on demand and supply, and thus on scarcity and utility, and considered land, labour and capital as 'sources of wealth', thus foreshadowing the neo-classical notion of 'factors of production' (also with an outline theory of capital and its returns, which was to be praised by Böhm-Bawerk). Above all, he proposed a theory of over-saving, in all likelihood taking up a point that had already made a passing appearance in Malthus's *Essay on population* – but for which he chose to make reference to Quesnay – centred on the idea that savings constitute an outflow from the circular flow of production and consumption, implying a reduction in spending, and hence in production and future income.

In his main work on economic theory, the *Principles*, published in 1820, Malthus showed himself far less hostile than Lauerdale to Smith, from whom he took the idea of labour commanded as a standard of value, which he contrasted with the Ricardian theory of labour bestowed on a commodity. The role of demand was stressed in respect of the determination of both the prices of commodities and the global level of production and income. More precisely, Malthus stressed the risk of inadequate demand, and hence the role in support of income played by the 'unproductive consumption' of the landlords.

However, we must stress that, unlike Torrens, or the John Stuart Mill of *Some unsettled questions*, or Marx and various others, Malthus did not derive the possibility of insufficient demand from the distinction between savings and investments, which may not in fact coincide in a monetary economy. For Malthus, as for Ricardo, investments and savings automatically correspond to one another.[32] Malthus's thesis concerned, rather, the possibility that the increase in productive capacity generated by investments exceeds the growth in demand; in fact, in the absence of unproductive consumption on the part of capitalists or landlords, the increase in wages due to the increase in employment associated with investments generates an additional demand, sufficient to keep pace with the increase in productive capacity. Here the Malthusian theory of value based on supply and demand entered the scene:[33] in the situation we have illustrated, the increase in production will found an outlet, but at decreasing prices, and thus with a decrease in profits and in the profit rate.[34] The result is a situation of generalised crisis.

All this, however, has nothing to do with Keynesian theory, which (as we shall see below, chapter 14) was based precisely on the distinction between savings and investments in a monetary production economy. The idea that Malthus was a precursor of Keynes (first suggested by Keynes himself, in the essay on Malthus in his *Essays in biography*, 1933) seems, rather, to find support in Malthus's opposition to the quantity theory of money. In particular, in the *Investigation of the cause of the present high price of provisions* (1800) Malthus maintained that the increase in prices is the cause, not the effect, of the increase in the quantity of money in circulation, which banks adjust to demand.

While Lauerdale was, especially in the latter part of his life, a diehard conservative (which among other things explains his hostility towards Smith) and while Malthus may be considered a moderate conservative, a third exponent of under-consumption theory, Jean Charles Léonard

---

[32] Cf. Meek 1950–1; Robbins 1958, p. 248; Corry 1959; Tucker 1960, pp. 123–56. Eltis, instead, proposes a reconstruction of the Malthusian theory of effective demand and growth based on the distinction between *ex ante* and *ex post* investments (Eltis 1984, pp. 140–81).

[33] More precisely, we can say that Malthus considered two separate elements: the 'difficulty of production', and the demand and supply that regulate the amount of profits to be added to costs in determining the price.

[34] This point was seen and developed by the anonymous author of *An enquiry into those principles respecting the nature of demand and the necessity of consumption* (Anonymous 1821a). On this work cf. Ginzburg 1976, pp. lxvi–lxxx.

Simonde de Sismondi (1773–1842), was undoubtedly a leftist, critical towards capitalism, upholding ideas of solidarity and social justice that in many instances anticipated theses characteristic of the socialist movement.[35] His main work was the *Nouveaux principes d'économie politique* (1819; 2nd edn., 1827).

Sismondi was an advocate of public intervention in the economy: a minimum limit to wages, a limit to working hours, public assistance for the sick, the old and the unemployed. At the same time, he was favourable to widespread private property and forms of worker participation in the profits of enterprises, with the objective of reducing inequalities in income distribution and favouring social mobility. His under-consumption theory was related to the thesis of the need to defend the purchasing power of consumers, and to favour a more equitable distribution of income; in particular, wages were seen as a source of demand, while the growth of income required an expansion of demand which was not automatically ensured by increasing production.[36]

As these summary remarks suffice to show, the economists considered that the major representatives of under-consumption theories were not lacking in interesting insights, even when they failed to detect one of the major weaknesses of the classical tradition, namely identification between savings and investments. However, their insights were not incorporated in sufficiently solid analytical schemes, and we can understand how relatively unconvincing their positions must have appeared at the purely intellectual level in the face of Ricardo's architecture, although we should not underrate how well they reflected pre-analytical viewpoints and political ideas widespread at the time.

5.   The debate on the poor laws

One of the fields in which the Malthusian principle of population played a central role, at least from the first decades of the nineteenth century, was the debate on the poor laws, which involved a number of other themes such as the role of the government in the economy and the risks of public interference with individual responsibility. Once again we are confronted with a problem that is continually cropping up, although in different forms, in the economic and political debate. It is, in general, the issue of

---

[35] The 'progressive' current of under-consumption theories was later to count among its major exponents such heterodox Marxists as Rosa Luxemburg and Hobson (cf. below, § 9.9). Denis (1965, vol. 2, pp. 40–1) considers Sismondi a precursor of the Marxian notion of surplus-value, and of the laws of increasing poverty and industrial concentration.

[36] Schumpeter 1954, p. 496, credits Sismondi with having been 'the first to practice the particular method of dynamics that is called period analysis'.

'what is to be done' about the poverty afflicting the lowest strata of the population.[37]

Obviously, the problem of poverty takes on different forms. Let us simplify: on the one hand, we have the orphan and the foundling, the old and the invalid: all those who, for one reason or another, are unable to work and do not have a family to look after them and provide for their subsistence. On the other hand, we have those who could work, but fail to find a job, or have a job yielding an income insufficient for survival. Finally, a third group includes those who prefer a life of privation and poverty like that of beggars, or a life fraught with risks like that of bandits, rather than work.

The importance attributed to this latter group is variable. In general, it is attributed greater importance by conservative economists, hostile to extending public intervention in favour of the poor from the first to the second category. On the other hand, the progressive economists favourable to public intervention consider the third group negligible, or include it in the first two groups.[38]

The problem of the poor is endemic, but it takes on particularly acute forms in periods characterised by marked technological change. Thus the radical technological changes characterising first the agricultural and then the industrial revolution led to impoverishment for masses of workers. In the sixteenth century, enclosures – delimiting the land reserved for stock raising – generated poverty-stricken masses, uprooted from lands their families had cultivated for generations. Thomas More (1516, pp. 65–7) ironically remarked in this respect that sheep, 'which are usually so tame and so cheaply fed, begin now [. . .] to be so greedy and wild that they devour human beings themselves and devastate and depopulate fields, houses, and towns'. In the second half of the eighteenth and in the first half of the nineteenth century, in England as in the more advanced countries of continental Europe, manufacturing industries arose to squeeze out traditional artisan activities, giving rise once again to mass pauperism.

We shall consider below (§ 7.7) the debate on 'compensation', or in other words the thesis that jobs lost with the introduction of machinery are 'compensated' for by the creation of new jobs, thanks to the new demand deriving from the improved standards of living generated by technical progress. In actual fact, however, pauperism was there for all to see: the 'compensation' was, at least, not immediate.

---

[37] For instance, towards the end of the seventeenth century Child maintained the necessity of deporting the able-bodied poor to the colonies or putting them to work in workhouses under public control.

[38] It is sufficient, for instance, to consider social deviancy as a psychiatric illness.

In Elizabethan England the poor laws had already contemplated not only systematic support for the first category of poor – the orphaned, old and invalid – but also more generally for all those unable to support themselves with their own work. The 1601 statutes introduced on a nationwide scale a tax going to the support of the poor; however, collection of the tax and distribution of the revenue were administered locally, under the surveillance of elected supervisors, and local administrations were left free to follow the direction of 'outdoor relief' (distribution of foodstuff, subsidies, public works) or 'indoor relief' (the assisted poor obliged to reside – and work – in public 'workhouses'), or a combination of the two.

The onus of intervention thus fell on the well-to-do classes of the local communities where the poor lived. Obviously this meant a tax burden differing from place to place, according to the proportion of poor in the local population; as a consequence, the communities were for ever seeking to encourage their poor to emigrate to other areas of the country, and to bar the poor from entering from other areas, with repeated attempts to regulate – and obstruct – the mobility of the poor. The 1662 Settlement Laws, for instance, imposed constraints that were not only absurdly rigid, but also extremely difficult to enforce. Moreover, the tax provoked continual complaints about the incentive to idleness offered by a system of assistance considered too generous to people who, although able-bodied, did not work.[39]

This twofold series of problems eventually gave rise, in the eighteenth century and in particular with the new Poor Law of 1772, to a set of rules that in practice prohibited the migration of the poor from one parish to another, and made the provision of food, as small as it was, dependent on living in a workhouse – and the workhouse thus became a sort of prison without bars.[40] Despite these constraints, assistance to the poor grew to considerable dimensions: according to some estimates, by 1803 it was reaching a million people, 11 per cent of the population of England and Wales, while in 1830 assistance was absorbing up to 2 per cent of the national income.[41] Assistance to the poor received a boost from, among other things, the so-called 'Speenhamland system' (from the name of the place where the magistrates of Berkshire used to meet), which began to spread in 1795, providing for supplementation of the lowest wages

---

[39] Among the advocates of this viewpoint in the eighteenth century we find Daniel Defoe and Bernard de Mandeville; it is, however, frequently met with in the literature of the time.

[40] An important contemporary reconstruction of the situation at the end of the eighteenth century and the road that had led to it is offered by Frederick Eden (1766–1809), *The state of the poor*, 3 vols., 1797.

[41] Williams 1981; cf. also Boyer 1990 and Oxley 1974.

to reach a minimum level determined on the basis of the number of dependants and indexed to food prices.

This was the background for the debate on the poor laws in England in the first half of the nineteenth century. As we saw above, great use of the Malthusian principle of population was made here to argue that aid to the able-bodied poor was useless – a thesis upheld by many classical economists, including Malthus himself and Ricardo. Others, like Senior, invoked the 'wage fund' theory to the same end: aid to the able-bodied poor reduces the work incentives, thus weakening the workers' efficiency and, as a consequence, the scale of production and availability of resources to pay wages.[42]

The debate between the conservative and progressive theses concerned whether disincentives to work arose with assistance to the able-bodied poor not made conditional upon compulsory labour in the workhouses. Thus the debate revolved not so much on the desirability of aid to the poor in principle as on the choice between outdoor and indoor relief. Problems of bad administration, of little interest from the point of view of theoretical economic debate, were mixed with issues including incentives for individuals to take an active approach, the role of public intervention and the idea that poverty was the inevitable lot of a great part of the population.[43]

6.   The debate on the colonies

The Malthusian principle of population, namely the idea that population growth exerts pressure on the means of subsistence, had every appearance of realism in England at the time of the Napoleonic wars, when the continental blockade obstructed imports from continental countries producing low-cost agricultural goods. In the years immediately following the 1815 Congress of Vienna, recollection of the war years could still account for the persistent and widespread acceptance of a theory already overtaken by the realities of the time. One field where the population principle was already quite clearly wearing thin was the debate on the

---

[42] Senior's preoccupations concerned industriousness, foresight (hence parsimony) and charity. More generally, Senior identified the progress of society with the gradual development of individual freedom and self-determination, which was obstructed by the constraints (on mobility, for instance) necessitated by administration of the poor law. Cf. Bowley 1937, pp. 288–90.

[43] In this respect, a characteristic example of the conservative view is offered by Senior. Cf. Bowley 1937, pp. 282–334, for ample illustration of Senior's participation in the debate. Among the economists who accepted the principle of assistance to the able-bodied poor we find a number of authors that we will be meeting again in chapter 8 among the Ricardians: McCulloch, Torrens, James and John Stuart Mill.

colonies, now largely ignored by historians of economic thought but a burning issue of the time.

This debate, too, had begun well before the period we are considering here. On the relations between colonies and fatherland, for instance, Adam Smith wrote some extremely interesting pages in the conclusion of his *magnum opus* itself, published in the same year as the Declaration of Independence of the American colonies. In these pages, and in a memorandum of February 1778, Smith not only appeared ready to recognise the rights of the colonies, but went so far as to delineate a 'commonwealth', similar to that which took shape only much later on, grasping the potentialities of North America as future leader of the world economy.[44] Even before Smith, we may recall Petty's participation in the American adventure of his friend Penn that led to the foundation of Pennsylvania,[45] or the role played by Cantillon and, above all, by the Scottish banker-economist John Law in the financial vicissitudes involved in the colonisation of Mississippi.[46]

But let us return to the debate on the colonies in the golden period of classical political economy. One of the main problems for countries across the oceans – both the recently independent United States and the new colonial frontier of Australia – lay in the extremely sparse population. The land available for cultivation was vast, the number of immigrants scant, which meant enormous difficulties for the newborn manufacturing firms seeking wage workers, thwarting the development of an integrated economic system with a manufacturing sector thriving on the division of labour between firms and within each productive process.

These problems were dealt with by authors such as Wakefield, Torrens and others. Without departing from the framework of the Malthusian principle of population, Torrens (we shall have more to say about him later: § 8.2) was among the first authors to present the colonies as outlets for the emigration that was to improve the conditions of the workers of the kingdom, and in particular of the Irish.[47] Soon, however, Torrens converted to Wakefield's ideas on systematic colonisation.

---

[44] Smith (1776, pp. 934–47), and above all (1977, pp. 377–85). On the sequence of countries acting as leaders in the world economy, cf. Kindleberger 1996.
[45] Cf. Fitzmaurice 1895.   [46] Cf. Murphy 1986 and 1997.
[47] Cf., for instance, Torrens 1817. Other authors, however, including Senior, utilised the Malthusian theory against the colonisation policies, maintaining that the 'void' left by emigration would soon be replenished by an increase in population, thus cancelling out the positive effects of emigration. A century and a half earlier, Petty (1691a, pp. 157; 1899, pp. 551 ff.; 1927, pp. 256, 262, 265–6) had repeatedly advanced a proposal of an opposite sign concerning the Irish 'colony': that 'transplantation', or mass deportation of the Irish people, would transform the island into an immense cattle-raising pasture with few workers.

Edward Gibbon Wakefield (1774–1854) argued that land in the colonies should be sold to the settlers at a price that not all could afford in order to guarantee the availability of wage labour; were they to take possession of land to cultivate freely, the settlers would scatter over vast areas and the division of labour would thus be rendered impracticable, with enormous loss in productivity and poverty looming for the new colonies.[48]

Once he embraced Wakefield's ideas, Torrens defended them with his characteristic vigour, playing an active role in the colonisation of South Australia, first (since 1831) as a founding member of the South Australian Land Company, then (since 1835) as chairman of a commission created by the British government to organise new provinces in South Australia.[49] Population theory thus turned away from the old, pessimistic views on the possibility of progress of human societies to form the basis for theoretical rationalisation of the expansionist forces leading to the formation of the British Empire.

7.   Bentham's utilitarianism

Let us now turn to another important stream of thought, Bentham's utilitarianism, which took shape and rose in influence in the period between Smith's *Wealth of nations* (1776) and John Stuart Mill's *Principles* (1848). In some respects – as we shall see in chapter 10 – it opens the way to the 'marginalist revolution'; in other respects, it may help us in understanding the transition – on many accounts a big step backward – from the Smithian notion of human beings as moved by a rich mixture of passions and interests to the Ricardian notion of economic man.

The 'utilitarian revolution' of the London-born philosopher Jeremy Bentham (1748–1832) fell within a different field from political economy, although on many accounts touching upon it, namely the field of ethics. Within this field, a centuries-long debate (mentioned above: § 2.1) saw the confrontation of two views: the deontological and the consequentialist approach. Bentham gave a crucial contribution to the development of the latter.

In a few words, the deontological approach maintained that actions are 'good' or 'bad' in themselves: the moral quality of any action is a characteristic intrinsic to it. For instance, to harm a person is surely

---

[48] Cf. Wakefield 1829 and 1833. On Wakefield's dominant role in this debate, cf. Winch 1965.

[49] Cf. Torrens 1835. On Torrens's contribution to the debate on colonies, cf. Robbins 1958, pp. 144–81. A large (5,700 sq km) lake in South Australia bears the name of Torrens.

'bad'. The consequentialist approach maintained instead that any action is to be judged within the specific context in which it takes place, that is, by looking at its consequences. Even to harm a person may be 'good', for instance if one is compelled to do so in order to prevent the person from killing somebody else.[50]

Deontological theories in ethics were commonly based on the principle of authority; they were traditionally associated with religious commandments, and were typical of societies oriented towards respect for traditions. Consequentialist theories of ethics, on the other hand, came to the fore with the new rationalistic orientation of the Enlightenment age. In different ways, many philosophers and social reformers (such as Beccaria and Verri in Milan: cf. above, § 4.8) contributed to the success of this approach; among them, Bentham undoubtedly played a crucial role.

Bentham summed up consequentialist ethics in the phrase 'the greatest happiness principle', or 'the principle of utility', which constituted his fundamental axiom from his first important work, the *Fragment on government*. According to this Bentham's maxim, 'it is the greatest happiness of the greatest number that is the measure of right and wrong' (Bentham 1776, p. 393). This principle derived from Francis Hutcheson and – through Beccaria – from Helvetius.[51] Literally taken, it implied two elements ('greatest happiness' and 'greatest number') to be simultaneously maximised. This is a crucial element to keep in mind when interpreting Hutcheson or Beccaria; however, Bentham's 'felicific calculus' seems to imply just one maximand: total social happiness.

The felicific calculus, which Bentham proposed as an essential component of his consequentialist ethics, consisted in quantitative evaluation and algebraic summation of pleasures and pains stemming from any action or set of actions (where pleasures obviously have a positive sign, pains a negative sign). Good is whatever gives as its result an algebraically

---

[50] Naturally, such a clear-cut dichotomy between deontological and consequentialist approaches is simplistic, and hides many a problem. As shown by Sen 1991, deontological theories in general are open to recognising, at least indirectly, the importance of the consequences of actions, while the consequentialist approaches commonly retain some elements of a priori judgements. On the whole, however, the distinction remains a most useful interpretative key. Much the same may be said of a dichotomy which displays a number of analogies with the one discussed above, but which differs from it in some substantive respects, namely the dichotomy between transcendental ethics and the hedonistic approach. In short, transcendental ethics maintained that the ultimate end of actions, which determines their moral worth, does not belong to this earth; the hedonistic approach maintained that the ultimate end is individual welfare. Together with consequentialism, this latter view characterised the so-called 'philosophical radicalism'.

[51] Cf. Halévy 1900, pp. 13 and 21. Schumpeter 1954, p. 130, recalled that Helvetius (in *De l'esprit*, 1758) 'compared the role of the principle of self-interest in the social world to the role of the law of gravitation in the physical world'.

positive felicific magnitude, and hence increases the 'amount of happiness' within human societies; bad is whatever gives as its result a negative felicific magnitude, and as a consequence decreases the amount of social happiness.[52]

The 'felicific calculus' was thus directed to evaluate the *social* impact of both individual actions and public policy choices; Bentham, however, concentrated attention on the latter.

Let us ponder this point. The private and the social impact of individual actions coincide if individuals, while pursuing their own personal interests, do not have an impact on the interests of others; in such a case selfish behaviour automatically also realises the common good and the so-called 'thesis of the natural identity of interests' holds. This was the thesis on which the most extreme ideas of *laissez faire* relied, holding that optimal social conditions are realised when individuals pursue their own personal preferences. This thesis, let us stress, was different from the position maintained, for instance, by Adam Smith, discussed above in §§ 5.3 and 5.8, according to which individual behaviour is to be guided by an adequate set of legal and moral norms upheld by public bodies – the police and the administration of justice. Smith's *laissez-faire* approach lay, rather, in the conviction that in an imperfect world we should abandon the dream of the 'enlightened prince', since each citizen can look after his or her own interests better than he or she can anybody else's. Bentham, on the other hand, wavered between the idea of the 'enlightened prince' and extreme *laissez-faire* views (implicit, for instance, in his defence of usury against Smith's proposal to set a ceiling on interest rates, Bentham 1787); indeed his faith in benevolent Reason, typical of the French Enlightenment, led him mainly in the former direction, with a central role attributed to the 'Legislator'.

Bentham's guiding aim with his researches was in fact the construction of a legal code such as to achieve the supremacy of Reason within human societies, the felicific calculus being the Legislator's main tool. With it the Legislator could take account of the behaviour of individuals motivated by their own self-interest, and intervene with laws setting rewards

---

[52] Among the precursors of utilitarianism – but not of felicific calculus – we may recall the English philosopher John Locke (on whom cf. above, § 4.2). In his *Essay concerning human understanding*, vol. II ch. 20, Locke 1689, p. 229, in fact said: 'Things then are Good or Evil, only in reference to Pleasure or Pain'; but this statement was then followed by an analysis of the different passions (ibid., pp. 229–33), which shows that pleasure and pain were not considered as one-dimensional magnitudes. John Stuart Mill's critique to Bentham, which revolves around this point and will be discussed below (§ 8.9), thus had deep roots: we might say that Bentham's felicific calculus and the connected one-dimensional view of man constituted a deviation from the English-language philosophical tradition, and rather showed signs of the influence of French sensism.

and punishments so as to modify individual behaviour in the direction of the optimal situation corresponding to the greatest happiness principle. Of course, the greater or lesser quantities of happiness stemming from different courses of actions were computed for society as a whole, and assessed by the Legislator himself. (It was not even necessary for individual behaviour to be strictly guided by individual felicific calculus: individuals could be guided by their habits more than by continuous rational computation of the effects of each action; what mattered was that the Legislator, if he wanted to modify individual choices, could do so by means of an adequate set of incentives and disincentives.) In other words, the Legislator's task consisted in producing harmony between private and public interests.

The Legislator's use of felicific calculus implied two prerequisites. First, the different pleasures and pains of each individual were assumed to be reducible to quantitative measurement along a one-dimensional scale. Second, it was assumed that felicific magnitudes referring to different individuals could be algebraically added up. Specifically, all individuals were assumed to be identical in their ability to experience pleasures and pains.

Bentham was in many respects a true believer in the powers of Reason and in the applicability of the felicific calculus to a homogeneous, one-dimensional human nature. However, in practice in his impressive output of manuscripts no example is to be found, at least to my knowledge, of factual computations of this kind, with numerical estimations of pleasures and pains. Bentham systematically limited himself to illustrating the elements which influenced the 'quantity' of pleasures and pains (such as 'intensity, duration, certainty, propinquity, fecundity, purity and extent'). This was sufficient for his purposes when dealing with specific issues, for instance to establish which criteria the laws (especially those relating to punishments, as in the debate on the death penalty) should follow. We may add that the idea of clearly specified, complete individual preference maps serving as a basis for factual quantitative evaluation of utilities and disutilities was far from Bentham's mind when considering the behaviour of economic agents. As we saw above, assessing social and individual preferences was the Legislator's task; the felicific calculus, we may stress once again, was introduced by Bentham in this context (and more generally in the context of the debate on ethics), not in the context of an analysis of consumers' behaviour.

Furthermore, though Bentham seems to incline towards a subjective theory of value (which, as we saw, had already a centuries-long tradition), between his utilitarianism and the later marginalist economics there is a difference in perspective. Bentham evaluated the outcomes of different courses of actions (and especially different legal rules: the distinction, typical of contemporary utilitarianism, between 'rule utilitarianism' and 'act utilitarianism'[53] is irrelevant here) by analysing their consequences, while marginalist economics aims at evaluating *commodities* through the connection between exchange value and use value. The notion of marginal utility, upon which this connection is based – as we shall see in chapter 10 – requires that the consumption of each successive dose of each commodity be considered as a different action. This (and in particular the postulate of decreasing marginal utility) was unnecessary from the perspective of Bentham's Legislator; indeed, it is likely that Bentham – and even more so some of the best-known among his followers, in particular John Stuart Mill – would have considered this line of argument as stretching application of the felicific calculus too far.

In fact, Bentham did not provide a systematic analysis of the notions of value and price. In his writings we find a number of emphatic enunciations to the effect that 'all value is founded on utility', but this simply means that 'where there is no use, there cannot be any value': that is, exactly as in Smith or in Ricardo, utility was considered a prerequisite for exchange value.[54] However, this did not necessarily imply attributing to utility a quantitatively measurable dimension, let alone relying on it for the determination of exchange values. True, as for so many other authors before him, Bentham indicated plenty or scarcity as factors accounting for prices, specifically while dealing with the water–diamond paradox; but it remains a very long stride ahead from this to the marginalist theory of prices, requiring clearly specified assumptions, including closely defined demand and supply functions, without which it was impossible to utilise the tools of differential calculus.

---

[53] Cf. Sen and Williams 1982, in particular John Harsanyi's essay, 'Morality and the theory of rational behaviour', pp. 39–62.

[54] Bentham 1801, p. 83. Hutchison 1956, p. 290, after quoting this passage, shows how Bentham differed from Smith in inclining towards a subjective theory of value based on comparison between scarcity and demand, but without going further than this, or than what was already present in 'the tradition of Galiani, Pufendorf and the Schoolmen' (ibid., p. 291).

7   David Ricardo

1.   Life and works

David Ricardo was born in London in 1772. He was the third of at least seventeen children of a well-to-do stockbroker, a Sephardic Jew. Following the family traditions, from eleven to thirteen years of age David studied in Amsterdam, an important financial centre that had recently lost its supremacy to London, and from where the Ricardo family came (although it seems that its original roots were in Portugal). Back in London at the age of fourteen, David began work in the stock exchange with his father. Soon, however, he was to become the protagonist of a romantic story: falling in love with a young Quaker girl, on reaching the age of twenty-one he married her against his family's wishes, and was disowned. Thus compelled to launch out on his own, thanks to his ability and the connections acquired while working for his father he soon succeeded in reaching an important position in the business community.

It was precisely his work at the stock exchange that prompted him to systematic consideration of the economic vicissitudes of the country.[1] An important stimulus, for instance, came with the suspension of gold convertibility by the Bank of England in February 1797. While on holiday at Bath, in 1799, Ricardo happened to read Smith's *Wealth of nations*, a book then twenty-three years old but established as the main reference work in the field of economic science. Ricardo was not a scholarly type, but he had a logical mind and sharp intelligence. His analytic penchant thus germinated around three elements: the immediate economic events of his time, debate revolving around them, and Smith's book.

---

[1] According to an anecdote circulating in Cambridge, Sraffa, editor of the monumental critical edition of Ricardo's works (Ricardo, 1951–5), summed up his personality in a single sentence: 'Ricardo was the son of a stockbroker.' In a letter to Gramsci's sister-in-law, Tatiana, dated 21 June 1932, Sraffa wrote: 'In general [Ricardo] never pursues a historical point of view and as has been said [by Marx] he considers as natural and immutable laws the laws of the society in which he lives. Ricardo was, and always remained, a stockbroker with a mediocre culture' (Sraffa 1991, p. 74).

His first economic writings (in 1809, *The price of gold*, three articles in the *Morning Chronicle*; in 1810, a short essay on *The high price of bullion, a proof of the depreciation of bank notes*, which reached four editions within the following year) entered upon the field of the monetary controversies of the time. However, his work left him little time for such endeavours. His main contributions to political economy came after his withdrawal from the stock exchange in 1815, when he was only forty-three years old but already a wealthy person, thanks in particular to successful speculations on the placing of public debt. Like Rothschild, Ricardo had bet on English victory over Napoleon and, after the battle of Waterloo (18 June 1815), he had a fortune estimated at more than £600,000 of the time behind him.

Ricardo moved to the countryside, at Gatcomb, and there led the tranquil life of a rich gentleman. Along with this he also got involved in politics, and from 1819 was a Member of Parliament representing Portarlington, a borough in Ireland with only twelve electors who, as was usual at the time, sold their vote to the highest bidder. Of course he also joined in the economic debates of the period, but more through correspondence with friends and parliamentary speeches than with publications. Among the latter, however, his *Essay on the influence of a low price of corn on the profits of stock*, published in 1815, met with a positive response. His main work is *On the principles of political economy, and taxation*, a book published in 1817; it had fair if not exceptional success in terms of readership (with two new editions – in 1819 and 1821 – in the author's lifetime), but helped to establish his standing as a leading figure in the politico-cultural élite of that period.

In his publishing and parliamentary activity Ricardo dealt with monetary, fiscal and public debt issues.[2] In 1816 he published the short essay *Proposals for an economical and secure currency*, in which he criticised the Bank of England, then a private concern, and proposed to reintroduce the convertibility of the bank notes in ingots rather than in coins, so as to favour circulation based on bank notes, with some saving on circulation costs. In an article on the 'Funding system', written in 1819 (but published in 1820) for a supplementary volume to the *Encyclopaedia Britannica*, Ricardo proposed recourse to wealth taxes in order to pay back over a four-to-five-year time span the public debt that had piled up

---

[2] Schumpeter's (1954, p. 473) well-known criticism, concerning the 'Ricardian Vice' seen as 'the habit of applying results of this character [i.e. based on simplifying assumptions such as the invariance of technology] to the solution of practical problems', did not refer to these aspects of Ricardo's thought, but to his theory of profits. Schumpeter's observation has, however, wider application; consider, for instance, Ricardo's acceptance of a strong version of Say's law (cf. above, § 6.3).

during the period of the Napoleonic wars. In 1823 he returned to monetary issues, with a short essay (published posthumously in the following year) on a *Plan for the establishment of a national bank*, in which he proposed that the issue of bank notes be entrusted to a National Bank, and that the Bank of England be limited to the activity of a commercial bank (let us recall that only in 1844, after long controversies, was the Bank of England compelled to accept internal separation between an issuing department and a banking department).

Ricardo died after a short illness, in 1823. He left a large estate to his wife and his surviving children, with bequests to his friends Malthus and James Mill.

Although he was acclaimed as the leading figure of classical political economy, in the years immediately following his death his scientific heritage was already gradually being dissipated, with increasing distortion of his original thought. With the rise of the marginalist approach, after 1870, the idea gained ground of Ricardo as a genius, but not worth reading; indeed, it was even suggested that with his extraordinary intelligence he had set political economy on a wrong track.[3] It was only with the ten-volume edition of his works and correspondence edited by Sraffa between 1951 and 1955 (plus a final eleventh volume with the indexes published in 1973) – an edition that constitutes a true master-work of philological rigour – that Ricardo and his scientific contribution were brought back to the attention of economists, freeing the field from an accretion of misinterpretations and awakening new, thought-provoking interpretative discussions relating directly to the contemporary theoretical debate on basic themes in the theory of value and distribution.

2.   Ricardo's dynamic vision

Ricardo substantially took over from Smith his 'vision' of the economic system, and upon it built an analytical construction admirable in its systematic and logically consistent character, aimed at supporting policies conducive to capitalistic development. Like Smith, Ricardo took into consideration a society based on the division of labour, with two broad sectors, agriculture and manufacturing, and three social classes – workers, capitalists and landowners – with three corresponding income categories: wages, profits and rents. According to Ricardo, wages correspond by and large to the subsistence consumption of the workers employed in the productive process, and therefore constitute part of the necessary expenses

---

[3] Let us recall Jevons's 1871, p. 72, resolute statement: 'that able but wrong-headed man, David Ricardo, shunted the car of economic science on to a wrong line'.

of production; rents and profits correspond to the surplus, namely to that part of the product that remains at disposal once the initial inventories of means of production and means of subsistence for the workers employed in production have been reconstituted. While the landlords allot their rents to luxury consumptions, the capitalists are induced by competition to invest practically the whole of their profits. Therefore economic development stems from accumulation, realised by capitalists on the basis of their profits.

Ricardo does depart from Adam Smith, however, in the broad lines of analytical construction. In his grand picture of the elements determining the wealth of nations, Smith had tried to keep account of the multifarious aspects of economic reality. The more analytical components were enclosed in a framework that we may define as historical analysis: within it, the economist brings to light the most important factors in play, but with continual reference to the other elements left in the background. Ricardo had an analytical mind, with an innate need for logical rigour and precision, which led him to construct an analytical building squared with an axe, even at the cost of excluding from analysis anything considered not directly relevant to the problem at hand.

Furthermore, Ricardo focused attention on a relatively less general field. Smith had illustrated the evolution of the economic system as a whole, connected to developments in the division of labour, and explored the different aspects of the issue. Ricardo, for his part, brought the main focus on the distribution of the surplus between rents and profits. This was indeed a central issue, since in Ricardo's view the share of income going to profits constitutes the crucial factor in determining the rhythm of capital accumulation in the economy. Moreover, with his analytical scheme it became possible to locate the impact on profits of constraints on international trade, and in particular of duties on corn imports – a burning issue both in the period of the continental blockade during the Napoleonic wars and in the period immediately after.[4]

---

[4] As a matter of fact, the problem of an increase in the price of corn – which in Ricardo's analysis appeared to be of a long-run nature – was there, and well perceived, in the years of the continental blockade; in the long run, before and after the 'hump' that characterised the beginning of the nineteenth century, thanks to technological change in agriculture the price of cereals turns out to have been relatively stable, as Smith had maintained, or even declining relatively to the general price level (cf. Sylos Labini 1984, pp. 31–6). Possibly it was Ricardo's poor historical culture and his point of view as a stockbroker that made him sensitive to the circumstances prevailing in a specific period of time and less sensitive than Smith to the long period tendencies, notwithstanding his well-known (and criticised) tendency to leave aside short period phenomena in his analysis. Another example of the influence played by the circumstances of the time can be seen in the change in emphasis in his monetary theory (cf. below, § 5): from an initial stage where the stress

At the basis of Ricardo's analysis there is thus the distribution of the surplus and its utilisation for accumulation. The size of the surplus – in a sense, the main object of analysis for Smith – changes over time as a consequence of the process of accumulation.[5] This means taking technology (thus leaving aside the problem of the evolution of the division of labour), levels of production and wage rate as given. Let us now focus on these latter two elements.

First of all, we need to clarify in what sense Ricardo may be attributed with the assumption of given levels of production. Within the framework of a dynamic conception such as the one we are describing, we certainly cannot assume that levels of production remain unchanged over time. In terms of Ricardo's analytic structure, however, this assumption stems from his acceptance of 'Say's law' (cf. above, § 6.3) in its strong version, implying the impossibility of general over-production crises, with the consequence that producers meet no difficulties in selling the commodities they have decided to produce. Thus, for Ricardo the level of production is given at any moment in time, the quantity that can be produced given the available production capacity being determined by the process of capital accumulation.[6]

As for the assumption of a given wage rate, Ricardo followed Malthus's theory of population (cf. above, § 6.2), and assumed the wage to be at subsistence level. Ricardo was ready to accept Torrens's critical remarks stressing the need to interpret the notion of subsistence wage not in a purely biological sense but as a historical-social minimum standard of

---

was mainly on the mechanisms of the quantity theory, while England adopted a regime of inconvertible paper money, to a stage (with the *Principles*) in which the labour theory of value came into play to explain the value of gold, while the return to convertibility of paper money into gold was under discussion.

[5] It was through connection with the introduction of new machinery that technological change made its appearance in Ricardo's analytical system, albeit in a relatively secondary position reflecting the under-valuation of technical progress of which Ricardo was accused in relation to his pessimism about long period economic trends due to the central role attributed to (statical) decreasing returns in agriculture.

[6] Note that this does not imply the assumption of full employment. In traditional marginalist theory (cf. below, §§ 11.4 and 17.5), full employment stems from a mechanism ensuring the automatic adjustment of demand for labour on the part of entrepreneurs: i.e. the flexibility in the capital–labour ratio. The decrease of wages that takes place (under competition) in the presence of unemployment leads entrepreneurs to adopt techniques that make a greater use of labour, and this renders the capital endowment available in the economy in a given moment of time compatible with full employment. This thesis is based on a notion of capital as 'factor of production' that not only is erroneous (cf. below, § 16.8), but that above all is totally alien to Ricardo's way of thinking. For him, as for the generality of classical economists, the capital endowment of the economy at a given moment in time depends on the accumulation that had taken place in the past, and implies specific technologies: those embodied in the available machinery. In any case, the very notion of full employment is absent from the analysis of the classical economists.

living acceptable for the workers; anyhow, he viewed wages as corresponding to the necessary consumption of the workers, and was therefore able to consider them as a given datum from the point of view of his own problem.[7] Thus the surplus turns out to be divided between rents – mainly utilised in luxury consumptions – and profits, mainly earmarked for investments.

The problem of rent is then solved with the differential rent theory: a theory often attributed to Ricardo (often we read of a 'Ricardian theory of rent'), but in fact proposed, during a short but lively debate on the duties on corn in 1815, by Malthus and (possibly) West before Ricardo, who however was ready to understand and use it.[8]

According to this theory, rent on the most fertile lands corresponds to the reduction in the costs per unit of output, as compared to costs computed on the less fertile lands. More precisely, for any plot of land the rent is equal to the difference between unit costs of production on the less fertile among lands in cultivation, and unit costs on the land being considered, multiplied by the quantity of product obtainable on it. Rent on the less fertile among lands in cultivation is nil and thus does not enter into the cost of production.[9] Profits thus turn out to be a residual magnitude, namely that part of the surplus which is not absorbed by rents.

---

[7] According to a different interpretation, known in the literature as the 'new view' (cf. Casarosa 1974 and 1978; Caravale and Tosato 1980; Hicks and Hollander 1977), the natural wage equal to subsistence level only prevails in the very long run, when the tendency to a stationary state has reached its conclusion. The market wage would instead be determined by a mechanism similar to the neo-classical one based on supply of, and demand for, labour. More precisely, according to Ricardo – if we follow the 'new view' – the market wage would be determined by comparison between rate of increase of population, namely of labour supply, which is an increasing function of the wage rate, and rate of capital accumulation, on which demand for labour depends and which in turn is an increasing function of the profit rate and hence, given the inverse relation between profit rate and wage, an inverse function of the wage. Income distribution thus proves to be determined by a moving equilibrium corresponding to equality between labour demand and supply. This is an interpretation clearly grounded on the neo-classical theoretical approach, attribution of which to Ricardo implies a thoroughly distorted reading of his writings. For criticism of the 'new view', cf. Roncaglia 1982; Rosselli 1985; Peach 1993, pp. 103–31.

[8] Cf. below, § 8.2. The theory of differential rent also has its precursors: Schumpeter 1954, pp. 259–66, recalled among others James Anderson (1739–1808), James Steuart's *Principles* (1767) and Turgot 1766.

[9] This aspect gave rise to wide debate in the following decades, until marginalist theory prevailed. According to this latter theory, as is well known, rent enters into cost of production since it corresponds to payment for the service of the productive factor land. Thus the authors who maintained around the mid-nineteenth century that rent should be included in the cost of production may be considered, on this account, precursors of marginalist theory.

We have seen that economic growth stems from accumulation, and hence from profits; therefore, whatever reduces profits constitutes a hindrance to accumulation. If we assume the size of the surplus as given, then profits fall when rents on land increase. According to Ricardo, *ceteris paribus* this happens automatically due to economic development itself: the growth of the economy is accompanied by population growth, which means an increase in food consumption, and hence in demand for agricultural products. This in turn leads to expansion in cultivation. Let us assume that the lands brought under cultivation are more fertile than the ones left uncultivated.[10] As new lands are brought under cultivation, the less fertile among the cultivated lands, namely the so-called 'marginal land' for the use of which no rent is paid, prove ever less fertile. Therefore, profits earned on the marginal land decrease, due to the increase in costs per unit of output. The rents increase on already cultivated lands, and as a consequence the profits of the farmers decrease. Such a decrease in profits is transmitted from agriculture to manufacturing, through the increase in the price of agricultural products, and hence in wages. All this hinders accumulation.

The policy implication is obvious. Imports of foreign corn are the best way to cope with increased demand for food due to the rise in population. Indeed, imports make it possible to avoid bringing under cultivation new, less fertile, lands with the consequent increase in rent, decrease in profits and in the pace of accumulation. It is thus opportune to eliminate all obstacles – such as customs duties – to the importation of agricultural products.

The theory of comparative advantages, which Ricardo developed in the *Principles* and which we shall consider below (§ 6), reinforces the policy conclusion, that obstacles to international trade, and customs duties in particular, are best removed. With this theory, indeed, Ricardo showed that the advantages of international trade stem from improvement in productive technology when all the countries involved in trade and hence in the international division of labour are considered as a whole. There is therefore a general improvement for every country, not an advantage for some at the expense of someone else, even if the problem remained open as to how the fruits of these improvements come to be distributed

---

[10] This assumption was criticised, as contrary to reality, by American writers of the time such as Henry Charles Carey (1793–1879); their criticisms are justified at the empirical level for the new colonies, but do not grasp the main point in Ricardo's analytical reasoning. In his *Principles of political economy* (1840), Carey also criticised Ricardo at the political level: 'Mr Ricardo's system is one of discords [. . .] its whole tends to the production of hostility among classes and nations' (quoted in Bharadwaj 1978, p. 25).

among the different countries.[11] Ricardo's analytical construction aimed mainly at showing that the abolition of duties on corn had positive effects on the rate of accumulation and hence on the 'wealth of nations'.

Ricardo thus expressed at the analytical level the clash of interests between the landlords, politically dominant in his times, and the infant manufacturing bourgeoisie: a clash of interests that found in the political contention over the expediency of duties on corn imports one of its central episodes.[12] The construction of a sound analytical structure for classical political economy constitutes Ricardo's main contribution both to the progress of economic science and to the gradual, difficult and partial victory of the political position he supported.

3.   From the corn model to the labour theory of value

We saw in the previous section how Ricardo was able to consider as a given datum in his analysis the size of the surplus and, within it, the share of rents. Profits thus appear as a residual magnitude: what is left once we subtract from the product both the rents and what was necessary to obtain it, namely the means of production and subsistence for the workers employed.

However, rather than the aggregate amount of profits, it is the rate of profits that is at the centre of the analytical edifice of classical political economy built by Ricardo. This is due essentially to two reasons.

First, in a capitalistic society driven by competition, in which capitalists are free to move their capitals from one investment to another, the return on the funds invested in the different sectors – the rate of profits – must be more or less equal. Hence, the rate of profits regulates the effort that society puts into the production of the different commodities, and it is this competitive mechanism based on the tendency to a uniform rate of profits which ensures that the quantities of different commodities produced more or less correspond to the quantities sold in the economy.

[11] John Stuart Mill some years later focused attention on this point, showing how the relative dimensions of demand coming from the two countries acquire importance in this respect. It was along this relatively secondary road that demand made its appearance as a factor determining relative prices in the analysis of classical economists; as we shall see, it was precisely by establishing a link between 'pure theory of foreign trade' and 'pure theory of domestic prices' that Marshall started development of his theoretical construction aiming at a synthesis between the classical and marginalist approaches (cf. below, § 13.2).

[12] Abolition of duties on corn imports in England occurred only many years later, in 1846, after fierce political battles in which the Anti-Corn Law League, founded in Manchester in 1838 by Cobden, played a central role. Hence the term 'Manchesterism', designating, as from this period, free trade ideology.

Second, the rate of profits is also – under the assumptions adopted by Ricardo – an indicator of the potential pace of growth of the economy. In fact, it is by definition equal to the ratio between profits and capital advanced; assuming that profits are wholly allotted to investments, the ratio proves equal to the ratio between investments and capital advanced, or in other words to the rate of accumulation. Furthermore, if we leave aside technical change (inclusive of non-constant returns to scale) and if we assume available productive capacity to be fully utilised, we find that the rate of profits is equal to the rate of growth of national income.[13] To be sure, Ricardo did not explicitly illustrate these relations, but they do express in analytical form the substance of his thinking (in particular, Pasinetti's 1960 'Ricardian model', followed by a large literature, was based on them). Furthermore, it is clear that for Ricardo to explain if and why the rate of profits tends to decrease in the course of the process of development, and to locate the factors that may counter this tendency, meant explaining the pace of development of the economy.

For these two reasons – its role in regulating the competitive working of the capitalistic economy and its role in the process of economic development – determination of the rate of profits constitutes a central aspect in Ricardo's analytical edifice and more generally in the whole classical tradition. In this field, Ricardo gave crucial analytical contributions, going much further than the vague Smithian idea of a normal rate of profits determined by the pressure of competition between the capitals available for investment, a thesis that Ricardo staunchly opposed.

According to the interpretation set out by Sraffa in the introduction to his edition of Ricardo's *Works and correspondence* (Sraffa 1951), we can distinguish two successive stages in the development of Ricardo's thought. The first, Sraffa conjectured, probably started in 1814, with a note on the 'profits of capital' since lost, and ended with the 1815 *Essay*;[14] the second stage began with Malthus's criticism of Ricardo's 'corn model', to conclude with the 1817 *Principles* (although Ricardo continued to ponder over the different aspects of the problem to the very last days of his life). Let us take a closer look at this issue.

---

[13] Let us denote with Y income, with P profits, with I investments, with K invested capital, with r the rate of profits and with g the rate of accumulation (which, if the capital–income ratio is constant, corresponds to the rate of increase of the economy). By definition, $r = P/K$ and $g = I/K$. If we assume that investments correspond to profits, namely that $P = I$, we have $r = g$.

[14] Sraffa's interpretation, which had it that in this first stage Ricardo determined the rate of profits as a ratio of physical quantities of one and the same commodity, corn, was questioned by Hollander 1973. This led to a close consideration of the point (cf. Bharadwaj 1983; Eatwell 1975a; Garegnani 1982; Hollander 1975 and 1979, pp. 123–90; Peach 1993, pp. 39–86, whose bibliography offers further references); from this debate, however, no at least equally convincing alternative interpretation emerged.

The rate of profits, we said, is equal to the ratio between profits and capital advanced. Obviously, in order to compute such a ratio it is necessary for profits and capital advanced to be expressed in terms of homogeneous magnitudes. In the first stage of his research, Ricardo attained this condition by interpreting profits and capital advanced in the agricultural sector as different quantities of the same commodity, 'corn'.[15] As we saw, the economy was subdivided into two sectors, agriculture and manufactures. Ricardo assumed that in the former sector only one commodity was produced, 'corn'. This commodity is also the sole means of production in agriculture, as seed, and the sole means of subsistence for the workers employed in cultivating the land. We saw that, according to the 'Ricardian' theory of the rent, on the marginal land (the less fertile among the lands under cultivation) rent is nil, and all the surplus goes to profits. Let us assume, for instance, that on the marginal land 100 tons of corn are produced, utilising 30 tons as seed and 50 tons as subsistence for the workers; the surplus, that goes entirely to profits, is equal to 20 tons of corn $(100 - 30 - 50 = 20)$, and the rate of profits is equal to 25 per cent $(20/80 = 0.25)$.

In this way we can circumvent the problem of value: that is, the need to determine the relative prices of the goods that enter into the capital advanced and surplus so as to be able to compute the value of profits and of capital advanced, and hence the rate of profits. Obviously, since under competition the rate of profits must be the same in the different employments of capital, a rate of profit equal to that computed on the marginal land will have to prevail not only in the whole agricultural sector, but also in all manufacturing activities. In this latter sector, 'corn' and manufactured goods are employed as means of production and means of subsistence in order to obtain manufactured goods, whose relative prices adjust in such a way as to ensure the uniformity of the rate of profits in all sectors of the economy.

In a letter of 5 August 1814, Malthus had objected to Ricardo that 'in no case of production, [therefore not even in the agricultural sector] is the produce exactly of the same nature as the capital advanced'.[16] In other words, Ricardo could not so blithely circumvent the problem of value

---

[15] According to Peach's (1993, pp. 39–86) interpretation, on the contrary, Ricardo *measured* costs in corn while assuming as given the ratio of exchange between corn and other means of production. Peach's reconstruction implies a rather more shaky Ricardo at the theoretical level, less systematic and less consistent than in general his contemporaries considered him to be, while Malthus gains stature. Peach's criticisms of the 'Sraffian' interpretation of Ricardo, however, while concerning important aspects, imply no substantive change to the description above (in § 2) of the core of Ricardo's picture of the functioning of the economy.

[16] Ricardo 1951–5, vol. 6, p. 117.

by determining the rate of profits as a ratio between different physical quantities of the same commodity, since in any productive process means of production are used that are heterogeneous among themselves and with respect to the product.

After pondering at length over these criticisms, the validity of which he was ready to recognise, Ricardo came up with a new solution in the *Principles*, adopting the labour embodied theory of value to explain relative prices. According to this theory, the exchange ratio between two commodities corresponds to the ratio between the quantities of labour directly and indirectly required to produce each of them. Ricardo considered this new solution a step forward from the previous one, although he did not see it as perfect since it was based on drastically simplifying assumptions – as many of his friends (in particular Torrens and, of course, Malthus, as usual, but not James Mill, too uncritical in his friendship) immediately reminded him.[17] However, from the point of view of his political objectives – attack on rents – Ricardo thought that his reasoning was sufficiently valid, and that the difficulties (the 'complications' that have to be introduced in order to deal with the problem of value) could be overcome.

Smith had already proposed this theory, also present in the Scholastic tradition, as holding in the 'early and rude state' that preceded separation between labour and the ownership of capital and land, and hence separation into the different social classes of capitalists, landlords and workers. Ricardo extends application of the theory to cover capitalistic economies too, assuming that for each commodity the amount of profits and rents that have to be added to the cost of labour in order to arrive at the price is roughly proportional to the amount of labour employed in the productive process. Once again, this is clearly an unrealistic assumption, as Ricardo himself recognised, discussing it in sections iv and v of the first chapter of the *Principles*, but this did not worry him too much. His main objective was, in fact, to work out not so much a theory of relative prices as a theory about how the surplus is distributed among the social classes and used for consumption or accumulation purposes, which thus

---

[17] Cf. Torrens 1818, Ricardo's correspondence with his friends and colleagues (Ricardo 1951–5, vols. 7–9; cf. for instance Malthus's letters in vol. 7, pp. 176, 214–15, and in vol. 8, pp. 64–5), and Malthus's *Principles* published in 1820 (in Ricardo 1951–5, vol. 2, pp. 55–79). James Mill gave a decisive contribution to publication of Ricardo's *Principles*, first of all by pushing and supporting his friend in the difficult enterprise of producing a book (especially difficult for Ricardo, because of his cultural background), and secondly with advice on specific points of exposition and possibly with compilation of the index (cf. Sraffa 1951, pp. xix–xxx). All this, however, does not imply any influence of Mill on the substantive content of the *Principles*; an exception, as suggested by Thweatt 1976, might be the theory of comparative costs.

does not concern the individual productive processes but the economic activities of a country as a whole.

Indeed, thanks to the labour theory of value Ricardo was able to measure both the product and the means of production and subsistence in homogeneous terms, as the quantities of labour bestowed on their production. More precisely, the value of the yearly produce of an economic system is equal to the quantity of labour spent as a whole in the same period of time (measured for instance in man-years and thus equal to the number of productive workers employed in the system).[18]

Computed as the difference between the value of the product and the value of the means of production, the value of the surplus also emerges expressed as a certain quantity of labour. Once the problem of rent is settled and done with, profits too turn out to be determined as a certain quantity of labour. The ratio between profits and capital advanced, both expressed as quantities of labour, is thus once again expressed as a ratio between different physical quantities of one magnitude (labour time).[19]

Thus, with his labour theory of value, Ricardo once again succeeded in circumventing the problem of value, but once again at the cost of drastic and unrealistic simplifications, so the solution he proposed cannot be seen as final. Ricardo was well aware of this and, as we shall see in the next section, continued to dwell on the subject of value to the last, but without getting appreciably further. Nonetheless, the structure of his analytic edifice, based on the notion of the surplus and centred on the relationship between accumulation and income distribution, remains a

---

[18] Let us recall here Ricardo's distinction between 'value' and 'riches' (in chapter 20 of the *Principles*, 1817: Ricardo 1951–5, vol. 1, pp. 273 ff.): whenever there is an improvement in technology and the quantity produced increases for a given amount of labour bestowed in production, the value of the national product (in terms of the labour theory of value) by definition remains unchanged; what we have is an increase in 'riches', which Ricardo defines as corresponding to Smith's notion of the 'wealth of nations', namely 'the degree in which [a man] can afford to enjoy the necessaries, conveniences, and amusements of human life' (Smith 1776, p. 47).

[19] Let us denote with L the number of employed workers (and hence the amount of labour, expressed in man-years, expended in a year). L thus corresponds to the value, in labour terms, of the yearly produce of the economy. Let us also indicate with Lw the value, again in terms of labour, of the commodities required for the subsistence of employed workers, which by assumption corresponds to the wages paid to them, and with Lc the value of means of production utilised overall within the year (under the assumption that only circulating capital is used). Let us disregard rents for the sake of simplicity. Let us assume that all productive processes last one year, and that wages and circulating capital are advanced by capitalists at the beginning of the year. The value of capital advanced on the whole is then equal to Lw/Lc, while the value of profits P is equal to the difference between product and costs of production, namely $P = L - Lw - Lc$. The profit rate r is equal to the ratio between profits and capital advanced, namely $r = (L - Lw - Lc)/(Lw + Lc)$.

landmark both for the debates of his times and for our understanding of the 'classical paradigm' of political economy.

4.   Absolute value and exchangeable value: the invariable standard of value

As we saw in the previous section, in the *Principles* the value issue appears settled in a way Ricardo considered acceptable for his own purposes, but relying on drastic, unrealistic simplifications. Over and above the criticisms of his contemporaries, from Malthus to Torrens, this constituted a challenge for one of Ricardo's rigorous mentality. To this challenge he devoted part of his time – side by side with his activity as a Member of Parliament and as protagonist in the current economic debates – throughout a period spanning from the publication of the first edition of the *Principles* to an essay on *Absolute value and exchangeable value* written in 1823, in the last few weeks of his life.

As early as the first edition of the *Principles*, as we have seen, Ricardo had pointed out the limits of the labour theory of value as an explanation of the relative prices of the different commodities; in the subsequent editions (1819 and 1821) these aspects are specified, also taking into account a critical blow by Torrens (1818), though without substantial changes in the original position.[20]

According to Ricardo, the relative prices determined as the ratio between the quantities of labour directly and indirectly required to produce the different commodities violate the condition of a uniform rate of profits in the different sectors of the economy for three reasons: different durability of productive processes; changing ratio between fixed and circulating capital; and different durability of fixed capital in the different sectors. More precisely, if for any commodity we choose as standard of measure the quantity of it that requires an hour of labour for its production, in order to ensure uniformity of the rate of profits in all the different sectors, profit per unit of output will have to be greater in sectors characterised by higher durability of productive process, or higher ratio between fixed and circulating capital, or higher durability of fixed capital.

---

[20] The thesis of a progressive move away from the labour theory of value on the part of Ricardo in the successive editions of the *Principles* was maintained by Jacob Hollander 1904 and by Cannan 1929, but was demolished by Sraffa 1951. Peach 1993, pp. 189–240, maintained instead the thesis of a Ricardo increasingly taken with defence of the labour theory of value, eventually attributing (in the third edition of the *Principles*, and especially in the essay on *Absolute value and exchangeable value*) to the labour bestowed on production a significance of absolute value, which becomes the necessary starting point to explain exchange value.

The labour theory of value may therefore be considered as at most an approximate theory of relative prices. For Ricardo, however, the problem was not so much that of establishing how wide the margin of approximation might be (an aspect that gave rise to debate between commentators, some attributing Ricardo with the idea of a 93 per cent approximation and thus having no difficulty in demonstrating that the error may in fact be much larger).[21] Rather, the problem revolved upon the possibility of finding rigorous anchorage, an 'invariable standard', for exchange values.[22]

In the search for such anchorage, Ricardo found himself clinging to a traditional term of reference, namely the labour time required to obtain a certain quantity of product. In this context, the use of the term 'absolute value' implies a certain ambiguity between, on the one hand, the choice to rely for his theory of natural prices on the relative difficulties of production of different commodities and, on the other hand, the vaguely metaphysical elements implicit in the traditional idea that the value of a commodity stems from the sacrifice required of the worker in order to obtain it.

The use of labour as a standard – that is, the choice to use as standard a commodity produced by a given and unchangeable quantity of labour – has the advantage that it provides precise answers when confronted with changes in technology. In this respect, it also satisfies the dialectical need to contrast a theory of exchange values based on the difficulty of production with the notion, ever present in economic debate, of a mechanism based on demand and supply. In Ricardo's thought, as already in Smith's (cf. above, § 5.6), the interrelationship between supply and demand only

---

[21] Cf. Stigler 1958; Barkai 1967 and 1970; Konus 1970. The references to the empirical robustness of the labour theory of value as an approximation to an exact theory of exchange values were inserted by Ricardo in the third edition of the *Principles*, but are clearly incidental to the main line of reasoning. The interpretation of Ricardo as a supporter of an 'empirical' labour theory of value appears forced and reductive at the same time. For criticism in depth of this interpretation, cf. Peach 1993, pp. 25–6 and 215–17.

[22] The search for a standard of value in Ricardo's analysis was connected, among other things, with the theme of money. Cf. below, § 5; and Marcuzzo and Rosselli 1994. Above all, we must bear in mind the importance, in that period, of attempts to unify physical measures within each country, and the theoretical debates that accompanied these attempts. In the case of the metre, introduced in post-Revolutionary France in 1793 with a decision of the National Assembly, the natural foundation for the definition of the standard was found in the length of a meridian arch at a given latitude. Today these measures are taken for granted, and it is rare to ponder the importance of a standard of measure common to all and the difficulties of its objective identification, but in the long phase of transition the question was well to the fore, both in intellectual debate and in the practice of daily life: cf. Kula 1970 for a history of the problem. We may well understand how, at a crucial moment in that transition, the idea of a natural standard of value should have appeared parallel to the idea of a natural standard for physical magnitudes. We should, however, add that many economists were aware of the error in drawing parallels between physical measures and value measures: cf. for instance Bailey 1825, p. 96 (quoted by Peach 1993, p. 227 n.).

concerns the adjustment of market prices to natural prices, not the determination of the latter:

It is the cost of production which must ultimately regulate the price of commodities, and not, as has been often said, the proportion between the supply and
demand: the proportion between supply and demand may, indeed, for a time,
affect the market value of a commodity, until it is supplied in greater or less
abundance, according as the demand may have increased or diminished; but this
effect will be only of temporary duration.

Ricardo then went on to highlight the contrast between his position
and that of his friend-adversary Malthus, who had it that not only market
but also natural prices are determined by demand and supply. The issue
is considered crucial:

The opinion that the price of commodities depends solely on the proportion of
supply to demand, or demand to supply, has become almost an axiom in political
economy, and has been the source of much error in that science.[23]

Thus Ricardo, in the first edition of the *Principles*, adopted as 'invariable
standard' a commodity produced by a year of labour without the help of
capital goods. In this way we have a clear criterion to determine the origin
of changes in exchange values. For instance, let us consider the exchange
value of two commodities, A and B, in terms of this invariable standard,
and let us assume that the technique for producing one of these two
commodities, A, changes, while the technique for producing B remains
unchanged. We can then unequivocally establish that the variation in
exchange value between A and B originates in commodity A, which has
changed in value in terms of the chosen invariable standard, while the
value of commodity B is seen to be constant. However, the standard
chosen by Ricardo proves inadequate when confronted with changes in
the distribution of income between wages and profits. Indeed, when two
commodities produced by the same quantity of labour are obtained over
different periods of production or with a different proportion between

---

[23] Ricardo 1951–5, vol. 1, p. 382. Cf. also the letter to Malthus of 30 January 1818 (in
Ricardo 1951–5, vol. 7, pp. 250–1) quoted by Peach 1993, pp. 258–9. Also interesting
is the argument with which Ricardo criticised the explanation of exchange value suggested by Malthus, based on the relative estimate of commodities on the part of buyers.
According to Ricardo (1951–5, vol. 2, pp. 24–5; quoted by Peach 1993, pp. 247–8),
'This would be true if men from various countries were to meet in a fair, with a variety
of productions, and each with a separate commodity, undisturbed by the competition
of any other seller. Commodities, under such circumstances, would be bought and sold
according to the relative wants of those attending the fair'; however, Ricardo went on,
this no longer holds when we have competition between different producers for each
commodity, since the prices are then governed by costs of production. Malthus's view
was clearly expressed in various passages of his *Principles* (1820), in particular in sections
i and iii of chapter 2 (reproduced in Ricardo 1951–5, vol. 2, pp. 36–54).

fixed and circulating capital, their relative value changes when distribution changes, and our invariable standard can give no indication of the origin of this variation in exchange value.

Initially, Ricardo applied his reflections on the standard of value in criticising a thesis he attributed to Smith. This was the idea that, if the wage or the rate of profits increases, as a consequence the natural prices of commodities should also increase. This thesis connects to the interpretation of Smith's theory of prices as an 'adding up of components theory'.

According to this theory, the cost of production of a commodity can be decomposed into labour directly necessary to its production, land and other means of production; with analogous breakdown of the production cost of the means of production we can proceed backwards, until the residuum of means of production disappears or becomes negligible, and all costs are reduced to labour and land invested for specified periods of time, and thus to wages, profits and rents computed at their natural rates. Given the technology in use (and therefore given the quantities of labour and land directly or indirectly necessary to produce a commodity, and given the length of the time intervals for which labour and land remain invested), knowing the natural wage rate, rent and natural rate of profits, it is easy to compute the natural price of the product.

The flaw in this theory lies in the assumption that wage rate, rent and rate of profits are independent of each other: only in this case, in fact, can the price be computed by adding up the three components. Furthermore, in such a case an increase in one of the three distributive variables automatically translates into a corresponding increase in the natural price of the product. This is precisely the point that Ricardo did not accept, in line with his basic thesis of the opposition between rents and profits. Precisely in order to show that the increase in one of the distributive variables is not necessarily followed by an increase in all prices, Ricardo chose as standard the commodity produced by a year's labour, with no capital advances and no land. If the wage rate increases, the prices of all other commodities decrease in comparison with the commodity chosen as standard of measure, since for them the ratio between indirect and direct labour, and hence the weight of profits (which decrease when wages increase), is higher.

Once again it was Malthus who criticised the excessive simplicity of Ricardo's assumption. Ricardo accepted the criticisms, while maintaining that they did not affect the substance of his position.[24] A number of

---

[24] See Malthus's letter of 10 September 1819, in Ricardo 1951–5, vol. 8, pp. 64–6, and Ricardo's answer (after an exchange of clarifications in other letters) of 9 November 1819, in Ricardo 1951–5, vol. 8, pp. 128–31.

commodities, Malthus said, may have a period of production shorter than a year, and as a consequence a weight of profits less than that of the commodity produced by a year's unassisted labour. The extreme case is that of a commodity produced by *a day*'s unassisted labour. Clearly, the reasoning Ricardo followed in criticising Smith applies to this case.

Malthus's criticisms led Ricardo to pursue a different line of research. Thus, in the third edition of the *Principles* and especially in his last work, *Absolute value and exchangeable value*, Ricardo referred to an 'average commodity' (an analytical tool that, as we shall see in § 9.7, would be taken up by Marx in a similar context), holding an intermediate position between the commodities whose prices rise and those whose prices decrease when the wage rate increases. If we take such a commodity as our standard, the variations in the prices of other commodities, some increasing and others decreasing, balance out. We thus have the advantage that the national product does not vary in size when income distribution changes, which brings out the fact that increase in one of the distributive shares (for instance, that of rents) has to be offset by decrease in another (for instance, that of profits). However, it is clear that such a choice does not eliminate the 'complications' connected to the theory of value: in order to verify whether increases and decreases in the prices of different commodities exactly cancel out (a point Ricardo does not worry about) we need to formulate an adequate theory of exchange ratios, keeping account of the condition of uniformity of the rate of profits in the different sectors.

Once these difficulties are faced up to, the path Ricardo took in his search for an 'invariable standard of value' appears a dead end. Let us try to see why. Like so many economists since Petty, Ricardo adopted a theory of exchange values based on the relative difficulty of production of the various commodities. The problem of value would then be solved, taking this approach, were it possible to find an exact measure of the difficulty of production. In order to fulfil this task, the invariable standard of value Ricardo was looking for should have a twofold characteristic, namely invariance both with respect to changes in technology and with respect to changes in the distribution of income. Labour required for production fulfils the first requisite, but as far as the second requisite is concerned, it contradicts the assumption – a crucial one for the whole of classical political economy – of a uniform rate of profits in the presence of competition.

Ricardo realised that his efforts in this direction were getting nowhere, but he remained convinced – at a pre-analytical level, we might say – that labour time must have something to do with such an invariable standard of value. This means that there was in Ricardo (as there would be, in still more acute form, in Marx) a metaphysical residuum: the purely analytical problem of a precise measure of value (and of the possibility or impossibility of finding it) was mixed up with the purely metaphysical problem of finding the foundation, the ultimate origin (or, as Marx said, the 'substance') of value: and such an ultimate origin cannot be found but in labour. The confusion between the two problems would only be sorted out by Sraffa, with his analysis of the standard commodity.[25]

The idea that it should be possible to find an 'absolute' measure of the difficulty of production corresponds, in a sense, to the desire to isolate a 'natural' aspect, side by side with the institutional one, in interpreting the functioning of a society based on the division of labour. In this sense, for instance, we may interpret Smith's 1776, p. 65, reference to the 'early and rude state of society' that precedes separation into the classes of workers, capitalists and landlords and in which the labour theory of value holds. However, any such attempt is vitiated by a basic flaw: the division of labour is only possible in the presence of a web of exchanges linking the different sectors of the economy and the different economic agents; the mechanisms of exchange then express not only the relative difficulties of production of the various commodities, but also the institutions, customs and social structure of the society under consideration, since all these elements concur in determining the way economic relationships are established and guarantee the sound functioning of the web of exchanges. No society exists devoid of social institutions, and the idea of an absolute value, grounded on exclusively natural foundations, is therefore a chimera. It is in exchange values that the relations between economic agents find expression, in a society based on the division of labour. Indeed, in all historically recorded human societies the institutional and social elements that govern the web of exchanges determine the rules of the game; exchange ratios, as expression of those rules, must obviously reflect a variety of elements, both technical and institutional. In the case of a capitalistic economy, alongside technology (difficulty of production, in Ricardo's terminology) it is essential to take into account also such elements as the assumption of a uniform rate of profits, expressing at the analytical level an essential characteristic of a capitalistic society, namely the 'competition of capitals'.

5.   Money and taxation

The classical economists, and so of course also Ricardo, are generally attributed with the quantity theory of money. According to this theory variations in the quantity of money in circulation – that are considered as

[25] On this point, cf. Roncaglia 1975, pp. 67–86.

exogenous, that is, independent of the other economic variables – determine variations in the general price level without influencing either the level of production (which, as we saw above in § 2, depends on available production capacity, and hence on the accumulation of capital realised over time) or the velocity of circulation of money, which depends on institutional and customary factors such as frequency in the payments of wages, rents and taxes.

Various elements of this theory already had a long tradition in Ricardo's times. For instance, the notion of velocity of circulation of money dates back as early as authors such as Petty or Locke (cf. above, §§ 3.3 and 4.2), who also considered it to be relatively stable, connecting it to a weighted average of the frequency of the different kinds of payments. The idea that the quantity of money in circulation influences prices was common amongst writers of the sixteenth and seventeenth centuries, confronted with the inflationary phenomena stemming from the discovery of new gold and silver mines in the New World (cf. above, § 2.7). In the eighteenth century David Hume considered the quantity theory of money (namely the hypothesis that prices move in accordance with changes in the quantity of money in circulation) as a well-established fact in his explanation of the automatic adjustment mechanisms of the trade balance (the so-called *flow-specie mechanism*: cf. above, § 4.9).

The different elements that compose the quantity theory of money – from 'Say's law' to the idea of a relatively stable velocity of circulation of money – are all present in Ricardo. However, it is difficult to attribute him with this theory *sic et simpliciter*. The difficulty is that alongside these analytical elements, in themselves sufficient to determine the relationship between money and prices, there are other elements, again concerning this relationship, which contribute to complicate the picture.

First, there is the idea that gold, or more generally precious metals, are produced commodities, so that it is possible to increase their quantity bearing certain costs of production. Therefore the price of gold relative to other commodities is, according to the labour theory of value, determined by the ratio between the quantities of labour directly and indirectly necessary to produce gold and the other commodities.

Second, there is the problem of the relationship between gold and the notes issued by the banks. This is the crux of Ricardo's theory of money. In fact, 'the role of gold in Ricardo's theory is not as money, but as the standard of money, i.e. the means to measure the value of money'.[26] By 'money' Ricardo meant the set of standardised financial

---

[26] Marcuzzo and Rosselli 1994, p. 1253. The interpretation of Ricardo's monetary theory adopted in this section is drawn from this work.

activities commonly used as means of payment, such as the notes issued by the main banks. It was to this notion of money that Ricardo applied the central tenet of the quantity theory: its value changes in inverse relation to their quantity. Such value 'is measured by the purchasing power of money over gold, which is the standard of money'.[27]

In other words, the purchasing power of money (bank notes) relative to commodities in general must be decomposed into two distinct relations: the exchange ratio between money and gold, i.e. the value of money, and the exchange ratio between gold and other commodities. As already noted above, this latter relationship is but a particular case of the general theory of exchange value for produced and reproducible commodities, while the former relationship is dealt with by recourse to the quantity theory.

Ricardo (like others among his contemporaries, and unlike the modern followers of the quantity theory) did not consider the problem of how to deduce the level of prices from the quantity of money. This would have implied not only simultaneous consideration of the two distinct relationships mentioned above, but also continuous information on the quantity of money in circulation. Now, such a quantity is quite difficult to observe, and above all the conditions of supply and demand that should determine the 'natural' quantity of money corresponding to an equilibrium (i.e. stable) level of prices are extremely variable. Thus, in Ricardo's analysis the crucial variable for monetary policy was not the price level of the commodities but the value of money, that is its ratio of exchange with gold: when this ratio is stable, then the quantity of money, which remains unknown, is at its natural level.[28] Furthermore, through the use of gold as the standard of money it is possible to determine, whenever the money price of a commodity changes, whether this happens for 'real' reasons, which can be traced to technology and income distribution, or for 'monetary' reasons, which can be traced to changes in the quantity of money: in the first case, it is the ratio of exchange between commodity and gold that varies, while in the second case it is the value of money that varies in terms of its standard, namely gold.

It was with this analytic structure that Ricardo tackled the monetary debates of his times, and in particular the bullionist controversy, which

---

[27] Ibid. In other terms, a rise of the market price of bullion above its natural value indicates over-issue of currency.

[28] As a corollary of this view, Ricardo displayed confidence in the automatic equilibrating mechanisms of the gold standard, and in any case a preference for fixed rules in economic policy rather than discretionary interventions, in contrast to those who (like Thornton) insisted on the possibility of crises of confidence and on the expediency, in such cases, of active interventions on the part of the central bank. Marcuzzo and Rosselli (1994, p. 1261), recalling this controversy, noted that the Bank Charter Act of 1844 drew more on Ricardo's ideas than on Thornton's.

had seen him playing a leading role since his 1809 contributions, and which moreover saw all the major economists of the time involved.[29]

The main contribution to the debate was the *Enquiry into the nature and effects of the paper credit of Great Britain* (1802) by Henry Thornton (1760–1815), banker and Member of Parliament.[30] Preceding Ricardo in this, Thornton considered the link between prices and quantity of money indirect and hence not automatic; in his case, however, the intermediary element was represented by the discount rate. Also, preceding Wicksell (cf. below, § 11.5), Thornton analysed the process of credit expansion, connecting it to the divergence between the bank rate of interest and the rate of profits. In this context, Thornton attributed an active role to the monetary policy choices of the central bank.

The debate on monetary problems took on new life a couple of decades later with confrontation between the *Currency School* and the *Banking School* over the way banks function and the rules which the issue of notes should be subjected (or not subjected) to. Culminating in the adoption of Peel's Bank Charter Act in 1844, the debate was fuelled by protagonists of the Currency School like Robert Torrens (cf. below, § 8.2), Lord Overstone (1796–1883) and Mountifort Longfield (cf. below, § 8.7), while on the opposite side, with the Banking School, we find Thomas Tooke,[31] John Fullarton (1780?–1849) and John Stuart Mill (cf. below, § 8.9). The distinction between the Currency School and the Banking School is traditionally based on the active or passive role attributed to

[29] The controversy concerned, among other things, the responsibility of the Bank of England for the inflation recorded in the immediately preceding years, following suspension – in 1797 – of the obligation to reimburse its notes in gold. This was obviously a controversy with an important political component. Critics of the Bank of England (among whom we may number Ricardo, though he was not a member of the committee) prevailed in the parliamentary committee which prepared the famous *Bullion report* of 1810, and were named 'bullionists'; their opponents were named 'anti-bullionists'. These latter accepted the so-called 'real bills doctrine', according to which notes issued by the banks corresponded to credit granted by discounting sound commercial bills, so that note issues corresponded to the needs of trade; however, this 'doctrine' left aside notes issued for financing government debt or banks' losses. The controversy ended with the return to gold convertibility at the pre-war parity, decided with Peel's Resumption Act of 1819, which among other things incorporated some of Ricardo's suggestions (such as the convertibility of notes into ingots, rather than coins) aiming at favouring the use of notes as circulating medium.

[30] Thornton was a leading member of the Bullion Committee, and a co-author of the *Bullion report*. His *Enquiry* was republished in 1939, in the series of the Library of Economics of the London School of Economics, with an extensive introduction by Hayek. On Thornton cf. also Beaugrand 1981.

[31] Thomas Tooke (1774–1858) is known for the extensive *History of prices, 1793–1856*, in six volumes (Tooke, 1838–57) and for the *Inquiry into the currency principle* (1844). A friend of Ricardo, Malthus and James Mill, he was among the founders of the Political Economy Club (cf. below, § 8.1). On his contributions to the debates of the time and on his life, cf. Arnon 1991.

banks in the process of creation of the circulating medium (or, in other terms, on the exogenous or endogenous nature – in response to variations in demand – of the money supply). In reality, however, the different positions were more varied, and the differences between authors traditionally classified as belonging to the two groups – which cannot be considered as 'schools' in the strict meaning of the term – were far less clear-cut than in the case of the bullionists and anti-bullionists, to the extent that some protagonists of the debate seemed to shift from one side of the field to the other.[32]

As with monetary issues, so it was with taxation: Ricardo took on practical issues of the day, and applied to them his analytical framework, with results that, thanks to their solid theoretical background, had far-reaching impact on the current policy debate. Let us briefly touch on two issues: direct and indirect taxes, public debt and the so-called 'Ricardian equivalence theorem'.

Taxes, however levied, ultimately fell on the surplus: thus, since Ricardo assumed natural wages to be at subsistence level, taxes ultimately fell on profits and rents. Since profits constituted the source of capital accumulation, and thus of economic development, while rents were commonly destined to luxury consumption, taxes on rents constituted a theoretically optimal solution. However, for policy reasons Ricardo favoured a wider tax base, embracing together with rents also wages (and so, indirectly, profits), and interest on government securities. This view ran counter to the prevailing opinion among the classical economists, mostly favourable to indirect taxes in view of practical considerations.[33] Ricardo also noted that taxes on specific commodities, but also a uniform tax on profits (which is bound to have differential effects on the various sectors for the very reasons that cause deviations of natural prices from labour values), give rise to costly readjustments through capital flows away from the trades hit by the taxes and consequent changes in relative prices.

[32] The debates between bullionists and anti-bullionists, and between the Banking School and Currency School, are illustrated in Schumpeter 1954, pp. 688 ff.; cf. also O'Brien 1975, ch. 6 and Rotelli 1982. Schumpeter 1954, p. 727, stressed that both the Banking School and the Currency School 'were equally averse to monetary management or any thoroughgoing control of banking and credit' and were 'staunch supporters of the gold standard'; however, while according to the Banking School 'convertibility of notes was enough to secure all the monetary stability of which a capitalist system is capable', according to the Currency principle 'convertibility of notes cannot be assured without special restrictions upon their issue'.

[33] In England, 'the *income tax* [. . .] introduced in 1799, abandoned in 1816, and then reintroduced in 1842 [. . . was] characterised by widespread fraud and evasion [. . .]. *Commodity taxes* were seen as the major source of revenue' (O'Brien 2003, p. 125; cf. also O'Brien 1975, ch. 9). McCulloch also thought that adequately structured indirect taxes could hinder consumption, especially luxury consumption, and stimulate savings, and hence accumulation.

As for the public debt, which had grown considerably during the Napoleonic wars, Ricardo was in favour of reimbursement, setting out various proposals to this end. At the analytical level, in chapter 17 of the *Principles* he maintained that taxation should be preferred to public debt for financing war expenditure because of the negative impact the latter had on savings, and hence on private investments. Thus, he did not believe in what was later dubbed the 'Ricardian equivalence theorem', namely the equivalence between taxes and debt as ways of financing public expenditure.[34]

6.   International trade and the theory of comparative costs

International trade was among the most keenly debated issues of the seventeenth century. However, the numerous tracts on trade, which we referred to above, in § 2.6, constitute a somewhat primitive stage in work on the problem; only with Antonio Serra and Thomas Mun, for instance, do we have a sufficiently precise notion of the balance of trade and the various items composing it. Overall, there was the idea that in international trade merchants of one country earn by importing at low prices and exporting at high prices, at the expense of producers of other countries. Recalling that precious metals constitute the basis for the monetary systems of all countries, we arrive directly at a theory of 'absolute advantages', according to which each country exports those commodities that it succeeds in producing at a lower cost than other countries.

In this respect Ricardo took a decisive step forward with his theory of 'comparative costs'.[35] According to this theory, each country specialises in the production of those commodities for which it enjoys a relative advantage in the cost of production. This means that there can be international trade between two countries even if, in terms of difficulty of production (expressed in terms of the hours of labour necessary for their production), all commodities have a higher cost in one country than in the other. For instance, if it takes ten hours of labour to obtain one measure of cloth and one hour for a litre of wine in Portugal, while in England the same cloth and wine take twenty and five hours respectively, England will therefore export cloth and import wine. In fact, international trade

---

[34] The equivalence theorem (Barro 1974) requires not only perfect foresight (rational expectations), but also the identification of the interest rate with the economic agents' rate of time preference – a notion which is wholly alien to Ricardo.

[35] There has been a debate on the extent to which Torrens 1815 may be credited with first publication of this theory (cf. below, § 8.2); as indicated above (note 17), an attribution of the theory to James Mill (while helping Ricardo with the writing of the *Principles*) has also been suggested.

is advantageous when it allows a country to obtain a commodity from a foreign country at a cost – in terms of commodities exported – lower than that necessary to produce it internally. Let us assume that, in the absence of foreign trade, in each of the two countries relative prices are determined, in accordance with the labour theory of value, by the ratio between the quantities of labour required to produce the different commodities. In such a situation, when considering the expediency of foreign trade, we see that an English merchant can acquire ten litres of wine in Portugal in exchange for one measure of cloth, which costs him twenty hours of labour; thus the English merchant pays two hours of labour for each litre of wine, while producing it in England would take five hours, that is, two and a half times as much.

Obviously, exchange ratios will not in general be so favourable to the English merchants; in any case, for any exchange ratio intermediate between that prevailing in England and that prevailing in Portugal in the absence of international trade,[36] both countries will benefit from trade, since they will obtain imported goods in exchange for the product of a number of hours lower than that required in the case of internal production. Both countries become richer thanks to foreign trade. This is the most important point in Ricardo's theory.

Ricardo's theory of comparative costs was based on the existence of differences between the technological structures of the different countries. Nothing was said on the origin of such differences (equally attributable for instance to climate, localisation, endowment of natural resources, workers' skills, technological knowledge, past capital accumulation). It would be up to marginalist theory, with the so-called Heckscher–Ohlin–Samuelson (HOS) theorem, to connect such differences with the different endowments of the 'factors of production': capital, land and labour.[37] It was, however, on a critique of the assumption of given technologies in the two countries that the defence of protectionism was based, pointing out the difficulties faced by countries lagging behind in the industrialisation process. This thesis, known as the 'infant industry argument', was already being argued around the mid-nineteenth century by

---

[36] The exchange values of the different commodities – determined on the basis of the labour theory of value – within each of the two countries constitute the extremes between which we find the relative prices at which international exchanges take place. The nearer the relative price of a commodity in foreign trade is to its internal exchange value, determined on the basis of the labour theory of value, the smaller is the advantage the country in question derives from foreign trade. On the subject of the determination of relative prices in foreign trade, which Ricardo did not take into consideration, there were subsequently important contributions by John Stuart Mill (cf. below, § 8.10) and Alfred Marshall (cf. below, § 13.2).

[37] Cf. Samuelson 1948b; for a critique of the HOS theorem, cf. below, § 16.9.

German and American economists; we may mention in particular Friedrich List (1789–1846), and his *Das nationale System der politischen Oekonomie* (1841).[38] Other, more recent, criticisms stressed the possibility that international trade influences the technological differences between the different countries, compounding them and rendering them permanent. These criticisms concern the presence of increasing returns to scale, such that the international division of labour itself becomes the cause of an increasing gap between the technological structures of countries involved in foreign trade (Krugman 1990). While constituting important qualifications to the free trade policies, however, these criticisms did not invalidate Ricardo's thesis on the immediate advantage that opening to foreign trade implies for the countries concerned – an advantage equivalent to an improvement in the technology in use.

7.   On machinery: technological change and employment

We have already discussed 'Say's law' and its variants. In the variant adopted by Ricardo, 'Say's law' states that supply and demand are equal for any level of income, hence for any level of employment. The background to this statement was, however, different from that of today's industrialised countries. As we have already noted, for a long period in the initial stage of capitalistic accumulation the capitalistic core of the economy coexisted with a large traditional sector in agriculture and artisan activities; the problem of the poor, already important in the sixteenth and seventeenth centuries, primarily concerned workers driven from the land, especially in the stage of the first agricultural revolution, characterised by enclosures, and subsequently also workers squeezed out from their traditional artisan activities. In substance, we may interpret 'Say's law' not as a statement on the absence of involuntary unemployment (which is the variant criticised by Keynes), but as stating the absence of demand difficulties hindering the growth of the capitalistic core of the economy.

Adam Smith, as we saw above, may be considered a precursor of 'Say's law', interpreted as a statement on the possibility of economic growth in response to the increasing division of labour and the increase in the productivity of labour stemming from it. To Smith we may thus attribute the idea that technical progress is not a source of occupational difficulties, in the sense that increase in per capita productivity was seen to translate into an increase in production, absorbed by a greater demand (corresponding

[38] List received attention for his support to the *Zollverein*, the customs union that constituted (Schumpeter 1954, p. 504) 'the embryo of German national unity'.

to an improved standard of living), and not into a decrease in employed workers, production remaining unchanged.

Smith's view gradually became a cornerstone of the classical school in its golden age. In fact, we may derive from it the more specific 'theory of compensation'. According to this theory, technological progress, when introduced in a given sector, generates unemployment not only in the sector itself, but also, in a first stage, in the economy as a whole. However, in a subsequent stage the jobs lost in the first sector are made up for by new jobs in other sectors, and the general standard of living improves. This is due to the fact that technical progress implies a reduction in costs in the sector where it is introduced, and hence a decrease in the price of the product; this brings out a generalised increase in real incomes all over the economy, which then generates an increase in demand. In turn, this induces an increase in production and hence in employment, since in the other sectors the technology is by assumption unchanged. In other words, the decrease in employment in the sector in which technical progress takes place is 'compensated' for by an increase in employment in other sectors.

The theory of compensation was accepted by Ricardo, too; in a long letter to McCulloch dated 29 March 1820,[39] Ricardo reproached him for having supported a contrasting thesis, developed by John Barton in a short pamphlet, *On the conditions of the labouring classes*, published in 1817. In the depressed conditions following the conclusion of the Napoleonic wars, Barton's argument – more at the level of applied economics than of a theoretical nature – had appeared sensible to many, notwithstanding the ideological reprimand of the extremists of classical political economy. Ricardo's authority in those years helped in no small measure to assert the compensation theory as an integral part of the body of classical political economy. However, on the occasion of the third edition of the *Principles* (1821), a *coup de théâtre* took place: Ricardo abandoned the theory of compensation, and analytically developed the thesis that introduction of machinery in a sector may imply reduction of employment in the economy as a whole.

The crucial point that we have to take into account is that, while Smith considered technological progress in general, Barton and Ricardo focused attention on a specific form of technical progress, that connected with the introduction of new machinery: a specific form but, in the context of capitalistic accumulation, such an important species as to be identifiable with the genus as a whole.

---

[39] Ricardo 1951–5, vol. 8, pp. 168–73.

Thus, in a chapter 'On machinery' added to the third edition of the *Principles*, Ricardo showed, with reasoning supported by arithmetical examples,[40] that the introduction of machinery may generate unemployment.

Ricardo's reasoning may be summarised thus. The capitalist introduces new machinery with a view to generating an increase in profits. Since the net product of the economy was identified by Ricardo with profits and rents, the increase in profits for an entrepreneur (or for a group of entrepreneurs) that does not stem from a decrease in the profits of some other entrepreneur or from a reduction in rents corresponds to an increase in society's net income. However, the investment in machinery implies the decision to employ a certain number of workers in the production of machinery. If such workers were previously employed in producing subsistence goods, the production of new machinery is accompanied by correspondingly lower production of subsistence goods and hence – in Ricardo's terms – by a reduction in gross income (corresponding to net income, that is, to the surplus – profits and rents – plus 'necessary consumption', that is, wages). As a consequence, the number of labourers that the economy can maintain necessarily decreases. Thus employment decreases, and this decrease, although destined to be reabsorbed by the higher rhythm of accumulation allowed for by the growth in net income, may be far from negligible in the immediate aftermath and may persist for a sufficiently long span of time as to be hard to dismiss as a temporary event.

The provocative stance taken by Ricardo, a typical manifestation of his intellectual honesty and passion for logical rigour, which left political implications at a secondary level, stirred up heated debate. The theory of compensation had assumed a central role within the substantially optimistic view of economic development supported by the classical school within what had in fact become a canonical view. Thus, apart from the immediate response (such as McCulloch's), Ricardo's argument was simply ignored, while the major protagonists of the economic debate in the decades immediately following his death restated in their most widely read writings a substantially unchanged theory of compensation.[41]

---

[40] Hicks committed a gross mistake in this respect in the first edition of his *An essay on economic history*, when he maintained (Hicks 1969, p. 168) that Ricardo's new chapter on machinery does not contain numerical examples: a mistake that was immediately corrected, and that we recall here because it constitutes a striking example both of the existence of objective criteria of evaluation of the different theses, also within the field of the history of economic thought, and of the need to constantly check in the original sources information given by secondary sources.

[41] Berg 1980 provides an account of the debate on mechanisation in the context of the economic situation of the time.

In any case, an interesting aspect of this episode worth stressing is a difficulty that brilliant economists evidently experienced in their efforts at analytical construction, that is, their efforts to adhere systematically to a canonical view which later, simplified reconstructions identify, *sic et simpliciter*, with their thoughts.[42]

---

[42] Something similar, as we shall see on various occasions below, also happens for the 'harmonic view of society', traditionally associated with the marginalist approach, while at least some of its major representatives – for instance Walras or Wicksell – supported theses that are far from conservative.

8   The 'Ricardians' and the decline of Ricardianism

1.   The forces in the field

Still admired for its clear, logical structure, Ricardo's theoretical construction constituted essential reference for anyone tackling economic issues after the publication of the *Principles*. However, this does not mean that a *pax ricardiana* then emerged, although a number of commentators see it precisely in these terms. Even Ricardo's followers, in the course of the controversies, often abandoned this or that aspect of his analysis, or introduced more or less important changes in the concepts utilised in the analysis, thus opening the way to a true change of paradigm with the so-called 'marginalist revolution'. Moreover, among the economists of the time we find many exponents of an approach radically different from Ricardo's, which looked to supply and demand, scarcity and utility, rather than the relative difficulty of production, to determine exchange values.

Ricardo's authority was undoubtedly very strong. His political goal – the abolition of customs duties – and his dynamic vision, including the profits–accumulation link, constituted a canonical model for more than fifty years after the publication of the *Principles*. His friends and followers, important as they were in their own right, and indeed intellectually autonomous, considered his analysis the light shining on their path, and even the critics of political economy (the 'dismal science' deprecated by Carlyle: cf. above, § 6.2) identified it with the 'Ricardian' school.

However, the debate waxed lively even within the walls of that quintessentially 'Ricardian' institution, the Political Economy Club (although its foundation, in 1821, and proceedings also saw the participation of Malthus, among others). Only a few years after Ricardo's death a question raised for debate at one of the meetings was just how much life was there still left in his theories.[1] Even the most important

---

[1] Cf. Political Economy Club 1921; this volume, published on the occasion of the centenary of the Political Economy Club, collects the most interesting material gathered from the volumes published in the 1880s and today somewhat rare, to which we refer in the following notes.

of his direct followers, like John Stuart Mill (author of the text – in 1848 – which Ricardianism had to thank for its lasting influence in the second half of the nineteenth century), modified certain crucial points in Ricardo's theoretical construction.

Of course, economic debate intersected with political debate, as comparison between the major cultural journals of the time clearly demonstrates: the *Edinburgh Review*, founded in 1802, showed a Whig leaning, favourable to reforms and supporting Ricardo's ideas, the *Quarterly Review*, founded in 1809, a Tory orientation, while the *Westminster Review*, founded in 1824 and close to Bentham's utilitarianism and the philosophical radicalism of his followers, was also favourable to Ricardo's ideas in the economic sphere.[2]

In the following sections we will summarise the debate as it progressed in the fifty years separating Ricardo from Jevons. The field saw many protagonists involved in a complex play of interrelations and confrontations of issues and theories centring, naturally, on Ricardo's thought. Lined up by his side were his most faithful friends: James Mill and McCulloch. On the right wing, after his friend and rival, Malthus, came Bailey and, above all, Senior, Lloyd, Scrope and various others. On the left wing, the 'Ricardian socialists' can be separated into two currents: the relatively moderate supporters of cooperativism and the rather more resolute advocates of ethical interpretations of the theory of labour value. On the inside right we can place Torrens, and possibly a sweeper like De Quincey; the corresponding role on the other side, the inside left, should go to John Stuart Mill (although precisely this fact shows just how schematic and reductive this linear representation of the positions in the field really is).

As we see, the debate took place largely in England: at least as far as political economy was concerned, the centre of European and world culture in the central decades of the nineteenth century was London, not Paris.[3] There are various reasons for this, but they cannot be reduced

---

[2] Articles published in these journals are commonly anonymous; for their attribution, and more generally to reconstruct the role of these journals in the economic debates of the time, cf. Fetter 1953, 1958, 1962a, 1965.

[3] Among the economists active in France in the first half of the nineteenth century, together with Jean-Baptiste Say and Simonde de Sismondi, already considered above (§§ 6.3 and 6.4), and Antoine-Augustin Cournot who will be discussed later (§ 10.2), we may mention here a few names, referring the reader for fuller analysis to Breton and Lutfalla 1991. Claude Frédéric Bastiat (1801–50) is known as a propagandist of liberalism and as a supporter of the thesis of 'economic harmonies' (which is also the title of his best-known work: Bastiat 1850), namely an optimistic view that liquidated social conflicts in the general tendency to economic progress; Schumpeter 1954, p. 500, considered him 'the most brilliant economic journalist who ever lived'; Spiegel 1971, p. 362, stressed his verve, recalling the ironic *Petition of the candlemakers*, in which the candlemakers ask the government to prohibit windows lest their activity be damaged by unfair competition

(although Schumpeter seems to have suspected it) to the Anglo-centrism of today's historians of economic thought. In part it was the economic conditions (namely the role of England as the leading country in the process of industrialisation), in part the presence of some exceptional personalities, like Ricardo himself, and the direct influence that such personalities exerted in the development of a culture flourishing on direct contacts (for instance through the Political Economy Club) – the various elements concurring to make English the language of political economy, in a measure unknown up to then.[4]

2.   Robert Torrens[5]

Among the first critics of the Ricardian theory of labour value, Robert Torrens (1780–1864), a heroic officer of the Royal Marines and for some years a Member of Parliament, merits a front-line position, both

from the light of the sun. Adolphe Blanqui (1798–1854), an economic historian and historian of economic thought, brother to Louis Blanqui known for his participation in the 1848 uprising, was teacher of political economy at the Conservatoire des Arts and des Métiers of Paris, holding the chair that had been Say's. Michel Chevalier (1806–79) held for many years a chair at the Collège de France. Also Charles Ganilh (1758–1836) and Joseph Garnier (1813–81) were mainly historians of economic thought and divulgers, authors of textbooks with no substantial theoretical novelty. Separate consideration must be given to Pellegrino Rossi (1787–1848), an Italian (born in Carrara, died in Rome) but professor in Paris (after Say and before Blanqui) and author of a tract and various economic writings in French. On the Italian economists of the time (among whom we may at least mention Melchiorre Gioja, 1767–1829, Francesco Fuoco, 1774–1841, and Carlo Cattaneo, 1801–69), see Faucci 2000, pp. 127–83. Cattaneo in particular would deserve attention, both for his personality, his ideas and the influence he had on European culture. Like Smith, he considered economic and political liberty as strongly connected; he was an active spokesman for economic reforms in agriculture, construction of infrastructures (railways) and the abolition of all feudal remnants, including special legislation on Jews; politically he upheld republican federalism, with projects for the United States of Europe, in opposition to all forms of centralised government, including that connected to socialist public ownership, and in opposition to nationalistic attitudes, thus to protectionism. His notion of the economic agent is connected to the idea of the good citizen; economic, cultural and civic progress appear in his writings as one and the same thing.

[4] Mention should also be made here of the divulgers of political economy, who wrote for a general readership, first place going to Jane Marcet (1769–1858), who followed a successful volume of *Conversations on chemistry* (1806) with the *Conversations in political economy* (1816), which went through many reprints: this lively, up-to-date text (it took into account the debate on the Corn Laws of 1815) expressed the mainstream opinion of the time and had considerable influence. The stories by Harriet Martineau (1802–76) also belong to the same kind of literature; her *Illustrations of political economy* (1832–4) were based on James Mill's Ricardian text, the *Elements of political economy* of 1821.

[5] Part of the material in this section is drawn from Roncaglia 1972. On Torrens's life, cf. Meenai 1956 and Fetter 1962b; on his work as an economist, Robbins 1958, who in a meticulous appendix (ibid., pp. 259–348) lists all the writings remaining to us, summarising their content. Cf. also the recent edition of Torrens's works, in eight volumes (Torrens 2000), and De Vivo's erudite and insightful editorial introductions.

chronologically and because along with his criticisms of Ricardo we find proposal of a different theory. Nevertheless, his theory remained within the conceptual framework of the Ricardian system, of which Torrens shared both the theory of accumulation and various specific aspects that we shall not dwell upon here, focusing rather on his contributions to the theory of differential rent and the theory of international trade.

In order to evaluate Torrens's role among the classical economists let us recall that in 1821, a few months before publication of his main work, the *Essay on the production of wealth*, he was among the founders of the Political Economy Club and chaired its first meeting, in the presence of Ricardo, Malthus, James Mill, Tooke and various other more or less well-known personalities of the time.[6] Conceived as a core of political pressure for the abolition of the Corn Laws,[7] the Political Economy Club was a vital centre of debate on the main themes of political economy, strengthening those personal connections that already existed among the various protagonists. Torrens participated in practically all the meetings, often proposing topics for debate; for instance, his was the theme discussed on 7 April 1823 – 'What are the circumstances that determine the exchangeable value of commodities?'[8] – which, together with publication of Malthus's *Measure of value* (1823), was possibly the immediate origin of Ricardo's last writing on *Absolute value and exchangeable value*.

Torrens first entered the field in 1808, intervening – with *The economists refuted* – in the debate on the economic effects of the continental blockade imposed by Napoleon. In the previous year Spence had maintained that the blockade, which hit the English foreign trade, could not have damaged the nation, whose wealth sprang solely from its agriculture.[9] Spence's theses were but a rigorous corollary of physiocratic theory; in order to criticise them, Torrens was led to attack the physiocratic stronghold. Returning to Smith's criticisms, Torrens pointed out among other things that the manufacturing sector, too, and not only the agricultural one, produces a surplus, adding that products of the former sector enter side by side with products of the latter among the means of subsistence, and that both groups of products are necessary to productive activity. Finally, coming to an aspect more directly relevant to the debate on the continental blockade, he stressed the advantages of trade in favouring the division of labour, formulating the fortunate expression 'territorial division of labour'. All

---

[6] On Torrens's participation in the foundation of the Political Economy Club, cf. Political Economy Club 1882, in particular pp. 35–54.

[7] At least this is what the official accounts of the Club say (ibid., pp. 11–22).

[8] Cf. Political Economy Club 1882, p. 59.

[9] William Spence (1783–1860), *Britain independent of commerce* (1807). Before Torrens's pamphlet, this work provoked a reaction from James Mill, and it was in this context that the latter proposed his version of 'Say's law' (cf. above, § 6.3).

such arguments were reproposed at length in the *Essay on the production of wealth*.

Torrens returned to the advantages of the territorial division of labour in 1815, with *An essay on the external corn trade*, which represented his contribution to the debate on the Corn Laws. A few days before Torrens's essay came out, two pamphlets by Malthus and one by West were published (respectively on 3, 10 and 13 February), and on the same day as Torrens's (24 February), Ricardo's *Essay on profits*. The near-simultaneity of these different publications gave rise to two problems of attribution for historians of economic thought, the first concerning the theory of rent, the second the theory of comparative costs.

As far as rent is concerned, the issue was finally settled by Sraffa,[10] attributing priority of publication to Malthus; West, and possibly Torrens (who quoted the second of Malthus's pamphlets in his essay), were credited with independent formulation, while Ricardo for his part explicitly declared his debt to Malthus. Unlike the other pamphlets, Torrens's only considered the cultivation of ever less fertile lands, and not the use of additional doses of capital on lands already farmed, showing a degree of caution that was to be shared by Ricardo in his *Principles*, and which might have been taken as a sign of remarkable theoretical rigour – as Sraffa observed in 1925 – had Torrens not abandoned it in his *Essay on the production of wealth*.

The second of the two problems of attribution, concerning the theory of comparative costs, was the object of lively debate at the beginning of the twentieth century. On the one hand, Seligman (1903) maintained Torrens's priority, among other things recalling a few passages from *The economists refuted*, while on the other hand, Jacob Hollander (1910), much more convincingly, vindicated the originality of the Ricardian formulation. Indeed Torrens, while relying on the advantages of the territorial division of labour in his theory of international trade, developed his analysis in terms of differences between the costs of producing the same commodity in the different countries, and not in terms of differences between countries in the cost structure for different commodities.[11]

---

[10] P. Sraffa, *Note on 'Essay on Profits'*, in Ricardo 1951–5, vol. 4, pp. 3–8.

[11] In other words, we may say that Torrens looked to the effects (the advantageousness of purchasing a given commodity in another country, and not within the national boundaries) rather than the causes (the comparison between the relative difficulty of production of a given commodity in the various countries). Also based on the territorial division of labour – Hollander 1910 remarks – was the chapter on 'Mercantile industry' in the *Essay on the production of wealth*, which came out four years after the publication of Ricardo's *Principles*. Sraffa 1930b shared Hollander's opinion; Viner 1937, pp. 346–9, and after him Robbins 1958, pp. 21–5, took up Seligman's opinion more or less explicitly, but brought nothing new to the debate.

The following years saw Torrens engaging in the debate on the theory of labour value. In October 1818, in a review of Ricardo's *Principles*, Torrens (1818) interpreted the theory of labour value set out in it as a rigid statement of proportionality between relative prices (or exchange values) and the quantities of labour contained in the various commodities. Against this 'law' Torrens remarked the importance of exceptions, due to different organic composition of capital in different industries and different lengths of active life of fixed capital goods. (In a personal note to Ricardo, Torrens also raised a third critical point concerning different velocities of rotation of circulating capital in different productive processes.)[12] Consequently the theory of labour value was to be rejected, and substituted with a theory endowed with general validity: 'When capitalists and labourers become distinct, it is always the amount of capital, and never the amount of labour, expended on production, which determines the exchangeable value of commodities.'[13]

Torrens returned to this statement in the closing pages of the first chapter of his *Essay on the production of wealth*. His solution lay in the thesis that products of equal capitals have equal exchange value. These are generic expressions, repeated again and again, with respect to which the charge of circular reasoning advanced by Ricardo appears justified: 'I would ask what means you have of ascertaining the equal value of capitals? [. . .] These capitals are not the same in kind [. . .] and if they themselves are produced in unequal times they are subject to the same fluctuations as other commodities. Till you have fixed the criterion by which we are to ascertain value, you can say nothing of equal capitals.'[14]

In other words, if we determine the relative prices of commodities on the basis of the values of capitals employed in producing them, how can we then explain the value of capital, made up of heterogeneous means of production? However, as we shall see, the arithmetical examples which Torrens used to illustrate his analysis contained precious pointers to go on beyond Ricardo's criticisms and develop a Sraffian theory of prices of production.

The first examples in the *Essay* seem to confirm Ricardo's strictures: the commodities produced are different from the commodities utilised as means of production, the prices of the latter and the rate of profit being assigned in a wholly arbitrary way. As we go on, however, the

---

[12] The note has not been found, but its existence and contents were reconstructed by Sraffa (in Ricardo 1951–5, vol. 4, pp. 305–6).

[13] Torrens 1818, p. 337.

[14] Letter by Ricardo to McCulloch, 21 August 1823 (in Ricardo 1951–5, vol. 9, pp. 359–60), quoted by Sraffa 1951, p. xlix. Cf. also the essay on *Absolute value and exchangeable value*, in Ricardo 1951–5, vol. 4, pp. 393–6.

examples become better fitted to the issue: in the chapter on agriculture a model with one basic commodity was generally utilised (corn produced by means of corn and labour, and corn was also the means of subsistence) until finally, discussing the effects of a technological improvement in the manufacturing sector on the levels of production in the agricultural sector, Torrens was compelled to utilise a model with two basic commodities.

The commodities taken into consideration were the produce of the agricultural sector and the product of the manufacturing sector. The workers' subsistence, according to a procedure common among classical economists and constantly adopted by Torrens, is directly included among the means of production. Given the wage rate in physical terms, there remain to be determined the rate of profits and the relative price of one of the commodities in terms of the other.

In Torrens's example, immediate determination of the unknowns was only possible thanks to some peculiarities of the example: the rate of profits may be determined as a physical ratio between the capitals employed in their production only because these capitals have equal proportional commodity composition in the two sectors.[15] It is understandable enough that Torrens chose to give this form to his example precisely for the sake of the simple computations it implies, although translation in terms of a system of equations raises no great difficulties for today's readers. Thus we see[16] that Torrens's example displays substantive analogy with the first example of production with a surplus which Sraffa presents in his book (wheat and iron produced by means of wheat and iron: Sraffa 1960, p. 7), and we may indeed wonder whether the theory of prices of production formulated by Sraffa might be taken as full, rigorous expression of Torrens's vague intuitions.

Thus Torrens circumvented the obstacle of different organic compositions of capital in the various sectors by including wage goods among capital goods and setting out a theory of prices based on difficulty of production expressed in physical terms, namely as quantities of the different means of production utilised to obtain a given output, rather than on the quantity of labour directly and indirectly required for production. Two other problems remained, which Torrens himself had recalled in his criticism of the theory of labour value: namely, the different velocities of rotation of circulating capital, and the existence of fixed capital goods.

---

[15] As far as the first aspect is concerned, Torrens foreshadowed Sraffa's 'standard commodity' (1960, ch. 4), while the second aspect brings us back to a one-commodity world, since the two goods are indistinguishable in the only relevant aspect here, the technique of production.

[16] Cf. Roncaglia 1972, pp. xx–xxi.

Torrens made only passing reference to the issue of the velocity of rotation of circulating capital: when for a given quantity of capital employed in production this velocity increases, there arises an advantage for society but – he added – the details are rather complex. More interesting is the way Torrens addressed the issue of the existence of fixed capital goods, first raised by Ricardo in his *Principles*. Torrens's method consisted in considering fixed capital as a specific kind of joint product; machines used in production appear among the outputs of the same production process, side by side with outputs proper, and reappear among the means of production in the following period.[17] This method was then adopted by Ricardo, Malthus and Marx; more recently, it reappeared in von Neumann's model (1945), while it is to Sraffa (1960, ch. 10), once again, that we owe a rigorous analysis of the problem.

Various other interesting theoretical pointers may be found in Torrens's pages, such as a suggestion on how to take account of commercial intermediation within a 'classical' model of price determination, or some references to price determination under non-competitive conditions, based on a shrewd distinction between what Sraffa (1960) was later to call basic and non-basic commodities.

In the 1830s Torrens focused mainly on colonial policy issues (cf. above, § 6.6) and international trade. In particular, elaborating on some ideas already present in the *Essay on the production of wealth* and developing them to their extreme conclusions, Torrens criticised the advocates of complete freedom in international trade.[18] He maintained, in fact, that by imposing customs duties a country is able to modify exchange ratios to its own advantage, and as a consequence criticised the unilateral abolition of customs duties, proposed in England by many free traders with particular reference to the Corn Laws. Rather, he favoured a policy of reciprocity, with customs abolished (or lowered) only towards countries adopting a similar policy. Moreover, since such reciprocity is more easily obtained with the colonies, whose local governments were emanations of the central government of the United Kingdom, the combative colonel of the Royal Marines advocated the creation of an imperial free trade area.

---

[17] Cf. Torrens 1818, p. 337: 'When capitals equal in amount, but of different degrees of durability, are employed, the articles produced, together with the residue of capital, in one occupation, will be equal to the things produced, and the residue of capital in another occupation.' The passage quoted and the numerical example that preceded it were taken up again in the *Essay on the production of wealth* (Torrens 1821, ch. 1).

[18] In so far as the theory of international trade is concerned, thus, in some respects Torrens preceded John Stuart Mill.

In the 1840s Torrens spent his energies above all on monetary theory and policy. The subject had attracted him since 1812, when he had published a long anti-bullionist treatise arguing that maintenance of a monetary regime based on metal alone could generate dangerous deflationary pressures, and showing preference for a regime of paper – even inconvertible – money.[19] However, in the 1840s we find Torrens holding just the opposite views as leading exponent, together with Lord Overstone,[20] of the Currency School. Opposing Tooke's and Fullarton's Banking School (cf. above, § 7.5), Torrens and his friends maintained that convertibility of paper money into gold was a necessary but not a sufficient condition to ensure the stability of the system. Therefore, they advocated rigorous limitations to issues of paper money, by means of which 'the currency would always be maintained in the same state, with respect both to amount and to value, in which it would exist were the circulation composed exclusively of the precious metals'.[21] In particular, division of the Bank of England into an issue department and a banking department was advocated; subsequently this was accomplished with the Peel Act of 1844.[22]

Torrens's radical change of opinion constitutes an interesting subject for debate among historians of economic thought; it is, however, undeniable that in both positions (and particularly in the more mature one) Torrens played a leading role.

3.   Samuel Bailey[23]

Torrens's criticisms of Ricardo's theory of value were in one important respect similar to, and in another different from, the criticisms advanced by a quiet provincial gentleman, Samuel Bailey (1791–1870), who was born, lived and died in Sheffield, joining in the economic debate of the time with some original ideas but remaining on the fringe of the circle associated with the Political Economy Club. In a work dated 1825, *A*

---

[19] Torrens 1812; cf. Robbins 1958, pp. 97 ff. and 265–6.

[20] Samuel Jones Lloyd, Lord Overstone (1796–1883) played a central role in the controversies leading to the Bank Charter Act of 1844 and for the following three decades. The three-volume edition of his correspondence, with some related papers (Overstone 1971) with the introduction and the rich critical apparatus provided by the editor, O'Brien, who discovered the Overstone papers in 1964, provides a wealth of material not only on the monetary and financial issues of the central decades of the nineteenth century, but also lively insights into English high-class life throughout the century.

[21] Torrens 1837, pp. 21–2.

[22] Torrens then returned to the subject repeatedly, in writings of 1844 and subsequently, always defending the Peel Act. Cf. Robbins 1958, pp. 101 ff. and pp. 324 ff.

[23] On Bailey, cf. Rauner 1961.

critical dissertation on the nature, measure and causes of value,[24] Bailey – like Torrens – reacted against the metaphysical intimations of absolute value lurking behind Ricardo's recourse to labour contained in *accounting for exchange values*. Of course, neither Torrens nor Bailey had been able to read the essay on *Absolute value and exchangeable value* that Ricardo had written in the last weeks of his life, since it remained unpublished until Sraffa's edition of his writings. However, it is clear that both economists – as well as many other protagonists of the debates of the time – perceived behind the choice of labour contained, aside from the analytical obstacles it involves, a misrepresentation of the issue of exchange value, which in their opinion was purely a matter of relations between different commodities in the market, and had nothing to do with the presence of a 'substance of value' within each commodity.

For the problem of exchange value itself, however, Bailey proposed a solution – albeit barely sketched out – drastically different from that of Torrens. The latter author, as we saw above, referred to the costs of production, with a theory that may be considered a way of reintroducing those 'physical costs' that, within the classical tradition from Petty onwards, expressed the relative difficulty of production of different commodities. Bailey, however, referred to a subjective theory of value, maintaining that in general exchange value depended on the evaluation of the economic agents taking part in the act of exchange; the very definition of value was 'the esteem in which any object is held' (Bailey 1825, p. 1). The causes of value concern the attitude of the human mind towards an object, and cannot be studied by considering such an object in isolation (ibid., p. 16); moreover, this evaluation is relative, in that it concerns relationships between different objects (ibid., p. 15), so that we can speak of money-values, corn-values, etc., according to the commodity with which the comparison is made (ibid., pp. 38–9). This means that it is impossible to compare commodities belonging to different moments in time; we may compare only the value relations (exchange ratios) between pairs of commodities taken at different moments in time (ibid., pp. 71–2). Bailey then distinguished (ibid., p. 185) three classes of goods: those that are the object of a monopoly, those whose supply can be increased, but only

---

[24] The reprint published by Frank Cass & Co. Ltd (London 1967) also contains a review of the book published in January 1826 in the *Westminster Review* and attributed to James Mill (for the attribution, cf. Rauner 1961, appendix II, pp. 149–57), and three other writings, only one of which (an answer to the above-mentioned review) is in fact attributable to Bailey. The attribution of the other two works, both published in 1821 – the *Observations on certain verbal disputes in political economy, particularly relating to value, and to demand and supply* (Anonymous 1821b), and *An inquiry into those principles respecting the nature of demand and the necessity of consumption, lately advocated by Mr. Malthus* (Anonymous 1821a) – is uncertain.

with an increase in costs, and finally those whose supply can be increased at will, costs remaining constant. Thus he maintained that Ricardo's theory (purged of references to absolute value, with the qualifications that Ricardo himself introduced for the principle of labour value, all too often forgotten by his followers, and with a great many further notes of caution in view of the heterogeneity of labour)[25] only held for the third category, which was far more limited than Ricardo's followers appeared to believe, while in the real world the second category was the most important. What mattered in this third category was the relation between the buyers' evaluation and the (relative) scarcity of supply. Here we find Bailey anticipating a current of thought that was to be taken up by John Stuart Mill before eventually finding its way into the Marshallian tripartition of constant, increasing and decreasing costs (cf. below, §§ 13.2 and 13.3).

Here Bailey departed from the line followed by a number of authors (such as Senior, Whately, Lloyd, Longfield, see below, § 7) who took a certain distance from Ricardo, stressing the difficulties he had come up against in developing his view of the economy, and returning to the viewpoint of scarcity and utility – a vision of society that survived from the times of the medieval fairs, whose essential characteristics it mirrored, to modern marginalist theory. Bailey followed his own path, in virtue of which we may classify him, albeit with some simplification, among the progenitors of the subjective theory of value,[26] but which above all opened the way to the 'Marshallian compromise'. At the time, however, the importance of his contribution was perceived as lying in his radical opposition to the metaphysical element that many economists, and not only the 'Ricardians', included in the notion of value. Bailey went so far as to criticise even Malthus on this point (while less subject to criticism in this respect were 'Ricardians' like De Quincey or McCulloch), although it was eventually to triumph in Marx's theory of value. It is precisely in this connection that we find an important element which, I feel, has not received all the attention it deserves, namely Bailey's criticism of economists who 'attempt too much' when 'they wish to resolve all the causes of value into one, and thus reduce the science to a simplicity

---

[25] It is precisely the heterogeneity of labour that makes it less suited than other commodities to act as a standard for the evaluation of other commodities. According to Bailey, the heterogeneity of labour should be placed on the same plane as the heterogeneity of land, which constituted the basis of the Ricardian theory of differential rent. An extension of the notion of rent to the case of superior personal qualifications was proposed a few years later by Senior and John Stuart Mill, who thus advanced on a road that was to lead to Marshall.

[26] This is, after all, the same kind of stretching the point needed to include the recalcitrant Marshall in the current of the subjective theory of value that took the lead with the 'marginalist revolution': cf. below, ch. 13.

of which it will not admit' (Bailey 1825, pp. 231–2): in other words, a warning against the pretence of *reductio ad unum* involved in metaphysical notions of value.

4.   Thomas De Quincey

While Torrens and Bailey were considered as more or less radical critics of Ricardo's theories, other front-line protagonists of the economic debate in the first half of the nineteenth century were considered 'Ricardians' – followers and defenders of the ideas of the master of the school (although it would be incorrect to speak of a Ricardian school in the strict sense of the term, i.e. with a cultural identity like that of the physiocrats during their short-lived splendour). Among them, side by side with Ricardo's friend and mentor, James Mill, and before his son John Stuart Mill, on whom we have more to say below, we find another Scottish economist transplanted in London, John Ramsey McCulloch (1789–1864), and a man of letters, Thomas De Quincey (1785–1859), best known for his *Confessions of an English opium eater* (1821–2). In this autobiographical novel the author tells how he was stirred from his drug-induced torpor thanks to the intellectual stimulus of reading Ricardo's *Principles*. Study of this work inspired him to publish (in the March, April and May 1824 issues of the *London Magazine* – just a few months after the death of the great economist) a brilliant illustration and defence of Ricardo's theory of labour value, the *Dialogues of three templars on political economy*. De Quincey (1824) insisted in particular on the fact that the labour contained in a commodity is a measure of its 'real value', not of 'wealth'; the latter, interpreted as the amount of commodities available, can increase without an increase in their real value when the productivity of labour increases. The distinction was already present in Ricardo's *Principles*,[27] but De Quincey brought the matter to life with a vivacity lacking in the master of the school, and accompanied it with a defence of labour contained as 'real value', all the more remarkable for an author who could not have read Ricardo's essay on *Absolute value and exchangeable value*. In some respects De Quincey here anticipated McCulloch's defence, presented the following year, which we will discuss in the next section.

De Quincey was the ideal representative of a stage of transition from the more intransigent Ricardianism to its gradual corruption and abandonment.[28] Indeed, his most important work in the economic field, *The*

---

[27] Ricardo 1951–5, vol. 1, pp. 273–8.
[28] Concise, accurate reconstruction of this process of transition is offered by Bharadwaj 1978.

logic of political economy (1844), in many respects constituted a step, even more decisive than that taken by John Stuart Mill in following years, in the direction of a theory of prices based on demand and supply and a subjective theory of value. Two elements above all need stressing in this respect. Firstly, we have the emphasis – achieved with a series of brilliant, lively examples that were repeatedly returned to in subsequent literature, in particular by Mill – placed on the role of utility in determining the value of scarce and non-reproducible commodities.[29] Secondly, but perhaps even more importantly, there was the interpretation of market prices no longer as empirical variables 'explained' at the theoretical level by natural prices, but as theoretical variables in themselves, whose *theoretical* process of gravitation towards/around natural prices based on supply and demand mechanisms could and should be studied.[30] This view, later taken up by John Stuart Mill in his *Principles*, together with Bailey's ideas discussed above (§ 3), opened the way to the Marshallian notion (§ 8.3) of different levels of analysis (very short, short, long period), characterised by the simultaneous presence of demand and supply, utility and costs in the determination of prices, with the first element decreasing in importance and the second element increasing when the length of the period of time allowed for adjustment increases.

De Quincey may not have had a great influence on the economic debate of the time (although John Stuart Mill's references to his works were significant), but his capacity for abstract reasoning ranks him high among participants in the debate of the calibre of James Mill and McCulloch, while his lively style appeals to readers well beyond the narrow world of the economists.

5. John Ramsey McCulloch

A prolific writer, the Scotsman John Ramsey McCulloch (1789–1864)[31] is known as one of the keenest advocates of Ricardo's ideas, whom he met after writing an appreciative review of the *Principles* not long before

---

[29] Cf. De Quincey 1844, pp. 129 ff. Edgeworth 1894 saw the limit to this exposition, from the point of view of the development of neoclassical theory, in the lack of a clear-cut distinction between total and marginal utility.

[30] Cf. De Quincey 1844, pp. 206–7. Side by side with natural and market prices, De Quincey introduced the category of 'actual prices', and criticised Ricardo for having left it out, while crediting Smith for its introduction (ibid., pp. 203–7). 'Actual prices' were the actual exchange ratios observed in the market; with the explicit introduction of this category, De Quincey implicitly stressed the nature of theoretical variables attributed to market prices. It goes without saying that the distinction between actual and market prices was absent in Smith: cf. above, § 5.6.

[31] A monograph was devoted to McCulloch by O'Brien 1970.

the author's death. Editor of *The Scotsman* from 1817 to 1821, journalist, professor of political economy at London University from 1828 to 1837, Comptroller of the Stationery Office from 1838 to 1864, McCulloch held the memorial lecture in honour of Ricardo in 1824 and in 1825 published *The principles of political economy* that enjoyed great success, notably in the United States, where – together with Say's text – it proved the most widely read.

As was the case with De Quincey, his subsequent writings (and subsequent editions, 1830 and 1838, of the *Principles*) showed – according to various commentators (in the forefront, O'Brien, 1970, but already Marx, 1905–10, vol. 3, pp. 168–76) – a corruption of Ricardian ideas and transition towards a notion of 'real cost' much like that of John Stuart Mill, which opened the way to Marshall. However, the first edition of the *Principles* is notable for a defence of the labour-contained theory of value so extreme as to appear a verbal trick, expounding the idea that 'accumulated labour' included a 'wage' that remunerated for the time during which the labour remained locked up, between the moment it was performed and the moment when the product could be sold on the market.[32]

Thus, McCulloch believed, he could render the labour theory of value (namely the explanation of exchange value based on the quantities of labour directly or indirectly required to produce the different commodities) compatible with the 'complications' already noted by Ricardo, arising over different periods of production, different ratios between fixed and circulating capital and different durability of fixed capital. It was, however, a purely verbal solution: an artificial redefinition of the notion of labour contained, which deprived it of direct correspondence with the quantity of labour actually spent and transformed it into something like a 'real cost', given by wages paid plus profits accrued on wage advances. It was precisely this element of 'real cost' that gradually acquired importance, to the point of transforming the Ricardian theory of value, related to the difficulty of production, into a theory of the cost of production.

McCulloch – as we have seen – exerted an important influence on the economic debate of the time, not so much thanks to his prestige, certainly nothing like Ricardo's, as, perhaps, to the eloquence of his exposition. Thus some aspects of his participation in the economic debates of the

---

[32] Schumpeter (1954, p. 658) proposed a more benevolent interpretation, when he suggested reading 'productive service' where McCulloch spoke of 'labour', and 'price of productive service' where he spoke of 'wages'; however, this interpretation implies too great a departure by McCulloch from Ricardo's conceptual and analytical system, where the idea (which would be typical of the marginalist approach) of placing the 'productive factors' – labour, land and capital – on the same plane could find no place.

time deserve to be mentioned, such as his support for a policy of high wages and opposition to the Combination Laws, which were against the workers' organisations, and his plea in favour of religious tolerance and education. Besides, McCulloch was among the first professional scholars of the history of economic thought, publishing various reprints of rare texts[33] and an important annotated bibliography, the *Literature of political economy* (1845).

6. The Ricardian socialists and cooperativism

In the economic debate arising in England on publication of Ricardo's *Principles*, a group of authors subsequently labelled 'Ricardian socialists' acquired some importance:[34] the group included William Thompson, Thomas Hodgskin, John Gray and John Bray. Some of these authors – Hodgskin, in particular – are commonly remembered (or at least have been since Marx)[35] for having utilised the Ricardian theory of labour value in support of the thesis that the equitable income for workers corresponds to the entire value of the product. More precisely, if commodities derive their value from the labour directly or indirectly necessary for their production, workers have a 'natural' right to the whole product of their work, without deductions for profits or rents going to social categories whose incomes derive from institutions typical of a market economy based on private property of land and means of production.

However, this picture of the Ricardian socialists is over-simplistic, making too direct a connection between Ricardo and Marx, between the labour theory of value and socialist ideas.[36] As a matter of fact, the

---

[33] The six volumes edited by McCulloch between 1856 and 1859 collect rare pamphlets of the seventeenth, eighteenth and early nineteenth centuries; they have recently been the object of a fine facsimile reprint, edited and with an introduction by O'Brien (McCulloch 1995).

[34] The term 'Ricardian socialists' was proposed by Foxwell (1899, p. lxxxiii), in the preface to the English translation of an essay (Menger 1886) on the history of socialist thought by Anton Menger (1841–1906), jurist and brother to the better known economist Carl, founder of the Austrian school. Foxwell (1899, pp. xxvi–xxvii) maintained that Menger's work 'conclusively proves that all the fundamental ideas of modern revolutionary socialism, and especially of the Marxian socialism, can be definitely traced to English sources'. (Actually, Menger only held – ibid., p. cxv – that 'Marx and Rodbertus borrowed their most important theories without any acknowledgement from English and French theorists'.) Menger's and, even more, Foxwell's statements are too categorical: the influence of English economists cannot be denied, and was recognised by Marx himself, but Hegel's influence was also very strong, as was that of the 'young Hegelians', and it remains absurd to deny the existence of original elements in the thought of the founder of scientific socialism, which will be the object of the next chapter.

[35] Marx 1905–10, vol. 3, pp. 263–325.

[36] An interpretation of these authors quite different from those offered by Marx and Menger is advanced by Cole (1953, pp. 102 ff.), who prefers the label of 'anti-capitalist

so-called Ricardian socialists were part of a current of socialist literature (in the pre-Marxian sense of the term 'socialism') which was not limited to England, and which was characterised by radical criticism of the institutional organisation of market economies. The main criticism was that such institutions guaranteed an income to the idle classes of landlords and capitalists in virtue not of their contribution to the productive process but of their social standing. The privileged tenet of this socialist literature was, at least in England, cooperativism, propounded variously on the local and national scale, in more or less utopian or realistic forms, often associated with a drive for the moral regeneration of social life.

The leading figure from this viewpoint – and as such recognised by his contemporaries – was Robert Owen (1771–1858), a successful textile manufacturer and supporter of cooperativism in practice and theory alike. His major writings (*A new view of society*, 1813, and the *Report to the county of Lanark*, 1820) took his textile factory at New Lanark as an example to advocate a policy of active involvement of workers in plant management and, more generally, cooperative organisation of the social aggregation that had the productive plant as its core.

The following years also saw great attention paid to a social experiment that Owen himself described in his autobiography (Owen 1857–8), with the formation of the community of New Harmony in Indiana, where he had in the meantime moved. Ricardo, among many others, had already had occasion to consider his proposals,[37] and Owenite cooperativism, despite a series of failures, represented a point of reference up to the mid-nineteenth century and beyond. It is this aspect – the centrality of the cooperativist view, both at the level of the productive unit and at the level of society as a whole – that we risk losing sight of if we focus attention on labour values and the 'natural right' of the worker to the whole produce of his labour.[38]

Both aspects – cooperativism and 'natural law' use of the theory of labour value – were present in the writings of William Thompson

economics' (ibid., p. 103). According to Cole, for instance, 'Hodgskin was not a Socialist. He was much nearer to what we should call nowadays an Anarchist' (ibid., p. 111); Thompson, whose work is considered 'an amalgamation of Utilitarianism and the Owenite doctrine', 'foreshadows the utilitarian structure of Jevonian theory' (ibid., p. 114).

[37]   In 1819 Ricardo was member of a committee chaired by the Duke of Kent, charged with the task of evaluating Owen's plan, and contributed to the proceedings a speech (Ricardo 1951–5, vol. 5, pp. 30–5, 467–8); Ricardo returned to Owen's ideas in his correspondence (for instance, cf. Ricardo 1951–5, vol. 8, pp. 45–6). Although somewhat sceptical about Owen's proposals, Ricardo also showed a real interest in examining them closely, and evident sympathy for their author.

[38]   Moreover, as Foxwell 1899, p. lxxxvi, pointed out, 'Ricardian socialism grew under the shelter of the Owenite movement.' Owen's influence declined only after the failure of the Labour Exchanges (a cooperativist experiment of 'labour banks') in the 1830s.

(1775–1833), an Irish landowner. Thompson propounded, notably in his book *Inquiry into the principles of the distribution of wealth* (1824), a notion of profits and rents as deductions from the value of the product of labour within the framework of an extensive discussion of the institutional forms in which distribution of the social product may take place, cooperativism emerging as a solution to potential conflict between productive efficiency and distributive justice (in the sense of social equality). Here it is worth noting that the idea of profits and rents as deductions can be traced back to Smith's influence even before (and possibly rather than) Ricardo's. Thompson enjoyed great prestige at the time, the influence of his cooperativist views being felt by John Stuart Mill, among others.

As for the productive efficiency of cooperativism (interpreted in a macroeconomic rather than microeconomic sense, although Owen greatly insisted on the latter aspect), we may mention a 'socialist political arithmetic' current, which tried to evaluate the labour time necessary to society net of the waste corresponding to subsistence of otiose classes or, more generally, deriving from a social system based on the distinction between workers, capitalists and landlords. Among these authors, we may recall Charles Hall (c.1740–c.1820) and Patrick Colquhoun (1745–1820), whose *Treatise on the wealth, power and resources of the British Empire* (1814) proposed an often-cited statistical table meant to illustrate the distribution of income among the different social classes.

It was Colquhoun's statistical analysis that prompted an early text by John Gray (1799–1883), the *Lecture on human happiness* (1825), maintaining that the 'productive' workers receive only one-fifth of the social product. After an initial cooperativist phase, in the second part of his long life Gray went on to uphold theses closer to the Marxist tenets of central planning for production.

In the same year that Gray's *Lecture* was published, the first important text appeared by another representative of this current of literature, *Labour defended against the claims of capital* (1825) by Thomas Hodgskin (1787–1869), whose theories found initial airing in a long letter to Place in May 1820 (Hodgskin 1820). Hodgskin was among other things the author of a manual entitled *Popular political economy* (1827) – and indeed popular it proved – as well as playing a leading role in the movement for education in political economy for the working classes, centred on the Mechanical Institutes.[39] Hodgskin rejected the Ricardian theory of rent, and proposed a distinction between 'natural price' and 'social price', the

---

[39] For an outline of the Mechanical Institutes movement and Hodgskin's role in it, cf. Ginzburg 1976, p. xxiv, and the literature quoted there.

former corresponding to what the capitalists paid the workers (including the cost for accumulated labour embodied in means of production), the latter to what the capitalists received from the sale of their products, thus also including the rents and profits through which the property-owning classes appropriated the surplus.[40] In Hodgskin's writings the cooperativist theses were left somewhat in the shade, and not explicitly criticised, greater attention being given to the role that workers' associations (the trade unions, which did not correspond exactly to the modern unions but represented their early forerunners) could have in combating expropriation of part of the product of labour in the form of profits and rents. Hodgskin also recalled the Smithian distinction between 'human institutions' (which may as such be modified) and 'the natural order of things'.[41]

Like Hodgskin, John Bray (1809–97) too, the author of *Labour's wrongs and labour's remedy* (1839) upheld the workers' right to the full product of their labour. Bray advocated common property, to be established through an intermediate stage of a network of cooperatives based on joint-stock companies. Like Proudhon, Bray supported the issue of money representing labour time.[42]

---

[40] The distinction between 'natural price' and 'social price' recalls that proposed by Petty (cf. above, § 3.5) between 'natural price' and 'political price', where the latter incorporated additional items of cost involved in non-optimal organisation of society.

[41] This was in fact the same distinction between 'human laws' and 'divine' or 'natural laws' that, in classical antiquity, fuelled the debate on the nature of private property, attributed by different authors to one category or the other: cf. above, ch. 2. Cole 1953, p. 111, remarks that Hodgskin 'favoured the existence of private property' and 'believed in the existence of a "natural law of property"'.

[42] However, both Proudhon (on whom cf. below, chapter 9, note 22) and Bray undervalued the problem of the compatibility of this system with the functioning of a market economy. If each worker receives a number of units of labour-money equal to the number of hours of actual work, and if this determines the price of the product, whenever the labour time actually spent did not correspond to the 'socially necessary labour' there would emerge once again the category of profit, positive or negative according to the sign of the difference. The same would apply to all instances of deviation of the market price from the natural price. Instances of firm bankruptcies would follow from this, which would make the situation unbearable for the banks that had lent labour-money to such firms, and the system would break down. Thus, for instance, despite the advantages intrinsic to an experiment constructed on a small scale and with an important ideal support, and despite the precautions (among which the reference not to actual work hours but to those usually required), the Owenite experience of the Labour Exchanges did not have a long life (from September 1832 up to the end of the 1830s). On the basis of this experience, the German Wilhelm Weitling (1808–71), an opponent of Marx in the International Working Men's Association who later founded the Communia community in Wisconsin, proposed a modified version, in which the state guarantees subsistence to every citizen in exchange for six hours' labour a day ('necessary labour'); any additional work ('commercial labour') is non-compulsory, and allows for the acquisition of useful but not necessary goods and services, on the basis of an exchange ratio between quantity

Another interesting figure belonging to this current of thought was Piercy Ravenstone (the pseudonym of a certain Richard Pullen).[43] *A few doubts on the correctness of some opinions generally entertaining on the subject of population and political economy* was published in 1821. Criticism of Malthus's law of population led Ravenstone to argue that poverty was due not to natural but to artificial causes, connected with the social institutions and in the first place the right to property, above all with respect to the means of production, or in other words capital, which was ultimately nothing but accumulated labour. Like Hodgskin and various others, Ravenstone also criticised the Ricardian theory of rent, maintaining that differences in productivity between different plots of land depended on 'artificial fertility' – a matter of investing in land improvement – much more than natural fertility; thus rent, like profits, also derived from 'accumulated labour'. Although his works appeared at the dawn of the golden age of this literature, Ravenstone represented an extreme case, and is considered by a number of commentators the most direct precursor of Marx.

These brief examples should suffice to show that British socialist literature, looming large in the debates of the time, displayed more Smithian[44] than Ricardian characteristics, centred as it was on analysis of the social division of labour and a dichotomy between productive labour and other forms of participation in economic life and product distribution. From this point of view, the literature offered a wealth of thought-provoking ideas, unfortunately lost sight of when it was, misleadingly, reduced to a pre-Marxian current. Actually, it may be considered useful precisely for reconstruction of non-Marxist socialist analyses of the present-day situation after the collapse of the centrally planned economies. Here, together with cooperativism we may recall analyses of the time that took the distribution of social income in connection with the productive organisation of society, and illustrated the waste intrinsic to an institutional system that left a great deal of room for forms of income corresponding to no productive contribution. Proceeding in this direction, some exponents of this

---

of 'commercial' labour and quantity of 'necessary' labour (or of 'commercial' labour lent in other sectors) determined by the market. Weitling was also a decided critic of private ownership of land, but not of the other means of production, anticipating here the American Henry George (1839–97), whose *Progress and poverty* (1879), with the proposal of a single tax on land (which in turn recalls physiocratic ideas) had enormous success, leading to the birth of a still active political movement.

[43] According to Sraffa's reconstruction; cf. Ricardo 1951–5, vol. 9, pp. xxviii–xxix.

[44] And, in some respects, Lockean (cf. above, § 4.2), especially in deducing from the expense of labour the right to ownership of the whole product. Cf. Ginzburg 1976, pp. xxvi–xl, who stresses, among other things, the frequent recourse to the distinction between 'natural' and 'artificial' institutions.

socialist literature (in particular Gray) went so far as to propose a society in which necessary labour was equitably shared among all, reducing the sacrifice each had to make in labour to a few hours a day. These ideas were taken up by Marxists like Paul Lafargue (1880), but above all by radical reformists like Ernesto Rossi (1946), although they had already been appearing in Utopian literature in various guises since Thomas More (1516) and Tommaso Campanella (1602).[45]

7.   William Nassau Senior and the anti-Ricardian reaction

It did not need the 'Ricardian socialists' to make the conservatives of the time wary of Ricardo's ideas (while their attitude towards Smith wavered between the direct opposition of, for instance, Lauerdale, and the sympathy shown by Malthus, albeit based on a softening reinterpretation). In various forms, a view alternative to Ricardo's – and Adam Smith's before him – held on, playing an important role in the debate of the time. At the political level, it was argued (by Lauerdale, for example: cf. above, § 6.4) that the landlords played a positive role in the economic process; at the analytical level, a theory of value based on scarcity and utility was proposed as an alternative to the theory based on the difficulty of production, summed up as labour contained. We saw above how some aspects of this view, already present in authors like Galiani and Turgot, were taken up by Samuel Bailey in 1825, in direct opposition to Ricardo's ideas. In the

---

[45] We are here compelled to leave aside the very broad – and in many respects extremely interesting – current of egalitarian political literature, which already found a place in classical antiquity and flourished during the birth of capitalism and the industrial revolution, with a number of important cases in eighteenth-century France. We may recall, for instance, the *Code de la nature* (1775) by Morelly, upholding a form of state communism; this book enjoyed a large circulation at the time, but we know practically nothing about its author, not even the first name. We may also recall the Abbé de Mably (1709–85), brother of Condillac, and the inspirer of the Conspiracy of Equals, François-Noël Babeuf (1760–97). Cf. Cole 1953 and, more recently, the fine book by Spini 1992, who stresses the role of the most radical currents of Protestantism in this literature, in Germany and England. Again in France, of the 'utopians' we may mention Charles Fourier (1772–1837), who proposed the constitution of 'phalanges', that is communities organised in such a way as to make labour attractive, through the rotation of tasks and freedom in the choice of occupation; of the 'socialists', Louis Blanc (1811–82), supporter of the constitution of public or cooperative firms; and, with a foot in both camps, Claude Henry de Rouvroy, Count of Saint-Simon (1760–1825), whose message sometimes took on semi-religious tones that waxed stronger in his disciples; a convinced supporter of industrialisation and of technical progress, he upheld a 'hierarchical socialism' extolling the role of the entrepreneur, who discovers and introduces new techniques. The critical attitude most of these authors had to private property did not stem from arguments about the theory of value, but from the negative effects that private property had on the character of men, favouring selfishness and pride rather than the spirit of cooperation and the sense of belonging to a social community.

following years, various other theoreticians worked on the same themes, throwing a bridge towards the marginalist edifice.

The best-known author in this tradition is William Nassau Senior (1790–1864), twice (1825–30 and 1847–52) holder of one of the most important chairs of political economy, the Oxford University Drummond Chair. In a series of writings – most notably the *Introductory lecture on political economy* (1827) and, above all, *An outline of the science of political economy* (1836) – Senior proposed a subjective theory of value based on scarcity and utility (considered a subjective judgement that differs from one person to another), and touched upon the principle of decreasing marginal utility[46] (although in terms much as can be found in various other, earlier, authors, from Galiani on). His own definition of wealth (the study of which constituted the object of political economy) included all goods and services that were useful and scarce; moreover, the objective of each person was 'to obtain, with as little sacrifice as possible, as much as possible of the articles of wealth' (1827, p. 30). Above all, Senior interpreted distributive variables as determined by the same mechanism as prices, locating behind the profit rate a cost (negative utility) borne by the capitalist, namely *abstinence*. This element, later embodied in Mill's *Principles*, constituted a decisive step for the transformation of the classical approach (where the 'difficulty of production' pointed to an objective element: technology) into the Marshallian 'real cost' approach, which, as we shall see, combined objective and subjective elements alike. Abstinence was in fact the capitalists' contribution to the productive process; as wages were the reward for the workers' toil, so profits were the reward for a specific sacrifice, the negative utility borne by capitalists.

The political content of this theory is clear, foreshadowing as it did the marginalist approach to distribution, taking wages, profits and rents as rewards for the services of the 'factors of production': labour, capital and land. Senior himself stressed, however, with creditable consistency, that if abstinence meant the right to a reward for those who bore it, this right did not extend to their heirs.

Another important element on the road leading to Marshall (although Bailey had reached it before Senior) concerned the role attributed to the cost of production in the framework of a subjective theory of value. When utility is confronted with scarcity, in order to define this latter we must bear in mind the possibility of increasing the supply of reproducible commodities, and with it the cost of production. Naturally, changes in supply come up against obstacles, and the shorter the time is for adjustment to the new production level the bigger they will be, moreover possibly

---

[46] 'The pleasure diminishes in a rapidly increasing ratio' (Senior 1836, p. 12).

aggravated by elements of monopoly; for this reason the cost of production is not the final cause of price, but only the 'regulator'.[47] Also worth noting on the subject of the cost of production is that Senior held increasing returns to scale to prevail in manufacturing, while in agriculture, given that land cannot be increased in the same proportion as the other means of production, labour productivity decreases when production increases.[48]

Wary as he was in distinguishing 'the art of government' from the 'science of political economy', Senior is also remembered for the part he took in the debate on the poor laws and for his contribution to the reforms these laws underwent in 1834, attempting to limit their scope of application to those accepting to work in public workhouses (cf. above, § 6.5). Despite his opposition to legal recognition of the workers' associations, which found him ever diffident if not downright hostile,[49] Senior cannot be considered a die-hard reactionary, as was in fact the stereotype assigned him by Marxist historiography on the basis of some celebrated pages by Marx. Actually, Senior was quite favourable to, among other things, social legislation ranging from housing and health to state-funded education, free elementary education for all and constraints on child labour (a terrible plague at the time).

Marx's criticism focused not only on the theory of abstinence, but also on the decidedly captious argumentation Senior lined up (in the *Letters on the Factory Act*, 1837) against the reduction of working hours by law (to 'only' ten hours a day!). Senior maintained that the whole profit – necessary for capitalists to be induced to bring productive activity under way – stemmed from the 'eleventh hour'. The thesis was not, however, set out as a theory of profit (a theory which would also have contradicted his own theory of value), but as empirical reasoning based on numerical examples assembled for the purpose, and here Marx's irony appears fully justified.[50]

---

[47] Ferrara criticised Senior for having distinguished scarcity from utility as an independent cause of value, while it is only a factor which influences marginal utility. Cf. Bowley 1937, pp. 103–4.

[48] Cf. Bowley 1937, pp. 122–4. Senior prefigures here the distinction between changes in the scale of production and changes in the proportions between productive factors, to which Sraffa later drew attention in his 1925 article.

[49] Cf. Bowley 1937, pp. 277–81.

[50] In substance Senior, apart from assuming that the weekly wage remains constant (hence that the hourly wage and, given the productivity per hour of work, the cost of labour per unit of product, increase in proportion to the decrease in the hours worked), forgot about the circulating capital and hence the fact that costs relating to it fall with the decrease in working hours. Cf. Senior 1837 and, for criticism, Marx 1867–94, vol. 1, pp. 222–8: cf. § 7.3. If the wage per hour of work remains constant (hence, assuming that the productivity per hour of work remains unchanged, if the cost of labour per unit of product remains unchanged), with fixed technical coefficients for circulating capital goods, and

In the wake of Senior, similar positions on the subject of value and distribution were upheld, for instance, by his successors to the Oxford chair, Richard Whately (1787–1863; his *Introductory lectures on political economy* are dated 1831) and William Forster Lloyd (1795–1852; his *Lecture on the notion of value* dates to 1837). Lloyd, in particular, clearly distinguished between what we now call total and marginal utility, and connected his subjective theory of value with a principle of decreasing (marginal) utility.

Once raised to the archbishopric of Dublin, Whately founded there a school of political economy faithful to the subjective view of value. The chair in political economy named after him at Trinity College, Dublin, had as its first holder Mountifort Longfield (1802–84). Those who entertain the illusion of a 'marginalist revolution', born in the space of just a few years, between 1870 and 1874, already adult and armed like Athena from the mind of Jupiter (in our case, from the mind of the trio Jevons–Menger–Walras), are advised to meditate on Longfield's *Lectures on political economy* (1834), where the essential elements of the marginalist theory of value were already all present, including the idea of wages regulated by the (marginal) productivity of labour. Moreover, in a work dated 1835, *Lectures on commerce*, Longfield developed the Ricardian theory of international trade along the lines later adopted by Ohlin and Samuelson (cf. above, § 7.6), taking endowments of labour and land as elements determining the international specialisation of labour.

1833 saw the publication of the *Principles of political economy* by George Poulett Scrope (1797–1876). This was a popular text, distinguished on the scientific level by the attention paid to the mechanism of supply and demand, as well as a theory of interest based on the productivity of capital and a proposal for a tabular standard anticipating the theory of index numbers for prices. Moreover, Scrope defended public works as a means to fight unemployment.

We may also recall here a Scottish economist, John Rae (1796–1872), who mainly lived in North America and authored a *Statement of some new principles on the subject of political economy* (1834). The theory of capital developed in this work foreshadowed the theory of Böhm-Bawerk (cf. below, § 11.4), focusing attention on the different evaluation of present

if the wear and tear of fixed capital goods depend on the quantity produced and not on the passage of time, the reduction in working hours leaves the profit per unit of product unchanged, while total profits decrease in proportion to the reduction in working time and the rate of profits falls more slowly (at a pace that depends on the proportion between fixed and circulating capital). If the reduction in working hours is accompanied not only by an unchanged hourly wage but also by a compensative increase in the number of workers employed and reorganisation of shifts such as to leave the degree of utilisation of the plant unchanged, neither total profits nor the rate of profits need change.

and future goods by economic agents, and comparing the investors' consequent sacrifice with the capital returns. Rae is also interesting for the importance he ascribed to technical progress, and the active role he attributed to the state in fostering innovations and technological change.

Although the influence these authors had in the economic debate of the time came short of Ricardians like McCulloch and, a little later, John Stuart Mill, we cannot consider it an underground literature (as indeed we can in the case of Gossen's work – below, § 10.2 – so widely celebrated now as a precursor of marginalism, so little known in his own time): the subjective theory of value then had even greater weight in the debate than the objective theory has today.[51]

Around the middle of the nineteenth century theoretical debate in England was characterised by the simultaneous presence of different lines of analysis, developed by authors who would confront one another in lively debate. In France, on the other hand, eclecticism was the rule (with Chevalier, Cherbuliez, Garnier, Ganilh and various others),[52] combining Say's theory of value based on utility and scarcity with Senior's theory of abstinence and Ricardo's stationary state, and elements of Smith's analysis of the division of labour with elements of theory of accumulation drawn from John Stuart Mill's manual. Germany, too, showed no lack of supporters of subjective theories of value at the time; indeed, authors like Gottfried Hùfeland (1760–1817) took up Say's torch, preceding the English subjectivists;[53] above all, a 'historical school' grew up, focusing on the institutional aspects of the way the economy works, but this is a line of research we will return to later on (§ 11.2).

8.   Charles Babbage[54]

Charles Babbage (1791–1871), an English engineer among Newton's successors to the Lucasian chair of mathematics at Cambridge, is

---

[51] Schumpeter 1954, p. 598, went so far as to state that 'the Ricardians were always in the minority, even in England'; his opinion is certainly correct, if the term 'Ricardians' is interpreted in a sufficiently restrictive way, and we limit ourselves to considering the number of authors or the pages published; however, things change if we take into account the political and cultural influence of Ricardo's theories, in particular his support for free trade, and all the more if we include among the 'Ricardians' John Stuart Mill with his *Principles*. Bowley 1937, p. 17, said that 'between 1823 and 1862 [. . .] there were two different and more or less contemporary schools even in England, the classical or Ricardian and the utility schools', unless we consider as classical 'all those economists before Jevons who drew inspiration directly or indirectly from Adam Smith'.

[52] Cf. above, note 3.

[53] So Bowley 1937, p. 114, was able to suggest that 'Gossen's statement of the law of diminishing marginal utility in 1854 was a brilliant, but not surprising, interpretation of the ideas generally current at that time.'

[54] On Babbage and his theory of the division of labour, cf. Corsi 1984.

considered a precursor of Taylorism, on the one hand, and computer science, on the other. His best known work is *The economics of machinery and manufactures* (1832; fourth edn. 1835), where Babbage combined close analysis of various productive processes and attention to technological change based on the introduction of machinery[55] with general reflections on causes and consequences of the division of labour. With respect to the latter, his contribution to the theory of the division of labour was twofold.

First of all, Babbage considered the division of labour a key element in reducing production costs. In particular, breaking a complex labour process down into simple operations allows for the utilisation of less qualified workers, who received less pay. In fact it sufficed for each worker to have only part of the qualifications necessary for completion of the whole set of working operations going into any given labour process.

For instance, if someone were to build houses by himself, he would have to be a super-qualified worker, with a degree in architecture and at the same time an able electrician, plumber, mason and painter: obviously his wage would have to be very high, far in excess of that of a simple mason or even architect. On the other hand, when the different tasks involved in building a house are assigned to different workers they need no such qualifications, and their wages will be correspondingly lower.

Babbage's thesis that division of labour allows for utilisation of less qualified workers suggests a theory of proletarianisation much like Marx's (cf. below, § 9.6), although Babbage then went in an opposite direction. His idea was that developing the division of labour, precisely because it means breaking down each operation into its elementary constituent elements, favours the invention of machinery able to perform these simple activities, thereby generating a process of continuous substitution of workers with machinery. Thus the more noble and complex activities involved in organising the work process and research for technological development are reserved for human beings, while the duller, more repetitive activities disappear from the scene. This was, after all, the same idea that lay behind the quest of his whole life, and which made him famous – a 'numerical computing machine', the distant progenitor of mechanical calculating machines which were, in turn, the forerunners of modern computers. The machine was in fact based on the principle of breaking down any computation into its elementary components, for which it is easier to substitute the mind of man with a standardised process that can be performed by a machine.

---

[55] Schumpeter 1954, p. 541 n., praised him for 'his definitions of a machine and his conception of invention'.

Essentially, Babbage conceived of a two-stage process. In the first stage, the division of labour (namely, gradual breakdown, over time, of the work process into more and more specific work operations) favours the substitution of qualified with non-qualified workers; in this stage we have a tendency to proletarianisation, much like the process later described by Marx.[56] In the second stage, however, a gradual substitution takes place of non-qualified workers with machinery, and hence a gradual reduction of the share of non-qualified workers over the total active population. This holds true, as the example of the computing machine shows, not only for manual workers but also for the 'white collars' on the less highly qualified jobs. One of the most interesting aspects of Babbage's analysis lies in the fact that it drew a direct connection between increasing division of labour and mechanisation.

Bearing in mind not only Babbage's first principle (the substitution of workers having manifold qualifications with specialised workers means saving on wage costs), but also Babbage's second principle (the division of labour favours the substitution of non-qualified labour with machinery), we find that division of labour and mechanisation interact in the process of development. As a result of the two contrasting forces, this interaction does not imply a tendency leading, as Marx foresaw, to the progressive impoverishment of increasing masses of the population, but rather towards progressive growth in the wealth of nations, which also allows, albeit in alternate stages, for the progressive enhancement of the role played by the workers in the productive process (thus at least in part compensating for what Smith himself considered as crucial negative aspect of the division of labour, namely the fragmentation of work tasks).

Less interesting than Babbage is Andrew Ure (1778–1857), the 'singer of mechanicism' (as Marx called him – it is in fact above all to Marx's criticisms that he owes his notoriety). An inventor, and professor of chemistry and natural sciences at Glasgow for a good many years, Ure extolled the mechanised factory and the division of labour on the basis of his analysis of certain productive processes, and the cotton industry in particular.

---

[56] It was on this stage, excluding the second, that the American Marxist Harry Braverman focused attention in his interesting analysis of modern trends in the division of labour (Braverman 1974). Decomposition of the working process into its elementary operations, to be then recomposed in such a way as to optimise the productive process, was brought to the level of scientific exactness by Frederick Winslow Taylor (1856–1915), an American engineer, with his *scientific management* (or Taylorism, from his name). The main essays are collected in Taylor 1947. Taylorism favoured the spread of assembly-lines, the first examples of which date from around 1860 (in the Chicago slaughter-houses and in the production of the Colt revolver); the triumph of the assembly-line came in 1912 when the famous model-T Ford went into production.

His best known book is *The philosophy of manufacture* (1835), but the analytical content of his works remained thin.

9. John Stuart Mill and philosophical radicalism

Important as he was as an economist – an exponent of the mature Ricardianism and author of an authoritative overview of the economic doctrine of the time – John Stuart Mill was the leading light of the political current of 'philosophical radicalism', a line of thought originating from Bentham. In the history of political culture, Mill is the main reference for a progressive view of liberalism: an advocate of a democracy where the minorities are not overwhelmed by the majority (*On liberty*, 1859), a staunch believer in the emancipation of women (and a propagandist of birth control),[57] open to suggestions of socialist cooperatives, a leader of the anti-slavery and anti-racist movement,[58] with his intellectual honesty and open-mindedness he was a key figure whose influence reached well beyond his own times.

The son of James Mill – already met as the friend who helped Ricardo in writing the *Principles* – and a pupil of Bentham, the young John Stuart grew up in an environment rich in cultural stimuli. Subjected by his father to a formidable educational *tour de force* (when three years old he began studying Greek and arithmetic), intelligent and cultivated, but also sensitive to the stimuli of Coleridge's poetry, after a period of psychological crisis which brought an end to a childhood and youth sadly lacking in human warmth and light-heartedness, at the age of twenty-five Mill fell in love with Harriet Taylor, two years younger but already married and mother to two children. John Stuart and Harriet married twenty years later, in 1851, after the death of her husband; but Harriet had by then long been, and would remain until her death in 1858, an important source of inspiration for John Stuart. Like his father James before him, he worked for the Company of the Indies, with positions of increasing responsibility, from 1823 up to his retirement when, in 1858, the Company was wound up and the administration of India became the direct responsibility of the British government.

---

[57] Cf. Schwartz 1968, pp. 26–30, and pp. 245–56 where the leaflets with contraception advice, probably distributed by the young Mill, are reproduced.

[58] Mill opposed the idea (supported by Carlyle, Ruskin and many others) that race, rather than institutions, explains under-development, condemning 'the vulgar error of imputing every difference which he [Carlyle] finds among human beings to an original difference of nature' (quoted by Peart and Levy 2003, p. 134). This is fully in line with Adam Smith's standing on the origins of the division of labour (cf. above, § 5.7).

We will consider here in outline two main aspects of his many contributions, regarding utilitarianism and (in § 10) political economy (thus disregarding, among other things, his important contributions on logic[59] and on liberty and democracy).[60] With regard to utilitarianism, we shall focus on the substantial differences between his view and the different approaches of Bentham and Jevons, discussed respectively in §§ 6.7 and 10.3. We shall also see that Mill's utilitarianism has nothing to do with the subjective theory of value developed by new-born marginalism, constituting rather a critique of it well ahead of its time.

Bentham's felicific calculus consisted in evaluation of the pleasures and pains (considered as positive and negative quantities in a mono-dimensional space) deriving from any given action. This provides the solution to the problem of ethics: an algebraically positive result for the felicific calculus indicates a good action, a negative result a bad action. Obviously, the calculus of pleasures and pains concerned the implications of the action under consideration for the whole of society. In his famous pamphlet on *Utilitarianism* (1861), Mill defended consequentialism as opposed to deontological morals. At the same time, however, he criticised the idea that human feelings could be reduced to different quantities of a one-dimensional magnitude, pleasure (or, in the negative, pain).

Abandoning the sensistic view of human nature underlying Bentham's theories,[61] Mill made a clear-cut distinction between utilitarianism as

---

[59] 'Mill was a radical empiricist – the only source of knowledge was sense experience; knowledge was obtained inductively; and scientific laws were simply empirical event regularities' (Hands 2001, p. 16).

[60] For a recent discussion of Mill's ideas on liberty and democracy and of their relevance to contemporary debate, cf. Urbinati 2002. Mill's viewpoint is characterised as 'liberty from subjection', rather than the traditional categories of 'liberty as non-interference' or 'liberty as autonomy'; this implies a sort of internal self-control on the democratic tenet of 'majority rule', requiring not suppression of dissent but openness towards it: 'a political order that thrives on publicity, speech, and judgement educates individuals to regard critical inquiry and dissent as political virtues rather than disruptive forces' (Urbinati 2002, p. 12). Despotism of 'the many' or 'the one' or 'the few' are equally condemned; public administration based on guidelines and a bureaucracy independent from party politics are important. Participation and representation (by elections) should be conceived 'not as two alternative forms of democratic politics, but as related forms comprising the *continuum* of political action in modern democracies' (ibid., p. 70). Contrary to Rousseau and the upholders of an absolutist view of the 'social contract', Mill was strongly averse to the idea that, once elections are done with, politics is the business of the elected; in this as in other respects, Mill declares himself in agreement with Tocqueville. What Urbinati 2002, p. 82, calls 'the agonistic model of deliberative democracy' implies a 'feeling of allegiance' (recalling Hume's 'common consent'), but with ample room for dissent and debate. We may also recall that 'Mill declared unequivocally that a social order based on nationalized means of production would be despotic' (ibid, p. 194); however, Mill 1848 favours nationalisation of monopolies.

[61] Indeed Condillac, supporter of a sensistic view, may be considered a common precursor to Bentham and Jevons.

a moral criterion and utilitarianism as interpretation of individuals' behaviour. There were two aspects in this distinction. First, Mill (1861, pp. 312–13) explicitly maintained that habit rather than conscious felicific calculus accounted for a large part of human actions.[62] Second, when we take into consideration those aspects of human behaviour upon which we wish to pass moral judgement, the utilitarian criterion was to be applied – again according to Mill (ibid., p. 324) – not to some immediate sensistic 'pleasure', but to a more complex mixture of feelings and reason, situated at a higher level.

This idea of a complex mixture of feelings and reason was connected to Mill's recognition that there are qualitative differences between different kinds of pleasures (and pains), which cannot be reduced to quantitative differences. Mill stressed, at times even scathingly, Bentham's failure to recognise this aspect (speaking for instance of 'the incompleteness of his own [Bentham's] mind' or, quoting Carlyle, of 'the completeness of limited men' or, again, recalling Bentham's declared indifference towards poetry).[63]

It was in this context, and referring to the strength of habit, that Mill (1861, p. 313) stressed that 'the will to do right ought to be cultivated', or (ibid., p. 289) 'that education and opinion, which have so vast a power over human character, should so use that power as to establish in the mind of every individual an indissoluble association between his own happiness and the good of the whole'. Another reason for education, in the sense of the development of an intelligent understanding of human nature and its 'many-sidedness', was that application of the utilitarian criterion in moral judgement requires such an understanding.[64] Indeed this application is no simple matter, mechanical and unambiguous: 'so many things appear either just or unjust, according to the light in which they are regarded. [. . .] Utility is an uncertain standard, which every different person interprets differently', and even 'in the mind of one and the same individual, justice is not some one rule, principle, or maxim, but many' (Mill 1861, pp. 328).

---

[62] We may discern David Hume's (and, derivatively, Adam Smith's) influence in this.

[63] Mill 1838, p. 148; 1840, pp. 173–4; 1861, pp. 279–83. We may perhaps detect an echo of Mill's criticisms in Schumpeter's invectives (1954, p. 133) against utilitarianism: 'the utilitarians reduced the whole world of human values to the same schema, ruling out, as contrary to reason, all that really matters to man. Thus they are indeed entitled to the credit of having created something that was new in literature [. . .], the shallowest of all conceivable philosophies of life.'

[64] 'Goethe's device, "many-sidedness"' (or, possibly better, a multiplicity of facets) was recalled by Mill in his *Autobiography* (Mill 1873, p. 98). Cf. also the essay on *Coleridge* (Mill 1840, p. 201).

As an example of different opinions Mill considered the issue of egalitarianism, where 'the equal claim of everybody to happiness, in the estimation of the moralist and the legislator, involves an equal claim to all the means of happiness', immediately adding, however, a qualification which opens the way to differences in judgement, 'except in so far as the inevitable conditions of human life, and the general interest, in which that of every individual is included, set limits to the maxim' (Mill 1861, p. 336).

It is clear, then, that Mill rejected the image of an all-embracing, univocal felicific calculus which individuals could safely apply as a criterion for moral judgement without different evaluations and controversies continually arising. As a consequence of the multi-dimensional nature of men, conflict is inevitable, and may even rise to the intensity of the conflicts underlying Greek tragedies. Incidentally, recognition of this fact – namely, the legitimacy of profound differences of opinion – played a crucial role in Mill's theory of politics, centred on the notion of liberty (to which he dedicated a famous essay, *On liberty*, published in 1859).[65]

Mill's 'modified utilitarianism', in short, did not reject consequentialist ethics, as opposed to the deontological a priori principles. However, it was even remoter than Bentham's position from Jevons's subjective theory of value. This latter theory was, as we shall see (§ 10.3), based on a one-dimensional notion of utility, in terms of which individual preferences were expressed; these were, moreover, assumed to be independent of one another and sufficiently stable as to allow for their use in analysis of economic agents' behaviour.[66] Even in Bentham, as remarked above (§ 6.7), consequentialist ethics did not imply the notion of 'rational economic agents' maximising a one-dimensional utility; in Mill, the cautions and qualifications with which the felicific calculus was surrounded sharply differentiated the classical notion of 'economic man' from the Jevonian conception. The classical notion of 'economic man' is nearer to the Latin idea of the good *paterfamilias* than to the sensistic idea of an automaton maximising happiness conceived as a one-dimensional magnitude. (As a matter of fact, the notion of the good *paterfamilias* is commonly applied by jurists precisely in order to circumvent the impossibility of determining optimal behaviour univocally and objectively, referring instead to such

---

[65] In this essay Mill underlined the need to guarantee to minorities areas of freedom which may not be suppressed by decree by the majority, stressing among other things that 'unity of opinion [. . .] is not desirable' (Mill 1859, p. 56).

[66] De Marchi 1973, pp. 78–97, points out that Mill, unlike the other classical economists, was acquainted with differential and integral calculus; his distance from the marginal utility view depended on his views on the method of science and on human nature, including his adhesion to associationist psychology.

behaviour as an impartial observer could deem justified by the circumstances, even if not necessarily such as to meet everybody's approval.)

It is important to stress here that Mill's view linked back with Adam
Smith's and, more generally, that of the Scottish Enlightenment, in at least
two important respects. The first was the idea of the 'impartial spectator' propounded by Smith in his *Theory of moral sentiments* and taken up
again by Mill in his formulation of the maximum happiness principle.[67]
The second element consisted in the view, common to Smith (and the
Scottish Enlightenment as a whole) and to Mill, of human beings as 'social
animals': a decisive element, in Smith as in Mill, for an understanding of
how the citizens of civilised society are able to perceive the existence of
common interests even as they pursue their personal interest, thus rising
above mere selfishness.

These elements, common to Mill and the Scottish tradition, have
been overlooked by commentators like Viner (1949), who saw in the
differences between Bentham and Mill the contrast between eighteenth-
century rationalism and nineteenth-century romanticism. Although this
interpretation does in fact correctly capture some important aspects of
Mill's thought, the contrast should not be stretched to the point of creating a gap between eighteenth- (and early nineteenth-) century rationalistic political economy and a new romantic trend whose point of arrival
would be the German historical school or its British equivalent, with a
final return to rationalism as economics came to be predominated by the
theory of rational choice based on the notion of the rational economic
agent.

In order to understand the eighteenth-century roots of Mill's thought
we must avoid any confusion between the Scottish Enlightenment and
the French Cartesian tradition, with its extreme exaltation of the goddess
Reason in the French Revolution. Bentham was in fact very close in spirit
to the latter persuasion, so much so that he was made an honorary citizen
of Republican France. Mill, on the other hand, followed the tradition of
the Scottish Enlightenment, which stressed the simultaneous presence of
different elements within human nature and, with Smith, distinguished
selfishness from personal interest, guided by sensitivity to one's fellow
human beings – the ethics of sympathy – and civic awareness.

We may thus conclude that the classical economists, from Smith to John
Stuart Mill, focused attention on a complex individual, simultaneously
guided by personal interest and social rules. The classical economists'

---

[67] 'The happiness which forms the utilitarian standard of what is right in conduct, is not
the agent's own happiness, but that of all concerned. As between his own happiness and
that of others, utilitarianism requires him to be as strictly impartial as a disinterested
and benevolent spectator' (Mill 1861, p. 288).

analyses certainly assumed that the economic agent behaved in a rational way; but this did not imply accepting the sensistic view – or at any rate a one-dimensional view – of human nature. In the context of classical political economy, 'rational behaviour' simply implied the absence of contradictions and the idea that, whenever there is a specific magnitude that measures the outcome of the choice between different alternatives, as happens with profits in the competition of capitals, more is preferred to less. But this possibility was certainly not generalised to embrace the whole of human behaviour. Specifically, in their analysis of consumption the classical economists eschewed the idea of measuring the outcomes of economic agents' choices in terms of a one-dimensional magnitude. In this field, individual choices were considered, rather, as the outcome of habits and customs, continuously modified by the appearance of new goods, so that producers were in fact considered the *primum movens* in determining consumption structures.

All this appears confirmed by Mill's definition of political economy, as limited to a specific aspect of human nature, namely the desire to possess wealth.[68] This definition is in fact equivalent to assuming 'rationality' in the sense that *ceteris paribus* individuals prefer more wealth to less (hence more wages, profits, rents to less). However, this had nothing to do with consumer choices or resort to the assumption of the measurability of use values to account for exchange values. As a matter of fact, consumer choice was an issue conspicuously absent from Mill's monumental *Principles*; he should, rather, be considered a typical exponent of classical political economy in that, as we have seen, he appeared to consider customs and habits the main element in an account of the structure of consumption and its evolution over time.

10.   Mill on political economy

Let us now sharpen the focus on Mill the 'Ricardian' and on his contributions to political economy.[69]

Mill's first writings in the economic field, the *Essays on some unsettled questions of political economy*, were written in 1829–30 but only published

[68] The issue was dealt with in the fifth (and last) of the *Essays on some unsettled questions of political economy*. Political economy was here defined (Mill 1844, p. 133) as 'the science which treats of the production and distribution of wealth, so far as they depend upon the laws of human nature'; as a consequence, political economy 'does not treat [. . .] of the whole conduct of man in society. It is concerned with him solely as a being who desires to possess wealth, and who is capable of judging of the comparative efficacy of means for obtaining that end' (ibid, p. 137).

[69] Studies on the different aspects of Mill's thought are numerous. For interpretation of his contribution to political economy, we may at least mention Hollander's 1985 extensive study, which favours a neoclassical interpretative key, in contrast to our approach here.

in 1844. Together with the definition of political economy outlined above, they contain a crucial contribution to the theory of international trade, namely the theory of reciprocal demand utilised to determine the exchange ratios between imports and exports. Ricardo's theory of comparative costs (cf. above, § 7.6) did not determine specific values for the exchange ratios between any pair of internationally traded commodities, but an interval the extremes of which are given by the exchange ratios between the two commodities within each of the two countries, namely – under the labour theory of value – the ratio between the quantities of labour respectively required for their production. In order to determine the specific international exchange ratio within this interval, Mill compared the demand from each country for the product exported by the other country, the international exchange ratio being determined at that level which ensures the equality in value between the reciprocal demand of the two countries. This means, among other things, that there is an advantage for a small country, whose demand is relatively small.[70] Furthermore, in these essays Mill developed an important critical evaluation of 'Say's law' (elaboration of which, as we saw above in § 6.3, saw the contribution of his father James) by assigning to the economic agents' state of confidence a leading role in accounting for economic vicissitudes.

After a deservedly famous treatise on logic (Mill 1843), in a couple of years' work eked out from his time at the India Company Mill produced what was for over forty years (up to the publication of Marshall's *Principles of economics* in 1890) to remain the standard text for the study of political economy, at least in the Anglo-Saxon world.[71] The *Principles of political economy* appeared in 1848, and went through eight editions before the author's death.

The text is an exposition of Ricardian thought, but not only this. Together with Mill's own contributions, it also incorporated some ideas

---

[70] The theory of reciprocal demand was taken up by Marshall in the elaboration of his theory of value (cf. below, § 13.2), and re-elaborated in a fully marginalist conceptual framework by Edgeworth 1894a.

[71] Moreover, the widely read text by John Elliott Cairnes (1823–75), *Some leading principles of political economy newly expounded*, 1874, clearly reflected Mill's influence. Cairnes himself was a leading exponent of the Anglo-Saxon academic world. We owe to him development of the Millian notion of 'non-competing groups' and the notion of 'commercial competition' which, unlike 'industrial competition', lacks territorial mobility of supply (that is, exchange must take place in a specific location, for instance the shop); with these concepts, Cairnes foreshadowed some elements of the 'imperfect' or 'monopolistic competition' notions of half a century later (cf. below, § 13.10). Another widely read university text, the *Manual of political economy*, was published in 1863 by another follower of Mill, Henry Fawcett (1833–84). From 1863 to his death, despite his blindness, Fawcett was professor of political economy at Cambridge, and was thus Marshall's predecessor in this role; moreover, as from 1865 he was an influential Member of Parliament (on Fawcett's interesting personality, cf. Goldman 1989).

developed by anti-Ricardian economists, such as Senior's theory of abstinence (cf. above, § 7). Mill also developed his own version of the positivism expounded by Auguste Comte (1798–1857; the *Cours de philosophie positive*, in six volumes, is dated 1830–42), who advocated a 'general science of society' able to capture the interdependencies linking up all social phenomena. Mill apparently chose to tackle the problem of interpreting human societies from different vantage points, applying a substantially inductive discipline (Comte's sociology) together with a substantially deductive discipline, political economy, and with a science still to be formed, namely ethology, or the science of national character.

With a step-by-step logical procedure that was to set the pattern, the *Principles* were divided into five books (possibly an echo of Smith's *Wealth of nations*): production, distribution, exchange, economic development and the role of the government.

Treatment of production, according to Mill, logically precedes distribution since the former is considered the field of 'natural laws', independent of the institutions, which by contrast are held to be relevant for the latter, subject to historically relative laws. There are implicit exceptions to this principle, however, since a number of issues concerning institutions are tackled in book one of the *Principles*.

The Smithian analysis of the division of labour constitutes the background for Mill's treatment of production; on machinery, and on the importance of increasing returns to scale, Babbage (1833) is also quoted. Mill thus suggests the thesis of a tendency to industrial concentration (increase in the size of firms), on which Marx would lay great stress. Among other specific topics dealt with by Mill under the general heading of production, there is the issue of natural monopolies (the remedy for which is nationalisation), and the separate treatment of agriculture, in which small-scale peasant farming is favoured.

Book two, on distribution, opens with a chapter on property. Mill provides here a balanced discussion of the pros and cons of different regimes. The judgement on private property depends on whether it is organised in such a way as to avoid excessive and arbitrary inequalities, which in turn depends on widespread education and checks on population growth, but also on progressive inheritance taxation and cultural and institutional safeguards against the abuse of property rights. Communism, identified with realisation of generalised equality, is considered inferior to socialism, which allows for individual differences according to merit. Cooperatives and profit-sharing, discussed in detail in book four, represent Mill's favoured solution.

As for income distribution itself, profits are identified with abstinence, following Senior, and are thus determined by society's evaluation of the present compared to the future. Malthus's population principle looms large in the discussion of wages: Mill insists on the need to contain population growth as a priority for improving the conditions of the working classes. Elements of a wage fund theory are also present, but not in the rigid form sometimes attributed to the whole of classical political economy by excessively simplified accounts focusing on Mill's 'recantation' (on which more below).

The theory of value made its appearance only in the third book, dealing with exchange – a choice that may have had something to do with a non-metaphysical interpretation of the notion of value (various other authors, from Ricardo to Marx, often retained a metaphysical element of 'intrinsic', or 'absolute' value), and which shows just what a distance lay between Mill and the marginalist approach (which took distribution as a particular aspect of the problem of value).[72]

Mill's theory of exchange value draws on Smith and Ricardo, but also on authors such as Bailey. Although never cited, the latter is the probable source of the distinction between commodities the supply of which is fixed, those the supply of which can be increased indefinitely without increases in the average cost of production, and those the supply of which can be increased but only at increasing costs. The theory of value can properly be applied only to the second category. Here, 'natural' prices correspond to costs of production (inclusive of rents, representing an opportunity cost, and profits, considered as the remuneration of abstinence); 'market' prices depend on supply and demand, and coincide with the natural price when supply equals demand. As already mentioned with respect to De Quincey (in § 8.4), this re-elaboration of the theory of value represents a transitional stage from the classical to the Marshallian approach – although we must remember that Mill is miles away from a subjective approach: as for Smith or Ricardo, value in use only represents

---

[72] It was precisely this that provoked Schumpeter's criticism (1954, pp. 542–3): 'The central theory of value, which should come first on logical grounds [. . .] is presented in Book III as if it had to do only with the "circulation" of goods and as if production and distribution could be understood without it.' Indeed, the role of the theory of value within the classical approach is a complex issue. On the one hand, it constituted the central core of the classical analytical structure and expressed the nucleus of its views of the functioning of a competitive economy. On the other hand, purged of the metaphysical elements, the classical theory of value, in so far as it concerned the determination of exchange ratios between sectors in an economy based on the division of labour and private ownership of the means of production, took technology as given, which stems from the evolution of the division of labour, and income distribution, which stems from institutional organisation and the relative bargaining strength of the contending social classes. Obviously, we must stress that in this context exchanges concern not only sale of consumption goods, but also and above all that network of relations among sectors that allows for the 'reproduction' over time of the economic system.

a (non-quantifiable) prerequisite for a positive value of exchange, but does not contribute to its determination.

Book four of the *Principles* concerns the trends of historical change; here we find an illustration of the tendency of profits to a minimum, and of the consequent tendency of the economy to a stationary state. But economic stagnation should not be confused with social and cultural stagnation: in fact, Mill returns to one of his favourite themes – constraints on population growth – to point the way to possible progress in the conditions of the working classes within a stationary economy; we also find references in this context to the issue of the ecological sustainability of economic progress. The book closes with a chapter on the probable future of the working classes, where cooperatives and socialism are discussed.

As in Smith's *Wealth of nations*, book five deals with the role of the government: taxation, public debt, areas of public intervention in the economy. Even more than in Smith, here espousing (political) liberalism does not imply rigid commitment to economic liberalism in the abstract, but a complex and well-argued case-by-case analysis of the opportune departures from the laissez-faire principle.

Mill was a prolific writer; but after the *Principles* his main contributions concerned political issues (liberty and democracy, the emancipation of women, socialism) and utilitarianism. However, historians of economic thought often recall as an important, late contribution his 1869 'recantation' of the wages fund theory.

In its most rudimental formulation, the theory of the wage fund stated that the wage rate is determined by the ratio between two independent magnitudes: the amount of capital available for the maintenance of the workers and the number of workers employed. The main defect of this theory, at least in its simplest formulation, is that it considered the numerator as a given datum of the problem, while it is clear that the amount of capital available for the maintenance of the workers (the wage fund) not only varies in the course of time as a consequence of accumulation, but can also vary at a given moment in time if the maintenance of productive workers involves making use of goods previously utilised for other purposes, such as luxury consumption. In an article appearing in the May 1869 issue of the *Fortnightly Review*, Mill declared that he had abandoned the wage fund theory after criticism raised in the same year by William Thornton (1813–80) in his book *On labour* (1869). Various historians of economic thought see a defining moment in this 'recantation' by Mill, reading into it the ultimate decadence of Ricardianism, but the fact is that the wage fund theory played no part in Ricardo's logical construction, nor any central role in Mill's analytical structure either, being mainly relevant to the debate – very important on the political level – on the power of the unions to raise the standard of living of the workers.[73]

Far more important from the point of view of the progressive decay of the Ricardian edifice, as already suggested above, together with acceptance of Senior's theory of abstinence was the transformation of the notion of market price into a theoretical variable, determined by demand and supply. It is precisely in this respect that we can say that Mill, attempting to reconcile in one analytical construction the Ricardian-classical principle of difficulty of production and the anti-Ricardian principle of demand and supply (hence, behind the scenes, of utility and scarcity), opened the way to the Marshallian synthesis,[74] although Mill kept his feet firmly in the classical field, rejecting any idea of bringing to the centre of the theory of value those elements – scarcity and utility – upon which the subjective approach relied.

---

[73] For a 'Lakatosian' (cf. above, § 1.3) reconstruction of the debate on the wage fund theory, cf. Vint 1994. On Mill's 'recantation', cf. Schwartz 1968, pp. 91–101.

[74] Schumpeter 1954, p. 530, went so far as to speak of a 'Smith–Mill–Marshall line'; in the same direction, cf. Dobb 1973, pp. 112–15.

9   Karl Marx

1.   Introduction

The analytic structure based on the notion of surplus and representation of the economic system as a circular flow of production and consumption, developed by the classical economists, and in particular by Ricardo, was taken up and utilised in an original way by Karl Marx (1818–83). He focused his analysis on the clash of interests between the bourgeoisie and the proletariat, his researches in the economic field being guided by a dominant political aim, namely radical criticism of the capitalistic mode of production. His frame of thought also reflected the influence of Hegelian philosophy (in particular that of the so-called Hegelian left – Ludwig Feuerbach, Bruno Bauer and Max Stirner) and French anti-capitalistic currents (from Babeuf and Buonarroti to Proudhon).

Thus, as we will see in more detail in the following pages, with his theory of alienation in the first phase, and later on with his theory of commodity fetishism, Marx proposed a critique of the division of labour in capitalistic society. Furthermore, with his theory of exploitation, Marx sought to show that profits stem from 'unpaid work' even in a system that adheres to the capitalistic criterion of justice – exchange of equals – where the two parties to exchange give and receive equal values.

In developing this thesis, Marx adopted the labour-contained theory of value. At the same time he was, like Ricardo, well aware of the limits of this theory; and he set out – unsuccessfully, as it proved – to demonstrate that the results obtained by recourse to it retained their validity when the analysis was instead based on 'prices of production', answering to the requisite of a uniform rate of profits throughout all sectors of the economy. The same weak foundations underlay the so-called law of the tendency of the rate of profits to fall and, more indirectly, that of the increasing impoverishment of the proletariat: two aspects central to Marx's politically crucial thesis that the overthrow of capitalism was inevitable.

Other aspects of Marx's theoretical constructions, such as the theories on the birth and development of the capitalistic mode of production (i.e.

244

the theories concerning primitive accumulation, simple and expanded reproduction schemes, the industrial reserve army, the tendency to industrial concentration), are however less directly connected to the labour-contained theory of value, and hence less conditioned by its shortcomings. Leaving aside his immense influence on politics, Marx's contribution to the development of economic science was probably most important in those fields of research where it had the least to do with his revolutionary project. Therefore, in evaluating his contribution to our field it is important to bear in mind the political context in which it was developed, but at the same time we should avoid making everything dependent on it, as if all the elements of the Marxian theoretical construction were to stand or fall together with his overall political design.[1]

2.   Life and writings[2]

Karl Marx was born in Trier, a small Prussian town, on 5 May 1818. His father, a lawyer, was a Jew converted to Protestantism. Karl attended the gymnasium in his native town, and the university – where in truth he showed no great application – first in Bonn (1835) and then in Berlin (1836–41), finally graduating in Jena in 1841 with a dissertation on Democritus and Epicurus. In 1843 he married Jenny von Westphalen, the daughter of a high-ranking Prussian civil servant.

During the university years Marx was influenced by the Hegelian left (Feuerbach, Bauer and Stirner). His initial ambition was to embark on an academic career as professor of philosophy, but he rapidly fell back on journalism. In May 1842 he became editor of the *Rheinische Zeitung*, a liberal newspaper of Cologne which was, however, closed after only a year by the Prussian authorities. Marx then emigrated to Paris, where he met Friedrich Engels (1820–95), his great friend and lifetime collaborator. Some notebooks, posthumously published as *Economic and philosophical manuscripts*, date from this period; they are important for reconstruction of the formative stage of Marx's thought, and above all for his theory of alienation.

In 1845 Marx was expelled from Paris, and moved to Brussels. From this period we have some mainly philosophical writings, in which Marx and Engels elaborated the theory of historical materialism. In short, the theory went that transformations in the mode of production (that is, changes in the economic structure of society) exert a decisive influence

---

[1] Of the numerous illustrations of Marx's economic theory we may mention Sweezy 1942.
[2] Of the many books on Marx's life, we may mention Riazanov 1927, Nikolaevskij and Maenchen-Helfen 1963.

on the 'superstructure', that is, on the political institutions and cultural environment. A voluminous manuscript, *The German ideology*, dates from 1845–6: it was written in the heavy, convoluted jargon of the Hegelian left; Marx and Engels left it 'to the stinging criticism of the mice' (as Marx himself recalls in the preface to *A contribution to the critique of political economy*, 1857, p. 86), and it was published only posthumously. Two other works developed a critique of Feuerbach's materialism: the *Theses on Feuerbach*, written in 1845, and the *Poverty of philosophy* written in 1847.

Entrusted by the League of the communists,[3] in 1848 Marx and Engels wrote their programme, the *Communist Party manifesto*, a literary masterpiece in the forcefulness of its language, which was to become one of the most influential writings of all times. The revolutionary project that Marx and Engels would remain faithful to for the rest of their lives, was set out there in incisive terms,[4] as a distillation of the fruits of their vast reflections on philosophical, political and economic issues. Thus, for instance, their formulation of historical materialism was expressed in a single sentence: 'The history of all hitherto existing society is the history of class struggles.'[5] The political programme of the *Manifesto* saw private ownership of the means of production overcome through expropriation, to be transferred under direct control of the state (which would obviously no longer be 'a managing committee for the common affairs of the entire bourgeoisie',[6] but the political expression of the proletariat).

1848 was a year of revolutions, all over Europe. Marx returned to Cologne to edit the *Neue Rheinische Zeitung* and play his part in the political upheavals of his country. The revolutionary fever soon died down, however; by April 1849 the *Neue Rheinische Zeitung* had already been closed and Marx, expelled from Prussia, moved to London. Here he

---

[3] The Communist League was born in 1847 as an evolution from the League of the Just, in turn founded in 1836 within the clandestine movement of expatriate workers, with which Marx and Engels came in contact in Paris. The League of the Just was affiliated to the French Society of Seasons, influenced by the ideas of François-Noel (Gracchus) Babeuf and Filippo Buonarroti (1761–1837; his *La conspiration pour l'égalité*, describing the events of 1796, dates from 1828). On the history of the Communist League, it is worth reading the pages by Engels and the Statutes published in the appendix to the Italian edition of Marx and Engels (1848, pp. 251–76).

[4] Let us recall, for instance, the opening and closing sentences of the *Manifesto*: 'A spectre is haunting Europe – the spectre of communism'; 'The communists [. . .] openly declare that their ends can be attained only by the forcible overthrow of all existing social conditions. Let the ruling classes tremble at a communistic revolution. The proletarians have nothing to lose but their chains. They have a world to win. Workingmen of all countries, unite!' (Marx and Engels 1848, pp. 48 and 82).

[5] Ibid., p. 48.   [6] Ibid., p. 51.

spent the rest of his days, leading a life of study centred upon the library of the British Museum, although maintaining an active involvement in politics through the First International (more precisely, the International Working Men's Association, founded in 1864).[7]

Marx's family lived in straitened circumstances: of his seven children, only the three daughters survived Karl. Marx lived on the royalties from his writings and occasional work as a journalist (from 1851 to 1861 he was European correspondent of the *New York Daily Tribune*), but mostly relied on financial help from Engels, who was the descendant of a family of German cotton entrepreneurs and worked in Manchester in the English subsidiary of the family firm.

Of the London years we shall consider four works. First we have the *Critique of political economy*, published in 1857. Here Marx illustrated, better than anywhere else, the materialistic conception of history, presenting it as the result of his reflections during the Paris years. We may quote here the celebrated passage in which Marx (1857, p. 84) summarised his views:

In the social production which men carry on they enter into definite relations that are indispensable and independent of their will; these relations of production correspond to a definite stage of development of their material powers of production. The sum total of these relations of production constitutes the economic structure of society – the real foundation, on which rise legal and political superstructures and to which correspond definite forms of social consciousness. The mode of production in material life determines the general character of the social, political and spiritual processes of life. It is not the consciousness of men that determines their existence, but, on the contrary, their social existence determines their consciousness. At a certain stage of their development the material forces of production in society come into conflict with the existing relations of production, or – what is but a legal expression for the same thing – with the

---

[7] The First International was dissolved in 1867, following increasing friction in the internal political debate, in particular between Bakunin, Lassalle and Marx. The Second International was born in 1889 as an alliance of the European socialist parties, and was dissolved when, on the outbreak of the First World War, nationalist feelings prevailed even within the socialist parties. The Third International or Komintern (1919–43), born in Moscow as an alliance of the communist parties all over the world after the Soviet Revolution, was dominated by the Soviet Union, to be followed after the Second World War by the Kominform (1947–89). There still exists a Fourth International, founded by Trotsky in 1931 in Paris. The Socialist International (or Fifth International), founded in Zurich in 1947, groups together the social-democratic parties.

Mikhail Bakunin (1814–76) brought to the fore the anarchist ideas latent in the writings of authors such as Godwin or Proudhon.

Ferdinand Lassalle (1825–64), a German, supporter of universal suffrage as means for the emancipation of the workers, also advocated cooperatives and was above all a political leader, founder of the General Association of German Workers, which led to the SPD, the German social-democratic party. He is also known as the author of the expression 'the iron law of wages'.

property relations within which they had been at work before. From forms of development of the forces of production these relations turn into their fetters. Then comes the period of social revolution.

In other words, the continuous change of technology (broadly interpreted as the development of the division of labour: what Marx called 'the powers of production') constitutes a dynamic, progressive element that generates increasing tensions within the static, conservative element represented by 'production relations', namely the set of institutions and habits within which economic activity takes place. The force of inertia represented by 'production relations' is in turn connected to the political, juridical and cultural 'superstructure'. The dynamic element – productive forces – is destined to overturn the system of production relations and the super-structure in a revolutionary stage. We then have the transition to a new system of production relations (in Marxian terminology, a new 'mode of production': from feudalism to capitalism, and then to socialism and subsequently to communism), with corresponding upheaval of the super-structure.

As can be seen in the passage by Marx quoted above, historical mate-rialism did not indicate a mechanical dependence of institutional and ideological superstructures on the economic 'structure'. Rather, we are confronted by a complex interrelation between the two terms: what Marx maintained, perhaps with excessive impetuosity, was that the causal link going from structure to superstructure is far stronger than the link run-ning in the opposite direction.[8] Be that as it may, history – the path of development of human societies – was conceived as a dialectical process in which stages of normal development inevitably lead to revolution-ary stages, marking the transition from one system of social relations to another.

The second important work of the London period consisted of the *Grundrisse*, a set of manuscripts written between 1857 and 1858 and pub-lished posthumously, which constituted the immediate premise of *Capital* and which, since their publication (1939–41), have proved particularly attractive to those interpreting Marx's thought from the philosophical rather than economic viewpoint.

The third and fundamental work was *Capital*. The first volume was published in 1867, the second and third volumes coming out posthumously, edited by Engels, in 1885 and 1894 respectively. What

---

[8] Marx's critics have, above all over the past few decades, commonly stressed that this thesis implies drastic underestimation of the role of nationalistic and religious feelings in determining the history of peoples and countries. Some political scientists maintain that it is precisely these elements that play a crucial role in the conflicts of the past decade around the world: cf. for instance the important essay by Huntington 1996.

Marx probably intended to be a fourth volume of *Capital*, that is, the *Theories of surplus value*, a survey of the history of economic thought left unfinished as little more than a set of preparatory notes, was edited by Kautsky and published in 1905–10. We now turn to this group of writings to illustrate Marx's contribution to economic science. Clearly, we are dealing here with the mature stage of Marx's thought; it is important to stress that, even though economic issues were already present in his research in the Paris years, Marx became involved in economic theory as a logical development of his philosophical and political investigations.

Finally, we may recall among the works of the London years the 'Critique of the Gotha programme' (1878), a brief but wide-ranging text that attracted considerable attention for its passing references to the characteristics of the socialist and communist societies that were to follow capitalism, but also important because it constituted Marx's (and Engels's) reaction to a political current, social-democratic reformism, that was taking on growing importance within the major workers' parties of the time: those in Germany and Britain.

Marx died in 1883: the same year in which Keynes and Schumpeter were born.[9]

3. The critique of the division of labour: alienation and commodity fetishism

The notion of alienation (from the Latin *alius*, the 'other') is a concept of Hegelian derivation, developed by Marx in the *Economic and philosophical manuscripts* of 1844. With this concept Marx intended to highlight the position of the worker in the capitalistic mode of production. The worker is alienated for three main reasons. Firstly, the workers do not own their means of production, which belong to the capitalists. Secondly, the workers do not own the product of their activity (also belonging to the capitalists, who advance means of production and wages in exchange for the right to the product). Thirdly, the workers do not control organisation of the productive process, where they play only a limited, specific role.

Thus, Marx remarked, tools, product and labour process appear to the workers as extraneous entities; as a consequence, the workers do not conceive them positively as ways and means for their active role in society and in relation to nature to find expression.[10] Work thus proves for the workers the means to one particular end – to earn a wage, and hence the

---

[9] The obituaries and the immediate reactions to Marx's death are collected in Foner 1973.
[10] 'What constitutes the alienation of labour? First, that the work is *external* to the worker, that it is not part of his nature; and that, consequently, he does not fulfil himself in his work but denies himself, has a feeling of misery rather than well-being, does not develop

means of subsistence – rather than self-fulfilment as individuals within society.[11] All this also implies the estrangement of the human being from other human beings.

The notion of alienation, so important in the *Manuscripts* and so revelatory of the influence of Hegelian philosophy, disappeared from the scene in the main work of the mature period, *Capital*, where it gave way to the concept of 'commodity fetishism'. Let us see what Marx meant by this.

Any society based on the division of labour, Marx argued, following Adam Smith's lead, is based on cooperation between producers. Once the stage of production for self-consumption is superseded, each worker performs a specific task the results of which are in general utilised for the satisfaction of others' needs and desires; thus the worker needs the product of the work of others for subsistence and means of production. As emerges from representation of economic activity as a circular flow of production and consumption, this network connecting separate productive activities cooperating for the survival and reproduction of the economy constitutes the very foundation on which the economy and the society rest. All the classical economists – and Marx, here following in their footsteps – consider the division of labour and its development as the basis for the wealth of nations, and so for social well-being. However, this does not mean that they ignored the negative aspects of the division of labour: as we saw above (§ 5.8), Smith himself addressed the issue, in some respects anticipating Marxian analysis of alienation. The open question here is whether recognition of certain negative implications of the division of labour must of necessity translate, as in Marx, into wholesale indictment of the social and political organisation of the market economy or rather, as in Smith, into comparative evaluation of the advantages and disadvantages, general approval counterbalanced by action against the negative effects.[12]

With the notion of commodity fetishism, illustrated in the first chapter of Book 1 of *Capital*, Marx took a step further in a precise direction,

---

freely his mental and physical energies but is physically exhausted and mentally debased. The worker, therefore, feels himself at home only during his leisure time, whereas at work he feels homeless. His work is not voluntary but imposed, *forced labour*. It is not the satisfaction of a need, but only a *means* for satisfying other needs. [. . .] Finally, the external character of work for the worker is shown by the fact that it is not his own work but work for someone else, that in work he does not belong to himself but to another person' (Marx 1844, pp. 124–5; italics in the original).

[11] 'Alienated labour reverses the relationship, in that man [. . .] makes his life activity, his *being*, only a means for his *existence*' (ibid., p. 127).

[12] It should be remembered that similar themes were present in various authors belonging to the Scottish sociological school, such as Adam Ferguson (cf. above, § 4.9), whose treatment of the subject Marx recalled with approbation.

explicitly framing his indictment of the division of labour in terms of the specific form it assumes in capitalistic economies. Here not only do the flows of exchanges connecting different productive units go through the market, but the workers themselves are compelled to sell their labour on the market, and buy their means of subsistence there. In this way the social relations of production – cooperation between workers active in different economic sectors and different productive units – are obscured by the fact that what is exchanged is not the labour time of one for the labour time of another, but different commodities. The market, while constituting the common ground for the necessary connection between separate workers, operates in such a way that commodities become fetishes, the ultimate end of production and exchange activity, and necessary condition (both as means of production and as means of subsistence) for the survival and reproduction of individuals, as indeed of the economic system as a whole. On closer critical scrutiny, however, a point emerges that is easily missed at first sight, namely that the exchange of commodities in the market constitutes the means for the exchange of labour time, or in other words for collaboration between workers, each performing a specific activity. In a society based on the division of labour, each worker contributes to the social product and hence to the common well-being with his or her activity. However, this social collaboration is obscured, and so diverted from its true end, by commodity fetishism, since it appears that the ultimate end of every economic agent is ownership of exchange values, in a situation characterised by social stratification where the productive processes are controlled by a specific social class – the capitalists – and not by society as a whole.[13]

4.   The critique of capitalism and exploitation

Together with commodity fetishism, the second – and main – aspect of Marx's critique of capitalism lies in the thesis that capitalist societies are based on the exploitation of the workers by the capitalists.

In order to demonstrate this thesis Marx introduced the distinction between labour and labour power. Labour is the exercise in real practice of some productive activity. Labour power, on the other hand, is the worker as a person, incorporating the potential to exercise a productive activity.

---

[13] 'We are concerned [. . .] with a definite social relation between human beings, which, in their eyes, has here assumed the semblance of a relation between things' (Marx 1867–94, vol. 1, p. 45).

The distinction between labour and labour power may be compared to the difference between heat and a specific source of heat, for instance coal. Coal is the commodity bought and sold on the market, at a price such as to cover its costs of production. The buyer then utilises coal to get heat, but could utilise it for other purposes, for instance writing on a wall or in any other way: once bought, the commodity belongs to the buyer, and can be utilised as she or he likes.[14]

Something of the sort happens in the relationship between worker and capitalist. The commodity sold by the worker is labour power, or work capacity; the capitalist pays for it at its value, or in other words she or he pays enough to cover the costs for its production. In the case of labour power these costs correspond to the means of subsistence required to keep the worker alive (together with the worker's family, so as to ensure substitution of the worker when she or he retires or dies). Thus the value of labour power corresponds to a minimum subsistence wage. On paying for it, the capitalist acquires the right to utilise the worker in the productive process, to get from her or him a given number of daily (or weekly) hours of labour which will in fact be as many as she or he possibly can obtain, and hence, given the length of the working day,[15] as a rule a number of hours in excess of the value of the labour power, or the number of hours of labour 'contained' in the worker's daily means of subsistence. As the use of coal gives us heat, so the use of labour power gives us labour or, more precisely, gives it to the buyer of the commodity, who in the case of labour power is the capitalist.

In an economic system where a surplus is produced, the quantity of labour daily provided by workers is higher than the quantity of labour required to produce their daily means of subsistence. The total amount of labour performed in our economic system may then be subdivided into

[14] Obviously, there is always a set of rules constraining our freedom of use of the commodity: for instance, we cannot use our coal to light a fire in the common courtyard of a condominium or to write on the white walls of somebody else's house, nor can we use a worker as a slave. Specifically, the capitalist has a right only to a given number of weekly hours of work from the hired worker, on the basis of the law and rules established with the trade unions in general labour agreements.

[15] There are different elements regulating the length of the working day, with results that differ from one sector of the economy to another, over time and in relation to different economic systems: first, we have social habits, embodied in the situation inherited from the past; second, there are laws and regulations; third, there are power relations between different social classes, and policies adopted by the relevant institutions, and above all the trade unions, that influence labour hours scheduled in collective labour contracts; finally we have the vagaries of the economic conjuncture influencing *de facto* labour hours. Yearly hours of work tend to decrease over time, in a gradual but systematic way, with significant effects in the long run: since Marx's times working hours have by and large halved, with revolutionary repercussions on lifestyles and life philosophies given the increasing importance of free time.

two parts. The first part, or *necessary labour*, is that required to produce the means of subsistence for all the workers employed within the economy. The second part, or *surplus labour*, is all the rest of the labour performed: i.e. *it is equal to the difference between total social labour and necessary labour*.

This representation of an economic system presupposes separation of the workers from ownership of the product.[16] As we have seen, in a capitalistic society this separation goes together with separation of the workers from ownership of their means of production. Capital, understood as the capacity to control means of production and labour power itself, is in Marx's opinion above all a 'social relation of production' – a category expressing class relationships in a capitalistic society, and in particular the subordination of the workers to the capitalists. The origin of capital in this sense of the term coincides with the formation of a class of workers dispossessed of their means of production, and is the result of a long social process that Marx called 'primary accumulation', and which marks the transition from feudalism to capitalism.[17]

Let us assume the labour theory of value (which Marx took up from Ricardo) to hold. The annual national product has, then, a value equal to the total social labour, L, which is the quantity of labour employed during the year. With a wage rate equal to the subsistence minimum, the total wage of all workers in the economy has a value equal to necessary labour, LN. The surplus has a value equal to the labour time exceeding necessary labour, or equal to surplus labour PL $(= L - LN)$, going to the capitalists in the form of profits P (and to landlords in the form of rent, but for the sake of simplicity here we will disregard this element, as also financial capital and interests, which Marx and the classical economists considered part of the profits). Thus, even if the workers receive the full value of the commodity they sell (namely their labour power, the value of which as we saw is equal to its cost of production, that is, to the amount of labour contained in its means of subsistence), or in other words even if what Marx considered the criterion of economic justice under capitalism – 'exchange of equal values' – does indeed hold, the surplus value going to

---

[16] In feudal societies surplus labour was (prevalently) utilised in unproductive ways, for the luxury consumption of the ruling classes (nobility and clergy); furthermore, and more importantly, the forms of appropriation of surplus labour were different from those prevailing in a capitalistic society.

[17] Primary accumulation was described by Marx (in chapter 24 of Book 1 of *Capital*: Marx 1867–94, vol. 1, pp. 790–847) as dissolution of the economic structure of the feudal society guided by the law of the fittest. On the transition from feudalism to capitalism, there has been keen debate among Marxian scholars. Cf. Dobb 1946; Dobb et al. 1954.

the capitalists corresponds to unpaid labour, and hence to exploitation of the workers by the capitalists.[18]

Marx defined the *rate of exploitation* s as ratio of 'unpaid labour' or surplus labour to 'paid labour' or value of labour power; hence $s = PL/LN$. The rate of exploitation therefore depends on both the length of the working day and the share of it corresponding to necessary labour, and so to the value of labour power. Marx distinguished in this respect between *absolute surplus value*, due to a lengthened working day, and *relative surplus value*, resulting from a reduction in the value of labour power.[19]

The rate of exploitation is equal to the rate of profits (given by the ratio between profits and capital advanced) only when the capital advanced consists solely of wages, or in other words when the workers do not utilise means of production (raw materials, tools and machinery). However, such an assumption contradicts the very nature of the capitalistic system, where the capitalists' role precisely derives from their control over the means of production. Thus, in general the capital advanced also includes means of production other than labour, and the rate of profits will be lower than the rate of exploitation. Therefore the rate of profits gives a reductive idea of the exploitation of the workers by the capitalists.

With his theory of exploitation Marx showed how the surplus emerges from the productive process, and not from the circulation of commodities. The latter thesis is described as *profit upon alienation*, the idea being that profits accrue from buying at low prices and selling at high prices. Marx attributed this thesis to the 'mercantilists' and, as noted above (§ 2.6), attacked it vehemently: 'The capitalist class of a country cannot, as a whole, overreach itself.'[20] According to Marx, in the sphere of circulation 'liberty, equality, property and Jeremy Bentham are supreme': liberty, since everybody enters freely into exchange agreements; equality, because 'the buyer and the seller [...] exchange equivalent for equivalent'; property, 'because each of them disposes exclusively of his own'; Bentham

---

[18] Extension of the category of exploitation from relations between social classes to relations between developed and developing countries, proposed by Marxian theories of imperialism (Luxemburg 1913; Lenin 1916), implies drastic overhauling of the Marxian theory of exploitation; in fact, the theories of imperialism are based to a greater or lesser degree on unequal exchanges resulting from drastic inequalities in economic and military power.

[19] 'I give the name of *absolute surplus value* to surplus value produced by a prolongation of the working day. On the other hand, to the surplus value that is produced by a reduction of the necessary labour time, and by a corresponding change in the relative proportions of the two components of the working day, I give the name of *relative surplus value*' (Marx 1867–94, vol. 1, p. 328; italics in the original).

[20] Ibid., p. 150.

(that is, utilitarianism) since 'the power [. . .] which makes them enter into relation one with another, is self-interest, and nothing more'.[21]

Marx aimed this criticism not only at mercantilist thought, but also at the various socialist currents that condemned profits as unjust deduction from the fruits of labour, a heterogeneous group including both the 'Ricardian socialists' (cf. above, § 8.6), who held that all the value of the product should accrue to workers, and anti-capitalistic writers like Proudhon (known for his saying: 'property is theft').[22] In order to distinguish his theory of exploitation from these theses, Marx stressed that his was a 'scientific socialism', which recognised that the equitable criterion of 'exchange of equals' was honoured in the capitalist system.

The *profit upon alienation* thesis can be represented by the scheme $M - C - M'$, where M indicates money and C commodities: money M buys commodities C, that are then sold again for a greater sum of money, M'. It is self-evident that this scheme violates the rule of exchange of equals: if C is equivalent to M in the first step, it cannot be equivalent to M' in the second step.[23] Marx, however, proposed a scheme that represented the process of circulation and the process of production simultaneously:

$$M - C \text{ (LP and MP)} \ldots C' - M'$$

In this latter scheme (where exchanges are represented by dashes and the productive process by a series of dots) money M buys commodities, and more precisely labour power LP and means of production MP; through the productive process we get a different set of commodities, C', which is exchanged for a sum of money, M', greater than the initial sum. The value of the means of production other than labour is transmitted unchanged in the value of the product;[24] the profit P $(= M' - M)$ originates from the fact that labour power transmits to the value of the product not only its own value (equal, as we have seen, to the value of its means of subsistence), but also the surplus labour or unpaid labour.

The exploitation characterising the capitalistic mode of production (and, even more directly, previous modes of production such as feudalism

---

[21] Ibid., p. 164.

[22] Pierre-Joseph Proudhon (1809–65), French typesetter and proof-reader, self-defined anarchist, supporter of projects for monetary reform and advocate of associationism, followed the 'Ricardian socialists' in deducing from the labour theory of value the thesis that profits, interests and rents are 'unearned income'. His main work, *What is property?*, was published in 1840. The answer to the question of the title, 'property is a theft', revives the definition by Brissot de Warville in 1782: cf. Cerroni 1967, p. xxx.

[23] To be precise, Marx used the scheme $C - M - C'$ (the commodity is sold in exchange for money, with which another commodity is acquired) to represent the process of circulation of commodities in general (Marx 1867–94, vol. 1, pp. 83 ff.).

[24] Obviously, for fixed capital this refers to depreciation.

and serfdom) can be overcome, Marx held, with transition to still more advanced modes of production, socialism first, and then communism. Socialism is characterised by collective ownership of the means of production, which Marx envisioned as a preparatory stage for communism. Marx considered transition from capitalism to socialism a necessary consequence of certain 'laws of movement of capitalism', more precisely the growing bi-polarisation of society between an increasingly vast, ever poorer proletariat (the 'law of increasing misery') and an increasingly strong but numerically small bourgeoisie (the 'law of capitalistic concentration'); such bi-polarisation must of necessity end in revolution. We will return to these points later on, in § 6.

As we have seen, a key element in the construction of the theory of exploitation illustrated above is recourse to the labour-contained theory of value to express in homogeneous terms the different magnitudes (product, means of subsistence, surplus). As we saw in the chapters on Smith and Ricardo, according to the labour theory of value the exchange value of commodities is proportional to the amount of labour contained in each of them, or in other words the quantity of labour directly and indirectly required to produce them. Like Ricardo, Marx too was conscious of the fact that exchange values determined on the basis of the labour theory of value do not correspond to the prices at which commodities are exchanged in competitive markets, when we have to assume that the rate of profits is uniform throughout all sectors of the economy. The labour theory of value can at best be utilised as an initial approximation, provided that it can then be shown, as a second step, not to have led to irremediable errors. As we shall see below (§ 7), Marx set out to tackle this crucial weak point in his theory in Book 3 of *Capital*, but the solution he proposed – the so-called transformation of labour values into prices of production – also proved insufficient, with the consequence that a number of crucial elements of the Marxian theoretical edifice must be called into question, including the theory of exploitation itself.

5.   Accumulation and expanded reproduction

In Book 2 of *Capital*, Marx illustrated two schemes for general analysis of the economic system, at the level of simple reproduction, and in terms of expanded reproduction, or accumulation.[25] Both schemes incorporate the reproducibility condition: for each commodity, the quantity produced must be equal to or greater than the quantity utilised in the productive process as means of production or necessary subsistence.

---

[25] In some important respects these schemes were forerunners of von Neumann's 1937 model of proportional growth.

In the case of *simple reproduction*, period after period the levels of production remain unchanged. If there is a surplus, it goes into luxury consumption or subsistence for the unemployed or unproductive workers.

In the case of *expanded reproduction*, on the other hand, at least part of the surplus is accumulated – added, that is, to the previous amounts of means of production and subsistence. In this way, period after period the number of workers employed in the productive process can increase, and with them the quantity of means of production they use. Without any change in technology, a progressive widening of the economy takes place. Over and above this process, there is technical progress generally taking the form of an increasing use of machinery, according to a representation of economic development common to both Marx and classical economists such as Ricardo.

Marx distinguished two sectors of the economy, one producing means of consumption, the other means of production. The relative activity levels of the two sectors are in equilibrium when the entire production of the two sectors can be absorbed by the economy.

In the case of simple reproduction, this happens when the quantity of means of production that are produced equals the quantity employed in the productive processes in the two sectors, while the quantity of consumption goods produced equals the requirements of means of subsistence for the workers employed in the economy plus the quantity utilised for luxury or unproductive consumption. In this case, the entire surplus consists of consumption goods.

In the case of expanded reproduction, the surplus must consist of both means of production and consumption goods. Furthermore, the ratio between consumption goods and means of production within the surplus must be equal to or higher than the corresponding ratio between means of subsistence and means of production available at the beginning of the production process. This is due to the fact that the surplus means of production can only be used for accumulation, while surplus consumption goods can be partly used for luxury or unproductive consumption. The rate of growth of the system is equal to the 'rate of surplus' of the means of production;[26] the maximum rate of growth of the economy obtains when there is no luxury consumption and the 'rate of surplus' of capital goods is equal to that of consumption goods – when the proportion, that is, between the two groups of goods in the surplus is equal to their proportion at the beginning of the production process, so that no waste of

---

[26] As the name suggests, the 'rate of surplus' for any commodity is given by the ratio between the quantity of that commodity included in the surplus and the quantity of the same commodity required as means of production and means of subsistence at the beginning of the production process.

consumption goods occurs, all going to 'necessary' consumption, for the maintenance of productive workers.

Here, too, applying a labour theory of value, Marx calls v the variable capital, i.e. the value of subsistence goods utilised in the productive process; c the constant capital, i.e. the value of means of production (labour excluded); s the value of the surplus. Let us call the sector producing means of production 1, and the sector producing consumption goods 2; C stands for the value of production in sector 1, and V for the value of production in sector 2. We may then express Marx's reproduction schemes as follows:

$$c_1 + v_1 + s_1 = C$$
$$c_2 + v_2 + s_2 = V.$$

In the case of simple reproduction, the equilibrium production levels of the two sectors are:

$$C = c_1 + c_2$$
$$V = v_1 + v_2 + s_1 + s_2.$$

In other terms, the level of production of sector 1 corresponds to the quantity of means of production utilised in both sectors; the level of production of sector 2 corresponds to the means of subsistence required for all the employed workers, plus the luxury consumption goods that capitalists buy with their profits, the latter being equal to the entire surplus of the economy. We can reduce these two equations to one equilibrium condition for the exchanges between the two sectors: the value of capital goods sold by sector 1 to sector 2 is equal to the value of means of subsistence sold by sector 2 to sector 1. Algebraically:

$$c_2 = v_1 + s_1.$$

In the case of enlarged reproduction, a share of the surplus, q, goes to accumulation of new capital goods; correspondingly, a share equal to $(1 - q)$ of the surplus thus consists of consumption goods. Algebraically:

$$C = c_1 + c_2 + q(s_1 + s_2)$$
$$V = v_1 + v_2 + (1 - q)(s_1 + s_2).$$

As we saw above, capital goods and means of subsistence serving to increase the number of employed workers must grow in the same proportion. Besides, the surplus may include a residuum of consumption goods to serve for luxury goods or the consumption of the unproductive workers; the rate of growth is at a maximum when this residuum is nil and the entire surplus goes into accumulation.

Marx's aim in using the analytical tool of the reproduction schemes was to show that given a certain set of conditions the system may grow endlessly, without any need for problems of realisation of the product to arise. Thus Marx finally demolished the under-consumption theories proposed by Malthus, Sismondi and Rodbertus.[27]

Refuting the under-consumption theories did not, however, imply for Marx adhesion to the so-called 'Say's law' (discussed above, in § 6.3), which states that any level of production can be absorbed by the market. Firstly, crises of disproportion between the two sectors may occur whenever equilibrium proportions do not hold (and growth in equilibrium, Marx said, can only come about by chance). Secondly, and more importantly, Marx did not rule out the possibility of general over-production crises: following up on the role Torrens attributed to financial intermediation, Marx clearly recognised the potential for crises intrinsic to a system based on investment decisions that are decentralised and distinct from decisions to save.[28] Nothing guarantees that surplus production is realised, or in other words that the commodities produced are sold at a price sufficient to recover costs and obtain a normal profit.

Another aspect that Marx clearly attributed a decisive role to in his theoretical construction had to do with fluctuations in production levels. In fact, his was one of the first theories of the trade cycle, still retaining interest for us today.[29]

Marx's theory of the trade cycle was based on the fluctuations in the *industrial reserve army* (a term by which Marx designated not only unemployed workers but also artisans and workers employed in agriculture but ready to change to employment in manufacturing).

---

[27] On Malthus and Sismondi, cf. above, § 6.4. Johann Karl Rodbertus (1805–75) was one of the so-called *Kathedersozialisten* (Chair Socialists): university professors who supported a system of social laws for the realisation of which they entrusted the state authority of the Prussian monarchy. They favoured active state intervention in the economy: tariffs on imports, subsidies to national industries and support to exports, regulation by law of hours of work and working conditions, dismantling of large landholdings and support to direct ownership of land on the side of small peasants, and diffusion of state ownership. Among them, Adolph Wagner (1839–1917), professor in Berlin from 1870, supported nationalisation of monopolistic industries and of real-estate property, and is known for the so-called Wagner's law, according to which as a consequence of development the public sector grows as a share of national income. This group had strong links (and many overlaps) with the 'young German historical school' led by Schmoller, on which see below (§ 11.2).

[28] On this aspect of Marx's thought, cf. Sardoni 1987 and the bibliography given there.

[29] This theory was again proposed, for instance, with the 'closed orbit oscillator' of Richard Goodwin (1967) based on the prey–predator cycle studied by the Italian Vito Volterra, and more generally by cycle theories based on the existence of a distributive conflict between wages and profits.

In the recovery phase, when income grows rapidly, unemployment falls and the industrial reserve army diminishes. As a consequence, the bargaining power of the working class increases, while the competition between entrepreneurs in search of workers for their factories grows tougher, and the real wage rate rises.[30] At the beginning of the recovery stage, wages increase slowly because the industrial reserve army is still large; subsequently, in the boom stage, production continues to grow and the industrial reserve army continues to shrink, eventually bringing about sharper increase in wages.

The increased cost of labour gives rise to a reduction in profits per unit of output. Firms then react to the increase in wages by trying to save on the labour utilised in the productive processes. To this end they mechanise production, stepping up the use of machinery in the production process. This favours technical progress, which forms the basis for economic development. Growth in national and per capita production thus constitutes a trend underlying cyclical fluctuations. What is more, the mechanism of economic development is, as we have seen, directly connected to the mechanism that gives rise to cyclical fluctuations.

The process of mechanisation allows firms to reduce the number of employed workers. The industrial reserve army thus grows, and this puts a brake on wage increases. Rising unemployment marks the beginning of the third stage of the trade cycle, crisis, and continues in the fourth stage, depression, when unemployment is above the average level (while income is below the trend level).

The growing size of the industrial reserve army halts wage increases while, thanks also to the productivity increases obtained with mechanisation, the cost of labour per unit of output decreases with a consequent rise in profits. Firms again expand and hire new workers, the increase in profits constituting both an incentive to increase production levels and a source of finance for investments to expand productive capacity. The industrial reserve army again shrinks. We thus have a stage of expansion, marking the beginning of a new cycle.

As we can see, this theory presents a number of interesting aspects: it is at the same time a theory of the trade cycle and a theory of economic

---

[30] By utilising as a central element in his analysis of the trade cycle an inverse relation between wages and unemployment, Marx anticipated the so-called 'Phillips curve', namely the inverse relationship between rate of change of money wages and level of unemployment empirically estimated for the United Kingdom between 1861 and 1957 by the New Zealand economist A. W. Phillips (1914–75), in a much-cited article published in 1958, which we will come back to later (§ 17.5). Furthermore, as already noted, Marx's analysis of income distribution was based on the relative bargaining power of workers and capitalists, as in Smith, and in contrast to the supporters of the 'iron law of wages' based on the Malthusian principle of population.

development; a theory of technical change and a theory of the evolution over time of employment and of the distributive shares. The connection between trade cycle and economic development may possibly be seen as Marx's main contribution to classical political economy; once the classical approach had lapsed into oblivion, this connection was practically ignored in twentieth-century theoretical analyses, while the tendency set in to analyse economic growth and the cycle separately.[31]

6. The laws of movement of capitalism

On various occasions and in various ways the classical economists addressed the close link between the division of labour and social structure. The connection between evolution in the division of labour (and hence in technology) and changes in social structure underlies the major attempts to single out the basic trends in human society, or in other words to understand 'where we are going'.

The most celebrated of such attempts must surely be that of Marx. In his opinion, capitalism is not the final stage in the history of human societies, but only an intermediate stage. Indeed, as it was preceded in the history of human societies by other forms of organisation of society (serfdom, feudalism), so capitalism will give way to new forms of social organisation (socialism first, then communism). Therefore we should study the laws of motion underlying capitalism, to understand how it came into being, how it has changed in the course of its evolution, and the reasons why it will have to give way to a new form of social organisation, namely socialism.

In this respect Marx noted the tendency of capitalistic societies towards increasing economic and social polarisation:[32] on the one hand, we have the growing misery, at least in relative terms, of an increasing proportion of population, and on the other hand, ever greater economic and political power concentrating in a few hands. In other words, Marx perceived, on the one hand, a growing *proletarianisation*, namely the formation of

---

[31] A theory dealing simultaneously with cyclical fluctuations and development was, instead, proposed by Schumpeter (cf. below, § 15.3). However, as we will see, in Schumpeter's contribution, too, the causes of cyclical fluctuations – the 'clustering' of innovations over time – appeared as a *deus ex machina* more than an endogenous element such as we find in Marx's theory. For illustration and comparison of the theories of the trade cycle by Marx and Schumpeter, cf. Sylos Labini 1954.

[32] This thesis was already present in the *Manifesto of the communist party* (Marx and Engels 1848, pp. 55–61). The elements composing it recurred repeatedly in Marx's (and Engels's) writings and were the subject of keen interpretative debate: some references to this debate are given in the following footnotes.

wider and wider masses of common workers,[33] and on the other hand, the tendency to increasing *concentration* of manufacturing production in a few big firms.[34] Such a tendency was due not only to the technological and organisational advantages involved in large-scale production, but also to the way the financial and credit system works and the mechanisms of capitalistic competition implying, among other things, obstacles to the entry of new firms in the arena. All this, Marx argued, leads to dwindling numbers of small entrepreneurs and independent artisans as they join willy-nilly the ranks of dependent workers. Hence the growing polarisation between a burgeoning proletariat and a capitalist class ever smaller, ever richer, ever more powerful. From this tendency Marx derived the thesis of inevitable collapse facing the capitalistic mode of production, and transition to a socialist society, when the proletariat – by then the overwhelming majority of the population – expropriate the capitalist class, economically dominant but numerically weak. Ineluctably capitalism will thus be superseded, and the way opened to socialism.

Another thesis developed by Marx takes much the same course, with the 'law of the falling rate of profits', illustrated in the third section of Book 3 of *Capital*.[35] This thesis was derived from the process of increasing mechanisation characterising technological change in capitalistic societies, which we have already seen in the context of Marx's theory of the trade cycle. The process entails progressive increase in the organic composition of capital, or in other words of the ratio between constant capital c (the value of means of production utilised in the productive process other than labour power) and variable capital v (the value of labour power employed in production), both expressed in terms of labour contained. More precisely, the rate of profits can be expressed $(s/v)/(c/v + 1)$, having as numerator the rate of exploitation and as denominator the

---

[33] A number of commentators pointed to a 'law of increasing misery' of the workers along with the 'law of proletarianisation'. Debate on the interpretation of it reached far and wide: cf. for instance Sylos Labini 1954, pp. 36–40; Sowell 1960; Meek 1967, pp. 113–28; and the bibliography given in these writings. Indeed, in Marx's writings passages have been identified supporting at least three different interpretations of the 'law': a 'thesis of increasing absolute misery', understood as a fall in real wages; a 'thesis of increasing relative misery', understood as a reduction in the wage share in national income; and, finally, a rather vague 'thesis of deterioration in workers' life conditions', that had to do with phenomena such as acceleration of the labour processes, increasing subdivision of operations within each labour process, and deterioration of the environment in the urban agglomerates of the time. In Marx's political and economic thought, the 'law of increasing misery' may have lined up alongside the thesis of proletarianisation in support of his deep conviction of the inevitability of revolution for capitalist societies, even if it cannot be considered a necessary condition for the validity of the latter.

[34] Cf. specifically chapter 22 of Book 1 and chapter 27 of Book 3 of *Capital*: Marx 1867–94, vol. 1, pp. 636 ff. and vol. 3, pp. 566–73.

[35] Marx 1867–94, vol. 3, pp. 317–75.

organic composition of capital plus one. Therefore, if the organic composition of capital increases and the rate of exploitation does not increase *pari passu*, the rate of profits necessarily decreases.[36]

Here, however, the reasoning is flawed by confusion between variables expressed in terms of labour values and underlying quantities of the various commodities. In fact, mechanisation does not necessarily imply an increase in the organic composition of capital. It is not the case, for instance, if a growing number of machines, thanks to technical progress, requires the same or a lower quantity of labour for their production, when the organic composition of capital will in fact remain constant or decrease. Furthermore, technical progress itself, by reducing the quantity of labour required for the production of subsistence goods, causes an increase in the rate of exploitation for a constant real wage.[37]

7. The transformation of labour values into prices of production

As we have had occasion to recall quite often in the previous sections, in *Capital* Marx adopted the labour theory of value, in the wake of a tradition well-established among economists in the first half of the nineteenth century, in particular with Ricardo. However, just like Ricardo, Marx, too, realised that such a theory was inconsistent with the assumption of a uniform rate of profits throughout all sectors of the economy: an assumption expressing in analytic terms the Smithian idea of the 'competition of capitals', which, in Marx's opinion too, represented a central feature of the capitalistic mode of production. Marx nevertheless set out to tackle the problem, in Book 3 of *Capital* (which, let us recall, was published posthumously under the editorship of Engels on the basis of notes left by Marx; thus we have no certainty about just how convinced Marx himself was of the solution he worked out) through the so-called 'transformation of labour values into prices of production'.[38] Marx's idea was to show

[36] For simplicity, it is assumed here that all capital be circulating capital.

[37] The law of the tendency to a falling rate of profits, too, like so many other aspects of Marx's thought, gave rise to wide-ranging interpretative debate. A number of authors (cf. for instance Sweezy 1942, pp. 147–55; Meek 1967, pp. 129–42) noted among other things that Marx himself referred to the elements mentioned above in order to criticise his own 'law'; such elements would represent 'counter-tendencies', that hinder but do not eliminate the basic trend. However, as Sweezy himself stressed, it is quite difficult to explain why the algebraic sign of the different forces and counter-forces should go in the direction indicated by Marx, rather than in the opposite direction. As a matter of fact, it is quite difficult to maintain that over the past century there has been a tendency to a decrease in the rate of profits – notwithstanding quite a sharp increase in real wages!

[38] Section 2 of Book 3 of *Capital* is devoted to the subject: Marx 1867–94, vol. 3, pp. 245–316.

that this 'transformation' did not modify the substance of the results reached on the basis of the labour theory of value, in particular in so far as the thesis of exploitation was concerned (but, for the purposes of his political construction, the tendency of the rate of profits to fall is also important).

In the following paragraphs we will illustrate the 'transformation problem' by utilising Marx's reproduction schemes; we will then briefly review the ensuing debate up to our own day. In the next section, where we attempt a provisional evaluation of Marx's contribution to economic science, we will take this aspect into account together with the 'metaphysical' importance of identifying value with labour contained and the 'laws of movement' of capitalism discussed in the previous section.

It will be remembered that Marx called v the variable capital, or in other words the value of labour power employed in the productive process, which corresponds to the quantity of labour contained in the means of production necessary to such workers; that he used c to indicate constant capital, or the value of means of production employed in the productive process (as circulating capital and as amortisation for fixed capital); and, finally, that s designated surplus value, or the value of the surplus corresponding to surplus labour, consisting in the labour employed in excess of the requirements to reconstitute the means of subsistence. Like the total labour employed in the economy, so also the working day of each individual worker is found to be made out of two parts: 'necessary labour' and 'surplus labour'. The 'rate of exploitation' is defined as equal to the ratio between surplus labour and necessary labour. If we assume that competition in the labour market brings out uniform working conditions in the different sectors of the economy, and in particular an equal length of working day, and if we go on to assume that the subsistence wage is the same for all workers,[39] then the rate of exploitation corresponds to the ratio between surplus value and variable capital, s/v, and is the same for each individual worker, for each sector and for the economic system as a whole.

However, the condition of a uniform rate of exploitation in all sectors of the economy is inconsistent with the assumption of a uniform rate of profits. Let us indicate the different sectors with $1, 2, \ldots, n$. The condition of equal rates of exploitation in the different sectors of the economy is expressed by:

$$s_1/v_1 = s_2/v_2 = \ldots = s_n/v_n. \tag{1}$$

---

[39] This means focusing attention on 'common labour': 'qualified labour' constitutes a complication to be dealt with in a subsequent approximation. Cf. Roncaglia 1973.

In conformity with the labour theory of value, let us measure in terms of labour contained both the value of the surplus (total profits) and the value of advanced capital. The assumption of equal rates of profit in all sectors of the economy (computed for each sector as the ratio between profits and value of capital advanced, which includes both constant and variable capital, or wages) is expressed by:[40]

$$s_1/(c_1 + v_1) = s_2/(c_2 + v_2) = \ldots = s_n/(c_n + v_n). \qquad (2)$$

Let us divide both numerator and denominator of the different terms of this series of equalities respectively by $v_1, v_2, \ldots, v_n$. We get:

$$(s_1/v_1)/(c_1/v_1 + 1) = (s_2/v_2)/(c_2/v_2 + 1)$$
$$= \ldots = (s_n/v_n)/(c_n/v_n + 1). \qquad (3)$$

At the denominator we thus have the ratio between constant and variable capital, c/v, which Marx called the 'organic composition of capital', plus 1. At the numerator we have the rates of exploitation of the different sectors, by assumption all equal. As a consequence, the series of equalities (3) – which, let us remember, we have just deduced from the assumption of uniform profit rates in all sectors expressed by the series of equalities (2) – hold if, and only if, the denominators, too, are all equal. Uniformity of profit rates hence requires that

$$c_1/v_1 = c_2/v_2 = \ldots = c_n/v_n, \qquad (4)$$

or in other words that the organic compositions of capital in the different sectors also be all equal. However, there is no reason for this to happen necessarily: in general, only by chance can we get uniform organic compositions of capital in all the sectors of the economy. In fact, each sector adopts a technology specific to it, the proportion between labour and means of production other than labour in general varying widely from one sector to another: take, for instance, the difference between a refinery and a vegetable garden. Thus, confronted with different organic compositions of capital in different sectors of the economy, the assumption of a uniform rate of profits, reflecting the crucial assumption of competition, contradicts the assumption that the quantities of labour contained are a correct measure of the exchange values of commodities produced and of means of production employed in the different sectors.

---

[40] Here we disregard the complications that might arise from the presence of fixed capital goods: that is, we assume that constant capital, namely means of production other than labour power, only includes circulating capital goods, wholly utilised in the course of the productive process.

Marx recognised this difficulty and, as we saw above, proposed 'transformation' of the magnitudes expressed in terms of labour values that do not comply with the condition of a uniform rate of profits into magnitudes expressed in terms of prices of production, thus complying with the condition. In order to do this, he added to the production costs of each sector (given by the sum of constant and variable capital employed in that sector) the profits for that sector. The latter are computed by applying the average rate of profit calculated for the system as a whole, expressed by $s/(c+v)$, to the capital advanced for the sector. Let us consider a two-sector economy; we then have

$$(c_1 + v_1) + r(c_1 + v_1) = Ap_1$$
$$(c_2 + v_2) + r(c_2 + v_2) = Ap_2$$

where A and B represent the quantities of product obtained in the first and second sector respectively, expressed in terms of labour values (that is, $A = c_1 + v_1 + s_1$ and $B = c_2 + v_2 + s_2$, while p_1 and p_2 represent the prices of production of the two commodities, and constitute the two unknown variables determined by the two equations, the rate of profits being known (since, let us recall, $r = (s_1 + s_2)/(v_1 + v_2 + c_1 + c_2)$).

However, the solution (which, as we have already seen, Marx only proposed in a manuscript left unpublished and clearly incomplete) cannot be considered satisfactory: costs and advanced capital are expressed in terms of labour contained, while it is obvious that capitalists compute their profit rate as ratio of profits and capital advanced *measured in terms of prices, not of labour values.*[41]

This objection to Marx's solution was raised on many sides immediately after the posthumous publication of the third volume of *Capital*, in particular by Böhm-Bawerk (1896). Some, like Ladislaus von Bortkiewicz (1868–1931), also tried to formulate a corrected version of Marx's proposal. In order to get round the error in this version, Bortkiewicz (1906–7, 1907) adopted as unit of measurement for each of the two commodities a and b the quantity of that commodity corresponding to a unit of labour contained. In this way the prices of production p_1 and p_2 can be interpreted as those multiplicative coefficients that allow us to move on from magnitudes measured in terms of labour contained to corresponding magnitudes measured in such a way to comply with the condition of a

---

[41] Marx (cf. 1867–94, vol. 3, pp. 261–72) recognised the existence of this difficulty, but ignored it, considering it as practically irrelevant when referring to aggregate magnitudes representing the economic system as a whole. In sum, Marx imposed a double constraint: (i) equality between total surplus value created in the economy, and total value of profits; (ii) equality of the total value of the product of the various sectors in terms of labour contained and its value in terms of prices of production. However, the two constraints are simultaneously satisfied only in very rare circumstances.

uniform rate of profits throughout all sectors of the economy. Therefore, not only the quantities of the two commodities, A and B, but also the quantities of constant and variable capital (that is, of capital goods and subsistence means) utilised in the two sectors, are to be multiplied by such coefficients. Thus we get:

$$(c_1 p_1 + v_1 p_2)(1 + r) = A p_1$$
$$(c_2 p_1 + v_2 p_2)(1 + r) = B p_2$$

that is, two equations in which, considering the technology and hence c_1, c_2, v_1, v_2, A, B as given, we have three unknowns: p_1, p_2 and r, which can easily be reduced to two by focusing attention on the relative price p_1/p_2 and on the profit rate r.[42]

Marx had also tried to demonstrate that the results reached on the basis of the labour theory of value do not change if we shift to reasoning in terms of prices, applying the notion of an 'average commodity'. In the transition from labour values to production prices, Marx said, we have a redistribution of surplus value among the capitalists in the various sectors: in the former case, surplus value is distributed in proportion to the amount of direct labour employed in each sector, in the latter in proportion to the capital advanced. However, we can assume that the total surplus value remains equal to total profits, and that at the same time the total product remains unchanged when measured in labour values or in prices of production. These properties hold for the 'average commodity', the productive process for which displays an organic composition of capital (c/v) equal to the average composition for the economy as a whole: for this commodity, moreover, the price of production proves equal to its value, and the sector profit equal to the sector surplus value.

Once again, however, the argument is flawed. Total profits may in fact be equal to total surplus value, if we choose this equality as our condition to set the unit of measurement for prices. But we cannot simultaneously impose the further constraint of equality between labour value and price for the total product, since the system of equations would thus become over-determined. The two conditions are consistent only if means of production, product and surplus are but different quantities of one composite commodity; only in this case – an exceptional case indeed – do the two conditions hold simultaneously also for an 'average commodity' representative of the system as a whole.[43]

[42] After Bortkiewicz, this line of reasoning was followed by Winternitz 1948 and Seton 1957; cf. also Morishima 1973; on the history of the 'transformation problem' cf. Meldolesi 1971, Vianello 1973 and Vicarelli 1975.
[43] Attempts at using Sraffa's 'standard commodity' to solve the problem that Marx tackled with the 'average commodity' were proposed by Eatwell 1975b and Medio 1972; for criticism, cf. Roncaglia 1975, pp. 76–9.

8.   A critical assessment

Marx's economic and political construction has given rise to debate on a vast scale, revolving around practically all aspects and generating a mass of literature of proportions far too voluminous to come fully to grips with. Here we will only consider, with a few brief remarks, certain aspects particularly relevant to our main theme, namely Marx's ideas on the 'laws of movement' of capitalism; the role of the labour theory of value vis-à-vis the theories of exploitation and of the tendency of the profit rate to fall; and Marx's critique of the division of labour and his idea of a communist society as the point of arrival for the evolution of human societies.

On the subject of the 'laws of movement' of capitalism, Marx stressed the process of industrial concentration, stimulated by large-scale production economies, and here he was right. The last few decades may indeed have seen a relative growth in importance of small- and medium-size firms, especially in the more technologically advanced sectors, but the fact remains that in a span of over a century from the publication of *Capital* the size of firms grew enormously, with the development of large financial groups and big multinationals.[44] However, all this has not led to bipolarisation between an ever smaller capitalist class and an ever vaster proletariat: other factors were at work in the meantime, leading to the formation of large and growing *middle classes*. Indeed, the trend proved so strong that the middle classes eventually outweighed the proletariat represented by unskilled workers.[45]

The growth of the middle classes was associated with a decreasing proportion of workers directly employed in the production of commodities, and an increasing proportion engaged in producing services, or only indirectly employed in the production of commodities (administrative employees, technicians and such like). This meant a relative increase in the weight of employees and qualified workers within the manufacturing sector, and of independent professionals in the services sector, as a share of the active population.

[44] On Marx's lead, the thesis of an increasing concentration of financial capital was developed by Rudolf Hilferding (1877–1941; his book, *Das Finanzkapital*, was published in 1910). Non-Marxian economists as well, such as Schumpeter (cf. below, § 15.4) and Kenneth Galbraith (b. 1908), considered the tendency to industrial and financial concentration as a central aspect in their analyses of capitalism.

[45] Cf. Sylos Labini 1974. We should stress here that while Marx's main theoretical model was based on the dichotomy between workers and capitalists, in Book 3 of *Capital* and especially in the historical writings (as 'The eighteenth brumaire of Louis Napoleon': Marx 1852) the picture had already filled out, a notable influence being attributed to the middle classes; in the background, however, the simple dichotomy remained the basic pillar for an understanding of the main trends in capitalistic societies.

The new political and economic strength enjoyed by employed workers favoured redistribution of income in the direction of wages and salaries. This increased the saving capacity of the workers, and with it a broad growth in shareholding, which meant the possession (through equities) of shares of ownership in big industrial companies. Thanks to broader-based shareholding, and above all thanks to the notable weight of the public sector in the economy, the process of industrial concentration did not – contrary to Marx's prediction – entail parallel concentration in a few hands of the totality or near totality of wealth and economic power.[46]

This fact sees the thesis of inevitable revolution looming up in the evolution of the capitalistic system deprived of one of its main pillars, and with it the thesis of the progressively increasing misery of the proletariat is undermined. Another pillar – the thesis of the tendency of the rate of profits to fall – also turns out to have shaky foundations (as we saw above, in § 6).

As for the theory of labour value, it is sufficient to consider how Bortkiewicz reformulated it to see it as nothing but a complicated and substantially useless way of measuring the quantities of the means of production to determine production prices. The 'transformation problem' seems to have found consummation in Sraffa's contribution on the *Production of commodities by means of commodities* (1960) – see below, § 16.7 – where relative prices and the rate of profits are determined, given the real wage rate, through a system of equations much like Bortkiewicz's, with the difference that any reference to quantities measured in terms of labour contained disappears from Sraffa's equations:

$$(A_a p_a + B_a p_b + \ldots + N_a p_n)(1 + r) + L_a w = A p_a$$
$$(A_b p_a + B_b p_b + \ldots + N_b p_n)(1 + r) + L_b w = B p_b$$
$$\ldots\ldots\ldots\ldots\ldots\ldots\ldots\ldots\ldots\ldots\ldots\ldots\ldots\ldots\ldots\ldots$$
$$\ldots\ldots\ldots\ldots\ldots\ldots\ldots\ldots\ldots\ldots\ldots\ldots\ldots\ldots\ldots\ldots$$
$$(A_n p_a + B_n p_b + \ldots + N_n p_n)(1 + r) + L_n w = N p_n$$

where $A_a, B_a, \ldots, N_a, L_a$ are the quantities of commodities $a, b, \ldots, n$ and of labour required to produce quantity A of commodity a; $A_b, B_b, \ldots,$ N_b, L_b are the quantities of commodities $a, b, \ldots, n$ and of labour

---

[46] The financial control structure of the major firms differs from one country to another. In some cases, e.g. the United States, investment funds have an important role; in others, e.g. Germany or Japan, a significant degree of concentration of economic power (far greater than can be deduced from the dispersion of share ownership) derives from a network of cross-shareholdings centring on banks and financial companies. The researches so far carried out on these subjects are quite insufficient, although the past few years have seen a certain revival of interest.

required to produce quantity B of commodity b; A_n, B_n, . . . , N_n, L_n are the quantities of commodities a, b, . . . , n and of labour required to produce quantity N of commodity n; r is the rate of profits; p_a, p_b, . . . , p_n are the prices of commodities. The equations are n, as many as the commodities, and allow us to determine $n - 1$ relative prices and one of the distributive variables, wage rate or rate of profits, given the other.

As we can see, then, there is no need to measure the different magnitudes in terms of labour contained. May it perhaps be, as Colletti (1969a, p. 431) said, that 'Sraffa has made a bonfire of Marx's analysis'? Actually, things are rather more complicated: it remains true, in fact, that profits can exist only in so far as the system is capable of producing a surplus that is not absorbed by wages; some economists (for instance Garegnani, 1981) have gone on to maintain that 'the fact' of exploitation remains evident even if we have to forgo the labour theory of value. However, curious problems arise (for which see Steedman 1977, whose work is an essential reference for a post-Sraffian criticism of Marx): for instance, in the case of joint production (when, as is commonly the case, each firm produces more than one single good), it may happen that for a given technology an increase in the rate of profits corresponds to a decrease in the rate of exploitation, or that a positive rate of profits corresponds to a negative exploitation ratio. Furthermore, as Lippi (1976) in particular stressed, abandonment of the labour theory of value can hardly be held painless from the Marxian point of view, since it takes labour to be the *substance* of value.[47]

This latter point is related to Marx's 'vision' in the broad sense, which focused on the necessity of overcoming not the division of labour in general, nor the form which it assumes in capitalism, but the compulsory aspect of the division of labour. On the evidence of the *German ideology* as indeed of the 'Critique of the Gotha programme', it is clear that Marx and Engels had in mind not the absolute disappearance of the division of labour, but the possibility of superseding compulsory labour.[48] They stressed that only when men (and women, we may add) are free to fish,

---

[47] These brief remarks are obviously insufficient to give an account of such a vast and varied debate as that on the meaning of Marx's labour theory of value; among the many writings on the subject, we may mention Althusser 1965; Colletti 1969b; Garegnani 1981; Napoleoni 1972, 1976; Meek 1956; Sweezy 1942; Rosdolsky 1955. It is, however, worth stressing that the idea of labour as a *substance* of value – while implying the idea of 'labour in the abstract', to be kept distinct from 'common labour' (cf. Colletti 1969b, pp. 28–30) – did not imply the idea (which we may, rather, attribute to certain among the 'Ricardian socialists') of labour as the *source* of the product; in the 'Critique of the Gotha programme', Marx (1878, p. 153) explicitly says: 'Labour *is not the source* of all wealth. *Nature* is just as much the source of use values.'

[48] 'In a higher phase of communist society, after the enslaving subordination of the individual to the division of labour, and therewith also the antithesis between mental and

philosophise or cultivate their gardens as they like, shall we have reached a really free society.[49] Until then, even with the crucial transition from capitalism to socialism, the division of labour retains the nature of a necessity imposed on the individual worker.

We may compare Marx's attitude to Smith's. According to the latter, the division of labour is a source of economic and civic progress, but also of social problems; the former aspect may be held to outweigh the latter, and the division of labour thus deemed desirable, but steps must also be taken against the negative aspects, to offset them as far as possible.[50] Marx, on the other hand, seemed to consider the liberation of men from the serfdom of compulsory labour a real possibility, which implied a more drastically negative judgement of the transitional stages before the target was reached, and readiness to bear the costs necessary to reach it, including the 'dictatorship of the proletariat' in the socialist stage preceding the ultimate construction of communist society.[51] Now, not only have the theoretical elements invoked by Marx in support of the thesis of the inevitable transition from capitalism to socialism (social polarisation, tendency of the profit rate to fall) proved faulty but, above all, the socialist mode of production has proved a fragile form of social organisation as compared with the market economies on the crucial evidence of historical

physical labour, has vanished; after labour has become not only a means of life but life's prime want; after the productive forces have also increased with the all-round development of the individual, and all the springs of cooperative wealth flow more abundantly – only then can the narrow horizon of bourgeois right be crossed in its entirety and society inscribe on its banners: "From each according to his ability, to each according to his needs!"' (Marx and Engels 1878, p. 160). For a survey of the debate on the subject and the main issues connected to it (as for instance the nature of state power), cf. Villetti 1978.

[49] 'As soon as labour is distributed, each man has a particular, exclusive sphere of activity which is forced upon him and from which he cannot escape. He is a hunter, a fisherman, a shepherd, or a critical critic, and must remain so if he does not want to lose his means of livelihood; while in a communist society, where nobody has one exclusive sphere of activity but each can become accomplished in any branch he wishes, society regulates the general production and thus makes it possible for me to do one thing today and another tomorrow, to hunt in the morning, fish in the afternoon, rear cattle in the evening, criticise after dinner, just as I have a mind, without ever becoming hunter, fisherman, shepherd, or critic' (Marx and Engels 1845–6, p. 295).

[50] In this respect Smith opened a current of social reformism within which we may find supporters of cooperative or public welfare schemes, 'industrial democracy' schemes, or proposals to attribute the less qualified, more oppressive tasks to a 'labour army' (Rossi 1946). It is significant that the revolutionary Marxist tradition always opposed such proposals, considering them at most as temporary palliatives that risked leading the working class astray from its 'true objectives', namely the overthrow of capitalism.

[51] Marx, in fact, only made brief reference to these themes, which became burningly relevant only after the October Revolution of 1917 and the birth of the Soviet Union. The harshness of the dictatorship of the proletariat, supported equally by Lenin and Trotsky as by Stalin, was, however, prefigured by Marx in the few passages he devoted to the subject in his writings.

reality, and precisely with respect to what Marx considered the decisive element, namely the development of productive forces. The apparently more modest Smithian perspective – a path of progress, but with no definite point of arrival – seems preferable then, both as an interpretation of the evolution of human societies and as a guide to action, to the more radical – in fact, substantially utopian – perspective within which Marx created his theoretical architecture.

9.   Marxism after Marx

Marx's influence, in the decades following the publication of Book 1 of *Capital* until recent times, has been enormous. His thought inspired great, highly organised communist movements in industrialised Western countries, and political regimes that long dominated the major developing countries, from the Soviet Union after the 1917 Revolution, to China after the Second World War. This explains the huge volume of Marxian literature and the importance it has had in cultural debate. However, we will limit ourselves here to a few brief references to certain authors and themes of major relevance to the economic debate, while also omitting some important lines of research already considered in the previous sections (such as the transformation of labour values into prices of production).

Marx's immediate successors – his friend Friedrich Engels and his pupil Karl Kautsky (1854–1938) – are to be recalled here above all as editors of important works by their master published posthumously: Books 2 and 3 of *Capital* for Engels, and the *Theories of surplus value* (Marx, 1905–10) for Kautsky. In his political activity Kautsky was also one of the first of the 'revisionists', stressing the importance of the market (and consequently of money) for political and social progress, showing a preference for a long phase of transition from capitalism to socialism rather than the abrupt revolutionary leap to a fully centralised system as happened in the Soviet Union after the Bolshevik Revolution of 1917.[52]

The same line was followed, with greater clarity and decision, by Eduard Bernstein (1850–1932); his best-known work is *The prerequisites of socialism and the tasks of social-democracy* (1899), where he developed an evolutionistic view of the construction of socialism (as shown by the title of the English translation, *Evolutionary socialism*). In contrast with Marxian theories on the necessity of dictatorship of the proletariat in the

---

[52] On Kautsky, and more generally on the debate of the time between the different currents of Marxist socialism, cf. Salvadori 1976.

socialist stage of transition towards communism, he stressed the central role of democratic institutions for political and social progress.

Bernstein set out to purge Marx's analysis of Hegelian dialectic; furthermore, he viewed with some diffidence the more strictly theoretical aspects of Marx's economic thought, from the labour theory of value to the 'laws' of the tendencies to a falling rate of profits and increasing misery of the workers, attributing decisive importance to what empirical observation of reality can tell us about them.

A somewhat similar line of thinking was followed by the socialists belonging to the Fabian Society, founded in 1884 by a group of British intellectuals that included George Bernard Shaw (1856–1950) and economic historians Sidney Webb (1859–1947) and his wife Beatrice (1858–1943).[53] Shaw, Webb and various others produced a collective work, the *Fabian essays in socialism* (Shaw 1889), departing quite sharply from Marxism in the direction of an evolutionistic socialism even less radical than Bernstein's. The very name of the group is indicative of their programme, recalling the Roman consul Fabius Maximus, dubbed the Cunctator for his victorious war tactic based on small steps rather than great battles.

As far as economic theory was concerned, the *Fabian essays* show traces of a controversy following on an article by Philip Wicksteed (on whom cf. below, § 10.6), '*Das Kapital*: a criticism' published in the periodical *To-Day* in October 1884. Wicksteed's criticisms of the labour theory of value and the Marxian theory of exploitation based on it won the attention of the 'Fabians', and particularly George Bernard Shaw. Reviewing the *Fabian essays*, Wicksteed was able to assert that 'The "Fabians" have been at work on political economy, and the result is the distinct and definitive abandonment of the system of Karl Marx.'[54]

With the Fabians evolutionary socialism, originally born as direct progeny of Marxism, broke sharply away. However, other currents that were placed under the heading of 'Marxist orthodoxy', essentially on account of their political success, can also be considered heterodox when we compare them with Marx's original thought.

---

[53] The Webbs supported, among other things, social security schemes to be financed through taxes rather than through compulsory contributions as was the case with the system adopted by Bismarck and the system that took root in Great Britain after the Second World War. They also founded the London School of Economics, in 1895, designed to favour the development of a progressive economic culture well rooted in empirical research and not conditioned by the conservative ideology prevailing in the traditional universities. (On the subsequent radical changes of the London School, cf. Robbins 1971.)

[54] *The Inquirer*, 16 August 1890, quoted by Steedman 1989, p. 131, who also provides an account of the debate (ibid., pp. 117–44).

The first name to be invoked here is that of Vladimir Ilich Ulyanov (1870–1924), also known as Lenin. Of his vast production on economic themes we may recall two works preceding the Soviet Revolution: *The development of capitalism in Russia* (1898) and *Imperialism, the highest stage of capitalism* (1916).

In the first of these two works Lenin stressed the role of growth in commercial relations in undermining the structure of economic power characterising agriculture, by far the dominant sector in Russia at the time, and the active intervention of the tsarist state in the industrialisation process, with the creation of great factories and large concentrations of workers. Clearly, in recognising the revolutionary potentialities of such a situation Lenin was departing from Marx's original thesis, which saw the proletarian revolution as the inevitable outcome of a fully developed capitalism.

The second work, a brief essay written under the impetus of the First World War, began by recognising an element that contradicted Marx's analysis and that had become clear with the war, namely the fact that the workers and socialist parties in different countries identified with their respective national interests. Lenin took up a thesis propounded by British economist John Hobson (1858–1940) in an essay on *Imperialism* published in 1902, which saw in colonial developments the quest for outlets for the population and capital that remained unused in the industrialised countries because of the tendencies to under-consumption always latent in them. Lenin combined this thesis with an interpretation of monopoly capitalism fusing the Marxian 'law of industrial concentration' with the theory of integration of financial and industrial capital propounded by the Austrian Marxist Rudolf Hilferding (1877–1941) in *Das Finanzkapital* (1910).[55]

As far as the post-revolutionary Soviet Union was concerned, Lenin's writings pointed in the direction of the New Economic Policy (NEP) based on recognition of a certain role to the market, above all for determination of the crucial exchange ratio between agricultural products and manufactures, within a centralised economy characterised by state ownership of the means of production.

A leading supporter of NEP was Nikolai Bukharin (1888–1938), who, after the failure of attempts to export the socialist revolution to Western European countries, and in particular to war-impoverished Germany, contributed to the debate on 'socialism in one country' maintaining

---

[55] In the area of reformist socialism, the Austrian current is particularly important; it included, together with Kautsky and Hilferding, also Otto Bauer (1881–1938) and various others. On the debate between Austrian socialists and Austrian marginalists, cf. Kauder 1970.

the expediency of postponing the stage of centralised planning, leaving greater leeway to market mechanisms. These should simply be 'guided' by the state authorities along the road to accumulation and industrialisation, through control over the nerve centres of the economy, which implied recognition of small-scale peasant agriculture, and gradualism in the industrialisation process. Subsequently Bukharin was converted to the Stalinist views of state agriculture and forced accumulation, but this did not save him from the Stalinist purges of the late 1930s.

Among other things, Bukharin was the author of an essay on the *Economic theory of the leisure class* (1917), criticising the subjective theory of value of the Austrian school (cf. below, ch. 11), interpreted as the manifestation of a freedom of choice in consumption open only to a small fraction of the population but extended, with ideological distortion, to represent the working of the whole economy. Less well known is his *The ABC of communism* (1919), written with Evgenii Preobrazhensky (1886–1937).

The latter author was, unlike Bukharin, critical of the NEP, advocating a 'primitive accumulation' that could be achieved in Russia only with systematic state extortion of the surplus produced by the agricultural sector. Preobrazhensky was therefore favourable to strongly centralised planning, state ownership in agriculture, and exchange ratios between agricultural products and manufactures set by the central planning authority in favour of manufactures in support of the industrialisation process. In a work of 1921, Preobrazhensky went so far as to foresee as inevitable the clash between the socialist state and the kulaks, the small independent farmers who were in fact to be exterminated by Stalin.

After the defeat of the NEP, Preobrazhensky turned his attention to the conditions of equilibrium growth, anticipating Harrod's theory (cf. below, § 17.6), and argued the possibility of 'over-accumulation crises'. Perhaps it was due to these ideas, despite the merits he had acquired in the NEP debate, that Preobrazhensky fell out of Stalin's favour: after a show trial one of the Soviet Union's best economists was shot in 1937.[56]

The theme of disequilibrium in the process of accumulation had already been subjected to Marxist analyses in relation to the capitalistic economies by Tugan-Baranovsky (1865–1919) and Rosa Luxemburg (1871–1919).[57] Both utilised Marx's simple and enlarged reproduction schemes (cf. above, § 5). Tugan-Baranovsky (1905) thus showed both

---

[56] On Preobrazhensky, cf. Ellman 1987.
[57] On Tugan-Baranovsky, cf. Nove 1970; on Rosa Luxemburg, cf. Sweezy's introduction and Luciano Amodio's meticulous bio-bibliographical note to the Italian edition of his 1913 book.

the error of under-consumption theories holding crisis from deficiency of aggregate demand to be inevitable, and just how difficult it is to follow a growth path so as to maintain equilibrium between the propensity to save and investment opportunities. Rosa Luxemburg, in her celebrated *The accumulation of capital* (1913), studied the conditions of product realisation by focusing on the relationship between accumulation and growth of demand in the presence of a continuous drive towards technological change. Her book is a mine of ideas – albeit not always fully developed – that prompted a profusion of interpretative studies. Among other things, Rosa Luxemburg stressed the monopolistic nature of capitalism, the role of political elements (and military violence) in the functioning of the economy, imperialistic tendencies and the internationalisation of capitalism.

All these thinkers were, however, in one respect or another heretical in relation to the orthodoxy that had, since the late 1920s, been established in the Soviet Union and the European communist parties by the political leadership of Joseph Stalin (1879–1953). We have already seen his political choices in favour of accelerated industrialisation and state economy.[58] As far as economic theory is concerned, mention must be made of his thesis on the 'validity of the law of value within the socialist economy', stated with increasing determination in the aftermath of the Second World War though previously it had been denied. Propounded in a cryptic form, the thesis was interpreted as grounds to attribute greater importance to the price mechanism within socialist economies.

After the end of Stalinism, in an intellectual climate less stifling, although respect for orthodox thinking still remained imperative, debate on the 'law of value in a socialist economy' saw the development of some courageous heterodoxies, especially in the 'Warsaw school' where Michal Kalecki (cf. below, § 14.8) was the leading figure, while Oskar Lange (1904–65) and Wlodzmierz Brus (b. 1921), among others, supported the development of a 'socialist market'. Among the most original contributions by Western Marxist economists we may mention publications by Paul Baran (1910–64) and Paul Sweezy (1910–2004). Baran wrote *The political economy of growth* (1957), an analysis of the processes of capitalistic development based on the notion of 'potential surplus' and singling

---

[58] The idea that compulsory accumulation, after helping the industrialisation process, would lead to the Soviet Union catching up with and possibly overtaking the economic power of the United States, was widespread among Marxist economists in communist and Western countries alike, after the end of the Second World War. With the fall of the communist regimes we now see, on the contrary, that Russia had remained a largely underdeveloped country: political totalitarianism (and Stalinist terror), apart from the damage they produced in terms of civic growth, brought precious little advantage even in terms of purely economic growth.

out the reasons – in particular political and institutional factors – in different countries and epochs standing in the way of full use of productive capacities. Sweezy, a pupil of Schumpeter, was not only responsible for the previously mentioned *The theory of capitalist development* (1942) – still the best illustration of Marx's economic theory – but also, together with historian Leo Huberman, founded the *Monthly Review* in 1949. In 1966 Baran and Sweezy together published *Monopoly capital*, a book that, together with the writings of philosopher Herbert Marcuse (in particular *One-dimensional man*, published in 1956), became one of the main points of reference in the student agitation that spread from California to Paris in 1967–8, which then swept the whole world over.

10 The marginalist revolution: the subjective theory of value

1. The 'marginalist revolution': an overview

The term 'marginalist revolution' is commonly utilised to indicate a sudden change of direction in economic science, with the abandonment of the classical – and, more precisely, Ricardian – approach, and the shift to a new approach based on a subjective theory of value and the analytical notion of marginal utility.[1] The outbreak of the 'revolution' is commonly located in the years between 1871 and 1874, when the main writings were published of the leaders of the Austrian marginalist school, Carl Menger (1840–1921), of the British school, William Stanley Jevons (1835–82), and of the French (Lausanne) school, Léon Walras (1834–1910). In fact, 1871 saw the appearance of both the *Principles of pure economics* by Menger and *The theory of political economy* by Jevons, while Walras brought out his *Elements of pure economics* in 1874.

Let us, however, once again reiterate that the 'marginalist revolution' had had important precursors, as we will see again below. Moreover, the differences between the Austrian imputation approach, the French general economic equilibrium and Marshallian partial equilibriums were quite important, as far as both method and the basic view of the functioning of the economy were concerned. Among the English economists, then, Alfred Marshall (1842–1924; his *Principles of economics* appeared in 1890) followed a path of his own, differing from the radically subjective line taken by the first author of a marginalist theory of value, Jevons; and the influence exercised by the ideas and the academic power of the former was far greater than that of the latter.

In this and the following chapters we will illustrate the main characteristics of the three principal research currents traditionally included under the marginalist label; we will thus see how different they are from one another, and how misleading it is to delineate a clear-cut break around

---

[1] Howey 1960, pp. xiii and xxvii, informs us that the term 'marginalism' was introduced by John Hobson in *Work and wealth* (1914), while the term 'marginal' was first utilised by Wicksteed in his *Alphabet* (1888), and Wieser utilised it in his *Grenznutzen* in 1884.

1870.[2] However, before doing so it may be useful to point out some basic elements common to these different lines of research, contrasting them with the classical approach illustrated in the previous chapters.

Sraffa (1960, p. 93) sums up the contrast with two images: the classical approach consists in the 'picture of the system of production and consumption as a circular process', while the marginalist approach aligns the perspective along 'a one-way avenue that leads from "Factors of production" to "Consumption goods"'. Thus Sraffa outlines the differences between the two approaches in terms of the view taken of the economic problem and the structure of the analysis, in particular in the field of value and distribution, which is where the basic nature of the different approaches finds its most direct expression.

Let us take a closer, albeit summary, look at these differences, which concern definition of the economic problem, the notion of value, the concept of equilibrium, the role of prices and the theory of distribution.

First of all, within the classical approach the economic problem was conceived as analysis of those conditions that guarantee the continuous functioning of an economic system based on the division of labour, and hence analysis of production, distribution, accumulation and circulation of the product. In the case of the marginalist approach, by contrast, the economic problem concerned the optimal utilisation of scarce available resources to satisfy the needs and desires of economic agents.

Secondly, the classical economists' objective view of value, based on the difficulty of production, contrasts with the subjective view of the marginalist approach, based on evaluation of utility of commodities on the part of the consumers.

Thirdly, as a consequence of these differences, the notion of equilibrium took on a central role in the marginalist approach, again marking it out from the classical approach: equilibrium corresponded to conditions of optimal utilisation of scarce available resources, and was therefore identified by a set of values for all economic variables, prices and

---

[2] On the 'marginalist revolution', together with the bibliography referring to Jevons, Menger and Walras which will be cited below, cf. Hutchison 1953, Howey 1960, Kauder 1965 and the articles collected in Black, Coats and Goodwin 1973. Howey stresses, among other things, that historians of economic thought at the end of the nineteenth century did not recognise the existence of a 'marginalist revolution'. Blaug 1973 entitles his paper 'Was there a marginal revolution?' and concludes (p. 14) that it 'was a process, not an event'. Stigler 1973, while attributing to Bentham the 'utility theory' (a thesis which, as we saw above in § 6.7, is rather superficial), stresses (p. 312) that the theory 'took no important part in any policy-oriented controversy up to World War I.' Hutchison 1953, p. 6, maintains that '"marginal" or neoclassical economics only really came into its own in the nineties' of the nineteenth century, while (1973, p. 202) only in the fourth quarter of the twentieth century did the different 'schools' merge 'into a general, cosmopolitan North American and western European melting pot'.

quantities simultaneously. The classical approach held the problem of relative prices distinct from the problem of decisions concerning accumulation and production levels; at the most, one might speak of equilibrium with reference to the levelling of sector profit rates stemming from the competition of capitals, while the term 'balancing', which did not imply a precise equality, was preferred when speaking of demand and supply (as in the expression 'The balance between supply and demand').

Fourthly, in accordance with the above points, prices acquired the meaning of indicators of relative difficulty of production for the classical approach, and of indicators of scarcity (relative to consumers' preferences) within the marginalist approach.[3]

Fifthly, and finally, income distribution was no more or less than a specific case of price theory in the context of the marginalist approach (where it concerned the prices of the 'factors of production'), while for the classical approach it was a problem with autonomous characteristics, concerning the role of different social classes and their power relations.[4]

As mentioned above, such common characteristics took on different forms in authors belonging to different currents within the marginalist approach. For instance, the French current of general economic equilibrium founded by Walras, taken up and developed at the beginning of the twentieth century by the Italian Vilfredo Pareto (cf. below, § 12.3) and subsequently, in the last thirty years, by authors such as Kenneth Arrow and Gerard Debreu, was based on the assumption of initial endowments

---

[3] Obviously, this means neither that the 'difficulty of production' did not play a role within the marginalist approach (indeed it did, as mediation between original productive resources on the one hand and final goods and services on the other), nor that 'scarcity' did not play a role within the classical approach (again, it did, through different kinds of constraints, concerning technology – as in differential rent – or levels of production, through the stage reached by the process of accumulation). It only means that, in the first case, scarcity played a central analytical role, in the basic model of pure exchange, while technology may be introduced in a successive stage of analysis; in the second case, instead, scarcity could play an indirect role in determining production levels and technology, but not a direct role in determining prices. On this latter point, cf. Roncaglia 1975, pp. 125–6.

[4] Also within this approach, however, the determination of prices and that of distributive variables were connected, as was to become evident in Sraffa's analysis. With some imprecision (within the general economic equilibrium approach, all variables are simultaneously determined), Walras 1874, p. 45, said that in opposition to the classical approach ('the school of Ricardo and Mill'), in the new theory 'the prices of productive services are determined by the prices of their products and not the other way round'.

Other characteristics common to the different currents of the marginalist approach (cf. for example Coats 1973, p. 338) were a consequence of those already noticed (such as attribution of an important role to demand vis-à-vis supply in the determination of prices, which stems from the subjective viewpoint), or were less clear-cut, concerning not the analytical and conceptual structure but the professionalisation of economics (greater precision of language) or the toolbox utilised (calculus).

of resources (different kinds of working abilities, lands, capital goods) considered as given in physical terms, and matched with economic agents' preferences.

The English current of Jevons and Marshall, by contrast, tended to consider the quantities available of the different resources also as variables to be determined within the theory, utilising as exogenous data utility and disutility maps of the various economic agents. In particular, it was the balance between the utility of goods obtainable through productive activity and the worker's toil and trouble, or in other words the disutility of work, that determined the amount of work done and hence, given the production function, the amount of product.

Finally the theorists of the Austrian school (together with Menger, we should also mention his pupils von Wieser and von Böhm-Bawerk: cf. below, § 11.4) adopted a radically subjective viewpoint according to which the value of each good or service was deduced from its utility for the final consumer, directly in the case of consumption goods and indirectly in the case of production goods. In this latter case a share of the utility that the produced good has for consumers was 'imputed' to the means of production, computing such a share in proportion to the contribution represented by the good or service under consideration to the productive process (hence the expression 'imputation theory').

2.   The precursors: equilibrium between scarcity and demand

As recalled in the previous section, side by side with the classical view of the economic system based on the idea of the circular flow of production and consumption, we have a different view involving the idea of scarcity of available resources with respect to potential demand. The former approach has prices derived from the conditions of reproducibility of an economic system based on the division of labour, while for the latter prices stem from the subjective evaluations of economic agents, and thus express the relative scarcity of the various resources and of the various goods obtained from them. Here it is worth stressing that this view was not born with the 'marginalist revolution' in the years between 1871 and 1874, but has accompanied economic science from its very beginnings.

Even in the prehistory of political economy we find discussion of the 'just price', with an important role acknowledged for the play between demand and supply. Here we also find conceptualisation, primitive though it may be, of the issue of prices in relation to the medieval markets, conceived as a place and time for encounter and comparison between supply and demand. Moreover, as early as the Scholastic writers we find the thesis being aired that utility is the true source or cause of value; in other words, the comparison between supply and demand was considered as an expression of the comparison between scarcity and utility. This view survived and developed over time, side by side with the idea that the value of commodities lay essentially in the difficulty of production, and particularly in labour requirements. While in the seventeenth, eighteenth and nineteenth centuries this latter view found its way into the classical approach of Petty, Smith and Ricardo, various authors took on and developed the alternative view, connecting prices with the comparison between scarcity and buyers' evaluation, and coming close, in some cases, to establishing a link between value in use and value in exchange based on the notion of marginal utility. The widespread acceptance of the quantity theory of money, with its analytical framework based on supply and demand, constituted an important help.

A brief survey shows that the subjective approach to the theory of value had important roots in England, Italy, France and Germany.[5] Here we limit ourselves to recalling some of the best-known authors, country by country.

In Italy, the most important exponent of the subjective approach was probably the Neapolitan Abbé Ferdinando Galiani, whose work is considered above, in § 4.8, where also his predecessor, Bernardo Davanzati, is discussed.

Half a century after Galiani, another Italian economist, Luigi Molinari Valeriani (1758–1828) proposed in even clearer terms a theory of value based on demand and supply against the theory based on production costs, and sought to develop for the first time a mathematical and geometrical analysis of the issue (*Del prezzo delle cose tutte mercatabili*, 1806).[6]

Various French economists who supported a subjective theory of value in the eighteenth and nineteenth centuries (apart from Jean-Baptiste Say, on whom see above, § 6.3) were recalled by Jevons, in the preface to the second edition (1879) of *The theory of political economy*. In particular, *Le commerce et le gouvernement* (1776) by Condillac was referred to by Jevons (1871, p. 57) as 'the earliest distinct statement of the true connexion between value and utility'. Jevons also recalled 'the French engineer Dupuit' and, quite naturally, the *Recherches sur les principes mathématiques*

---

[5] Some authors (for instance Bowles 1972; Blaug 1973) explicitly deny, on these grounds, the revolutionary character of the marginalist 'revolution'.

[6] (About the price of all things subject to commerce). On Valeriani, cf. Schumpeter's 1954, p. 511 n., laudatory remarks, and Faucci 2000, pp. 165–6. Other eighteenth-century authors worthy of mention here are Beccaria and Verri (cf. above, § 4.8). Schumpeter 1954, p. 307 n., attributes to the latter a 'hyperbolical demand law'; according to Verri's law, $pq = c$, where c is a constant.

de la théorie de la richesse (1838) by Antoine Augustin Cournot (1801–77), who, however, while building his analysis of price determination on demand and supply, considered as functions of price, 'does not recede to any theory of utility' (Jevons 1871, p. 59) and to whom, as a consequence, it was not possible to attribute a subjective theory of value.[7] Indeed, Cournot was more a child of French rationalism than of utilitarianism.[8]

'A theory of pleasure and pain' was attributed by Jevons (1871, p. 60) to a German, Hermann Heinrich Gossen (1810–58), author of a book that fell quickly into oblivion, *Entwickelung der Gesetze des menschlinen Verkehrs* . . . (The laws of human relations and the rules of human action derived therefrom, 1854), who had developed a marginalist theory of consumer equilibrium.[9] Again in Germany, Johann Heinrich von Thünen (1783–1850), a landowner active in land improvements, produced a work in two parts, *Der isolierte Staat* (The isolated state, first part, 1826; second part, 1850),[10] in which he not only developed a theory of rent connected to the distance from the place of consumption, but also and above all proposed an analysis of substitution between land and labour, when rent decreases, substantially based on equality between marginal productivity and price for each of these productive factors.[11]

Jevons did not, however, dwell on the interesting contribution of the Swiss mathematician Daniel Bernoulli (1700–82). This latter author had

---

[7] Arsène Dupuit (1804–66), Piedmontese by birth, engineer in the famous French Corps des Ports et Chaussées, is known for his writings on how to determine the usefulness of public works. In these writings, relying on demand functions, he measured what was later to become known as the notion of consumer's surplus. In this context we must also recall various other French authors, such as Turgot and Cantillon (whom we consider here among the French, since this was the language in which his work appeared, although he was of Irish origin: cf. above, § 4.5). In an essay on Cantillon, Jevons (1881) considered him the founder of political economy precisely for his analysis of prices. Also, Leon Walras's father, Auguste Walras, in his book *De la nature de la richesse, et de l'origine de la valeur* (1831) stated with decision that 'value depends upon *rarity*' (quoted by Jevons 1871, p. 64).

[8] Note that Cournot did not show traces of the influence of French sensism. Streissler (1990, pp. 56–7), however, stresses that Cournot was the first who explicitly introduced a demand curve, in his 1838 book, preceding by three years the German Karl Heinrich Rau (cf. below, § 11.1). Walker 1996, p. 3, instead stresses that, as remarked above, Cournot did not provide theoretical foundations for the demand function (commonly located by marginalists in individual preferences), but simply presupposed it. Blaug 1962, p. 43, notices that Cournot 'first laid down the modern notion of perfect competition in which firms face a horizontal demand curve because their number is so large that none can influence the price of the product'.

[9] On Gossen, cf. Georgescu-Roegen's introduction to the English translation of his book (Georgescu-Roegen 1983), and Niehans 1990, pp. 187–96.

[10] A third part was published posthumously in 1863, bringing together unpublished writings of various types. Cf. Schumpeter 1954, p. 465.

[11] On von Thünen, cf. Niehans 1990, pp. 164–75.

tackled, within the theory of probability, the so-called St Petersburg paradox, that is, the aversion to risk manifested by individuals who prefer a sure sum to an equal sum given by the actuarial value of a bet (who for instance prefer 1,000 euros for sure to the possibility of winning 0 or 2,000 from tossing a coin, according to which side of the coin shows up, while the actuarial value of the two cases is identical). To solve such a paradox, Bernoulli assumed that the increase of individual wealth is accompanied by an increase in utility that is an inverse function of the wealth already owned; in other words, he invoked a specific instance of the principle of decreasing marginal utility.[12]

In England, from Petty to Smith, up to Ricardo and his followers, the subjective approach to value was decidedly confined to a secondary plane. We can, however, recall the statements of principle by Samuel Bailey on the nature of value (cf. above, § 8.3), the writings by Senior, Whately, Longfield and above all a lecture on value in 1833 by William Forster Lloyd (1794–1852), professor of political economy at Oxford University, and published together with other lectures in 1837 (cf. above, § 8.7).

Thus, in the development of a subjective analytical construction, a central role was played by explanations of consumers' choices, and hence by demand. In this field we have the main innovation of the 'marginalist' approach, in comparison with the tradition of the classical school, namely the idea of explaining exchange value on the basis of use values. Within the classical approach, the distinction between value in use and value in exchange was already explicit, for instance, in Adam Smith (cf. above, § 5.5), who was followed slavishly in this by many others, including David Ricardo and John Stuart Mill. Value in use – the fact of being useful to some purpose – was considered a quality of commodities, an indispensable characteristic (a prerequisite) for goods to have a positive exchange value; not a measurable characteristic, however, and hence not an element to rely on when explaining exchange values.

It is, of course, true that the classical economists also spoke of large or small value in use, but in very generic terms. This happened, for instance, with the well-known paradox of water and diamonds: the former, it was said, has a large value in use but a small value in exchange, while diamonds have a modest value in use but a considerable value in exchange. As we saw above (§ 4.8), the paradox was solved before Smith, by Galiani

---

[12] The importance of Bernoulli's work is stressed by Schumpeter 1954, pp. 302–5, and, in his wake, by Spiegel 1971, pp. 143–4. Schumpeter considered Bernoulli also a precursor of the modern von Neumann–Morgenstern theory of games (cf. below, § 17.2). Spiegel recalls that Bernoulli's work was originally (1738) published in Latin, and only much later translated into German (1896) and English (1954), thus escaping the attention of economists.

in particular, recalling that the most useful good may also be the most abundant one, while it is scarcity vis-à-vis the demand from potential buyers which determines the price.[13]

This argument foreshadowed the key element of marginalist theory, namely the idea that value in use (assumed as capable of measurement) decreases when the quantity consumed of each commodity increases. Value in use thus became a decreasing function of the quantity consumed of each commodity and, as we will see in more detail below, value in exchange could be derived from the value in use of the last dose consumed of the good under consideration. To be developed on the analytical plane, the subjective theory of value, i.e. the approach which derived the value in exchange of commodities from the consumer's subjective evaluation, thus required a notion which some of the subjective theorists' forerunners of marginalism foreshadowed, namely the notion of marginal utility.

The Jevonian approach was made up of other elements side by side with the simple subjectivist orientation in the explanation of the theory of value. Firstly, there was a reinterpretation of classical utilitarianism, originally developed by Bentham with different aims and meaning. Secondly, there was a twin methodological choice: methodological individualism, and the search for 'scientific rigour' conducted through the application of the mathematical tool in the economic field. These elements will be discussed in the next sections.

3.   William Stanley Jevons

Some historians of economic thought have spoken of a Jevonian revolution, in order to stress, on the one hand, the break with the tradition of classical political economy and, on the other hand, differences with the other currents of the so-called marginalist revolution, namely the French current initiated by Walras and the Austrian one starting from Menger.[14]

What characterised Jevons in his break with the classical tradition were, on the one hand, his views on the psychology of the human being and, on the other, his aim to mathematise economic theory: two aspects which we will examine in § 4. Another interesting aspect, for which Jevons was representative of his times, concerned the professionalisation of economics. This tendency will be discussed below, when illustrating

---

[13] Within the classical approach, where attention focuses on reproducible commodities, scarcity can be overcome through production of additional units of the commodity; as a consequence, as seen above, exchange value is brought back to the relative difficulty of production. We may speak of scarcity, in substance, only when the available quantity of a commodity is given.

[14] Cf. Schabas 1990: an essential contribution to our understanding of Jevons.

Marshall's contribution to the construction of a specifically economic curriculum of studies. Here we will only stress that Jevons's own life was indicative of a clear-cut change: personal success coincided with publication of new theories and their acceptance on the part of colleagues – university professors – while for Petty or Cantillon, Quesnay or Smith, Ricardo or John Stuart Mill, success was revealed in the wider circle of men of culture or in acceptance of their ideas in the political arena.

Jevons was born in Liverpool in 1835 to a Unitarian family, followers of a religious creed characterised by concern with realities rather than form, and in particular by compassion for the derelict. Personal and public vicissitudes influenced the formation of the young Jevons: the death of his mother in 1845, the terrible Irish famine of 1847, and the economic crisis of 1848 with the collapse of railroad companies and bankruptcy of the small family firm. Further stages in his life were marked by the Great Exhibition of 1851, in London, and his father's death in 1855. At that time, one of his brothers had moved to New Zealand, while one of his sisters had been committed to a lunatic asylum; the relatives with whom Jevons was closest were his younger brother Thomas, who was to become a banker in New York, and his sister Lucy; it is clear that Jevons had to fend for himself to find his way through life.

After junior school, in 1850 Jevons went to University College, London, where he studied natural sciences, chemistry and mathematics. As a chemist he was hired by the Australian mint, and at the age of nineteen he moved to Sydney, where he resided from 1854 to 1859, dedicating his spare time to the study of botany and meteorology. In 1857 he began to cultivate an interest in social and economic issues, and soon decided to make the 'study of Man' his mission in life. To this end, he forewent a tenured job and returned to London to register again at University College, where he took a first degree in 1860 and graduated in 1862. At the same time he tried to eke out a living as a journalist; in 1863 he accepted a job as general tutor in Manchester, the lowest rung on the academic ladder. He had already presented (in 1862) a memoir to the British Association, without obtaining any reaction, although his paper already contained the essential elements of his subjective theory of value. An applied economics essay on the fall in the value of gold, published in 1863, met with a better reception. In the same year he published a work on logic; to this field Jevons returned repeatedly in subsequent years.

Jevons achieved fame with *The coal question* (1865). This was again an applied economics work, in which he maintained the thesis of the impending exhaustion of coal reserves, hence the existence of an insurmountable constraint to the development of British manufactures, since coal constituted the energy source for the entire productive system. This was a Malthusian idea, in which a scarce natural resource – coal – took up the role that food products had in Malthus. The dire predictions of the latter had not come true, according to Jevons, because of the abolition of the Corn Laws, and hence of duties on corn imports. As a matter of fact, both Jevons and Malthus were way off the track in their pessimistic forecasts of thwarted development through purblind undervaluation of technological change.[15]

The fame thus acquired, together with his works concerning logic, brought him nomination to a professorship in logic and mental and moral philosophy at Owens College, Manchester, in 1866. Finally, after publication of his major contribution to economic theory, the *Theory of political economy*, in 1871, and the treatise on the *Principles of science* in 1874, in 1876 he became professor of political economy at University College, London.[16] In 1880 Jevons decided to resign, in order to work full time on his researches; but in 1882 he drowned while swimming during a seaside holiday.

Jevons's personal itinerary helps us to understand the background to his 'subjective revolution'. Behind it there was in fact adhesion to a view of political economy no longer as a moral science, much like history or politics, but as a science like physics or mathematics. This choice of perspective coincided with the cultural path followed by Jevons himself: a student of chemistry and mathematics first, then author of essays on method in science and formal logic (together with the writings on economics that brought him fame). His views on human psychology, relating to Condorcet's sensism, pointed in the direction of necessary quantitative connections ('laws') also in the field of the social and human sciences. Faith in the natural sciences thus combined with belief in the objective nature of perception. Logic, as a purely formal and abstract science, provided the tools for analysis of 'laws' in the field of both the natural and human sciences.

Though not important in themselves, in this respect it is worth noting Jevons's contributions to formal logic, where he followed in the wake of De Morgan and Boole (who conceived logic as a sector of algebra), but with a wider perspective, maintaining that while mathematics considers

---

[15] In the case of energy sources, the history of the last centuries records an opposite tendency to the one sketched out by Jevons, with the transition from less efficient and more costly sources (first wood, then coal) to more efficient and less costly sources (oil, natural gas). Cf. Roncaglia 1983a.

[16] Jevons's papers and correspondence have been published in seven volumes, edited by Black and Könekamp: Jevons 1972–81. The (few) reviews of the *Theory of political economy* are summarised by Howey 1960, pp. 61–9. Among them, the one with which Marshall began his career as an economist was considered by Jevons as scarcely deserving attention.

quantities, formal logic concerns the relations between qualities. The laws of probability are conceived of as a priori. Fundamental in particular was Jevons's view – in this respect following a tradition going at least from Petty to Condorcet – that numbers are capable of expressing everything.[17]

In the field of research, the scientist must pursue agreement between theory and facts through a procedure consisting in inventing hypotheses and comparing the deductions drawn from them with experience.

We find many of these aspects in the *Principles of science*, which Jevons published in 1874 and, in a largely revised second edition, in 1877. Actually, Jevons dedicated rather more time to this line of research, before and after publication of *The theory of political economy*, than to research in the field of economics, and these themes are therefore significant for an understanding of how one of the fathers of the 'subjective revolution' reasoned. From our viewpoint, the point to be stressed is that Jevons was very far from pursuing an axiomatic method, where what mattered was the logical construction of the theory and not its realism: had he not embraced a sensistic view of man, it is unlikely that Jevons would have gone in the direction of building a subjective theory of value.

4.   The Jevonian revolution

Jevons's subjective theory of value was thus the joint product of the project of relying on the mathematical method in economics and on a sensistic view of human psychology.

In developing this theory Jevons modified the meaning of some key concepts, thus breaking with the earlier tradition. Such modifications, essential to build the marginalist analytical edifice, mainly concerned the notion of utility inherited from Bentham, which Jevons oriented in the opposite direction to that suggested by John Stuart Mill.

As remarked above, Bentham with his felicific calculus proposed to consider pleasures and pains in quantitative terms. Closer to Jevons (who quoted him as a forerunner) and to the economics field, was Richard Jennings (1814–91) who, in his essay on the *Natural elements of political economy* (1855) and in some other writings, also took this path. Jevons brought the line to an end, building a subjective theory of value on the basis of a quantitative, one-dimensional view of value in use.

---

[17] Schabas stresses this aspect in the very title of her book on Jevons, *A world ruled by number*. Cf. also Mays 1962, p. 223: 'following Boole and De Morgan, he believed that any rational system of ideas could be put into symbolic form. The system could then be operated on according to the laws of logic to produce a chain of deductions.' Cf. also Black 1973.

Firstly, the quantification of pleasures and pains as one-dimensional magnitudes was developed by Jevons with greater rigour than in Bentham. The latter, as remarked above (§ 4.8), had pointed to a number of elements – seven, for the sake of precision: intensity, duration, certainty, propinquity, fecundity, purity and extent – which determine the quantity of pleasure or pain connected to a given action. Jevons reduced these elements to two – intensity and duration – and considered the quantity of pleasure as determined by their product. Time, hence duration, was treated as a continuous variable and, symmetrically, so was intensity. In this way the quantity of pleasure, namely utility, turned out to be itself a continuous variable. These were obviously necessary features for the applicability of differential calculus or, in other words, for the formulation of the Jevonian notion of the 'final degree of utility', nowadays commonly known as marginal utility.

Secondly, Jevons stressed that utility is an abstract relationship between object and person, not a property intrinsic to the object.[18] Any object may, in fact, have a different utility for different persons or in different moments of time. In any case, what matters is not so much total utility, but rather the increment of utility when the quantity available of the commodity increases, namely the final degree of utility. Each individual signals such a magnitude with readiness to pay for the commodity itself.[19] This allows us to compare through the market the valuations of a given individual for different goods, but also – through the amount of money each of them is willing to pay – those of different individuals for the same good; however, this fact is not in itself sufficient to ensure the possibility of a social felicific calculus, since nothing guarantees that every individual will attribute the same utility to any given quantity of money.

These aspects are essential for an understanding of the differences between Jevons's views and those of the utilitarian tradition going from Bentham to John Stuart Mill discussed above. Jevons built a 'utilitarian' economics in direct opposition to Ricardo's and Mill's classical school; in doing so, he reduced economic science to a theory of rational choice, under the postulate that each individual is able to compute in a one-dimensional space all consequences of any action, at least within the economic sphere. Thus Jevons explicitly postulated the possibility of a felicific

---

[18] In this respect Jevons, implicitly focusing on *complacibilitas* and totally neglecting *virtuositas*, differed from a large part of the Scholastic tradition which took into consideration both aspects (cf. above, § 2.4) and from authors such as Galiani, while taking up Bailey's relativism.

[19] The idea that individuals signal their valuation of the commodities through the sum that they are ready to pay for them had already appeared in Verri and in Bentham: cf. Faucci 1989, p. 79.

calculus for each individual. At the same time, in his main contribution to economic theory, the 1871 volume, he explicitly and emphatically denied the possibility of interpersonal comparisons.[20] Consequentialist ethics, requiring interpersonal comparisons, was thus made to disappear. Each individual may identify 'good' in whatever increases his or her personal utility; but all this is completely different from the utilitarian ethics of Bentham and Mill, where social, not individual, consequences are what matter for the moral assessment of any action.

Jevons's definition of economics also differed from Mill's idea of political economy. As we saw above (§ 8.9), Mill considered political economy as limited to a specific aspect of human nature, i.e. the desire to possess wealth. Jevons, on the other hand, recalling a characteristically Millian point – namely that 'the feelings of which a man is capable are of various grades' – limited economics to a specific subset of feelings, 'the lowest rank of feelings'. In this way, according to Jevons, 'The calculus of utility aims at supplying the ordinary wants of man at the least cost of labour.'[21]

It is worth stressing that this definition is only apparently obvious and unproblematic. For instance, it would relegate my demand for Bach recordings to the lowest rank of feelings, exactly on the same level as my demand for chocolate (both, recordings and chocolate, being part of my ordinary wants); on the other hand, were it not so, economics would take into account only part of the consumer's expenditure decisions, and it would be impossible to define univocally a budget constraint. In fact, the reason why Jevons found himself compelled to give such an obviously controvertible definition of economic science lay in the fact that such a definition was essential for his crucial aim, the formulation of economics as a mathematical science. In fact, in Jevons's own words, 'It is clear that economics, if it is to be a science at all, must be a mathematical science [. . .] *our theory must be mathematical, simply because it deals with quantities.*'[22] It was this crucial aim which led Jevons to assume human feelings

---

[20] Not even Menger or Walras, considered together with Jevons as the fathers of the marginalist revolution, resorted to interpersonal comparisons, even if they did not feel compelled to explicitly reject them. In fact, while in England it was impossible not to take Benthamite utilitarianism into account, there was hardly any need for this in France, and even less in Austria.

[21] Jevons 1871, pp. 92–3. Bukharin 1917, instead, maintained that marginalist theory, by attributing central importance to consumer's choice, concerned the behaviour of the leisured classes more than that of the mass of the population which, living at or near simple subsistence level, has a largely constrained consumption structure.

[22] Jevons 1871, p. 78; italics in the original. As a matter of fact the last sentence should be inverted: 'our theory should deal with quantities – namely with variables defined in such a way as to be liable to be treated as one-dimensional quantities – because only in this way are we able to work it out in mathematical terms'. We may also recall here that the use of differential calculus was by no means an absolute novelty; for instance, it

as a one-dimensional quantitative variable: a point which was stressed again and again.[23]

All this involved both explicit and implicit shifts in the way the economy was viewed and in the conception of human nature. First of all, the core of the theory consisted in the analysis of individual choices between different pleasures (consumption) and pains (labour); the feelings (preferences) of each individual had to be assumed as an independent datum of the problem. Only under these conditions could the summation of individual behaviours constitute a theory of the whole economy. In other terms, methodological individualism[24] was a necessary requisite for the subjective theory of value. But the assumption of independence of individual preferences was in no way justified by Jevons: it was simply postulated, as implicit in the very structure of his theory.[25]

Second, Jevons viewed economics not as the science of the wealth of nations – its growth, its distribution among the different social classes – but as a problem concerning the maximum satisfaction obtainable from the allocation of a given amount of resources. In Jevons's own words

had already been recommended – even if not utilised in practice – by Malthus, and had subsequently been utilised by Thomas Perronet Thompson (1783–1869), Bentham's ally in the launch of the *Westminster Review* (Spiegel 1971, pp. 507–8).

[23] Naturally, as noted above, utility was not measured directly, but through its manifestation in individual choices. The core of the issue does not, however, lie in the *direct* measurability of utility, but rather in the fact that it is conceived, as recalled above, as a one-dimensional magnitude.

Recourse to indirect measurement of utility, through observation of consumer's behaviour, raises a different issue, concerning the circularity of reasoning: cf. Roncaglia 1975, pp. 106–11. However, if we accept a sensistic view of the individual, and if we assume stability over time of consumer's preferences, the charge of circular reasoning falls as far as comparative static analyses are concerned. This is why it is important to stress the limits of the utilitarian-sensistic view, connected to a one-dimensional representation of human nature.

[24] There are a number of definitions of methodological individualism. (For a critical survey, cf. Donzelli 1986, pp. 33–113.) Here by methodological individualism we mean the assumption that society is nothing but a sum of individuals, and that the preferences of every individual are independent from those of any other individual, so that we have the thesis according to which 'all social macro-laws are reducible to the theory of individual behaviours' (Donzelli 1986, p. 38).

[25] John Stuart Mill's thesis, on the need to build an 'ethology' in the sense of a science of the national character (cf. above, § 8.9), implicitly pointed out how far from obvious (and how alien to the classical economists' view of the world) was the assumption of independence of individual preferences. It contradicts the idea of man as a 'social animal' on which, for instance, Smith relied in his ethics of sympathy and in his analysis of the origins of the division of labour. To introduce such an assumption, without an explicit evaluation of its foundations, means meeting a need imposed by the chosen theoretical structure without considering the costs it implies in terms of distortions in the representation of reality. Common recourse to this procedure within the marginalist approach should lead us to ponder the shaky foundations of the marginalist theoretical construction (especially when continuous confrontation of theory and reality is considered necessary, as indeed it was by Jevons).

(1871, p. 254; italics in the original): 'The problem of economics may [. . .] be stated thus: *Given, a certain population, with various needs and powers of production, in possession of certain lands and other sources of material: required, the mode of employing their labour which will maximize the utility of the produce.*'

Third, Jevons's economics applied perfect rationality to an aspect of individual behaviour (identification of which, as we saw above, is not so simple): 'the lowest rank of feelings'. Not only was each individual isolated from all the others, interdependence of preferences being ruled out, but this specific aspect was also isolated from all other aspects of human nature, and in particular from what is essential in civilised human beings, their very nature as social beings. Jevons (ibid., p. 102) remarked that 'In the science of economics we treat men not as they ought to be, but as they are.' However, this was precisely the crucial point of difference. The Scottish Enlightenment – the tradition, that is, within which Smith developed his notion of political economy – considered 'men as they are' as something more complex than mere sensistic machines, certainly endowed with natural proclivities to socialising; it was precisely because of this, as we saw above, that Smith was able to focus on self-interest, restrained by the 'moral of sympathy', rather than on sheer selfishness, as a motivation driving human actions.

In other words, his decision to formulate economics as a mathematical science compelled Jevons to redefine as measurable magnitudes the motivations of human actions, at least in so far as choices of rational economic agents were concerned. In this way, however, the richness and subtlety of the Smithian notion of the economic subject were drastically impoverished, with the risk of gross misunderstandings of the way human societies operate. In a sense, in so far as it relies on conceptual foundations similar to Jevons's, it is the whole of the marginalist tradition based on the view of economics as a theory of rational behaviour that may be considered as a wrong line in the history of economic thought: a deviation from the laborious progress of a social science that endeavours to take into account the complex nature of human beings and human societies, forking off along the path of 'economics' built on the model of physical sciences – at the price of substituting the real world with a fictitious one-dimensional picture.

5.   Real cost and opportunity cost

The subjective theory of value developed by Jevons was thus based on a specific reformulation of Bentham's 'calculus of pleasures and pains'. It was a theory of the choices of the individual economic agent considered in isolation. Pleasure was identified with consumption of economic goods (inclusive of services), to which a positive utility was attributed. The magnitude of utility depended on the preferences of the economic agent under consideration; for each good, it decreased when the quantity of the good consumed increased. Conversely, 'pain' was represented by labour, to which a negative utility was thus attributed; labour is identified with 'any painful exertion of mind or body undergone partly or wholly with a view to future good' (ibid., p. 189).

Jevons, as we saw above, developed the notion of the 'final degree of utility (or disutility)', which corresponds to marginal utility (or disutility). The exchange value of each good was thus equal, on the one hand, to its marginal utility, and on the other hand, to the marginal disutility of the labour necessary to obtain it (even indirectly, i.e. through exchange with a good directly produced by the economic subject under consideration).

In this way, for each good the quantity produced and/or consumed was determined simultaneously with its exchange value.

Under the simplifying assumption that production of each good required only labour, and in the absence of different temporal profiles of the labour inputs required to obtain the different commodities, at first sight this approach gave a result analogous to the classical theory of labour value. In fact each individual attributes the same disutility to the last dose of labour employed in the production of each commodity; as a consequence, the exchange ratio between different commodities is equal to the ratio between the quantities of labour necessary to produce each of them. We should recall, however, that each economic subject was seen as an island: 'labour differs infinitely', Jevons (1871, p. 187) said, between one economic agent and another, in terms of quality and efficiency; furthermore, different individuals may have different evaluations of the pain intrinsic to the same dose of labour. For these reasons, labour cannot be the cause or the origin of value.

Also when introducing the notion of capital, Jevons was inclined to clearly distinguish it from accumulated labour. According to Jevons, in fact, capital is not accumulated labour, as the classical economists considered it: 'capital [. . .] consists merely in the *aggregate of those commodities which are required for sustaining labourers of any kind or class engaged in work*'; thus, 'Capital simply allows us *to expend labour in advance*' (ibid., pp. 226–7; italics in the original). Jevons introduces here a distinction 'between the *amount of capital invested* and the *amount of investment of capital*. The first is a quantity of one dimension only – the quantity of capital; the second is a quantity of two dimensions, namely, the quantity of capital and the length of time during which it remains invested' (ibid., p. 229; italics in the original). A notion of 'average time of investment of the whole amount' (ibid., p. 231) is then obtained as a ratio between the second and the first of these two quantities. Thus, such a notion foreshadows Böhm-Bawerk's average period of production (cf. below, § 11.4), it too being connected by an inverse relationship to the rate of interest in such a way as to provide some sort of theory for the determination of a demand for capital function and hence for the determination of the interest rate. However, such a theory cannot hold in a world characterised by heterogeneous capital goods, fixed capital and compound interest.[26] Jevons is apparently unaware of these complications; his argumentations can only be rigorously constructed as referring to a one-commodity world. What must matter for him, it seems, is that his notion of capital was defined in such a way that it could be referred to the isolated individual as well as to society as a whole. According to Jevons (ibid., p. 229), indeed, division of labour and exchanges were 'irrelevant complications', which could not substantially modify his theory of value, based on individual choices.

As for natural resources, these were considered an external constraint on the conditions in which the choice of the economic subject takes place. Their treatment followed the line of the 'Ricardian' theory of differential rent.

Jevons's theory of value thus presented profound differences in comparison to the approach of classical economists like Smith, Ricardo or Marx, especially because it was a theory of individual choices rather than a theory concerning the connections among different sectors of a society based on the division of labour. At the same time, however, it displayed an important analogy with the latter, as well as with the subsequent Marshallian theory, because it connected value to the 'real cost' required to obtain a given commodity, even if the 'real cost' was meant as disutility rather than as labour time.

6.   Philip Henry Wicksteed and Francis Ysidro Edgeworth

Following a path noticeably different from Marshall's, frontal opposition to the classical approach was to be developed by Philip Henry Wicksteed (1844–1927), described by Sraffa (1960, p. v), significantly enough, as 'the purist of marginal theory'. A Unitarian minister between 1867 and 1897, then a freelance writer and lecturer, Wicksteed had a solid classic culture and was known as a scholar of Dante and Thomas Aquinas, Greek tragedy and Aristotle. Initially a follower of Henry George's land nationalisation schemes, on reading Jevons he became 'Jevons's only disciple'

---

[26] On Jevons's theory of capital and distribution, and on the analytical difficulties intrinsic to it, cf. Steedman 1972.

(Steedman 1987, p. 915). Here we will briefly recall three aspects of his economic contributions: his purism within the marginalist approach, his marginalist theory of distribution and his critique of Marx's theory.

First, Wicksteed 'the purist': in his main contribution, the 700 pages-long book on *The common sense of political economy* (1910), he took to its logical consequence the subjective approach, applying it to all fields of human activity and conceiving the theory of value as one of individual choices. In other terms, he connected value to the 'opportunity cost' of each good: namely, to the fact that, in the presence of scarce resources, to obtain utility along a certain road (by producing and consuming a given good) implies forgoing obtaining utility in some other way (producing and consuming some other good). Indeed, '"cost of production" [. . .] is simply and solely "the marginal significance of something else"' (Wicksteed 1910, p. 382). Thus, the supply curve for any commodity is in fact nothing else but a reverse demand curve – the demand curve for the set of all other commodities. Along these lines, Wicksteed explicitly criticises the 'real cost' approach proposed by Marshall and his school: 'utility [. . .] is the sole and ultimate determinant of all exchange values' (ibid., p. 392). Interpersonal comparisons of utility are rejected; Wicksteed's leaning towards egalitarianism is more a matter of ethics than of economic analysis.

Second, the theory of distribution: among Wicksteed's other writings, *An essay on the co-ordination of the laws of distribution* (1894) has been considered one of the first organic illustrations of the marginalist theory of the wage rate, the profit rate and rent based on the marginal productivity of the 'factors of production', labour, capital and land. Wicksteed took into account the issue of exhaustion of the product, which is only guaranteed under constant returns to scale (on this point, as on Clark's independent contribution, cf. below, § 13.7). Let us add that Wicksteed's analysis should be considered an early example of partial equilibrium marginalist theory, since input supplies are taken as given (Steedman 1992, p. 35).

Third, his critique of Marx's theory of value (already hinted at above, § 9.9): in his first contribution on economic issues, a review of *Das Kapital* (Wicksteed 1884), he remarked that it is 'abstract utility', and not 'abstract labour', the common element for goods which are the object of exchange acts, since these can be both reproducible and non-reproducible goods. It is then a comparison of (marginal) 'abstract utilities' which determines exchange ratios between goods in exchange; in the case of reproducible goods, and with some additional assumptions, exchange ratios may turn out to be equal to the ratio of labour values, but this is due to the fact that 'labour will be so allocated as to produce those quantities of the commodities which imply marginal utilities proportional to the given labour costs' (Steedman 1987, p. 916). This kind of allocation does not hold in the case of the production of 'labour-force', so that Marx's theory of exploitation does not hold either.

Another convinced utilitarian, who worked alongside Jevons in building the analytical foundations of the marginalist approach, was Francis Ysidro Edgeworth (1845–1926), author of a volume of *Mathematical psychics* (1881) and numerous articles, collected in three volumes in 1925 under the title of *Papers relating to political economy*. His main theoretical contribution concerned the 'contract curve', illustrated for the case of two individuals and two commodities available in given quantities, and defined as the set of allocations of the two commodities among the two individuals which could not be modified without worsening the condition of at least one of the two individuals.[27] Edgeworth thus anticipated the notion of 'Pareto optimality'; furthermore, in building the contract curve he utilised contour lines to represent preferences, christening them with the name which has since become familiar: 'indifference curves'. With respect to these curves, we also owe to Edgeworth explicit introduction of the assumption of convexity towards the origin of the Cartesian axes (and demonstration that this assumption, while stemming from the postulate of decreasing marginal utility, is not necessarily implicit in it). In his analysis Edgeworth began with the case of bilateral monopoly to go on to competition, and demonstrated that the indeterminacy of equilibrium in the case of two participants in the exchange recedes when the number of economic agents participating in the exchange increases.

As holder of the Drummond chair at Oxford from 1891 to 1922 and as editor and then co-editor (with Keynes) of the *Economic Journal* since its foundation in 1891 up to his death, Edgeworth played an important role in the professionalisation of economics and the rise to dominance of the new theories of value and distribution. However, the extremely convoluted style of his writings, together with his proverbial reservedness and modesty, made his role appear decidedly subordinate to that of Alfred Marshall, the great academic leader of England in those times, whom we will discuss below (ch. 13).

---

[27] For illustration of Edgeworth's theory, cf. Niehans 1990, pp. 279–86.

11   The Austrian school and its neighbourhood

1.   Carl Menger[1]

The founder of the 'Austrian school' was born in Poland, then part of the Austro-Hungarian empire, in 1840. He attended university in Vienna and Prague, and went on to take his doctorate in Cracow. His first job was as a journalist, and by 1871, when he published the book he owes his fame to, the *Principles of political economy*, he had become a civil servant. Thanks to this book he had a rapid academic career, obtaining the *Habilitation* (the qualification to teach) and a teaching appointment (*Privatdozent*), and by 1873 he was already professor. In 1876–8 he was made tutor to Crown Prince Rudolf of Austria, and from 1878 to 1903 he held the chair of political economy at the University of Vienna. Until his death, in 1921, he worked on a second edition of his *Principles*, which was published posthumously by his son Karl in 1923.[2]

The *Principles of political economy* are hardly what a modern reader would expect of a key text for the marginalist approach, and the differences to Jevons and Walras are significant.[3] Menger had studied law, which, in the continental European tradition, implied an approach with a strong emphasis on history and great pains taken over the definition/illustration of concepts, often proving pedantic and prolix. Menger thus appeared quite distant from the project – shared by Jevons and Walras – to construct economic theory as a quantitative science, to be developed in mathematical terms. Not only was his text devoid of mathematical formulas, but on various – albeit informal – occasions Menger made no secret

---

[1] Renewed interest in Menger emerged recently, thanks also to the availability of his papers, deposited in 1985 at Duke University: cf. Barnett 1990. On Menger, cf. Streissler 1973, the essays collected in Caldwell 1990, especially the essay by Streissler 1990a, Alter 1990, and the bibliography given there.

[2] The second edition differs from the first one in important respects; I am aware of no systematic analysis of the changes, which might prove very interesting.

[3] Menger himself was aware of such differences: see his letter to Walras of February 1884, in Walras 1965a, vol. 2, pp. 2–6. On many accounts Menger's pupils, particularly Böhm-Bawerk, appear to have significantly reduced the distance from the 'Lausanne school': see Böhm-Bawerk's letters in Walras 1965a.

of his profound scepticism regarding the use of mathematical tools.[4] His aim was, rather, to construct a theory transcending simple description of economic phenomena while retaining strong links with empirical reality. It is worth noting, also in the light of the debate on method of the 1880s, that his *Principles* had been dedicated to Wilhelm Roscher (1817–94), one of the leading exponents of the 'old' German historical school. Moreover, Menger's subjectivism in the field of value theory, unlike Jevons's, owed little or nothing to utilitarian concepts.

Rather, the tradition that Menger settled into was that of Austro-German universities, where a subjective approach to a theory of value based on comparison between supply and demand, value in use and scarcity, was very much the rule. This tradition had its roots in medieval Scholastic doctrines (cf. above, § 2.4), and had dominated German universities in the fifty years preceding publication of Menger's book, with Karl Heinrich Rau (1792–1870) at Heidelberg, Friedrich B. W. Hermann (1795–1868) in Munich, and Roscher in Leipzig.[5] The latter's textbook on political economy, published in 1854, was the most widely utilised in German universities (with twenty-six editions up to 1922) at the time Menger started his career. The approach implied systematic rejection of Ricardian labour-value theory, but not of the theory of differential rent or the Smithian theory of the growth of the 'wealth of nations' associated with the division of labour.

Menger's *Principles* thus followed the tradition of the great German textbooks, taking on their structure: extensive discussion of goods and needs led up to the theory of value, exchange and price, after which attention turned to topics such as distribution, development and money.[6] Menger, too, opened his text with meticulous illustration of the fundamental notions of goods and economic goods. The objective of economic theory was, he asserted, to analyse the causal relations between goods and human values; significantly, while Jevons stated his concern for a specific aspect of human activity, relating to the satisfaction of needs of the lowest level (cf. above, § 10.4), and Walras declared his subject matter to be an economic life which 'by its very nature, is obviously passive and limits

---

[4] Menger's diffidence towards mathematics was made explicit in an 1889 review (in the *Wiener Zeitung* of 8 March) of a work by Auspitz and Lieben, *Untersuchungen über die Theorie des Preises* (1889), and may be ascribed to his adhesion to the epistemology of intuitionism: mathematics, being a deductive science, cannot contribute to our understanding of economic phenomena. Cf. Alter 1990, pp. 15, 85, 91, 95.

[5] As was shown by Streissler 1990a.

[6] Streissler 1990a, p. 51, reconstructed the structure of a typical German manual of the time, and showed that the structure of Marshall's *Principles of economics* practically coincides with it. Curiously, an echo of the structure can still be perceived today in the economics syllabuses of Italian secondary (technical and professional) schools.

itself to adapt to natural and social influences acting over it',[7] Menger defined economic activity as a search for knowledge and power.

This was in fact one of the most innovative aspects of Menger's text, marking a real departure from the previous tradition. We shall be returning to it later on. Another significant element was his interest in the interrelations between the different goods within the economic system, which saw Menger advancing beyond the traditional tendency (again dating back to Scholastic thought) to consider the formation of value, or price, of each good in isolation. Let us now see the place these elements found in his argumentation.

Menger's subjectivism was indeed radical, his analysis starting from the evaluation that each individual makes of his own situation[8] – hence also his methodological individualism. Thus, according to Menger, value is given by the way human beings assess the varying importance of their various needs, and the suitability of the different goods to satisfy such needs. The value of each good or service was deduced from the agent's evaluation on its fitness to satisfy some need.[9] More precisely, the different needs were classified in order of importance, and it was assumed that the intensity of each progressively decreased when it was satisfied; a certain degree of satisfaction had to be reached for the most pressing need before tackling the immediately successive one in order of importance.[10]

---

[7] At least, this is what Schumpeter, in the preface to the Japanese edition of his *Theory of economic development*, said was the common opinion, confirmed by Walras in a private conversation with him (Schumpeter 1912, preface to the Japanese edition, translated in the Italian 1971 edition, p. xlvii).

[8] Spiegel (1971, p. 531) referred to a possible influence of German idealism: while it 'interpreted the phenomena of the external world as creations of the human mind', the subjective theory of value 'derived economic value from man's state of mind'. We should also recall that the individual's evaluations take place in conditions of uncertainty and (severely) limited knowledge: Menger's agent is quite different in this respect from the later mainstream notion of the rational economic agent.

[9] Let us recall that according to Menger value had to do with the essence, and price with the phenomenic manifestation, of economic activity: a distinction which had some affinity with Marx's, and which was conversely absent from Walras's French approach or from the Anglo-Saxon line followed by Jevons or Marshall.

[10] In contrast to what happens in the canonical marginalist theory of the consumer, where substitutability among goods plays a central role, Menger did not admit substitutability among needs (that is, the possibility that a lower degree of satisfaction of a need be compensated by a higher degree of satisfaction of some other need, leaving the situation of the consumer unchanged). According to Alter 1990, ch. 3, this fact determines a lexicographic ordering of preferences, which in turn gives rise to insurmountable difficulties for the 'transformation of values into prices' in the framework of Menger's theory (that is, for transition from a theory taking the standpoint of the economic agent – his evaluation of needs and of the fitness of goods to satisfy them – to a theory taking the standpoint of the scientist, who tries to understand the functioning of the economic system and thus, among other things, the exchange ratios between different goods).

The determination of value then required that, along with the value in use of the goods, their scarcity be taken into account. Scarcity determined the measure in which needs could be satisfied, and their evaluation did not therefore concern the absolute importance of each need, but its importance 'at the margin'. This evaluation was made directly in the case of consumption goods ('goods of the first order') and indirectly in the case of production goods ('goods of the second, third, etc. order'). In the latter case, in fact, the means of production was 'imputed' with part of the value that the produced good held for the consumer, this portion being computed in proportion to (the entrepreneurs' evaluation of) the contribution made by the good or service to the productive process (hence the name 'imputation theory').[11]

Clearly, this was a view of the economic system that attributed the role of *primum movens* to the consumer. The idea of the consumer as sovereign had at the same time a normative and a descriptive content, thus implying a justification for economic liberalism, in the sense of 'leaving it to the market'.[12]

The subjective view of value in use proposed by Menger departed from the dominant line followed by German economists of the time, seeking objective foundations for the measurement of use values. To use Bernardine from Siena's terminology (cf. above, § 2.5), we might say that Menger focused on the goods' *complacibilitas* (that is, on their correspondence to the individual users' preferences), while the German tradition of the time looked to their *virtuositas* (capacity to satisfy human needs). In fact, Menger sought a compromise between these two aspects based on the simultaneous presence of two elements: the subjective evaluation of own needs on the part of each individual, and the objective capacity of the goods to satisfy such needs. As it turned out, it was, however, the subjective element that prevailed.[13] Finally, we should stress that, possibly in order to mark his distancing from utilitarianism, Menger

[11] Here too, through entrepreneurs' evaluations on the prospective role of inputs, the subjectivist perspective is reaffirmed. As a consequence, some commentators argue, at least in its Mengerian formulation 'the Austrian version of marginalism is not easily captured by equilibrium constructions' (Horwitz 2003, p. 269). The analytical structure of the subjective approach, based on utility and scarcity, needs the equilibrium notion and attributes to it a central role – as will be shown by subsequent developments even within the Austrian school, in particular with Böhm-Bawerk.

[12] For evaluation of Menger's economic liberalism, his lectures to Crown Prince Rudolf, now deposited among his papers at Duke University, are useful. Cf. Streissler 1990b, 1994. Menger stressed among other things the negative effects of public intervention on the spirit of initiative and self-sufficiency of economic agents.

[13] Despite the intuitive connection between needs and the use values of goods, Menger's subjectivism distinguishes his approach from the modern theory of consumption based on the demand for characteristics, developed by Lancaster 1971.

avoided the term 'utility', preferring to speak of the 'importance of satisfactions'.

In his analysis of the value of exchange – which, as pointed out above, remained on a discursive level – Menger started from the case of two goods and two parties to the exchange, or bilateral monopoly.[14] In this case there is a range of values compatible with realisation of the act of exchange coming between the two extremes at which one of the two parties loses interest in the exchange. In general, then, Menger saw the exchange as a matter of unequal values[15] implying an advantage for both participants.

Menger outlined, but did not fully develop, generalisation of this analysis to cases of more than two goods and two parties to the exchange. In fact, his analysis was seriously flawed by his refusal to apply mathematical tools, falling far short of the analyses produced by other authors of the time, or even of earlier times. His original contribution is to be found elsewhere, in the attempt to delineate a conceptual framework such as would allow the theoretician to keep account of crucial aspects of the real world. Among such aspects, a central role was occupied by the limits of human knowledge and the uncertainty consequentially surrounding the decisions of economic agents. Moreover, Menger stressed the role of the market (and in general of economic interrelations) in favouring subjective evaluations of the situation and the diffusion of factual data. However, it proved difficult to relate these data to mathematical analyses of value within the subjective approach, based on a restrictive view of *homo oeconomicus* and the techniques of constrained maximisation. As a consequence, elements of conceptual analysis central to Menger's contribution were tacitly disregarded in the 'marginalist *vulgata*' which came to dominate universities worldwide from the early decades of the twentieth century.

Unlike Jevons or Walras, as mentioned above, Menger did not assume utility functions to be maximised under budget constraints; value did not depend on objective elements or the systematic, sufficiently stable, preferences of economic agents: rather, it depended on the subjective

---

[14] The role attributed by Menger in his analysis to the monopolistic market form contrasts with the dominance of perfect competition in the analyses by his pupils, Wieser and Böhm-Bawerk, who came closer in this respect to the approaches of the French and Anglo-Saxon marginalist theoreticians.

[15] Here the difference surfaced with the classical approach, which expressed with value the 'difficulty of production', and thus considered exchange of equal values the rule in competitive conditions. Marx in particular insisted on the fact that exchange of equal values corresponds to the 'criterion of justice' of a capitalistic society. The idea of the exchange of unequal values has, in any case, an important tradition within the subjectivist approach to value, going back as far as the Scholastic period and Classical antiquity.

evaluations people made of their needs and the way to satisfy them, and such evaluations could change in unexpected ways.[16] Although he developed a subjective view of value, Menger appeared more interested in 'dynamic' aspects (in the generic meaning of change, and not as in modern growth theory), like the study of how goods *tout court* become economic goods, the related issue of the original development of private property and, above all, the active way economic agents set out to increase their knowledge and consequently modify their preferences. In this context, Menger stressed the elements of inequality, irreversibility and gains from exchange. We might say, in fact, that while he applied the notion of equilibrium to the choices of the individual economic agent, the ambit in which economic activity took place (limited knowledge, learning) rendered the coordination of such choices a very complex process indeed, so that the notion of equilibrium proved difficult to apply to the economic system as a whole.

Similarly, Menger stressed the existence of transaction costs, practically ignored in the tradition of the Lausanne school, and thus the theoretical and not only practical importance of elements such as knowledge and distance. Hence the role attributed to the intermediaries, who help the economic agents towards fuller knowledge and better organisation of the market, and the role attributed to money, considered the most easily tradable of all commodities. From here we finally come to Menger's conception of the process of civilisation itself, identified with the reduction of ignorance and development of institutions that help human beings get to grips with an uncertain future. Institutions such as money, but also the market and the division of labour, were explained – in accordance with methodological individualism – as undesired effects of individual uncoordinated choices, which, however, in the course of time are modified as a consequence of learning processes in response to the experience gradually acquired. On the whole, Menger had an optimistic view of economic progress, decidedly closer to Smith than to Malthus's *Essay on population*; as in Smith, progress was related to improvements in the division of labour and to capital accumulation.[17]

---

[16] Closer to the canonical representation of the marginalist approach we find another German author, Hans K. E. von Mangoldt (1824–68), with his 1863 university textbook: Streissler (1990a, pp. 53–5) recalls his theory of prices, 'full of demand and supply diagrams, diminishing marginal utility as a reason for the falling demand curve, substitution and complementarity of commodities, and even a discussion of the question whether market equilibrium will be unique'.

[17] Menger made reference to Malthus with regard to the notion of economic good and value theory, but not to his 'principle of population'. Menger's theory of economic progress was illustrated in § 6 of ch. IV of his *Principles*, 2nd edn. Along with improvement in technological knowledge, Menger repeatedly stressed as a factor for progress improvement

2. The 'Methodenstreit'

Historicism is commonly seen as rebellion against the rationalism of the Enlightenment, and had much to do with the then newborn nationalistic spirit particularly strong in Germany. Indeed, by extolling the specific nature of each concrete historical situation, historicism opposed universalism, or the claim that it is possible to derive, from a few general principles, rules endowed with validity at all times and in all places. Outstanding among the fathers of German historicism was the philosopher Georg Wilhelm Friedric Hegel (1770–1831), while in the specifically economic field, in the same generation as Hegel, we may mention Adam Müller (1779–1829), a follower of the British Tory Edmund Burke (1729–97) and supporter of an 'economic romanticism' that called for revival of the corporative state and other medieval institutions, but also advocated the absolute state. Not much younger was Friedrich List, whose economic nationalism meant among other things the defence of customs duties (as we saw above, in § 7.6) as a means to help infant industries in countries lagging behind in the process of industrialisation.

The 'old German historical school' flourished in the decade of 1843–53, when the major contributions by Roscher, Bruno Hildebrand (1812–78) and Karl Knies (1821–98) were published. Roscher, a professor at the University of Leipzig for a period of forty-six years and, as we have seen, author of an influential textbook, defined political economy as the science which studies the natural laws of economic development, without implying opposition to the approach of classical economists like Adam Smith. Hildebrand and Knies, active liberals, both driven to exile in Switzerland for a few years, were subsequently professors respectively in the University of Jena and the Universities of Freiburg and Heidelberg. Supporters of statistical enquiry, they considered the 'economic laws' deduced from empirical enquiry to be historically relative.

As pointed out above, Menger saw no opposition between his theoretical contribution and the approach of the 'old' German historical school. To the eyes of a contemporary economist, indeed, the very structure of Menger's *Principles* may appear to be permeated with historicism. However, with transition to a new generation more radical views emerged. The 'new historical school' led by Gustav von Schmoller (1837–1917), who dominated the German academic scene from his chair in Berlin

in the knowledge of needs and how the economic goods available can satisfy them. The 'principle of the marginal productivity of capital' which Menger referred to at the end of the chapter mentioned above may be interpreted as an axiom in the theory of choice: in the presence of a positive interest rate, a more 'indirect' technique must be more productive, otherwise it would not be utilised (cf. Streissler 1973, p. 170).

(held from 1882 until retirement in 1913), was characterised by a more decided opposition to abstract theoretical deductions. Furthermore, the possibility of distinction between political economy and politics, laws and institutions, and customs, was denied.[18]

Followers of the new historical school looked on political economy as an essentially empirical science. A priori assumptions and deductive reasoning were to be rejected, until a degree of knowledge was reached sufficient to constitute a solid basis for the generalisations through which the abstract assumptions were obtained to constitute the necessary starting point for economic theory. Thus not even the 'new German historical school' rejected a priori the deductive techniques of economic theory. The thesis defended with fierce certainty was that abstract theory had – in the concrete situation of the time – insufficient foundations, and was therefore a tottering building, to escape from before it collapsed. The aim of the historical school was precisely to provide such foundations through systematic analysis based on coordinated empirical investigations. To this end, in 1873 the 'Verein für Sozialpolitik' was founded, and work promptly began on the systematic collection of data on the most diverse aspects of economic reality.[19] Moreover, the 'Verein' generated a movement towards social reform policies which was christened 'socialism of the chair' – a sort of 'socialism from above', whereby the high bureaucracy of the Hohenzollern empire, Chancellor Bismarck in particular, tried to appease the working classes, thus isolating the rising bourgeoisie,

---

[18] In this respect, the German historical school exerted significant influence on the so-called institutionalist school, still alive today, above all in the United States, where its main representative was Thornstein Veblen (cf. below, § 13.8). Among the contemporaries of Roscher's first German historical school in England were Richard Jones and Cliffe Leslie, already referred to above. To them we should add the Irish economist John K. Ingram (1823–1907), whose *A history of political economy* (1888) was translated into various languages. More generally, the British culture of the time responded to the influence of the biological evolutionism of Charles Darwin (1809–82; his *Origin of species* was published in 1859) and its extension to human society by the individualist philosopher Herbert Spencer (1820–1903). In Italy, extreme economic liberals such as Francesco Ferrara (1810–1900; cf. Faucci 1995) were followed by the supporters of a less rigid approach (such as Augusto Graziani, 1865–1944), but this opposition, rather than mirroring the contrast between Menger and Schmoller, resented the influence of French and Anglo-Saxon culture, on the one hand, with reference to Adam Smith and the study of Say's text, and on the other hand the influence of the German law school and, in the economic field, of Roscher's moderate historicism.

[19] Schumpeter (1954, pp. 803–4) attributed importance to a number of empirical studies carried out in the 'Verein', although criticising their anti-theoretical attitude. Outside the 'Verein', we may classify as belonging to the same cultural framework the investigations by Ernst Engel (1821–96), director of the Prussian statistical institute, into the differences in consumption structures at different income levels (the so-called 'Engel's law', one of the strongest empirical regularities, which stated that the share of food consumption in a family's total expenditure decreases when income increases).

by adoption of social insurance policies which in fact represented the first experiment of a 'welfare state'.[20]

In 1883 Menger published *Enquiries on the method of economic science*, a review of Schmoller, and in 1884 a pamphlet, *The errors of historicism in German political economy*, written in the form of sixteen letters to a friend. These works marked the beginning of a harsh clash, perhaps the first clash between rival academic schools in which the ideological conflict was exacerbated by the struggle for baronial power within universities.[21] In a clash of the kind it was not enough to persuade readers that one's own theses were sound, but it was also necessary to show the erroneousness – indeed the total absurdity – of the rival's theses. This implied stretching, often actually distorting, the opponent's views while illustrating them, searching out the weak points rather than addressing and assimilating the points of strength, and the very reason for the existence of the rival approach. In the *Methodenstreit* none of the participants was immune from these defects, and the defeat of the historical school in the rhetorical confrontation for many years obscured the importance of an approach that tied in theoretical work with historical research, which Menger himself had endeavoured to practise.

Menger distinguished three components of political economy: the historical-statistical aspect, theory and economic policy.[22] Theory in particular was attributed with a special role, and Menger proposed a causal-genetic approach, which consisted in starting from the simplest elements to arrive at enquiry into the composite laws. Thus political economy arrived at exact laws, but they only concerned a subset of human actions; Menger insisted in particular on the fact that the notion of economic man was a fictitious construction. He too, however, stressed the importance of a close connection between theory and reality, guaranteed by the fact that the assumptions at the basis of the theory were considered data known from direct experience, and hence true with no need for empirical verification: for Menger the intuitionist it was indeed the very essence of economic reality that manifested itself directly in the economists' reflections, from which he deduced the nature and characteristics of economic phenomena.[23]

---

[20] Cf. Maddison 1984.

[21] It has been maintained (for instance by Alter 1990, pp. 83–4) that Menger was irritated by what he considered a failure to recognise the value of his work on the part of Roscher and his school. However, brief and superficial as they may be, Roscher's references to Menger's *Principles* can be considered neither mistaken nor malicious.

[22] A somewhat similar distinction between the components of economic research is proposed by a heterodox disciple of the Austrian school, Schumpeter, in the first chapter of his *History of economic analysis* (Schumpeter 1954, pp. 12–24).

[23] On Menger's intuitionism, cf. Alter 1990, pp. 91 ff.

The view of the economic system thus proposed by Menger was not that of a static equilibrium between supply and demand. What Menger described was the development of an organic order as a process of discovery and accumulation of new knowledge through imitation, motivated by economic interest: an intrinsically dynamic view, imbued with historicism. Opposition to the historical school did not revolve around an axiomatic theory like general economic equilibrium as an alternative to a historical approach, but rather the possibility of utilising analytic reasoning to build a theoretical structure declaredly open to an evolutionary, dynamic view.

It is this methodological approach that helps us to evaluate the results reached by the Austrian school. As a matter of fact, while in principle we cannot but agree with Menger's position (once purged of rhetorical overtones) on method, and hence the essential, central role of analytic reasoning in economic theory, perplexities arise – as we shall see in more detail below – over the compatibility between a dynamic, explicitly evolutionary, approach and the marginalist analytic structure on which it rests, based as it was on the notion (which at the time had already enjoyed a long tradition) of equilibrium between demand and supply. The very problem of tension between the stage of the formation of concepts and the stage of model-building which characterised the Austrian school, from Menger to Hayek, arose, as we shall see, in the case of Marshall. The tension between a dynamic view of the economy and the analytic structure was, by contrast, tolerable within the classical approach, where the notion of equilibrium was less relevant and was in any case based not on the condition of equality between supply and demand but, rather, on the condition of a uniform rate of profits in the different sectors as a consequence of the 'competition of capitals'.

3.   Max Weber

The 'debate on method' also serves to prompt a few, brief remarks on some developments now considered external to the field of economics, but which were originally considered part of the economists' research work. Among these,[24] the most important is undoubtedly represented

---

[24] Let us recall in this context at least three names. Georg Simmel (1858–1918) studied the social implications of the monetary economy, among which he stressed development of individual freedom. Werner Sombart (1863–1941), professor in Breslaw and then in Berlin, studied the development of capitalism as based on the spirit of enterprise, and anticipated some Weberian theses concerning mature capitalism and the transition to socialism; he also stressed the influence of Protestantism, but on workers' discipline rather than on entrepreneurs. Arthur Spiethoff (1873–1957), professor in Bonn from

by Max Weber. Indeed, while Weber is now considered the most famous among the sociologists, if not the founder of sociology as a science (a role commonly attributed to Comte), he was in fact the holder of a chair in political economy, and was on many accounts closer to the economists of the Austrian school than to those of the historical school.

Max Weber (1864–1920) was professor of political economy first at Freiburg and then at Heidelberg, and was concerned among other things with strictly economic issues (such as the foundations of the marginalist theory of value, in a review dated 1908 of a book by Lujo Brentano, 1844–1931). He also took part in research projects on agricultural labour and on the stock exchange. However, his main work remains *Economy and society*, published posthumously in 1922, while his *Protestant ethic and the spirit of capitalism* (1904–5) is also widely known.[25] The common theme of these writings is enquiry into the factors that determine the origin and dominance of certain economic behavioural patterns, thus navigating between sociology and political economy in an area now commonly attributed to the field of economic sociology.

Weber is considered 'the Marx of the bourgeoisie': like Marx, he focused on interpretation of the capitalistic mode of production and its process of evolution, but unlike Marx, he held that in the historical process of development the main causal link did not go from the material conditions of economic reproduction to the sphere of institutions and culture, but rather in the opposite direction. Thus he tried to delineate some general ideas on the relationships between religion, the political and legal set-up, different forms of organisation of economic and social life. One of the ideas concerned the transition from a market, competitive capitalism to a regulated capitalism. In other terms, Weber saw in the evolution of capitalism a gigantic process of rationalisation concerning not only economic activity but society as a whole, on this basis developing his forecast of a progressive bureaucratisation of the state organisation and the productive process, with the growth of middle ranks of clerks and technicians – a forecast that attributed crucial importance to the middle classes, thus contrasting with the process of proletarianisation heralded by Marx. The rise of the bureaucracy, within the firm as within the state,

1918 to 1939, was the author of researches on the business cycles and above all of the notion of 'economic styles', each characterising a specific historical epoch and each requiring a separate 'historical theory', with the set of all such historical theories constituting general economic theory.

[25] A critical edition of Weber's writings is being published in many volumes since 1984 as *Max Weber Gesamtausgabe*, with the publisher J. C. B. Mohr (Paul Siebeck) of Tübingen. In particular, much new material (and a reorganisation of already published material) is being made available in the critical edition of *Wirtschaft und Gesellschaft* (Economy and society), in six volumes, three of which have appeared between 1999 and 2001.

implies a weakening of the dynamic role played in the initial stage by entrepreneurs, with their attitude towards risk-taking and change (innovations) and towards personal responsibility. On the origins of capitalism, Weber also followed a route different from Marx, maintaining that a crucial role was to be attributed to the assertion, with Protestantism, of a specific culture favourable to concrete engagement in society (against the ascetic attitudes of the medieval Catholic Church and the Counter-Reformation).[26] Foreshadowing Schumpeter (cf. below, § 15.4), Weber considered as worrisome the advent of socialism (in the Marxian variety of nationalised means of production and central planning), since it implies a drastic increase in bureaucratisation, with the accompanying outcomes of economic stagnation and limits to individual liberty.

Weber's method – which, in comparison with Marx, distanced him from the British classical economists, and particularly from Ricardo, showing the influence of the German historical-juridical tradition – was based on the definition of 'ideal types', or categories abstracted from concrete historical evolution. Conceptualisation was the dominant phase in this approach, while construction of abstract models based on these categories was conducted without recourse to mathematical tools, in opposition to the trend then coming to dominate the various currents of the marginalist approach (although less markedly than elsewhere within the Austrian school – the school with which Weber was in closest contact). Weber also favoured wide pictures of reality, where a plurality of influences on social phenomena and reciprocal relations between them are considered.

4.   Eugen von Böhm-Bawerk

Among the most direct followers and collaborators of Carl Menger, we find Friedrich von Wieser (1851–1926) and Eugen von Böhm-Bawerk

---

[26] In the line of Weber, cf. Tawney 1926. On Marx's ideas, again concerning the transition from feudalism to capitalism, cf. Dobb 1946; however, the issue gave rise to heated controversies in the Marxian field: cf. Dobb et al. 1954; Brenner 1978 and the bibliography given there. For a position similar to Weber's, in that the importance of the cultural debate for the evolution of political and economic institutions is stressed, but different with respect to the thesis proposed, since the driving role is attributed to Scholastic thought rather than to Protestantism, cf. Schumpeter 1954, pp. 78–82, and, more recently, Chafuen 1986. Important critical discussion of Weber's and Tawney's ideas is offered by Viner (1978, pp. 151–92), who points out that various authors before Weber had already connected the birth of capitalism with Protestantism, and in particular with the role it attributes to direct study of the Bible by the faithful (in contrast to the hierarchical organisation of the Catholic Church), and hence to education and individual thinking; Weber's distinctive thesis is the importance attributed to the doctrine of predestination and to the idea that success in business is a sign distinguishing the elect.

(1851–1914), who went on from being fellow-students to become brothers-in-law. A subsequent generation included Ludwig von Mises (1881–1973), originator of the theory of 'forced saving' and significant debate on the sustainability of a planned economy,[27] and Joseph Schumpeter. The latter will be discussed later on (ch. 15), while Friedrich von Hayek (1899–1992) will be the subject of the final section of this chapter.

Wieser is generally recognised as the first to have used the term 'marginal utility' (*Grenznutzen*), utilised in his work on the *Origin and fundamental laws of economic value* (1884). In this work Wieser used the theory of imputation to determine the value of the means of production. On this basis, he interpreted the cost of production as a sacrifice of the utility which could have been obtained through a different use of the factors of production (with a theory analogous to the opportunity-cost theory developed in the same years in England by Wicksteed, but differing from it in the subjective nature of the opportunity costs, since these are derived from entrepreneurs' evaluations rather than from objective technological data). Among Wieser's other writings, *Natural value* (1889) proposed application of the marginalist approach to the field of public finance; his *Theory of the social economy* (1914) was a systematic economics treatise, which enjoyed wide circulation and exerted great influence, becoming the main point of reference for the teaching of the doctrines of the Austrian school; finally, *The law of power* (1926) was a sociological work. In 1903 Wieser was Menger's successor to the economics chair at the University of Vienna.

Böhm-Bawerk was by far superior to both Menger and Wieser in analytical powers. He was a pupil of the economists of the first German historical school (after graduation, he studied for two years at Heidelberg with Karl Knies, at Leipzig with Roscher, and at Jena with Hildebrand), to become professor of political economy at Innsbruck from 1880 to 1889. The two volumes of *Kapital und Kapitalzins* (Capital and interest, 1884 and 1889) belonged to this period. Subsequently he went on to important posts in the Austro-Hungarian administration, thrice as minister of finance (1893, 1896–7, 1900–4), eventually causing a government crisis when he resigned in protest against a decision by Parliament for a sharp increase in military expenditure. In the same year Böhm-Bawerk joined forces with Wieser as professor of political economy at the University of Vienna on being appointed to a chair instituted specially for him.

---

[27] Cf. Mises 1912 and 1920 respectively. See also, on this economist's personality and thought, the extensive introduction and the biographic and bibliographic notes to the 1999 Italian edition of Mises 1912, edited by Riccardo Bellofiore.

His fame as an economist derives mainly from his writings of the Innsbruck period, and in particular his extensive work on *The positive theory of capital* (1889), where Böhm-Bawerk developed an original theory of interest, and then set out to bring the problem of accumulation within the Austrian theory of value.[28]

The key notion for Böhm-Bawerk's theoretical construction was that of the average period of production, which will now be briefly illustrated. The Austrian economist took up ideas already long present in the theoretical debate, like the notion of abstinence proposed by Senior and revived in a modified form at the time by Marshall as 'waiting'. Böhm-Bawerk thus considered the rate of interest as the price which compensated for the waiting intrinsic to recourse to more indirect but more fruitful methods of production. In other words, considerable cost is involved in building machinery (and machinery to produce machinery) to be utilised in the place of rudimentary tools, because there is a longer interval of time between the moment the work is performed and the moment when the final product is obtained, but production is thereby increased.[29]

In order to measure the capitalistic intensity of production processes, Böhm-Bawerk proposed reference to the average period of production, or in other words an average of all the intervals of time during which the hours of labour expended to obtain a certain product are immobilised. Thus both the hours of labour directly employed in the production of the commodity under consideration and those indirectly employed for the production of the required means of production, and of the means of production of such means of production, are taken into consideration. The result was a series of dated quantities of labour; which was then reduced to a single magnitude, a weighted average of the different intervals of time, with weights proportional to the hours of labour immobilised during the different intervals of time. For example, if to obtain 100 litres of wine an hour of labour performed ten years ago is necessary, together with an hour performed five years ago and an hour one day ago, the 'average period of production' proves equal to five years, and this average period of production constitutes the quantity of time-capital utilised in the productive process together with a given quantity of labour-time (three hours all together, in our example).

---

[28] On Böhm-Bawerk's life and thought cf. Hennings 1997 and the extensive bibliography given there.

[29] We thus have two elements which, according to Böhm-Bawerk's theory, concur in determining the rate of interest: on the one hand, a psychological element, namely the tendency of human beings to over-estimate the utility of present goods compared to that of goods available in the future (and in parallel to over-estimate the disutility of a present cost compared to a future one); on the other hand, a 'technological' element, namely the higher productivity of indirect methods of production.

As the overall quantity of labour employed increases, the amount of wages paid increases; equally, when the capital-time (namely the average period of production) increases, the payment of interest also increases. Moreover, when confronted with an increase in the unit wage (that is, in the price of labour), firms tend to reduce the quantity of labour utilised; equally, according to Böhm-Bawerk, when the rate of interest (that is, the price of 'capital') decreases, firms tend to utilise a greater amount of time-capital, lengthening the duration of the productive processes. More precisely, applying the postulate of decreasing marginal productivity, we may say that when confronted with a reduction in the rate of interest, the average period of production is lengthened up to the point at which the marginal productivity of a further lengthening of the integrated productive process has come down to the new, lower, level of the interest rate.

This theory was less of an approximation than the simple theory of labour value, which completely ignored the magnitude of the intervals of time during which the quantities of labour expended remain immobilised, but it was still an approximation. In fact, it failed to take the phenomenon of compound interest into account; the fact is that the cumulated interest on an hour of labour performed ten years ago is far greater than the interest on ten hours of labour one year ago; nor is it possible to redefine the weights in order to take account of compound interest, since the 'average period of production' would thus prove no longer independent of income distribution, and it would no longer be possible to utilise it to determine the value of a distributive variable such as the rate of interest.

As we shall see, Böhm-Bawerk's theory was taken up again in the Austrian school by Hayek and earlier on, at the very beginnings of the Swedish school, by Wicksell. However, within the ambit of a widely defined Austrian school it was criticised by Schumpeter, while Wicksell himself, in the course of his investigations, appeared increasingly dissatisfied with the solution proposed by the Innsbruck professor.

Böhm-Bawerk's contribution to the development of the Austrian school was crucial: both positively, in so far as it allowed for Menger's original formulation to be embodied in an extensive and, indeed, fascinating analytical construction, including that essential phenomenon of modern capitalist economies represented by the accumulation of capital; and negatively, because of the limits displayed by the analytical construction, which obviously only become evident when we proceed from representation of the conceptual picture to the stage of analytical theory.[30] Even

---

[30] It is worth recalling that, according to Schumpeter 1954, p. 847 n., the shaky nature of the foundations of Böhm-Bawerk's theoretical building had already been perceived by

today, however, the limits of the Austrian approach are often ignored: circumventing the difficulties that Böhm-Bawerk's contribution came up against also means glossing over the necessary analytical specification of an approach which otherwise remains suspended in the air. But, as we shall see, Sraffa's 1960 book showed that a solution to these analytical difficulties along the lines indicated by Böhm-Bawerk himself, later taken up by Wicksell and then by Hayek, is simply impossible

5.   Knut Wicksell and the Swedish school

Swedish Knut Wicksell was contemporary with Böhm-Bawerk and Wieser, like them born in 1851. However, his career as an economist began later: while for Böhm-Bawerk university teaching preceded a brilliant career in public administration, in the case of Wicksell teaching (and research in the field of pure economic theory) followed a stage of lively activity as a neo-Malthusian polemicist, freelance lecturer and journalist. Wicksell's fame among his contemporaries derived above all from his role as a radical opponent of the prevailing moral beliefs, from his repeated challenges to the traditional ideas of family, religion, motherland and state authority. His provocative attitudes made it hard for him to embark on an academic career, arousing widespread hostility and even landed him in prison – at the ripe age of fifty – on charges of offence against the state religion.[31]

His interest in economic issues concentrated for a long time on the population problem. Wicksell was a passionate neo-Malthusian, accompanying study of the subject with intense propaganda activity. His studies in economic theory were at first collateral to this interest, and were seriously tackled only when, in 1887, thirty-six-year-old Wicksell gained a scholarship abroad. He was thus able to study at the British Museum in London, and to attend lectures by Knapp and Brentano at Strasbourg, by Menger at Vienna (where he studied among other things Böhm-Bawerk's book) and by Wagner in Berlin. In 1889 he married a Norwegian law student, Anna Brugge. In 1890 he also began seeking employment with some Swedish university (Stockholm, Uppsala, Lund) as economics lecturer,

Menger, who considered the theory of capital based on the average period of production as 'one of the greatest errors ever committed'. In particular Menger was averse to recourse to aggregate concepts, especially as far as capital was concerned (cf. Streissler 1973, p. 166).

[31] These aspects of his life dominate the fascinating biography by Gårdlund 1956. Wicksell thus constitutes clear proof of the erroneousness of the thesis, typical of the Marxian tradition, of an opposition between a politically progressive classical approach and a politically conservative marginalist approach. However, Wicksell is no isolated exception in this respect: recall for instance Walras's social reformism, with his support for land nationalisation, and the British Fabians. On this issue, cf. Steedman 1995.

but succeeded in getting a provisional appointment as professor at Lund only in 1899, having satisfied the legal requirement of a law degree and overcome the hostility of the conservative academic environment. Only in 1905 did he become full professor, after fierce controversy. He died in Stockholm in 1926.

His main works in economic theory were a small book on *Value, capital and rent* dated 1893, an essay on *Interest and prices* dated 1898, an article on 'Marginal productivity as the basis for distribution in economics' dated 1900, and the two volumes of *Lectures on political economy* (volume 1, *Theory*, 1901, and volume 2, *Money*, 1906, translated into English in 1934–5). The English edition of the *Lectures*, edited by Lionel Robbins, also collected the main articles of the same period, among which are a work dated 1919 criticising Cassel's theories[32] and an important work in capital theory dated 1923, in the form of a commentary on an essay by Ackermann. Other important contributions by the Swedish economist were on the theory of public finance, but they are beyond our scope here.

Wicksell made two major contributions to economic theory. Firstly, in the 1893 essay on *Value, capital and rent* Wicksell developed a marginalist theory of income distribution between capital, labour and land based on their respective marginal productivities, which came out a few years before Wicksteed's (cf. above, § 10.6). In this work, and in the first volume of the *Lectures*, Wicksell utilised the theory of the average period of production developed by Böhm-Bawerk. However, having initially accepted it, he eventually took a certain distance from it and set out to develop it in such a way as to take into account the heterogeneity of the means of production. Thus, in essence, Wicksell wavered between an aggregate notion of capital and a disaggregated notion, which he adopted when

---

[32] Gustav Cassel (1866–1945), professor at Stockholm, a typical lord of academia, egocentric and presumptuous, Wicksell's rival and even more diehard conservative, is known above all for his simplified version of Walrasian theory, the *Theory of social economy*, published in German in 1918 and in English in 1923. It was thanks to the mediation of this work that Walrasian ideas found circulation in the German and Anglo-Saxon cultures (the translation by Jaffé of Walras's book, *Elements of pure economics*, appeared only in 1954). Cassel is also known for his contributions to the theory of international economic relations, such as the PPP (purchasing power parity) theory, according to which, in the presence of free international trade of goods, exchange rates are set at a level such as to guarantee the parity of purchasing power in the different countries, given the internal price level (that is, ten dollars buy the same amount of goods in Italy, Germany, France or in any other country: if this did not hold, an outflow of goods from countries with relatively low prices towards countries with relatively high prices would take place, and the consequent disequilibria in the balance of trade would bring about readjustment of the exchange rates). The theory became the object of much theoretical debate, failing to stand up to the numerous empirical verifications which, rather, appear to confirm the typically Keynesian thesis that financial flows dominate over commercial flows in the determination of exchange rates, causing non-transitory deviations from purchasing power parities.

identifying capital with the entire temporal structure of the direct and indirect labour flows necessary to obtain a given product.[33]

Secondly, within the framework of the monetary theory illustrated in the 1898 essay and re-elaborated in the second volume of the *Lectures*, Wicksell developed a distinction between the money interest rate and the natural interest rate. The latter was determined by the 'real' variables which concur to determine equilibrium for the economic system; more precisely, it corresponded to the marginal productivity of 'capital', as indicated by the marginalist theory of income distribution. The money rate of interest was, instead, determined on the money markets, with some degree of autonomy with respect to the natural rate. The relationship between money and natural rate of interest was then utilised to explain the cyclical oscillations of the economy and the inflationary or deflationary pressures on the general level of prices. Whenever the money rate of interest is lower than the natural one, entrepreneurs find it advantageous to take out loans and invest, thus giving rise to inflationary pressure; conversely, whenever the money rate of interest is higher than the natural rate, investments are discouraged and deflationary pressure is generated.[34]

This theory takes its place in a current of monetary explanations of the cycle and inflation that tried to have it both ways, on the one hand safeguarding the marginalist theory of value and distribution, in terms of which to determine the equilibrium values for prices and distributive variables, and on the other hand recognising a fact obvious to any empirical economist, namely the existence of 'disequilibria' and of a certain influence which monetary vicissitudes have on the trends followed by real variables. Wicksell's approach was taken up and developed by a number of economists, including Hayek.

The so-called Swedish school (Erik Lindhal, 1891–1960; Gunnar Myrdal, 1898–1987, Nobel prize in 1974; Bertil Ohlin, 1899–1979) emerged in the late 1920s developing various aspects of Wicksell's theory, but above all, in contrast with Keynes's analysis, taking up once again the tool of sequential analysis (already present in the Austrian tradition, and later re-embraced in England by Hicks).[35]

---

[33] For illustration and criticism of Wicksell's theory of capital, cf. Garegnani 1960, pp. 123–85.

[34] In his theory on these (inflationary and deflationary) cumulative processes Wicksell assumed that no changes took place in production techniques; as a consequence, neither income distribution nor production levels or relative prices can change, and the disequilibria can only translate into changes in the monetary variables, or in other words the price level. On this point, and on the ambiguities of the Wicksellian definition of the natural interest rate, cf. Donzelli 1988, pp. 67–71.

[35] For illustration of Wicksell's monetary theory and the debate it aroused, cf. Chiodi 1983. On the relations between the Swedish school, the Austrian school, Hayek and Hicks, cf. Donzelli 1988 and the bibliography given there. For illustration of the reasons why Keynes rejected sequential analysis, cf. below, § 14.6.

In Italy, elements of Wicksell's monetary theory were utilised by Marco Fanno (1878–1965) in a work published in 1912, *Le banche e il mercato monetario* (Banks and the money market). Fanno, however, criticised Wicksell's assumption of completely endogenous money, characterised by supply totally elastic to demand. With this and other writings, among which was a contribution (in German) to a volume edited by Hayek, Fanno obtained international fame; he also produced various important theoretical contributions, especially in the field of trade cycle theory, following an approach similar to Hayek's, which we consider in the next section. Suffice it here to add that the approach took account of the active role played by financial phenomena while avoiding criticising the marginalist theory of long run real equilibrium.[36]

6.   Friedrich von Hayek

Friedrich von Hayek (1899–1992), winner of the Nobel prize in economics in 1974, is possibly better known for his extreme economic liberalism than for his theoretical contributions to economics. However, in the 1930s he appeared to many as the champion of the continental school, a point of reference of great theoretical strength to set against the 'Cambridge school' for those who did not share the political implications of Keynesian theory.

We may distinguish four components in his thought: an individualistic methodology; a conceptual approach which took up and developed that of the Austrian school, in particular the elements of uncertainty and learning mentioned in our discussion of Menger; a theoretical approach based on Böhm-Bawerk's theory of capital and Wicksell's theory of money; and contributions to the political and social theory of economic liberalism, opposing the collectivistic propensities which, many held, characterised not only Soviet planning but also Roosevelt's New Deal and Keynesian interventionism. Our main interest here is in the first three of these components, and discussing them we shall see how the difficulties Hayek came up against in the field of pure theory led him to an interesting revision of the conceptual foundations of traditional marginalist analysis, in particular as far as the notion of equilibrium was concerned.

A pupil of Wieser and Mises at the University of Vienna after the First World War, in 1927 Hayek was made the first director of the newborn Austrian institute for the study of the trade cycle.[37] In 1931, after a series of conferences on the theory of the trade cycle which attracted widespread

---

[36] On Fanno, cf. Realfonzo and Graziani 1992, including the biographical note, list of writings and bibliography given there.

[37] The Österreichische Konjunkturforschungsinstitut was founded on von Mises's initiative, in order to propose an approach based on integration between theory and empirical

attention, Hayek moved to the London School of Economics, on the invitation of his friend Lionel Robbins. Like him, Hayek was also a refined scholar of the history of economic thought.[38] After the Second World War, he moved to Chicago in 1950, and returned to Europe (at first Freiburg, in Germany, then Salzburg, in Austria) in 1962. A provisional bibliography of his writings (in Gray 1984) included 18 books, 25 pamphlets, 16 books as editor or author of the introduction, and 235 articles.[39] An edition of his writings, which will eventually run to nineteen volumes, has been coming out over the last few years.[40]

Methodological individualism, i.e. the idea that the functioning of an economic system must be explained starting from the choices of the individuals making up the system, was already present in Menger and constituted a dominant tradition within the different currents of the marginalist approach. For Hayek, as for many other authors sharing his approach, this was not only a rule of method, but also a veritable political dogma, given the connection between holism (namely the idea that social aggregates should be studied independently of the behaviour of the individuals making them up) and political organicism (the state, the community, is 'more' than the individuals making it up) which is at the basis of dictatorial regimes such as nazism or Stalinist communism.[41]

The behaviour of individuals expresses itself through actions which, in Hayek's view, stem from rationally selected plans of action. Methodological individualism thus dictated that the theory of the behaviour of the economic system be based on consideration of plans of action of all the agents in the system. Hence the central role of the notion of equilibrium, which identifies within the set of such plans of actions those that

analysis in the study of the trade cycle, against the purely empiricist approach of the National Bureau of Economic Research at New York, which focused on the search for regularities in the behaviour of the economy.

[38] A collection of his writings on the history of economic thought is in Hayek 1991.

[39] Hayek was an economist with an exceptional cultural background. Vienna in the 1920s was in this respect a unique melting pot: Konrad Lorenz the ethologist was a playmate in infancy, the philosopher Ludwig Wittgenstein was a relative and comrade-in-arms in the last year of the First World War, the physicist Erwin Schrödinger a family friend, and we might go on.

[40] Edited by W. W. Bartley III, *The collected works of F. A. Hayek* is being published by the University of Chicago Press. Up to now eight volumes have appeared, plus a special volume including a lengthy, lively interview with Hayek, where he recounts much of his life (Hayek, 1994).

[41] An important 'political' critique of holism, from Plato and Aristotle to Marx, was provided by Hayek's friend, Karl Popper, in *The open society and its enemies*, 1945. However, we can fully share Popper's critique of totalitarianism and its cultural roots without necessarily accepting the identification between political individualism, namely the defence of individual freedom in the political sphere, and methodological individualism. This distinction was clearly stated by another representative of Austrian economic culture, Schumpeter: cf. below, § 15.2.

are compatible among themselves and with the given conditions in which economic activity takes place (technology, endowments of resources of each agent).[42] Given the limits to the knowledge of economic agents, it is realistically impossible for *ex ante* planning to ensure the coordination of individual plans of action. Coordination is entrusted to the market, which operates as an adjustment mechanism ensuring equilibrium.

A typical feature of Menger's view, as of Hayek's, is that subjective knowledge was included among the variables undergoing adjustment processes induced by market operation, along with prices and quantities produced and exchanged. Moreover, as he became aware of the unsolved problems in the theory of value and distribution he had adopted, Hayek gradually attributed growing importance to the role of the market as an instrument of diffusion of information and adjustment of individual knowledge.[43] These are stimulating ideas, and they fascinated a number of contemporary economists. However, the proposal of interesting concepts should be accompanied by demonstration of their analytical fecundity, and the demonstration should have included, given Hayek's views, a theory of equilibrium (or, in other terms, a theory of value, distribution, employment and the choice of techniques) such as to prove the equilibrating efficacy of market mechanisms. It was to this field of research that Hayek dedicated the first decades of his long activity.

Hayek took up from Böhm-Bawerk the idea of capital as a flow of dated labour quantities. Investment and production decisions thus have effect in a period subsequent to the period of adoption (here the sequential framework of the Austrian approach reappeared, as developed especially by the Swedish school), and problems of intertemporal coordination of decisions arise. The subject of Hayek's analysis was thus the emergence of a spontaneous order from the decisions of economic agents coordinated, in a market economy, by the invisible hand of competition.[44] Hayek considered the different obstacles to the emergence of such a spontaneous

---

[42] It may be useful to stress that the notion of equilibrium proposed by Hayek differed from the traditional marginalist concept based on equality between supply and demand. This was an important conceptual shift, which has failed to attract the attention it deserves. Moreover, Hayek stressed that equilibrium relations do not stem from objective data, but from the agents' subjective evaluations which determine their plans and their actions, and that such evaluations are formed in an uncertain world and under conditions of limited knowledge.

[43] Moreover, as Hayek recalled, the market embodies in its customary ways of functioning important elements of 'tacit knowledge'.

[44] Donzelli 1988, pp. 37 ff., stresses that the notion of 'spontaneous order', present in embryo in Hayek's early writings, came to the fore – to the extent of substituting the traditional notion of equilibrium – with the conclusion of the debate on capital theory (hence beginning with Hayek 1941). With this notion Hayek referred 'to a structure of relations or a system of inter-individual connections which display a relative stability or persistence' (Donzelli 1988, p. 38).

order, particularly scarcity of knowledge, but maintained that a market economy is superior to a planned economy precisely because the information needed in a market economy is far, far less than the information necessary (and certainly not available) to a planned economy.[45]

Hayek's political writings also insisted on these aspects. He maintained the superiority of economic liberalism in comparison not only with centralised planning but also with mixed economies (such as Roosevelt's New Deal), which imply active state intervention in economic life. These writings – much more than his texts on economic theory – especially *The road to serfdom* published in 1944 (which sold hundreds of thousands of copies, thanks partly also to a condensed *Reader's Digest* version, and was translated into more than twenty languages) made Hayek one of the most famous political scientists of the twentieth century. For our purposes, there are two aspects of this series of writings to note. Firstly, even in works aiming at the general public rather than specialists, Hayek retained and divulged the main elements of the 'vision' of the Austrian school: uncertainty, economic activity as quest for power deriving from knowledge – an approach that saw the analytical notion of equilibrium fuse with the notion of spontaneous order, and that offered characterisation of the economic agent far more complex than the one-dimensional view of Benthamite utilitarianism which led to the notion of *homo oeconomicus*. Secondly, in the political writings the idea of the spontaneous order emerging from the functioning of the market was transformed from an analytical result to be proved into a simple assumption or postulate.

The latter point brings us back to the field of economic theory. Here Hayek's contributions had dwindled by the beginning of the 1940s when, after the unfortunate controversy with Sraffa and Keynes in the early 1930s, Hayek seemed stuck in the blind alley he had ended up in with his theory, as finally witnessed by Kaldor's scathing attack.[46]

---

[45] The controversy on the vitality of a planned economy, the possibility of which had been shown by Enrico Barone (cf. below, § 12.3) as early as 1908 in the framework of a general economic equilibrium theory, was revived by Ludwig von Mises (1920), who appears not to have taken account of the answer already provided by Barone. Hayek, instead, insisted on the impossibility of obtaining the necessary information in practice. Oskar Lange (1904–65) answered them in a famous article of 1936–7, proposing a trial and error approach to the planning process, which embodies elements of a 'socialist market'. A different answer was offered by Maurice Dobb (1900–76), a British Marxist, who maintained in a series of writings (for instance Dobb 1955) the superiority of planned economies not in so far as resource allocation is concerned, but in terms of the *ex ante* coordination of investments.

[46] Kaldor 1942 discussed the evolution of Hayek's theory in the decade following publication of *Prices and production* (1931), up to *The pure theory of capital* (1941), and showed how the difficulties Hayek had met with from the beginning, and which had been the object of Sraffa's criticisms in 1932, found no solution with the variations on the theme Hayek went through in later years.

In order to illustrate Hayek's theoretical views let us take a look at *Prices and production* (1931), a slim volume collecting lectures given the previous year at the London School of Economics, which had aroused wide interest. Here Hayek presented a theory that he had gradually devised through a series of previous writings, a theory that – as we saw above in connection with Wicksell – combined the marginalist foundations of a real equilibrium of prices and quantities with the recognition of short run disequilibria connected to essentially monetary phenomena. As far as the marginalist foundations were concerned, Hayek drew in particular on the notion of the average period of production proposed by Böhm-Bawerk, grafting on to it the Wicksellian mechanism of the relationship between natural and money interest rate, together with the theory of forced saving proposed by Mises in 1912 and also utilised by Schumpeter (1912) in his theory of the trade cycle.[47]

In short, the mechanism described by Hayek went thus: when the natural rate of interest is higher than the money rate, entrepreneurs are induced to ask for bank loans in order to enact investment expenditures above the equilibrium level. Since the starting situation is – by the very definition of equilibrium – characterised by the full utilisation of resources, the additional investments can only be made through the increase in prices brought about by the excess demand financed by bank loans; inflation deprives consumers of purchasing power, while entrepreneurs find advantage in it given the time lag between acquisition of the means of production and sale of the product. Furthermore, the additional demand for investment goods generates an increase in their relative prices as compared with consumption goods; this in turn corresponds to an increase in the real wage rate, which enhances the advantage of 'deepening' of the technique, or in other words lengthening the average period of production. These elements constitute the ascending stage of the trade cycle. However, the increased incomes of the productive factors are transformed into greater demand for consumption goods; the relative prices of these goods increase, and the real wage rate decreases. Thus it becomes more advantageous to shorten the average period of production, and the capital goods characterised by higher duration lose in value. Hence the descending phase of the trade cycle. Given the sequence of cause and effect linkages determining the latter stage, a policy in support of demand for consumption goods as proposed in under-consumption theories (which Hayek took to include Keynes's

---

[47] Schumpeter 1954, pp. 723–4, making reference to Hayek, attributed Wicksell with the theory of forced savings, while pointing to Bentham and above all Thornton (1802) as precursors; Hayek himself (1931, pp. 18–19) also looked back to Malthus.

theory) proves counterproductive. According to Hayek, in fact, the capital accumulated in the ascending stage of the trade cycle (corresponding to forced saving) is economically destroyed in the descending stage, so that the economic system returns to its original equilibrium.

Hayek's theory clearly constituted a step forward from Wicksell since it overcame the dichotomy between real and monetary factors, while Hayek's analysis considered changes in technique, income distribution and relative prices. Thus it appeared the most solid alternative to the Keynesian research programme.

So we come to Sraffa's reaction (probably prompted by Keynes himself). In a weighty review of *Prices and production* published in the *Economic Journal* in 1932, Sraffa attacked the foundations of the analytical edifice built by Hayek (and, before him, by Wicksell) and showed the non-existence of a 'natural rate of interest': in a world in which the structure of relative prices changes over time, there are as many 'natural rates of interest' as there are commodities (and, for each commodity, as many intervals of time are considered). According to Sraffa, Hayek had not fully understood the difference between a monetary and a barter economy, so that the monetary factors proved superimposed on the real ones, and any assumption of an influence exercised by the latter over the former clashed with the theory of value developed with reference to a real economy, with its simultaneous determination of equilibrium prices and quantities, techniques and distributive variables.[48]

Hayek's response (1932) was feeble. As a matter of fact, the impact of Sraffa's criticism was more general, concerning the impossibility of reconciling the influence of monetary factors over real variables within the trade cycle with acceptance of a marginalist theory of value for the 'real' equilibrium: a theory which implied a clear-cut dichotomy between real and monetary factors. Thus Sraffa's controversy with Hayek took on crucial importance for subsequent developments in economic theory. With the publication of Sraffa's book in 1960 the final blow was delivered to the foundations of the notion of the average period of production, and Hayek's approach lost even its initial appearance of solidity. However, some new directions in Hayek's work concerning sequential analysis and the question of intertemporal consistency may be seen as seminal contributions to the origin of modern research currents focusing

---

[48] Keynes's support for Sraffa in the face of Hayek's reaction, precisely on this point, was revealing. Hayek concluded his reply by stating that Sraffa 'has understood Mr. Keynes' theory even less than he has my own' (Hayek 1932, p. 249); taking advantage of his position as editor of the *Economic Journal*, Keynes added a sharp footnote: 'With Prof. Hayek's permission I should like to say that, to the best of my comprehension, Mr. Sraffa has understood my theory accurately' (ibid.).

on the sequential analysis of disequilibria, temporary equilibrium and general intertemporal equilibrium.[49]

On various occasions Hayek took up from Menger ideas about the functioning of the economic system departing from the traditional marginalist ones, and worked on them. In particular, the act of choice performed by the economic agent was conceived as an experiment in conditions of uncertainty, the result of which modifies expectations and the initial knowledge, as part of a continuous process. Indeed, competition was conceived as a dynamic process which favours the diffusion of information and emergence of tacit knowledge embodied in rules of conduct, as a process of discovery. Differing in this respect from the French and Anglo-Saxon marginalist approach, the notion of equilibrium thus lost its traditional role of analytical reference central to interpretation of the functioning of the economy.

In conclusion, to sum up Hayek's achievement we may distinguish once again between the interest that lies in his conceptual representation of the market economy and the limits to his analytical construction. The success of Hayek's political writings may perhaps be accounted for not only by their close accord with the cultural climate of the Cold War period, but in particular by the line implied by many aspects of his conceptual representation, as well as reflecting his own choice – followed by many – to leave aside the most controversial aspects of his strictly economic theory in presenting his political ideas on the role of the market. As for the elements of Hayek's 'vision' which aroused the widest interest in contemporary debate – such as the role attributed to economic agents' learning when confronted with the market's responses to their actions – incorporating them in a coherent body of economic theory still remains a challenge which should be tackled on new foundations.[50]

---

[49] In particular we may credit Hayek with the analysis of intertemporal equilibriums, Hicks 1939 with the analysis of temporary equilibriums, and Lindahl and the other representatives of the Swedish school with the sequential analysis of disequilibria. Hayek, in any case, adhered to a stationary view of equilibrium. Cf. Milgate 1979; Donzelli 1988.

[50] In fact, it is quite difficult to give a precise characterisation to the 'Austrian school' in the second half of the twentieth century: cf. Boettke and Leeson 2003.

12   General economic equilibrium

1.   The invisible hand of the market

Among contemporary economists the idea is widespread that general economic equilibrium theory is to be identified with theory *tout court*, and is to be taken as a yardstick by which any other theory can be considered as a particular case.[1] To anyone sharing this viewpoint, the history of economic thought appears as the path of progressive development and consolidation of this theory. Along this route, in interpreting classical economists the economic issue they dealt with is identified in the functioning of the 'invisible hand of the market'. The latter would ensure not simply a sufficiently regular working of the economy but, more than this, a systematic tendency towards an equilibrium with perfect equality between supply and demand for each commodity (market clearing), even in the presence of many commodities and many economic agents.

As a matter of fact, such an extreme idea cannot be attributed to the economists of the classical period; it was originally developed by only one of the 'schools' which concurred in the so-called marginalist revolution, the 'Lausanne school', founded by Léon Walras. In order to clarify this point, let us first consider which elements enter the view of the economic system underlying the general economic equilibrium approach; we shall then see whether these elements were present among classical economists or in the other marginalist 'schools'.

As will emerge clearly when we consider Walras and his followers in greater detail, two elements above all should be considered essential: the idea of general interdependence among all the parts that compose an economic system, and the idea of the market as an equilibrating mechanism between supply and demand. Side by side with these two crucial elements,

[1] Recently this idea appears somewhat in decline, due to increasing fragmentation of economic research, increasingly accepted as a fact, for which no explanation is attempted. Cf. below, chs. 17 and 18.

322

and in part stemming from them, we find a specific view of the economic problem (as a problem of optimal allocation of scarce resources) and of the economic agent (the *homo oeconomicus*).

We have already seen that each of these two crucial elements was present in the history of economic thought and among economists contemporary with Walras. However, this may happen in a context quite different from the Walrasian one. Thus the idea of interrelations among the different parts that compose an economic system was at the centre of Quesnay's analysis, with his *tableau économique*. His immediate precursor, Cantillon, though without developing a formal model, also proposed a representation of the economic system based on interdependencies between social classes, economic sectors and territorial zones (countryside, villages, cities). Subsequently, we may recall the simple and expanded reproduction schemes developed by Marx in volume 2 of *Capital* (which, however, appeared only in 1885, after the publication of Walras's main work). More recently, the idea of a general interdependence in production, among the sectors in which an economy based on the division of labour is subdivided, was at the centre of Leontief's input-output tables. None of these analytical contributions, however, included, or imposed as a logical necessity, a mechanism of adjustment of prices and quantities based on the reactions of agents in the market to disequilibria between supply and demand. Furthermore, these analytical contributions all focused attention on interdependencies among sectors in production, while interdependence (substitutability) in consumption choices was not considered, or anyhow remained in the background.

The role of demand and supply in determining the price of a good (and behind it its value, interpreted as the expression of the good's scarcity in comparison to the utility attributed to it by economic agents) was conversely at the centre of a widespread tradition of economic thinking, which in representing the working of the market initially took as ideal reference points medieval fairs, then stock exchanges, both considered institutions which ensure a meeting place, in time and space, for buyers and sellers. However, we should be hard-pressed to find in the writings of Galiani an integration of the two aspects which in his exposition remained separate: on the one side, the outline of a subjective theory of value; on the other, the idea of a general interrelation among the various parts of the economic system. Analogously, the French economists Cournot and Dupuit, unanimously considered as precursors of the marginalist approach (cf. above, § 10.2), totally overlooked economic interdependencies, with one focusing on the equilibrium of the firm and the other on the evaluation of public works.[2] Jevons's utilitarian approach also focused on the analysis of individual behaviour, with the comparison between disutility (labour) and utility (consumption), while interrelations among different economic agents in the market constituted a superstructure in many respects only outlined cursorily. Somewhat later Marshall, though taking into account Walras's work, demonstrated – as we shall see in the next chapter – his preference for 'short causal chains', hence the method of analysis of partial equilibrium, in comparison to general economic equilibrium analysis, which he considered too abstract.

If we take all this into account, we are better able to understand the major distortion of those who view even classical economists as precursors of the analysis of general economic equilibrium.[3] There are three aspects to which reference is usually made in doing this: the notions of the 'invisible hand of the market', of competition, and of 'convergence' of market prices towards natural prices. Briefly recalling what we have already seen above (in particular in ch. 5), we may stress that none of these elements implies a subjective view of value or the choice of the medieval fair (or of the stock exchange) as paradigm for representing the working of the economy. In particular, the idea of the convergence of market prices towards natural prices did not imply, for classical economists such as Smith or Ricardo, the idea of market prices as theoretical variables univocally *determined* by an apparatus of demand and supply curves (nor the idea that it is possible to define – and consider as a given datum for the treatment of the theoretical problem – sufficiently precise and stable relations connecting quantities demanded and supplied to prices, nor the idea that such relations can be deduced as representing economic agents' behaviour). The same may be said for the thesis of the tendency

[2] Walras anyhow recognised that it was Cournot (cf. for instance the letter of 20 March 1874, n. 253, in Walras, 1965a, vol. 1, pp. 363–7) who had the merit of maintaining that economists must work with mathematical tools: according to Walras as well as Jevons (but not Menger or Marshall), this was a decisive point of distinction of the 'new school' from classical political economy in its wider definition and its varied progenies, from Smith to John Stuart Mill, from Say to the 'socialists of the chair'. Cournot's influence was especially important for 'the idea that application of mathematics to economics should not regard numerical calculations, but the application of functional analysis in order to deduce theorems of a general nature' (Ingrao and Israel 1987, p. 91). Obviously, as far as the mathematisation of economics was concerned, the influence of mathematical physics developed in Newton's wake is essential, as stressed by Ingrao and Israel (ibid., pp. 33 ff.) amongst others. In this context, Ingrao and Israel (ibid., pp. 38–40) also stress the Newtonian derivation of the notion of equilibrium of social forces introduced by Montesquieu (1689–1755). On Dupuit and Cournot as precursors of Walras, cf. Ingrao and Israel (ibid., pp. 72–5). On the role of physics as a paradigmatic model for economic theory cf. Mirowski 1989.
[3] Cf. for instance Hollander 1973 on Smith; Hollander 1979 on Ricardo; Morishima 1973 on Marx.

to a uniform rate of profits through which Smith's or Ricardo's 'competition of capitals' was expressed, based on the freedom of movement of capital among different sectors of the economy. Finally, the notion of the 'invisible hand' was originally used by Smith in different contexts; in general, we can attribute to him the idea that individual actions driven by personal interest may have positive effects on society: a thesis typical of eighteenth-century Enlightenment optimism, which in Smith referred among other things to the good functioning of an economic system in which individuals are driven by personal interest; but we most certainly cannot attribute to him the idea of the optimality of a competitive market based on the mechanism of demand and supply.[4]

In conclusion, we must recognise that the idea of an economic system driven by the tendency of all its parts towards equilibrium between supply and demand (market clearing) is simply one of the viewpoints on which we can build a 'system of concepts' of political economy, on the basis of which we can then construct theories and models.[5]

The history of this specific approach is considered in this chapter. First of all, we shall consider Walras's (§ 2) and Pareto's (§ 3) contributions, that is, the Lausanne school in what we may call the heroic stage of the general economic equilibrium approach. The generation following Pareto, but still within the heroic stage, included the United States economist Irving Fisher (§ 4). Then we pass on to the 'critical stage', when it was realised that equality between number of equations and number of unknowns is not sufficient for ensuring existence of economically meaningful solutions (which in the minds of the founders of this approach also meant stable solutions). The redefinition of the analytical model which took place in this stage – briefly illustrated in § 5 – implies a considerable reduction in the heuristic value of general economic equilibrium theory. However, from here the story went on to a new heroic, or rather totalitarian, stage: general economic equilibrium analysis was identified with the project of an axiomatic economic science. When one forgets the specific nature of the conceptual system on which it is built, the axiomatic model of general equilibrium, discussed in § 6, naturally becomes the all-inclusive reference

---

[4] On the use of the expression 'invisible hand of the market' on the part of Smith, cf. above, § 5.6. Let us also recall, anticipating what will be illustrated below in this chapter, that the thesis of the re-equilibrating capacity of the market came out decidedly weakened, if not rejected, by the enquiries on stability of general economic equilibrium models.

[5] Fecundity of this viewpoint for the interpretation of the working of economic systems, in comparison with other viewpoints, should then be judged on the basis of the greater or lesser success of the research programmes which originate from them. In this respect, we cannot certainly consider as a triumph the outcomes of the attempts to connect the subjective theory of value and the idea of general interdependence within the economy: cf. below, §§ 12.7 and 17.2, and ch. 18.

theory, from which any theoretical analysis of specific issues should stem, at least in principle. The analytical rigour of the model is fascinating, but obscures its basic limits as interpretation of the actual economy. In particular, the very work of strengthening the analytical structure and extending the basic model leads to leaving aside the idea of the 'invisible hand of the market' where the long path of general economic equilibrium theory had started.

2.   Léon Walras

The general economic equilibrium approach, in so far as it implied the insertion of the mechanism of supply and demand in a context of general interdependencies in production as in consumption, arose with Walras. Naturally, this does not mean that there were no precursors. We may recall in particular Turgot (cf. above, § 4.7), especially for the metaphors with which he connected economic equilibrium to the equilibrium of forces in the field of mechanics. We should also mention Achylle Nicholas Isnard (1749–1803), author of a *Traité des richesses* (Treatise of wealth, 1781) present in Walras's library, and author of a theory of relative prices based on a system of simultaneous equations of exchange. Isnard stressed the fact that the requirement of equality between the number of independent equations and number of unknowns made it necessary to choose a standard of measure, thus limiting the price unknowns to relative prices.[6]

Isnard's influence was, however, mediated by that of Walras's main precursor, his own father, Antoine Auguste Walras (1801–66), author of a number of economic writings among which *De la nature de la richesse et de l'origine de la valeur* (About the nature of wealth and the origin of value, 1831) and *Théorie de la richesse sociale ou résumé des principes fondamentaux de l'économie politique* (A theory of social wealth or summary of the fundamental principles of political economy, 1849), and supporter of the thesis that value stems from scarcity (or, in other words, that social

---

[6] On Isnard, cf. Ingrao and Israel 1987, pp. 61–6, and the bibliography quoted there. Among Walras's precursors, Ingrao and Israel (ibid., pp. 66–72) also recall Nicolas-François Canard (1750–1838), mathematician by training and winner of an Institut de France prize for a work (Canard 1801) in which marginal analysis was used for analysis of economic equilibrium, a notion considered close to that of mechanical equilibrium; in relation to it Canard also considered the adjustment process. Walras (like Cournot) might not have quoted Canard because of 'resentment [. . .] for the obscure high school math teacher who had obtained the recognition constantly denied to them by the prestigious scientific institution' (Ingrao and Israel 1987, p. 67). Jaffé 1983, pp. 297–9, also recalled Jean Jacques Burlamaqui (1697–1748), professor of law in Geneva, widely quoted in the writings of Walras's father; but at the same time stressed the limits of all these anticipations (including those by Turgot, Condillac and Nassau Senior) in comparison to a rigorous formulation of the marginal utility principle.

wealth is the sum of the goods which are simultaneously useful and available in limited quantity). Walras's father developed, among other things, some of the concepts later used by his son, such as that of the standard of measure,[7] the distinction between capital goods and their services, and the distinction between capitalist and entrepreneur. The capitalist is the owner of capital goods; the entrepreneur operates as an intermediary between the market of productive factors and that of products, buying the services of factors of production, coordinating their utilisation, and selling the product thus obtained (a view of the entrepreneur which Walras senior took over from Say).[8]

Apart from his father, the main precursors for the development of the Walrasian theory of general economic equilibrium are to be found in a completely different field of research, namely physics, in particular mechanics, with its theory of static equilibrium. Well recognised is the importance, in Léon's studies, of the text *Éléments de statique* (1803) by the physicist Louis Poinsot.[9]

From father to son. Marie Esprit Léon Walras, one of the best-known and least widely read economists of all times, was born on 16 December 1834 at Evreux in France, and died on 5 January 1910 at Clarens in Switzerland.[10] His father put him down for the renowned École polytechnique, but Léon failed to gain admission (due to shortcomings in mathematics, it seems), and registered at the École des mines. Quite soon, however, he abandoned his studies in engineering to dedicate himself to literature and journalism; he published a novel (*Francis Sauveur*, 1858), worked on the *Journal des Économistes* and *La Presse*, was a clerk with the railways, co-editor with Léon Say of a cooperativist review, *Le Travail* (1866–8), administrator of a cooperative bank (which went bankrupt in 1868), and a paid lecturer. Finally, after many failed attempts in France, in 1870 he obtained a position as a teacher at the Academy (then University) of Lausanne in Switzerland and the following year he was nominated to the chair of political economy. Married in 1869 after a long period of cohabitation from which two daughters were born, Walras had to undertake various additional jobs (collaboration with journals and

---

[7] The numeraire is the commodity chosen as standard of measure for prices. The term 'money' designates the means of exchange; it may be the same commodity chosen as numeraire, or a different commodity, or inconvertible paper money.

[8] On the influence of Walras's father, cf. for instance Howey 1989, pp. 28–32. Howey stressed, however, that the problem tackled by Walras's father is that of the *cause* of value, not that of the determination of relative prices or that of the allocative role of prices.

[9] On Poinsot's influence, cf. Walker 1996, pp. 4 and 36. Walras used the eighth edition of Poinsot's text, published in 1842.

[10] On his life see the 'Notice autobiographique' written in 1909 (Walras 1965b).

encyclopaedias, consultancy with an insurance firm) in order to add to his meagre salary as professor during the long illness of his first wife, who died in 1879. Five years later Walras married again, finally reaching a sound economic position; but only in 1892, thanks to an inheritance from his mother, was he able to pay back the debts contracted to finance publication of his writings.[11] At the same time, aged only fifty-eight, Walras resigned from his chair both because he felt tired and to concentrate on research; he favoured Pareto's nomination as his successor.

Léon's main work were the *Éléments d'économie politique pure* (1874; second part, 1877; fourth edition, 1900; the edition commonly used today is Jaffé's 1954 English translation of the 'definitive' French edition of 1926, which in many important aspects is quite different from the first).[12] The original research programme of the French economist entailed two other volumes after that dealing with pure theory: one concerning applied economics and the other on social economy. In their place, we have two collections of essays: the *Études d'économie sociale* (1896) and the *Études d'économie politique appliquée* (1898).[13]

The original work plan derived from a distinction, in the field of economic phenomena, between (a) the 'laws of exchange', assimilated to natural laws similar to those studied by physics even if concerned with 'facts of humanity' rather than with 'natural facts', which were the subject of pure economics; (b) the production of wealth (division of labour, industrial organisation), which was the subject of applied economics; and (c) problems of distribution, involving also ethical issues, which were the subject of social economics. The three fields in which the economist's work were thus subdivided imply three different kinds of analytical work, with different levels of abstraction and different connections with other fields of research: greater proximity to natural sciences and particularly to physics for pure economics, to social sciences for applied economics, and

---

[11] In 1901, Walras estimated he had spent 50,000 francs, more than ten times his highest annual salary, for the diffusion of his theories: cf. Walras 1965a, vol. 3, p. 187.

[12] The differences between the various editions of the *Éléments* are vigorously stressed by Walker 1996, a volume which draws with revisions on a series of articles on Walras originally published between 1984 and 1994. In the development of Walras's thought, Walker distinguishes a first creative stage (1872–7), a mature stage (from 1878 to the middle of the 1890s, which includes the second and third edition of the *Éléments*, 1889 and 1896 respectively) and finally a stage of decline (which includes the fourth edition of 1900 and the 'definitive' edition of 1926). Walker remarks that only in this latter stage did Walras introduce the so-called written pledges; the French term used by Walras was *bons*; Jaffé's English translation uses *tickets* and the Italian one by A. Bagiotti *buoni*, with some imprecision; on the meaning of the French term cf. Walker 1996, p. 331. Written pledges are important in so far as they allow avoiding disequilibrium production decision.

[13] For a bibliography of Walras's writings, cf. Walker 1987. Publication of a complete edition of the economic writings of Auguste and Léon Walras is under way, in fourteen volumes, with the publisher Economica of Paris; vol. 8 (1988) is a critical edition of the *Éléments* which indicates the variants between successive editions.

to philosophy for social economics. Parallel to this tripartition, among other things, was the distinction between the theoretical assumption of absolute free competition, the competitive conditions of real markets and, finally, the 'principle' of free competition (meant not only as inclusive of the theoretical optimality of perfect competition, but also of its concrete realisation and its equity).

In the 'definitive' edition, the *Éléments* were divided into three parts. After an introductory part on the definition of political economy and social economy, we have a step-by-step sequence: part two concerns the theory of exchange between two commodities,[14] part three extends analysis to the case of more commodities; subsequently we find production (part four), accumulation and credit (part five), money (part six), growth and the critique of previous theories (in particular, the 'English' theory – that is, Ricardo's and John Stuart Mill's – concerning price, rent, wages and interest: part seven), monopoly and taxes (part eight).

Underlying this construct there was a stylised representation of the market economy, which assumed the Paris Bourse as archetype (already studied in Walras 1867, and then again in Walras 1880, where he stressed in particular the absence of exchanges at non-equilibrium prices). The tradition of continental stock exchanges, which up to a few years before had differed from that of Anglo-Saxon ones, was based on an auctioneer who was to call out in succession the various stocks, proposing a price for each of them and ascertaining the corresponding demand and supply. The price was then adjusted, increasing it when demand was higher than supply and reducing it in the opposite case. Such an adjustment process continued until an equilibrium was reached between supply and demand; actual exchanges only took place when this situation was reached.[15]

---

[14] Unlike what Niehans 1990, p. 211, maintains, this is not a partial equilibrium analysis, but a general equilibrium analysis referred to an over-simplified system.

[15] Anglo-Saxon stock exchanges are instead based on *continuous trading*, a mode of operation recently adopted by continental stock exchanges as well (the Italian stock exchange converted to it between 1992 and 1993), and which as we will see constituted the term of reference for Marshall's theory as for that of Hicks. Anyhow, we should stress that in the framework of Walras's theory exchanges only took place once the prices which ensure equilibrium between demand and supply simultaneously on all markets were reached; since demand functions depend on the prices of all goods simultaneously (while within the model of pure exchange the available quantities of the various goods are given data of the problem), we cannot consider the equilibrium price of a commodity to have been reached simply because equality between demand and supply for that commodity has been established, if equilibrium has not been established for all other commodities as well. Passing over these difficulties, Walker 1996 repeatedly stresses the wealth of details which Walras provided on the market mechanisms considered in his analysis, especially in comparison to the quick treatment Marshall gave of the 'corn market' in his *Principles* and to the totally abstract nature (in the sense of absence of any reference to the concrete world) of modern general economic equilibrium axiomatic theory.

The working of the stock exchange was taken as the archetype of the freely competitive market, which according to Walras constituted at the same time an analytical assumption and a normative ideal whose optimality had to be demonstrated.[16] There is a tension between the interpretative and the normative side in Walras's analysis (as in most of those of his followers). Some readings of his work focus on one aspect alone, thus sacrificing the other. The majority of Walras's interpreters, however, take a middle path between the two extremes, with only differences of emphasis on the relative importance of normative and interpretative analysis.[17]

Let us try to provide a sketchy representation of Walras's analysis; in doing so, however, fidelity to Walras's text is in some respects sacrificed to simplicity of exposition.[18]

As far as the *model of pure exchange* is concerned, the data of the problem consist in the number of commodities and of economic agents, in their preferences and in the endowments of each commodity for each agent. Preferences are expressed by individual demand functions for the different goods, which Walras derived from utility functions.[19] For

---

[16] On the political plane, Walras was a progressive thinker, who proposed cooperativism rather than class struggle and pursued ideals of social justice, for example with the proposal to nationalise land and attribute rent to the state. On the relationship between competition and the role of the state in Walras, cf. Ingrao and Ranchetti 1996, p. 284.

[17] Thus, for instance, Jaffé stressed the normative aspect (see the essays collected in Jaffé 1983), while Schumpeter 1954, Morishima 1977 and Walker 1996, pp. 31–52, focused attention on the descriptive nature of Walras's analysis. These differences also extend to the analysis of *tâtonnement*, interpreted alternatively either (with great caution) as an essentially atemporal construct or as analytical representation of a real process; the latter interpretation possibly undervalues (or leaves aside) the analytical difficulties which appear along this road. If we bear in mind such difficulties, of which Walras was not completely unaware, we can hypothesise a third interpretation, intermediate between the first two: namely, that Walras had started from the analysis of real processes, and had then shifted gradually (and partially) in the direction of an a-temporal construct.

[18] This is anyway true for practically all illustrations of Walrasian theory, many of which are mainly concerned with building a bridge between it and subsequent theoretical developments. Among these, we should recall at least the important writings by Napoleoni 1965 and Morishima 1977.

[19] With the help, in this respect, of a colleague of the Académie de Lausanne, Antoine Paul Piccard: cf. Walras 1965a, vol. 1, pp. 309–11, and Jaffé 1983, pp. 303–4. Walras considered utility as measurable: a point on which his successor Pareto differed from him. He also assumed 'that the utility a consumer derives from any commodity is independent of the amount he or she consumes of other commodities' (Walker 2003, p. 279). Howey 1989, p. 38, anyhow, stressed Walras's tendency to pass as much as possible over the problem of the measurability of utility. Ingrao and Israel 1987 stress that for Walras 'while not numerically measurable, "satisfaction" is a quantitative magnitude' (ibid., p. 157; cf. also p. 147 and pp. 166–8, where the distinction drawn by Walras between 'physical data' and 'psychic data' is recalled; to this distinction – or, better, to the distinction 'between external facts and intimate facts' – Ingrao and Ranchetti, 1996, pp. 306 ff., connect that 'between analytical application and numerical application of mathematics';

each individual we then have a budget constraint, which ensures equality between the value of goods he or she demands and the resources he or she commands. The equilibrium solution for the relative prices of the different commodities and for the quantities of each of them acquired and sold by each individual is defined both analytically, as a solution to a system of equations, and through the illustration of an adjustment process (*tâtonnement*) which is meant as an idealised representation of what takes place in reality under competitive conditions.[20] According to such a process, the system begins with an initial price *crié au hazard* (given at random by the auctioneer); then the corresponding levels of demand and supply are compared, and the 'cried out' price is changed until an equilibrium is reached; only then do exchanges take place.[21]

The analytical model is simple. First of all, as hinted above, for each individual we have as many demand functions as there are commodities; each function expresses the demand of that individual for that commodity as a function of the price of the commodity itself and of all other prices – which are unknowns to be determined – in addition to the initial endowments of the different commodities which the individual commands (and which, multiplied by their prices, determine the individual's disposable income). These functions are by assumption independent and remain unchanged in the course of the process of adjustment to equilibrium; moreover, the quantity demanded decreases when the price of the commodity under consideration increases, all other variables remaining unchanged. For each commodity, the demand functions of the different individuals are added up; we thus arrive at defining aggregate demand functions, one for each commodity. To the individual's budget

they also stress that Walras always appeared hostile to the application of numerical computation in pure economics, hence to Benthamite utilitarianism, while in the wake of Descartes he believed mathematics to constitute the necessary form of any true scientific knowledge). A clearer grasp of the limits of the cardinal notion of utility – Ingrao and Ranchetti 1996, pp. 310–14, notice – was proposed by the famous mathematician Jules-Henri Poincaré (1856–1912), in a letter to Walras (Italian translation in Ingrao and Ranchetti 1996, pp. 336–7) of September 1901; Poincaré in particular 'identifies the two fundamental postulates of Walras's economic theory [. . .] in the assumptions of perfectly selfish behaviour and of perfect foresight, and concludes: "The first assumption may be admitted only as a first approximation, but the second possibly calls for some reservations"' (Ingrao and Ranchetti 1996, p. 312).

[20] Competition is here identified with absence of obstacles or frictions to the flow of orders of purchase or sale that converge on the market: cf. Jaffé 1983, p. 291.

[21] The traditional interpretation attributes to an 'auctioneer' responsibility for indicating the initial price and for changing it; Walker (1996, pp. 55–7, 82–9, 263–7) maintains that in Walras's opinion all professional agents in an authorised market may assume this role, exchanging oral options (promises) to sell or purchase in case the price 'cried' by the auctioneer is the equilibrium one (as already hinted, written pledges were introduced only in the fourth edition of 1900).

constraints there corresponds a system of equations expressing the aggregate equilibrium conditions: that is, for each commodity the quantity demanded is set equal to the quantity supplied. We thus have two groups of equations: the demand functions and the conditions of equilibrium; in each of the two groups, the number of equations is equal to the number of commodities. 'Walras's law' then reminds us that one of these equations can be deduced from the others (namely that if n-1 markets are in equilibrium, the same necessarily holds true for the n-th market). If there are n commodities, hence, the independent equations are $2n$-1. We then have a number of independent equations equal to the number of unknowns to be determined (the n-1 relative prices, that is, the prices of the various commodities in terms of one of them chosen as standard of measure, and the n quantities of the different commodities demanded in the system as a whole). Obviously, once prices are determined, the quantities of each commodity acquired or sold by each individual are also determined on the basis of the individual demand functions. The result, analogous to that published three years earlier by Menger and Jevons, is that the prices of the various commodities are proportional to their *raretés*, or marginal utilities.

Walras was aware of the fact that simple equality between number of equations and number of unknowns did not ensure by itself economically meaningful solutions for the variables to be determined; this essential function was in fact implicitly attributed to the illustration of the *tâtonnement* process which purported to ensure the stability of equilibrium. In the case of pure exchange, as in the following steps in which gradually exchange and production, accumulation and money were considered, the analysis of stability was an integral part of Walrasian theory: in Walras's opinion, as for all the other founders of the marginalist approach, an unstable equilibrium did not constitute an acceptable solution to the problem of representing the working of the markets. In each case then the analysis of equilibrium and of its stability was followed by comparative statics analysis, aimed at identifying what happens when some data of the problem – the initial endowment of some commodity, or consumers' preferences – change.[22]

In the case of the *model of production and exchange*, each individual has at his or her disposal given endowments of what we may call capital goods at

---

[22] Analysis of stability, and in general of disequilibria processes, is essential according to Walras. On this point cf. for instance Walker 1996, pp. 26–7, 263, 271–2. Ingrao and Ranchetti 1996, p. 281, also stress that according to Walras convergence towards equilibrium takes place with extreme rapidity. Walker 1996, p. 67, shows that Walras, after declaring himself 'certain' of convergence in 1874, following an epistolary discussion with Wicksteed in 1889 shifted to consider convergence only 'likely'.

large: land, capital goods in the real sense, personal capital goods (skills). Moreover the production functions are known, which express the quantities produced of the different commodities as increasing functions of the quantities used of the services of the various productive factors. Initially, for the sake of simplicity, such functions are based on the assumption of fixed technical coefficients, which implies absence of substitutability among different factors of production and constant returns to scale. Side by side with the markets for commodities we now have the markets for services of productive factors, which are 'hired' by their owners to entrepreneurs. The role of the latter is to acquire such services, organise the productive process and sell the commodities produced. Competition ensures that entrepreneurs do not obtain any profit, apart from the 'wage of direction' which is included in the costs of production.[23]

We thus have a new group of equations, as many as there are commodities, which ensures for each consumption good equality between its cost of production and product value. Moreover, we have a group of demand functions for the services of capital goods, as many as there are capital goods; the demand for each service corresponds to the quantity of it employed in the productive processes on the whole, and is therefore expressed as a function of technology (more precisely, of technical coefficients of production) and of levels of production of different consumption goods. Another group of equations (once again as many as there are capital goods) expresses the equilibrium condition for the markets for the services of capital goods as equality between quantity demanded and quantity available for each service.[24] The additional equations correspond in number to the additional unknowns: the prices of the services of capital goods, in terms of the commodity chosen as standard of measure, the quantities demanded for each service, and the quantities produced of the different consumption goods.

The process of adjustment to equilibrium, or *tâtonnement*, is in this case obviously much more complex than in the case of the model of pure exchange. Walras tried to outline with precision the different aspects of this process, and in subsequent editions of the *Éléments* his analysis underwent important changes. Thus, for instance, the third edition (1896) envisages exchanges of the services of capital goods even at prices different from the equilibrium ones: production may take place in disequilibrium,

---

[23] On the role of entrepreneurs in Walras's model, cf. Walker 1996, pp. 280–7.

[24] Let us recall that in the model of production and exchange there is no production of new capital goods, which are assumed to last for ever and to have an efficiency independent of their age. Let us also recall that in Walrasian terminology capital goods include both capital goods properly called, land and personal capital goods (working abilities).

with price and average cost which may differ from one another, generating profits or losses for the different firms, which as a consequence expand or contract, enter or exit the market, even if the endowment of the different capital goods remains constant.[25] Probably it was precisely in order to overcome the shortcomings that such a solution presented when moving on to the model with accumulation that Walras was induced to introduce the mechanism of the 'written pledges' in the fourth edition of 1900. However, this mechanism, apart from being decidedly less realistic, since it excluded any transaction outside the situation of full equilibrium, created more problems than it solved.[26]

Walras then tackled the third model, with *accumulation and credit*. In other words, he moved on to the case in which capital goods may be produced as well, hence to the issue of capital accumulation. It was in this stage, before money was taken into account, that the problem of credit was introduced: we are thus confronted with demand and supply of credit in real terms, that is, in terms of the commodity chosen as standard of measure.

In order to deal with this problem, Walras introduced a commodity E (*épargne*, that is savings), which has the characteristic of yielding an annual perpetuity equal to a unit of the commodity chosen as standard, and which thus has a price equal to the inverse of the rate of interest. This commodity is demanded by those who desire to invest in the purchase of new capital goods (the entrepreneurs), and is supplied by those who decide to save (the capitalists). Demand and supply of this commodity thus depend, on the one hand, on the preferences of economic agents for current consumption over future consumption and, on the other, on the return on investment in new capital goods. The condition of equality between demand and supply of the commodity E constitutes an additional equation, which corresponds to the additional unknown represented by the price of the commodity E (or by its inverse, the rate of interest).

[25] Cf. Walker 1996, pp. 129–54. Absence of markets for capital goods (in addition to the markets for their services), as well as absence of savings and accumulation, are necessary in order to avoid contradictions in this analytical representation of the adjustment process, especially so as to avoid the equilibrium values of the variables turning out to depend on the path of adjustment followed by prices of services of capital goods (Walker 1996, p. 153).

[26] Cf. Walker 1996, pp. 321–95. Walker considers the model of the fourth and fifth editions of the *Éléments* decidedly inferior to that of the third edition, undervaluing the limits of the latter, recalled in the previous note. He moreover stresses that the economists of the generation immediately subsequent to that of Walras, particularly Pareto and Edgeworth, used as reference mainly the model of the third edition, while the model with the written pledges acquired a dominant role only in the subsequent stage of axiomatic general equilibrium theory; Edgeworth is also one of the first authors to stress the problems of path dependency implicit in the representation of a dynamic model allowing for exchanges also outside of the full equilibrium situation. On the debate between Walras and Edgeworth on this point, cf. Walker 1996, pp. 302–15.

In equilibrium, moreover, the supply price of the capital goods which are produced (which is given by their cost of production) must be equal to their demand price, which corresponds to their net return, discounted on the basis of the rate of interest implicit in the price of the commodity E. Alternatively, it is possible to define, for each capital good, a rate of return, which is given by the net income (equal to gross income, namely to the price of the service of the capital good under consideration, less the costs for amortisation and insurance) divided by the price of the capital good. Investment in different capital goods must yield the same rate of return, in turn equal to the rate of interest which brings to equilibrium demand and supply of the commodity E, namely savings. Furthermore, for each capital good in equilibrium demand must equal supply. If in the initial situation a capital good yields a higher rate of return than that of other capital goods, it proves profitable to increase its production, hence its supply. This brings about a reduction in its price, up to the point at which its rate of return has decreased to the same level as the rates of return of other capital goods. Conversely, those capital goods for which the demand price turns out to be lower than the supply price will not be produced, and their price will be equal to the present value of the rents expected from sale of their services.[27]

This model too underwent major changes, with more detailed analysis in the transition from the first to the second and third edition, and with additional modifications in the fourth and fifth editions.

Money was introduced in a fourth stage of analysis as a bridge required by economic agents to cross the time intervals between outlays and takings. Money was thus considered one of the two kinds of circulating capital, side by side with non-durable means of production. Net demand for money balances depended on the level of the interest rate which represented their opportunity-cost.[28] In this stage of development of his theory too, Walras stuck to the assumption of absence of uncertainty in equilibrium states. As a consequence, Walras's monetary theory did not lend itself to analysing the trade cycle as a sequence of disequilibria with its origin in the monetary phenomena: a kind of analysis which characterised the oral tradition of Marshall's Cambridge and then the works of Marshall's pupils, as well as the Austrian school with Mises and Schumpeter, and later with Hayek. On the whole, an insurmountable

---

[27] On this model, already criticised by Bortkiewicz and Edgeworth (cf. Walker 1996, pp. 211–34), there has been in Italy an interesting interpretative-theoretical debate, with contributions by Pierangelo Garegnani, Augusto Graziani, Domenico Tosato, Enrico Zaghini and others. For an overview of this debate and the bibliographical references, cf. Tiberi 1969.

[28] Also the discussion of money underwent drastic changes in the transition from the third to the fourth editions of the *Éléments*; for an illustration of the two stages, cf. Walker 1996, pp. 235–55 and pp. 399–419 respectively.

contradiction arises between the static nature of Walrasian general economic equilibrium analysis and the attempt to allow for a notion of money which is something different and wider than a simple standard of measure.[29] It is worth stressing that this is not a secondary aspect: as a matter of fact, it brings sharply into focus the heuristic limits of the Walrasian approach and of the whole line of research originating from it.

Despite many years' work devoted by Walras to completing and refining his great theoretical edifice, even apart from the issues concerning the definition of the institutional assets and the behaviours underlying the formal systems of equations,[30] various crucial problems remained unsolved. These concerned not only the difficulties Walras met in what for him were only successive approximations, the introduction of accumulation and money. As we shall see in the next sections, crucial analytical issues remained open: demonstration of the existence, uniqueness and stability of the solutions. Indeed, in his attempts in this direction Walras appeared to confound the questions of existence and uniqueness of equilibrium. Overall, Walras built the conceptual and analytical foundations of general economic equilibrium theory, but did not succeed in even provisionally bringing his analysis to a close.

This task was attempted by successive generations of scholars. However, as we shall see, the results will be some way from the hopes that had nurtured Walras's efforts: neither stability, nor uniqueness of general economic equilibrium, not even for the simplest model of pure exchange, can be proved under sufficiently general conditions.[31] Given the objectives he had set for himself, we might say that, despite the sophistication of many later contributions, if Walras had known this outcome, he would have had to consider that he had lost his wager by starting the new research stream centred on general economic equilibrium.

3.   Vilfredo Pareto and the Lausanne school

When he withdrew from the Lausanne chair in 1892, Walras ensured that a forty-five-year-old engineer, Vilfredo Pareto, was nominated in his place.

Born in Paris in 1848, the son of a Genoan marquis in exile as a follower of Mazzini, Pareto studied engineering at Turin University, where he graduated in 1870. Subsequently he worked as a railway engineer and

---

[29] An accurate analytical reconstruction of Walras's (and Pareto's) attempts to introduce money in general economic equilibrium theory and their failure is provided by Bridel 1997.

[30] This is an aspect repeatedly considered by Walker 1996.

[31] Uniqueness of equilibrium is important in order to maintain the general validity of comparative static analyses, otherwise limited to a limited contour of the equilibrium solution.

then as assistant director and general director of the Ferriere Italiane in Florence. Compelled to resign in 1890 when the company underwent a crisis, he began taking an interest in economics by reading the *Principii di economia pura* by Pantaleoni, and then Walras's writings; only in 1892 did he publish his first articles in the *Giornale degli economisti*. Activity as a full-time scholar only began with the Lausanne appointment. In 1896–7, collecting and expanding his lectures, he published, in two volumes, the *Cours d'économie politique*, largely devoted to erudite digressions which foreshadowed his sociology writings, while only the first part was devoted to an illustration of Walras's theory. His main work in our field is the *Manuale di economia politica* (1906), in particular the mathematical appendix to the 1909 French edition. The other best-known writings concern sociology: *Les systèmes socialistes* dated 1901–2, and the two volumes of the *Trattato di sociologia generale* dated 1916.[32]

Greatly enriched by an inheritance in 1898, Pareto married a countess of Russian origins a year later, only to be deserted two years later when she ran away with their young cook. The Lausanne professor then moved to Céligny in Switzerland and in 1907 resigned from his chair, living in isolation up to his death in 1923.[33] He had just been appointed senator by Mussolini, but though his opinions had become increasingly conservative with age, he was too much of an aristocrat to accept trooping with the fascist herd. Only two days before his death he married the companion of the last seventeen years of his life, the young Parisian Jeanne Régis, treated for a long time more as a governess than as a wife.

His contributions to economic theory essentially, but not exclusively, consisted in the able application of mathematical tools to the general economic equilibrium approach developed by Walras.[34] Intermediate

---

[32] Pareto's *Oeuvres complètes* have been published in thirty volumes, edited by Busino (1964–89). A bibliography of Pareto, prepared by Gabriele De Rosa, has been published as an appendix to Pareto 1960, vol. 3, pp. 471–542. Pareto's correspondence fills five volumes: Pareto 1960, 3 vols. (his correspondence with Pantaleoni) and Pareto 1973, 2 vols., which includes a careful chronological bibliography (ibid., vol. 1, pp. 101–43).

[33] Another Italian, Pasquale Boninsegni (1869–1939) succeeded him on the Lausanne chair. Among the (rare) followers of the general economic equilibrium approach in its initial stages, let us recall the first French disciple of Walras, Albert Aupetit (1876–1943); and the Italian Enrico Barone (1859–1924), known for his 1908 article on the 'Ministro della pianificazione nello stato collettivista' (The ministry of planning in the collectivist state), but also responsible for introducing the analytical tool of the 'budget line' (Spiegel 1971, p. 557) and unsuccessful supporter of a reconciliation between Walras and Pareto who since 1893 had come into conflict on political and methodological – rather than theoretical – issues (Pareto's extreme liberalism).

[34] In this field Pareto mainly developed comparative static analysis and with him 'for the first time, the slope of the demand curve was derived from the characteristics of the utility function' (Niehans 1990, p. 266). Pareto was also the first economist to study the (semi-centennial) 'long waves', christened by Schumpeter 'Kondratieff cycles': cf. Sylos Labini 1950.

between economics and sociology was the widely known 'Pareto's law' concerning personal income distribution. The 'law' (Pareto 1896) was summarised in a famous formula:

$$\log N = \log A - \alpha \log x$$

where N is the number of families with an income at least equal to x, A is a parameter indicating the size of the population, α is an estimated parameter, generally equal to 1.5. The apparent applicability of this formula to different populations and different epochs seems to indicate independence of income distribution from historical and social vicissitudes. A moral teaching seems implicit in this, analogous to that drawn from the Malthusian 'population law': policies aimed at improving the living conditions of the poor classes are useless, since they cannot modify an income distribution which is a 'law of nature', depending as it does – according to Pareto – on innate differences of personal abilities, distributed casually among the population. It is important to recall this theory not only for the fortune it had, giving rise to a significant stream of research,[35] but also in order to stress the importance that the economist and sociologist Pareto attributed to the experimental method of natural sciences, in particular of physics to which he referred on more than one occasion, in opposition to the 'humanitarian sociologies' of Comte, Spencer and many others.[36]

The main analytical contributions connected to the name of Pareto are the abandonment of the cardinal notion of utility in favour of an ordinal notion, and the notion of the 'Pareto optimum'. While the cardinal utility notion assumed utility as a quantitative, measurable, magnitude, 'ordinal utility' only implied an ordering of the economic agent's preferences, such as to be represented by a series of indifference curves. For pairs of goods,[37] each such curve indicates the locus of all combinations of quantities consumed of the two goods considered equivalent by the

---

[35] On this theme cf. Corsi 1995.

[36] On these themes Pareto also had, in 1900–1, a polemic with Benedetto Croce, conducted through contributions to the *Giornale degli economisti*. Croce maintained that 'economics does not know things and physical objects, but only actions', namely choices, facts 'of (positive or negative) valuation'; therefore, pure economics cannot be assimilated to rational mechanics, as Pareto tried to do. The latter answered by correcting Croce's various terminological inaccuracies; he also recalled that he had started from the utilitarian principle, but then had replaced it with the fact of choice, after having realised that nobody was able to measure a pleasure: following the deductive method he had then construed on the basis of a few principles a pure theory. Pareto equated Croce's position to that of Platonic ideas, and concluded the polemic by stating: 'I am not an enemy of metaphysics, but do not understand it and hence do not argue about it.' Cf. 'La polemica Croce-Pareto', in Pareto 1960, vol. 2, pp. 391–3.

[37] For n goods, we have indifference surfaces with dimension n-1, in the n-dimensional space of commodities.

consumer. In other terms, the curve indicates by how much consumption of one of the two goods should increase in order to compensate a given reduction in the consumption of the other good.

Actually there were precursors for both notions: Irving Fisher for the ordinal notion of utility, and Francis Ysidro Edgeworth, with his 'contract curve', for the notion of the 'Pareto optimum'; Pareto returned the favour by christening 'Edgeworth box' an analytical tool developed by himself, which Edgeworth had never used.[38]

In the *Cours* (1896–7) Pareto proposed the term 'science of ophelimity' (derived from the Greek, and indicating the ability of a good to satisfy needs) to designate the subjective theory of value. In this way Pareto wanted to stress – possibly in Menger's wake – that his theory did not deal with a value in use considered as an intrinsic property of the economic good, but rather with a subjective evaluation of the results of given actions in the framework of a pure theory of rational agents' choice (in the sense of the *homo oeconomicus*, the analytical role of which was assimilated to that of the material point in mechanics).[39] However, only in the 1906 *Manuale* do we find a systematic illustration of general economic equilibrium theory, on the lines of a rational mechanics textbook. Around 1898, Pareto abandoned the idea of measurable utility (cardinal utility). Taking on the notion of indifference curves, introduced by Edgeworth in 1881, Pareto fulfilled decisive steps towards construction of a complete analytical system, in particular by outlining those which were later called the fundamental theorems of welfare economics, aimed to prove the optimality of the market economy in conditions of perfect competition.[40]

---

[38] Cf. Niehans 1990, p. 265.

[39] Cf. Donzelli 1997. Abandonment of the notion of cardinal utility ('the hedonistic assumption') was a manifestation of Pareto's anti-metaphysical tendency; with his ordinal notion of utility, he thought he was able to focus attention on 'the material fact of choice'. Cf. Tarascio 1973, pp. 145–51. Tarascio (ibid., p. 156) also recalls Pareto's distinction between utility (used in the psychological field to indicate the satisfaction stemming from economic and non-economic sources alike) and ophelimity (used in economic theory to designate the satisfactions stemming exclusively from economic sources).

[40] Later developments include Slutsky's famous 1915 article, followed by Hicks and Allen 1934, providing all the main elements of a demand theory based on indifference curves, and showing that it does not imply measurability of utility. Samuelson's 1938 theory of 'revealed preferences' sought to indicate how consumers' preferences could be derived from observation of consumers' behaviour, so as to provide an 'operational' theory of demand; this implied, of course, a strong assumption of stability over time of consumers' preferences, so that different observations of the behaviour of a consumer could be interpreted as stemming from the same 'map of preferences'. On the empirical side, Schultz 1938 analysed consumption of agricultural goods; among other things, he tried to test the assumption of rational behaviour, but the results were not positive; in general, 'the project of establishing quantitative demand relations appeared unsuccessful' (Backhouse 2003, p. 313). On the story of demand theory up to 1950 cf. Stigler 1950.

The notion of 'Pareto optimum' designates a situation (more precisely, a specific utilisation of the initial endowment of resources) such that it cannot be modified in order to improve the position of some economic agent without worsening the position of at least one other economic agent. Pareto demonstrated that competitive equilibrium corresponds to an optimum in this sense.

Naturally, given a multiplicity of competitive equilibriums, hence a multiplicity of Pareto optimums, a criterion would be necessary for inter-personal comparisons in order to locate an absolute optimum. Moreover, the subsequent debate, up to the works of Arrow and Debreu illustrated below (§ 6), pointed out the conditions required for the validity of the two 'fundamental theorems of welfare economics'. Such theorems, specifying the connection Pareto established between competitive equilibrium and optimal position of the economy, stated (a) that each competitive equilibrium is Pareto-optimal; and (b) that each Pareto optimum corresponds to a competitive equilibrium. Among the assumptions used to prove the two theorems, let us recall absence of externalities, completeness of markets, perfect information and foresight; the second theorem moreover requires absence of increasing returns to scale. The debate on Pareto optimality (or efficiency) constituted for decades the central core of so-called welfare economics.

However, these developments mainly concerned the stage of construction of an axiomatic theory of general economic equilibrium (cf. below, § 6). As far as Pareto is concerned, we may stress as a conclusion that, like Walras, also his successor to the Lausanne chair did not succeed in fulfilling the crucial steps with respect to the decisive issues of existence, uniqueness and stability of general economic equilibrium. Perhaps it was this outcome, his increasing awareness of the limits of pure economic theory – limits which grew more evident the more rigorous the theory became – that decisively shifted Pareto's interests towards sociology.

4.   Irving Fisher

Among the first American economists of international fame, we find both a representative of the Marshallian approach dominating in England (John Bates Clark, whom we will discuss below, in § 13.7), and a representative of the mathematical orientation typical of the French–Italian school of general economic equilibrium, Irving Fisher (1867–1947). The latter had a mathematical training; gradually his interests moved towards economics, and this intellectual path was favoured by the connections he established when, after his marriage, he spent a year travelling throughout Europe. His first works concerned application of mathematics to the economic theory of value (as in his dissertation of 1892 on *Mathematical investigations in the theory of value and prices*, reprinted in 1925).[41] Gradually, his passion for social and political themes grew, and Fisher became an ardent supporter of monetary stability (developing in this context his theory of index numbers and becoming, in 1930, the first president of the Econometric Society) and of many other causes, from Esperanto to defence of the environment.

In the theoretical field, Fisher contributed on different fronts. First of all, he developed an analysis based on the distinction between stocks and flows, and proposed a definition of income connected to the flows of services and which excluded savings. This led him to support the thesis (which dates back to William Petty, and which in Italy was to find a supporter in Luigi Einaudi) of a taxation focused on expenditure.

Secondly, though using for the sake of exposition a cardinal notion of utility (with the name of *utils* for units of utility), Fisher anticipated Pareto in proposing a theory of consumer equilibrium based on the ordinal notion of utility, remarking that to locate the equilibrium position what matters is only the shape of the indifference curves (a tool, as was said above, already utilised by Edgeworth). In this context, it seems that Fisher was the first to use 'the familiar graph of the convex indifference curves intersected by the budget line'.[42]

Thirdly, Fisher developed a theory of the rate of interest in the framework of a model of general economic equilibrium, deducing it from the comparison between the rate of intertemporal preference of economic agents and the marginal rate of temporal substitution on the production side. In this framework, Fisher proposed the idea of a system of interest rates, as many as there are commodities, connected among themselves and to the monetary interest rate by expected changes in relative prices: a view later developed in an original way by Sraffa (1932) in his polemic with Hayek, and by Keynes in chapter 17 of the *General theory*, but which at the same time foreshadowed the models of intertemporal general equilibrium of the Arrow–Debreu type.

Finally, the best known of Fisher's contributions is the so-called equation of exchanges, or Fisher equation, which constituted the foundation of the modern quantity theory of money: $MV = PQ$, where M is the supply of money, V the velocity of circulation (that is, the number of times in which money changes hand within a unit interval of time), while PQ

---

[41] We should stress that with these works Fisher opposed the then dominant orientation of American economists, among whom historicism and institutionalism prevailed, characterising for instance the birth in 1885 of the American Economic Association.

[42] Niehans 1990, p. 273.

designates the value (equal to price P multiplied by quantity Q) of the commodities exchanged during the same unit interval of time. Written in terms of flows of transactions (with a difference in this respect relative to the 'Cambridge (or Marshall's) equation', as we shall see in § 13.5), this equation is by itself an identity which says that money flows going from one hand to another have the same value as the flows of goods and services which move in the opposite direction. In order to transform this identity into a theoretical relation connecting the price level to the money supply, three assumptions are then necessary: independence of the velocity of circulation and of the volume of exchanges from the amount of money in circulation, and dependence of this latter on the decisions of monetary authorities.

The American economist thus worked 'at the frontier' in various areas of research; in particular, confronted with the increasing use of mathematics in pure economics, his training as a mathematician allowed him to formulate with a rigour, precision and completeness unusual at the time a number of elements of the theoretical construction now prevailing in university textbooks all over the world.

5.   The debate on existence, uniqueness and stability of equilibrium

Walras, the founder of general economic equilibrium theory, attributed great importance to stability. Indeed, he considered analysis of stability an essential part of the very analysis of equilibrium; furthermore, in the absence of stability, even comparative static analysis, to which he also attributed great importance,[43] would prove meaningless. However, as recalled above, simple equality between number of independent equations and number of unknowns is not by itself sufficient to guarantee the existence of economically meaningful solutions (that is, non-negative solutions, for prices as well as for quantities), even less their uniqueness and stability. Generations of mathematical economists tackled these themes, and the debate still goes on.

The debate reached a climax in the early 1930s in Vienna. Pareto had rephrased the Walrasian theory in terms which could be directly used by professional mathematicians.[44] A schematic presentation of the Walrasian theory, widely known in German-speaking countries, was that of the Swede Gustav Cassel (1866–1945): it too brought to attention the problems left unsolved after the first fifty years of work on general economic

---

[43] As later did Schumpeter, who went as far as to consider it the real fulcrum of general economic equilibrium theory: cf. below, § 15.2.

[44] In particular, Pareto utilised the Hessian determinant.

equilibrium.[45] Simultaneously, within the Austrian school, von Wieser's formulation of imputation theory (cf. above, § 11.4) re-proposed, though in a different context, the problem of the solution of systems of economic equations.

Debate on the mathematical aspects of general equilibrium theory was also influenced by the axiomatic programme that within the mathematical field was fervently pursued by David Hilbert (1862–1943). The mathematical language, from a tool to be utilised within specific theories worked out by economists as well as by physicists or by applied scientists in some branch of knowledge, became the unifying element of the different theories, which were conceived more as abstract formal structures than as representations of the world.

Among Hilbert's pupils we find John von Neumann (1903–57), who contributed to the debate on general equilibrium not only with important results, but also and mainly by favouring the acquisition in economic theory of the language of topology, to which he had recourse in his proofs, using in particular Brouwer's (or the 'fixed point') theorem.

In Vienna, the most active caucus of discussion on the themes of general economic equilibrium was the seminar organised by Karl Menger (1902–85), mathematician, son of the economist Carl who had founded the Austrian school. Insufficiency of the mere equality between number of equations and number of unknowns had been stressed in a series of contributions by Hans Neisser (1932), Friedrich Zeuthen (1933) and Heinrich von Stackelberg (1933), after Remak (1929) had recalled that in economics only non-negative solutions can be accepted as meaningful. Spurred by the banker Karl Schlesinger, an active participant at Menger's seminars, an initial solution to the problem of existence of equilibrium was offered by Abraham Wald (1902–50). All these works used the distinction between free goods (that is, goods available in a quantity superior to that demanded at any non-negative price), the price of which is zero, and economical goods, for which equality between demand and supply is reached in correspondence with a positive price. The trick consisted in replacing the equalities of the Walrasian equations with feeble inequalities, so as to determine endogenously which goods are free and which are not free, which goods are produced and which are not produced. Wald (1936) went so far as to demonstrate the existence and uniqueness (but not stability) of equilibrium; however, this result was obtained through recourse to the restrictive assumption, which cannot be justified

---

[45] Cassel simplified Walras's theory by assuming as given the individual demand functions, thus giving up their derivation from utility functions; he also assumed fixed coefficients of production.

at the level of economic interpretation, that for the economy as a whole the so-called feeble axiom of revealed preferences holds, concerning the non-contradictory nature of individual choices.[46]

Immediately after this, in 1937, in an essay originally presented at Princeton in 1932, von Neumann provided a decisive contribution with his famous model of balanced growth. This model was formulated in terms of inequalities: for each good, the quantity supplied must be greater than or equal to the quantity demanded; moreover, the price must be lower than or equal to production costs. As a consequence, some goods may prove 'free', that is, available in quantities superior to demand for any positive price: their price will be zero, and their production will be nil. By the same token, production of each commodity whose price proves lower than production costs will be nil. In other words, the solution to the system of equations, which include equalities and inequalities, defines a nucleus of goods for which both prices and produced quantities are positive.

A peculiarity of von Neumann's model, which on this account followed the same lines as Cassel's contribution, is the strict relationship between rate of growth and rate of interest. In von Neumann's model, these two variables were defined as solutions of distinct but 'dual' problems: the rate of growth emerged as the solution of the problem of quantities considered as a problem of maximisation under constraint, while the rate of interest emerged as the solution of the problem of prices considered as a problem of minimisation under constraint.

A crucial aspect of this group of contributions, hence of Karl Menger's seminar, was the use of topology in economic theory. We may recall particularly the central role, in the proofs of existence of equilibrium, of Brouwer's fixed point theorem: a contribution which seems to have also had an influence on the development of philosophy, by inducing Ludwig Wittgenstein to reconsider his opinion that his 1921 *Tractatus logico-philosophicus* constituted the definitive solution to all philosophical problems, and thus to go back to philosophy.

Karl Menger's seminar had already been dispersed, even before Austria's annexation to Germany, by the rise of fascism and nazism, which induced many of its protagonists (and all leading Austrian economists) to choose the path of exile. (Schlesinger instead chose suicide.) The subsequent point of reference was, after the conclusion of the Second World War, the Cowles Commission at Chicago. With it, however, we enter the field of the development of the axiomatic theory of equilibrium on the one side, and of econometric models on the

[46] Cf. Ingrao and Israel 1987, pp. 202 ff.

other – that is, themes which will be discussed respectively in the next section and in § 17.7.

Here we merely touch on a theme which will be taken up in chapter 17: the development of game theory *in primis* by von Neumann and Morgenstern, as a method which allowed the interrelations which connect the decisions of different economic agents to be taken into account. Their volume, *Theory of games and economic behaviour*, was published in 1944; its authors presented game theory as a better tool than the Walras–Pareto theory for interpreting the complexity of interrelated social phenomena, in particular the cases of intermediate market forms between competition and monopoly. Game theory gave rise to different streams of research within economic theory, among them the reconstruction of cardinal utility functions on the basis of a probabilistic-subjective approach which dates back to Daniel Bernoulli and his solution to the St Peterburg's paradox[47] and develops through Ramsey (1926) and De Finetti (1930, 1931) and then Savage (1954); Nash's notion of equilibrium and of a core of the economy (Nash 1950);[48] industrial organisation theory; and, in more recent times, evolutionary theories based on repeated games.

6.   The search for an axiomatic economics

As we have already hinted in the previous section, a decisive step towards the mathematical solution of the problem of existence of a general economic equilibrium was accomplished in the 1930s, particularly thanks to the use of topology. This mathematical tool became established among economists only after the Second World War; Hicks's *Value and capital* (1939), the most influential reworking of general economic equilibrium theory of that period,[49] still used only the tools of differential calculus,

---

[47] For a synthetic illustration, cf. Niehans 1990, p. 405 ff.

[48] A Nash equilibrium is, in essence, that situation in which no agent can improve his or her own position, given the strategies – not simply the already known choices – of other agents. In relation to traditional theory, here the possible reactions of agents to the moves of other agents are taken into account: The 'core' of the economy consists of the set of Nash equilibriums.

[49] As Ingrao and Israel 1987, p. 178, recall, 'it was the assimilation and the methodological filter proposed first by Hicks and then by Samuelson to spread the theory of general economic equilibrium among professional economists and give it an unchallenged key position.' This happened despite the relative backwardness of the analytical toolbox used and insufficient attention to the problems of uniqueness and stability of equilibrium, or perhaps precisely thanks to this delay with respect to the Vienna debate of the late 1920s and early 1930s. Again Ingrao and Israel (ibid.) recall that 'in a little read and soon forgotten review, Morgenstern accused Hicks's book [. . .] of lacking rigour and of being outdated.'

dating back to Newton and Leibniz. However, together with topology another element made its entry in economics, the method of axiomatic theorising. This is a way to organise analysis which is typical of mathematical economists: indeed, the first to adopt it and to impose it in economics – to become Nobel prize winners for economics, like Arrow or Debreu – were mathematicians by training who turned to work on economic issues, for different reasons, in the intermediate stage between university studies and the beginning of an academic career.

The method of axiomatic theorising consists in formulating a precise set of basic assumptions expressed in formal terms (like the axioms of convexity of isoquants on the production side and of indifference surfaces on the consumption side), in expressing the problem itself in formal terms, commonly in the economic field in terms of constrained maximisation or minimisation (maximisation of utilities, minimisation of costs), and in defining again in formal terms the desired result (for instance, determination of a set of non-negative values for price and quantity variables such as to satisfy the problem under consideration). In other words, the issue of what economic meaning should be attributed to the variables and to the results of the analysis is rigorously distinguished from the search for an analytical solution to a problem which in this context only features as a mathematical problem.[50]

Kenneth Arrow (b. 1921, Nobel prize winner in 1972) adopted both the method of axiomatic theorising and the mathematical tool of topology in his first famous contribution, *Social choice and individual values* (1951). In this work the important 'impossibility theorem' was proposed, according to which no decisional procedure exists such as to satisfy simultaneously two requirements: first, to guarantee the transitivity of social choices among three or more alternatives (if A is preferred to B and B is preferred to C, A too is preferred to C); second, to satisfy some requirements of 'democracy' (expressed in formal terms: for instance, if one of the alternatives goes up in an individual's ranking, while all other individuals' rankings remain unchanged, that alternative cannot go down in ranking for society as a whole).

---

[50] It is precisely this clear-cut separation between the stage of conceptualisation, in which the assumptions are chosen to be used as a basis for analysis, and the stage of model building, together with the (unjustified) choice of focusing attention exclusively on the latter, which explains the absolute absence of attention on the side of modern general economic equilibrium theoreticians for such an essential aspect as the total unrealism of the assumptions of convexity in technology or of completeness of consumers' preferences. Confronted with the persistent refusal to tackle such issues, Debreu's statement (quoted by Ingrao and Israel 1987, p. 288) according to which 'the axiomatization [. . .] facilitates the detection of conceptual errors in the formulation of the theory and in its interpretation' appears devoid of content.

When Arrow tackled the problem of existence of solutions for the general economic equilibrium model, there already existed the solutions by Wald (1936) for Cassel's simplified version, and by von Neumann (1937); there also existed a solution by Nash (1950) for an n-person game in the framework of a variant of game theory proposed by von Neumann and Morgenstern (1944). The 1954 solution by Arrow and Debreu[51] (like a similar solution, published in the same year by Lionel McKenzie) jointly adopted axiomatic method and topology. The conditions under which existence of a solution was proved were given by the starting axioms; one of them, concerning the initial endowments of each economic agent (who must have positive quantities available of each good), was immediately considered too restrictive, and a few subsequent works were devoted to replacing it with other axioms, held to be less restrictive. Conversely, the axiom of convexity of production isoquants was quietly accepted, even though it corresponded to an assumption – constant or decreasing returns to scale – already considered unacceptable by Marshall, who devoted much of his theoretical activity searching for a way to circumvent it (cf. below, § 13.3). In more recent years, the attempts to introduce local concavities in production sets originated more in the search on the part of some mathematical economists of little-developed fields of enquiry than in the real perception of the importance of this limit in Arrow–Debreu analysis.

Another development, along the same lines, of general economic equilibrium theory was the slim volume by Debreu, *Theory of value* (1959), and a number of other writings culminating in the wide systematisation by Arrow and Hahn (*General competitive analysis*, 1971). A first important step consisted in the introduction of 'dated' commodities: a ton of corn available at a certain date is different from a ton of corn available at a different date. The main step then consisted in the introduction of the notion of 'contingent goods': the same good, for instance an umbrella, is considered as a different good according to the 'state of nature' (whether it rains or not) in which the economic agent finds himself. Economic agents, in this context, maximise expected utility (a notion illustrated by

---

[51] Gerard Debreu, French, born in 1921, Nobel prize in 1983, was at the beginning of the 1950s a colleague of Arrow at the Cowles Commission at Chicago, then remained in America as professor first at Yale and then at Berkeley. A feature of Debreu's work is that the issue of the stability of equilibrium is left aside, while attention is focused on existence proofs. Arrow and Hahn, instead, follow Wald's approach in trying to specify less and less restrictive sets of axioms but such as to allow for a proof of both existence and stability of equilibrium. Cf. Ingrao and Israel (1987, pp. 278 and 300–1) on this difference of approach, and (ibid., pp. 280–8 and 299–305) on Debreu, whose approach involves 'emptying the theory radically and uncompromisingly of all empirical reference' (ibid., p. 285).

von Neumann and Morgenstern in an appendix to their book on the application of game theory to economics), attributing (subjective) probability distributions to the different 'states of nature'. We can thus represent a general economic equilibrium in which there are as many markets as there are dated and contingent goods, thus dealing with the issue of uncertainty (or rather, of risk); it is also possible to interpret contingent markets as markets for insurance certificates relative to different possible events.[52]

Axiomatic general economic equilibrium theory has been considered by many, possibly by the majority of mainstream economists, as the frontier of basic research in the field of economics. The label 'general', in particular, has been used not simply in the original meaning of 'inclusive of the totality of the economic system in its interrelations', but also, implicitly if not explicitly, in the meaning of compulsory reference for any economic enquiry. Indeed, as should be evident if we consider not only the basic assumptions, always very restrictive, but also and especially the specific operating mechanisms based on the omni-pervasive rule of market clearing equilibrium between supply and demand, the 'Arrow–Debreu model', though most useful for dealing with well-defined issues along a specific research path, is only one of the possible analytical representations of economic reality.

In other words, we may perhaps say that the method of axiomatic theorising was used by Arrow and Debreu in the local meaning of analytical procedure for specific issues, but was then interpreted in a wider sense: the same sense in which Hilbert, at the end of the nineteenth century, proposed a programme of complete axiomatisation of mathematics.[53] The analysis of general economic equilibrium has thus been considered a programme for the reduction of the whole of economic theory to a central core: a precise set of axioms from which, with the addition of further assumptions which could change from case to case, we can deduct a series of theorems constituting a 'complete' representation of economic reality or at least, according to the famous thesis of the early Wittgenstein, of everything in economic reality which is capable of scientific expression.

Thus, on a number of accounts the 'substantive' result of the long research work on general economic equilibrium takes us backwards:

---

[52] In doing this it is assumed, among other things, that economic agents are averse to risk.

[53] The influence of 'Bourbakism' (from Bourbaki, the nickname under which an important association of French mathematicians published their results in the immediate post-Second World War period, trying to reconstruct the foundations of mathematics) was also important, especially – through Debreu – at the Cowles Commission: cf. Mirowski 2002, pp. 390–4. 'The lesson derived by Arrow, Debreu, and Nash from Bourbaki was that questions of existence of equilibrium were really just demonstrations of the logical consistency of the model; there was no pressing commitment to models as a calculative device that mimicked reality' (ibid., p. 410).

further backwards than the problems already tackled by Marshall (such as in particular increasing returns to scale) or the debates in the 1930s on Gödel's theorem and the impossibility of Hilbert's programme for a complete axiomatisation of mathematics, or of the abandonment, on the part of Wittgenstein, of the stand adopted in the *Tractatus* when confronted with Sraffa's criticisms. But we will return to these issues in the coming chapters.

13   Alfred Marshall

1.   Life and writings

Alfred Marshall (1842–1924) was not among the protagonists of the 1871–4 'marginalist revolution': his first major writings belong to the end of the 1870s, and his main contribution, his *Principles of economics*, appeared in 1890, nearly two decades after the works of Jevons, Menger and Walras. Marshall himself was averse to considering the new road taken by economic analysis as a 'revolution' or a clear-cut break with the past: in his opinion, this was instead a step forward, although certainly an important one, relative to the classical economists' (in particular Ricardo's and the Ricardians') approach. Indeed, his personal contribution, in his own opinion, consisted in the synthesis between the great tradition inherited from the past and the new yeast of the subjective approach. Yet, we must recognise that Marshall contributed more than anyone else, possibly at least in part against his own intentions, to 'shunt the car of economic science' in the direction of that approach (which Hicks, Stigler and Samuelson preferred to call 'neoclassical', rather than 'marginalist' or 'subjectivist', in order to stress that the turn-around implied an important element of continuity with the past) which still today dominates the teaching and thinking of economists all over the world.

Marshall was born in London, on 26 July 1842, to a modest bourgeois family.[1] His father, authoritarian if not tyrannical within the family, was a modest clerk of the Bank of England. Alfred studied in a school in the periphery of London, the Merchant Taylor's School; he distinguished himself and was awarded a scholarship to Oxford, aimed at financing classical studies as a basis for an ecclesiastical career. However, he felt more

---

[1] There are two main references for Marshall's biography. The first is the classical portrait of Marshall provided by Keynes immediately after the death of his master, in the obituary (Keynes 1924) later reprinted in the *Essays in biography* (Keynes 1933, pp. 150–266) with a number of changes and without the second part, the 'Bibliographical list of the writings of Alfred Marshall'. Let us also mention the monumental, richly documented, biography by Groenewegen (1995), to which we defer also for the references to the multitude of other writings on the subject.

inclined to mathematics and, thanks to a loan from an uncle who had migrated to Australia and had become rich, decided to defy his father's pressures and choose Cambridge's mathematical curriculum, as a student of St John's College. In 1865 he brilliantly passed his examinations, second wrangler (that is, ranking second among the mathematics graduates, only surpassed by Rayleigh, future lord and Nobel prize winner for chemistry in 1904).

Thus Marshall's career began, first with a fellowship at St John's, then (in 1868) as lecturer of moral sciences in the same college. Around the middle of the 1870s, perhaps in connection with his preparations for a trip to America in 1875, his interests shifted from mathematics and moral sciences towards political economy. Participating in a scheme to promote the admission of women to university, Alfred taught political economy to Newnham Hall's female students.[2] There he met Mary Paley, whom he married in 1877.

After a review in 1872 of Jevons's 1871 book, Marshall's first important contribution to economic theory was a collection of essays, published in 1879 for private circulation by Henry Sidgwick, on *The pure theory of foreign trade. The pure theory of domestic values*.[3] In the same year he published, together with his wife, a declaredly didactic text, *The economics of industry* (Marshall 1879a), which had good sales and also constituted a most important original contribution in outlining a representation of economic life which we may define as evolutionary.

Following his marriage, Marshall was compelled to resign from St John's College, which required celibacy of its fellows. Marshall was able to go back to Cambridge only when elected professor of political economy, as a successor to Fawcett, in 1884.[4] In the meantime the Marshalls spent some difficult years in Bristol. Here Alfred, who appeared exhausted in body and in spirit, struggled under the workload – which

---

[2] The lecture notes, taken by Mary Paley and revised by Marshall himself, have been published, with a broad introductory apparatus setting them against their historical background, edited by Raffaelli, Biagini and McWilliams Tullberg (Marshall, 1995).

[3] Marshall 1879b; nearly 100 years later, in 1975, an edition of *The early economic writings of Alfred Marshall, 1867–1890* appeared, edited (and with an extensive introduction) by J. K. Whitaker, including among other things the manuscript of a volume on foreign trade from which the two chapters published by Sidgwick were drawn. On the first stage of development of Marshall's economic thought, cf. also Dardi 1984.

[4] On Henry Fawcett (1833–84), one of the most popular figures of Victorian times, cf. the collection of essays edited by Goldman 1989. Fawcett became blind when twenty-five years old due to a hunting accident, after having been one of the most brilliant students at Cambridge, but reacted with energy and courage. A follower of John Stuart Mill and an exponent of the most radical stream of liberalism, he published a *Manual of political economy* (Fawcett 1863), became professor of political economy at the University of Cambridge and, in 1865, Member of Parliament.

included administrative tasks in addition to teaching – connected to his role as professor and simultaneously as principal of the University College. In 1881 he resigned, and the Marshalls spent a year largely travelling, with a long stay in Palermo where it seems the writing of the *Principles* began. Back in England, in 1882 Marshall became professor of political economy at Bristol, but in the following year he moved to Oxford, as the successor to Arnold Toynbee, lecturer at Balliol College.

The prestigious Cambridge appointment, which came unexpectedly, marked a turning point in his life. Marshall held the political economy chair for twenty-four years, up to 1908, but remained in Cambridge until his death in 1924, and retained a strong interest in the vicissitudes of the economics curriculum created by his impulse in 1903.

From Cambridge, Marshall exercised significant influence over the teaching of economics in the rest of England. In 1890, with his active intervention, the British Economic Association was founded and the *Economic Journal* was launched. His *Principles of economics* (eight editions, from 1890 to 1920)[5] soon became the reference text for generations of economics students: years later, Keynes said that the formation of a good economist only requires the *Principles*, accompanied by the careful reading of the economic pages of a good newspaper. Among the students, the small guide published by Marshall in 1892, *Elements of the economics of industry*, was widespread; it replaced the widely read (and in many respects much more interesting) *Economics of industry* (1879a),[6] which had been written in collaboration with his wife.

Marshall's influence was exercised, perhaps mainly, through his pupils: without ever taking on the presidency of the British Economic Association or the direction of the *Economic Journal*, Marshall influenced the selection for these positions, and likewise influenced the nomination of the economics professors in the major English universities, among which Cambridge had come to dominate; there Alfred imposed Arthur Cecil Pigou as his successor. Marshall's mark was so strong as to be perceptible decades later in post-Second World War Cambridge as well as in today's textbooks.

[5] The eighth edition had ten reprints between 1922 and 1959, and still others subsequently; the ninth (variorum) edition, dated 1961, was edited by Marshall's nephew, C. W. Guillebaud, in two volumes, of which the first contains the text of the eighth edition and the second the variants of previous editions and other materials.

[6] See Becattini's (1975) wide-ranging introduction to the Italian edition. In the new book of 1892, Marshall put 'the most original results of his researches on the labour market' (Becattini 2000, p. 32). As noted by Keynes (1924, pp. 628, 632, 633), while the two editions of the *Economics of industry* represented, with their ten reprints, 15,000 copies in all, the *Elements of the economics of industry* reached four editions with nineteen reprints and 81,000 copies. The *Principles* had eight editions and one reprint, 37,000 copies overall, before Marshall's death.

Side by side with the oral tradition of his lectures and the vast correspondence with interlocutors worldwide,[7] an important component of the Marshallian theoretical legacy is represented by his *Official papers*, mostly testimonials to parliamentary commissions,[8] and a group of articles collected after his death in a volume of *Memorials*.[9] Considered as less important are the two volumes originally intended as the completion of the great design begun with the *Principles*, which Marshall published only in the final years of his life: *Industry and trade*, dated 1919, and *Money, credit and commerce* dated 1923. Marshall died, aged eighty, in 1924.

2.   The background

In order to study Marshall's thought it is worth focusing on his *magnum opus*, the *Principles*. Yet, not even in this way is it possible to reach a univocal representation of his thought. Indeed, through a multiplicity of qualifications and shades of meaning Marshall brought together different elements, even contradictory ones, such as an evolutionary view and static equilibrium analysis. Moreover, in time (hence in subsequent editions of the *Principles*) there were numerous and often major changes to the meaning of key notions and the very analytical structure of Marshallian theory. Thus, it may be useful to begin by considering Marshall's background and his first writings.

Marshall always maintained that he had developed his approach autonomously, based on a substantially subjective theory of value and on equilibrium between demand and supply, but also on an attempt to safeguard what he considered as vital in the classical tradition. His thesis was that the results subsequently developed in the *Principles* had already been reached by him at the end of the 1860s, by translating John Stuart Mill's theories into mathematical terms. Indeed, it is clear that when Jevons's *Theory of political economy* appeared in 1871, Marshall was ready – as was shown by his review of the book, which constituted one of his first printed works (Marshall 1872) – to understand its elements of novelty, and to evaluate them in the light of an already sufficiently developed view of his own. However, this does not deny Jevons's priority of publication, as regards the main innovative elements of the marginalist revolution

---

[7] Cf. *The correspondence of Alfred Marshall, economist*, 3 vols. (with an accurate critical apparatus) edited by John K. Whitaker, Marshall 1996a.

[8] The volume collecting these *Official papers* was published posthumously, in 1926, edited by J. M. Keynes. Further material collected by Peter Groenewegen has been published recently, like the first volume under the auspices of the Royal Economic Society, with the title *Official papers of Alfred Marshall. A supplement* (Marshall 1996b).

[9] The *Memorials of Alfred Marshall*, edited by Pigou, were published under the auspices of the Royal Economic Society in 1925.

within the subjectivist tradition, in particular the derivation of demand curves and the determination of prices connected to marginal utility. This fact impressed on Marshall the need to clearly distinguish his ideas from those of the 'founding father' of English marginalism: a need reinforced by his personal vicissitudes, typical of a university man, determined to progress in the career which he had undertaken.

Differentiation from Jevons, systematically pursued in all of Marshall's subsequent scientific work, consisted first in stressing the one-sidedness of a purely subjective theory of value, as Jevons's utilitarian one was, and in countering it with the equally one-sided objective theory of the classical economists, based on cost of production; then in presenting his own contribution as a synthesis which included what was valid in each of the two opposing approaches. As we shall see, this implied a somewhat misleading reinterpretation of the classical approach, as if it were based, like the marginalist one, on the pillar of the static notion of equilibrium between supply and demand.

Marshall's first enquiries in the economic field, as already stated, were published in 1879 for private circulation by his friend Sidgwick, under the title *The pure theory of foreign trade. The pure theory of domestic values.* It seems, however, that the initial writing of the two essays collected in this small volume dated back to 1869–73, which lends support to the idea that Marshall's theories developed independently of those of the founding fathers of the marginalist revolution, in particular Jevons.

Marshall's thesis of an autonomous development of his thought, gradual and not in frontal opposition to the classical school, is made plausible by these first writings. Here Marshall began with analysis of equilibrium in foreign trade, and as a logical development arrived then at a theory of internal prices. The starting point concerned the following issue which classical theory had left open. On the one hand, the labour-value theory adopted by Ricardo and his immediate followers provided a univocal – though not satisfactory – answer to the problem of determining relative prices; on the other, the theory of comparative costs proposed by Ricardo in order to explain the flows of foreign trade left the exchange ratios between imported and exported commodities indeterminate (though within an interval whose extremes are determined for each pair of imported and exported commodities by the ratios between their costs of production in the countries of origin and destination of the flows of exchange). This problem had attracted John Stuart Mill's attention in one of his *Essays on some unsettled questions of political economy* (published in 1844), and he had proposed a solution based on recourse to the role of demand. In the simplified case of two countries and two commodities, we may thus reach conclusions such as 'the advantage of small dimensions', by which the smallest country obtains better terms of exchange, thanks to the reduced dimension of its demand for the imported commodity relative to the demand for the exported commodity coming from the larger country, or such as the forecast of a worsening of the terms of trade for that country in which demand for the imported commodity increases.

This is the line of research that Marshall developed in his *Pure theory of foreign trade*, determining equilibrium terms of trade on the basis of a comparison between the demand curves for imports of the two countries. Marshall took full advantage of his mathematical training, in particular by recourse to the 'graphical method'. In considering the case of two goods and two countries, the graph analysed by Marshall had on the two axes the quantities of the two commodities. For each of them it is already known, from comparative cost theory, which is imported and which exported by each of the two countries. The two demand curves (one for each country) indicate, for any given quantity of imported commodity, the maximum quantity of exported commodity which the country being considered is ready to give in exchange. The intersection of the two curves determines the equilibrium point, which indicates the quantity exchanged of the two commodities, hence the corresponding exchange ratio between them.

The results that Marshall thus reached included, first of all, attributing a central role to the notion of equilibrium between demand and supply as the basis for determining exchange ratios; secondly, the proposal of the themes of multiplicity and possible instability of equilibrium, to which detailed discussion was devoted.

The same method, the same notion of equilibrium and the same themes concerning multiplicity and possible instability of equilibrium were then developed in *The pure theory of domestic values*. Here we also find the problem of increasing returns to scale with which Marshall was so concerned in his mature formulation of the theory of equilibrium of the firm in his *Principles*. Finally, we also find systematic use of the temporal specification of the notion of equilibrium; in particular, Marshall distinguished between very short, short, long and very long period equilibriums.[10] Such equilibriums are connected to the assumption of given supply (very short or market period), variable supply but on the basis of a given productive capacity (short period), variable supply also through the adaptation of productive capacity but on the basis of a given technology (long period), variable supply in a context in which also technology and the whole state of the economic system change, including consumer incomes and tastes (very long period).

---

[10] Of course the distinction does not concern actual (historical) time, but what has been called 'operational' time: cf. Blaug 1962, p. 354.

The same year, 1879, saw the publication of the work Marshall wrote with his wife Mary Paley, *The economics of industry*, based on his aptly revised university lectures. While the essays edited by Sidgwick reflected Marshall's mathematical formulation, and decidedly pointed in the direction of a 'neoclassical' view based on static equilibrium between supply and demand, *The economics of industry* more strongly reflected Marshall's studies in the social sciences (at the time included in the area of moral sciences). It was thus a contribution that, whilst not seeking to build a rigorous analytical structure, was more receptive to aspects of historical evolution, aiming to represent a complex and constantly changing economic reality. Even if the influence of Darwin's evolutionism was not explicitly recognised, it is much more visible in this work than in the theoretical essays collected by Sidgwick (let us recall that *The origin of species* was published in 1859 and *The descent of man* in 1871, and that Darwin's influence was quite strong in Cambridge university circles).[11]

Marshall expressed both a gradualist view to evolutionism summarised in the motto prefixed to the *Principles*, 'Natura non facit saltum', and a complex view of economic progress which laid stress more on the quality of life than on per capita income. Also the idea of time as an irreversible flow was repeatedly stressed. Finally, at least partly connected to the evolutionary view is the shift from the classical notion of 'natural' prices to that of 'normal' values (for prices as well as for produced and exchanged quantities). Such a shift reflected with some delay the diffusion of lognormal (or Gaussian) curves in statistics, and the connected idea that such curves represent laws of distribution for the phenomena of society as well as for those of the natural world. In substance, deviation from the 'norm' was considered, at least within limits, a most common event which did not constitute a violation of the norm itself. Such a norm emerged as a statistical average from a large number of cases observed; as a consequence, the element of 'corresponding to what it should be' or 'perfect expression of a law which is intrinsic to the nature of things' was lost, while it was implicit in the notion of natural value. Furthermore, according to Marshall the presence of technological change accentuated the indicative character of normal value as defined by the theory, and thus the margin of imprecision with which the theoretical law could be applied to the real world.[12]

---

[11] Becattini 2000, p. 7, also recalls the influence of the 'revolution' of non-Euclidean geometry.

[12] Carl Friedrick Gauss (1777–1855) used the lognormal curve to represent the likely distribution of error in the theory of measure. Subsequently Adolphe Quetelet (1796–1874) used the same curve to represent biological or social phenomena, interpreting the results as manifestations of natural or social laws, whose average (or median: in

We thus have, since Marshall's first publications, a twofold line of research: on the one side, the attempt to build a rigorous theoretical system, based on a static notion of equilibrium between supply and demand; on the other, the attempt to work out a system of concepts such as to represent economic reality in a way that allowed for historical developments and evolution. Rather than the problem of a synthesis between the subjective marginalist approach and the objective approach of classical economists, it is the continuous overlapping of these two lines of research and the impossible reconciliation between the two distinct research aims which is the true key to understanding and interpreting Marshall's path, his contributions to economic science and the limits of his economics construct.[13]

3.   The *Principles*

When in 1890 the first edition of the *Principles of Economics* appeared, after many years' work, the ground had already been prepared to ensure the book had a major impact on the economic culture of the time. Marshall was then settled in the Cambridge chair, which thanks mainly to his prestige had become the main economics chair of the country, and his pupils occupied important positions in the English academic world (as we have noted, the same year saw the birth of the Royal Economic Society and the *Economic Journal*). Moreover, the influence of the classical tradition

the lognormal distribution the two coincide) represents in synthesis the property of a population of cases, and the 'law' thus represented is not violated by individual cases differing from the average. We may consider as 'anomalous' only the cases which differ from the average by more than a pre-set amount (bearing in mind that in the case of a Gaussian distribution, a difference higher than twice the mean square deviation has a probability of about 5 per cent). On the importance of this view for the development of social sciences and on its rapid spread, cf. Hacking 1990, in particular pp. 105–24. With some excess of emphasis, we might say that the idea of human sciences as concerning arguments to be deduced from 'human nature' was replaced by that of statistical laws about what is 'normal'. In this sense, we might add, the view of economic science as a theory of the behaviour of the rational agent (or *homo oeconomicus*) is the extreme descendant of the old view of human sciences; substitution of the term 'natural' with the term 'normal' on the part of Marshall is an indication of his persistent attempt to escape such a view.

The motto 'natura non facit saltus', 'nature does not proceed by jumps' (not 'saltum', as Marshall wrote), had already been utilised in the mid-eighteenth century by the great naturalist Carolus Linnaeus (1707–78).

[13] Becattini 2000 offers a fascinating reconstruction of Marshall's 'vision', stressing the 'anomalies' in this author relative to the marginalist tradition. Among such anomalies, a view of 'man as a varied and variable entity' (ibid., p. 11), already hinted at in the previous note, is prominent. Becattini (ibid., p. 50) goes so far as to conclude, agreeing in this with Dardi 1984, that 'Marshall should not be placed as more advanced or lagging behind on the path of neoclassical economics, but elsewhere.' This interpretation implies considering the *Principles* as 'only an introduction to the introduction of the book "on the world" which [Marshall] always longed for writing' (ibid., p. 32).

was still strong, while the marginalist heterodoxy attracted indeed the most brilliant minds but still less consensus than Cliffe Leslie's English historical school.[14] In such a situation, Marshall offered a set of elements designed to attract the convergent interest of the different streams of economic culture existing at the time: insistent reference to the classical tradition, from the Smithian theory of the division of labour to the 'Ricardian' theory of rent; acceptance of the basic elements of the marginalist revolution, with attribution of a central role to demand, hence to economic agents' preferences, within a theory of value in which prices were determined by the mechanism of equilibrium between supply and demand;[15] insertion of this analytical structure in the context of broad discussions (which cannot be reduced to simple digressions) on the meaning of the concepts used in the analysis and on the historical evolution of society; and references to Darwinian evolutionism, which conferred an element of scientific modernity on the work and provided a flexible, open response – also in methodological terms – to historical evolution in comparison to the reference to physics (more precisely, to static mechanics) prevailing in the theories of equilibrium of authors of stricter marginalist faith.

The *Principles* were presented as the first of two volumes; the second volume, however, was never completed, and since the sixth edition (1910) the label 'first volume' disappeared. The second volume was originally planned to deal with foreign trade, monetary and financial issues, trade cycle, taxation, collectivism and a synthesis of tendencies of the economy towards social progress; only part of this ground corresponds to that covered in the two last works by Marshall, *Industry and Trade* (1919) and *Money, credit and commerce* (1923).[16] From the first (1890) to the eighth

---

[14] Thomas Edward Cliffe Leslie (1827–82), professor of law and political economy at Queen's College, Belfast from 1853, proposed and used in various writings a historical-deductive method of analysis, recalling Smith and John Stuart Mill in opposition to Ricardo's deductive method. His was a relatively moderate historicism, especially if compared with the positions that were to be taken up by Schmoller's German historical school (cf. above, § 11.2). Occupying slightly more radical positions than Cliffe Leslie's was the other first-rank exponent of the English historical school, John Kells Ingram (1823–1907), follower of Auguste Comte's positivism, hence of an integration of political economy with other social sciences, whose best-known work (*A history of political economy*, 1888) illustrated to the English public the contributions of the continental historical school.

[15] More precisely, for each commodity the normal price is determined by the point where two curves meet, graphically representing the demand and supply functions. These respectively connect the supply price (cost plus normal profit) and the demand price (the maximum price which the purchaser is ready to pay) to the quantity of the commodity under consideration.

[16] Cf. Whitaker 1990. When eighty years old, when he had completed *Money, credit and commerce*, Marshall still planned a collection of essays on *Economic progress* as a partial substitute for an original volume on the subject, which he felt he was no longer able to write.

(1920) edition, the *Principles* remained at the centre of Marshall's theoretical work, undergoing substantive revisions; this is especially true for the fifth edition (1907), the last before his resignation from the Cambridge chair. The voluminous *variorum editio* (1961), promoted by the Royal Economic Society and edited by Marshall's nephew, Charles Guillebaud, allows us to reconstruct this path.

The importance of Marshall's revisions to his *Principles* testifies to the difficulties he met in his work of synthesis between different approaches and in his attempt to build a theory of value which was to include simultaneously the objective (cost of production) and the subjective (utility) element, and which was to be at the same time rigorous, realistic and open to historical evolution. Before discussing the difficulties Marshall met, it may be useful to run over the main aspects of his approach: the method (complexity of the real world and short causal chains); the notions of equilibrium and competition; and the concepts of the firm and the industry. We will then consider the problem of increasing returns and the two solutions suggested by Marshall, the representative firm and external–internal economies.

Marshall's methodological standpoint was simple in its objective: to recognise the extreme complexity of the real world. Theory cannot but be abstract, but must keep its feet on the ground. Hence his tenet, which underlay his 'partial equilibrium method', that 'short causal chains' should be privileged. At each step, theory proceeds by isolating a logical nexus of cause and effect held to be the main one, and thus leaves aside other effects held to be secondary, though not non-existent. This is legitimate, indeed necessary, for construction of each individual analytical piece. However, when we put together many logical links and generate long causal chains – as happens for instance in general economic equilibrium theory – the secondary effects left aside may in reality have repercussions which amplify step by step, and this may cause the conclusions drawn from the theoretical analysis to be misleading. Hence Marshall relegated to a mathematical note, in appendix to his *Principles*, his illustration of general economic equilibrium (an exposition which, compact as it is, is one of the most rigorous of the time). Instead, in the text Marshall preferred to focus on the 'short causal chains', in particular on the method of partial equilibriums. The latter consisted in considering demand and supply of each good – that is, the conditions which concur in determining equilibrium in the corresponding market – as independent of what simultaneously happens on other markets for the other goods.

The same awareness of the complexities of the real world – an awareness which is demonstrated in the wealth of footnotes and qualifications he makes, that on occasion dominate the logical thread of the exposition – may also be perceived in the attention Marshall lent to the construction of the system of concepts by which to represent reality.[17] In the first books of the *Principles*, step by step the concepts introduced are discussed by illustrating for each the shades of meaning and the 'penumbra' – to use Georgescu-Roegen's evocative term – which rendered their contours imprecise.[18]

This is true in particular for the key notions of equilibrium and competition to which, in the intertwining of text and notes, affirmations and qualifications, it is very difficult to attribute a univocal meaning. We can point to two terms of reference, between which Marshall's position oscillated, in the impossible attempt to absorb both: on the one side, the notions which subsequently took the textbooks by storm, and which constitute what we might call the Marshallian *vulgata*; on the other, the esoteric notions, disseminated among the circle of pupils and direct followers, connected to an evolutionary view which drew more on Lamarck rather than on Darwin's original theories.[19] In the first case – the Marshallian *vulgata* – the notion of equilibrium corresponds to the static notion of equality between demand and supply, and the notion of perfect competition to the presence of a large number of firms in each industry, so large as to render the size of each firm irrelevant to the dimensions of

---

[17] Perhaps in this respect the influence of Austrian and German economists was important. One could recall, for instance, the attention lent to these aspects in Menger's *Principles*. Streissler 1990a, p. 51, shows that the structure of Marshall's *Principles*, like those of Menger, reproduced the structure of a typical German textbook of the middle of the nineteenth century, such as those by Rau or Roscher (cf. above, § 11.1). Streissler (ibid., p. 57) stresses also that Rau's text, one of the first economics books read by Marshall, preceded the latter's *Principles* in representing the demand curve with the price on the horizontal axis.

[18] It was also in this way that Marshall succeeded in realising an uncertain compromise between the 'objective' approach of classical economists and the 'subjective' one of the theoreticians of the marginalist revolution. Thus, for instance, the wage was sometimes considered as the material subsistence of the workers and sometimes as an incentive to their 'effort and sacrifice'. Bharadwaj 1978, p. 98, in stressing this point, recalled that it was suggested to her by Sraffa. Analogously, in the case of profits the notion of 'abstinence' proposed by Senior was softened by Marshall into the notion of 'waiting'. When from the concepts we move on to the theory, the pendulum decidedly tends towards marginalist theory.

[19] Cf. Ridolfi 1972. The thesis which characterised the position of Jean-Baptiste de Lamarck (1744–1829) and which was rejected by Darwin, was the heredity of the characteristics acquired in life by an organism as response-adaptation to the environment in which it lives. Darwin's well-known thesis was that the characteristics best adapted to existence (and above all to reproduction) in the end prevail because of a process of natural selection. Lamarck's theses had been reproposed, confounded with Darwin's evolutionism, as a tool for the analysis of society by the sociologist Herbert Spencer (1820–1903), very influential at the time; his importance in the development of Marshall's thought is stressed by both Ridolfi 1972 and Groenewegen 1995.

the industry as a whole, and the choices of each individual firm irrelevant for the industry as a whole (hence for the equilibrium price level). In the second case – the evolutionary view – the notion of equilibrium takes on dynamic features, in the attempt to take account of the irreversibility which characterises the actual movements of the firm and the industry along demand and supply curves;[20] the notion of competition is softened by attributing to each firm some room for manoeuvre which among other things includes the possibility of violating the so-called law of the one price.[21] Theoretical analysis – construction of well-structured models – is inevitably led to refer to clear-cut concepts of the first kind; in the case of the evolutionary view, as we shall see below, we remain instead in the field of metaphors, which are evocative but certainly not rigorous.[22] In other words, in the oscillation from the first to the second pole of the Marshallian construct, what is gained on the side of realism is lost on the side of analytical rigour.

The very notions of industry and firm constituted a bridge between the complexity of the real world and the requirement of simplicity of abstract theory. Marshall thereby distanced himself from the extreme methodological individualism of the first marginalist theoreticians, and privileged instead a classical feature, by which each commodity ('good', in the subjectivist terminology, which thus lays stress on their utility to the consumer) corresponds to a category which includes objects not identical between themselves but sufficiently similar to warrant unitary treatment,[23] and in parallel each industry includes the firms (complex productive units) which operate in one of such commodity categories.

[20] Marshall derived the 'evolutionary' notion of equilibrium from the theory of population, which can tend to a stationary state through birth and death flows. Cf. Ridolfi 1972. In the *Principles* Marshall seemed to prefer this notion to the 'mechanical' one derived from physics, which dominated before and after him among marginalist theoreticians.

[21] Competition was rather identified with freedom of manoeuvre. Marshall 1890, p. 347, explicitly stressed that his notion of 'normal' did not coincide with that of 'competitive'. Hart 1996, p. 360, remarks that 'In *Principles*, competition was essentially seen as a behavioural activity rather than as a market structure.'

[22] Obviously, an evolutionary view too can give rise to mathematical models and a well-structured analysis. We may ask, in this sense, what shape the *Principles* would have taken if Marshall had known Alfred James Lotka's (1880–1949) writings on mathematical population theory. However, a development in this direction may well have brought to light the numerous elements of unrealism of too strict a comparison between biological populations and sets of economic subjects like firms, even aside from confusion between Lamarck's and Darwin's evolutionism. A debt towards the difference equations used by Lotka to define dimensions and the age structure of the population in the case of the stationary state was recognised by Samuelson in his *Foundations* (1947).

[23] In this respect Marshall (1890, p. 509 n. 2) quoted Petty approvingly, who had recalled (in Petty 1662, p. 89) that in the Lord's Prayer the term 'bread' designates food in general. We may also recall the use of the term 'corn' in Ricardo and many other classical economists to designate the set of agricultural products.

Quite naturally, various problems arise when the categories thus defined are related to the real world: from the case of joint production to the problem of differences in the technologies adopted by different firms belonging to the same industry, up to the problem of greater or lesser similarity between the products of different firms belonging to the same industry. The latter aspect in particular is important, for it renders less clear-cut, and more flexible, the Marshallian notion of competition; in such a way, indeed, this notion was bent so as to allow for some degree of independence between the 'markets' of the different firms belonging to an industry, hence some degree of autonomy in the price choices of the different firms.

As hinted above, within this conceptual framework Marshall's analytical structure was based on (short or long period) equilibrium between demand and supply. The demand function for each commodity is assumed to be derived from individual preferences;[24] overall, however, Marshall tended to skate over the relationship between utility maps and demand functions: this aspect did not constitute one of his original contributions.[25] For the purpose of determining equilibrium, it is sufficient to assume as given (and decreasing, on the basis of the decreasing marginal utility postulate) the demand functions for the different goods.[26] Attention is rather focused on supply functions: it was in this field that Marshall tried to provide an innovative contribution in comparison to the theories proposed by the first protagonists of the marginalist revolution, particularly by Jevons. The latter had recourse to a principle symmetrical to that of decreasing utility, the principle of the increasing sacrifice or painfulness of labour; this allowed him to obtain increasing supply curves, since producers ask for higher and higher prices as a condition for increasing their contribution (the amount of labour spent), hence for increasing the quantity produced. Such an approach, however, cannot easily be extended from the study of the behaviour of individuals to the analysis of industries and firms in competitive markets, the more so if we stick to the method of partial analysis: each firm or industry considered

[24] For derivation of demand curves from utility functions, cf. Marshall 1890, pp. 92 ff. and 838 ff. In the context of partial analysis, the marginal utility of money is assumed to be constant: income effects are thus ruled out. This is justified by assuming that the market for the commodity under consideration is very small, compared to the economy as a whole; this must be true for each individual economic agent.

[25] Following in this the exponents of the 'old' German school, Marshall attributed importance to the analysis of needs: the objective element of the ability to satisfy needs (Bernardine from Siena's *virtuositas*: cf. above, § 2.5) was thus placed side by side, as in Scholastic thought, to the subjective element (*complacibilitas*) in determining the demand function.

[26] Recalling John Stuart Mill, Marshall in this respect stressed the need to develop a new science, ethology, or the study of human habits and customs and of their gradual changes in the course of time.

in isolation, in fact, can easily obtain (in a competitive labour market) additional hours of labour simply by subtracting them from other firms or industries without changing the marginal disutility of labour for the individual worker.[27]

Marshall thus proposed the road of partial equilibrium for supply side analysis, hence for constructing supply curves referring to individual firms and industries. To this purpose he took two elements of the classical tradition and reworked them in a context quite different from the original one. The first was the Smithian theory of the connection between enlargement of the market and division of labour, and consequently productivity increases. The second was the 'Ricardian' theory of differential rent. Newly christened as 'laws of returns to scale', these two theories were simultaneously used to explain the variations of costs in response to changes in the quantity produced, respectively identified with the case of increasing returns to scale and with the case of decreasing returns.

Clearly this is an artificial construct, which puts together quite different things.[28] Furthermore, even if considered one at a time, the transposition of the Smithian and 'Ricardian' 'laws' into the ambit of the theory of the firm and the industry gave rise to difficulties which Marshall saw or perceived, but to which he did not attribute the importance they deserve.

Let us consider first of all the reference to the 'law of decreasing returns' used by Ricardo in the theory of rent with reference to the productivity of a means of production of a particular kind, such as land, taken to be available in a given quantity and with distinctive features for each unit of land. The Ricardian theory of differential rent in fact did not revolve around decreasing returns for individual firms or industries, but around the problem of the distribution of national income among the social classes of workers, landlords and capitalists, and in particular around the problem of determining the rent accruing to the landlords. In the modified form which Marshall gave it, the theory of decreasing returns instead concerned the means of production utilised by specific industries. The case in which an industry is the sole subject to use a given

---

[27] On the other hand – we may now add on the basis of Sraffa's 1925 remarks – if we were to take account also of infinitesimal changes in the painfulness of labour, stemming from changes in production levels of a single firm or industry, such changes would equally affect all industries and firms in the economy. As a consequence, it would not be possible to use the *ceteris paribus* clause which is the basis of partial analysis; in particular, when faced with generalised changes in prices it would not be possible to assume as given the demand curve for the individual industry.

[28] This point will be considered again later, when illustrating Sraffa's critiques of this construct: cf. § 16.4. Here we will merely stress that in the first case increasing returns correspond in a first approximation to proportional changes in all the means of production used; in the second case, instead, decreasing returns are connected to changes in the proportions in which the different means of production are utilised, since the quantity of 'land' utilised remains fixed while the quantities of labour and 'capital' change.

means of production is, however, a very peculiar one. Once again, outside this case, which was the one to which the Ricardian theory referred, the *ceteris paribus* clause (hence the method of partial analysis) should be abandoned.

Already in his first writings, moreover, Marshall considered a further problem, crucial for his approach: the existence – and importance – of increasing returns to scale, which are considered as the source of economic development in the Smithian theory of the division of labour. Cournot's 1838 theory of the equilibrium of the firm – a crucial point of reference for the development of the marginalist theory – falls apart if the assumption of decreasing returns is abandoned in favour of that, decidedly more realistic, of increasing returns to scale. A stable equilibrium is possible in this case only if the demand curve decreases more rapidly than the supply curve; but this cannot hold in the case of competition, where the price is by assumption independent of the quantity produced by the individual firm. In other words, the assumption of perfect competition is incompatible with the case of increasing returns to scale.

As stated above, Marshall had already recognised the existence of this dilemma in his essays on *The pure theory of domestic values*, published in 1879; much of his analytical effort in the *Principles* and in subsequent revisions of the book was devoted to solving the dilemma. In this case too, due to the complex interplay of affirmations and qualifications, cross-references and oppositions between text and notes, it is quite difficult to define univocally the solution proposed (which moreover evolved over time); it may be better to focus on two distinct reference points.

First, we have the solution that was developed by some among Marshall's followers, in particular Pigou and Viner, and then adopted in most textbooks.[29] This solution was based on the assumption of U-shaped curves representing the relationship between average and marginal costs on the one hand and quantity produced on the other. Initially, cost curves are decreasing because increasing returns prevail; from a certain point (a certain level of the quantity produced) onward, decreasing returns take the lead, and costs start increasing. Under competition and in the long run, the equilibrium point for the firm corresponds to the minimum of the average cost curve, namely the point where the average cost curve terminates its descent and begins to increase. The weight of the development of the industry is then put on the shoulders of

---

[29] Cf. Ridolfi 1972 for a critique of the idea, rather widespread in the literature, that this solution was present in Marshall's *Principles*, and for a reconstruction of its origin. Bharadwaj 1989, pp. 159–75, following a suggestion given her by Sraffa, used Marshall's manuscript notes at the margin of Pigou's *Wealth and welfare* (1912) to show how Marshall in effect considered with extreme diffidence the line of research on which his successor to the Cambridge chair had embarked.

a specific kind of economies of scale: those internal to the industry itself (since for the industry the demand curve is decreasing, so that an equilibrium is possible even if the supply curve is also decreasing, provided that the speed of decrease is lower than that of demand), but external to the individual firms which compose the industry (so as to retain for them the possibility of a competitive equilibrium which needs cost to increase with the quantity produced, from a certain point onwards). Such a construct, thus, may be criticised both for its lack of realism and its connection to a static notion of equilibrium.[30]

Marshall, while hinting at the line of reasoning just sketched above, suggested a second path to solving the dilemma between assumption of competition and increasing returns: a path to which he seems to have adhered with increasing confidence in the editions of the *Principles* subsequent to the first, at least up to the fifth. This second road consists in the theory of the representative firm and in recourse to biological metaphors. The core of the argument is this: the industry is made up of many firms which, like trees in a forest, are at different points of their 'life cycle': some, the 'young' ones, experience increasing returns and develop though in a competitive environment; others, the 'mature' ones, have already reached dimensions at which the elements of growth and decay balance out; still others are decaying. In a world composed of individual firms distributed among the different stages of development, the 'representative' firm, of average dimensions, turns out to be at the middle of its development process, and can thus be identified with a firm experiencing increasing returns, even if overall the population of firms is stationary.

The weakness in this construct is not simply the difficulty of translating it into a well-structured analytical model; it rather lies in the difficulty of accepting the assumption of the 'life cycle'. Justification of such an assumption was given by referring to the sequence of three generations in control of the firm: the founder, endowed with above-normal organisational and innovative ability; his immediate heirs, grown at the hard school of the founder and used at least to a rigorous management of the family business; the third generation, grown up in prosperous conditions and less ready to make the sacrifices which are often necessary in a competitive environment characterised by continuous technological change and hence by the need to save and invest in order not to lose ground to their competitors.[31] Such justification clearly refers to a world of small

---

[30] Sraffa 1925 provided sufficient material for a critique of this approach.

[31] In that period (eleven years after the first edition of Marshall's *Principles*, but six years before the fifth edition, in which the idea of the representative firm reached its full development) the idea of the life cycle of firms found literary expression in the famous novel by Thomas Mann, *Buddenbrooks* (1901).

firms managed by their proprietor. In the last editions of the *Principles* published in his lifetime, Marshall himself stressed the growing importance of public companies, in which the assumption of the life cycle does not seem acceptable, and appeared conscious of the difficulties stemming from this. Various among his followers nonetheless remained faithful to the construct of the representative firm, like Robertson who reproposed it in 1930, provoking Sraffa's (1930a) sarcastic reaction.

The *Principles* thus constituted a failure, at least with respect to what Marshall himself considered a crucial element of his personal contribution to the development of a neoclassical theory of value. However, various other elements of Marshall's edifice are fully entitled to remain part of modern economic theory: let us recall for instance the notion of elasticity. And it should be added that Marshall's greatness as an economist lies also (and perhaps mainly) in his awareness of the limits of his analytical constructs, which instead have been accepted without critical scrutiny by many of his followers, even in recent years.

4.   Economics becomes a profession

Among Marshall's contributions to the development of economics we should also recall his role in the transformation of the economist into a profession, with specific autonomy in the areas of research and teaching.

When Marshall began his professional career, within university studies it was possible to distinguish two general curricula: human sciences and natural sciences. Within the first curriculum, philosophy (with a dominant role for moral philosophy), history and morals coexisted. Political economy had a smaller role; the economic lectures that Marshall gave to the female students of Newnham College were on many accounts lessons in civic education.

In this sense – as a contribution to a sound moral education – we should interpret the support which the young Marshall gave to the movement for admission of women to university studies: support which was subsequently to change to heated opposition – with a shift in attitude that biographers and scholars have found difficult to explain.[32] This change of attitude may have been due to Marshall's impression that the connection originally perceived between university instruction and civic and moral education (a connection consistent with the role he attributed to women as enlightened vestals of the family and society) had transformed into a link between getting a university degree and starting a professional career, such as to favour a growing assimilation of men and women. Apart from

---

[32] Cf. Groenewegen 1995, pp. 493–530. The chapter is entitled 'A feminist *manqué*'.

an undoubted evolution of his position, Marshall in fact appears a traditionalist Victorian, favourable to cultural enhancement as instrumental
to moral enhancement in the case of women as in that of workers, but
poles apart compared to the pro-women position manifested for instance
by John Stuart Mill some decades earlier or the – often quite moderate –
contemporary supporters of women's accession to university, like his old
friend Henry Sidgwick.

Creation of professional education in the economic field required that
economics be made to emerge from the wider field of study of the moral
sciences, taking on decidedly the character of a technical tool of analysis
of an important aspect of social reality. In substance, economics was no
longer to be seen as one of the possible fields of learning of a generic social
scientist, but was to be considered itself a set of connected specialist fields
of work.

As already stated, Marshall made a decisive contribution in this direction. First of all, there was the foundation in 1890 of the British Economic
Association (subsequently the Royal Economic Society) and of its publication, the *Economic Journal*.[33] Second, we should recall the long struggle
for the institution of a specialised curriculum of studies at the University
of Cambridge, independent of the generic one in moral sciences.[34] Economics (no longer 'political economy') was conceived as a science whose
development was entrusted to specialists, on the model of natural sciences, and no longer as a branch of knowledge entrusted in part to those
who could ponder on their own practical experiences (from Cantillon the
banker to Ricardo the stockbroker) and in part to persons endowed of
good general culture and with a political interest for an understanding of
economic and social events (from the physicians Petty and Mandeville to
a professional revolutionary such as Marx).

The professionalisation of economics had both positive and negative
effects on its evolution. Among the positive effects, there was no doubt
the diffusion of more refined techniques of analysis, which called for
greater rigour and greater control of the logical consistency of arguments. The development of mathematical economics and especially the
collection and systematic analysis of statistical information were aspects of

---

[33] We should not be misled by the fact that Marshall preferred to remain behind the scenes,
leaving to others the official roles of president and secretary of the British Economic
Association and of editor of the *Economic Journal*. His *de facto* control over the association
and the journal, and more generally on the selection of economists in English universities,
was nonetheless quite strong. Cf. Groenewegen 1995, pp. 464–68; Maloney 1991; Hey
and Winch 1990, in particular the essay by Kadish and Freeman.

[34] The history of this battle, which culminated in 1903 with the institution of a new economics tripos, is told in Groenewegen 1995, pp. 531–69; cf. also Maloney 1985, 2nd
edn. 1991.

this process. As for the negative elements, research activity lost its nature of participating in cultural and political life, and became an instrument of academic careers. The importance attributed to originality and priority of publication of one's own ideas, on the part of Marshall as well as of Jevons or Walras, can thus be better understood.[35] However, at this point the theoretical debate acquired a dangerous autonomy with respect to the constant confrontation with the real world: to show one's own 'scientific' ability, essentially through use of refined analytical tools, gradually became more important than a good 'practical' understanding of the real issues.

Through the process of professionalisation of economics Marshall made a decisive contribution to the rise to dominance of neoclassical theory: not only in the version he himself had proposed in the *Principles*, but also in that of general economic equilibrium. Moreover, if we bear in mind the negative effects recalled above, it was perhaps natural to expect that, relative to the ambivalence of the theses presented in the *Principles*, the more simplistic even if analytically more precise theoretical construct of the *vulgata* of static equilibrium should have come to prevail. By the same token, the axiomatic version of general equilibrium theory was to prevail over the more concrete, but less 'scientific', Marshallian analysis of partial equilibrium and 'short causal chains'.

5.   Monetary theory: from the old to the new Cambridge school

In his main work, the *Principles*, Marshall did not deal with money: as stated above, the subject was set aside for a subsequent volume of the great treatise initially planned; when Marshall, already eighty years old, succeeded in publishing *Money, credit and commerce* (1923), his analytical vigour had disappeared. His contributions to the field of monetary theory are rather to be found in his participation (mainly in the form of

---

[35] Episodes of conflict on pretended plagiarisms, or on priority of publication, had also taken place previously; let us recall for instance the famous controversy between Adam Smith and Ferguson on the division of labour (but we may stress that, not by chance, both Ferguson and Smith were professors!). However, there is a qualitative leap in the attention in these aspects. Let us recall, for instance, that in the seventeenth century William Petty, certainly not a model of altruism, quietly made a gift of at least some ideas to his friend John Graunt, if not the whole text of the famous work on London's mortality tables to which the origins of demography are usually traced (Graunt 1662); in the eighteenth century the proclivity to plagiarism of the Marquis de Mirabeau or of Postlethwayt are well known; thanks to the latter we now have what is in all probability the original English text of Cantillon's book (1755).

testimonials) in some commissions of enquiry into the subject,[36] and in the oral tradition stemming from his teaching.

Two aspects of Marshall's theory of money deserve mention here. First, Marshall transformed Irving Fisher's quantity equation (cf. above, § 12.5), $MV = PQ$, into the so-called Cambridge equation, $kY = M$.[37] Second, there was the role of 'monetary disturbances' in explaining the cyclical oscillations of the economy around the long period equilibrium determined by the 'real' factors considered within the neoclassical theory of value.

As far as the first aspect is concerned, at first sight it might seem a simple change in symbols: 'Cambridge's k' corresponds in fact to the inverse of the velocity of circulation of money V in Fisher's equation. However, behind this formal change a different notion of the demand for money shone through. This is connected not so much to financing requirements for exchange as to economic agents' choices on the share of their income (or, in a different formulation, later to be developed by Keynes, on the share of their wealth) that they desire to keep in the form of money.[38] In this way precautionary demand for money (and later, with Keynes, speculative demand) was made to appear explicitly side by side with demand for money for transaction purposes. In other words, the formal change in the equation of exchanges allowed Marshall to stress a new perspective from which to tackle the issue of the role of money: a potentially revolutionary perspective, as was to be seen when his pupil Keynes accomplished decisive steps forward.

With respect to the role of money in the determination of the real variables of the economy, Marshall advanced further interesting ideas, admitting the influence of liquidity conditions on income and employment as well, together with its influence on money prices. However, in this case as well the decisive step forward was accomplished later, by Keynes. Marshall limited the 'non-neutrality' of money to the short period, as after him his pupils or followers, from Hawtrey to Robertson, and more or less the whole of the neoclassical tradition, up to Hayek and beyond were also to do.[39]

---

[36] Cf. Marshall 1926 and 1996b.

[37] Let us recall that M indicates the quantity of money in circulation in the economy, V its velocity of circulation, P the price level, Q an index of quantity produced, Y national income in money terms (so that $PQ = Y$), k the share of income that economic agents desire to keep in money.

[38] On this point Marshall had been preceded by Senior. Cf. Bowley 1937, pp. 214-15, who illustrates how Senior opposed (J. S. Mill's version of) the quantity theory of money.

[39] Cf. above, § 11.4, for Hayek's theory of the trade cycle; and below, ch. 14, for the developments of this line of analysis by Keynes. On Marshall, cf. Eshag 1964 and Tonveronachi 1983, pp. 15–24.

6.   Maffeo Pantaleoni

Maffeo Pantaleoni (1857–1924) was a key protagonist of the development of Italian economic thought at the end of the nineteenth century and the beginning of the twentieth century. 'The prince of [Italian] economists', as Sraffa (1924, p. 648) called him, played on various accounts a decisive role: first of all, as the master to more than a generation of economists and as influential friend of others, like Pareto;[40] secondly, because of the impulse he gave to the founding of one of the research lines in Italy which had the largest influence internationally, the Italian school of public finance;[41] thirdly, for his passionate participation in the debates of the time in theoretical and applied economics;[42] fourthly, for his most influential textbook, *Principii di economia pura* (Principles of economics, 1889); and last but not least, for his combination of scientific and moral rigour demonstrated in the course of an often tormented life.

After graduating in Rome, Pantaleoni became professor of political economy at the University of Camerino when twenty-five years old, and subsequently moved to Macerata, Venice and Bari. In 1890, however, he resigned in response to the controversy arising from his critiques of the government and his statements in favour of banking reform: a very harsh campaign, which among other things contributed to the bankruptcy of the Banca Romana. In 1895 he went back to the university as a professor in Naples, but after two years, again in polemic with the government, he resigned and moved to Geneva. In 1900 he went back to Italy, as professor at Pavia and then (from 1902 up to his death) at the University of Rome, holding the chair that thanks to his prestige became the most important economics chair in Italy: a role it lost after the Second World War, when the focus of economic teaching shifted out of the faculties of

[40] The correspondence between Pantaleoni and Pareto (Pareto 1960) is a most useful document (as, in a subsequent stage, is that between Loria and Graziani, in Allocati 1990) for reliving from 'behind the scene' the theoretical debates and the academic vicissitudes of Italian economists at the time.

[41] In particular with an essay published in 1883, *Contributo alla teoria del riparto delle spese pubbliche* (A contribution to the theory of allotment of public expenditure). Among the economists who, after Pantaleoni, contributed to the development of an Italian school of public finance we should at least mention Antonio de Viti de Marco (1858–1943), who among other things is one of the eleven Italian holders of a chair who refused the oath of loyalty to fascism. This school originated the stream of 'public choice theory' which has been revived in the last few decades by the 1986 Nobel prize winner, the American James Buchanan (b. 1919).

[42] Cf. the essays collected in *Erotemi di economia* (Economics questions, 1925), and the book on *La caduta della Società Generale di Credito Mobiliare Italiano* (The fall of the SGCMI, 1895), which Sraffa (1924) compared to the famous influential work on *Lombard Street* by Bagehot (1873).

law. From 1900 he was Member of Parliament; but was soon the object of false accusations (in his opinion, made by those whose interests he had damaged at the time of the bankruptcy of the Banca Romana). Compelled to a long and difficult defence which ruined him financially (moreover, his wife, after attempting suicide, became mentally ill), he resigned from Parliament as soon as he emerged victorious from the scandal. Minister of finance with D'Annunzio at Fiume, he adhered to fascism and in 1923 was appointed to the Senate; his death the following year makes it difficult for us to settle the issue of his reactions to the political assassination of Matteotti, a leading anti-fascist Member of Parliament – an assassination for which Mussolini was to claim full moral responsibility.

The book to which he owes his fame as an economist is, as mentioned above, the text on *Principii di economia pura*, published in 1889 and translated into English in 1898. Publication preceded by a year that of Marshall's *Principles*, and was the fruit of largely independent research, but shared a substantially similar orientation.

In his *Principii*, Pantaleoni decisively adopted the subjectivist approach of Jevons and Menger (Jevons was there the most frequently quoted author, although in Italy the influence of the Austrian school was probably stronger). Such an approach was connected in an original, only apparently eclectic way to the contributions of the classical tradition, with marked sensitivity to the concrete applicability of theoretical argumentations. Many ideas, including his analysis of predatory and parasitic phenomena, indicate an inclination on the part of Pantaleoni towards an evolutionary approach which was in line with the cultural climate of the time and similar to that which we find in Marshall's *Principles*.

Pantaleoni remained substantially faithful to this approach in his subsequent teaching when, though attracted by the developments of general economic equilibrium theory, he remained perplexed by its rarefied abstract nature, while he appeared annoyed at the classificatory manias to which the Marshallian *vulgata* had given rise, with the distinction between increasing, constant and decreasing returns industries. However, his influence led to the rise of a Marshallian–Pigovian stream within Italian universities, with among its epigones some of his successors to the Rome chair, like Giuseppe Ugo Papi (1893–1989) and Giuseppe Di Nardi (1911–92).

We cannot know what the new textbook would have been like, on which Pantaleoni was working in his latter years while he refused to let his old *Principii* be reprinted. However, despite his famous statement according to which there are only two schools of economists, those who understand economics and those who do not (a statement which implies the existence of an objective truth in our field), 'his teaching, far from being aimed at imposing ready-made theories upon his pupils, was solely concerned with urging them to think for themselves' (Sraffa 1924, p. 652).

7.   Marshallism in the United States: from John Bates Clark to Jacob Viner

The rise to dominance of the neoclassical *vulgata* in the teaching of economics and in economic culture in the first half of the twentieth century was due not only to developments in England and in particular in Cambridge with Pigou, but especially to the increasing role of American universities (favoured when Italian and then middle-European culture was upset by the rise of fascism and nazism) and the influence of a few protagonists there, who systematised economic theory in the simplified versions of partial or aggregate equilibrium.

Let us focus attention on two key figures: John Bates Clark (1847–1938) and Jacob Viner (1892–1970).[43] J. B. Clark was, with Richard Ely (1854–1943) and Henry Carter Adams (1851–1921), one of the three promoters of the American Economic Association in 1885, and was from 1895 to 1923 professor at Columbia University in New York. After studying at Amherst, in the 1870s he had spent two years at Heidelberg, feeling the influence of Knies's German historical school; but already his first book (*The philosophy of wealth*, a collection of articles published in 1886) contained 'a totally original and quite sophisticated statement of the principle of marginal utility ("effective utility" in Clark's vocabulary)'.[44] His main work, *The distribution of wealth*, published in 1899 after long years of elaboration, offered an organic illustration of the neoclassical theory of value and distribution based on the aggregate notion of capital, and had a wide impact.

Let us briefly examine this theory. Clark considered an economic system with only two factors of production, labour and capital (land, and any other productive input different from labour, were reduced to capital). Within such a system, the quantity of product obtained depends on the quantity utilised of the two factors of production and on their combination; rate of interest and wage rate correspond, in equilibrium, to the marginal productivity of the two factors, capital and labour, and constitute their prices or 'natural values'.[45]

---

[43] In the previous chapter we have already discussed Irving Fisher, who worked at the boundary between the general economic equilibrium approach and the aggregate approach on which we focus attention here.

[44] Dewey 1987, p. 429. Cf. also the essay by John Bates's son, John Maurice Clark 1952.

[45] Clark left open the issue of the conditions under which the distributive rule based on the marginal productivities of the factors of production wholly exhaust the value of the

Clark was a strong supporter of aggregate analysis, for the possibility it offers to achieve concrete and analytically robust results.[46] Therefore, he rejected as irrelevant the attempts to develop a disaggregate theory of capital such as that of the mature Wicksell, derived from Böhm-Bawerk, based on the periods of production of the different capital goods (cf. above, §§ 11.4 and 11.5). Moreover, Clark proposed a 'universal measure of value' based on a combination of utility and labour. On the conceptual plane, his main contribution consisted in the distinction between statics and dynamics; at the analytical level, in the demonstration, though based on a simple graphical apparatus – in the framework of the aggregate neoclassical theory recalled above – of the erroneousness of considering the share of income going to capital or to land as a surplus, because of the symmetry between the determination of the wage rate and that of the interest rate, which correspond to the marginal product of the two factors of production, labour and capital.[47]

In the generation following Clark's, Jacob Viner taught at the University of Chicago, with very short breaks, from 1916 to 1946, and subsequently moved on to Princeton up to 1960. His main fields of research were the theory of international trade and the history of economic thought.[48] His most influential contribution, however, was an article on 'Cost curves and supply curves' published in 1931. Therein Viner offered systematic treatment in four graphs of the determination of short run and long run equilibriums of the firm and the industry based on pairs of U-shaped curves representing average and marginal costs as functions of quantity

product: the same thing which Wicksteed had done in his *Essay on the co-ordination of the laws of distribution* published in 1894. However in a review of this work, published in the *Economic Journal* in June 1894 (hence five years before the publication of Clark's book), Flux had stressed the need to assume constant returns to scale for the applicability of Euler's theorem to the aggregate production function, hence to guarantee the correspondence between sum of the distributive shares and value of the product. Cf. Steedman 1992; on the history of marginal productivity in general, and on the role of Euler's theorem within it, cf. Stigler 1941. Later important contributions on the line of a marginalist theory of distribution based on an aggregate production function are Hicks 1932 and Douglas 1934.

[46] Already Wicksell (cf. above, § 11.5) had remarked that such concreteness and robustness were only apparent, and this was to become finally evident in the debate which followed publication of Sraffa's 1960 book: cf. below, § 16.8.

[47] Clark was also the author, in the second stage of his research activity, of works which constitute the theoretical foundation of antitrust US policy (let us recall in particular *The control of trusts*, published in 1912 and written in collaboration with his son, John Maurice Clark, 1884–1963, who was also an influential economist, professor at Chicago from 1912 to 1926 and then at Columbia University up to 1952). Finally we should recall his contribution, which also concerned organisation, to the peace research sponsored by the Carnegie Endowment for International Peace.

[48] Cf., respectively, Viner 1937 and the essays collected in Viner 1991. Viner's huge erudition may be likened perhaps only to Schumpeter's or Sraffa's.

produced. The long period supply curve for the firm, in particular, was obtained from the envelopment of short run supply curves.[49]

This systematic treatment was taken on substantially unchanged in economics textbooks of the subsequent half-century and beyond. In particular it was accepted – together with Clark's aggregate neoclassical version of the theory of value and distribution – as the central core of the famous textbook *Economics* (1948a) by Paul Samuelson (b. 1912, Nobel prize in 1970), not only the best selling textbook of the last fifty years (more than three million copies sold in subsequent editions and in numerous translations), but also a model for various other authors.[50]

8.   Thornstein Veblen and institutionalism

In the United Kingdom, Marshall's fight was more with the historical school than with the remnants of Ricardianism in the endeavour to establish the dominance of his particular brand of economics; in the United States, the spread of Marshallism also took place in a context where historical-institutionalist views were widespread, although by no means all-pervasive. In fact, the main representative of institutionalism, Veblen, perhaps also due to his unconventional personality, was never considered as belonging to the academic establishment.

Thornstein Veblen (1857–1929), the son of Norwegian immigrants, born into a farming community, a student of John Bates Clark and subsequently of the pragmatist philosopher Charles Peirce,[51] often felt out of place in university life, due to his unconventional lifestyle and also to his religious scepticism in a period in which most American colleges

---

[49] In this respect there is a well-known story about Viner, who asked his readers to excuse the inability of the draughtsman of the graphs of his article to make the long period average cost curve pass through the minimum points of the short run average cost curves: Viner's request was one which it is impossible to satisfy, as algebraic treatment of the problem can show. It is to Viner's credit that in the reprints of the article, after his mistake had been spotted, the footnote on his disagreement with the draughtsman recalling the latter's mathematical doubts then not understood by Viner himself, was not omitted.

[50] In this new synthesis, analytical techniques drew increasing attention, while issues concerning the representation of the world receded in the background. Thus, 'consumer theory ceased to explain choices and merely described them: rationality came to be equated with consistent, transitive preferences [. . .] Competition came to be understood in terms of the inability of agents to influence prices in markets that were devoid of any institutional features, defined only by the existence of a single price. The result was that process views of competition were ignored. [. . .] A common feature [. . .] was the neglect of all arguments that could not be expressed using formal equilibrium models' (Backhouse 2003, p. 321).

[51] Another of his professors was William Graham Sumner (1840–1910), a conservative evolutionist and leading representative of so-called Social Darwinism, supporter of elitist individualism and extreme economic liberalism. Sumner, like Marshall, was strongly influenced by Herbert Spencer's social evolutionism (cf. above, note 19).

and universities were church-affiliated. A prolific writer, hired as a junior teacher at the University of Chicago in 1892, in 1896 he became the first managing editor of the *Journal of Political Economy* and in 1899 published a provocative and successful book on *The theory of the leisure class*, in which he discussed the influence of economic values on customs and fashion with heavy irony. He also showed how the business mentality came to dominate even within the institutions of learning, with a retrogression of cultural values.

According to Veblen, modern capitalism is characterised by persistence of old modes of thought, such as ancient predatory instincts and the use of conspicuous consumption to assert social superiority. In *The theory of business enterprise*, published in 1904, Veblen contrasted the men of industry (inventors, engineers, technical experts) with businessmen become salesmen or focusing on financial management rather than production.[52] As an implication of this, in later writings he foresaw 'the coming domination of the economy by an oligopolistic nucleus of giant corporations' (Diggins 1999, p. 57).

There are many other insights in Veblen's writings, and many of them resurface here and there in later American economic thought. For instance, the separation between ownership and management of firms and the growth of giant corporations are at the centre of Berle and Means's famous 1932 book; there are shades, in Veblen's writings, of Galbraith's 'technostructure' (cf. below, § 17.4); more recently, the dominant role of finance and the ideas on cyclical financial fragility resurfaced in Minsky's notion of 'money managers capitalism' and in his theory of endogenous financial crises (cf. below, § 17.5). But two central aspects of Veblen's institutional approach disappear from American economic culture with the rise to dominance of marginalism, both in the Marshallian and in the general equilibrium varieties, namely the idea that human nature should not be taken as given, but is an endogenous variable in economic analysis;[53] and the idea of a decisive role played by cultural and

---

[52] It is Veblen, following then customary habits, who writes 'men' where today we prefer to write 'persons'; but he was certainly not an anti-feminist. In fact, he considered 'the barbarian status of women' (an expression on which he insisted, quoted by Diggins 1999, p. 141) 'as an anthropological artifact, a residue that reflected the persistence of custom and the continuity of habit' and saw 'in human evolution the descent of women as well as the ascent of men' (ibid.). On Veblen's position on the gender issue, cf. Diggins 1999, pp. 139–66.

[53] 'The hedonistic conception of man is that of a lightning calculator of pleasures and pains, who oscillates like a homogeneous globule of desire and happiness under the impulse of stimuli that shift him about the area, but leave him intact. He has neither antecedent nor consequent. He is an isolated, definitive human datum, in stable equilibrium except for the buffets of the impinging forces that displace him in one direction or another.

institutional change in the process of economic development.[54] In contrast with the optimism of Sumner, who saw social evolution as a path of progress, Veblen's evolutionary views, which concerned both social institutions and human culture, focused on the tensions stemming from the lag in cultural adaptation to the changing economic environment.

Veblen was too much of an outsider to belong to any 'school', but the important institutionalist current in the United States, with protagonists such as Wesley Clair Mitchell (1874–1948) and, at least in part of his researches, John Maurice Clark,[55] can be seen as largely inspired by his writings and teaching.[56]

Another important, at least partly independent, influence was that of John Rogers Commons (1862–1945), co-founder with Richard Ely of the Wisconsin institutional school, which had a not insignificant influence on the New Deal in the 1930s.[57] Among other things, Commons gave important contributions to the industrial relations field: recognising the reality of conflicts, he pressed for institutions ensuring mediation and governance for them.

Mitchell was the leading protagonist of another institutional school active in the interwar period, based in Columbia University and the National Bureau of Economic Research in New York, of which he was the director for a quarter of a century (1920–45), making important contributions to study of the business cycle and, more generally, to empirical studies, statistics collection and the elaboration of national accounts.[58]

9.   Welfare economics: Arthur Cecil Pigou

Among Marshall's pupils, two emerged above the others: John Maynard Keynes, to whom the next chapter is devoted, and Arthur Cecil Pigou

---

Self-imposed in an elementary state, he spins symmetrically about his own spiritual axis until the parallelogram of forces bears down upon him, whereupon he follows the line of the resultant' (Veblen 1919, quoted by Diggins 1999, p. 50).

[54] This did not imply a leaning towards an anti-theoretical attitude such as adopted by the historical school, which Veblen criticised precisely on this account. His critique of neoclassical theory concerned, rather, its restricted scope, with its neglect of the wider issues of social evolution and its interrelation with cultural-institutional change, and its static, non-evolutionary method.

[55] Clark's 1923 book on overhead costs stressed the role of a high ratio between fixed and circulating capital, intrinsic to modern technologies, for a tendency away from competition and towards oligopolistic and monopolistic market forms. Another important contribution is the 1926 book on market failures and the need for a 'social control of business'.

[56] For an overview of American institutionalism in the first half of the twentieth century, cf. Rutheford 2003 and the bibliography quoted there.

[57] On Ely's central role in the founding of the American Economic Association cf. Barber 2003, pp. 240–2.

[58] On subsequent developments of institutionalism in the United States cf. below, § 17.4.

(1877–1959). Six years older than Keynes and by temper better suited to the university environment, although he was then very young Pigou was chosen by Marshall in 1908[59] as his successor to the economics chair in Cambridge, a position he held up to his retirement in 1943.

Here there is only space to mention three of his contributions: his 'orthodox' version of the Marshallian theory of the firm and the industry; his most innovative contribution: the development of the research stream of welfare economics; and his analyses of employment and macroeconomic equilibriums, characterised by his torn relationship with Keynesian theory.

As we have already suggested in § 3, Pigou chose to adopt, within the varied corpus of Marshall's analysis, the approach that at least seemed better suited to rigorous analytic treatment, that of partial analysis of short and long period equilibriums based on U-shaped cost curves, dropping Marshall's suggestions for an evolutionary analysis ('the trees and the forest'). This also provoked some rigorously private reservations on the part of his mentor (cf. Bharadwaj 1989, pp. 159–75) and a growing isolation even with respect to his more strictly Marshallian colleagues, like Robertson and Shove. Despite his active participation in the debate started in 1922 by the publication of an article by Clapham in the *Economic Journal* (cf. below, § 10), and especially despite his systematic application of Marshallian tools in different fields of analysis, we cannot consider this the field of his main analytical contribution. Though he preceded Viner in utilising a graph with U-shaped cost curves (Pigou 1928, p. 246), more important for the systematic construct of the Marshallian *vulgata* was in fact Viner's 1931 article mentioned in § 7 above.

Pigou's main contribution is commonly considered to be his recourse to notions of external economies and diseconomies, illustrated by Marshall in the *Principles*, for the development of a new field of theoretical research: welfare economics. Let us recall that we have external economies (or diseconomies) whenever an economic activity – be it production or consumption – generates indirect effects on third parties, from which they reap a benefit (or a loss), without having participated in the decision of the economic agent directly concerned. For instance, we have a case of external economies when the roses I decide to cultivate at my expense in my garden gladden not only myself but also my neighbours; we have a case of external diseconomies whenever the car I drive pollutes the air and contributes to a traffic jam. When the (assumedly selfish) economic agent decides how much to produce and consume, he or she considers the effects of the action which directly concern him or her, but not the effects on others; this implies that too little is consumed and produced

---

[59] With a harsh academic battle, on which see Deane 2001, pp. 247–52.

of what generates external economies, and too much of what generates external diseconomies. Hence the desirability of public intervention in the economic field, aimed at stimulating with subsidies the first kind and hindering with taxes the second kind of activity. Welfare economics is precisely the field of analysis which studies the nature and measure of such interventions, aimed at driving the economy towards optimal situations for the community as a whole.

Pigou's main contribution to this line of research is *Wealth and welfare* (1912), which in the widely revised second edition took on the title of *The economics of welfare* (1920). In these writings Pigou systematically used the analytical tool of 'consumer's surplus', proposed by Marshall in the *Principles* in the context of partial equilibrium analysis. Such a notion designates the gain of total utility obtained by the buyer from exchange thanks to the fact that, while for the last (infinitesimal) dose purchased the price paid corresponds to the additional utility obtained (marginal utility), the utility of the preceding doses was greater than the price paid. The difference between these two magnitudes (assuming that utility is measured in terms of money, under the assumption of constant marginal utility of money), added up for all units purchased, gives the consumer's surplus. Obviously the choice between different situations is easily derived by comparing the consumer's surplus realised within the economy in different cases: this is in fact the road taken by welfare economics.[60]

Finally, Pigou was known as the representative of that orthodoxy that Keynes attacked in his *General theory*. In this work, the critiques to the

---

[60] The use just illustrated of the notion of consumer's surplus is vitiated by the fact that such a notion can be derived exclusively in the context of partial analysis, since it assumes the demand curve does not shift when the quantity produced or consumed changes, so that this construct cannot be applied rigorously in the context of general analysis. Moreover, partial equilibrium analysis does not constitute a solid theoretical background for welfare economics: as the so-called 'second best theorem' shows (Lipsey and Lancaster 1956), in a multi-sector economy a movement towards optimality in one sector does not necessarily imply a general move towards Pareto optimality.

   Another dubious aspect of welfare economics concerned the issue of interpersonal comparability of utilities and disutilities, which is circumvented – but certainly left unsolved – by recourse to an aggregate social welfare function (Bergson 1938), and which was to become essential for later developments (the so-called new welfare economics). Such developments concerned the analysis of cases in which some agents gain from a change in the situation while others lose. There is said to be an increase in welfare if the former can pay the latter 'compensation' which is lower than the advantage they derive from the change in question, but sufficient to render the change acceptable to the agents who bear a loss.

   A more recent development in welfare economics is connected to Rawls's 1971 ideas on justice, according to which an equitable distribution of resources is that which would be agreed on by the agents involved in it before they knew which position they will occupy in it.

'classical theory' were indeed aimed at Pigou and his *Theory of unemployment* (1933). In the debates which followed publication of Keynes's *General theory*, too, Pigou's name was connected to the defence of the idea of re-equilibrating power of competitive markets confronted with unemployment. The idea is that, even when the traditional re-equilibrating mechanism based on the reduction of the real wage rate is abandoned, since it does not work when the reduction in the money wage rate induced by unemployment induces a parallel reduction in the price level, we may resort to the so-called 'Pigou effect' or 'real wealth effect'. This mechanism is set in motion by the effect that the price decline, induced by unemployment through the reduction of money wages, has on the real value of money balances (or balances anyhow denominated in money terms) held by families. The increased value of such balances, hence of the real value of the families' wealth, induces an increase in consumption, hence in aggregate demand, which leads to reabsorption of unemployment.

Even when, in one of his last writings (*Keynes's General theory: a retrospective view*, 1950), Pigou declared that he had favourably revised his judgement on Keynes's theory, he was in fact suggesting a reabsorption of the theory within the traditional neoclassical framework. Pigou thus took sides with Hicks (1937) and Modigliani (1944, 1963) in developing the so-called 'neoclassical synthesis' within which, as we shall see better below (§ 17.5), the truly original elements of Keynes's thought were abandoned. Keynes's thesis on the possibility of persistent unemployment was taken up only in so far as it is connected to rigidities in the market for labour; such rigidities were attributed the role of impeding operation of the adjustment mechanisms outlined by traditional neoclassical theory which should have led the economy to its 'true' full employment equilibrium.

10.   Imperfect competition

As we have already hinted, the notion of competition within Marshall's theory was more nuanced – hence less restrictive – than in other marginalist theoreticians, in particular Jevons and Walras. In the theories of these latter, as in the textbook *vulgata*, perfect competition was that situation in which the economic agent is too small, relative to the dimensions of the market of a clearly defined and homogeneous product, to be able to influence with his behaviour the determination of the price: at the limit, it is necessary to assume that the dimension of each firm, or of each consumer, be infinitesimal compared to the dimension of the market, hence that the number of firms, or of consumers, be infinite. In technical terms, the price is considered an externally given parameter for the theory explaining the behaviour of the individual firm or consumer, while the unknown to be determined is the quantity respectively supplied or demanded. In Marshall's theory, conversely, many arguments presupposed some degree of freedom for firms in price setting.

This margin of freedom of action, which disappeared in Pigou's and Viner's *vulgata*, was present in the evolutionary metaphors with which Marshall illustrated the behaviour of the representative firm, in the attempt to strike a compromise between theoretical rigour and realism. In the Cambridge school we will find subsequently an analogous notion of competition, for instance in Keynes's theory (notwithstanding Kahn's efforts to bring it into the more 'rigorous' forms of the *vulgata*). The main manifestation of a representation of the working of the economic system which left firms some margins of freedom – the price should not necessarily be the same for all firms within an industry – was represented by the theory of imperfect competition, for which the traditional reference is Joan Robinson's book published in 1933. Behind this book, however, we must recall the long series of contributions which constituted its background.

We might say that the story begins with a famous controversy on the theory of the firm started in 1922 by an article by Clapham, 'On empty economic boxes', in the *Economic Journal*. The 'empty boxes' to which Clapham pointed in the title of his article were the categories of increasing, constant and decreasing returns to scale: categories which appeared to be inapplicable to the case of real industries. Among the responses of the orthodox Marshallians (with Pigou in the front line), who occasionally provided novel contributions, and the critical voices who added to Clapham's criticisms, a contribution by Sraffa published in 1926 came to dominate the scene. The first half of this article summarised the critiques of the Marshallian theory of the long run equilibrium of the firm and the industry under competitive conditions, which had been illustrated in a long essay published in Italian the previous year (cf. below, § 16.3); the second part proposed a way out of the difficulties by recalling the non-competitive elements commonly present in reality (and already variously illustrated by Marshall in the *Principles*), which allow us to consider each firm as endowed with a distinct market of its own within the industry. The imperfect nature of real-world competition allows us to assume that each firm is confronted with a demand curve which is not horizontal, but rather decreasing, so that within certain limits the firm can increase the price of its product without losing all of its clientele (or can decrease it without having to absorb all the demand previously directed to the other firms in the same industry). In a situation of this kind, equilibrium of the firm is possible even in conditions of constant, or slowly decreasing, costs when the quantity produced increases.

As we shall see (§ 16.4), Sraffa was soon to abandon this line of research. However, the notion of competition on which it relied corresponded, as we stated above, to Marshall's original orientations and to a well-established attitude in the oral tradition of the Cambridge school. Thus a view of the way the economy worked which stressed the role of market imperfections resurfaced, for example, in Kahn's 1929 fellowship dissertation (*The economics of the short period*), which remained unpublished at the time and was published only recently, first in Italian in 1983, then in English. The same direction was perhaps taken by Gerald Shove (1888–1947) who, however, published only two articles, one in 1928 and a contribution to the 1930 *Economic Journal* symposium on the Marshallian theory of the representative firm.[61]

Robinson's 1933 book thus represented the point of arrival of a line of research to which various representatives of the Cambridge school had contributed. By utilising an analytical tool commonly attributed to Kahn, the notion of marginal revenue, Joan Robinson provided a *vulgata* of the theory of imperfect competition, in which static equilibrium is determined, for the short and the long run, the firm and the industry.

Joan Robinson's book remained within the traditional Marshallian framework, relying on the notions of the firm and the industry. The work by Chamberlin[62] on monopolistic competition, published in the same year and commonly placed side by side with that of Joan Robinson, constituted instead a different contribution on important accounts. In stressing the margins of freedom enjoyed by each firm because of the widespread presence of market imperfections, Chamberlin remarked that in this way the very notion of industry loses meaning, since its boundaries had been established artificially on the basis of the assumption of homogeneity of the product of firms included in the same industry. In the place of groups of firms (the industry) producing an identical commodity, we now have a continuum of qualitative variations among products of different firms. In this sense, Chamberlin's contribution (as was to be better shown by a subsequent contribution by Robert Triffin, 1940) represented a shift in the direction of the modern axiomatic theory of general economic equilibrium, in which each economic agent represents a case by itself.

---

[61] On Richard Kahn and Joan Robinson, cf. below, § 14.9.
[62] Edward Chamberlin (1899–1967), student and then professor at Harvard, focused all his research on the theme of monopolistic competition.

11.   Marshall's heritage in contemporary economic thought

Marshall had an exceptional impact on the development of economic thought, stronger than is commonly recognised. The reason for this under-valuation is that his contribution embraced two distinct if not opposite streams of economic culture. On the one side, the Marshallian *vulgata* still played in the second half of the twentieth century, and often still plays today, a central role in basic economic instruction in secondary schools and undergraduate university textbooks, with an impact which is felt not only in the theory of prices (equilibrium of the firm and the industry) but also in collateral disciplines, from industrial economics to public finance. With its apparent greater generality and rigour, the general economic equilibrium approach, despite frequent references, often remained in the background, due to its sterility for concrete applications. On the other side, the Marshallian approach to economic development as an evolutionary process, its nuanced notion of competition and the attribution to monetary disturbances of a key role in determining the cyclical swings of the economy, constituted a strong call for important streams of contemporary thought, intermediate between heterodoxy and orthodoxy.

Apart from references to Schumpeter, indeed, it was to Marshallian evolutionism that theories of the firm like those by Nelson and Winter (1982) referred; these theories considered the firm as an organism whose genes consist in a set of routines. Technological progress takes place, according to such theories, through substitution of old routines with new ones, more adequate to the tasks of the firm and the environment in which it operates. The spreading of such routines then takes place through a mechanism of spreading and selection, in which latecomers are doomed to succumb. (Once again, the reference here was more to Lamarck's genetic theories than to Darwin's: exactly as had already happened for Marshall, through the intermediary of Spencer's sociology.)

This approach had an important role in bringing attention to dynamic processes and technological change[63] with a wealth of empirical research. However, at the theoretical level it remained trapped in the same blind alley in which Marshall had found himself. Indeed, the promises of a vague conceptual apparatus, which precisely because of its imprecision seems ready to take into account different aspects of the process of economic development, cannot be kept when one seeks to formalise in rigorous models a theoretical approach which tried to circumvent the need

---

[63] It thus favoured the development of research streams with similar orientation, albeit with important differences: cf. the survey by Dosi 1988.

for a frontal critique of the neoclassical notion of equilibrium and the tradition of which this notion is a constituent element.

As for the Marshallian notion of competition, the idea of economies of scale external to the individual firm but internal to the industry (or rather to a local industrial system) found an important outlet in the recent flourishing of studies on local economies, in particular on the notion of the industrial district, already hinted at in Marshall's work.[64] In this case too, however, apart from throwing light on the concrete importance of a particular form of territorial aggregation of small and medium firms and on the factors which favour them, the theory of the industrial district did not manage (nor did it aim) to develop an analytical apparatus endowed with sufficient generality to allow a theory of prices and distribution to be built on top.

Finally, in so far as monetary theory is concerned, Marshall's influence was flanked by similar influences from other theoretical streams, such as the Austrian one of Wicksell and Hayek, who also sought an explanation for cyclical phenomena and unemployment in monetary 'disturbances'. Thus reinforced, the impact of the Marshallian monetary tradition on economic culture was very strong, but the main result was to favour sterilisation of Keynes's theory within the so-called neoclassical synthesis which, as we shall see below, tried to render compatible the long period equilibrium of traditional marginalist theory on the one side with the cyclical swings and unemployment on the other, relegating the latter to the short period.

On the whole, therefore, the undoubted conceptual richness of Marshall's thought had a far-reaching, lasting impact on economic thought, with important ramifications which persist in contemporary economic thought. However, the problem which Marshall himself had encountered remains unsolved: that of translating such an intrinsically dynamic conceptual apparatus into theoretical models which, linked to the marginalist tradition, remain based on the irremediably static key concept of equilibrium between demand and supply.

[64] Cf. Becattini 1989; Brusco 1989.

14   John Maynard Keynes

1.   Life and writings[1]

John Maynard Keynes was born in Cambridge, England, on 5 June 1883, the first son of John Neville Keynes (1852–1949) and Florence Brown (1861–1958). His father, a pupil of Marshall, was a scholar of logic and economics, author of *The scope and method of political economy* (1891), but had preferred an administrative career to prospects of a professorship, reaching the top of the Cambridge University administration; his mother was one of the first female graduates of that university, and the first woman to be elected mayor of Cambridge.[2]

Maynard's curriculum was in keeping with the highest standards of the bourgeoisie: secondary school at Eton, university at King's College, Cambridge. Here he studied mathematics and classical humanities; he was also elected into the elitist secret society of the Apostles, devoted to 'the pursuit of truth'. In a generation shortly preceding that of Keynes, another Apostle, the philosopher George Edward Moore (1873–1958), had rejected the utilitarian identification between 'to be good' and 'to do good', proposing an ethics of inner self-searching for truth and personal coherence. In the climate of cultural renewal characterising the Edwardian period, to Keynes and his friends this meant a radical reappraisal of Victorian culture and ethics, manifested also in their personal conduct (marked by extreme intellectualism and the pursuit of aesthetic pleasures), while, departing from Moore, they rejected the idea of general rules of conduct, substituted by confidence in the ability of the 'elect' to evaluate case by case what the right behaviour would be.

This society enlisted among others the novelist Lytton Strachey and philosophers Bertrand Russell and Alfred Whitehead. Some of the

---

[1] The main biographies are those by Skidelsky (1983, 1992, 2000) and Moggridge (1992); now outdated is the biography by Harrod (1951). The *Collected writings of John Maynard Keynes*, in thirty volumes, edited by Donald Moggridge and (vols. 15–18) Elizabeth Johnson, were published at the initiative of the Royal Economic Society between 1971 and 1989 (Macmillan, London).
[2] On John Neville Keynes (with a wide recourse to his personal diaries), cf. Deane 2001.

Apostles, in particular Strachey, with other leading protagonists of English literature such as Virginia Woolf and Vanessa Bell, gave life in the following decades to the Bloomsbury circle (from the name of the residential area of London where the protagonists of the circle lived). Keynes maintained close relations with this group, at least up to his marriage.

After graduating in mathematics, in 1906 Keynes took the civil service entrance examinations but, coming in second, had to content himself with a job at the India Office (while the top of the list traditionally went to the Treasury). There was little work to be done, and Keynes had the time to write a treatise on the Indian monetary system (published in 1913, under the title *Indian currency and finance*), and a long essay on the theory of probability. Thanks to this essay, after a first, unsuccessful attempt, in 1909, he obtained a fellowship at King's College, Cambridge. Keynes was to continue active involvement with his college for the whole of his life; elected Bursar in 1924, he topped up the college coffers with a series of shrewd real-estate investments and adventurous speculation on the stock exchange.

In 1908, before obtaining the King's fellowship, Keynes resigned from the India Office and accepted a post as lecturer in economics at Cambridge; his modest salary was paid by Pigou out of his own pocket, thus continuing a tradition started by his master, Marshall. In that year Pigou had succeeded Marshall to the economics chair; later, in the 1930s, he was to become a theoretical adversary of Keynes and the Keynesians. As from 1911, with Marshall's support, Keynes took over editorship of the *Economic Journal*; two years later he also became secretary of the Royal Economic Society. He was to hold these two appointments for more than three decades, in a period of exceptional vitality, especially for the *Economic Journal*, which rose to be the most prestigious economic journal of the time.

During the First World War, following the example of his Bloomsbury friends, Keynes declared himself a conscientious objector, although working – with some inconsistency, which drew criticism from his more intransigent literary friends – at the Treasury on issues connected with financing the war effort. In 1919 he was a member of the English delegation at the peace conference in Versailles, but opposed the 'reparations' imposed on Germany, considering them an unsustainable burden on the German economy and society: thus he resigned and, once back in Cambridge, addressed the subject in his most successful *The economic consequences of the peace*.[3]

---

[3] Keynes's criticisms were not based on the 'internal' sustainability of reparations, i.e. on the fiscal burden they implied, but on their 'external' sustainability, i.e. the chances of

By now a widely recognised writer, Keynes contributed on the main themes of economic policy with a series of articles; he also published some books, among which were the *Treatise on probability* in 1921 (a revised version of his 1909 fellowship dissertation, to which Keynes dedicated more years of work and more care than to any other of his publications) and the *Tract on monetary reform* in 1923.[4] To his various academic responsibilities he then added that of chairman of an insurance company and, in partnership, launched into speculation on the exchange markets on his own account and on behalf of relatives and friends (although the results were not always happy). In 1925, having spent a great part of his life cultivating male friendships, Maynard married a famous Russian dancer, Lydia Lopokova, notwithstanding the ill-concealed opposition of his Bloomsbury friends.

In 1930 and 1936, respectively, he published the two works – the *Treatise on money* and the *General theory of employment, interest and money* – to which he principally owes his fame as a theoretical economist. Other important contributions were the lively and provocative essays collected in the *Essays in persuasion* (1931), and the well-documented and incisive biographies collected in the *Essays in biography* (1933). In the same year that saw the *General theory* published, Keynes inaugurated in Cambridge the Arts Theatre, built almost entirely from his own private funds; his wife Lydia was prima ballerina in the inaugural performance. In the following year he had a heart attack and was obliged to scale down his workload.

In 1940 he was appointed adviser to the Treasury and plunged once again into problems of war finance, negotiating loans from the United States. In 1941 he also joined the board of the Bank of England. In the

---

realising a surplus in other items of the balance of payments sufficiently large to offset unilateral transfers for reparations. Keynes's attention focused on the impossibility of generating a sufficient surplus in the balance of trade, and thus gave rise to a wide-ranging debate centred on export and import elasticities to the exchange rate and to income. As a matter of fact, Germany actually showed a substantial capital inflow, thanks also to loans from the United States. Keynes was thus considered responsible for too benevolent an attitude towards Germany: a thesis which took on renewed vigour after the rise of nazism and the outbreak of the Second World War, as was testified for instance by the essay by Belgian Étienne Mantoux, *The Carthaginian peace, or the economic consequences of Mr. Keynes*, published posthumously in 1946, a year after its author died in the war (cf. Skidelsky 1983, pp. 397–400).

[4] In this work Keynes distinguished between internal and external stabilisation of the value of money (a distinction probably suggested by Sraffa: cf. below, § 16.1) and declared preference for stabilisation of internal prices rather than of the external value of the national currency; he was therefore critical of the idea of the pound returning to the gold standard – decided, however, a few months later, on 28 April 1925. Moreover, by the decision of the then Chancellor of the Exchequer Winston Churchill, return to the gold standard took place at the pre-war parity; this implied an over-valuation of the pound and a loss of competitiveness for English manufactures. Keynes criticised the decision scathingly in a brilliant pamphlet, *The economic consequences of Mr. Churchill*, 1925.

following year he was made a lord, with the title of Baron of Tilton. During the war Keynes had already begun to produce a series of plans to reform the post-war international economic order; in July 1944 he played a leading role in the Bretton Woods conference, although the greater bargaining power of the United States led to final results that were closer to the US position (the 'White Plan', from the name of the American delegate) than to his own. Suffering a further heart attack, he died in his country house (at Tilton in Sussex) on 21 April 1946.

There is an immense literature on Keynes's thought: we might say that there is no aspect of his theories which has not seen a variety of interpretations. This holds true also for the relationship between his analysis and the times he lived in. Many – indeed the overwhelming majority – concur in drawing a parallel between Keynes and the 1929 Great Crisis (or, more precisely, with the recession in the United Kingdom after return to the gold standard in 1925). There can in any case be no doubt that the conditions of high and persistent unemployment in the 1930s at least favoured the spread of Keynesian ideas. Some commentators stress other aspects, such as the distinctly British viewpoint of Keynes, who saw his country losing ground to the United States, both in manufacturing and in the financial markets, but more rapidly in the former, which appears to account for the greater interest he took in the latter. At the same time, as far as problems of reconstructing the international monetary system were concerned, Keynes outlined schemes which took into account the interests of the less strong currencies, as in fact the British pound was likely to be in a world dominated by the US dollar.

Indeed, in laying out the foundations of his theoretical analysis Keynes, whose exceptional pragmatism was repeatedly stressed by his contemporaries, mirrored the main economic events of a period of time which included the Great Crisis, but which was not limited to the 1930s. Keynes's basic commitment was as an economist whose profession coincided with his civic sense. His great design was to contribute to a reformed system of capitalism, which should guarantee increasing fairness together with an ample degree of freedom and efficiency. The design emerged in fuller definition when confronted with the rise of totalitarian systems: fascism and nazism in Italy and Germany and Stalinism in the Soviet Union. Hence his recognition of the end of the ideology of economic liberalism in its most simplistic and extreme form: *The end of laissez-faire*, as he entitled a pamphlet published in 1926. Reconsidering from this perspective the role played by the state in the economy, a twofold need emerged: on the one hand, to provide a critique of the then dominant theory, showing how insufficient were the equilibrating mechanisms of the free market; on the other hand – on the positive side – to construct a theory of state intervention and hence of economic policy. This is the project which, with his scientific activity and his direct involvement, Keynes endeavoured to carry out.

For ease in exposition we may distinguish three historical stages, and three corresponding stages in Keynes's research work. The first stage embraced the first decades of the twentieth century, up to the Wall Street crash in 1929; the second stage reached the outbreak of the Second World War, thus corresponding to the years of the Great Depression; the third stage began when the economic problems connected with the war brought the pattern of international economic relations to general attention. In parallel, the first stage in the development of Keynes's analysis went from the tract on the Indian monetary and financial system (1913) up to the end of the 1920s; the second period was that which led from the *Treatise on money*, published in 1930, to the *General theory* (1936), including the immediately subsequent writings which defended the approach proposed in the latter work and stressed its novelty; the last stage was that of *How to pay for the war* (1940) and of proposals such as the Clearing Union, for a new international economic set-up. In general, commentators focus attention mainly, if not exclusively, on the second stage, since the writings belonging to this period are rightly considered Keynes's main contributions in the theoretical field. However, much is lost on the way, both in so far as interpretation of Keynes's thought is concerned, and with respect to his 'programme for action'. In particular, his contribution to the theory of probability, with his notion of uncertainty, merit treatment in their own right, before considering his contributions to the theory of money and employment.

2.   Probability and uncertainty

As mentioned above, Keynes's original specialisation was that of a mathematician with a leaning to logic. Between 1906 and 1911 Keynes devoted most of his research work to an essay on the theory of probability. This work, taken up again in 1920 when Keynes had already acquired fame as an economist, was further revised and finally published as the *Treatise on probability*.

In order to understand this work we must approach it in terms of the culture of Cambridge at the time. The tradition inherited from the past was that of John Stuart Mill's logical inductivism. In this tradition we also find Maynard's father, John Neville Keynes, who attempted in his 1891 book an eclectic synthesis between it and German historicism, the influence of which was mediated in Cambridge by Marshall; fusion of an abstract-deductive approach and historical-inductive approach was attributed to a tradition which went from Smith to Mill, while Ricardo was considered too unilateral in his adherence to abstract models of reasoning. In the same years that saw Keynes at work on probability theory, another Apostle, the philosopher Bertrand Russell (1872–1970), laid the foundations of analytic philosophy and together with Alfred North Whitehead (1861–1947) went ahead on the project of deducing mathematics from purely logical premises, publishing between 1910 and 1913 the three volumes of the *Principia mathematica*.

Keynes thus tackled the theory of probability in the cultural context of a lively debate on the themes of inductive knowledge and the role of deductive logic. His ambition was to build a general theory of knowledge and rational behaviour, with respect to which the cases of perfect certainty and full ignorance are the extremes. For this reason Keynes rejected the frequentist interpretation of probability, which is applicable only to that class of phenomena for which we can assume the possibility of an infinite series of repetitions under unchanged conditions (as with dice throwing). He proposed instead a 'rationalist' approach, centred on the degree of confidence which it is reasonable to have in a certain event, given the state of knowledge.

Let us mention briefly some aspects of this approach. In the first place, its importance lies in the fact that it deals with the problem of rational behaviour in a context in which the subject is devoid of certainties. In other terms, humans pursue rational behaviour even if they know that they do not have objective foundations sufficient for a full and certain evaluation of the outcomes of their actions. Rational behaviour is then connected to subjective evaluations based on experience as well as on personal intuitions; probability calculus is the technique by which these evaluations are screened. 'The probable [. . .] is that which it is rational for us to believe. [. . .] The probable is the hypothesis on which it is rational for us to act' (Keynes 1921, p. 339).

Secondly, Keynes distinguished between the proposition which expresses the probability of a given event, and the confidence which one can have in such an evaluation, named 'weight of the argument'. When relevant empirical evidence – understood as the set of information directly or indirectly useful for our assessment of the event – increases, then the weight of the argument increases, while the probability attributed to the event may increase or diminish or remain unchanged.

Thirdly, Keynes rejected the idea that it is possible in general to attribute a numerical value to the probability of events. In his opinion, we should distinguish three classes of events: in the first we have those events for which it is possible to define probability as a rational number coming between zero and one (for instance, in the game of dice, or mortality tables: in general, in all cases of actuarial risk); in the second class we have those elements for which we have a sufficient basis of knowledge to express non-quantitative opinions on partial ranking of events (for instance, on the basis of our model of the working of the economy, we may say that the rate of interest is more likely to increase than to diminish in the next three months); in the third class we have those events for which the knowledge basis is insufficient for us to formulate even relative judgements of this kind (is it more likely that the president of the United States in 2050 will be called Mary, or that the Italian president will be called Paola?). When confronted with events belonging to the second or third class, it may be rational to rely on 'conventional' forms of behaviour, conforming to or possibly anticipating the behaviour of the majority.[5]

Fourthly, for these very reasons Keynes's approach should be kept distinct from the subjective one developed a few years later by Ramsey (1931), De Finetti (1930, 1931, 1937) and Savage (1954), who saw probabilities in terms of subjective evaluations expressed through bets, and thus generally quantifiable. While Ramsey viewed the existence of probability relations such as those described by Keynes with scepticism, the latter – notwithstanding his admiration for the intelligence and exuberant personality of his young friend[6] – showed no signs of modifying his position in the face of criticism and of the development of the new

---

[5] Cf. Pasquinelli and Marzetti Dall'Aste Brandolini 1994, p. xxiv. According to these commentators, uncertainty of short run expectations (those which entrepreneurs rely on when deciding on production levels) may be connected to the 'known probability' of the *Treatise on probability*, while uncertainty of long run expectations (those relevant for entrepreneurs' decisions on investments) may be connected to 'unknown probability'. This is considered to be the origin of Keynes's reference to the role of entrepreneurial 'animal spirits' in investment decisions, taken by rational agents more on the basis of an 'urge to action' than of actuarial comparison between risks of losses and possibilities of gains. However, this interpretation appears to be too drastic. The animal spirits were based on, or at any rate went side by side with, a rational evaluation of the situation, in which alternatives existed for the employment and accumulation of wealth that fell within the second class of events. Indeed, the first and third classes of events may be considered extreme cases of relatively low interest in the economic field. Keynes took up and gradually re-elaborated in his works, on the implicit basis of the *Treatise on probability*, a notion of expectations already present in the economics literature, and thus arrived at the 'canonical' systematisation of the notion in the *General theory*: the meaning of the notion of expectations and their analytical role only became clear once the theoretical framework the notion was to find a place in had been specified.

[6] To Frank Ramsey (1903–30) Keynes dedicated fond and eulogistic pages, collected with other biographical writings (including the two substantial essays on Malthus and Marshall) in the *Essays in biography* (1933). In the economic field, we may recall Ramsey's model of growth based on intertemporal maximisation (Ramsey 1928) and, in the context of his work on the theory of probability, the axiomatisation of preferences connected to subjective expectations (Ramsey 1931).

approach, which drew upon Bernoulli's insights (cf. above, § 10.2) to go on, with Savage, to combine axiomatic treatment of probabilities and preferences.[7]

As may be seen from these broad outlines, the Keynesian notion of uncertainty, which played a crucial role in his theory of money, income and employment, has rather more substance than the famous distinction drawn by Knight (1921) between 'probabilistic risk' and 'uncertainty', useful as it may be. The same holds for the question of the limits of economic agents' knowledge, in connection with which the Austrian school is often associated, although it received bare mention from Menger (1871) in this context, to be developed by Hayek only in the second stage of his research activity (cf. above, § 11.6), hence a couple of decades after Keynes.

3. The *Treatise on money*

As we have seen, the two great economic works by Keynes are the *Treatise on money* and the *General theory*; we will now focus attention on them. Various other works of his played an important role in the economic debate of the time and are relevant to interpretation of his thought, but on these aspects we refer readers to the many commentaries and the edition of his *Collected works*.[8]

Of all his economic works, the *Treatise* was the one on which Keynes worked the longest – over six years. This was also a period of great intellectual ferment in Cambridge. Beginning in 1922, the *Economic Journal* (edited by Keynes) published a series of important contributions to the debate on the Marshallian theory of the firm, while again within the framework of Marshallian theory – but referring more closely to Marshall's *Official papers* and the oral tradition of his teaching than to the *Principles* – a number of works were published on the relationship between monetary phenomena and short period production levels, such as the books by Dennis Robertson (1890–1963), *A study of industrial fluctuations* (1915) and *Banking policy and the price level* (1926); by Ralph

---

[7] In effect, the notion of animal spirits seems to have been meant to stress the existence of a residuum of unavoidable, accepted imprecision in subjective evaluations of the situation in which economic decisions are taken, hence the unsuitability of the scheme of quantitative bets to describe such situations. The distinction between short and long period expectations indicated that the dimension of such a residuum – significantly larger in the latter case – had notable analytical relevance.

[8] Among the many works on interpretation of Keynes's thought, let us recall Asimakopulos 1991; Kregel 1976; Minsky 1975; Moggridge 1976; Pasinetti 1974, ch. 2; Tonveronachi 1983; and Vicarelli 1977.

Hawtrey (1879–1975), *Currency and credit* (1919); and by Arthur Cecil Pigou on *Industrial fluctuations* (1927a).[9]

Keynes was always involved with the economic policy debate. In his 1923 *Tract on monetary reform*, he confronted the post-war tensions – the sense of instability, mainly connected to inflation and unemployment – opposing the then dominant recipe of a return to stable rules of the game, namely to automatic equilibrating mechanisms such as the gold standard. Keynes perceived that stabilisation of the exchange rate, at which the gold standard aimed, did not necessarily ensure internal price stability; keeping into account the conflicting interests of savers, entrepreneurs and workers he considered both inflation and deflation as damaging for the economy. Thus, money should not be considered neutral, and should be managed with an eye to internal price stabilisation. Neutrality of the return to the gold standard was also ruled out by the different behaviour of two sectors within the economy, one subjected and the other not subjected to foreign competition. All this ruled out the simple policy of *laissez-faire* predicated by the political establishment.

In an important 1926 pamphlet, *The end of laissez-faire*, Keynes remarked that the dogmatic laissez-faire principle, though adopted as the foundation of the then current liberalism, was not upheld in the writings of the great classical economists. Moreover, an efficient social organisation – as under certain circumstances capitalism could be – should not be considered as an end in itself, and care should be taken that it did not run counter to our basic system of values. Equity, besides efficiency, was needed for the very stability of society.

All this is very similar to the distinction between economic and political liberalism: the first one taken in isolation – namely dogmatic laissez-faire – was found to be both anachronistic in the circumstances of modern capitalism, and not a moral value in itself. A new economic wisdom, on which to rely for the governance of modern capitalism, was called for; its construction was the task that Keynes set himself.

Such, then, was the background that saw the birth of the *Treatise*. In a number of respects, it too may be considered as a work within the Marshallian tradition; at the same time, however, the innovative elements constituted a bridge to the radical novelties of the *General theory*.

---

[9] In very broad outline, Robertson focused attention on monetary elements in so far as short cycles were concerned, and on the crowding of purchases for the renewal of plant and machinery and for durable capital goods caused by the alternation of 'swarms' of innovations with periods of relative stagnation in technological change in so far as cycles of medium duration were concerned (following Schumpeter 1912, in this respect: cf. below, § 15.3); Hawtrey stressed the role of movements in interest rates on short-term loans, hence on the 'inventory cycle'; Pigou dwelt upon the sequence of waves of optimism and pessimism.

Keynes avoided head-on criticism of the theoretical nucleus of the marginalist tradition, consisting in the idea of a long run equilibrium characterised by full employment of resources, labour included, and by the neutrality of money (that is, by the fact that the quantity of money in circulation affects the level of prices but not the 'real' variables of the system, such as production and employment levels). This view of the long period thus remained in the background, especially for readers untrained in the subtle qualifications of Marshall's teaching.

As far as the interpretation of the working of the monetary and financial sector was concerned, the *Treatise* took up and developed the Marshallian critique of the quantity theory of money, in the version proposed by Irving Fisher, with his mechanical relationship between money supply and general price level. On the positive side, Keynes developed the approach based on the 'Cambridge equation' for liquid stocks demand. As far as the real sector was concerned, Keynes proposed a two-sector model, which we shall now take a closer look at. The most interesting novelties of the *Treatise* concerned the connections between monetary and financial aspects on the one hand and real aspects on the other. Following the Marshallian methodological principle of focusing attention on short causal chains, Keynes set out to locate, link by link, the cause-and-effect connections in the interrelations between changes in prices and produced quantities, the aim being to gain insight into the working of a monetary economy in perennial movement.

Keynes, then, utilised in his analysis a two-sector scheme: one sector produces investment goods, the other consumption goods. The problem thus arises of price index numbers, and Keynes showed that there could be no univocal answer, but only approximate ones. In other words, it is not possible to attribute to the notion of a general level of prices that analytical rigour which would be indispensable if we were to rely on it as one of the central elements in a theoretical construction. This observation may be seen not only as a stricture on the conceptual foundation of the quantity theory itself, but also as expressing diffidence towards aggregate notions: a diffidence typical of the Marshallian tradition, which should be kept in mind when confronted with interpretations of Keynes's theory based on the opposition between an aggregate 'macro' analysis and a disaggregated 'micro' one.

The 'fundamental equations' constitute the analytical core of the *Treatise*. They express, through the effects that may cause prices to diverge from their equilibrium levels, the relations between prices and demand and supply levels in the two sectors. Moreover, they provide a sequential scheme that connects production levels and realised profits. Keynes utilised here notions of income, profits and savings at variance with those normally used in modern national accounting, and with those that he himself was to utilise in the *General theory*. These notions are in fact defined in the *Treatise* so as to allow for their use within a sequential analysis. At the centre of the analysis – and this is an element which anticipated a crucial aspect of the *General theory* – there was the distinction between investments and savings. In so far as they are an effect of the decisions of two different groups of economic agents (entrepreneurs and families), investments and savings may differ; their difference determines disequilibria between demand and supply in the two sectors, with price changes which generate unforeseen profits or losses,[10] to which entrepreneurs react with changes in production and employment levels.

Savings are assumed to be connected to wealth, and hence relatively stable in the face of short period changes in income. Cyclical dynamics, interpretation of which was the object of the book, thus depends on the variability of investments. Given the scant influence of investments in inventories, Keynes focused attention on investments in fixed capital, mainly connected to Schumpeterian processes of innovation-imitation, although the rate at which they are enacted depends on long run interest rates.

This is the theoretical core of the work. We should add that Keynes devoted many pages – most of the book, in fact – to description of the different channels of liquidity creation and decisions on holding financial assets, with a study in applied economics that remains a model of its kind to this day. Although it develops a line of argumentation proposed by Marshall with his analysis of demand for monetary stocks, this is an aspect commonly overlooked by commentators. It is, however, interesting not only in itself, suggesting a system of interrelations between financial stocks and real flows, and as an anticipation of the *General theory*, but also as an indication of anti-cyclical economic policy lines. From this latter point of view, in particular, Keynes analysed the transmission mechanisms of impulses from short run interest rates, influenced by the central bank, to long run interest rates, which in their turn impact on fixed capital investment decisions.

In the context of an open economy, to those already mentioned above other reasons for disequilibria are added. Again with reference to the

---

[10] In the *Treatise* terminology, profits corresponded exclusively to such unforeseen gains or losses, and were not included in the definition of income. Interest on capital advanced, usually included in the category of entrepreneurial income, was instead considered as part of production costs and included in income. (The category of profit normally utilised by Keynes thus mirrored the marginalist and Marshallian view of the rate of interest as the price for the service of the 'factor of production capital', while the wage was the price for the use of the productive factor labour.)

fundamental equations, a different relationship between average productivity and wages in different countries, and in particular in countries at different levels of development, generates disequilibria in the balance of trade, and hence in internal demand. Thus it follows that the exchange rate is a crucial policy tool in the absence of adjustment in internal money wages and/or productivity.

The *Treatise* also included analysis of international monetary relations, a usual theme for Keynes both in the 1920s, when he took part in the debate on the return to the gold standard, and in the 1940s, as we shall see below (§ 5). Keynes stressed the desirability of an international monetary standard, and in the place of gold proposed (in the wake of Irving Fisher's tabular standard and analogous proposals advanced by Marshall and others) a currency issued by an international central bank constrained by the obligation to keep its value stable in terms of a basket of sixty internationally tradable goods. In this context, characterised by fixed exchange rates among national currencies, national monetary policies lose any autonomy, and it then becomes necessary to resort to fiscal policies, and in particular to public works, in order to support employment – another theme which then appeared on the scene, to assume a central role later in the *General theory*.

4.   From the *Treatise* to the *General theory*

There has been much debate among Keynes's commentators on the crucial stage of transition from the *Treatise* to the *General theory*, regarding both definition of the main innovative elements of Keynes's theory and evaluation of the contribution of ideas and suggestions from that group of young economists who constituted the so-called 'Cambridge Circus'.

The process of transition began when the *Treatise* was about to appear. Keynes, characteristically, succeeded in viewing his own ideas with critical detachment as soon as he had put them forward, and even while correcting and revising the proofs of the *Treatise* he arrived at the conclusion that a different analytical structure would have been better fitted to support his main ideas on the governance of the market economy. The key moment in the transition was the passage from analysis of disequilibria to analysis of underemployment equilibrium. While the causal nexus going from interest rate to investments and from these to income remained, the possibility – indeed, the likelihood – was recognised that the marginal propensity to consume might take on values lower than one, which opened the way to attributing investments with a crucial role in determination of the equilibrium level of income. Choice between the many possible equilibriums then required a theory of interest rates.

However, Keynes did not build a new theory of value as the foundation for his analysis but settled for the more familiar confines of short period analysis, tried and tested and – thanks to the diffusion of Marshallism in England – more readily understandable to his readers. Among other things, he was driven in this direction by Richard Kahn, his pupil and closest collaborator as well as being animator and 'messenger-angel' of the Circus.[11]

Between the *Treatise* and the *General theory* there are thus certain crucial differences in analytical structure. The key ideas, however, remained unchanged: as Keynes said in the preface to the second of the two works (Keynes 1936, p. vi), between them there is a 'natural evolution', not a 'change of view'. The crucial idea, diametrically opposed to a central tenet of traditional marginalist theory, was that in a monetary economy entrepreneurial decisions on production levels are not necessarily consistent – or automatically made so by market mechanisms – with the equilibrium situation characterised by full utilisation of available resources. In the *Treatise* we find an analysis of disequilibria; the idea of long run equilibrium remained in the background, but with a markedly reduced heuristic value because of the central importance attributed to the analysis of disequilibria, in the absence of relevant equilibrating mechanisms. In the *General theory*, the main thesis – as we shall see in greater detail in the next section – was precisely this: the persistence of equilibriums characterised by unemployment is possible, since market economies do not have reliable automatic mechanisms to bring them to equilibriums characterised by higher levels of income and employment. Hence the importance of active management of the economy primarily with the monetary-financial lever in the *Treatise*, with both it and the fiscal lever (public expenditure in particular) in the *General theory*.[12]

Between publication of the first and second of these two works, as we have seen, the analytical structure supporting this thesis changed. In this

[11] In other words, Kahn was the intermediary between Keynes and the group of young economists who, grouped in the 'Circus', discussed the *Treatise on money*: cf. Keynes 1973, vol. 13, pp. 337–43. (The expression 'messenger angel' was Meade's: cf. ibid., p. 339.) On this stage of transition see the reconstruction by Kahn himself (1974, 1984). On the same lines, cf. also Moggridge 1976. Patinkin 1976, 1987, was of a different opinion, rather inclined to isolate the development of Keynes's thought from the extreme positions of his young followers and to bring it back to the neoclassical tradition.

[12] In the *Treatise* and in various other works of the period Keynes seemed to suggest recourse to an anti-cyclical fiscal policy with the balancing of the public budget ensured as an average over the cycle, when monetary policy was ineffective; in the *General theory* the connection between long run deficiencies of aggregate demand and policies of public expenditures became clearer. Over time, Keynes seemed to have become more and more sceptical about the use of public works as a tool of anti-cyclical policy, especially in the presence of short cycles. (These aspects have been pointed out to me by Mario Tonveronachi.)

respect, the influence of the 'Circus', and in particular of Richard Kahn, appears important. The contribution of the latter consisted not only, nor indeed prevalently, in the multiplier mechanism,[13] although it constituted one of the three analytic pillars of the *General theory*, together with the notion of effective demand and the theory of the rate of interest based on the speculative demand for money. For good or ill, Kahn's main contribution in all likelihood consisted in suggesting reliance of the *General theory* on the Marshallian short period equilibrium. This was, as we have seen, a tried and tested analytical system (developed in particular by Kahn in his fellowship dissertation and in other respects by Joan Robinson in her 1933 book: cf. above, § 13.10) which, after all, constituted the live core of the Marshallian tradition in Cambridge when Keynes was writing. At the same time, the variant of this approach developed by Kahn focused on a system of firms under strong competitive pressure but endowed with some margins of strategic autonomy and some decision-making power, not necessarily characterised by decreasing returns but constrained in their growth by difficulty in finding market outlets for their products. It was thus an approach which saw a crucial role played by market imperfections, and which thus differed substantially from the Marshallian *vulgata* of perfectly competitive equilibriums based on the pairs of U-shaped cost curves (average cost and marginal cost as a function of quantity produced, for the firm and the industry, for the short and the long run) proposed by Pigou that found their way, through Viner and others, into the textbooks (cf. above, § 13.7). Actually the theory had already come in for devastating criticism from Sraffa in his 1925 and 1926 articles; moreover, it implied a passive role for entrepreneurs, alien to Keynes's conceptual framework that had them playing an active role with respect to decisions both on production levels and on investments in new productive capacity.

Within the 'Circus' a variety of positions were represented alongside Kahn's. At one extreme we find (with Meade and Austin Robinson) a more traditional view, closer to Pigou's *vulgata*, even if not identifiable with it, and in any case significantly more open to the developments of the 'neoclassical synthesis' (cf. below, § 17.5). At the other extreme we have a view largely external to the marginalist approach as a whole (with Sraffa, who in those crucial years had already laid the foundations of *Production of commodities by means of commodities*: cf. below, ch. 16). With the committed support of Joan Robinson and the influence of Marshall's teachings, Kahn's central role and intelligent devotion eventually prevailed, and indeed determined the analytical framework in which Keynes

---

[13] Among other things, Kahn's 1931 was an employment multiplier; its transformation into an income multiplier, as in the *General theory*, required development of a general analytical scheme. I owe this remark to Mario Tonveronachi.

presented his view of the monetary production economy. The question still remains tantalisingly open as to which theory Keynes would have developed if a different influence had prevailed over the analytical framework serving as the setting for his ideas. Thus, on the one hand we may wonder whether Keynes's ideas would have been distorted if they had been oriented more internally within the mainstream of marginalist theory, which is tantamount to asking whether Hicks's and Modigliani's 'neoclassical synthesis' (cf. below, § 17.5) was a natural development or a radical distortion of Keynes's analysis. On the other hand, we may question the legitimacy of a reformulation of Keynes's theory based on a classical approach or – what amounts more or less to the same thing – just how compatible Sraffa's and Keynes's analyses actually were and what scope there is to develop a 'Sraffian–Keynesian' approach as an alternative to the dominant marginalist theories. What is certain is that the 'compromise' suggested by Kahn (but also undoubtedly prompted by the Marshallian background of Keynes himself), despite its immediate success, showed significant limitations in the long run.[14]

5.   The *General theory*

The *General theory of employment, interest and money* appeared in February 1936. It immediately found a wide readership, although not quite repeating the success of *The economic consequences of the peace*. However, it had a more solid influence, concentrated in the field of professional economists and already in the air before publication thanks to a shrewd circulation of proofs among Keynes's colleagues and pupils. The impact was especially strong among the young scholars: from Harrod to Hicks, from Lerner to Samuelson, from Reddaway to Tarshis, hundreds of budding economists who were to occupy important positions in universities all over the world, but especially in the Anglo-Saxon world, rapidly adopted the new theory as a basic reference point in their own research work and teaching.

The *General theory* is not an easy book, and many 'Keynesian' economists did not read it. Philologically untenable interpretations, like the idea that Keynesian theory was based on the downward rigidity of wages and prices (when chapter 19 of the book discussed precisely the case of a reduction in money wages, showing that not even it guarantees an

---

[14] This is not to deny the unorthodox nature – relative to the marginalist approach – of the theoretical structure of the *General theory*. In this respect, the crucial point is the monetary and financial nature of the rate of interest, which implied abandonment of the traditional theory of the rate of profits. In chapter 17 of the *General theory*, indeed, Keynes went so far as to indicate, though in a not fully developed way, an inverse causal relation going from the rate of interest to the rate of profits.

increase in employment), could never have enjoyed the circulation they actually did if direct acquaintance with Keynes's book had been more widespread.[15]

First of all, let us take a look at the background to the *General theory*: what Keynes was aiming at and the crucial aspects of what he called 'the monetary theory of production'.[16] As we have seen, defence of a liberal political system based, among other things, on freedom of individual initiative in the economic arena required, according to Keynes, that the limits of the pure *laissez-faire* system be recognised; hence the need for active intervention of the state in the economy, in the interests not only of fairness but also of overall efficiency. Interpretation of the functioning of the 'monetary production economy' revolved upon the central characteristic represented by the conditions of uncertainty – as defined in the *Treatise on probability* – in which economic agents take their decisions. At the methodological level, this led to rejection of deterministic omni-comprehensive models and a preference for 'open' models, specifically designed for the problem under consideration, to be built with caution, and pondering the conditions under which individual causal relations hold.

Various other aspects of the set of concepts on which the more strictly analytical part of Keynes's theory was built also derived from uncertainty. This applied in particular to the role of the financial markets, which not only played an intermediary part between the active and passive financial positions of the different economic agents but also, and above all, provided an element of flexibility that allowed consumers to avoid choices too binding for the future, while meeting the need for entrepreneurs to take decisions on production levels and investments concerning the future. It is in this context that we find the distinction between short and long run expectations, the former concerning choices on current production, such that they can be promptly adjusted to results, the latter concerning future production, and hence decisions on investment in fixed capital; for these immediate adjustment is impossible without significant costs, so the impact which uncertainty has on them is indeed strong. Hence the relevance of the theory of investment and, within it, of financial factors (the influence exerted on investments by the interest rate simply summing them).

---

[15] Naturally, this does not mean that the assumption of downward rigidity of wages and prices could not be utilised within a reformulation of Keynes's theory in a different analytical framework, as was the case with the so-called neoclassical synthesis, but not to interpret 'what Keynes really meant'.

[16] 'The monetary theory of production' was the title of the lecture courses which Keynes gave in 1932 and 1933: cf. Keynes 1973, vol. 13, pp. 411–12 and 420–1.

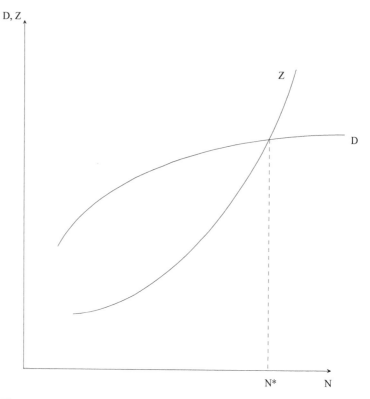

Figure 14.1

The analytical structure of the *General theory* rested on three pillars: the notion of effective demand, the multiplier mechanism and the theory of interest.[17] All these are well-known aspects, but they occasionally suffer some distortion – the first and third in particular – when illustrated in university textbooks, so let us take a brief look at them here.

The third of the twenty-four chapters of the *General theory* is devoted to the principle of effective demand. The 'point of effective demand' (figure 14.1) is defined by Keynes as the point of encounter of two curves: an aggregate supply function and an aggregate demand function. A point

---

[17] One might with good reason maintain that the theory of effective demand – which among other things left unsolved various analytical difficulties – was not essential to the result constituting the central objective of Keynes's analysis, namely the possibility of underemployment equilibrium. Rather, it was the theory of investments and savings which was crucial in this respect. However, in Keynes's argument the notion of effective demand did in fact play a crucial role.

to stress here is that these two curves are conceptually different from traditional supply and demand curves. At first sight, they are still two functions relating price and quantity; as a matter of fact, however, these two functions relate the number of employed workers to the entrepreneurs' evaluations regarding costs, on the one hand, and receipts on the other. More precisely, the aggregate supply function relates N, the number of employed workers, represented on the horizontal axis, to a Z variable, represented on the vertical axis, and defined as 'the aggregate supply price of the output from employing N men', while the aggregate supply function relates N to a variable D (represented like Z on the vertical axis), defined as 'the proceeds which entrepreneurs expect to receive from the employment of N men' (Keynes 1936, p. 25).

In other terms, Z indicates the minimum expected proceeds necessary to persuade entrepreneurs to employ N workers. For each given value of N, Z is thus equal to the total cost that entrepreneurs expect to have to bear if they employ N workers. Total cost obviously includes not only wages but also raw material costs, and overheads including amortisation of fixed capital, augmented by a profit sufficient to induce entrepreneurs to continue their activity. Conversely D indicates how much entrepreneurs expect to earn by selling on the market the product they hope to obtain through the employment of N workers. Both curves thus express the point of view – the evaluations – of the same category of economic agents, the entrepreneurs, not of two distinct and opposed groups of buyers and sellers (consumers and producers).[18]

Both expected costs and expected proceeds increase with the number of employed workers. Thus both functions are increasing ones, that is both Z and D increase with N. However, Z increases ever more rapidly (its second derivative is positive), while D increases ever more slowly (its second derivative is negative). This feature of the two functions may be justified in various ways. As far as effective demand D is concerned, Keynes remarked that it is made up of two components, consumption and investment; because of a 'psychological law', the first component increases but less than income, and hence than employment, while the second component depends on the entrepreneurs' long run expectations, so it may be considered as given in the context of determination of the point of effective demand. As far as Z is concerned, in the Marshallian context of Keynes's theory it was natural to assume that when the number of employed workers increased (while, in the short period context,

---

[18] It is clear that Keynes's construct left open the crucial problem of the construction of aggregate curves, referring to the evaluations of all entrepreneurs as a whole and not of an individual entrepreneur.

it is assumed that the productive equipment remains unchanged), the marginal cost turned out to be increasing.[19]

The 'point of effective demand' is the one at which $D = Z$. It thus tells us which is the expected level of employment, and hence of production, given the entrepreneurs' short run expectations regarding costs and proceeds.[20] Assuming short period expectations be fulfilled, analysis focused on the notion of aggregate demand and its constituent elements, consumption and investment.[21] To these elements Keynes devoted book 3 (chapters 8–10) and book 4, i.e. the central part of the *General theory*, after a book 2 devoted to 'definitions and ideas' and before two conclusive books devoted to 'money-wages and prices' and 'short notes suggested by the general theory'.

As we have seen, Keynes made a sharp distinction between decisions concerning consumption and decisions concerning investment. The two kinds of decisions are taken by different categories of economic agents

[19] This implied an inverse relation between real wage and employment analogous to the one postulated by all versions of marginalist theory. This was an assumption that Keynes derived from Marshall, who maintained that in the course of the trade cycle the real wage would increase in periods of crisis and diminish in periods of recovery. Within marginalist theory, as we know, this assumption played a central role since the mechanism of adjustment ensuring automatic tendency to full employment equilibrium is based on it. Within Keynes's theory, which rejected this adjustment mechanism, the assumption of an inverse relation between real wage and employment was not essential, and could have been abandoned, as in fact Keynes was ready to do when confronted with Dunlop's 1938 and Tarshis's 1939 empirical criticisms. Indeed, as is obvious, abandonment of that assumption (following a sizeable mass of empirical evidence on the pro-cyclical nature of real wage movements) reinforces the Keynesian critique of the thesis of an automatic tendency towards full employment equilibrium.

[20] Therefore, it should not be interpreted as a point of equilibrium between two opposite forces of demand and supply, let alone as a stable equilibrium. In order to proceed in this direction, as all macroeconomics manuals have long done, it is necessary to substitute entrepreneurs' evaluations with an aggregate demand function (consumption plus investments, in the simplified case of an economy closed to the outside world) opposed to an aggregate supply function (production). To the left of the point of equilibrium, aggregate demand is higher than supply, with a resulting fall in inventories; entrepreneurs are then induced to increase production, thus moving in the direction of equilibrium. In this situation it is usual to distinguish between *ex post* investments (which include the undesired change in inventories, and are those considered by national accounting statistics) and *ex ante* investments (those planned by entrepreneurs). As far as the former are concerned, equality with savings is an accounting identity; instead, when we refer to the latter, the accounting identity becomes a condition of equilibrium which may be verified or not, and we have a theory aimed at explaining the equilibrium level of employment. All this constitutes a reformulation of Keynes's theory in a context which may perhaps be similar to, but certainly does not coincide with, the original one. The connection may be realised through the assumption that short period expectations are always fulfilled. In this way expectations exit the scene, while Keynes's thesis that supply (production) adapts to demand remains.

[21] The *General theory* analysed the simplified case of a closed economy, and hence ignored exports. As an initial approximation, moreover, public expenditure is also ignored.

(respectively, families and firms), and thus follow two completely different logics. Consumption (and savings, defined as their complement
to income) essentially depend on income, and are thus endogenous to
the circular flow going from firms to families (income) and back to
firms (expenses).[22] Investments, on the other hand, depend on the
entrepreneurs' decisions (hence on their expectations), and are thus
exogenous to the circular income flow. As a consequence, it is investment decisions which determine the equilibrium level of income. More
precisely, equilibrium income has to be such as to generate an amount
of savings corresponding (in the simplified system without taxes and
public expenditure, and with no relations with foreign countries) to the
amount of investments generated by entrepreneurs' decisions. It thus
depends both on the level of investments I, and on the propensity to save s
($s = S/Y$, where S are savings and Y is income); more precisely, on the
equilibrium condition $I = S$ (equality between inflows and outflows in the
circular income flow) and on the definition of the propensity to save we
get $Y = I/s$. The multiplier, namely that multiplicative coefficient which,
when applied to the level of investment, gives equilibrium income, is
equal – as can be seen from the above equation – to the inverse of the
propensity to save.[23]

We have already seen that the multiplier may be considered as the
second of the three pillars of the *General theory*. Those who maintain
this thesis, in effect, are not simply referring to the equation connecting
the level of income (or its changes) to autonomous expenditure (or to
its changes), but to the (active) role attributed to investments and the
(passive) role attributed to consumption and savings in determination of
income.

For the theory of investment, as for that of effective demand, Keynes
based his argument on illustration of the entrepreneur's point of view. The
latter decides whether to invest, attempting to evaluate expected returns
on investment and comparing them with the monetary rate of interest

---

[22] Other factors which influence overall consumption, such as income distribution within
the economy (consumption grows with the increase of distributive equality), wealth, and
facility of consumer credit, Keynes saw as complications which could have been added
without difficulty to the simplified basic representation of the circular flow, without
modifying its essential features.

[23] Kahn's 1931 original work concerned effects on employment (not on income) of
increases in public expenditure. In the Keynesian representation of the circular income
flow, public expenditure may be assimilated to investments, since it does not depend
on income. The change in income ΔY will then be equal to the change in autonomous
expenditure ΔI multiplied by a coefficient (the 'multiplier') equal to the inverse of the
marginal propensity to save, defined as the ratio between change in savings and change
in income, $\Delta S/\Delta Y$, as we may readily see from the condition of equilibrium $\Delta S = \Delta I$.

indicating return on financial investments, which constitute an alternative employment of available funds.[24] As pointed out above, expectations relevant to investment decisions are qualitatively different from those relevant to decisions on production and employment levels. The former concern the 'long period', since they cover the whole foreseen life of the productive equipment the acquisition of which is under consideration, and decisions taken on their basis may be revised within such a time interval only at high costs, while the latter concern the 'short period', in the sense that decisions adopted are open to ready revision with relatively low if not zero costs. Note that Keynes did not consider long period expectations stable for sufficiently long intervals of time; on the contrary, precisely because they concern so long an interval of time as to elude sufficiently precise and reliable evaluation, they may be considered far less stable than short period expectations.

The third pillar of Keynes's *General theory* was, as we saw, represented by the theory of monetary and financial markets, and more precisely by the theory of the rate of interest conceived as premium for forgoing liquidity. Here, too, many commentators and, above all, the traditional line dominant in macroeconomic textbooks, have misinterpreted at least one of the crucial aspects of the Keynesian analytical construction. Essentially, these crucial aspects boil down to two. Firstly, once again, we have the selection of a group of protagonists: behind the mass of large and small savers deciding in what form to keep their financial assets loom financiers (and financial institutions), and to them the decision-making process described by Keynes should more properly be referred. The decision-making process itself – and this is the second crucial aspect of Keynes's monetary theory – does not concern flows, but the allocation of stocks. It is thus dominant in relation to the element (transaction demand for money) regarding flows, which traditional theory focused on.

Once again, it is the expectations of the decision-making agents that play the leading role. Indeed, in this case changes in expectations produce their effects immediately, or at any rate in a very short time span. On well-developed financial markets transaction costs are very low, and it is possible to revise daily, or even from one hour to the next, decisions on the allocation of financial holdings between the various possible assets. Simplifying the issue, Keynes considered two kinds of assets: money,

---

[24] Obviously the monetary rate of interest also indicates the cost of financing investment. However, the point Keynes focused attention on, in his analysis, was the relation between different ways of moving wealth into the future available to economic agents in a monetary production economy: investment in productive assets, in financial assets, and in non-reproducible goods. Hence the role of indicator of the opportunity-cost attributed to the rate of interest.

extremely liquid since commonly accepted for all kinds of transactions but not yielding income, and bonds yielding a predetermined yearly coupon. As we know, the market price of pre-existing bonds increases when the rate of interest decreases, and vice versa. As a consequence, those who expect a fall in interest rates by the same token also expect an increase in bond prices, and will be buyers on the bond market, while those expecting an increase in the interest rate operate in the opposite direction, offering bonds in exchange for money. In the presence of different opinions on the prospects facing the monetary and financial markets, the rate of interest is set at each instant at that level which corresponds to equilibrium between the two opposite ranks, the 'bulls' and the 'bears'.

Thus, everything depends on the expectations of the financial operators. If for a moment we assume that these remain fixed, it is clear that when the rate of interest decreases, the number of operators who expect a subsequent increase (and thus offer bonds in exchange for money) rises: the demand for money thus turns out to be an inverse function of the interest rate. However, this relationship has very thin foundations, since expectations regarding financial events are extremely volatile. It is quite possible, for instance, for a reduction in the interest rate to induce many operators to revise their expectations and foresee further interest rate reductions, preferring bonds to money even more than before: a direct, rather than inverse, relationship would then hold between changes in the rate of interest and changes in the demand for money.

The important place occupied by this theory in Keynes's theoretical edifice lies in an aspect largely misunderstood in the tradition of macroeconomic textbooks. The point is this: within Keynes's analytical framework, the theory of speculative demand for money – far more realistic than the traditional theories in interpreting the working of monetary and financial markets – distanced interest rate determination from the traditional mechanism of comparison between savings and investments, respectively understood as supply of and demand for loanable funds. According to Keynes, decisions to save should be kept logically distinct from those concerning the kind of financial asset (money or bonds) in which to invest the savings. Contrary to the interpretation advanced by many commentators, the main point was not that the amount of savings depended more on income than on the rate of interest – a point also acknowledged by a theoretician like Pigou, chosen by Keynes as paradigm of the traditional theory he was attacking.[25] The point was the separation between the two kinds of decisions concerning, respectively, the amount of savings and the

---

[25] Cf. Roncaglia and Tonveronachi 1985.

financial asset to invest the savings in; it was this latter decision which, according to Keynes, concurred together with the monetary policy followed by monetary authorities in determining the current level of the interest rate. Thus, if we wish to include this latter variable among the factors determining the amount of savings, we should in any case consider it as exogenously given relative to savings decisions.

Hicks's idea, embodied in his famous IS-LM model (Hicks 1937), to set transaction demand and the speculative demand for money side by side, coordinating them, or in other words treating them as if they were on the same plane, lost sight of the fundamental difference in nature between the two kinds of decisions. In fact the 'speculative' choices concern the allocation of the stocks of savings cumulated over time, and thus clearly dominate over liquidity requirements to finance the flow of current exchanges. This is all the more evident when the stocks of savings to be allocated between bonds and money are confronted not with yearly income and exchanges but, as is in the nature of continually revised financial choices, with daily flows. We thus have a hierarchy of influences: financial expectations dominate the scene concerning the allocation of the stock of savings, and hence the determination of interest rates, relegating to a secondary level all other factors, including the transactions demand for money. It is, then, the interest rates thus brought about, together with long run expectations, which determine the level of investments, while the latter in turn, through the multiplier mechanism, determines income and employment.

This scheme of hierarchical relations was in sharp contrast to general economic equilibrium schemes, in which each variable depends on all other variables and on all the parameters of the system. It is precisely in this aspect that Keynes's theory, following through with the 'short causal chains' methodology, fully revealed its deep Marshallian foundations, emphasised by the pragmatism characterising all Keynes's work. And, indeed, it is this aspect which has been submerged in the interpretations of Keynes's thought dominating successive generations of macroeconomics textbooks, from the Hicksian 'general equilibrium' scheme to recent insistence on the microfoundations of macroeconomics. But these are points we will return to later on.[26]

---

[26] Cf. below, § 17.5. We will also be making some reference later, in § 7, to Keynes's ideas concerning the international economic institutions. Let us recall here, only briefly, alas, that many of Keynes's writings concerned issues of economic policy: examination of them would show how limited is the identification of 'Keynesian policies' with fiscal and monetary policies aimed at the control of aggregate demand (even if these are undoubtedly part of the economic policy toolbox considered by Keynes). In particular, Keynes paid great attention to the problem of institutions and customs which regulate the working of

6.   Defence and development

As we have seen, the *General theory* immediately aroused great interest. In contrast to the response accorded to the *Treatise on money* on publication, there was no head-on criticism: Hayek, whose lengthy review of the *Treatise* (Hayek 1931–2) had given rise to significant debate despite, or perhaps also thanks to, the harsh polemical tones, forbore reacting to the *General theory*. In the environment of the London School of Economics, where Hayek's influence had kindled an attitude favourable to the 'continental' approach of general economic equilibrium among young economists more inclined to pure theory, we find not direct criticism but a most insidious reinterpretation of Keynes's analysis in terms of a simplified general equilibrium model, namely the famous IS-LM model (Hicks 1937) mentioned above, which we will return to later on.

A more complex debate arose between Keynes and the Keynesians on the one hand and the main representatives of the Swedish school, successors to Wicksell, on the other. This series of discussions prompted further contributions from Keynes in clarification and elaboration of his analysis, albeit to the limited extent allowed by the sheer multiplicity of his interests and the slower pace his work took on after a heart attack in May 1937.

Let us briefly recall here two elements. Firstly, an article published in 1937 in the *Quarterly Journal of Economics* illustrated in broad outline the core ideas of the *General theory*. A particular feature of this article is the sharp focus Keynes brought to bear on the crucial role of expectations and the hierarchy of causes and effects mentioned at the end of the previous section.

Secondly, there is the problem of Keynes's relations with the Swedish school of Lindahl, Myrdal and Ohlin, who had developed a system of

the market and condition the degree of uncertainty in which economic agents operate. Another of Keynes's proposals was the 'socialisation of investments': a formula he used to refer to the advantages of keeping ready to hand investment projects in infrastructures, often characterised by relatively modest and above all greatly deferred returns, to be implemented – possibly by public firms, managed with entrepreneurial criteria, seeking maximum productive efficiency – in periods when it was found opportune to provide public support for aggregate demand. These are but a few examples of Keynes's fervid imagination, ranging from issues such as the temporary reduction of working time to 'financial engineering' proposals to facilitate the realisation of large-scale investments. So-called 'functional finance', i.e. application of the monetary and fiscal lever to control aggregate demand, was developed only after Keynes's death, in the context of the 'neo-classical synthesis', in particular by Abba Lerner (1905–82), an enthusiastic advocate of Keynesism and 'functional finance'. Lerner himself, however, saw fiscal and monetary policies supported with other tools, such as ingenious anti-inflationary schemes based on automatic disincentives to price and money wage increases (cf. Lerner and Colander 1980).

sequential analysis based on the distinction between *ex ante* and *ex post* in the 1920s and 1930s. This was a line of research which shared with Keynes (albeit more with the Keynes of the *Treatise on money* than the Keynes of the *General theory*) rejection of the equilibrium method in favour of process analysis. However, Keynes rejected the technique of sequential or period analysis out of hand, 'owing to my failure to establish any definite unit of time'.[27] In other terms, sequential analysis would presuppose the possibility of establishing the boundaries of successive periods of time in a sufficiently objective way (for instance in the sequence of a week for labour and a final day of the week for the market, as in the Marshallian–Hicksian model of the fish market), while in reality not only do productive processes have different durations, but also the very decisions of the entrepreneurs and financial operators, the moments in time in which expectations are revised and new decisions adopted, cannot fit into a fully specified sequential scheme.

An element commonly attributed to sequential analysis, but in fact independent of it, was, however, central to Keynes's analysis. This was the distinction between fulfilled and unfulfilled expectations – a distinction that within sequential analysis was connected to the distinction between *ex ante* and *ex post* magnitudes. For Keynes (as Kregel 1976, showed) the distinction between the different situations might be organised around a logical sequence of models: the static equilibrium model, the stationary equilibrium model, and the shifting equilibrium model. In the first, short run expectations (those influencing decisions concerning production levels) are fulfilled, while long run expectations (those determining investments) are considered as given and constant, and do not interact with short run expectations. In the stationary equilibrium model, the assumptions concerning long run expectations still hold, but short run expectations may prove unsatisfied, with the consequent need to revise decisions previously taken. Finally, in the shifting equilibrium model, not only do short run expectations prove erroneous in general, but long

---

[27] Cf. Keynes 1973, vol. 14, p. 184; the passage is quoted by Kregel 1976, p. 223. In a different context (that of the Austrian theory discussed above, chapter 11), the technique of sequential or period analysis, already utilised by Hayek and Hicks in the 1930s and 1940s, was taken up by Hicks 1973 and in his wake by a group of 'neo-Austrian' authors in the 1970s and 1980s. Sequential analysis, with its alternation of stages of production and market, implicitly referred to the notion of the market as a moment in time and space in which supply and demand meet, a notion which – as we have already remarked – opposed the classical one which considered the market as consisting in a web of relations and repetitive flows of exchange, connected to the productive interrelations among economic sectors within a system based on the division of labour. Keynes's remark, considering also the context in which it was presented, implied this wider notion of the market.

run expectations may change over time, and interdependence may exist between them and the short run expectations.

The distinction between these three kinds of models not only indicates a line of research already present in the *General theory* and taken up again in the discussions immediately following its publication, but also the extraordinary scope of Keynes's theory in its original version, proposing a complex method of analysis of the actual vicissitudes of a capitalist economy, with the focus on the evaluations and decision-making processes of its active protagonists.

7.   The asymmetries of economic policy in an open economy and international institutions

The *General theory* analysed the case of a closed economic system – a world economy, useful both as a theoretical simplification and to establish some principles holding for the industrialised countries in general.[28] However, at the level of economic policy, results concerning a closed economy cannot automatically be extended to an open economy. In particular, in an open economy a reduction in real wages can have a positive effect on employment, by enhancing the competitiveness of national over foreign products. In this way the inverse relationship between wages and employment could be re-established, and under the assumption that unemployment leads to reduction in real wages we again have at our disposal a mechanism of convergence to full employment. That is, a country can favour its own development by subtracting market outlets from other countries with the so-called beggar-thy-neighbour policies – a zero sum game, with advantages for one country corresponding to losses for some other country.

Policies of this kind had been followed by a number of countries coming up against formidable difficulties in the years of the Great Crisis. Keynes himself had occasionally adopted this point of view when discussing the policies most suited to Great Britain in the 1920s and 1930s. However, as the Second World War drew to a close and the leaders of the major Western countries were at last able to look beyond it, Keynes found himself involved in an 'enlightened' attempt to outline rules for the international economic game favouring cooperation among countries. The debate came to its celebrated culmination with the conference held in Bretton Woods, a small town in the United States, in July 1944:

[28] While still assuming a closed system, Keynes developed the notion of 'inflationary gap', proposed in *How to pay for the war* (1940) in order to explain the inflationary pressures arising when aggregate demand overshoots aggregate supply, as happens in a country in a period of war, with conspicuous military expenditures.

here Keynes's ideas were watered down, if not defeated, by American conservatism.

Keynes's central idea, as outlined in various memoranda and secondary contributions of the 1930s and 1940s, was that the unemployment problem is recurrently and inevitably raised in a capitalist economy by technical progress, making it possible to obtain the same quantity of product with an ever decreasing number of workers.[29] Waxing acute, the problem can become socially explosive in the absence of adequate policies to manage the economy. In other terms, Keynes perceived unemployment as a 'systemic' problem, which persists and recurs again and again over time. Moreover, the thought experiment of the closed economy adopted in the *General theory* allowed Keynes to maintain that beggar-thy-neighbour policies involve a simple redistribution of the costs of a world crisis without offering any contribution to its solution, and indeed with the risk of bringing to a head nationalistic antagonisms that had already been seething in the pre-war and war years.

Keynes's idea was that the international economic system should be organised not only in such a way as to facilitate the development of commerce (hence in a context of free trade, currency convertibility, stable exchange rates and mechanisms for financing international transactions applied by international organisations to help overcome temporary disequilibria in trade balances), but also to provide systematic support to world production levels. To this end, the rules of the international game should avoid any asymmetry in stimulating corrective action on the part of countries with a positive balance of trade or with a negative one. Countries with a negative balance of trade are driven by dwindling currency reserves to adopt deflationary measures in order to reduce imports and favour exports, or restrictive monetary policies in order to stimulate capital imports, but with the additional result of discouraging investments in new productive capacity. Conversely, the countries with an active balance of trade could look on calmly as currency reserves accumulated, or might limit themselves to low interest rate policies to favour capital outflows. Keynes thought that a balanced international monetary system should govern international liquidity (through the issue, on the part of a super-national organisation, of an international currency, the Bancor) by lightening the pressure for adoption of deflationary policies on countries with a negative balance of trade; conversely, countries with an active balance of trade should be stimulated by the rules of the international game (for instance regulations on foreign currency reserves) to adopt reflationary policies.

[29] Cf. Guger and Walterkirschen 1988.

Among the projects following in the wake of Keynes's we may also recall the 'buffer stocks' of raw materials, serving mainly to avoid heavy repercussions on the growth process of the developing countries deriving from oscillations in the world demand for raw materials, which represent an important share of their exports. Working in a similar direction were the projects for a 'link' between the issue of a supranational currency and exploitation of the rights of issue to finance development in the third world countries. It was no mere chance that both proposals were made by Keynes's pupils and followers, in particular by Richard Kahn, Nicholas Kaldor and Joan Robinson.[30]

8. Michal Kalecki

When Keynes published the *General theory*, a young Polish economist, Michal Kalecki (1899–1970) bought the book and realised that his famous English colleague had rediscovered a theory of employment and the trade cycle that he had published in Polish a little earlier. This interpretation of the events, put into circulation by Joan Robinson,[31] certainly has an element of truth, but it obscures substantial differences of approach between the two great theoreticians.

Kalecki grew up in the Marxian tradition and was influenced by the growth schemes of the second book of Marx's *Capital*, taken up by Tugan-Baranovsky (1905), and by Rosa Luxemburg's (1913) underconsumption theories. It was thus easier for him than for Keynes to escape the hold of traditional marginalist analysis based on the notion of equilibrium between supply and demand, and as a consequence on the thesis of an automatic tendency, under competitive conditions, towards full employment. The set of relations between income, consumption, savings and investments that Kalecki proposed thus offered a theory of the level of income and employment very similar to Keynes's, both in considering full employment as a borderline case rather than the general one, and in attributing the driving role to autonomous expenditure and in particular to investment decisions. The necessity of active policy interventions in favour of full employment is another important similarity.[32]

---

[30] On the Keynesian derivation of buffer stocks proposals cf. Sabbatini 1989. On the 'link', cf., for instance, Kahn 1973.

[31] Cf., for instance, Robinson 1977.

[32] In this context, let us recall Kalecki's important role in the preparation of *The economics of full employment* (1944), a book made up of six essays written by six different authors at the Institute of Statistics of Oxford University.

The differences were, however, significant. The role of uncertainty and expectations, crucial in Keynes, was virtually absent in Kalecki's work, where a fully worked-out theory of financial markets was also lacking.[33] Conversely Kalecki, despite showing signs – especially in his early writings – of a Marshallian influence, embodied in his analysis mechanisms such as the full cost principle[34] which allow for links with modern theories of non-competitive markets. Moreover, Kalecki extended his formal structure to deal with problems of trade cycle and development, and connected such theories with analysis of income distribution among the social classes.[35]

Many of Kalecki's main contributions concerned the planned and mixed economy.[36] Though he was a moving spirit of the liveliest economics research and teaching centre of Eastern European countries, namely Warsaw, Kalecki spent the last years of his life marginalised by the political authorities of his country. Comparison with Keynes shows just how much importance nationality, conditions of birth and 'degree of political antipathy' may have in determining the impact of an economist's ideas and analysis.

[33] Kalecki proposed a 'principle of increasing risk' to account for the limits to the possibilities of financing investments on the side of each individual firm. This theme was taken up and developed by Kalecki's collaborator, the Austrian Josef Steindl (1912–93), in his theory of the firm: cf. Steindl 1945 and the writings collected in Steindl 1990, pp. 1–73. Steindl developed Kaleckian themes also in his best-known work, *Maturity and stagnation in American capitalism* (1952; 2nd edn 1976), where he maintained the thesis of a tendency to stagnation in capitalistic economies due to the gradual emergence of oligopolistic market forms. A similar thesis (transmission of the effects of technical progress generates development in a competitive system, but not in a system of oligopolies) was presented by Sylos Labini 1956. A tendency to stagnation was also maintained by the American Alvin Hansen (1887–1975) on more directly Keynesian grounds (Hansen 1938); in effect, Hansen played an important role in circulation of Keynesian ideas in the United States, both in the universities and in economic policy institutions.

[34] Cf., for instance, Kalecki 1943. The full cost principle is a pricing criterion frequently adopted by firms enjoying some market power, hence especially in oligopolistic sectors, and consists in setting the prices of their products on the basis of variable costs, adding to these a proportional margin destined to cover fixed costs and general expenses and to guarantee the margin of profit usual within the sector. Studied by Philip Andrews (1914–71; see the writings collected in Andrews 1993), the full cost principle was then integrated within oligopoly theory by Sylos Labini 1956.

[35] Particularly interesting is his theory of the 'political cycle' (Kalecki 1971, pp. 138–45).

[36] A selection of Kalecki's main writings, edited by the author himself but published posthumously, is divided between two slim volumes, one on capitalistic economies (Kalecki 1971, which includes the three articles in Polish of 1933, 1934 and 1935 which anticipated important aspects of Keynesian theory), and one on socialist and mixed economies (Kalecki 1972). On Kalecki and on his relationship with Keynes there is an extensive literature; cf., for instance, Chilosi 1979, the works quoted there, and subsequently the essays collected in Sebastiani 1989, and Sebastiani 1994.

9. The new Cambridge school

Naturally enough, the impact of Keynes's *General theory* was particularly strong in Cambridge. It was not a case of total conquest: at least at the beginning, apart from 'the professor', Arthur Cecil Pigou (cf. above, § 13.9), the Marshallian orthodoxy still found defenders of the calibre of Dennis Robertson, who in 1939 moved to London but then returned in 1944 as Pigou's successor to the economics chair, which he held up to retirement in 1957. However, the role of Keynes's direct pupils, like Kahn and Joan Robinson, gradually grew, and it was reinforced, after the end of the Second World War, by other 'converts', such as Nicholas Kaldor who arrived from the London School of Economics where, in an early phase, he had followed Hayek's star. A separate case was that of Piero Sraffa who, though nearer to Keynes than many commentators recognise, followed an autonomous research path (illustrated below in chapter 16). All these protagonists, and many others, from the British Marxist Maurice Dobb (1900–76) to the American Richard Goodwin (1913–96),[37] constituted the 'new Cambridge school' (so called to distinguish it from the 'old Cambridge school', of Marshall and his pupils), a highly lively intellectual group, particularly in the 1950s and 1960s.

Keynes's closest collaborator, his pupil and subsequently literary executor, was Richard Kahn (1905–88). A student and then teacher in Cambridge, in the early 1930s Kahn was the moving force of the 'Circus' which, as we saw above, stimulated Keynes's transition from the *Treatise on money* to the *General theory*. He also contributed a crucial element (Kahn 1931) to Keynes's analytical apparatus with his theory of the multiplier, which connected changes in employment to changes in autonomous expenditure (investments, public expenditure, exports) and to the propensity to save: a relationship which presupposed the existence of unemployed workers. This was, for all the economists of those times, a

---

[37] Dobb, Sraffa's collaborator in the final stages of the work for the edition of Ricardo's works, was the author of important writings on theory, economic history and history of economic thought, including a volume on the Soviet Union (1928 and subsequent editions), a volume of *Studies in the development of capitalism* (1946) in which, among other things, the issue of the transition from feudalism to capitalism was discussed, and a volume of history of economic thought (Dobb 1973). By Goodwin (whose papers are kept at the University of Siena, where he taught after his retirement from Cambridge) we may recall the works on the multiplier and the cycle; in particular, Goodwin 1967 presented a model of economic cycle based on the evolutionary scheme prey–predator originally studied by the mathematician Vito Volterra (1860–1940); we may also consider as a compendium of his view a volume with the ironic title, *Elementary economics from the higher standpoint* (1970), which makes use of highly refined graphic illustrations (Goodwin was also a refined painter); for an autobiographical interview and a biography, cf. Goodwin 1982.

fact of life, but it was also an element that – let us repeat once again – contradicted a central tenet of the dominant theory, namely the automatic tendency under competitive conditions towards full employment. Kahn had begun a gradual departure from this theory through his researches on 'the economics of the short period' (the title of his 1930 fellowship dissertation, which was to remain unpublished for more than fifty years: Kahn 1983), where he had taken up the theme of market imperfections, already present in Marshall's work but left somewhat in the background in Pigou's Marshallian *vulgata*. The author of relatively few, deeply pondered pages,[38] Kahn also made important contributions on monetary theory, both with signed works (as in the paper entitled *Some notes on liquidity preference* published in 1954) and through his influence on the famous *Radcliffe Report* (1959), which developed a Keynesian view of the working of financial markets and the role of monetary policy tools. Kahn's influence could also be seen in Joan Robinson's research on the theory of imperfect competition.

Joan Violet Robinson née Maurice (1903–83; her husband was Austin Robinson, 1897–1993, a Keynesian as well and an influential economics professor in Cambridge, but more interested in applied policy issues) was the standard-bearer of Keynesianism: a lively and prolific writer, passionate and brilliant orator, vigorous polemist, she left her mark in universities all over the world. Among her contributions, together with various expositions of Keynesian theory, we may recall *The economics of imperfect competition* (1933). As we have seen (§ 13.10), it was with this work that Joan Robinson started what has been called 'the imperfect competition revolution', albeit with some exaggeration since it substantially remained within a Marshallian framework; so much so, indeed, that Robinson herself took a certain distance from it in the preface to a new edition in 1969. Robinson also attempted to extend Keynes's analysis to the long period, in particular with *The accumulation of capital* (1956). An aspect of the book that attracted particular interest was the taxonomy of growth models, while the analysis of the interrelation between effective demand and productive capacity remained in the shade, although it occupied a central position in Robinson's work, as indeed it had in Harrod's famous model (1939).

A 'convert' to Keynesianism, as we saw above, was Nicholas Kaldor (1908–86), born in Budapest in the Austro-Hungarian empire and subsequently a British citizen and lord for merits acquired as economic counsellor to Labour governments. Before Keynes published the *General theory*, the young Kaldor was already able to boast some important articles on

---

[38] The main contributions are collected in Kahn 1972.

the theory of capital and the firm (with an original synthesis of Hayek's and Marshall's ideas). An expert on the UN Commission for Europe in the immediate post-war period, consultant to many developing countries and, on various occasions, to the British government, Kaldor contributed to the theoretical corpus of the Cambridge school a theory of income distribution, in which distribution between wages and profits depended on the capitalists' propensity to save and the growth rate of the economy.[39] This theory was then flanked with theories of accumulation based on Keynesian and classical (Ricardian) ideas in successive versions of a growth model (Kaldor 1957, 1961) where he set out to represent the main 'stylised facts' of developed capitalistic economies. Kaldor also contributed to the development of Keynesian monetary theory (from the 1959 *Radcliffe Report*, to a long series of contributions where he criticised Friedman's monetarism and its Thatcherite *vulgata*).

On the applied side, Richard Stone (1914–91, Nobel prize in 1984) gave a decisive contribution to the development of national accounting on Keynesian lines (cf. below, § 17.7). International trade theory, also along Keynesian lines, is a field of research to which James Meade (1907–94, Nobel prize in 1977) gave important contributions.

The 'Cambridge team' also included, in successive stages, many Italians attracted there by the Keynesian tradition and by the fame of Sraffa: from Luigi Pasinetti to Pierangelo Garegnani, from Luigi Spaventa to Mario Nuti, protagonists in the debate on the theory of capital which in the 1960s saw Cambridge, England victoriously opposed to Cambridge, Massachusetts. This debate stemmed mainly from Sraffa's contribution, as we shall see below (§ 16.8). Cambridge constituted for years a centre of attraction for economists all over the world: Geoffrey Harcourt from Australia, Amit Bhaduri, Krishna Bharadwaj, Amartya Sen and Ajit Singh from India, Tom Asimakopulos from Canada, Bertram Schefold from Switzerland, Jan Kregel from the United States, and many others among the contemporary economists mentioned in this book.

---

[39] Originally presented in an article of 1956, this theory was taken up and developed by Pasinetti 1962; in subsequent debates with Samuelson and Modigliani, Kaldor 1966 connected it to the financial choices of the firm, and hence to the new stream of researches on managerial capitalism (cf. below, § 17.3). For a survey of the debate and of other aspects of Kaldor's thought, and for a bibliography of his writings, cf. Targetti 1988.

15   Joseph Schumpeter

1.   Life[1]

Joseph Alois Schumpeter (1883–1950) is one of the most frequently quoted economists in our days. Above all, many recall his idea that the process of economic development is generated by a succession of innovations achieved by entrepreneurs with the purchasing power supplied to them by bankers.

The attractiveness of Schumpeter's ideas stems, at least in part, from their twofold political implications. On the one hand, they bring to the fore entrepreneurs and bankers, the leading actors of the development process; at the same time, Schumpeter opposed Keynesian-type policy activism and considered crises a necessary evil, needed to stimulate the very vitality of capitalism. On the other hand, the view of a dynamic process endogenous to the economy and society, and of the decay of capitalism as the inevitable outcome of such dynamics, seems to align Schumpeter with Marx against the traditional theorising of economic equilibrium.

Schumpeter's thought is, however, far more complex and richer in lights and shadows than these contrasting evaluations might suggest. What remains truly alive today is the objective he propounds for economic science, namely to start from solid theoretical foundations and accomplish a theory of social change. As we shall see in § 2, in order to make headway along this road Schumpeter proposed as methodological canon the maximum possible flexibility: his theoretical building, extensive and complex, is made up of 'analytical bricks' bound together by a common pre-analytical view: not by a formally unified scheme, but by a broad representation of economic life. Thus he was free to apply in his theoretical building a range of tools: from those of economic analysis strictly

---

[1] Various biographical and bibliographical studies have been devoted to Schumpeter; let us mention here the lively biography by Swedberg 1991 and the meticulous bibliography by Augello 1990. The interpretation presented in the following pages draws on Roncaglia 1987.

speaking, to those of sociological analysis, economic history and the history of economic analysis. It is precisely the proposal of this objective and method that accounts for the deep fascination of Schumpeter's thought, together with the subtle heterodoxy marking him out from the tendencies prevailing in economic research in the second half of the twentieth century.

Like his contribution to economic science, his personality was also rich and complex. Albeit with many vicissitudes, Schumpeter traversed the first half of the twentieth century in the role of a leading protagonist of economic debates.

Schumpeter was born in Triesh, in Moravia (then part of the Austro-Hungarian empire), on 8 February 1883. His father, a small entrepreneur in the textile sector, died when Joseph was only four years old. His mother, the daughter of a doctor and a woman of strong character and considerable culture, found herself a widow when twenty-six years old; she married again in 1893 with a high-ranking officer in the Austrian army, already retired and thirty-three years older than her. This marriage ended in divorce thirteen years later; but in the meantime the stepfather had a noticeable influence on the formation of the young Joseph, who was sent to study in the Theresianum in Vienna, the school of the young aristocrats. Here he received an education centred on humanistic studies, including Greek and Latin alongside French, English and Italian: all useful tools for Schumpeter's research work up to his last venture, the *History of economic analysis*.

From 1901 to 1906 he attended the Faculty of Jurisprudence at Vienna University. Here Böhm-Bawerk was one of the professors; at his seminars Schumpeter came into heated debate with Otto Bauer and Rudolf Hilferding, two future leaders of Austrian socialism, and one of the champions of liberalism, Ludwig von Mises.

After graduating, Schumpeter visited England, where he met Marshall and Edgeworth. He also met his first wife, the daughter of an Anglican priest, his elder by twelve years; however, the marriage lasted only a few years.

In 1907 Schumpeter moved to Cairo, earning his living as a lawyer and managing the estate of an Egyptian princess. In the meantime he worked on the first of his books, *The essence and the principles of theoretical economy*, published (in German) in 1908. He then became ill with Maltese flu, and in 1909 had to go back to Vienna. Here, thanks to the book he had just published and the help of his professor, Böhm-Bawerk (a few years later they would be wrangling over interest theory), he was appointed to a professorship at Czernowitz University. Then the capital of Austrian Bucovina, on the far eastern fringe of the empire, today part of Ukraine, the town was certainly no centre of cultural life: years later, Schumpeter recalled its balmy nights and beautiful women, but in 1911 he was quite happy to move to Graz University, where he held a chair up to 1921.

The years before the war were characterised by intense scientific activity: in 1912 Schumpeter published (in German) *The theory of economic development*, and in 1914, again in German, the *Epochs in the history of doctrines and methods*; in 1913–14 he visited the United States, where he gave lecture courses and seminars at Columbia University in New York and received an honorary degree when only thirty years old.

Decidedly a non-conformist, during the war Schumpeter displayed pacifist and pro-Western views; in 1918–19, notwithstanding his own conservative views, he took part in a committee chaired by Kautsky and instituted by the Austrian socialist government to organise the nationalisation of private firms.[2] In 1919 he became member of the Austrian government led by Renner, a socialist, and supported by an alliance between socialists and social-Christians (Catholics and conservative): as an expert external to both parties, he took the unpopular office of minister of finance, charged with the impossible task of solving the problem of the public debt inherited from the war. His experience as minister lasted only a few months, from 15 March to 17 October, but gave rise to heated debate, on the one hand raging over points in his policy (extraordinary wealth tax, incentives to the influx of foreign capitals, inflation aimed at reducing the real value of the public debt) that drew the fire of the middle classes, and, on the other hand, over his opposition – bordering on boycott – to the nationalisation programme officially adopted by the government he belonged to, thus arousing the hostility of socialists. Indeed, the socialists accused Schumpeter of having favoured acquisition of the biggest Austrian iron firm, the Alpine Montan-Gesellschaft, by foreign (Italian) interests, and secured his resignation.

Schumpeter went back to the university, but by 1921 he had already resigned from his professorship to become chairman of a small private bank of solid traditions, the Biedermann Bank, and headed it until bankruptcy struck in 1924. The bank was ruined by the financial crisis following upon the stabilisation policy enacted by the government. Many of its clients were hit by heavy losses; Schumpeter lost all his estate and his past savings, and, in addition, over the following years part of his income had to be used to pay back debts incurred as a result of the bankruptcy.

---

[2] Schumpeter's own justification (as reported by Haberler 1950, p. 345) was that 'if somebody wants to commit suicide, it is a good thing if a doctor is present'; on his standing within the commission, however, there are different interpretations (cf. Swedberg 1991, pp. 55–8).

At the age of forty-two, with the controversial experiences of minister and banker behind him, Schumpeter went back to university teaching. The first offer came from a Japanese university, but Schumpeter chose the University of Bonn. Here he taught (with some interruptions: one year at Harvard, in 1927–8 – returning there in autumn 1930 – and some months in Japan, where many of his writings were translated and where he enjoyed considerable prestige) up to his final move to Harvard in 1932.

The first year in Bonn was possibly the happiest in his life. Before leaving Vienna he married a most beautiful young lady, daughter of his mother's door-keeper, whose studies his mother had contributed to financially. But after only one year, in 1926, his young wife died in childbirth, and the same period also saw the death of his beloved mother. These events left Schumpeter's character marked by a dark vein of pessimism.

In the Bonn years Schumpeter worked among other things on a lengthy treatise on money; however, it remained incomplete, and was published posthumously only in 1970. Schumpeter put it aside after five years' work when, in 1930, Keynes's *Treatise on money* appeared – a contribution setting out a line of thinking completely different from his own. Most likely, Schumpeter believed that without further intensive research his work would pale in comparison with Keynes's, and preferred to wait for new fruits from his researches.

After his move to the United States in 1932 Schumpeter's life became more regular, measured out by the publication of his new writings. In 1939 the monumental work on *Business cycles* appeared, in 1942 the provocative and successful *Capitalism, socialism, democracy*, while at his death the great *History of economic analysis* was still incomplete (it was to be published posthumously in 1954, edited by his third wife, the economist Elisabeth Boody, whom he had married in 1937).

Along with his impressive research activity, Schumpeter took on a heavy load of teaching and academic work. Among his students we find many of the greatest economists of the twentieth century, from Leontiev to Samuelson, from Sweezy and Goodwin to Minsky, from Tsuru to Sylos Labini. Sweezy (1951, p. xxiv; italics in the original) recalled: 'He didn't care *what* we thought as long as we *did* think.' In his research work, however, he remained a 'lone wolf'. Notwithstanding academic recognition (president of the Econometric Society in 1937–40,[3] of the American

Economic Association in 1948, designated first president of the International Economic Association at the moment of its foundation), his public image bore the weight of his position as an ultra-conservative, opposed to Roosevelt's New Deal and, above all, considered too soft on nazi Germany during the war years.

Lonely and worn out by work, Schumpeter died of a stroke in his country house at Taconic in Connecticut, in the night between 7 and 8 January 1950.

2.   Method

The question of method is not only the first theme that Schumpeter tackled in his scientific production, but also the necessary starting point for any interpretation of his views. One of his very first writings (Schumpeter, 1906) was a brief article on the crucial importance of the mathematical method in economic theory; questions of method occupied many pages in his first important work, the volume on *The essence and the principles of economic theory*, published in 1908.

In this volume Schumpeter was already taking a position that would be refined, but not substantially changed, in his mature works: a sort of methodological liberalism that has many affinities with some of the most recent developments in epistemology (for instance, in one aspect or another, with the positions of a variegated range of authors including Kuhn, Lakatos and Feyerabend: cf. above, § 1.3), while also reflecting ideas circulating in the cultural context of his education. To sum up, with Schumpeter's own words (1908, p. 156, italics added), it is 'advantageous not to set the methodological assumptions once and for all our purposes, but to adapt them to each objective and, once such specific assumptions appear adequate to the purpose, *to be as liberal as possible*'.

Schumpeter (1908, p. 3) started from the statement that 'all sciences are nothing but [. . .] forms of representation' of reality, and emphatically declared: 'we do not accept *a priori* the statement that economic reality shows a systematic regularity and that therefore the formulation of exact "laws" is possible' (ibid., p. 12). This methodological position was not very different from Keynes's: it conceived theories and formalised models as tools for orientation within reality. Above all, this methodological position was radically different from the one prevailing in the initial stage of development of modern science, when it was believed that mathematical laws expressed the intrinsic essence of things, and that the theoretician's task was to 'uncover' such laws from the accidental phenomena enshrouding them (cf. above, § 3.1): a view still widespread at the time.

A controversial aspect in Schumpeter's methodological position concerned the need to check theory against empirical reality. Schumpeter recalled the limits to the arbitrary character of the theoretician's activity: 'in constructing our system we proceeded arbitrarily, but also rationally drawing up hypotheses with the facts always in mind'. 'This does not mean [. . .] that such statements are "laws" prescribed for the universe or, even, that they regulate the world of phenomena [. . .]; it only means that they give good results in an appreciable measure, in so appreciable a measure as to be worth having been formulated' (Schumpeter 1908, pp. 424–5). The second of the two passages quoted finds an echo in Friedman (1953), who argues that assumptions can be unrealistic provided that the results are useful (in particular, provided that the forecasts deduced from the assumptions thanks to the theoretical construction prove correct); but the first of the two passages contradicts such an interpretation.

It was from the viewpoint of his 'methodological liberalism' that Schumpeter criticised as sterile the famous debate on method still under way in those years (cf. above, § 11.2) between those who (like Menger) considered economics an 'exact' science and those who (like Schmoller, the leader of the historical school) saw it as closer to the historical-social sciences: 'the historical school and the abstract one are not in contrast and [. . .] the only difference between them is their interest in different issues' (ibid., p. 22) or, perhaps better, in different aspects of the same reality – an extremely complex reality that cannot be reduced exclusively to one problem or another.

Schumpeter reproposed this methodological position in various writings, also of his mature period, stressing again and again that economic life has so many different aspects that it may usefully be analysed from a multiplicity of viewpoints.

A corollary of Schumpeter's 'methodological liberalism' was his cautious attitude towards methodological individualism, or in other words that method of analysis which starts from the individual – from his or her preferences and endowments – and which was at the root of neoclassical economic theory. Schumpeter (1908, p. 83) stressed in a clearcut way the distinction between individualism in scientific method and political individualism (liberalism), stating that 'there is no particularly close relationship between individualistic economic science and political individualism' and that 'from theory in itself we can draw arguments neither in favour nor against political individualism'. In this he followed the separation, repeatedly asserted in his writings and strongly advocated by

Weber as well, between theoretical propositions that fall within the field of science and value judgements that fall within the field of politics.[4]

3.   From statics to dynamics; the cycle

In the 1908 book, in fact, methodological issues were a secondary concern. Schumpeter's main aim was to illustrate what he considered the foundations of economic theory, namely the static system of economic equilibrium, or – in his own words – 'the fundamental concepts that constitute the present of pure economics' (ibid., p. 6). In his opinion, it was necessary to bring order again in a picture that 'appeared confused, almost chaotic and not at all satisfactory' (ibid., p. 7).

Schumpeter adopted the 'principle of value' from the marginalist tradition, according to which the value of economic goods is expressed by demand for them relative to their scarcity. However, he rejected Jevons's utilitarianism, based on the definition of economic goods 'as things of the external world that are in a causal relation with the satisfaction of needs' (ibid., p. 64), and hence with the identification of value with the (subjective) measure of the ability of goods to satisfy such needs. In fact, 'psychological deduction is simply a tautology. If we say that somebody is prepared to pay something more than somebody else because he values it more, with this we do not give an explanation, since it is precisely from his evaluation that we infer the fact that he offers to pay a higher price' (ibid., p. 64).

As a consequence, the so-called principle of decreasing marginal utility according to Schumpeter 'in economics [. . .] is not a law [. . .] but a basic assumption for the generalisation of given scientific facts. As such this assumption is in principle arbitrary' (ibid., p. 71). Similarly, and in conformity to the methodological principles illustrated in the previous section, 'the *homo oeconomicus* – the hedonistic computer – [. . .] is a construction the hypothetical character of which is now known' (ibid., pp. 80–1).

Schumpeter considered the theory of prices as 'the core of pure economics' (ibid., p. 106), describing it with grandiloquent overtones: 'A chain of equations surrounds the sphere of the economic activity of

---

[4] This is also the background for the distinction between economic liberalism and political liberalism. The former is identified with 'the theory that the best way of promoting economic development and general welfare is to remove fetters from the private-enterprise economy and to leave it alone', while political liberalism is identified with 'sponsorship of parliamentary government, freedom to vote and extension of the right to vote, freedom of the press, divorce of secular from spiritual government, trial by jury, and so on' (Schumpeter 1954, p. 394).

the individual' (ibid., p. 116). However, his illustration of this theory is not without defects; in this respect Pantaleoni's judgement is indicative: according to him the book 'is very useful for the Germans most of whom know nothing of the new economics', but 'is prolix, not new, elementary, often also imprecise'.[5]

In Schumpeter's opinion, the point of arrival of the theory of economic equilibrium is what he called 'the method of variations'. In fact, 'we can never explain an *actual* state of equilibrium of the economy' (ibid., p. 361); what the theory can explain is what consequences a change in one of the data has on equilibrium: 'This is the only reason for which such laws have been constructed' (ibid., p. 360).

Such a method – what is nowadays called comparative statics analysis – may be used only in a very limited ambit, with respect to infinitesimal changes: 'rigorously speaking, our system excludes any change whatsoever' (ibid., p. 375). However, the economic equilibrium approach is useful because with it light can be shed on a particular aspect of economic realities subject to continuous change: habit, repetitiveness, the thousands of 'mechanical' actions of everyday life.

In order to clarify his position, Schumpeter used a number of metaphors: the photograph (ibid., pp. 123–4), the centre of gravitation, the sea and the waves (ibid., p. 458). For example, he writes:

The state of equilibrium is a centre of gravity of 'economic forces', abstract, yes, but always existing perpetually. In fact we do not describe an actual state of the economy, but only a formal state of affairs which we may always observe even in any of the most active moments of development, and which in reality remains unchanged even when the actual data change. However, we cannot say that our state of equilibrium resembles the surface of a sea which is always in motion although always tending to resettle, and which, if observed at a sufficient distance, always appears flat: the waves of the sea in fact always return to the same level, but not the waves of economic life.[6]

The main point of differentiation between Schumpeter and traditional marginalist theory emerged in a debate on the theory of interest. Schumpeter criticised the theory developed by his professor Böhm-Bawerk, who 'defines interest as the premium of present goods over future goods' (ibid., p. 329). Schumpeter opposed this theory not so much with

---

[5] In a letter to Pareto, in Pareto 1960, vol. 3, p. 360. For instance, the demonstration (in words, not symbols) of the theorem of the equalisation of weighted marginal utilities is wrong (Schumpeter 1908, p. 115); for other examples cf. Roncaglia 1987, p. 53.

[6] Schumpeter 1908, p. 458. The metaphor of the level of the sea and the waves, to which Schumpeter makes critical reference, is utilised for instance by Walras 1874, p. 381. To be precise, Walras, professor at Lausanne, looking out of the window of his study spoke of a 'lake [. . .] stirred to its very depths by a storm'.

a new theory as with a different, 'dynamic', approach: 'The essential phenomenon is the interest deriving from credit which serves for the creation of new industries, new forms of organisation, new techniques, new consumption goods' (ibid., p. 355). And again: 'The origin of the phenomenon of interest lies in development and in credit; here we must look for its explanation' (ibid., p. 338). In the static system, according to Schumpeter, the money market plays only a secondary, passive role, while it becomes an actor with an important role only within the process of economic development. Interest, as a monetary phenomenon, can only be explained within the field of a dynamic theory.

This thesis was developed by Schumpeter in his *Theory of economic development*. The first edition of this famous work – a massive volume in German, prolix and rich in disquisitions on historiography and methodology – was published in 1912; a second decidedly slimmer German edition appeared in 1926. The popularity of the work is, however, mainly due to the English edition, prepared by Redvers Opie under Schumpeter's direct control and published in 1934. This edition was yet further shortened, although Schumpeter maintained in his preface that no substantial change had been made to it.

The dichotomy between statics and dynamics was substituted in this work with a dichotomy between theory of the circular flow and theory of development. The circular flow corresponds to the stationary state, in which the economy reproduces itself, period after period, without structural change; Schumpeter also admitted in this context a purely quantitative growth, from which changes in production technologies and consumers' tastes were excluded by definition.

Development, by contrast, is characterised by change. The role of active agent in the process of change is attributed to the producer, while consumers follow passively and 'are educated by him if necessary' (Schumpeter 1912, p. 65). Having recalled that 'to produce means to combine materials and forces within our reach' (ibid.), Schumpeter notes that 'Development in our sense is then defined by the carrying out of new combinations' (ibid., p. 66), namely by 'the introduction of a new good', by 'the introduction of a new method of production', by 'the opening of a new market', by 'the conquest of a new source of supply of raw materials or half-manufactured goods', and by 'the carrying out of the new organisation of any industry, like the creation of a monopoly position [. . .] or the breaking up of a monopoly position' (ibid.).

The introduction of new productive combinations is the work of the *entrepreneurs*, who are such only in so far as they realise innovative choices. The notion of the entrepreneur is a key category within the Schumpeterian theory: as the originator of change, the entrepreneur generates capitalistic development (while within the classical economists' approach it is the process of development that generates the drive to change, and consequently the very figure of the entrepreneur); his motivation is not that of the *homo oeconomicus* (among other things, because he may not be the owner of the firm or the person who appropriates the profits deriving from the innovation) but rather 'the dream and the will to found a private kingdom [. . .] the will to conquer [. . .] the joy of creating, of getting things done, or simply of exercising one's energy and ingenuity' (ibid., p. 93).

Alongside the leading role of the entrepreneur in the process of development Schumpeter extolled the role of the banker, considered equally necessary. This thesis stemmed from two crucial assumptions in the basic Schumpeterian model. First, innovations – at least the most important ones – are not realised by diverting to such an end the resources previously used according to traditional schemes by the same entrepreneur-innovator. Secondly, in conformity to traditional marginalist equilibrium theory, there are no unused resources on which entrepreneur-innovators can rely. Thus entrepreneurs can realise their innovations only if they have at their disposal some ad hoc purchasing power, with which they are able to draw the resources required to start new productive processes from 'old' firms (that is, from the set of traditional productive activities) and from consumers. According to Schumpeter, such purchasing power is created *ex novo* by the banks: thus, the innovative and executive capacity of entrepreneurs needs to be accompanied by the far-sightedness and ability of bankers to evaluate aright the potentialities of new initiatives. Bankers too, like entrepreneurs, have to accept the challenge of uncertainty (and the consequent risks of losses and failures) that accompanies anything which is new.

Entrepreneurs set on innovation apply to bankers who, if they decide to finance the innovation, agree to the loan and thus create the means of payment with which entrepreneurs can enter the markets for productive resources. By assumption, in equilibrium all available productive resources are already utilised; as a consequence, the additional demand cannot be satisfied by an increase in supply. Thus, there is an increase in prices, which automatically reduces the purchasing power of consumers and the 'traditional' firms: namely, those firms that, operating along the traditional lines of the circular flow, go on restoring the stocks of productive resources through current receipts. The inflationary process allows new firms, financed by banks with newly created means of payment, to draw productive resources from their traditional uses. This is a theory of 'forced saving': an element common to various theories developed within the Austrian school, from von Mises to Hayek who, as we saw

(§ 11.6), made use of it in his theory of the trade cycle. Such theories are connected to the idea that the economy tends to full employment. Monetarist theories maintaining that private investments are 'crowded out' by public expenditure, developed in the 1950s and 1960s as a reaction to Keynesian theories favouring active fiscal policies in support of aggregate demand, are but variants of the theory of forced saving.

The trade cycle is linked to the process of development. The phases of expansion take place when the innovation is imitated by a swarm of new firms attracted by the temporary profits realised by the entrepreneur-innovator, and when the inflation induced by the bank's creation of new purchasing power stimulates productive activity. The phases of recession arrive when repayment of the loans provokes credit deflation; furthermore, if firms are able to pay back the banks, it is thanks to sale on the market of products obtained with new technologies, but this exerts a downward pressure on the demand for, and prices of, the old products, which leads to bankruptcy for firms that have remained anchored to old production technologies, and especially those most directly hit by competition from the new products. In fact, within the sector where innovation has taken place, prices fall below production costs for those firms that have not adopted new production techniques (and costs have increased in the meantime, as a consequence of increases in the prices of productive resources caused by excess demand for them); thus, those who fail to keep pace by adapting to the innovations are expelled from the market.

If innovations were uniformly distributed over time, taking place now in one sector of the economy, now in another, the phases of expansion and recession would concern different sectors in different periods of time, as they come to be affected by the innovative process, while on average development would follow a regular path for the economy as a whole. However, according to Schumpeter the development process is discontinuous. In fact, innovation implies a break in the traditional way of proceeding: in other words, the barriers represented by the force of tradition should be overcome in order to implement the innovative change, and such barriers are easier to overcome the more widespread the change is within the economy. Thus innovations do not constitute a regular flow over time, but appear as grouped in 'swarms'.[7]

Schumpeter's trade cycle theory thus has an essential characteristic: the endogenous nature – that is, internal to the theory – of the relationship between cycle and development. In this respect the Schumpeterian theory is analogous to the Marxian one, in that within both theories the

---

[7] Schumpeter 1912, p. 223. 'Schumpeterian' mathematical models of the trade cycle have been worked out assuming an irregular flow of innovations: cf. for instance Calzoni and Rossi 1980.

same mechanism behind the cycle – in the case of Marx, the alternating vicissitudes of the conflict between capitalists and workers; in the case of Schumpeter, the irregular flow of innovations – also lies behind the process of economic development. Within both theories, the connection between cycle and development is shown by the fact that the situation at the end of a cycle must be different from the situation at the beginning because of technological change, which is an essential part in the cyclical movement of the economy.

The basic model of development theory presented in the 1912 book did not change in substance in the ponderous work on *Business cycles*, published in English in 1939, in two volumes and more than a thousand pages packed with text and footnotes. As a matter of fact, the fame of Schumpeter's theory of the cycle owes more to his youthful work than to *Business cycles*. In this latter work, substantially the same theories are repeated, illustrated and discussed from different points of view, as the very subtitle of the work indicates: 'A theoretical, historical and statistical analysis of the capitalist process'. There are, however, some new contributions worth noting.

One of these contributions dealt with analysis of market forms other than perfect competition, which Joan Robinson (1933) and Chamberlin (1933) had worked on after Sraffa's 1926 article (cf. below, § 16.3).[8] In their wake, Schumpeter recognised the existence of unused productive capacity but did not come round to accepting the Keynesian ideas: as in his 1912 book, analysis in the 1939 work was also carried out as if the assumption of full utilisation in equilibrium of available resources did in fact always hold (and indeed the 'reserve' productive capacity recalled by Schumpeter is *desired* by entrepreneurs).

Another contribution concerned an aspect of the development process stressed by Schumpeter, namely the simultaneous presence of many cycles. In his historical-statistical analysis, in particular, Schumpeter utilised a scheme with three cycles, short, long and very long run (respectively named Kitchin, Juglar and Kondratieff cycles from the names of the scholars who – according to Schumpeter's own reconstruction – had first identified and analysed them), the fifty-year or Kondratieff cycle having to do with 'epoch-making innovations' that affect the whole of the

---

[8] With an article Schumpeter intervened in the debate on the theory of the firm, started by Clapham's 1922 article in the *Economic Journal*, and in which Sraffa also took part with his 1926 article. Schumpeter's 1928 contribution was essentially an attempt to present to English readers his own theory; however, the need to abridge his reasoning in a few pages and to include reference to the debate on Marshallian theory and returns to scale, together with the rather German style, made for a convoluted exposition and limited the impact of the article.

productive system: railways with the transport revolution, electricity, or electronics in our own times.[9]

4.   The breakdown of capitalism

The second among the three main works of Schumpeter's maturity, *Capitalism, socialism and democracy*, published in 1942, is possibly his now most frequently quoted work: even those who have not read it often recall its main thesis, according to which capitalism cannot survive and is destined to be supplanted by socialism. However, all too often it is forgotten that, unlike Marx, Schumpeter did not see this as a triumphal march of human progress, but rather as an advance on the road to decadence.[10]

Political scientists and sociologists mainly focus attention on Schumpeter's prophecy, while modern economic theory, which seems to consider the possibility of mathematical formalisation as crucial, appears to place the decay of capitalism thesis outside its field of enquiry.[11] However, this means undervaluing the role that Schumpeter attributed to an essentially economic element in his argumentation, namely change in the market forms dominating the economy.

The central thesis of the book had already been foreshadowed by Schumpeter in his 1928 article in the *Economic Journal*:

Capitalism, whilst economically stable, and even gaining in stability, creates, by rationalising the human mind, a mentality and a style of life incompatible with its own fundamental conditions, motives and social institutions, and will be changed, although not by economic necessity and probably even at some sacrifice of economic welfare, into an order of things which it will be merely matter of taste and terminology to call Socialism or not.[12]

---

[9] As a matter of fact exaltation of the 'long waves', commonly attributed to Schumpeter, and by him to Kondratieff, was originally due to Pareto, as Sylos Labini 1950 remarked. This theory recently came back into vogue, first as an explanation of the long stagnation of the 1970s and 1980s and then, in the opposite direction, to extol the potentialities of the 'microelectronics revolution'.

[10] McCord Wright 1950, pp. 195–6, considered the book 'one of the most able defences of capitalism ever published', and maintained that in it Schumpeter adopted the technique of Mark Antony's speech, 'by coming first "to bury Caesar not to praise him" (capitalism is doomed)', while ready to state that '"Brutus" moreover is "an honourable man" (socialism is "workable").' The correctness of this interpretation is confirmed by a relatively unknown article of 1946 (brought to my attention by Paolo Sylos Labini), in which Schumpeter summarised the theses of his 1942 book and proposed that 'free men' react to the tendencies therein illustrated, which risk leading to the 'decomposition' of society and the victory of 'centralised and authoritarian statalism', with a 'moral reform' drawing on the corporative principles of the encyclical *Quadragesimo Anno* of Pope Pius XI (Schumpeter 1946, pp. 103–8).

[11] There is, however, a considerable literature on this issue. Cf. for instance the essays collected in Heertje 1981.

[12] Schumpeter 1928, pp. 385–6.

Thus, Schumpeter's thesis had already taken shape before the Great Crisis: it had nothing to do with the stagnation theories based on the dissolution of investment opportunities, which after Keynes were taken up and developed by Hansen (1938), but rather looked back to the Weberian view of capitalism (cf. above, § 11.3) as an all-embracing rationalisation process affecting both productive activity and culture.[13] According to Schumpeter, there is a contradiction between the 'economic' and 'political' components of capitalistic development: the 'economic stability' of capitalism requires incessant development, but this creates growing difficulties for its 'political stability': beyond a certain point such difficulties make the breakdown of capitalism inevitable.

The core of Schumpeter's argument is the connection between the process of economic development and destruction of the politico-social foundations of capitalism. The connection has two aspects: on the positive side, growth of an opposition to capitalism associated mainly with the spread of rationalistic ways of thinking and the swelling ranks of intellectuals; on the negative side, the weakening of capitalism's 'protective strata', consisting mainly of the ranks of small and average-sized entrepreneurs, faced with the growth of the big bureaucratised firms. The former aspect concerns what the Marxist tradition considers the 'superstructure' of capitalistic societies, the latter the 'structure'; as is customary in Schumpeterian analysis, the two aspects interact in the process of social transformation.[14]

Bureaucratisation of the economy hinders both the innovative action of entrepreneurs and the 'creative destruction', i.e. bankruptcy of slow-moving firms, which frees resources for the innovating firms and continuously selects the ranks of firm owners and managers and indeed characterises the process of development in a competitive economy. Bureaucratisation is the result of changes in dominant market forms through a process of industrial concentration (an aspect already stressed by Marx) which implies, among other things, transformation of the activity of technological innovation into routine. (Much the same had already been argued by Karl Renner and Rudolf Hilferding, leading representatives of Austrian socialism and companions of Schumpeter's at Vienna University).

The Schumpeterian theory of market forms is not well specified but, given its intrinsically dynamic character, it stands out distinctly from the

---

[13] Let us recall that Weber's 1904–5 fundamental work had been reprinted only six years earlier, and had had considerable immediate impact on German culture.

[14] Schumpeter followed Weber in rejecting Marxian materialism, according to which the evolution of the 'superstructure' is essentially determined by what happens within the 'structure' of human societies; the causal relation was not, however, inverted, but left room for recognition of a complex interdependence between the two aspects.

traditional marginalist theory. Against 'the traditional conception of the *modus operandi* of competition', which takes place in a static context and leads to the so-called law of the one price, Schumpeter (1942, pp. 84–5) argued,

the competition from the new commodity, the new technology, the new source of supply, the new type of organization (the largest-scale unit of control for instance) – competition which commands a decisive cost or quality advantage and which strikes not at the margins of the profits and the outputs of the existing firms but at their foundations and their very lives. This kind of competition is as much more effective than the other as a bombardment is in comparison with forcing a door [. . . It] acts not only when in being but also when it is merely an ever-present threat. It disciplines before it attacks. The businessman feels himself to be in a competitive situation even if he is alone in his field.

Competition, as we can see, is associated with the freedom of entry of new innovative firms into the market. This means attributing little importance to the barriers to competition stemming from market differentiation, upon which Schumpeter's colleague at Harvard, Edward Chamberlin (1933), so much insists. It also foreshadows a radical critique of anti-monopolistic policies based on the number of firms active in the market.

The process of industrial concentration also generates drastic change in the social structure: 'The perfectly bureaucratized giant industrial unit not only ousts the small or medium-sized firm and "expropriates" its owners, but in the end it also ousts the entrepreneur and expropriates the bourgeoisie as a class which in the process stands to lose not only its income but also what is infinitely more important, its function' (ibid., p. 134).

Economic and social transformations are accompanied by equally radical changes in culture and ideology: 'Dematerialized, defunctionized and absentee ownership does not impress and call forth moral allegiance as the vital form of property did' (ibid., p. 142). 'The social atmosphere of capitalism' thus changes: 'capitalism creates a critical frame of mind which, after having destroyed the moral authority of so many institutions, in the end turns against its own; the bourgeois finds to his amazement that the rationalist attitude does not stop at the credentials of kings and popes but goes on to attack private property and the whole scheme of bourgeois values' (ibid., p. 143).

In this respect Schumpeter offered some provocative remarks on the 'sociology of the intellectual' (ibid., p. 145), often invoked in recent years – particularly since 1968 – in attempts to interpret waves of student uprisings: 'Intellectuals are in fact people who wield the power of the spoken and the written word, and one of the touches that distinguishes them from other people who do the same is the absence of direct responsibility for practical affairs' (ibid., p. 147). However, 'from the criticism of a text to the criticism of a society, the way is shorter than it seems' (ibid., p. 148). In this situation, intellectuals favour the spread of critical attitudes towards capitalist society, and in particular an attitude of rejection towards the heroic role of the entrepreneur and that basic institution of capitalism which is private property. 'That social atmosphere or code of values affects not only policies – the spirit of legislation – but also administrative practice' (ibid., p. 155); hence the 'decomposition' (ibid., p. 156) of the capitalistic society.

Such an analysis clearly moves along the borderline between economics, sociology and political sciences, but this is not a sufficient reason to consider it alien to the field of scientific research; on the contrary, precisely in virtue of its interdisciplinary nature it still constitutes an important reference point for reflections on the possible paths of evolution of market economies.

5.   The path of economic science

After *The essence and the principles of economic theory* and after *The theory of economic development*, the third great work of the young Schumpeter is a long essay published in 1914, on *Epochs in the history of doctrines and methods*. In this work, Schumpeter set out not only to retrace the path followed by economic enquiry from the beginning to his own times, but also, and mainly, to interpret the path, or in other words to offer a theory of the development of economic science.

Similarly, in his maturity, after *Business cycles* and *Capitalism, socialism and democracy*, the third great work is the *History of economic analysis*, left unfinished and published posthumously in 1954. (Another important contribution in this field is the volume, published posthumously in 1951, *Ten great economists: from Marx to Keynes*, which collected biographical essays written in different periods.) Again, having moved forward in his analysis of capitalism and its prospects, Schumpeter felt the need to turn his mind to the path followed by economic science. In this case, however, the dimensions of the work afforded him the scope to pursue a twofold objective: both a *history* of economic analysis, in the traditional sense of illustrating the path followed by economic enquiries, and a *theory* of this history, in the sense of *interpretation* of the path, as we saw above referring to the *Epochs*.

With his historical enquiry Schumpeter (1954, p. 6) also set out to tackle an epistemological issue: to study 'what may be called the process of the Filiation of Scientific Ideas – the process by which men's efforts to

understand economic phenomena produce, improve and pull down analytic structures in an unending sequence'. The study of such a process is
an essential part of the effort to push science ahead: Schumpeter considered simplistic the thesis that 'current work [. . .] will preserve whatever
is still useful of the work of preceding generations' (ibid., p. 4), and maintained, on the contrary, that 'we stand to profit from visits to the lumber
room provided we do not stay there too long' (ibid.; the qualification
seems ironical if we consider the sheer magnitude of his effort).

The reason why the 'visits to the lumber room' are useful does not
reside in the fact that 'to a large extent, the economics of different epochs
deal with different sets of facts and problems' (ibid., p. 5); in fact, for the
field of economic analysis Schumpeter saw no good reason to stress the
historically relative nature typical of social sciences (although he recognised that 'economic analysis and its results are certainly affected by historical relativity', ibid., p. 13). The reasons in favour of an enquiry into
the history of the theoretical developments hold for economic analysis as
for any other science: if we limit ourselves to the study of the most recent
treatise, without any historical reflection whatsoever, 'a sense of *lacking
direction and meaning*' will spread among the students (ibid., p. 4).

According to Schumpeter (ibid.),

Scientific analysis [. . .] is not simply progressive discovery of an objective reality
[. . .] Rather it is an incessant struggle with creations of our own and our predecessors' minds and it 'progresses', if at all, in a criss-cross fashion, not as logic,
but as the impact of new ideas or observations or needs, and also as the bents
and temperaments of new men, dictate.

The closing lines of the quotation stress the role of the human element:
an element that Schumpeter emphasised in his biographical essays, but
that was also relevant in the *Epochs* and in the *History*. We might even
suggest a parallel between the hero in Schumpeter's theory of development, the entrepreneur-innovator, and the economist who contributes to
the progress of her or his science.

In studying the zigzag path of economic science, Schumpeter focused
attention on theories and analytical tools, leaving aside visions or ide-
ologies, or 'systems of political economy'.[15] Indeed, it is only when we

---

[15] Schumpeter 1954, p. 38, explicitly stressed his choice to produce a 'history of economic
analysis', not a history of 'systems of political economy' (that is, 'an exposition of a
comprehensive set of economic policies that its author advocates on the strength of
certain unifying (normative) principles such as the principles of economic liberalism,
of socialism, and so on'), nor a history of 'economic thought' ('that is, the sum total of
all the opinions and desires concerning economic subjects, especially concerning public
policy bearing upon these subjects that, at any given time and place, float in the public
mind').

succeed in isolating the analytical aspect in economic enquiries from the elements of vision and ideology – Schumpeter maintained – that we can speak of ' "scientific progress" between Mill and Samuelson' in 'the same sense in which we may say that there has been technological progress in the extraction of teeth between the times of John Stuart Mill and our own' (ibid., p. 39).

As was pointed out in chapter 1, according to Schumpeter the analytical work does not consist solely in working out formal theorems, but also in working out a conceptual apparatus for the representation of reality, and indeed this latter aspect comes first in importance. As we saw, 'conceptualisation' constitutes the second stage of research work, after the pre-analytical stage in which the problem to be tackled and the direction of analysis are more or less vaguely defined, and before the stage of construction of formal models.

Let us now turn to another question: what interpretative line do we find running through Schumpeter's researches on the history of economic thought and economic analysis? To answer the question let us start from some anomalous evaluations of the Austrian economist: his admiration for Aristotle and the Scholastics (of whom he said: 'it is they who come nearer than does any other group to having been the "founders" of scientific economics': ibid., p. 97), his underestimation of Smith's contribution,[16] and his positive appraisal of both Marx and Walras at the same time. There is a parallel here with his methodological liberalism, and with his idea that we should study as two distinct aspects equilibrium (Walras) and economic development (Marx); similarly, concerning the Scholastics we may recall (as Stolper 1951, p. 176 does) 'the belief that one could understand Being only by simultaneously understanding its Order and Motion'.

However, this is only one among the interpretative lines that Schumpeter offered in his historical reconstruction. Another important interpretative line, explicitly indicated by him, is that which identified in the chain 'physiocrats–Smith–John Stuart Mill–neoclassical theory' the dominant line of development in economic research. Schumpeter contrasted with this chain the Ricardo–Marx line, considered a deviation along which sight is lost of the central role played by demand and supply in the determination of equilibrium, and of the fact that the issue of

---

[16] 'The *Wealth of nations* does not contain a single *analytic* idea, principle, or method that was entirely new in 1776' (Schumpeter 1954, p. 184; italics in the original). Schumpeter's statement seems to repeat, with a somewhat excessive generalisation, a remark made by Marx (1867–94, vol. 1, p. 367 n.): 'Adam Smith did not bring forward a single new proposition concerning the division of labour.'

income distribution in essence concerns determination of the prices of productive factors.[17]

A central element in the chain connecting the classical (including David Ricardo, in this respect) to the neoclassical economists is constituted by the notion of *homo oeconomicus*:

The conscious will of the individual, fleeing from pain and seeking satisfaction, is the scientific nucleus of this strictly rationalist and intellectualist system of philosophy and sociology which, unsurpassed in its baldness, shallowness and its radical lack of understanding for every thing that moves man and holds together society, was with a certain justification already an abomination to the contemporaries and to an even larger extent to later generations in spite of all its merits.[18]

The Austrian economist was implicitly suggesting here what in other writings became his central contribution: the possibility of a different – and more attractive – view of the economic agent, namely the active figure of the entrepreneur-innovator (and of the banker). As was the case with many theoreticians (beginning with Smith in book IV of the *Wealth of nations*), so too for Schumpeter reconstruction of the history of economic thought was in a sense part of his theoretical contribution, in the twofold sense of clarifying its methodological and conceptual foundations through contrasts and analogies, while stressing the innovative qualities marking it out from the whole of the previous tradition.

[17] The interpretative line adopted by Schumpeter is clearly quite different from the line taken in the present volume.

[18] Schumpeter 1914, p. 87; cf. also p. 97 and pp. 177–8.

16   Piero Sraffa[1]

1.   First writings: money and banking

Piero Sraffa (1898–1983) is one of the leading intellectuals of the twentieth century: not only for his strictly economic contributions, but also for his influence on others, from Antonio Gramsci to Ludwig Wittgenstein.

In the field of economic sciences, Sraffa's cultural project is an extremely ambitious one: 'to shunt the car of economic science' in a direction opposite to that indicated by Jevons, one of the protagonists of the 'marginalist revolution'. With his writings, in fact, Sraffa aims to expose the weak points of the marginalist approach as developed by, for instance, Jevons, Menger, Walras, Marshall, Böhm-Bawerk, Hayek and Pigou and at the same time to repropose the classical approach of Adam Smith, David Ricardo and, in certain respects, Karl Marx. In order to better understand its nature and impact, it may be useful to follow the gradual development of this cultural project, from the first writings on money and banking to the edition of Ricardo's works and the small but dense volume on *Production of commodities by means of commodities* (1960).

Piero Sraffa was born in Turin on 5 August 1898. His father, Angelo Sraffa (1865–1937), was a well-known professor of commercial law and subsequently (from 1917 to 1926) Dean of the Bocconi University in Milan. Following his father as he moved from one university seat to another, the young Sraffa studied in Parma, Milan and Turin. Here he attended the classical lyceum (at the Liceo D'Azeglio, a forge of antifascist youth) and then (since 1916) the faculty of law. From March 1917 to March 1920 he did his military service; in November 1920 he graduated with a dissertation on *L'inflazione monetaria in Italia durante e dopo la guerra* (Monetary inflation in Italy during and after the war), discussed with Luigi Einaudi.[2]

---

[1] In the following pages the results of previous works are summarised; the reader is referred to them for a wider treatment of the issues discussed in this chapter: cf. Roncaglia 1975, 1983b, 1990a, 2000.

[2] Luigi Einaudi (1874–1961), a pragmatic liberal, professor of public finance at Turin since 1902, member of the Senate since 1919, withdrew from public life under fascism and was

The degree dissertation also constituted his first publication (Sraffa 1920). The rapid increase in prices was associated with the expansion in the circulation of money, in line with the dominant tradition of the quantity theory of money. However, Sraffa's empirical analysis differentiated itself pragmatically from the quantity theory of money (in the then dominant Fisherian version), to consider the diverse evolution of different price indexes, the meanings of which were connected to the different viewpoints of the various groups of protagonists of economic life, in particular the social classes of workers and entrepreneurs. Implicit in this position was the idea that a general price index (a crucial notion not only for the Fisherian version of the quantity theory of money, but more generally for all theories that conceive money simply as a 'veil', with no influence on real variables) is misleading precisely in that it obscures the central role of social conflicts in economic life.[3] This point is worth stressing since, as we saw above (§ 14.3), it was precisely the non-univocal nature of the concept of the general price level (and thus of its inverse, the purchasing power of money) that underlay Keynes's criticism of the quantity theory of money in the opening chapters of his *Treatise on money* (Keynes 1930).

The most significant original contribution offered by Sraffa's thesis, anyhow, lies in the distinction between stabilisation of the internal and

in exile to Switzerland during the final stages of the Second World War; he then became Governor of the Bank of Italy in 1945, minister for the budget in 1947, and president of the Italian Republic (1948–55). On him see Faucci 1986. Here we limit ourselves to recalling two aspects: his policy – a very drastic one, and crowned with success – of stabilisation of the internal value of the lira in 1947–8; and his controversy with Croce on the relationship between economic and political liberalism. On this latter case cf. Croce and Einaudi 1957; the writings by Croce to which we refer date from 1927, those by Einaudi date from 1928 and 1931. Einaudi and Croce agreed on the fact that economic liberalism cannot be an absolute tenet, differently from political liberalism, but only a practical rule. However, Einaudi stressed the instrumental role of economic liberalism in favouring the diffusion of economic power (that otherwise would be concentrated in the hands of the state, or of the political elite). The fact remains that no one could call himself a liberal if he were exclusively interested in the most widespread *laissez-faire* in the economic arena. Though holding conservative views, Einaudi thus opened the way to the development of a reformist or socialist liberalism, such as that of Piero Gobetti, Carlo and Nello Rosselli, and the political movement 'Justice and freedom' (Giustizia e libertà). Sraffa, as a student at the D'Azeglio Lyceum and a cousin of the Rosselli brothers, participated in this cultural climate and, though oriented towards Gramsci's Marxism, always had very good relations with many protagonists of the democratic streams of anti-fascism.

[3] In a similar direction went, a few years later, one of the critiques that Sraffa (1932) developed of Hayek. According to the theory of forced savings utilised by Hayek, a period of inflation may correspond to an accumulation of capital quicker than what is justified by the basic parameters of the economy, but the system then automatically goes back to its long period equilibrium through a deflationary process. In criticising this theory, Sraffa stressed that the re-establishment of a situation of monetary equilibrium does not bring back each individual economic agent to the initial conditions.

the external value of money, or in other words between stabilisation of the average level of domestic prices and stabilisation of the exchange rate. The two things coincide, according to the traditional theory of the gold standard; however, at least in principle they should be kept separate. The distinction becomes essential, then, when considering both short run problems and inconvertible paper money systems. Such a distinction thus had crucial importance for the policy choices of the time.[4] Moreover, it was also connected to the development of Keynesian theory: we may recall, in fact, that Keynes did not use it in *Indian currency and finance* (1913), but did bring it into his *Tract on monetary reform* (1923), having in the meantime (in August 1921) met Sraffa.[5]

Sraffa's early publications again addressed monetary issues: an article of 1922 in the *Economic Journal* on the crisis of the Banca Italiana di Sconto, and one on the bank crisis in Italy – again of 1922 – in the *Manchester Guardian Supplement on the Reconstruction in Europe*. The two articles reveal a thorough command of the institutional and technical aspects of banking (probably thanks at least in part to the practical experience the young Sraffa had acquired in a provincial branch of a bank immediately after graduating) and a strikingly well-informed approach and awareness of the interests at stake.

The first of these two articles (Sraffa 1922a) reconstructed the vicissitudes of the Banca Italiana di Sconto from its birth at the end of 1914 to its bankruptcy in December 1921. Sraffa concluded with some pessimistic remarks on the risks involved in direct relations between banks and enterprises, on the inevitability of such relations given the backwardness of Italy's financial markets and on the difficulty of bringing about a change in the situation, due in the first place to a lack of real will at the political level.[6] The second article (Sraffa 1922b) highlighted the weakness of Italy's three leading commercial banks (Banca Commerciale, Credito Italiano and Banca di Roma), casting serious doubts on the correctness of their official accounts and of the institutional expedient (resorting to a 'Consorzio per sovvenzioni sui valori industriali') adopted to side-step the law setting limits on the support issuing banks could give to commercial banks.[7]

---

[4] Cf. De Cecco 1993; Ciocca and Rinaldi 1997.

[5] Among other things Sraffa was the editor of the Italian edition of the *Tract*, published in 1925 under the title *La riforma monetaria* by the Fratelli Treves publishers in Milan. Keynes and Sraffa met in Cambridge in August 1921: Sraffa in that period was staying in London for a few months, attending courses at the London School of Economics.

[6] Explicit in this sense was the conclusion of the article: 'But even if these laws were not futile in themselves, what could be their use as long as the Government is prepared to be the first to break them so soon as it is blackmailed by a band of gunmen or a group of bold financiers?' (Sraffa 1922a, p. 197).

[7] The publication of this article provoked a harsh reaction from Mussolini: cf. Roncaglia 1983b and Naldi 1998c.

Monetary issues were subsequently to re-emerge among Sraffa's interests. A brief, biting attack on an article in *Popolo d'Italia* on the movements of the exchange rate of the lira was published in Piero Gobetti's (1901–26) *Rivoluzione liberale* in 1923; two important letters on the revaluation of the lira were published by Angelo Tasca (1892–1960) in *Stato operaio* in 1927; from 1928 to 1930 Sraffa gave courses at Cambridge University on the Italian and German financial systems, along with his more celebrated lectures on the theory of value. The 1932 controversy with Hayek, to which we shall return, was also about problems in monetary theory.

Apart from their intrinsic value, Sraffa's first publications stand as a testimonial to his personality as an all-round economist, in whom the dominant interest in pure theory was accompanied by a solid knowledge of the institutional details and by exemplary analyses of specific real-world issues.

2.   Friendship with Gramsci

In May 1919, at the University of Turin, Sraffa met Antonio Gramsci (1891–1937). They were introduced by Umberto Cosmo (1868–1944), who had been Sraffa's teacher of Italian literature at upper secondary school, and Gramsci's teacher at the university. In 1919 Gramsci founded *L'ordine nuovo* (The new order); Sraffa collaborated with some translations from German and three short articles which he sent from London on the occasion of his visit there in 1921. The same year of 1921 saw the foundation of the Italian Communist Party in Livorno; Gramsci became its secretary in 1924. Sraffa never joined the party, fully maintaining his independence of views, while keeping up a close intellectual relationship with his friend.

An important piece of evidence documenting the two friends' political exchanges is offered by a letter from Sraffa that Gramsci published (unsigned, initialled S.) in the April 1924 issue of *L'ordine nuovo* with his reply (Gramsci and Sraffa 1924). In his letter Sraffa stressed the function played by bourgeois forces of opposition in the struggle against fascism and the importance of democratic institutions for the social and political development of the proletariat. In Sraffa's opinion, in the situation of the time, characterised by the rise of a fascist dictatorship, the working class was absent from the political scene. The unions and the Communist Party were incapable of organising political action, while the workers were compelled to face their problems as individuals, rather than as organised groups. 'The main issue, taking first place over any other, is one of "freedom" and "order": the others will come later, but for now they can be of no interest to the workers. Now is the time for the democratic forces of opposition, and I think we must let them act and possibly help them' (ibid., p. 4).

In his answer, Gramsci rejected Sraffa's suggestions, maintaining that they would bring the liquidation of the Communist Party, subjected as it would have been to the strategy of the bourgeois forces of opposition, and criticised his friend for 'having so far failed to rid himself of the ideological residue of his liberal-democratic intellectual background, namely normative and Kantian, not Marxist and dialectical' (ibid.). We should keep in mind, though, that Gramsci's position necessarily mirrored that taken by Amadeo Bordiga, then secretary of the Communist Party: a party in which the principle of centralist leadership prevailed, with the exclusion of any dissent from the official party line.

Indeed, the very fact that Sraffa's letter was published, probably after heart-searching discussions between the two friends, amounted to a recognition of the importance of the problems there discussed and of the political ideas proposed by the young economist. To these ideas Gramsci drew attention, displaying greater openness towards them, in a letter reserved for comrades closer to his position, and thus less subservient to the Bordiga orthodoxy.[8]

The episode suggests that Sraffa played some role in the development of Gramsci's political thinking, away from Bordiga's line, at least away from the idea of the total opposition of the Communist Party to all the other political forces for the sake of the Bolshevik Revolution. Years later, Gramsci's political reflections appeared close to the position Sraffa had taken up as early as 1924, when Gramsci in turn proposed a pact between the anti-fascist political forces for the reconstruction of a democratic Italy after the hoped-for fall of the fascist regime. Indeed, we may consider significant in this respect the fact that, apparently in their last meeting in March 1937, it was to Sraffa that Gramsci entrusted a verbal message for the comrades still enjoying freedom, and one that he attached great importance to – the watchword for the constituent assembly, which synthesised the proposal hinted at above.

Along with this fundamental point in the political debate, we must also recall the help Sraffa gave Gramsci after his arrest in 1926. It was he who took pains to get books and magazines to his friend in prison; it was he who explored the possible paths to freedom (on the binding condition, that Gramsci insisted on, and which Sraffa adhered to, that no concessions be made to the fascist regime, such as a petition for pardon would have implied); it was he who liaised with communist leaders in

---

[8] Cf. Togliatti 1962, pp. 242 ff.

exile and gave Gramsci further food for thought (through the latter's sister-in-law, Tatiana Schucht) in the reflections that were to take shape in the *Quaderni del carcere*. Some documentation of these activities can now be found in a posthumously published volume of letters from Sraffa to Tatiana (Sraffa 1991).

3.   Criticism of Marshallian theory

Thus, in the years following graduation Sraffa's interests ranged from politics to questions of applied economics, in particular, monetary economics. His interest in theoretical issues probably developed after the beginning of his academic career, in November 1923, as lecturer in political economy and public finance at the University of Perugia, Faculty of Law. We may hypothesise that, having to give a general, introductory course of lectures in political economy, Sraffa found himself having to confront the academic framework then dominant in Italy, namely marginalism in the Marshallian version of Maffeo Pantaleoni (cf. above, § 13.6), whom Sraffa himself (1924, p. 648), in a beautiful obituary, called 'the prince of [Italy's] economists'.

The fruits of Sraffa's reflections – a radical critique of the Marshallian theory of the equilibrium of the firm and the industry – were set out in a long article published in Italian in 1925, 'Sulle relazioni fra costo e quantità prodotta' (On the relations between cost and quantity produced). Five years had passed since publication of the eighth edition of Marshall's *Principles of Economics*, and one year since his death.

Sraffa's article fell within a debate on the 'laws of returns' sparked off by a paper by John Harold Clapham (1873–1946) published in 1922 in the *Economic Journal*. The point in question was of vital importance for the Marshallian theoretical construction and more generally for the theories of value based on equilibrium between demand and supply. Within this approach, in particular within the Marshallian method of partial equilibriums, a decisive role is played by construction of a supply curve for each product, expressing production costs as a function of the quantity produced, both for the individual firm and for the industry as a whole.

Marshallian theory singled out three cases accounting for all eventualities: constant, increasing or decreasing returns, according to whether the average unit cost remains constant, decreases or increases when the quantity produced increases. Clapham, a professor of economic history, tackled the problem of the concrete application of these theoretical categories, and came to a provocative conclusion: the theoretical apparatus under consideration is sterile, since the three categories of constant, increasing and decreasing costs are 'empty economic boxes' (this was also the title of his article), impossible to fill with concrete examples of real industries.

Clapham's article provoked immediate response, with an article in the following issue of the *Economic Journal* by Arthur Cecil Pigou, paladin of a line of Marshallian orthodoxy that had led to the 'geometrical method' of demand and supply curves for the firm and the industry, for the short and the long period. This construct, as we saw above (§§ 13.3 and 13.7), did not fully correspond to Marshall's view of the world; in fact, walking a tightrope rich in ambiguities and corrections of direction, in subsequent editions of his *Principles* Marshall had attempted to reconcile an evolutionary, and thus intrinsically dynamic, conception with an analytical apparatus based on the requirement of equilibrium between supply and demand, and thus necessarily static. Greater fidelity to Marshall's ideas was shown by Dennis Robertson (1890–1963), who in a contribution to the debate (Robertson 1924) raised further doubts about Pigou's analytical apparatus.

In the following years the debate went on in the *Economic Journal*, with contributions, among others, by Allyn Young, Arthur Cecil Pigou, Lionel Robbins, Gerald Shove, Joseph Schumpeter and Roy Harrod.[9]

With his 1925 article, Sraffa joined the debate Clapham had begun by arguing that the problem of the 'empty boxes' does not concern how to apply the categories of constant, increasing and decreasing returns to real situations, but rather the existence of theoretical insurmountable difficulties within the theory of firm and industry equilibrium. Underlying all this, Sraffa pointed out, there was a conceptual confusion: in classical

---

[9] Allyn Young (1876–1929) was the author, in 1928, of an important contribution on 'Increasing returns and economic progress', but his influence on the development of economic thought was often an indirect one; for instance, the celebrated books by Knight (1921) and Chamberlin (1933) were born as doctoral dissertations under his supervision. Gerald Shove, Marshall's pupil, notwithstanding the few pages he had published, was an influential member of the 'Cambridge school'. Lionel Robbins (1898–1984) dominated the London School of Economics (where he was a professor from 1929) in the central decades of the twentieth century; a supporter of Hayek against Keynes, he participated as a protagonist in the policy debates of the period; from 1960 he was chairman of the *Financial Times*; his best-known work is *An essay on the nature and significance of economic science* (1932), famous for his definition of economics ('economics is the science which studies human behaviour as a relationship between ends and scarce means which have alternative uses': ibid., p. 16), but he was also the author of important works in the history of economic thought. He also had important roles as arts administrator (at such institutions as the National Gallery and the Royal Opera House), and chaired the Committee on Higher Education which produced, in 1963, the so-called 'Robbins Report', with far-reaching proposals for, among other things, a strong expansion of university education which, Robbins maintained, could take place without a lowering of the standards (on these experiences, cf. Robbins 1971, pp. 241–67 and 272–83). On Pigou, Schumpeter and Harrod cf. respectively § 13.9, chapter 15 and § 17.6.

political economy the 'law' of decreasing returns was associated with the problem of rent (namely, with the theory of distribution), while the 'law' of increasing returns was associated to the division of labour, or in other words general economic progress (namely, with the theory of production). Marshall and other neoclassical economists tried to put these two 'laws' on the same plane, co-ordinating them in a single 'law of non-proportional returns'. They were thus able to express costs as a function of the quantity produced, for firm and industry alike, and then to use these functions in the theory of prices. We thus get a supply curve for each product, to be set against the corresponding demand curve deduced from the 'law' of decreasing marginal utility (where each of these two curves 'may be compared to one blade of a pair of scissors', as Marshall 1890, p. 820, said). However, this meant transposing increasing and decreasing returns to an ambit different from the original ones; and this fact made it difficult to apply in the new ambit the justifications originally used to account for the variations in costs following from the variations in the quantities produced. Sraffa illustrated these difficulties analysing the literature on the subject.

In particular, Sraffa stressed that decreasing returns are connected to changes in the proportions of factors of production, while increasing returns stem from expanding production and increasing division of labour. The former case – decreasing returns – occurs when a factor of production is scarce. Now, unless we identify the industry with all the firms using a scarce factor, variations in average cost associated with increased production in the industry under consideration will be of the same order of magnitude as variations in costs simultaneously experienced by other industries using the same factor of production. The *ceteris paribus* assumption that underlies partial equilibrium analysis is thus violated.

As for increasing returns, they cannot be present at the same time in both the industry and the firms within it, since otherwise firms would go on expanding, until they reach a size incompatible with the assumption of competition; nor can they be found in various industries at the same time, otherwise the *ceteris paribus* clause would be breached once again. Marshall, well aware of this, had developed the category of economies of production external to the individual firm but internal to the industry; generalising such a category might have ensured consistency between increasing returns, the assumption of competition and the partial equilibrium method. However, Sraffa, with good reasons, considered such a generalisation to be wholly unrealistic. In conclusion, the theoretical building of the Marshallian tradition cannot comply with the requirement of logical consistency except by recourse to unrealistic ad hoc assumptions, that obviously constitute a wholly inadequate foundation for a theory designed for general interpretative application.

4. Imperfect competition and the critique of the representative firm

Sraffa's 1925 Italian paper attracted the interest of Edgeworth, co-editor – together with Keynes – of the *Economic Journal*. At the suggestion of the first of the two co-editors, the second asked Sraffa for an article for their review, and the young Italian economist was ready and happy to accept their offer.

The English paper (Sraffa 1926) is much shorter than the Italian one, and correspondingly much less rich in collateral elements of noticeable importance; the first half of the article consists of a summary of the main points in the Italian article, while the second half elaborates an original line of research. As we already saw above (§ 13.9), the idea is that, as a consequence of the imperfections present in all markets in the real world, within every industry each firm is confronted with a specific, negatively sloped, demand curve, even when many firms are simultaneously present in the industry. There is thus a crucial difference with respect to the traditional theory of competition, according to which each firm should confront a horizontal demand curve. The theory propounded by Sraffa was thus a theory of imperfect competition, that had the advantage of being compatible also with the cases of constant or increasing returns, and among other things took over various real world elements suggested here and there in Marshall's work. However, Sraffa stressed the limits of this approach already in the closing lines of his article. He remarked in fact 'that in the foregoing the disturbing influence exercised by the competition of new firms attracted to an industry the conditions of which permit of high monopolist profits has been neglected'. Basically, this meant neglecting competition in the classical sense of the term, consisting in the shifting of capital from one sector to another in pursuit of the maximum returns.

In the following years the theory of imperfect competition constituted a flourishing field of research (cf. above, § 13.9). Sraffa however, though originating this line of research (still influential today), soon abandoned it. As already said, it was based on a notion of competition – the one on which the marginalist approach focused attention, connected to the presence of many firms in the same industry – that was quite different from the notion developed by classical economists, concerning the free movement of capitals among the various sectors of the economy. It was in fact the conclusion of Sraffa's 1926 paper that paved the way for the modern non-neoclassical theory of non-competitive market forms, and in particular Paolo Sylos Labini's 1956 theory of oligopoly, based on the presence of obstacles to the entry of new firms into the economic sector under consideration.[10] The classical notion of competition, furthermore, constituted the basis for the line of research that Sraffa was already developing in a first draft (discussed with Keynes in 1928) of his 1960 book on *Production of commodities by means of commodities*.

Sraffa's radical departure from the traditional framework of the theory of the firm and the industry was then evident in his contributions to the symposium on 'Increasing returns and the representative firm' published in the *Economic Journal* in March 1930. The conclusion of these brief contributions was a clear-cut break with the then mainstream views: 'Marshall's theory [. . .] cannot be interpreted in a way which makes it logically self-consistent and, at the same time, reconciles it with the facts it sets out to explain'; thus, 'I think [. . .] that [it] should be discarded' (Sraffa 1930a, p. 93).

It is worth noting that here Sraffa's criticism was directed against a version of the Marshallian theory more faithful to Marshall's own original framework than Pigou's, namely the evolutionary version Robertson presented in his contribution to the symposium (Robertson 1930), based on the concept of the firm's 'life cycle' which Marshall had employed in an attempt to make increasing returns compatible with the firm's competitive equilibrium (cf. above, § 13.3). Like a biological organism, the firm goes through successive stages of development, maturity and decline; the 'representative' firm is half-way through the process of development, thus at a stage of increasing returns to scale. As Marshall himself pointed out, a concept of this type, that sees the expansion of firms depending on the 'life cycle' of entrepreneurial capacities, may be plausible in the case of directly family-run concerns, but cannot apply to modern joint stock companies.

Thus biological analogies prove a false exit to the blind alley Marshallian analysis had got into, hemmed in by the contradiction between increasing returns and competitive equilibrium. Sraffa had an easy task in pointing out the *deus ex machina* nature of the biological metaphors that Robertson used on Marshall's wake, which cannot fill in the gaps in logical consistency intrinsic to these analytic structures: 'At the critical points of his argument the firms and the industry drop out of the scene, and their place is taken by the trees and the forest, the bones

---

[10] Baumol's 'contestable markets' theory, which took into account the 'barriers to exit' consisting in 'sunk costs' together with the barriers to entry (cf. below, § 17.3), may be considered as a variant to this theory.

and the skeleton, the water-drops and the wave – indeed all the kingdoms of nature are drawn upon to contribute to the wealth of his metaphors' (Sraffa 1930a, pp. 90–1).

5.   Cambridge: Wittgenstein and Keynes

The 1926 paper published in the *Economic Journal* had considerable impact, especially in Cambridge. Keynes was thus able to offer Sraffa a job as lecturer at the university, which was then the most prestigious centre for economic theory in the world. In 1926 Sraffa was also awarded a chair in Italy, at Cagliari, but after Gramsci's imprisonment and the threats he himself received as an anti-fascist,[11] he decided to move to England, where he lived from 1927 until his death on 3 September 1983.

As lecturer in a foreign university, Sraffa was allowed to retain his chair in Italy; he did so, passing his salary to the economics library of Cagliari University. When Italian professors were called upon to swear loyalty to fascism, he resigned, wishing neither to take such an oath nor to dissociate himself from the line chosen by the Communist Party, which was to fulfil what might be seen as a purely formal obligation in order to keep channels of communication open with the younger generations (a line that meant a painful *volte-face* for the famous Latinist, Concetto Marchesi, a militant communist who took the oath after a public declaration that he never would).[12]

After a year spent settling in Cambridge (despite his previous stays in England, his English was by no means perfect when he arrived), Sraffa lectured for three years on the German and Italian financial systems and on the theory of value. This latter course made a great impact: Sraffa discussed the theories of classical economists, Ricardo in particular, and the general economic equilibrium theories of Walras and Pareto – little of which was known in the rather provincial England at the time – as well as advancing his own criticisms of the Cambridge (Marshall–Pigou) tradition, in particular the theory of the firm. However, Sraffa – who was increasingly shy of speaking in front of a public, hence of giving lessons as well – became an assistant director of research and finally librarian of the Marshall Library at the Economics Faculty. Since his arrival he had been attached to King's College, where Keynes reigned; in 1939 he became a fellow of Trinity College, and remained so until his death.

In the quiet Cambridge environment, Sraffa developed his researches along three lines connected in one great cultural design: the work on the critical edition of Ricardo's writings, entrusted to him by the Royal

[11] Cf. Naldi 1998a.   [12] On Sraffa's academic vicissitudes, cf. Naldi 1998b.

Society at the initiative of Keynes in 1930; researches in the field of the theory of value, which were to lead after thirty years' labour to *Production of commodities by means of commodities* (Sraffa recalled in the preface showing Keynes an outline of the central propositions as early as 1928); and a collateral interest in the development of Keynesian theory, in particular in the early 1930s. Moreover, in Cambridge Sraffa made the acquaintance of the Austrian philosopher Ludwig Wittgenstein (1889–1951), who became his friend and on whom Sraffa was to have a significant influence.

Sraffa met Wittgenstein in 1929. The Austrian philosopher had just arrived in Cambridge, called there by Bertrand Russell, who a few years before had organised the publication of a basic contribution to the development of modern philosophy, the *Tractatus logico-philosophicus* (1921). This book is generally considered the culmination of logical neo-positivism; Wittgenstein had conceived and written it during the war, that he had fought first on the Russian and then on the Italian fronts, and during a brief period of imprisonment in Italy at the end of the war. In the opinion of Wittgenstein himself, his contribution should have constituted the point of arrival of philosophical enquiry; therefore, after completing it, he considered that he had no other work to do in the philosophical field. A withdrawn, difficult character, Wittgenstein then retreated to teach in an Austrian small village primary school and to work as a monastery gardener. His contacts with the world of philosophical research were scant: a few letters and occasional meetings with Bertrand Russell or with the young Frank Ramsey, another Cambridge philosopher and mathematician who was also a friend of Sraffa's, and who died at the early age of twenty-six in 1930; above all, Wittgenstein retained some links with the so-called Vienna Circle animated by Moritz Schlick.

It may well have been the Viennese discussions – in particular a celebrated lecture by Brouwer on the foundations of mathematics – that finally persuaded Wittgenstein that after all there was still some work to be done in the philosophical field. Thus, early in 1929 Wittgenstein arrived in Cambridge, to become fellow of Trinity College after a few months; there he remained, except for a few brief intervals, until his death in April 1951.

When they were both in Cambridge, Wittgenstein and Sraffa generally spent an afternoon each week together, talking not so much about economics and philosophy directly but rather about a wide range of issues, from gardening to detective stories. These talks had a crucial influence on the Austrian philosopher, and on the transition from the logical atomism of the *Tractatus* to the mature positions set out in the *Philosophical investigations*, published posthumously in 1953.

Georg von Wright, a pupil of Wittgenstein, reported him as once having said 'that his discussions with Sraffa made him feel like a tree from which all the branches had been cut' (Wright 1955, pp. 15–16). Wittgenstein himself is still more explicit in his preface to the *Philosophical investigations*: 'I am indebted to [the criticism] which a teacher of this university, Mr. P. Sraffa, for many years unceasingly practised on my thoughts. I am indebted to *this* stimulus [the italics are Wittgenstein's] for the most consequential ideas of this book' (Wittgenstein 1953, p. viii).

Between Wittgenstein's initial and final positions there was a clear change, long thought out. With drastic simplification, let us focus attention on the methodological results that are of more direct interest to us, even at the cost of abstracting from elements quite important in other respects. The *Tractatus* argued that there was a correspondence between the world and the elements that constitute it (the 'facts') on the one hand, and our representation of the world (whose constituent elements are the 'thoughts', expressed in 'propositions') on the other. On this basis Wittgenstein argued that it is possible to build a logical, axiomatic set of propositions, each describing a 'fact' while together they describe the world, or rather, if not all the world, all that can be described in a rational form. On that for which no rational description can be provided (sentiments, religious beliefs, aesthetic judgements, etc.), said Wittgenstein, 'one must be silent'.

However, in the *Philosophical investigations* Wittgenstein abandoned the idea of language as 'mirroring' the world, and the idea of the 'unspeakable'. Discussions with Sraffa seem to have played a role in this. There is an anecdote that Wittgenstein himself told his pupils. One day, as they were travelling together on the train between Cambridge and London, 'Sraffa made a gesture, familiar to Neapolitans and meaning something like disgust or contempt, of brushing the underneath of his chin with an outward sweep of the finger tips of one hand.' The gesture can only acquire a specific meaning from the context in which it is performed; thus it contradicted Wittgenstein's idea that every proposition has to have a precise place in the axiomatic order of rational language, independently of the context in which it may be employed.[13]

Following this critique, in the *Philosophical investigations* Wittgenstein developed a new theory of language, and of the relations between it

---

[13] According to Malcolm (1958, p. 69), who related the anecdote, the object of the discussion was Wittgenstein's idea 'that a proposition and that which it describes must have the same "logical form", the same "logical multiplicity"'; according to von Wright, as Malcolm reported in a footnote, the object of the discussion was the idea that each proposition should have a 'grammar'. In a conversation with the present author (21 December 1972), Sraffa confirmed the anecdote, telling me that von Wright was right.

and the world it should describe. There is not just one type of language, Wittgenstein (1953, p. 21) asserted, 'but there are *countless* kinds: countless different types of use of what we call "symbols", "words", "sentences". And this multiplicity is not something fixed, given once for all; but new types of language, new language-games, as we may say, come into existence, and others become obsolete and get forgotten.' In general, Wittgenstein went on, 'the meaning of a word is its use in the language' (ibid., p. 33). However, words do not correspond to simple elements of reality, and these simple elements cannot be defined; nor is it possible to produce a general theory of language.

Wittgenstein demonstrated these theses with a series of examples of 'language games' – namely, theoretical models that focused attention on particular aspects of the real language, presenting them as the general language of a group of people. From these examples we may conclude that 'there is not [. . .] any unique analysis of propositions into their intrinsically unanalyzable elements. What sort of analysis will be useful and provide a real clarification depends on the circumstances, on just what is problematic about the propositions under examination' (Quinton 1968, p. 13).

We do not have any textual support for maintaining that Sraffa agreed with the point of arrival of Wittgenstein's reflections. We only know that the initial position of the Austrian philosopher had provoked criticisms on the side of the Italian economist, and that these criticisms had played a crucial role in Wittgenstein's subsequent thinking. Perhaps we may perceive Sraffa's political interests behind his opposition to an a priori theory of language and his preference for a theory open to recognising the role of social factors (the environment in which the 'linguistic game' takes place), of rules and conventions. Moreover, we may perhaps also perceive here a methodological choice: the rejection of all-embracing theories that pretend to describe any and all aspects of the world, starting from its elementary constituting elements; the choice instead of flexibility in theoretical constructions, aimed in each case at the specific problem under consideration.

After Gramsci and Wittgenstein, a third protagonist of twentieth-century culture to have fecund exchange with Sraffa was John Maynard Keynes, fifteen years older. Keynes was a great help to Sraffa on various occasions: in 1921 he asked Sraffa for a contribution for the *Manchester Guardian Supplement*; in 1922 he decided to publish in the prestigious *Economic Journal* a paper by the then twenty-four-year-old Italian economist; in 1926 he asked – though acting at Edgeworth's suggestion – for the paper criticising the Marshallian theory of the firm which was to be written in a few months and published in the same year, in the December issue of the

Economic Journal; in 1927 he brought Sraffa to Cambridge as lecturer and in the following years helped to establish his Italian friend in the Anglo-Saxon world; in 1930 he had the Royal Economic Society entrust Sraffa with the task of preparing the critical edition of Ricardo's writings; and in 1940 he had Sraffa released from the detention camp which the Italian had been sent to as an 'enemy alien' when Italy entered the war. The only publication Sraffa signed jointly was with Keynes: both keen bibliophiles, in 1938 they edited the reprint of an extremely rare booklet, *An abstract of a treatise on human nature* (Hume 1938), complete with a learned introduction containing decisive proofs for its attribution to Hume, rather than to Adam Smith as was generally supposed.[14] Sraffa also took care of the Italian edition (1925) of Keynes's *Tract on monetary reform*.

More relevant to our immediate concern is the cultural exchange in the field of economic theory. Four episodes may be recalled in this respect; we have already hinted at three of them: the likely influence on Keynes of the distinction between stabilisation of money in relation to the level of domestic prices and in relation to the exchange rate proposed by Sraffa in his graduate thesis (cf. above, § 1); his participation in the 'Cambridge Circus' and more generally in the debates that stimulated Keynes's transition from the *Treatise on money* to the *General theory* (cf. above, § 14.4); and his critical intervention (Sraffa 1932) on Hayek's theory (cf. above, § 11.6), from which Keynes derived the theory of own interest rates that is at the centre of the analysis in chapter 17 of the *General theory*.

The fourth episode was recalled by Sraffa himself in his preface to *Production of commodities by means of commodities*. Sraffa (1960, p. vi) stated that 'when in 1928 Lord Keynes read a draft of the opening propositions of this paper, he recommended that, if constant returns were *not* to be assumed, an emphatic warning to that effect should be given'. Keynes was the only economist to be thanked in the preface (Sraffa's thanks also went to three mathematicians – Ramsey, Watson and Besicovitch – and, in the Italian edition, to Raffaele Mattioli, a banker who long played a leading role in the Banca Commerciale Italiana as well as being a very close friend of Sraffa's and a moving force in the preparation of the Italian edition of the book). The point Keynes intervened on is of fundamental importance, since the absence of an assumption on returns constitutes a crucially distinctive feature of Sraffa's book, implying among other things the abandonment of the marginalist notion of equilibrium (cf. below,

---

[14] An interesting point in this introduction concerns the stress laid on Hume's thesis that "Tis not [. . .] reason, which is the guide of life, but custom' (Hume 1938, p. xxx).

§ 7): thus it seems quite likely that his discussions with Keynes played an important role in the development of Sraffa's ideas.

6.   The critical edition of Ricardo's writings

The difficulties economists like Robertson (in the 1930 symposium) and Hayek (in the 1932 controversy) had in understanding just what Sraffa was aiming at, and more generally speaking the widespread idea of Sraffa as a critical spirit but not reconstructive reveal the extent to which the marginalist approach had encroached on the classical tradition in the first half of the twentieth century. Hence the need for the rediscovery of the classical approach that Sraffa pursued with his critical edition of Ricardo's works: Sraffa's long-celebrated philological rigour was not an end in itself, but the tool for a critical enquiry on the very foundations of political economy. Sraffa began work on Ricardo's writings in 1930, and went on with it for over a quarter of a century, side by side with the theoretical work that was to lead to *Production of commodities by means of commodities*.

Once again it was Keynes, in his capacity as the secretary of the Royal Economic Society, who determined the assignment to Sraffa of editing the critical edition of Ricardo's writings. Repeatedly, in the following years, Keynes intervened to defend Sraffa from the publisher's protests at the delays in the completion of the work. Finally, it was with Keynes's help that Sraffa started a meticulous detective search for the manuscripts, and the fruits of this soon arrived. Already in 1930 a chest containing many letters which Ricardo received from his correspondents was found in the house of one of his heirs. Many other searches proved unsuccessful, but still others were fruitful, and Sraffa succeeded in amassing a huge amount of material thanks to which he was able to draw an extremely rich and precise picture of the cultural and human environment in which Ricardo had lived.

Then, in July 1943, after thirteen years' work and when six volumes were already at proof stage, a number of extremely important letters from Ricardo to James Mill were discovered in an Irish castle, together with other manuscripts among which was the fundamental essay on 'Absolute value and exchangeable value', on which Ricardo had been working on in the last weeks of his life. The lead proofs, part of which had been for years in the warehouses of Cambridge University Press, had to be melted due to changes in the work connected to the addition of the new material.

In the final stages of the work, while pressure from the Royal Society and the publisher was mounting, Sraffa was helped by Maurice Dobb, a Marxist economist and one of his best friends, whom Keynes and Austin

Robinson saw as the only one who could stand up to the meticulousness and the working hours (late into the night) of the Italian economist. At last, between 1951 and 1955, the ten volumes of the *Works and correspondence of David Ricardo* appeared, to be followed in 1973 by a painstakingly compiled volume of indexes.

Sraffa's philological rigour played a decisive role in the rediscovery of the classical economists' framework, centred on the notion of the surplus, after a century of oblivion and misleading interpretations. Let us recall that when Sraffa began his work the most commonly accepted interpretations were that of Marshall (1890, Appendix i), according to whom Ricardo was a somewhat imprecise and unilateral precursor of modern theory (since he takes account of the cost of production, i.e. supply, but not of demand, in the determination of prices), and that of Jevons (in the preface to the second edition of the *Theory of political economy*), who considered Ricardo responsible for perniciously diverting economics from the path of true science.[15] From either interpretation, there was no reason to waste time on Ricardo's works. At most, one could have recalled his theory of rent as forerunner of the principle of decreasing marginal productivity, or his theory of money, or his theory of international trade based on the principle of comparative costs.

Nevertheless, expectations grew around Sraffa's work. Publication was signalled as imminent on a number of occasions: by Luigi Einaudi in *Riforma sociale* in 1931; by Keynes in his 1933 essay on Malthus; by Sraffa himself in a letter to Rodolfo Morandi in 1934; in his *History of economic analysis* published posthumously Schumpeter (1954, p. 471) expressed the hope that 'Some day, perhaps, we may see completion of Professor Sraffa's comprehensive edition of Ricardo's works, which we have been eagerly awaiting these twenty years.'

Such expectations were more than justified. Sraffa's critical edition of Ricardo's *Works and correspondence* is unanimously recognised as a model of philological rigour. It was above all for this that Sraffa was awarded in 1961 the gold medal of the Swedish Academy of Sciences: an honour that among the economists had been given also to Keynes and Myrdal, and that may be considered as an anticipation of the Nobel prize, awarded only from 1969 on. The writings published in this edition, together with the apparatus of notes and, above all, Sraffa's introduction

---

[15] In a subtler way, Jacob Hollander (1904, 1910) spoke of a gradual retreat on the side of Ricardo from the labour theory of value towards a theory of prices based on costs of production, hence in a direction open to the marginalist developments connected to the principle of decreasing marginal productivity, in turn considered as a development of the 'Ricardian' theory of differential rent. In his Introduction to Ricardo's *Principles*, Sraffa 1951 criticised in a destructive way both this interpretation and that given by Marshall.

to the first volume, restored Ricardo – and through him the whole classical approach to political economy – to a central position in economic theory, freeing the interpretation of his thought (in substance, that illustrated above in chapter 7) from the accretions of misleading marginalist readings.

Sraffa stressed in particular the importance of the notion of the surplus, and of the conception of the economic system as a circular flow of production and consumption. The size of the surplus (the Smithian problem of the wealth of nations), its distribution among the various social classes (the problem on which Ricardo focused attention in his *Principles*), and its utilisation in unproductive consumption or accumulation, constituted the issues upon which the classical economists focused their analyses. Division of labour, surplus and the circular flow of production and consumption were thus the elements that characterised classical political economy: 'in striking contrast' – as Sraffa 1960, p. 93, pointed out – 'to the view presented by modern theory, of a one-way avenue that leads from "Factors of production" to "Consumption goods"'.

7.   *Production of commodities by means of commodities*

As we saw above (chapter 7), the analytic representation Ricardo offered had a weak point in the assumption that relative prices are proportional to the quantity of labour required for the production of the various commodities. In *Production of commodities by means of commodities* (1960) Sraffa came up with a solution to the problem framed in terms of the classical conception.

There is therefore a close link between the critical edition of Ricardo's writings and the theoretical research Sraffa himself was engaged on. In the 1930s and 1940s work proceeded in parallel on the two fronts; in the latter half of the 1950s, once the work on Ricardo was completed (apart from the volume of indexes, published only in 1973), Sraffa concentrated on preparing for publication his more strictly analytic contribution, published almost simultaneously in English and Italian in 1960.

In analogy to the line of enquiry followed, according to his own interpretation, by classical economists, Sraffa put at the centre of his analysis an economic system based on the division of labour. In such a system, the product of each sector does not correspond to its requirements for means of production (inclusive of the means of subsistence for the workers employed in the sector). Each sector taken in isolation is not able to continue its activity, but needs to get in touch with other sectors in the economy by obtaining from them its own means of production, in exchange for part at least of its product. We thus have the web of exchanges that characterises the economies based on the inter-industry division of labour. As Sraffa showed, the problem of quantitative determination of the exchange ratios that get established among the various sectors is to be tackled, in a capitalistic economy, simultaneously with the problem of income distribution between the social classes of workers, capitalists and landlords. The intersection between these two problems constitutes what in the classical tradition was called the problem of value.

In this respect it may be useful to stress the specific meaning that the concept of value implicitly assumed within the Sraffian analysis. Value does not stand for the measure of the importance that a certain good has for man (as happens for instance within marginalist theory, where value is connected to utility); neither does it take on ethical elements as in the notion of the just price; nor an optimality character, as the result of the maximisation of some target function under constraints. The value of the commodities mirrors the relationship that connects among them sectors and social classes within the economy. Moreover, Sraffa's analysis suggests an implicit reference to a specific mode of production: capitalism. In fact, it is based on assumptions (the 'law of the one price'; division into the social classes of workers, capitalists and landowners; a uniform rate of profits) that mirror its fundamental characteristics. In particular, the last among these assumptions – the equality of the rate of profits in all sectors of the economy – expresses in the simplest possible analytic terms a central aspect of capitalism: connection among the different parts in which the economic system articulates itself (a necessary connection, since as we saw no sector can subsist in isolation from the others) is ensured by the market not only for what concerns exchange of products, but also for what concerns partition of profit flows among the different sectors. In other terms, the internal unity of a capitalistic system is guaranteed both by the productive interdependence connecting the different sectors and by the free flow of capital from one sector to another in pursuit of the most profitable use.

The problem that Sraffa tackled presented an analytical difficulty the failed solution of which was fatal for the very survival of classical political economy: when commodities are at one and the same time products and means of production, the price of one commodity cannot be determined independently of the others, nor the set of relative prices independently of income distribution between profits and wages. We must therefore consider the system as a whole, with all the interrelations connecting the various sectors on account of required means of production, and we must consider simultaneously income distribution and the determination of relative prices. This was precisely the line of enquiry developed by Sraffa in his 1960 book.

In the preface to *Production of commodities by means of commodities* Sraffa stressed that his analysis of the relations connecting prices and distributive variables did not require the assumption of constant returns to scale. This fact, as we shall see more clearly below, is crucial for understanding the meaning that Sraffa attributed to the relations he analysed, in particular to the notion of prices of production (and at the same time agrees with the criticisms Sraffa formulated in his 1925 and 1926 articles of the Marshallian attempts to utilise 'laws of returns to scale', namely functional relations connecting cost and quantity produced, in the determination of equilibrium prices and quantities). However, also in the preface Sraffa stressed that, 'as a temporary working hypothesis', 'anyone accustomed to think in terms of the equilibrium of demand and supply may [. . .] suppose that the argument rests on a tacit assumption of constant returns in all industries' (Sraffa 1960, p. v). Thanks to the assumption of constant returns, in fact, Sraffa's analysis of the relationship between relative prices and income distribution may be considered as part of a marginalist model of general economic equilibrium, in which the initial endowments of productive factors are given in such a way as to be compatible with the final demand of economic subjects. It is precisely in this way, thanks to the possibility of 'translating' it into a particular case of the marginalist analysis, that Sraffa's analysis may serve as the foundation for an internal criticism of logical inconsistency of the traditional marginalist theories of value and distribution. As a matter of fact, however, in Sraffa's book nothing is said on the relationship between demand and supply for each commodity: the assumption that equilibrium prices correspond to the equality between supply and demand, which characterised marginalist economic theory, is absent from Sraffa's exposition.

In other terms, Sraffa's analysis should not be interpreted as an enquiry aimed at the determination of a static equilibrium for prices, which would require either simultaneous determination of prices and quantities or the assumption of constant returns to scale. It is rather an enquiry into the 'conditions of reproduction' of a capitalist economy, based on the assumption of a uniform rate of profits and on the 'photograph' of the productive structure of the economy at a given moment in time.[16]

---

[16] On this point, cf. Roncaglia 1999, ch. 2; more generally on the interpretation of Sraffa's work, and on the debates it aroused, cf. Roncaglia 1975, where the metaphor of the 'photograph' was first published (ibid., p. 119). The interpretation of Sraffa's scheme as a 'photograph' (or as a 'snapshot', as my Italian was at first translated) is opposed both to interpretations of Sraffa's scheme as the supply side of a general equilibrium model (cf. for instance Hahn 1982a) and to Garegnani's 1976b notion of 'long period positions'.

Let us now see the line of enquiry followed in *Production of commodities by means of commodities*. When commodities are at one and the same time products and means of production, the price of one commodity cannot be determined independently of the others, nor the complex of relative prices independently of the distribution of income between profits and wages (which are expressed in terms of the commodity chosen as the unit of measurement, and are thus real wages). One must therefore consider the system as a whole, with all the interrelations running between the various productive sectors, tackling simultaneously income distribution and determination of relative prices.

As a first step, Sraffa (1960, p. 3) showed that in a system of production for mere subsistence, 'which produces just enough to maintain itself', and where 'commodities are produced by separate industries and are exchanged for one another at a market held after the harvest' (i.e. at the end of the production period), 'there is a unique set of exchange values which if adopted by the market restores the original distribution of the products and makes it possible for the process to be repeated; such values spring directly from the methods of production'.

If the economic system under consideration is able to produce a surplus, also 'the distribution of the surplus must be determined through the same mechanism and at the same time as are the prices of commodities' (Sraffa 1960, p. 6). If the wage can exceed subsistence level, relative prices and one or other of the two distributive variables – wage or rate of profits – are jointly determined, once the technology and the other distributive variable are known; the higher the wage is, the lower the rate of profits will be.[17]

Sraffa (1960, pp. 12–13) then went on to analyse 'the key to the movement of relative prices consequent upon a change in the wage'. As the classical economists and Marx already knew, it 'lies in the inequality of the proportions in which labour and means of production are employed in the various industries'. Indeed, 'if the proportion were the same in all industries no price-changes could ensue', while 'it is impossible for prices to remain unchanged when there is inequality of "proportions"'.

Sraffa (1960, pp. 18–33) also constructed a particular analytical tool, namely the 'Standard commodity', thanks to which he was able to solve the Ricardian problem of an invariable measure of value, after having aptly redefined it. Ricardo had in fact attributed two meanings to the notion of a standard measure of value, which must not be confused: that of having invariable value (in relation to the complex of the means of production necessary to obtain it) when changes occur in the distribution of income

---

[17] The system of equations corresponding to this case is given above, in § 9.8.

between wages and profits, the technology remaining unaltered; and that of having invariable value in relation to the changes the technology goes through in the course of time (cultivation of ever less fertile lands on the one hand, and technological progress on the other).

Having made the distinction between the two problems clear in his Introduction to Ricardo's *Principles* (Sraffa 1951, pp. xl–xlvii), in *Production of commodities by means of commodities* Sraffa went on to show how the former can only be solved in terms of the 'Standard commodity'. This is a composite commodity (i.e. a set of commodities taken in particular proportions) so determined that the aggregate of its means of production has its same composition. In other words, in the Standard system – the abstract economic system the product of which consists in a certain quantity of Standard commodity – the aggregate means of production also correspond to a certain quantity of Standard commodity. Thus, with the Standard system (and under the assumption that wages are included in the costs of production) it is possible to determine the rate of profits, analogously to what happens in the 'corn model' that Sraffa attributed to Ricardo, as a ratio between two physically homogeneous quantities: the surplus, i.e. the quantity of Standard commodity given by the difference between product and means of production, and the means of production advanced by the capitalists. Coming to the second problem – namely invariance in the face of changes in technology – measurement in terms of labour embodied clearly retains significance as a broad indicator of the difficulty of production, but there is also an evident risk of bringing metaphysical or subjectivist nuances into play within the economic discourse (labour as 'toil and trouble').

With the distinction he drew between the two problems Sraffa offered a precise indication of the limits circumscribing any analytical solution to the question of the standard measure of value, and by so doing he implicitly pointed out the impossibility of establishing a scientific basis for any metaphysical notion of labour as absolute value: that is, as a substance embodied in the commodities which characterises univocally the difficulty of production. Proceeding along this road, Sraffa perhaps could have hoped to stimulate a reinterpretation of Marx by freeing him from the residual Hegelian elements.

The analysis of prices of production is completed with the case of joint products and, within this category, fixed capital goods and scarce or non-reproducible means of production such as land. The book closes with a chapter on the choice between economically alternative methods of production in relation to variations in the rate of profits, and with four appendices including the 'References to the literature', where Sraffa explicitly associated his analysis with that of classical economists.

8.   Critique of the marginalist approach

While advancing a theory of production prices within the framework of the classical conception of the functioning of an economic system, Sraffa's book also offered the tools for a radical critique of the foundations of the marginalist theory of value and distribution. In this respect we can concentrate on two chapters: one on the average period of production, and the final chapter on the choice of techniques.

Preliminarily, however, we need to clear the path from a serious misunderstanding: namely, the interpretation of Sraffa's contribution as a general equilibrium analysis conducted under the assumption of constant returns to scale, in which it would have been possible to explain prices by focusing attention on production costs – the side of supply – and dropping the side of demand, thus the subjective element of consumers' preferences.

Sraffa rejected explicitly and repeatedly – three times, in the preface to his book – the idea that his analysis would require the assumption of constant returns. 'No question arises as to the variation or constancy of returns. The investigation is concerned exclusively with such properties of an economic system as do not depend on changes in the scale of production or in the proportions of "factors"' (Sraffa 1960, p. v). Sraffa immediately afterwards stressed that 'This standpoint, which is that of the old classical economists [. . .], has been submerged and forgotten since the advent of the "marginal" method.' Between the classical and the marginalist approaches there are basic differences (synthesised by Sraffa 1960, p. 93, by opposing the 'circular flow' of the first one to the 'one-way avenue' of the latter as an illustration of the functioning of the economy). We can, however, with an apparent but not substantive ambiguity, admit that the analytical results reached with regard to prices of production may be transposed into the conceptual picture of the marginalist approach, so as to serve as the foundation for an internal criticism of logical inconsistency of the marginalist theory of value and distribution. Thus Sraffa recognised, as it was recalled above, that for readers brought up within the marginalist tradition the assumption of constant returns to scale may be helpful. With respect to such readers, indeed, the most important aspects of Sraffa's analysis are those concerning the critique of the traditional marginalist approach, and such an assumption allows us to read Sraffa's results as criticisms of logical inconsistency internal to the marginalist analytical structure. However, as a theory of prices of production, and hence as a contribution to the reconstruction of the classical approach, Sraffa's analysis does not imply any assumption whatsoever concerning returns to scale.

As already hinted above, the results in Sraffa's book that can be directly used as the foundation for a criticism of the marginalist theories of value and distribution concern the average period of production and the choice of techniques. The concept of the average period of production had been propounded by a leading representative of the Austrian school, Böhm-Bawerk (1889), as a measure of the capital intensity of production, interpreting capital as 'waiting time' (cf. above, § 11.4). Sraffa showed that, depending as it does on the rate of profits, the average period of production cannot be used to measure the quantity of the factor of production capital in the ambit of an explanation of the rate of profits taken as the price of this factor (cf. also Garegnani 1960). The difficulty had already been sensed by Wicksell (1901–6), but modern exponents of the Austrian school, including Hayek 1931, were later to return to the notion of the average period of production (cf. above, § 11.6). Harrod, too, in a review of *Production of commodities by means of commodities* (Harrod 1961), persisted in defending the Austrian theory of value, but Sraffa's 1962 brief reply suffices to clear up the point once and for all.[18]

With regard to the problem of the choice between alternative techniques of production when the rate of profits changes, Sraffa (1960, pp. 81–7) pointed out the possibility of a 'reswitching of techniques'; in other words, a given technique that proves the most advantageous for a given rate of profits may be superseded by another technique when we raise the rate of profits, but may once again be preferable when the rate of profits rises still higher. The implication of this fact is that, however the capital intensity of the two techniques (or in other words the ratio between the quantities utilised of the two 'factors of production', capital and labour) is measured, the general rule that the marginalist theory of value rests on remains contradicted. Such a rule takes the distributive variables, wage rate and rate of profits, as prices of the corresponding factors of production determined by the 'law' of demand and supply, so that the quantity of capital employed in production should diminish (and the quantity of labour increase) as the rate of profits rises (and the wage consequently falls). With the 'reswitching of techniques', if this happens when one technique gives way to another with a rising rate of profits, the contrary occurs when from the second technology the economy turns again to the first as the rate of profits rises yet higher.

[18] Harrod 1961 recalled that for any level of the rate of profits we may univocally define the average period of production, though in the presence of the mechanism of compounded interest. Sraffa 1962 replied that this fact is not sufficient to rescue the marginalist theory of income distribution based on the average period of production, since we fall here into a vicious logical circle: the rate of profits must be known in order to determine the average period of production to be utilised, as a measure of the capitalistic intensity of production, in determining the rate of profits.

Wide debates have taken place around this criticism,[19] while the crucial question of its relevance received relatively scant attention. Contrary to the opinions many seem to entertain, it applies not only to the aggregate production function: a tool which continues to be used, however, in all the various versions of mainstream macroeconomic theory, from the 'real cycle' theories to the overlapping generations models (cf. below, § 17.5). Sraffa's critique also applies to all those cases in which, while acknowledging the fact that capital is in reality a collection of various, heterogeneous means of production, the attempt is still made to determine the rate of profits as the price of a factor of production 'capital', however it be defined (aggregate of value, 'waiting', average period of production). In particular, Sraffa's critique undermines the very foundations of the idea – crucial to marginalist macroeconomic theory – that a competitive labour market in a closed economy would automatically tend towards full employment equilibrium since the decline in real wages which should stem from unemployment would prompt an increase in the labour–capital ratio and hence, given the endowment of capital, an increase in the quantity of labour employed. This is a result that undermines the very foundations of practically the whole of contemporary macroeconomic theory, based as it is on the assumption of a trade-off between real wage rate and the level of employment.

[19] More or less simultaneously to the publication of Sraffa's book, Garegnani 1960 developed a direct critique of some among the main theoretical contributions in the marginalist tradition. The publication of Sraffa's book was then followed by a lively debate. A first skirmish (Harrod 1961; Sraffa 1962), already recalled in the previous note, clarified that the possibility of measuring capital, once the profit rate is given, did not constitute a reply to Sraffa's strictures, since these referred to the necessity, for the traditional marginalist theories of distribution, to measure capital independently of income distribution between wages and profits (a point which Garegnani 1960 stressed as well). A second clash began with Samuelson's 1962 attempt to depict the aggregate production function (already criticised by Joan Robinson in 1953) as a 'parable' not betraying the essential characteristics of a market economy; and by Levhari's 1965 attempt to show that the problems raised by Sraffa (such as the possibility of the 'reswitching of techniques') referred only to the single industry, and not to the economic system as a whole. These propositions were immediately refuted: Samuelson's by Garegnani 1970 and Spaventa 1968; Levhari's by Pasinetti 1966 followed by other authors; Samuelson 1966 and Levhari (with Samuelson, 1966) were themselves to recognise the erroneousness of their theses. This notwithstanding, in the following years some other skirmishes took place, without, however, adding anything substantial to the previous debate: cf. for instance Gallaway and Shukla 1974; Garegnani 1976a; Burmeister 1977, 1979; and Pasinetti 1979a, 1979b. Let us also recall that Pasinetti 1969 criticised the recourse on the side of Solow 1963, 1967 to the Fisherian notion of the rate of return, considered by Solow himself (1963, p. 16) as 'the central concept in [neoclassical] capital theory', since it was assumed as index of the 'quantity of capital' definable independently from the profit rate and thus utilisable for explaining the latter one; for the discussion ensuing Pasinetti's critiques, cf. in particular Solow 1970; Pasinetti 1970; Dougherty 1972; and Pasinetti 1972. For surveys of these debates, cf. e.g. Tiberi 1969; Harcourt 1969, 1972; and Kurz and Salvadori 1995.

Taking an overall view of Sraffa's work, we can see it as the sum of three parts: the reconstruction of the real nature of the classical approach with his edition of Ricardo's works; the critique of marginalist theory, whether in the Marshallian version (with the papers of 1925, 1926 and 1930) or in Hayek's macroeconomic version (with the 1932 paper), or as based on a theory of capital as a factor of production (with the 1960 book and the reply to Harrod of 1962); finally, an analysis of value and distribution that is both analytically consistent and rooted in the classical conception of the functioning of the economic system. As far as this latter element is concerned, we may add that various elements lead us to think that this reproposal of the classical theory should be developed so as to take into account the Keynesian contribution.[20]

Thus with his research Sraffa pursued the objective of favouring a radical change in the path of economic science: away from the marginalist tradition, and in favour of a return to the classical tradition. Sraffa alone contributed all the basic pointers necessary to the pursuit of such an objective: he revived the classical approach, freeing it from the misinterpretations accrued from marginalist readings; he provided a logically self-consistent solution to the problem of exchange values to which Ricardo – and, following him, Marx – had given an insufficient answer, constituting one of the causes that led to the abandonment of the classical framework and the rise of the marginalist approach; and he showed that to this problem the marginalist approach offered a solution that was only apparently more 'scientific', but that in reality was vitiated in its foundations in so far as the theory of value and distribution is concerned.

9.   The Sraffian schools

For reasons of space, it is not possible to illustrate here the work done by many economists in the wake of Sraffa's contribution (for a survey, cf. Roncaglia 1990a). We can only mention a few elements. This work initially follows three distinct lines of development, corresponding to the three main paths of Sraffa's research. We have first a number of researches into the history of economic thought, contributing to a reconstruction of

---

[20] Two elements in particular should be stressed in this respect. First, the abandonment of the approach based on the comparison between supply and demand for the simultaneous determination of equilibrium prices and quantities allows us to separate as distinct analytical issues the determination of production prices and the determination of activity levels; this opens the way to a Keynesian explanation based on the notion of effective demand for this latter issue. The second element is Sraffa's (1960, p. 33) cryptic reference to the influence of the interest rate on the rate of profits, with which Sraffa hinted at the importance of monetary and financial factors for the evolution of the real economy, namely to one of the main tenets of the Keynesian approach.

the precise nature of the classical approach and of its differences with respect to the marginalist approach.[21] Second, we have the debates concerning the marginalist theory of value and capital,[22] and the critiques to the marginalist approach in the different fields of economic research, as the pure theory of international trade.[23] Finally, we have analytical development and transposition into rigorous mathematical terms of Sraffa's analysis of prices of production.[24]

Sraffa's work is also, directly or indirectly, the origin of various contributions to the reconstruction of political economy that have followed different tracks. For the sake of simplicity, we may distinguish three main orientations, that for ease of exposition we will associate with the names of the three leading representatives of the classical approach: Smith, Ricardo and Marx.

(a)   Pasinetti's 'Ricardian' reconstruction

We may consider as the first wide-ranging development of Sraffa's analysis the one propounded in particular by Pasinetti in a number of writings, culminating in his 1981 volume on *Structural change and economic growth*.

Pasinetti's main reference is to Ricardian analysis. On methodological grounds, Pasinetti follows the principles of logical deduction, leaving to historical references a purely illustrative role: similarly to Ricardo, and in direct opposition to Smith's predilection for historical generalisations as opposed to the analysis through models. Moreover, Ricardo's 'model' was the subject of a well-known essay (Pasinetti 1960) that may be considered as the ideal starting point for the development of his growth model (Pasinetti 1965). This latter also incorporated Pasinetti's 1962 formulation of the post-Keynesian theory of distribution, connecting income distribution between wages and profits to the level of investments, once the saving propensities of workers and capitalists and the growth rate are given. Subsequently, the development of the theory of vertically integrated sectors (Pasinetti 1973) constituted a decisive analytical step for moving on from Sraffa's analysis of the relationships between relative prices and income distribution to analysis of economic growth. The text of *Lectures on the theories of production* (Pasinetti 1975) can then also be considered as a reinterpretation of the history of economic thought, especially recent history (Sraffa, Leontief, von Neumann). This set of writings

---

[21] Cf. for instance Dobb 1973; Roncaglia 1977; and Bharadwaj 1978. The present book also goes in this direction.
[22] Cf. above, note 19.   [23] Parrinello 1970; Steedman 1979.
[24] Lippi 1979; Schefold 1989; Kurz and Salvadori 1995.

contributed to providing the basis for a specific view of the nature and role of economic science: a view which cannot be considered as opposed to that implicit in Sraffa's writings, but which can neither be identified with, nor logically deduced from, the latter.

Pasinetti's (1981, p. 19) purpose was 'to build a unifying theory behind all the new contributions to economics': Keynes and Kalecki, theories of the firm, Leontief and Sraffa, theories of the cycle, the Harrod–Domar model and the post-Keynesian theories of income distribution. Such a unifying theory had its main pillar 'not in the caprice and scarcity of Nature, but in the progress and ingenuity of Man', namely in the classical approach interpreted as the reproducibility view (ibid., p. 23).[25]

Proceeding from this basis Pasinetti (ibid., p. 28) aimed to develop 'a theory which remains neutral with respect to the institutional organisation of society', focusing attention on 'the "primary and natural" features' of the economic system, by which he meant 'the conditions under which it may grow and take advantage of exploiting all its potential possibilities' (ibid., p. 25). A model of non-proportional growth based on the full employment assumption was utilised for identifying such conditions, interpreted as 'necessary requirements for equilibrium growth' (ibid., p. 25). Specifically, in any vertically integrated sector the 'natural' rate of profits – which differs from sector to sector – must be such as to ensure an amount of profits equal to the 'equilibrium' value of investments, that is, to the amount of investments required for expanding productive capacity at a rate equal to 'the rate of population growth' plus 'the rate of increase of per capita demand for each consumption good' (ibid., p. 130). In order to explain the changes over time in the structure of demand, Pasinetti drew on 'Engel's law', thus avoiding any reference to subjective elements such as utility maps and consumers' preferences. The increase in per capita income and demand corresponds in equilibrium to the increase in per capita product due to technical progress (which can proceed at different speeds in different sectors).

In this context the notion of equilibrium assumed a normative meaning, connected as it was to the assumption of full employment of the available labour force and of productive capacity (cf. also ibid., pp. 96–7, where the 'dynamic' equilibrium corresponds to the conditions allowing for continuous full employment over time). In other words, Pasinetti's analysis focused on what should happen to ensure full employment, not on the actual behaviour of an economic system necessarily tied to specific institutions.

[25] Cf. Roncaglia 1975, pp. 5–7 and 124–6, on the limits of this interpretation of the marginalist and the classical approaches.

From this viewpoint the issue of the relationship between the short and the long period was discussed: '*the very nature* of the process of long run growth requires a structural dynamics which leads to difficulties in the short run'. Hence the methodological suggestion 'of singling out first the fundamental structural dynamics which must take place and then of trying to facilitate them' (ibid., pp. 243–4): a suggestion which tended to affirm the priority of the normative analysis.

Obviously all this is not intended to deny the possibility and usefulness of a direct analysis of short period issues, and more generally of the – certainly not optimal – way of functioning of concrete economies. In fact, various hints in Pasinetti (ibid., especially the four closing chapters) point in this direction. But there is no doubt that, compared to the long run normative analysis discussed above, such hints are far less developed: they appear to constitute for Pasinetti a second stage of analysis, subsequent to that decisive first stage which was the object of systematic formal analysis in his work.[26]

(b) Garegnani's 'Marxian' reconstruction

Some economists are convinced that the potentially most fruitful way to pursue the reconstruction of classical political economy along the lines started by Sraffa consists in bringing to the fore Marx's vision. As Garegnani (1981, p. 113) stated, 'a revival of the Classical economists' theoretical approach cannot [. . .] take place but starting from the highest point of development which such an approach received in the past: the point which was reached with Marx'.

Naturally the Marx thus reproposed was a specific Marx: not necessarily a travesty, as many orthodox Marxists maintained (cf. e.g. Medio 1972), but certainly a Marx in which some elements were given emphasis, while others – though undoubtedly present in his writings, such as materialistic dialectic – were played down. Also, Sraffa's own analytical contribution could not have left untouched Marx's vision (in the wider sense of the term).[27]

---

[26] On the limits of this approach (the normative character of the analysis, the exogenous nature of technical progress, the exclusion from the analysis of the role of market forms and of monetary and financial factors, as well as on the role of 'short period' elements in 'long period' evolution) cf. Roncaglia 1990a, pp. 207–9.

[27] For instance, the use of Sraffian analytical tools shows that the Marxian 'law of the tendency of the falling rate of profits' is devoid of general validity (cf. Steedman 1977, ch. 9; the issue was debated in various articles collected in Screpanti and Zenezini 1978). Furthermore, contrary to what various authors maintained (Meek 1961; Medio 1972; Eatwell 1975b), the Standard commodity does not constitute the analytical tool capable of connecting the world of labour values to the world of prices of production

The analytical core common to classical economists, to Marx and Sraffa, was located by Garegnani (cf. in particular Garegnani 1981 and 1984) in the set of relations concerning production prices and distributive variables analysed in Sraffa 1960. More precisely,

the surplus theories have [. . .] a *core* which is isolated from the rest of the analysis because the wage, the social product and the technical conditions of production appear there as already determined. It is in this 'core' that we find the determination of the shares other than the wage as a residual: a determination which [. . .] will also entail the determination of the relative values of the commodities. Further, as a natural extension of this, we shall find in the 'core' an analysis of the relations between, on the one hand, the real wage, the social product and the technical conditions of production (the independent variables) and, on the other hand, the shares other than wages constituting the surplus, and the relative prices (the dependent variables).[28]

The analytical core which Marx shared with classical economists and Sraffa is taken as the foundation on which to rely in developing the analysis in different directions, corresponding to the elements considered as exogenous data in Sraffa's book (income distribution, production and employment levels, technology).

However, it is stressed that the analysis of the relations internal to the core and of those external to it constitute 'distinct logical stages' (Garegnani 1984, p. 297), and that the nature of the analysis is substantially different in the two cases. Garegnani (1990) characterised this difference in a clear-cut way. He pointed to a 'distinction between two fields of analysis: a field where general quantitative relations of sufficiently definite form can be postulated', i.e. the 'core'; 'and another field where relations in the economy are so complex and variable according to circumstances, as to allow not for general quantitative relations of sufficiently definite form', i.e. the rest of economic theory: 'The relations pertaining

---

(cf. Roncaglia 1975, pp. 76–9); the widely debated issue of the 'transformation of labour values into prices of production' (for a history of which cf. for instance Vicarelli 1975) was solved, in the light of Sraffa's analytical results, by concluding that in general the results arrived at in terms of labour values cannot be confirmed by an analysis conducted in terms of prices of production (cf. in particular Steedman 1977).

[28] Garegnani 1981, pp. 13–14. The notion of the 'core' is connected to the 'method of long period positions', considered as centres of gravitation for the economy: cf. Garegnani 1976b. Two notes of caution are to be stressed. First, side by side with the relations considered internal to the core, the variables under consideration (both dependent and independent) can also be connected by other relations, which 'were left to be studied outside the "core"' (Garegnani 1984, p. 297). Secondly, the notion of a core of the surplus theories remains substantially unchanged when the profit rate replaces the wage as the independent distributive variable determined exogenously, that is, outside the core (Garegnani 1984, pp. 321–2); the importance of this modification was stressed in Roncaglia 1975, 1990a.

to this second field had accordingly to be studied in their multiplicity and diversity according to circumstances.'[29]

(c)   Sylos Labini's 'Smithian' reconstruction

A 'Smithian' interpretation of the central aspects of classical political economy has been developed in a long series of writings by Paolo Sylos Labini (see, in particular, Sylos Labini 1954, 1956, 1972, 1974, 1976, 1983, 1984, 2000). In these writings Sylos Labini brought to the centre of the programme of reconstructing classical political economy started by Sraffa the role of market forms in their interaction with the division of labour and the process of accumulation. This meant bringing to the centre of the analysis a causal chain that draws from Smith more than from Ricardo or Marx: the causal chain that goes from changes in the division of labour (or, more specifically, from technological changes) to changes over time in market forms and hence in the pace of accumulation. Developments in income distribution are then made to depend on these elements, together with aspects concerning public policy and the politico-institutional setting. In this way, while the notion of the surplus retains a central role in economic analysis, the functional relations connecting production prices and income distribution lose their role as the central pillar of economic theorising.

More generally, Smith's vision of a development process characterised by both positive and negative elements, but fundamentally positive, and conditioned by institutional reforms (from the elimination of customs barriers to free elementary education) was reproposed by Sylos Labini as an alternative, if not in opposition, to the traditional Marxian view of a progressive deterioration of capitalism (law of increasing misery, proletarisation, tendency to a falling rate of profits) up to the inevitable breakdown and the unavoidable revolutionary outcome.[30]

In dealing with such issues, it is clear that the problem of the relationship between production prices and income distribution, which was at the centre of Sraffa's analysis, constitutes a crucial knot – in fact, *the* crucial one – for the construction of a theoretical system based on the notion of the surplus. However, it did not constitute for classical economists, and should not constitute today, the main objective of economic enquiry.

---

[29] Garegnani 1990, pp. 123–4; the expressions used are more cautious in the form, but not in substance, than those used in the original text distributed on the occasion of the Florence conference in 1985. For a critique of this distinction, cf. Roncaglia 1990a, pp. 209–11 and 1990b.

[30] This opposition is particularly clear in Sylos Labini's writings on social classes (1974) and on under-development (1983).

Such an objective should rather be located in the 'wealth of nations' and the factors determining its development over time and in different countries, especially the distribution of income and wealth (and – too often forgotten – the distribution of power, which has also to do with the role of market forms) among different groups of economic agents. In other terms, in order to repropose a 'classical' interpretation of the development of the economic systems in which we live it is not sufficient to 'build on' the analysis developed by Sraffa in *Production of commodities by means of commodities*: neither in the sense of gradually extending a basic formal model, nor in the sense of gradually extending a restricted analytical nucleus of causal relations.

The connection between the different lines of research contributing to the reconstruction of classical political economy (and in particular the connection between two lines of enquiry such as that on the relationship between relative prices and income distribution, and that on market forms) must be found in the reference to a common conceptual framework: the representation of the economy as a circular process, centred on the causes which allow the production of the surplus and determine its distribution among the different social classes and the different sectors of the economy and its utilisation. But within this common conceptual framework it is possible to distinguish a whole series of analytical issues, obviously connected but best dealt with if subjected to separate analysis (though without losing sight – 'at the back of our minds', as Keynes said – of their interconnections). The 'analytical separability' of the different issues (propounded in Roncaglia 1975, ch. 7, as a possible interpretation of the method implicit in Sraffa 1960) thus opens the way to the use of different analytical areas for dealing with different analytical issues.

For instance, Sylos Labini 1956 revived the classical conception of market forms, based on the difficulty of entry of new firms into a sector rather than on the number of firms present in that sector, and analysed the factors determining the 'barriers to entry' facing new firms. Such factors were viewed as determining a deviation of the sectoral profit rate from the 'basic' profit rate that would prevail under free competition, i.e. in the case of unrestrained freedom of entry. Such an analysis of market forms is clearly compatible with the idea of a tendency to a uniform rate of profits in the case of free competition in all sectors of the economy, and is thus compatible with Sraffa's analysis: in comparison to the assumption of a uniform rate of profits, the introduction of non-competitive market forms can be considered as a 'second approximation'. However, the objective of the analysis (namely, to locate the factors determining the size of the barriers to entry into the different sectors of the economy) can be pursued independently of an analysis such as that presented in Sraffa 1960. Among other things, a too direct link between the two lines of analysis could limit the horizon of the study of the barriers to entry to the determination of the sectoral profit rate differentials, since these represent the formal link connecting the analysis of market forms to the analysis of the relationship between natural prices and income distribution. On the contrary, side by side with sectoral profit rate differentials and possibly more importantly, the analysis of market forms throws light on issues such as the influence of barriers to entry on the pace of technological change, on the rhythm of accumulation, and on income distribution (especially when the nature of the barriers to entry and their size are different in the different sectors of the economy: cf. Sylos Labini 1956, 1972, 1984).

Maintaining that this stream of research opens the way to the reconstruction of a renewed classical political economy is clearly a bet, in the present situation of economic research. However, the bet may be not excessively risky. More generally, it is surely difficult to foresee which developments the different streams of research illustrated in this section will have; their variety anyhow testifies to the vitality and attractiveness of the research project started by Sraffa, perhaps not yet fully assimilated in the contemporary debate.

17   The age of fragmentation

1.   Introduction

Over the past fifty years or so we have seen a veritable fragmentation of economic theory. Research has ramified in different directions and its very foundations – methods and techniques of analysis, crucial concepts and simplifying assumptions, central problems – have undergone broad diversification. This has led to a division of labour among substantially autonomous groups of economists who often ignore, or in any case do not take into account in their own research, what happens in other areas of research. This trend has been reinforced by the high level of technicality that, together with diversification in the techniques of analysis, makes the studies required for any given field of research increasingly specific and time-consuming. For instance, the new evolutionary theories of the firm have no relation to research on the microeconomic foundations of macroeconomics; it would be quite difficult to find some common ground between research on the institutional evolution of financial markets and the so-called 'new growth theory' which seeks to make technical progress endogenous to the theory itself. Economists become ever more specialised and increasingly limit their readings and their professional contacts to researchers active in the same field and pursuing a similar research orientation; increasing numbers of specialised journals and professional societies are created; the very processes of academic selection favour the fragmentation of economists into separate corporations.

It is thus quite difficult, in this situation, to provide a reasonably balanced and complete illustration of the different streams of economic research. The path that we will follow not only suffers from many omissions, but also the fact that the more recent contributions have not yet been subject to the usual process of selection through debates that are still under way; as a consequence, the relative importance attributed to different research streams depends on the subjective evaluation of the present writer (and on a certain randomness in his readings) more than in the case of the preceding chapters.

The interval of time considered in this chapter covers more or less the last fifty to sixty years. Some aspects of this period have already been considered in the last few chapters, devoted to the greatest economists of the second half of the nineteenth and the first half of the twentieth century: in the concluding sections of those chapters we have already hinted at the more recent developments of the research streams there taken into consideration. These elements are now recalled, side by side with aspects not already dealt with in the preceding chapters, in the context of an extremely brief survey of the contemporary economic debate.

We begin by considering, in the next section, the recent developments of general economic equilibrium theory, already outlined above (§ 12.7). In its self-declared generality, the project of building an axiomatic micro-economic theory is presented by its proponents as a necessary prerequisite for any other field of research. Then in each specific case it would be a question of adding appropriate specifications (such as the hypothesis of asymmetric information) for dealing with problems cropping up in the different branches of economics.

In some cases this methodological design is clearer, in others it is much less clear – the less so the further we move away from the traditional core of the marginal theory of value. In each case, it soon meets limits that appear impossible to overcome. The crucial difficulty is the contradiction between the requirement of logical consistency and the requirement of realism. Already in itself, general economic equilibrium analysis implies crucial assumptions that are clearly unrealistic, such as that of market clearing (precise balancing between supply and demand) as the funda-mental mechanism in the functioning of markets, or that of absence of exchanges out of equilibrium, or that of completeness in consumer pref-erence maps, or that of convexity in the technology frontier. Then, when we get into any particular field of analysis, it is necessary to introduce other assumptions in order to specify the theoretical model helpfully. Above all, simplifying assumptions are needed if the model has to yield definite solutions. Of these, the most common consist in going back to one-commodity models (as is typical, as we shall see, in mainstream macroeconomics) or to the Marshallian clause of *ceteris paribus* and to partial equilibrium analysis.

Bearing these difficulties in mind, we will examine – once again briefly – some fields of research. First, in § 3, we will consider Coase's theory of the firm, that constitutes the point of departure for the so-called 'new theories of the firm'. Such an approach relies on the existence of ambits characterised by high transaction costs, which favour adoption of the hierarchical organisation prevailing within the firm; vice versa, the market prevails when transaction costs turn out to be lower than the costs of a centralised management of productive activity. The modern theory of the firm is at any rate a varied field, in which we also find managerial theories concerning the separation between firm ownership and control, and the modern theories of market forms, from Bain's and Sylos Labini's oligopoly theory based on the barriers to entry into a market, to Baumol's contestable markets theory based on sunk costs.

We shall then discuss, in § 4, a group of 'neo-institutional theories', that tackle the problem of the microfoundations of economic institutions. Within this approach institutions are conceived of as a rational answer given by the market to the imperfections always present in the real world (mainly consisting in transaction costs and asymmetric information). This approach is quite different from that of evolutionist or historical theories, in which – as in Adam Smith – institutions are considered the result of a historical process. In this field there has been wide recourse to the theory of games (to which we shall return in § 8), with a predominance of one-shot games in the case of neo-institutional theories and repeated games in the case of evolutionary theories. In both cases, institutions show the prevalence of cooperative behaviour over non-cooperative behaviour.

A substantially different path is taken by the debate on macroeconomic theory. Even when speaking of micro-foundations of macroeconomics, in fact, the connection with general equilibrium theory is a spurious one. The simplifications on which the main streams of research rely (from Friedman's monetarism to Lucas's real cycle theory, up to the overlapping generations models utilised for instance in the recent debates on the sustainability of public debt) imply as a matter of fact a one-commodity world, and therefore – even if this is often far from clear to the researchers in this field – point in an opposite direction to that of the Walrasian research project. Explicitly external to it, of course, are the streams of research that spring directly from Keynes's original ideas.

Modern growth theory, discussed in § 6, has also had a substantially aggregate character since Solow's seminal model. Attempts to introduce in it endogenous technical progress and increasing returns to scale violate – in this case as well, often without researchers active in this field being aware of this basic defect – the microeconomic consistency of such a model, even though it met with favour, in Romer's version, as supposedly overcoming the traditional limits of neoclassical theory. Paradoxically, the original formulation of the dynamic problem proposed by Harrod, though explicitly based on aggregate variables, remains open to developments not constrained to the one-commodity world, as is shown for instance by Pasinetti's model.

Macroeconomics and the theory of growth are exemplary cases of a theoretical retreat induced by the desire to get models adequate for empirical analysis, which is thriving, favoured as it is by developments in the collection of statistical data and more recently in computers, but also in national accounting and in econometrics. These aspects are the object of a brief excursus in § 7. Then, in § 8, we will consider the use in the economics field of some techniques of analysis developed in the collateral field of applied mathematics: the theory of repeated games, the theory of stochastic processes, chaos theory. In the latter case, the results seem to favour different research orientations from those based on the traditional notion of rationality (and of maximisation of an objective function by individual economic agents) on which general economic equilibrium theory also relies. We thus have, for instance, the ideas of path dependence in the new analyses of technological change.

The debate on the different possible notions of rationality leads us to a series of other research streams. Some of them (discussed in § 9) deal with central issues for the evolution of modern societies: ethics and new utilitarianism, growth and sustainable development, economic democracy and globalisation. In such fields at the boundary with other social sciences, economists who leave behind them the conceptual apparatus of equilibrium theories, offer a variety of useful contributions both for understanding contemporary societies and for the development and extension of economic theory.

2.   The microeconomics of general economic equilibrium

We have already seen, in § 12.6, how in the 1950s an axiomatic formulation of general economic equilibrium theory was developed, with the so-called Arrow–Debreu model. Let us now briefly recall some aspects of this research project and the lines of evolution that it shows in the most recent stage.

The axiomatic formulation of general economic equilibrium theory has an analytical core consisting of few assumptions. There is a given number of economic agents and a given number of commodities. The initial endowments of economic agents and their preferences are taken as given, and preferences are assumed to be convex (which is equivalent, in our context, to the postulate of decreasing marginal utility). Moreover, some rules of the game are assumed as given: essentially, one price for each commodity. On the basis of such data and assumptions, the problem consists in determining the set of exchange ratios that emerge from the interaction between the various agents, when they seek to improve their own position through exchange.

Rigorously defined, the problem is a purely formal one: to establish whether (and under what conditions) there are solutions, whether (and under what conditions) such solutions are unique and stable, and to locate an algorithm for determining them.[1] An interpretation – in fact already implicit in the choice of terminology (economic agents, commodities, preferences) – is then superimposed on the formal problem: the theory is thus presented as representing the mechanisms of a competitive market. This interpretation opens the way to considering further issues, extending the original scheme through redefinition of the basic concepts and/or introduction of further assumptions.

For example, as was suggested above (§ 12.6), the notion of economic good may be extended to include 'dated' and 'contingent' goods: a commodity with specific physical features, for instance steel of a specific quality, is considered as so many different goods as the possible delivery dates (thus giving rise to as many forward markets), and as the possible 'states of the world' (for instance different conditions in international policy relations). We thus have intertemporal equilibrium models, which deal with 'dated' goods, and models of equilibrium with contingent markets: the simple redefinition of a concept opens up new perspectives to the analysis.[2]

Another development of the basic model, already proposed by Walras (cf. above, § 12.2), consists in introducing the possibility of productive processes, which transform originally available goods into other goods: it is then necessary to introduce among the data of the problem the 'production functions' (generally assumed to be concave, in conformity to the postulate of decreasing marginal productivity). It is also necessary, at the conceptual level, to attribute to economic agents an additional role: that of coordinators of the productive process, who seek opportunities for gain by acquiring means of production and selling the products.

Over time, the research stream on general economic equilibrium has used different analytical tools: the differential calculus utilised by the first theoreticians of the marginalist revolution, then topology from the 1920s; in the 1950s the theory of games entered the scene and gradually came

---

[1] In order to deal with the problem of stability it is obviously necessary to introduce assumptions on how the system behaves out of equilibrium: for instance, assuming that, if for a given commodity supply exceeds demand, its price should decrease. As a matter of fact, stability can only be guaranteed under very restrictive assumptions: for a survey of the issue, cf. Hahn 1982b. On the statics–dynamics and stability–instability dichotomies, cf. Weintraub 1991.

[2] For instance, the markets for different 'states of the world' referring to a given variable, everything else remaining the same, may be interpreted as markets determining insurance premiums against specified contingencies.

to dominate.[3] The advantage of the latter is that it considers interactions among economic agents: while within traditional theory each economic agent in taking his own decisions considered those of others as given parameters, expressed in the market price and in the overall quantity supplied and demanded, in the case of 'strategic behaviour' each economic agent takes account of the possible reactions of others. In this way it is no longer necessary to assume that each economic agent has an infinitesimal size in comparison to the overall dimensions of the market for each commodity: quite a difficult assumption to swallow, the more so if we consider that in the transition to the intertemporal model with contingent markets the number of commodities is multiplied by a very high factor while the number of economic agents remains unchanged.

In the most recent period, research within the general economic equilibrium approach has focused on the limits set to the optimal functioning of the market by different circumstances. Thus, the impossibility of fully specifying all aspects of an agreement gives rise to the so-called 'principal-agent problem', that is, the possibility that the person who accepts responsibility for a job (for accomplishing a certain task, the agent) utilises the margins of freedom of action available in his own interest rather than in the interest of the person who entrusts the task (the principal). A vast literature discusses then the problem of designing incentive structures such as to induce the agent to adopt the principal's interests as his own.[4]

The 'principal-agent problem' is but a species of a wider genus, the research into the effects of imperfections in the knowledge of economic agents. In the field of finance, for instance, asymmetric information is used for justifying stability of relations between house-bank and firm. The different availability of information between seller and buyer on the good being exchanged is then at the centre of the theory of 'lemons' proposed by George Akerlof (b. 1930, Nobel prize in 2001) in 1970: a mechanism of adverse selection in which – with a generalisation of Gresham's

---

[3] A decisive step in this direction was von Neumann's and Morgenstern's 1944 book; cf. above, § 12.5. An important recent book, Mirowski 2002, illustrates the path of mainstream microeconomic theory since von Neumann and Morgenstern 1944 up to our days, highlighting among other things the role of the Cowles Commission and the Rand Corporation, together with that of military grants, in the formation of a dominant consensus around axiomatic general equilibrium theory. Mirowski also points to the germs of a different line of research present in von Neumann's and Morgenstern's thought, particularly the first of the two, with his opposition to the notion of Nash equilibrium (cf. above, § 12.5) and his propensity towards evolutionary developments of game theory.

[4] Among the first works on the problem let us recall Ross 1973; for an illustration of the results reached by this stream of research see for instance Mas-Colell et al. 1995, pp. 477–510; in general, this text constitutes a reference for a survey on the state of the art in the microeconomic field, thus also for other aspects hinted at in this section.

law – the bad commodity squeezes the good commodity out of the market.[5]

It is to be stressed that, despite the references to the methodology of general economic equilibrium, quite often the models used to analyse the various cases of asymmetry or imperfect information fall in the category of partial equilibriums. Indeed, without simplifications it is practically impossible to extract meaningful results from the analysis. Use of extremely simplified models in order to deal with specific issues, with recourse to ad hoc assumptions, has indeed been the most common path for research in the past twenty years. Often it is maintained that this provides rigorous microeconomic foundations for the treatment of concrete issues, originally dealt with in conceptual frameworks different from that of general economic equilibrium theory. The outcome, however, is quite different: the attempt to avoid absolute indefiniteness of results imposes opportunistic choices. The most often adopted paths are those of return to partial equilibrium analysis, or to the assumption of a one-commodity world: either analytical rigour or realism is sacrificed. The conclusion is that, despite the efforts expended on it, the research stream of general economic equilibrium did not overcome its basic limits (from the assumptions of convexity recalled above, to the difficulty of excluding multiple equilibriums or instability of equilibrium): it thus remained an abstract exercise, an end in itself, devoid of any utility for understanding the economic systems in which we live. Indeed, reference to the general economic equilibrium approach is often used deviously, on the one hand as a rhetorical trick to enhance the value of models with a low theoretical content, on the other as Caudine Forks for students of advanced economic courses.

3.   The new theories of the firm

General economic equilibrium theory considers relations among legally independent economic agents and tries to show how, under certain assumptions, equilibrium solutions may be reached. A problem thus arises: why should the firm exist?

Let us recall that while within the market legally independent agents enter in relation with each other, within each firm organisational set-ups

---

[5] Akerlof's example is that of the used cars market: the buyer is unable to exactly evaluate the conditions of the used car offered for sale, and it is likely that if the price demanded is the average one for a car of that age, the specific car offered for sale is of an inferior quality compared to the average one. The cases to which this theory is applicable are numerous: from selection among loan applications to selection among potential insurance clients, up to selection among workers on hire.

prevail based on 'command', that is on hierarchy and on centralisation of decisions and control over their execution. What is it then that determines the boundary between these two different forms of organisation of economic life, market and command?

Within the neo-classical tradition, the most widely accepted answer may be traced to an article published in 1937 by the American Ronald Coase (b. 1910, Nobel prize in 1991), whose ideas have been taken up and developed by others mainly over the past twenty years, after a long period of near oblivion. Coase stressed that market transactions have a cost for participants: it is necessary to collect information, search for a counter-party ready to exchange, negotiate over prices and other conditions. All this implies time and expense. In the absence of the organisational structure of the firm, each worker would have to bargain to acquire a variety of inputs – the semi-finished products and raw materials he himself uses, his working tools, engineering services, and so on – and then to bargain for the sale of his own product, which in general will only be a semi-finished product or part of the final product. The firm allows for simplification, drastically reducing the number of necessary transactions and replacing the bargaining over all aspects of the productive process with an organisation based on command (that is, on a hierarchical decisional structure). When the size of the firm grows, its internal organisation becomes more and more complex, less and less efficient; once a certain point – corresponding to the optimal size of the firm – is passed, the costs of expanding relations based on command become higher than the costs of recourse to exchange, that is, to the market.

A quite different answer to the question concerning why the firm exists is provided by radical economists looking to economic power relations. The American Stephen Marglin (1974) maintained, for instance, that the superiority of the firm – in particular, of the large firm – as a form of organisation of production is based on technological choices (mass production of standardised goods) which were not necessitated. An alternative line of technological development would have been possible, based on flexible production; such an alternative would have favoured organisational forms more similar to artisan shops than to large-size modern manufacturing industry. The technological line of mass scale production of standardised goods, thus the big corporation, prevailed – according to Marglin – mainly because this favours appropriation of the surplus on the part of the dominant classes, thanks to control over the productive process made possible by the organisational form of command and by division of labour within the firm.

Marglin's ideas have been severely criticised by the American historian David Landes (1986). The latter reproposed Smith's original answer:

the modern firm prevailed over artisan shops because it allowed cost reductions, by exploiting economies of scale obtainable through division of labour in the productive process and through the consequent introduction of machinery. However, it should be noted that such an answer lies outside the approach based on the traditional notion of equilibrium. Indeed, according to Smith's line of argument, firms do not have an optimal size: their growth takes place in time, in the course of a dynamic process which cannot be interpreted by the static analysis of traditional theory.

Growth in firm size, which brings big corporations to the fore, leads to another problem: who controls the firms? Public companies have top managers who are in general not the proprietors, who are often very numerous.

American economists Adolf Berle (1895–1971) and Gardiner Means (1896–1988), in a book published in 1932, indicated in the public company and in the separation between owners and managers the characteristics of a new form of society, *managerial capitalism*. In an initial stage of the process of industrialisation, *competitive capitalism*, small firms directly managed by their owners prevailed. Subsequently, with the rise of big firms organised as public companies, ownership is subdivided among many small shareholders; the managers of the firm acquire sufficient autonomy to become the real protagonists of economic life, assuming responsibility for all decisions relative not only to the current life of the firms but also to strategic long period choices.

Many economists (among them the American William Baumol, b. 1922, in a book published in 1959), sharing Berle's and Means's ideas, inferred from them a change in firm objectives: the objective of profit maximisation had prevailed in the stage of competitive capitalism, when firms were directly managed by their owners; in the stage of managerial capitalism other objectives prevail, especially sales maximisation, which better corresponds to the interests of the firm's managers.

Obviously the managers have to consider the risk of being replaced, at the shareholders' annual meeting, if a new group of owners takes over the firm. This may happen when many shareholders, dissatisfied with the management of the company and in particular with their dividends and the share price, sell their shares on the stock market; in this case the firm's takeover by a new group is favoured, since this new group can more easily acquire a sufficient number of shares to gain a majority in shareholders' meetings. It is on this constraint on managers's freedom of action that the 'theory of managerial capitalism' is based, as developed by the English economist Robin Marris, in a book published in 1964.

Another stream of research concerns the market power of large firms. The Italian Paolo Sylos Labini (b. 1920) and the American Joe Bain (1912–93), in two books both published in 1956, developed a theory of oligopoly (focusing attention respectively on the cases of concentrated and differentiated oligopoly), considered as the common market form, compared to which pure competition and monopoly constitute two polar limit-cases. In the case of oligopoly, the firms present in the market are partially protected from competition of potential entrants by a 'barrier to entry', the study of which is the subject of the theory. Such a barrier is not insurmountable (in which case there would be monopoly, while the case of a non-existing barrier corresponds to perfect competition); its size, hence the difficulty in overcoming it, depends on a series of factors discussed in the writings of Bain and Sylos Labini and in subsequent literature on the subject. For instance, in the case of concentrated oligopoly, the size of the barrier to entry depends on the minimal technologically optimal size of the plant, and in general on economies of scale, which require the new firm to enter the market with a rather sizeable minimum production, such as not to find a market outlet at current prices; in the case of differentiated oligopoly, it depends on advertising expenses necessary to impose the new trademark on the market. Defended by these barriers, firms already active in the market may enjoy profits well above the competitive level and a certain freedom of action, though within the limits determined by the risk of entry of new competitors into the sector.[6]

Theories of the behaviour of the large firm which display noticeable similarities to those of Marris, Bain and Sylos Labini have been developed by some Keynesian economists. Let us recall in particular the Austrian Josef Steindl (1952), the American Alfred Eichner (1976) and the Englishman Adrian Wood (1975). These economists took over the Keynesian view according to which investment decisions by the firms constitute the *primum mobile* in the evolution of the economy. Once the level of investments to be realised has been decided, firms must decide how to finance them; for a number of reasons, they prefer to use internal sources (profits not distributed as dividends to shareholders) rather than debt.[7] Therefore, according to the post-Keynesian theory of the firm,

---

[6] This theory was reformulated by Modigliani 1958 in terms compatible with traditional neoclassical analysis, with a 'neoclassical synthesis' parallel to that realised by himself concerning Keynes's theory.

[7] The 'Modigliani–Miller theorem', according to which under conditions of perfect competition and perfect knowledge the different sources of financing are equivalent (cf. Modigliani and Miller 1958), is considered inapplicable, explicitly or implicitly, by these economists, who in general consider non-competitive market conditions and imperfect knowledge as prevalent.

entrepreneurs set product prices so as to obtain a profit margin sufficient to finance the desired level of investments.

Quite naturally this theory may refer only to firms endowed with some market power, which are able to set autonomously their product prices and which in doing so are not rigidly constrained by competition with other firms. However, even in the case of oligopolistic firms it is to be doubted whether prices may be set freely, so as to generate an amount of profits sufficient to finance any amount of investments the firms desired to enact. We may thus interpret Keynesian theories of the firm as concerning utilisation of margins of choice which top managers enjoy in the presence of strong elements of uncertainty and of oligopolistic conditions.

A development of the theories of market forms based on barriers to entry is the contestable markets theory developed by Baumol and others (1982). Perfectly contestable markets are those for which there is no cost of entry or exit. In such markets, no firm can enjoy extra-profits. Indeed, any opportunity of extra-profits, even temporary ones, immediately attracts new firms into the market. Absence of exit costs allows new firms to avoid any risk, for instance due to reactions of firms already present in the market: if market conditions change and the extra-profits turn negative, the new firm can immediately exit without having to bear any cost (with what is commonly called 'hit and run' behaviour). Exit costs mainly derive from existence of fixed capital goods which cannot be reutilised once the activity for which they had been acquired has been abandoned: the so-called 'sunk costs'. This element constitutes the main novelty of contestable markets theory relative to the theory of market forms based on barriers to entry.

Completion of this quick survey of the modern debate on the theories of the firm requires at least recalling evolutionary theories, which we have already mentioned in the conclusion of the chapter on Marshall. These theories have been proposed to explain in particular the behaviour of the firm and the industry in the process of technological change. In the approach proposed by the Americans Richard Nelson (b. 1930) and Sidney Winter (b. 1935) in a book dated 1982, the industry structure in any moment in time is considered as the result not of a process of maximisation (of profits or sales), but of an evolutionary process. Some firms may grow more rapidly than others, some go bankrupt while others are started up; the industry evolves over time as the result of the vicissitudes of firms within it. As in biology, recourse is proposed to mathematical stochastic models, which are able to allow for the random element always present in economic events, but also the different probabilities of different events. The 'genes' of firms – which determine the identity of each of them, transfer from one to the other the main behavioural features and undergo 'mutations' over time – consist of 'routines': standard procedures adopted by the firm in production, product commercialisation, financial management, and so on. In a market economy the routines which prevail, and thus determine the dominant features of firms, are those which ensure success, namely those which in the long period ensure profit maximisation.

4. Institutions and economic theory

In the previous section we discussed Coase's approach for explaining the existence of the firm on the basis of transaction costs. From this other streams of research originate, which consider property rights and political institutions in general as the outcome of rational processes of choice in the presence of transaction costs (and of information asymmetries which give rise to 'principal-agent' problems).

Among the main exponents of this stream of research, called neo-institutionalism, let us recall the Americans Douglass North (b. 1920, Nobel prize in 1993) and Oliver Williamson (b. 1932).[8] In substance, neo-institutionalism may be considered as yet another case of neoclassical synthesis: the problem of institutions, traditionally tackled with historical-sociological analyses, is brought within the field of the theory of rational behaviour of maximising economic agents.

Neo-institutionalism is thus opposed to the institutionalist school which, under the influence of Thornstein Veblen (cf. above, § 13.8), had wide success in the United States at the beginning of the twentieth century, among other things inspiring the foundation of the American Economic Association in 1885. In the wake of the German historical school (cf. above, § 11.2), study of institutions and of the social structure which underlie an economic system, with even profound differences among countries, is opposed to abstract theory and to the 'Ricardian vice' consisting in applying theory without due caution to direct interpretation of reality.[9] The institutionalists' writings are today often classified as external to the field of economics, or at most as falling on the boundary between economics, sociology and history. However, they are rich in

[8] Cf. for instance North 1990, Williamson 1975, 1986, and the wide survey by Eggertsson 1990.
[9] American institutionalism was strengthened, in the period immediately following the Second World War, by the influx of Austrian and German scholars compelled to exile by nazism. This was the origin, among other things, of the New School for Social Research in New York. After the Second World War, the institutionalist approach, while losing ground to the diffusion of Samuelson's neoclassical synthesis, still has a journal of its own, the *Journal of Economic Issues*. For a brief survey of institutionalism in the second half of the twentieth century, cf. Hodgson 2003.

extremely useful hints for economic analysis, which occasionally emerge in heterodox research streams, as in the case of analysis of firms' actual pricing practices.

In the second half of the twentieth century, the best-known exponent of the institutionalist tradition was John Kenneth Galbraith (b. 1908); some of his works, such as *The affluent society* (1955) and *The new industrial state* (1967) have attracted widespread attention. According to Galbraith, the paradigm of perfectly competitive equilibrium is wholly inappropriate for interpreting contemporary economies, the evolution of which is mainly determined by interaction among big players such as government (especially the military), the largest corporations and trade unions.

With Galbraith, who was among the protagonists of the Kennedy administration, institutionalism met with post-Keynesianism, which will be considered in the next section. The same direction is taken by the debate on the different financial systems developed since the 1970s: the Japanese *keiretsu* system, the German system based on universal banks and the Anglo-Saxon system based on the market.[10] Post-Keynesian theory of finance[11] constitutes in this respect fecund mediation between the anti-theoretical attitude of institutionalists and Keynesian theories.

In Europe, renewed debate on the relationship between economic institutions and social structure recently concerned the so-called welfare state: essentially education, medical care and state-supported pension schemes. In this case too the debate takes place in territory bordering economics, sociology and politology; for a brief but dense illustration of the problems in this sphere see Dahrendorf 1995.

5.   Macroeconomic theory after Keynes

Among the different groups of economists taking part in the varied contemporary theoretical debate on macroeconomic themes of employment and money, many refer to Keynes's ideas, in order either to revive (albeit in a suitably modified version) or to criticise them. Let us distinguish three main groups: neoclassical synthesis economists, dominating for more than thirty years after the end of the Second World War, characterised by the insertion of Keynesian elements – particularly concerning economic policy – in the marginalist tradition; monetarists and the rational expectations school, who more or less radically reject public intervention and, on the strictly theoretical level, Keynesian theory, considered

---

[10] Among the roots of this debate we should also recall Hilferding's 1910 book, though he retained a Marxist perspective, more precisely the Austro-Marxism recalled above, in § 9.9; Hilferding discussed the dominance of financial capital over manufacturing capital.

[11] Cf. for instance Davidson 1972; Minsky 1982; Kregel 1996; Tonveronachi 1988.

contradictory with the analytical structure of the marginalist approach; and finally, the post-Keynesians who, diametrically opposed to the other groups, repropose the distinctive elements of Keynes's original thought, *in primis* uncertainty.

(a)   The neoclassical synthesis[12]

Confronted with the experience of the Great Depression of the 1930s, many economists had been induced to lend an attentive ear to Keynes's ideas on the opportunity of public interventions in support of demand in order to counter unemployment, even if they were unwilling to abandon the marginalist theory of value and distribution which constituted the foundation of their own education. In order to reconcile these two aspects, Keynes's theory was reinterpreted inserting it within the framework of the marginalist approach, while ad hoc assumptions, such as the downward rigidity of wages, were added to the core of the marginalist theory of value and distribution, so as to render unemployment a possible outcome.

Along this road we find in particular John Hicks (1904–89, Nobel prize in 1972). In an article of 1937, Hicks proposed the so-called IS-LM scheme, which translated Keynes's theory into the more traditional terms of a simplified general economic equilibrium model, with the presence of three markets: for goods, money and bonds (though the latter, thanks to 'Walras's law' – cf. above, § 12.3 – only plays a purely passive role, and attention may focus on the first two).

The goods market is in equilibrium when supply, that is production, is equal to aggregate demand (which under the simplifying assumption of a closed economy with no government expenditure and no taxes corresponds to demand for consumption and investment goods). The equilibrium condition, that is equality between aggregate supply and demand, holds when savings, which are an increasing function of income, are equal to investments, which are considered a decreasing function of the rate of interest.

The money market is in equilibrium when demand and supply of money are equal. According to the exogenous money assumption, the supply of money is determined by monetary authorities who directly control the issue of legal money, and indirectly control the amount of credit money that banks are allowed to create. Demand for money is equal to the sum of two components: transactions demand for money, which is an increasing function of income, and speculative demand for money – the

---

[12] 'The "neoclassical synthesis" was a label coined by Samuelson in the fifth edition of his *Economics* (1955)' (Blaug 2003, p. 407).

one on which Keynes focused attention, and which expresses the choice of the form, money or bonds, in which wealth is held – considered a decreasing function of the rate of interest.

Following the same lines as Hicks we find Franco Modigliani (1918–2003, born in Italy, then emigrated to the United States – like many other Italian, Austrian and German economists – to escape racial persecution, Nobel prize in 1985). In an article dated 1944, subsequently developed in another article dated 1963, Modigliani extended the IS-LM scheme to explicitly consider the labour market too. As for other markets, in the labour market as well changes in price lead towards equilibrium between demand and supply. More precisely, changes in the wage rate, that is in the price of labour services, bring into equilibrium labour demand and supply, thus ensuring full employment. In order to obtain the 'Keynesian' result, namely the possibility of a situation of persistent unemployment, it is then necessary to introduce some obstacle hindering the free operation of the labour market. Such an obstacle is located in the non-competitive nature of the market, due to trade unions' bargaining power, which determines the downward rigidity of wages.

Patinkin's 1956 book is another important contribution to the construction and the rise to dominance of the neoclassical synthesis, drawing attention to the non-neutrality of money out of equilibrium: when real wages are sticky because the fall in money wages provoked by unemployment is accompanied by a fall in prices, another adjustment mechanism comes into play, the so-called Pigou effect, by which the increase in the real value of money holdings due to the fall of prices provokes an increase in consumption, which depends not only on current income but also on real wealth.

In this way Keynesian theory is presented as a particular case of marginalist theory: that case in which full employment equilibrium cannot be reached, because the labour market is not a competitive market. We thus have the neoclassical synthesis, that is a synthesis between the neoclassical theory of value and Keynes's theory of employment,[13] which in the second half of the twentieth century dominated macroeconomics teaching all over the world.

The neoclassical synthesis absorbs the Keynesian thesis of the possibility of under-employment equilibriums in the framework of the traditional marginalist approach based on the notion of markets in which price variations ensure equilibrium between supply and demand. This opens

---

[13] Or better, as already stated, a specific case of neoclassical theory based on ad hoc assumptions, while Keynes's theory was modified in essential respects such as the role of uncertainty and expectations.

the way to recognising the utility of public intervention in the economy: unemployment can be countered through recourse to fiscal and monetary policies, useful in general to regulate the economy avoiding or reducing its cyclical oscillations.

Naturally, in the presence of some market power on the part of trade unions, public intervention aimed at reducing unemployment can simultaneously lead to an increase in the rate of growth of money wage rates, which in turn generates an increase of inflation. The trade-off between unemployment and rate of inflation was reproposed in an often quoted 1958 article by the New Zealand economist A. W. Phillips (1914–75). The decreasing curve representing such an inverse relationship (the so-called 'Phillips curve') represents, according to neoclassical synthesis economists, the set of possible economic policy choices. However, as we shall see below, such a view has been subjected to a number of criticisms over the past thirty years.

Let us briefly discuss here three lines of research that we may consider variants of the neoclassical synthesis. The first was originated by Robert Clower (b. 1926) and by Axel Leijonhufvud (b. 1933), who interpreted Keynes as a disequilibrium theory, whose microfoundations are to be found not in the Walrasian approach but rather in the Marshallian one, taking into account the problems of information diffusion and intertemporal coordination of real economies.[14]

The second line of research is the so-called 'new Keynesian economics', whose main representative is Joseph Stiglitz (b. 1943, Nobel prize in 2001), who tried to locate in different kinds of market failures the origin of unemployment. In other words, microeconomic explanations are sought for the rigidities which at the macro level cause the presence of unemployment. We thus have models based on 'menu costs' (costs of adjusting prices on the part of the firms, as a result of which the adjustment to demand takes place through levels of production and hence of employment rather than through prices), 'insider–outsider' models (in which those already employed enjoy a margin of market power which they use to get higher wages, at the expense of higher employment levels), 'efficiency wages' models (in which firms prefer to avoid reductions in

---

[14] In the absence of a Walrasian auctioneer, transactions may take place at out of equilibrium prices; moreover, quantity adjustment is assumed to be speedier than price adjustment; as a consequence, both buyers and sellers are subject to quantity constraints. Cf. Clower 1965; Leijonhufvud 1968. Subsequently, the models by Barro and Grossman 1971 and Malinvaud 1977 reformulated this line of research in terms of Walrasian schemes in which prices and money wages are fixed and transactions may take place at disequilibrium prices. The result is the possibility of 'rationing' either demand or supply, hence a 'classical' unemployment provoked by downward wage rigidity or a 'Keynesian' unemployment provoked by insufficient effective demand.

money wages, in order to retain experienced workers, presumably more efficient than potential new employees), and the list might go on. Success of this line of research is quite difficult to understand: in order to reproduce the notable results of Keynesian analysis within the neoclassical tradition, ad hoc assumptions are introduced, often rather implausible ones, on the sandy theoretical foundations of one-commodity and/or partial equilibrium models with their inverse relationship between real wages and unemployment.

The third line of research concerns extension of the neoclassical synthesis to the field of monetary theory. Let us recall here James Tobin (1918–2002, Nobel prize in 1981), who explains demand for money as a portfolio choice on the part of a rational economic agent in the presence of risk.[15]

(b)   Monetarists and rational expectations theoreticians

Within the marginalist tradition since the 1950s there has been a lively debate on the plausibility of the assumptions necessary for ensuring the Keynesian result of persistent unemployment. This debate impinges on the greater or lesser confidence attributed on the one hand to the ability of the market to ensure equilibrium between demand and supply of labour, on the other on the efficacy of fiscal and monetary policies.

Among those who show faith in the equilibrating powers of the market and hostility to state intervention in the economy, the Chicago school is prominent. Milton Friedman (b. 1912, Nobel prize in 1976) is the recognised leader of this school.[16] He worked out a different theory of money from Keynes's, taking on and developing the theses of the old quantity theory.[17] In particular, in the long if not in the short run, the equilibrium

---

[15] In this context Tobin proposed the useful notion now known as 'Tobin's q', defined as the ratio between current market evaluation of a given capital stock and its replacement value (which for physical capital goods is given by their cost of production). In some respects this line of research may also include the Modigliani–Miller theorem already mentioned above (note 7) and the CAPM (capital asset pricing models) which now dominate the theory of finance. This line of research has already yielded a few Nobel prizes: apart from Modigliani, who also gave important contributions in various fields, and Tobin, Nobel laureates were Harry Markowitz (b. 1927), Merton Miller (b. 1923) and William Sharpe (b. 1934) in 1990 and Robert Merton (b. 1944) in 1997.

[16] Occasionally Friedman's is called the 'second' or 'new' Chicago school, in order to distinguish it from the 'old' Chicago school, whose protagonists were Frank Knight (1885–1972), Henry Simons (1899–1946) and Jacob Viner (1892–1970). The 'old' Chicago school adhered to economic liberalism as well, although in a somewhat different sense: cf. Tonveronachi (1990) and the bibliography quoted there. In particular Simons considered a priority a liberal reform of the institutional set-up, which the market power of large firms and of trade unions had made non-competitive: cf. Tonveronachi 1982.

[17] Cf. in particular Friedman 1956.

level of income depends on 'real' factors such as resource endowments, technology and preferences of economic agents; the velocity of circulation of money is considered a stable function of the rates of return of various kinds of assets (money, bonds, goods, human capital). Friedman therefore maintained that monetary events, in particular the money supply (which is assumed to be exogenous, that is, sufficiently independent from demand for money) may influence income and employment only in the short run; in the long run changes in money supply only influence the general price level. In other words, the Phillips curve turns out to be negatively sloped only in the short period, but becomes vertical in the long period.[18]

Moreover, Friedman criticised monetary and fiscal policy measures aimed at supporting aggregate demand, hence income and employment: not only because efficacy of such interventions is limited to the short period, but also because the short period effects are uncertain and may well be negative. Indeed, Friedman recalled, economic policy measures are subject to three kinds of lags and uncertainties: those concerning evaluation of the situation in which to intervene; those concerning transition from such evaluation to choice of policy measures and their application; finally, those concerning the very impact of the policy adopted. Due to these lags and uncertainties it is possible, for instance, that policy measures exert their foreseen impact in a situation quite different from the one which had led to their adoption, even in a situation in which policies of an opposite sign would have been necessary. Economic policy measures may thus have a destabilising impact, widening rather than reducing income fluctuations.

A still more extreme thesis is proposed by rational expectations theoreticians, among whom is the American Robert Lucas (b. 1937, Nobel prize in 1995). In a 1972 article, Lucas joined the assumption of markets in continuous equilibrium with that of rational expectations, originally formulated by Muth (1961), according to which 'expectations [. . .] are essentially the same as the predictions of the relevant economic theory'.[19] As a consequence, economic agents learn to take account of public intervention in the economy, discounting its effects beforehand. Thus, for instance, deficit public expenditure, that is not financed by a contemporary increase in taxation, adopted by the government to stimulate aggregate demand, is counterbalanced by a reduction in private consumption, decided by private economic agents to put aside the savings with which to pay for the taxes which sooner or later will have to be introduced to pay for the public debt with which public expenditure is

---

[18] Cf. Friedman 1968; Phelps 1967.   [19] Muth 1961, p. 316.

financed. In this context, the Phillips curve turns out to be vertical also in the short run: expansionary monetary and fiscal policy interventions may only produce an increase in the rate of inflation, not in the level of employment. (We may also remark that these assumptions presuppose that all economic agents share the same model of the working of the economy, and are endowed with an economic culture and an ability to forecast the future that it would be an understatement to call unrealistic.)[20] Only 'surprise' policy measures unforeseen by economic agents may have an impact, though a temporary one, on real variables.

The only kind of economic policy admitted by rational expectations theoreticians is that aiming to reduce frictions in the working of the market: so-called 'supply-side policies', consisting for instance in facilitating the workers' mobility from one job to another, or in ensuring that the qualifications of which the labour force of the country is endowed correspond to the economic system's requirements. Among these policies there is also a reduction in fiscal pressure, since increase in income net of taxes is accompanied, in equilibrium, by an increase in the amount of 'sacrifice' (under the form of productive effort) that economic agents are ready to make, hence by an increase in production.

The rational expectations assumption, in the usual context of a one-commodity model, also underlies a new theory of the trade cycle, the 'real cycle theory'.[21] According to this theory, fluctuations in income and employment around long run equilibrium values are determined by unforeseen shocks on the side of supply, such as changes in technology, and by consequent reactions of economic agents (for whom the economic system is always in equilibrium, in any stage of the trade cycle it may be). As in Marx's and Schumpeter's theories of the trade cycle (cf. above, §§ 9.6 and 15.3), the same factors – as in Schumpeter, changes in technology – simultaneously explain cycle and trend.

After dominating the scene in the 1980s, in the following decade rational expectations theory gradually lost ground, even if in the theoretical confrontation with representatives of the neoclassical synthesis the shaky nature of its theoretical foundations – the one-commodity model, common to their rivals too – has not been stressed.

---

[20] In fact, the crucial defect of this theory is not so much the assumption of rational expectations, as rather the model to which such an assumption is appended: a one-commodity model, in which an inverse relationship between real wage rate and employment may be easily deduced so that, under competitive conditions, a stable full employment equilibrium exists. As we have repeatedly recalled, in a multi-commodity model in general existence of such an equilibrium cannot be proved. The rational expectations assumption applied to a model of this kind would thus give quite different results.

[21] The original contribution is Kydland and Prescott 1982.

(c)   The post-Keynesians

In opposition to the reinterpretation of Keynes's theory proposed by the neoclassical synthesis and to monetarist critiques, there has been a decided reaction on the side of 'post-Keynesians': exponents of the 'new Cambridge school' which we have already mentioned (§ 14.9), like Richard Kahn, Nicholas Kaldor and Joan Robinson; and some American economists like Sidney Weintraub (1914–83), Hyman Minsky (1920–96) and Jan Kregel (b. 1944).

These economists maintain that the IS-LM scheme proposed by Hicks and utilised by neoclassical synthesis economists relegates to a secondary role the salient feature of Keynes's view of the economy: uncertainty, which dominates economic agents' decisions. In the case of the investment function, much more important than the interest rate are entrepreneurs' expectations on the return of different investment projects: expectations considered 'volatile' by Keynes, since they change continuously, depending, for example, on the political climate and on general economic conditions. In the case of the demand for money, Keynes considered expectations on the future (to be exact, on the future path of interest rates) – they too being extremely volatile, even more than those concerning the expected yield of investment projects – essential for determining the speculative demand for money. Moreover, the latter was considered as the main component of the demand for money – both for its dimensions and its instability – since it is connected to the choice, continuously revised by economic agents, on the form in which to keep the stock of cumulated wealth, while the transaction demand for money is connected to the flow of income.

Confronted with the relevance of uncertainty, volatility of expectations and consequent variability of relations connecting investments and speculative demand for money to the interest rate, post-Keynesian economists consider as misleading the representation of markets in equilibrium both for goods and for money, based on well-defined and sufficiently stable demand and supply functions, which is the view that underlies the IS-LM scheme.

Instead of the simultaneous equilibrium of various markets, typical of the marginalist approach and taken on in the IS-LM scheme, post-Keynesian economists[22] propose a characterisation of the economic system based on a sequence of cause and effect relations: speculative demand for money affects the interest rate; this in turn, together with expectations, affects the level of investments; in turn investments, through the

---

[22] Cf. for example Pasinetti 1974, ch. 2.

multiplier, determine income and employment. Thus the influence exercised by monetary and financial markets on income and employment is stressed, in opposition to the thesis of the neutrality of money accepted in the classical and marginalist tradition. Moreover, various post-Keynesian economists maintain that the supply of money is endogenous: that is, the quantity of money (in particular bank money) in circulation is not rigidly controlled by monetary authorities, but depends at least in part on the decisions of other agents.[23]

6.   The theory of growth

The history of modern growth theory begins soon after the publication of Keynes's *General theory*, with a famous 1939 article by Roy Harrod (1900–78). Harrod used Keynes's approach to define an equilibrium growth rate, the 'warranted rate of growth', which corresponds to continuous equality between growth rate of productive capacity and growth rate of aggregate demand. Harrod's model is very simple, based as it is on three equations: the first defines savings as a function of income, the second follows accelerator theory in setting investments equal to the product between change in income and capital-output ratio, the third expresses the Keynesian condition of equilibrium between aggregate supply and demand as equality between savings and investments. Substitution in the third equation of the expressions for savings and investments defined by the first two equations makes the 'warranted' rate of growth equal to the ratio between propensity to save and capital-output ratio.

A similar model, but with a somewhat different interpretation, was proposed in 1946 by the American (of Russian-Polish origin) Evsey Domar (1914–98), leading many to refer to a Harrod–Domar model. The subsequent debate originated in a problem raised by Harrod in the concluding section of his article. This is the so-called 'knife edge' problem, concerning instability of the actual growth rate as soon as it diverges from the warranted rate of growth. Harrod recalled that whenever actual growth, determined by aggregate demand, is higher than warranted growth, productive capacity lags behind. This implies an increase in investments, hence in aggregate demand, in the following period, which generates new increases in the growth rate. Conversely, if actual growth is lower than that corresponding to the warranted rate, investments will be reduced

[23] In particular Minsky – cf. the essays collected in Minsky 1982 – developed on this basis an 'endogenous' theory of financial crises, which had wide success: among other things, it was utilised by Kindleberger 1978 as theoretical reference in his historical investigation, and has been continuously referred to in interpreting the most recent financial and currency upheavals.

and the consequent decrease in aggregate demand will provoke a further slowing down of growth.

This instability may lead to cyclical oscillations in the economy, if coupled with a system of 'roofs' and 'floors'. The 'roof' is given by full employment; the absence of a 'floor' endowed with sufficient justifications reproposes Keynes's thesis of the possibility of persistent unemployment. Moreover, a continuous increase in unemployment may take place when the actual growth rate corresponds to the warranted one, but the latter is lower than the 'natural' rate of growth, equal to the rate of growth of productivity plus the rate of population growth.

On this theme – possibility of persistent differences between natural and warranted growth rates, and existence of equilibrating mechanisms – there has been considerable debate. Following an important review article by Hahn and Matthews (1964), this multiplicity of contributions may be boiled down to three approaches. In the first place we have the classical (more precisely, Malthusian) approach, according to which adjustment takes place through the growth rate of population, which falls when increasing unemployment brings down the wage rate. We then have the Kaldorian approach (cf. Kaldor 1956), based on an adjustment of the propensity to save, brought about by a change in income distribution: when unemployment grows, the wage falls and, since the workers' propensity to save is lower than the capitalists' one, the average propensity to save increases, which corresponds to an increase in the warranted growth rate. Finally we have the neoclassical approach, based on an adjustment of the capital-income ratio: the fall in wages brought about by increasing unemployment leads firms to adopt production techniques which use relatively more labour, the factor of production whose price has fallen; thus the capital-income ratio falls; once again, this corresponds to an increase in the warranted growth rate.

These equilibrating mechanisms, however, are not without defects. For instance, it is doubtful whether in present-day conditions population growth depends on the wage level, according to an inverse relation, as required by the classical approach. The Kaldorian theory requires that increases in unemployment provoke a change in distributive shares in favour of profits, while in general during a crisis or a depression profits may well decrease more than wages. Finally, Sraffa's 1960 critique and the ensuing debate (cf. above, § 16.8) definitely showed that the capital-income ratio cannot be considered as an increasing function of the wage. We thus return to Harrod's original thesis, a typically Keynesian one: growth in a capitalistic economy is intrinsically unstable.

The neoclassical approach to the theory of growth, originally proposed in an article by Solow (1956) and, simultaneously, in a contribution by the Australian Trevor Swan (1918–89; cf. Swan, 1956), notwithstanding its basic feebleness stimulated various streams of research.[24] In the first place, the very simple original Solow model, based on an aggregate production function in which the capital-labour ratio is a continuous and increasing function of the wage, has been extended to consider different aspects, such as taxation or a two-sector model, without, however, this modifying the original approach. In particular, in a variant proposed by Solow himself (1957), the original model was enriched by introduction of exogenous technical progress. In the second place, we have a rich stream of empirical research which, often in connection with this latter variant of the model, seeks to determine the relative contribution of capital, labour and technical progress[25] to economic growth in different countries; the best known among such research is Denison 1967.

To identify technical progress with the 'residuum', that is with that part of income growth which is not justified by increase in labour and capital inputs, means failing to explain what empirical analyses show to be the major component of economic growth. After some attempts at reducing the size of the 'residuum' by inserting accumulation in 'human capital' alongside accumulation in fixed capital, a new stream of research was opened by Romer 1986 by extending Solow's basic model to render technical progress endogenous, namely connected to income growth, through introduction of increasing returns or 'learning by doing' mechanisms which allow for 'augmentation' of human capital given the physical inputs of capital and labour.[26] This stream of research had a lukewarm reception which appears incredible, considering its unstable foundations: indeed, increasing returns are known to be incompatible with competitive equilibrium of individual productive units, except for the case of economies of scale external to individual firms but internal to the industry (that is, to the economic system as a whole, in the 'one-commodity world'

---

[24] Cf. Solow 2000 for a survey, and Pasinetti 2000 for a critique. Robert Solow (b. 1924) received the Nobel prize, in 1987, precisely for his contribution to the theory of growth.

[25] In fact the contribution of technical progress is determined not directly, but residually, that is it corresponds to that part of income growth which is not explained by increase in the factors of production. Therefore some prefer to speak of a 'residuum' (which for instance may stem from improvement in 'human capital' due to investments in education and professional training) rather than of technical progress.

[26] 'Learning by doing' phenomena appear when unit costs of production decrease as experience is acquired, that is in proportion to cumulated amount of product. The object of a famous article by Arrow (1962), though playing an analogous role in the context under discussion, these effects should not be confused with the connection between growth of production and technical progress (a dynamic form of increasing returns to scale) named 'Verdoorn's law' (cf. Verdoorn 1949) and utilised in his models of growth by Kaldor (1957, 1961).

formalised in endogenous growth models); as Sraffa already remarked in his 1925 and 1926 articles, this is a very specific case.

More faithful to the Keynesian inspiration of Harrod's model and more theoretically solid, not being limited to the case of a one-commodity world (or, even worse, to a one-firm world), is the model of disaggregated growth developed by Pasinetti (1981), already discussed above (§ 16.9). Apart from the normative implications proposed by Pasinetti himself, the model shows how only by chance actual growth of employment may correspond to growth of labour supply, exogenously determined by demographic factors, and how a technological change differing from one sector to another leads to continuous change in relative prices as an unavoidable feature of a capitalistic development process.[27]

7.   Quantitative research: the development of econometrics

Economic growth is a field in which theoretical and empirical analyses go hand in hand and often interact. The idea that economic issues are to be studied by analysing quantitative relations between different variables is more general, and is as old as the study of economic phenomena. William Petty's political arithmetic, as we saw above (§ 3.2), was precisely based on the view that the structure of the economy was constructed according to mathematical laws, 'in terms of weight, number and measure'. True, this is not the view that prevailed in subsequent centuries. With Adam Smith, the idea of political economy as a moral science prevailed: an idea more or less shared by protagonists of the nineteenth and twentieth centuries such as Marshall and Keynes. The quantitative view was, however, always present, accompanying the development of collection of statistical material (Hacking 1990); consider for instance work by Gauss, Pearson and, on more specifically economic themes, Engel and Pareto. A renewed vigorous proposal of the quantitative view then arrived, on the theoretical level, with Jevons's and Walras's marginalist revolution.

Walras was directly referred to by Wassily Leontief (1906–99, Nobel prize in 1973) concerning his input–output tables. These are a representation of the economy through matrices, that is squares of numbers: each column indicates the means of production utilised in a given sector

---

[27] Within growth theory, let us recall here also two lines of research sharply different from that originated by Solow: one, at the boundaries with economic statistics, due to Simon Kuznetz (1901–85, Nobel prize in 1971) and another, at the boundaries with economic history, due to Walt Rostow (1916–2003), with his theory of 'stages of economic development' (cf. Rostow 1960).

distinguished by sector of origin; each row indicates the sector-by-sector destination of the product of a given sector (cf. Leontief 1941). However, if we consider the formative period of Leontief's studies, the origin of input–output tables should rather be found in the schemes of reproduction studied by Marx in book II of *Capital* (cf. Gilibert 1990). This twin ascendancy suggests that Leontief's tables may be considered a technical tool for statistical analysis, in itself open to use within different approaches, whether classical or marginalist ones. On the theoretical level, too, Leontief's tables, by focusing attention on formal elements of analysis of relative prices and quantities produced common to Marxian and Walrasian theories, constitute a contribution which may be developed either in the direction of a theory of prices such as Sraffa's (1960), if this aspect is isolated from the determination of production levels; or of modern general economic equilibrium theory, if we 'close' the model by adding consumer preferences on the one side and choice among alternative techniques of production on the other.

Leontief's input–output tables have been extensively used in applied economic research; their construction has become routine for national statistic institutes, and it is frequently attempted also by private research centres. A wide input–output multiregional model of the world economy was developed in the framework of a research project directed by Leontief himself and organised by the United Nations (Leontief et al. 1977).

Apart from the use of individual input–output tables for analysis of the productive structure of an economic system, recourse to comparisons between input–output tables relative to different countries or to different years has been made to study differences among national productive structures and technological change; moreover, statistical information organised according to the Leontief model has been used within linear programming. Under the assumption of constant returns to scale in all sectors of the economy, input–output tables allow us to compute technical production coefficients (that is, the quantity of each means of production required for each unit of product); on this basis, linear programming techniques allow us to deduct the quantity of gross output of the different sectors corresponding to a given set of net products (and analogous techniques are moreover applicable to a series of analogous issues: cf. Dorfman, Samuelson and Solow 1958). At the theoretical level, the system of determination of gross production levels thus arrived at turns out to be the 'dual' (in the mathematical meaning of the term) of a system of determination of relative prices based on relative difficulties of production of the various commodities; hence the thesis, advanced by many, of an affinity between Leontief's input–output analysis and Sraffa's analysis of prices discussed above, in chapter 16.[28] However, also the relationship between linear programming and general economic equilibrium theory is very strict indeed. As stated above, Leontief's tables may be related, with the necessary caution, both to the one and the other approach.

Another tool of empirical analysis, worked out under the stimulus of theoretical developments of the time but whose subsequent worldwide use proved largely independent of its cultural roots, is the system of national accounting. In this case the main stimulus came from Keynes's theory and the macroeconomic categories it used. However, at least in the case of the major protagonist of this line of research, Richard Stone (1913–91, Nobel prize in 1984), we should also recall the influence of the long tradition of research on measurement of national income, from political arithmeticians like William Petty in the seventeenth century to the economic historian Colin Clark (1905–89). The national accounting system offers a set of categories, defined in such a way as to be susceptible of precise statistical computation and to accord with the principles of double entry bookkeeping, which represent the working of the economic system as a web of flows of goods and money connecting different economic agents or rather, within the aggregate representation of the economy, different groups of economic agents. Initiated by the United Nations and under the direction of Stone, a system of national accounts (SNA) has been worked out (for the first time in 1953, and subsequently revised a number of times) which constitutes a compulsory reference point for the national statistic institutes of various countries.

Increasing availability of statistical information, sufficiently reliable and organised in categories defined according to sufficiently general criteria, undoubtedly favoured development of applied economic research. But developments of statistical theory, in particular inferential statistics, also played an important role. These elements (and others, such as – especially – computer advances) combine to explain the impetuous development over the past decades of econometrics (from the Greek *metron*, measurement): the science that aims at identifying quantitative relations among economic variables, as a basis for interpretation of economic phenomena. A relatively modest role in this direction was instead played by the 'marginalist revolution' and the ensuing mathematical

---

[28] Duality between price and quantity system lay at the centre of the model of homothetic growth proposed by von Neumann 1937, which also stressed another correspondence, that between profit rate and rate of growth. Both Leontief's and von Neumann's models, however, were developed on the basis of the assumption of constant returns to scale: an assumption which instead is external to Sraffa's approach, whose analysis focuses on the problem of the relationship between relative prices and income distribution (cf. above, § 16.7).

reorientation of economic theory. Attempts to estimate precise numerical values for economic relations, between the end of the nineteenth and the beginning of the twentieth century, mainly concerned aspects external to the core of value theories: this is the case of the consumption curves studied by Ernst Engel (1821–96)[29] or of Pareto's studies on personal income distribution (cf. above, § 12.4). Moreover, there is a qualitative jump between simple use of statistical data for descriptive purposes, and systematic search of precise quantitative relations between variables. It is this second aspect which marks the birth of econometrics.

The Italian Rodolfo Benini (1862–1956), statistician, demographer and economist, was among the first (cf. Benini 1908) to utilise advanced statistical methods such as multiple regressions in economic analysis. The American Henry Moore (1869–1958) and his pupils (among whom we may recall Paul Douglas, 1892–1976, and Henry Schultz, 1893–1938) systematically pursued quantitative analysis through statistical estimates of economic relationships.[30]

Ambitious methodological foundations for the newly-born econometric science were then provided by the Norwegian Ragnar Frisch (1895–1973), in his editorial to the first issue of the new journal *Econometrica* (Frisch 1933), edited by him up to 1955 and conceived as the organ of the Econometric Society, founded in 1930.[31] According to Frisch, econometrics constitutes the unification of statistics, economic theory and mathematics necessary 'for a real understanding of the quantitative relations in modern economic life'.

Crucial contributions to the development of new econometric techniques came from economists grouped in the Cowles Commission, amongst whom were Jacob Marshak (1898–1977), Tjalling Koopmans (1910–84, Nobel prize in 1975), Don Patinkin (1922–97) and Lawrence Klein (b. 1920, Nobel prize in 1980).[32] The Norwegian Trygve Haavelmo (1911–99, Nobel prize in 1989), in an essay published in 1944 as a supplement to *Econometrica*, proposed the insertion in a stochastic context of the estimate of econometric relations. In this way, among

---

[29] 'Engel's law' states that when family income grows, food expenditure grows less than proportionally. On the history of this 'law', cf. Kindleberger 1989, First Lecture.

[30] To Douglas, together with the mathematician Charles Cobb, we owe in particular the construct of the aggregate production function – the so-called Cobb–Douglas – widely utilised not only in statistical analyses but also in theoretical analysis, notwithstanding the demonstrated limits of its foundations (because of the aggregate capital notion it employs). In fact, on the theoretical level the aggregate production function may be traced back to Wicksell (even if he himself was aware of its limits: cf. above, § 11.5).

[31] In 1969 Frisch shared with the Dutch Jan Tinbergen (1903–94), another key figure in the field under consideration, the first Nobel prize for economics.

[32] For an illustration of the role of the Cowles Commission in this respect, cf. Klein 1991.

other things, Haavelmo defended the econometric approach against the criticism that Keynes (1973, pp. 295–329) had levelled at Tinbergen's research on economic cycles and the construction of macroeconomic models.[33]

Development of quantitative analysis received an impulse, in particular in the United States, from its utilisation in support of the war effort during the Second World War. This, however, mainly holds true for operational research, utilised for solving planning problems in transport and in similar issues. Modern econometrics, aimed at constructing large econometric models, emerged instead in the immediate second post-war period, at the Cowles Commission; the first econometric model of the US economy is Klein's.[34] Partly due to the growth of public intervention in the economy, at the time the necessity of forecasts on macroeconomic trends was strongly felt, and this favoured development of new analytical methods to that end. Cold War political tensions and expectations of a new Great Crisis in market economies after the end of war expenditure, created an atmosphere in which the optimistic forecasts of the Cowles Commission economists came to constitute a crucial test for the new analytical techniques, which were soon to be widely adopted.[35]

Among the most recent developments of the new econometric techniques, let us recall those concerning methods of time series analysis, with the ARMA models (autoregressive moving average: cf. Box and Jenkins 1970). Still more recently, the VAR method (vector autoregressive: cf. Sims 1980, 1982) has been proposed as an alternative to traditional econometrics. The latter had been the target of radical critiques; in particular Lucas 1976, on the basis of rational expectations theory (cf. above, § 5), had maintained that the structural parameters of

[33] Contrary to a widespread *vulgata*, Keynes's critiques did not stem from generic hostility to use of mathematical or statistical tools in the economic field, but from a conscious evaluation of their limits: let us recall that Keynes was the author of an important *Treatise on probability* (Keynes 1921)!

[34] The model was then developed at Michigan University. Klein subsequently headed two other projects aimed at constructing large-scale macroeconomic models: the so-called 'Brookings model' and the 'Project Link', which aimed to link among them econometric models built by research centres of different countries (for Italy, Beniamino Andreatta's Prometeia model), in essence arriving at a world model articulated by large geographical areas and where possible by countries.

[35] Among others let us recall the FED-MIT model, built from 1964 under Modigliani. He also collaborated, from 1966, to build an econometric model for Italy at the Bank of Italy. Among the models of the Italian economy, let us also recall that developed by Sylos Labini 1967: a model whose distinctive feature was distinction among the main economic sectors (industry, agriculture, commerce) as characterised by different market forms. Explicitly targeting economic policy is instead the 'Modellaccio' built at the University of Ancona under the guide of Fuà (cf. Fuà 1976).

macroeconomic models are subject to change when confronted with discretional economic policy measures, so that the models themselves cannot be used to predict the consequences of adopting policy measures. An avalanche of econometric exercises followed, aimed at 'verifying' or 'falsifying' rational expectations theory (or specific propositions within it, such as public debt neutrality) in opposition to models of the neoclassical synthesis. Sims instead proposed an 'atheoretical econometrics', in which the structure of the model is not predetermined: econometric analysis is intended to specify case by case the most suitable model, rather than to test pre-assigned hypotheses. Thus, the distance between economic theory and econometrics widens, since economic theory appears to lose the role of 'prompter' of hypotheses to submit to econometric testing, while on its side it was already – or it should have been – obvious that econometric enquiries cannot in any case discriminate between 'correct' and 'incorrect' theories, since in each case verification would simultaneously concern the theory itself and the auxiliary assumptions needed to translate it into an econometric model.[36]

8.   New analytical techniques: theory of repeated games, theory of stochastic processes, chaos theory

As already hinted above (§ 2), game theory played an important role in development of modern general economic equilibrium theory. This new technique was also widely utilised in the field of the theory of the firm. The so-called theory of industrial organisation proposed, indeed, a turnaround of the analytic structure of traditional analysis: that is, it proposed to derive market forms from the firms' behaviour, rather than building a different theory of the firm for each market form. This is a 'revolution' parallel to the one simultaneously taking place in macroeconomics, where recourse to game theory also spread rapidly: in both cases, the idea is abandoned that economic agents follow a 'parametric' behaviour, that is choose their actions by assuming as a datum – as a parameter of the function to be maximised – the behaviour of other agents, and the reactions of other agents to one's own decision are taken into account. At the same time, in both cases – in the theory of industrial organisation as in macroeconomic theory – the aim is to develop microfoundations from which to derive analysis of market forms or the theory of economic policy. In both directions, game theory favoured production of new theoretical contributions, but relying on concepts that remained substantially those

---

[36] Cf. Cross 1982.

developed within the framework of the traditional neoclassical view of individual rationality.[37]

Conversely, development in the late 1970s of the theory of repeated games, though at first sight it might seem a simple extension of a technique whose application in economic theory has reached maturity, opens up interesting perspectives for a more complex view of the notion of rationality and for an understanding of cooperative behaviour within economic systems.

Within the traditional approach various developments take place, such as use of the notion of 'reputation' within the theory of economic policy:[38] if non-cooperative behaviour may be 'punished', but punishment has an immediate cost higher than forgiveness also for those who administer it, punishment may nonetheless be chosen systematically within a repeated game, since reputation of non-acquiescence thus acquired will induce others to adopt a cooperative behaviour.

Less traditional results are obtained instead when analysis is conducted on the basis of experiments of 'computer tournaments', a tool which is used increasingly frequently due to the difficulties of solving mathematically problems with more than two players.[39] In these tournaments each player is represented by a computer program, which may be equal to, or different from, those chosen by other players; the computer then makes the different 'players' interact according to the predetermined rules of the game. In a case which soon became a classic (Axelrod 1984), the players meet in a series of direct encounters; as in the famous 'prisoner's dilemma', the choice not to cooperate gives a higher pay-off than cooperation, whatever is the choice of the other player; but if both players decide not to cooperate, the result is worse than if both decide to cooperate. In the case of a non-repeated game, the equilibrium solution is the choice not to cooperate. In the case of repeated games, instead, if each player recalls how the other behaved in previous encounters, cooperation may emerge. Indeed, the tournament experiments studied by Axelrod showed that in the spectrum between altruism and asocial selfishness the

---

[37] Cf. Tirole 1988 for the 'new theory of industrial organisation'; more generally, cf. Fudenberg and Tirole 1991 for an illustration of game theory from the economists' vantage point.

[38] The notion of reputation has for instance been used in order to justify systematic adoption of restrictive monetary policies on the part of central banks when confronted with increasing inflation.

[39] In this case, too, progress in computer sciences favoured diffusion of this technique of analysis. Indeed, recourse to computer simulations is frequent for all problems in which it is difficult to find sufficiently general mathematical solutions: thus, in applications to economics of the theory of non-ergodic stochastic processes as in chaos theory, which we will mention later in this section.

mechanism of economic (and social, in general) interactions rewards an intermediate position, the so-called 'tit for tat' strategy, in which the agent is ready to cooperate but reacts negatively to those who answer with a non-cooperative behaviour, though being ready to pardon whoever goes back to cooperation. In a sense, we may see here a return to the Smithian theory of self-interest, differing on the one side from benevolence and on the other from sheer selfishness (cf. above, §§ 5.3 and 5.4). We may perhaps see in these developments also a hint of some sort of microfoundation of an evolutionary theory of customs (but not of the institutions that sustain and drive them, to which instead Smith had already attributed great importance).

Like game theory, another mathematical technique, that of stochastic processes (applied to economics for instance by Steindl 1965 in the analysis of the size distribution of firms), has been used in the most recent debate both within the mainstream approach (for instance in macro-economics, in real cycle models) and within heterodox approaches, in particular in pursuing evolutionary research lines. In the latter case, the stochastic element plays an essential role, since the outcome depends on the path randomly adopted (so-called 'path dependence'). In the now-famous example of the typewriter (Paul David 1985) as in Brian Arthur's theoretical contributions (cf. Arthur 1994), learning by doing or increasing returns to scale – that is, essentially, the presence of cumulative phenomena in the process of economic development – generate outcomes which depend on historical, even random, vicissitudes. A technique which for any random reason is chosen more often than another in an initial stage – for instance, one keyboard arrangement rather than another, or gasoline motors for cars rather than electric motors – is progressively advantaged in comparison to the rival technique, up to the point at which 'lock-in' phenomena intervene, namely the practical impossibility of changing the technological paradigm: a minimum initial advantage becomes insurmountable because of the presence of cumulative effects.

This type of phenomenon was initially utilised, as the examples just recalled show, in the field of research into technological change. Subsequently it also gave rise to so-called 'new economic geography' (cf. for instance Krugman 1990) which aims to explain phenomena of spatial concentration of specific productive activities. In substance, an initial random distribution of firms over the territory may evolve over time, driven by cumulative mechanisms due to increasing returns of localisation present in different productive sectors; the result is a progressive differentiation of the productive structure of different countries and regions, hence specialisation in the flows of international trade, with 'lock-in' phenomena in the geographical division of labour.

In all these cases, we are confronted with stochastic processes of a non-ergodic kind, in which it is not possible to invert the arrow of time, as it is instead possible to do in the case of ergodic processes. This distinction is used by Davidson in the context of the macroeconomic debate (cf. for instance Davidson 1994) to distinguish the role played by time within the post-Keynesian approach and within mainstream theory. On the whole, analysis of non-ergodic stochastic processes appears to give rise to interesting results for the study of cumulative processes, particularly whenever some form of increasing returns to scale is present: that is, precisely in those cases which mainstream theory, even in its most sophisticated versions of general economic equilibrium theory, finds it difficult if not impossible to consider, but which already in Adam Smith's 1776 view appear as a central aspect of reality and economic theory.

Chaos theory, too, has been used both within mainstream theories and in support of theoretical approaches which attribute a central role to uncertainty and to history.[40] Indeed, chaos theories are difficult to use in the positive;[41] in the negative, they allow us to show a high sensitivity of the temporal pattern of the variables under consideration to starting conditions, such that even a small difference in such conditions brings out totally different patterns (according to a famous example, the flutter of a butterfly's wing in Peking may provoke a storm in New York). In this sense, among other things, chaos theory has been used for critical evaluation of problems concerning stability, in particular the hypothesis of convergence of market to natural prices.[42] In the macroeconomic field, use of the mathematical tools of chaos shows how easy it is to obtain non-regular cyclical patterns in the economy. However, this analytical tool, whilst it allows us to criticise results previously arrived at on the basis of simple models consisting of a single differential or first difference equation, does not by itself allow the location of elements responsible

---

[40] Chaos theory is, in essence, a mathematical theory in which the pattern followed by a variable (or by a set of variables) is determined – in general univocally – by non-linear differential equations. This theory has been applied to different research fields within natural sciences, for instance meteorology (where the theory of fractals was born, a fascinating theory for the beauty of geometrical objects which it produces, in which the dimensions of space vary continuously rather than by whole numbers: as yet, a theory little applied to economic issues, but which might prove useful, for instance, in critique of deterministic theories in macroeconomics). For a simple illustration, cf. Gleick 1987; for a more advanced illustration specifically directed to economists, cf. Brock and Dechert 1991; cf. then the bibliographical references provided there for examples of applications of chaos theory in economics.

[41] Let us anyhow recall Goodwin's 1990 attempt to present chaos theory as a positive interpretation of capitalism alternative to the mainstream equilibrium approach.

[42] Cf. for instance the essays collected in the monographic issue of *Political Economy* (vol. 6, no. 1–2, 1990) devoted to 'Convergence to Long-Period Positions'.

for the cycle or the behaviour of prices and thus construct a positive explanation of these and other phenomena.

9.   **Interdisciplinary problems and the foundations of economic science: new theories of rationality, ethics and new utilitarianism, growth and sustainable development, economic democracy and globalisation**

The quick survey of the last sections indicates the simultaneous presence of different lines of research in contemporary economic debate. In particular, there is an evident clash between the view of the economic problem characterising mainstream theory, based on the notion of equilibrium between demand and supply, and the view implicit in evolutionary approaches, or at least approaches open to recognising the role of path dependence. In essence, the clash concerns two different views. On the one side we have a restricted vision of economic theory, which through the axiomatic approach aims to maximise rigour, while it tackles with simplified ad hoc constructs the different problems arising from confrontation with actual economic systems. On the other, we have a broader view, which abandons the objective of a monolithic, all-inclusive construct, and follows a varied set of research strategies sharing greater attention for the realism of assumptions, hence for instance by recognition of the necessity to allow for the cumulative nature of crucial economic processes.

In this second direction, among the problems to be dealt with, those relative to the stage of 'conceptualisation' acquire relevance: definition of the concepts of rationality, welfare, development, equality and so on. Often research becomes interdisciplinary, due to the importance that other social sciences such as psychology, ethics, ecology and politics have for investigation of these notions. Still, subdivision into separate fields of investigation on society and man is a relatively recent phenomenon, perhaps an unavoidable one but certainly not a positive one in every respect.

Let us quickly recall some aspects of these research lines. As early as the eighteenth century the notion of rationality was implicitly a subject for investigation within the debates on passions and interests (cf. above, § 4.3); we saw among other things that the notion of rationality, connected to pursuit of personal interest in the sense of Adam Smith (that is, distinct from benevolence as well as from selfishness), is wider and more flexible than that which took the lead with the Jevonian interpretation of utilitarianism (cf. above, § 5.3 and ch. 10). This latter notion, however, prevailed within mainstream economics and axiomatic general economic equilibrium theory. Rational behaviour is here interpreted as a choice among a given set of alternative actions maximising a target function (more specifically, the expected value of a given utility function) taking account of the expected outcome of each course of action.

Perplexities already present in past centuries with respect to this notion have resurfaced, in various forms, in the past fifty years as well. First of all,[43] we have a series of specifications, such as distinction between rationality meant as internal consistency of the choice set, or as systematic pursuit of personal interest on the part of the economic agent. A specification of the latter category is given by the notion of 'substantive rationality', meant as the pursuit of personal interest definable in an 'objective' way, namely independently of individual choices. We have instead 'instrumental rationality' whenever the economic agent pursues a given purpose, however identified.

These specifications, and a series of logical problems connected with them, lead us to stress the distance separating the notion of rationality typical of axiomatic theory from actual behaviour of individuals. Yet, the assumption of irrational behaviour appears unreal too. Herbert Simon (1916–2001, Nobel prize in 1978; cf. Simon 1957, 1979) proposed as a solution to this dilemma the notion of bounded rationality. We must abandon, in their rigidity, the prerequisites of the mainstream notion of rationality: the assumption of a predefined set of alternative actions among which to choose; the assumption of knowledge of the outcomes of the different actions (which may admit conditions of probabilistic uncertainty – or risk, in Knight's terminology – but not uncertainty *tout court*); finally, the assumption of a given utility function (as an objective datum) to be maximised. We thus recognise that most of the time spent choosing an action involves collecting information, never complete, on the main available lines of action and their outcomes, which in any case remain uncertain. Moreover, when confronted with a multiplicity of objectives it appears reasonable to adopt a 'satisficing' behaviour to reach an acceptable result for each of the different objectives simultaneously pursued, rather than maximising a function which incorporates, adequately weighted, the different objectives.[44]

Another stream of research tries to analyse the actual behaviour of economic agents through experiments in which the working of the market is

---

[43] For a brief survey of these aspects and connected bibliographical references, cf. Sen 1987.

[44] A related distinction is that between 'instrumental rationality' (adequacy of the chosen strategy of action to a given target) and 'substantive rationality' (where choice of the target is also part of the problem, so that the target is somehow justified as corresponding to the 'nature' of the actor). Behavioural theorists, such as Cyert and March 1963, look for empirical evidence on which to rely for analyses of the decision procedures of complex organisations.

simulated. Among the leaders of experimental economics, let us recall Vernon Smith (b. 1927), Nobel prize in 2002 together with Daniel Kahnemann (b. 1934). The latter authored, in collaboration with Amos Tverski (1937–96), some important works which utilise hints drawn from psychological research in the field of the analysis of economic behaviour, and in particular of decisions under uncertainty.[45]

Enquiry into the relation between economics and ethics is obviously connected to the debate on rationality and the objectives of human action. In various respects, debate in this field draws on the old debate between consequentialist and deontological ethics. As we saw above (§§ 6.7 and 8.9), prevalence of utilitarianism and of philosophical radicalism between the end of the eighteenth and the nineteenth century had led to the dominance of consequentialism, even though the connection with maximisation of individual utility appears in many respects questionable. However, growing dissatisfaction stemming from the contrast between prescriptions of such approach and common sense[46] led to renewed interest for deontological ethics, especially with Rawls (1971). The new consequentialism developing between the end of the 1970s and the beginning of the 1980s also broke any rigid connection with utilitarianism: see for instance Sen's contributions, based on the distinction between rights, functions and capabilities.[47]

Thus, in the debate on the concept of rationality as in that on ethics, in recent years a richer and more complex view than that inherited from the neoclassical tradition has prevailed. The same happened for the debate on the notion of *sustainable development*. Here critiques concerned identification of economic development with simple quantitative growth of national income. Indeed, in this way there was the risk of ignoring the multiplicity of aspects which concur in determining the 'quality of life', in particular environmental aspects,[48] and the analysis of the relation between economic growth and civic development, which we will consider below, risks being left aside.

These aspects should not be confused with the debate on the limits to growth, which had greater resonance but also less substance. Malthus's

---

[45] On the relationship of their contributions with the recent economic debate, cf. Mirowski 2002, pp. 300–1, 546 ff.

[46] Hausman and McPherson 1996, pp. 9–21, offer some examples of such conflicts.

[47] See for example the essays collected in Sen 1984; the Italian edition contains an appendix with an extensive bibliography of his writings up to then. As an example of the recent debate on utilitarianism, see the essays collected in Sen and Williams 1982.

[48] Critiques of 'growthmania' (cf. for instance Mishan 1967; Fuà 1993) revived attention to the different elements which comprise economic and social development, behind monodimensional growth of national income. Thus indicators such as life expectancy at birth, infant mortality, instruction, income inequalities, political democracy, and territorial disequilibria (which, in the context of the global economy, take the form of the terrible disequilibria between the North and the South of the world) acquire importance.

conservative pessimism (and, before him, Necker's: cf. above, §§ 6.1 and 6.2) surfaced again in many writings over time, from Jevons's essay on coal (Jevons 1865) to research on *The limits to growth* stimulated by the Club of Rome (Meadows et al. 1972), progressively acquiring greater attention for ecological issues.

Indeed, environmental issues were already present in economic debate since John Stuart Mill's *Principles* (1848). However, ecology within the classical tradition has little to do with the fears, typical of the marginalist approach, of the limits to development set by impending exhaustion of natural resources. The problem rather concerns the set of interrelations between economic activity and natural environment. The notion of 'sustainable development' (Brundtland 1987) is a progressive response to this problem, with the proposal of a multidimensional view of economic growth. Conversely, the theses on 'the limits to growth', in the context of a world economy characterised by dramatic problems of misery and underdevelopment, have represented in some instances a conservative stance, analogous to that represented in other respects by the thesis concerning the claimed existence of an inverse relationship between rate of growth of the economy and some measure of equality in income distribution or, even worse, development of democracy and political freedoms.

Debates on these issues have followed different streams. In investigations on dualism between developed and developing countries, after a great mass of writings had maintained the most different theses, it clearly appears that neither inequalities in income distribution nor authoritarian political systems constitute prerequisites for sustained economic growth; on the contrary, we can maintain that progress in conditions of civic life (education, hygienic-sanitary conditions, morality and efficiency of public administration, public order and correct administration of justice, up to active involvement of citizens in political life in a context of democratic freedoms) constitute a fundamental prerequisite for a socially sustainable development process.[49]

In the debate on industrialised countries, analyses of internal power structure (to which also belong recent debates on property and

---

[49] An enormous mass of data, together with interesting analyses, is provided in the yearly reports of the World Bank, and in the yearly *Human development report* of the United Nations Development Programme (UNDP), stimulated by Mahbub ul Haq. On the connection between civic and economic development, cf. Sylos Labini 2000. A group of debates in some respects connected to this one and which here we may only mention, concerns the conditions of transition to the market of the ex-planned economies; we are confronted in this field with a frontal clash between the thesis of the 'big bang', that is of immediate liberalisation, and the thesis of a gradual transition, based on previous construction of institutional preconditions for the good functioning of the markets (inclusive for instance of efficient surveillance and anti-trust authorities) and accompanied by policies aimed at reducing the social costs of change.

governance of firms: cf. for instance Barca 1994) are accompanied by only apparently utopian proposals on democracy within the firm: a stream particularly rich in Europe (for a survey cf. Tarantelli 1986), which includes debates on worker-management (Vanek 1970), on profit-sharing (Meade 1972), on joint management with trade unions (Tarantelli 1978), and on the working army, which among other things implies sharing the less skilled and most unpleasant jobs among all (Rossi 1946).

Difficulties encountered by these proposals concern not so much their practicability within a given economic system, but rather their incompatibility with the maintenance of competitive conditions in international markets, in an increasingly integrated world economy. This leads us to recall – even if only by name – a final stream of research which is acquiring increasing importance, that on globalisation and the 'new ICT (information and communication technologies) economy'. Enormous progress in information transmission connected to development in telecommunications and in computers, fall in transportation costs, growing integration of financial markets in a single world market, and practical impossibility of controlling migration flows, all lead to a more direct connection of each country with the rest of the world. In a regime of non-perfect but less and less difficult transferability of technologies, competition of economies with low labour costs (hence downward competition not only in wages, but also in working conditions) exerts growing pressure on workers in developed countries, especially on less skilled workers. Economic problems intersect here with political and social ones, bringing to the fore difficult choices which have little to do with textbook economic theory, and concern the economic and social set-up of the different countries and hence, more generally, the different forms that life in common takes in such diverse cultural traditions as the European, the American, the Japanese, the Muslim, the Chinese or the Indian one.[50]

---

[50] Dahrendorf (1995, p. 4) stressed, with happy synthesis, that 'The overriding task of the First World in the decade ahead is to square the circle of wealth creation, social cohesion and political freedom. Squaring the circle is impossible; but one can get close to it, and probably that is all a realistic project for social well-being can hope to achieve.'

18 Where are we going? Some (very tentative) considerations

1. How many paths has economic thought followed?

In the introductory chapter I pointed out that the history of economic thought is useful both to get a 'sense of direction' in contemporary theoretical enquiry and to explore the conceptual foundations of theoretical models now in use. This means following the process of abstraction underlying such models and so being better equipped to evaluate them. What conclusions does this lead us to at the end of our journey?

Let us address the question taking three aspects into account. The first point is whether the path followed so far by economic research runs in a precise direction of progress. Second, we will briefly consider one of the main tendencies in contemporary economic research: the tendency to subdivision, or rather fragmentation, of research into an increasing number of specialised fields. Third, and the answer here will inevitably be largely provisional and personal – little more than a bet – starting from the reconstruction of the history of economic analysis set out in the preceding chapters I shall try to gauge the direction in which we might most profitably proceed.

The first aspect constitutes a necessary premise for dealing with the other two. Happily, the answer is sufficiently clear: the path followed up to now by economic research is far from linear. Historians of thought inevitably simplify their subject matter, focusing on what they see as the most significant features. However, not even simplifying to the very limits can we trace out in our summary account a single, logical path, let alone a straight one, such that we might speak of a clear and continuous ascent of economic science towards ever fuller understanding of reality.

This is, of course, not to deny the sustained endeavour to explore realities characterising each of the different currents of research. As we saw in the previous chapter, however, the foundations of economic research – methods of research implicitly or explicitly adopted, concepts utilised, the very definition of what an 'economic problem' is – not only change both in the course of time, from economist to economist, and across different groups of economists in the same historical period, but above all they do not display univocal tendencies. Moreover, we have also seen that it is hard to speak of 'progress' without due qualification, even within one given line of research. Let us recall two examples discussed in the previous chapters: the more robust analytical structure realised by Ricardo within the surplus approach was accompanied by, in comparison to Smith, a more simplistic representation of both the notion of *homo oeconomicus* and the complexities of development processes; the advance in analytical rigour from the original Walrasian theory represented by the modern axiomatic theory of general economic equilibrium also entails a drastic loss in heuristic power for the theory itself.

In the preceding chapters we have seen at least two rival ways of conceiving the functioning of the economy. On the one hand, we have a subjective view of value, considered as stemming from the opposition between scarcity and utility: a view that has its roots deep in the prehistory of economic thought and that, from Galiani and Turgot down to the axiomatic theory of general economic equilibrium, has always played a leading role in economic debate (only briefly obscured – but never completely cancelled – by the triumph of Ricardianism). On the other hand, we have an objective view of value,[1] based on the notion of the surplus, which expresses the conditions of reproduction in a capitalistic system founded on the division of labour, in which each sector has to recover through sale of its product the means of production required to carry on the productive process, plus the wherewithal to pay the wages of the workers employed and yield the competitive rate of profits. This view, too, from Petty to Ricardo up to Sraffa, has a central role in the history of economic thought and in contemporary debate.

Again, however, it would be too drastic a simplification to represent the evolution of economic science as a continuous confrontation between two rival views, always clearly distinct.[2] As a matter of fact, these two

---

[1] By 'objective' view we do not mean here the idea of value as a characteristic intrinsic to the commodity (as in a sense Marx does with his labour theory of value, considering labour as the 'substance' of value: cf. Lippi 1976; and as is also the case with subjective theories when based on a sensistic view of the economic agent, in which utility is considered as a characteristic intrinsic to the good to which the *homo oeconomicus* reacts in a mechanistic way). We refer, rather, to the idea that no role should be attributed to the 'mutable minds, opinions, appetites and passions of particular men', as Petty (1690, p. 244) said, and that we should rather deduce value from the structure – the 'skeleton', Sraffa would have said – of an economy based on the division of labour, the market and private property.

[2] Moreover, it should be borne in mind that it would be incorrect to represent the confrontation between the two views as a political opposition, with the neoclassical-marginalist approach on the conservative/reactionary side and the classical approach on the progressive/revolutionary side. We can find representatives of either approach scattered across the whole political spectrum.

views are rarely encountered in a 'pure state'; rather, it is the historian of thought who – with good reason, we should add – isolates them to offer a clearer picture of the multifaceted reality that confronts us with all its light and shade and manifold positions finding no place in too rigid a dichotomy. Along with 'purists' such as William Petty on the one hand or Philip Wicksteed on the other, we also see attempts to throw bridges to the other side of the river (albeit with perfectly recognisable foundations on one side) as in the Smithian analysis of market prices (and even more, subsequently, in the analyses of John Stuart Mill and Thomas De Quincey) or, on the other side, in the Marshallian notion of 'real costs'. The two views do not remain continuously opposed: they intersect (we may recall, for instance, the attempt to devise a marginalist Marxism!),[3] assay compromises (to tell the truth, in general doomed to failure), and occasionally – as ever more frequently happens in contemporary debate – hide round the corner, leaving the way clear for declaredly atheoretical approaches (as in the most recent econometrics).

In these conditions progress – should there be any[4] – advances in many different directions: so different, indeed, that viewed from one path advance along the other paths may appear as regression. We are far from a clear, unambiguous line of development: confusion ever reigns sovereign!

However, it is precisely this confusion that makes the economist's work so interesting today. Among the different components of the economist's work, this is particularly true of the work of the historian of economic thought. In fact, the confusion comes not from minds turning blank before the complexity of the real world, but from the wealth of analyses developed in the course of time. In this age of extreme fragmentation in research, with communication technologies showing dramatic progress while the economists seem increasingly incapable of communicating among themselves, there is all the more need to trace out if not a single line, at least some main lines along which economic analysis can proceed, and to evaluate their potentialities in the light of their developments. In this endeavour the historians of economic thought have a crucial contribution to offer. The fact that there are no obvious, cleancut answers makes the challenge even more interesting.

---

[3] Some examples are recalled in Steedman 1995.

[4] This has repeatedly been doubted by those who speak of a 'crisis in economics'. In fact, there appears to be some decline of interest in economics whenever it is interpreted as by and large applied mathematics, in comparison – for instance – with business studies or political sciences. The history of economic thought could play an important role not only in providing a unifying ground against tendencies to internal fragmentation of the economics field, but also in bringing to light its foundations – the different ways in which reality is represented – and hence its connection to (and importance for our understanding of) the real world.

2.   The division of labour among economists: can we forge ahead along different paths?

The second question to be considered in these concluding notes has to do with an evident characteristic of contemporary research that contrasts with experience in the early stages of development of economic science: the division of intellectual labour has led to the formation of specialised fields, each now enjoying a life of its own. The range of these fields appears to expand over time: macro and microeconomics; history of thought, public finance, economic policy; monetary economics, industrial economics, the economics of energy sources, labour economics and so on.

It is a situation that may well in part respond to the didactic need to divide an ever vaster corpus of knowledge into various courses for teaching at university level (and if this were all, there would be no need to worry, provided some form of rotation of lecturers among the various courses were brought in to keep the necessary connections between them alive). In a large measure, however, the phenomenon has its origin in the activity of research itself. In this case, too, we may be faced with an inescapable answer to a real problem, namely the multiplication of analysis techniques and research results and thus a dramatic increase in the quantity of written material we must take into account when dealing with any specific issue. However, the tendency to a growing division of economic research into separate sectors increases the sense of confusion mentioned in the previous section; nor is it exempt from risks.

We thus have, on the one hand, 'lowbrow' economic analyses, which make indiscriminate use of analytical tools whose theoretical foundations have come in for destructive criticism (for instance, the inverse relation between wage rate and employment in macroeconomics) but which pretend to provide 'scientific' economic policy advice on such flimsy foundations. Frequently, policies tricked out in scientific guise actually derive from a priori opinions and may arouse reasonable perplexity on the grounds of plain common sense, while recourse to unnecessarily complex theoretical apparatus is essentially for rhetorical effect. On the other hand, we have 'highbrow' theories, sophisticated exercises within axiomatic schemes based on processes of abstraction that are never subjected to critical scrutiny. The element of pure intellectual challenge is dominant here, but there is a significant cost in terms of lost heuristic power and hence of a meaner market share for economic science in the political and cultural debate.[5]

---

[5] The distinction between 'highbrow' and 'lowbrow' theories was propounded by Samuelson (1962, pp. 193–4): on the one hand, the more rigorous theorisations of general economic equilibrium do not need an aggregate notion of capital; on the other hand, the

In substance, the division of labour in economic research between specialised subfields often facilitates uncritical acceptance of the *mainstream* approach in any specific economic field. The economic problem is conceived of as search for an equilibrium emerging from confrontation between scarcity and utility, or between demand and supply. Behind this view lies the stylised representation – derived first from medieval fairs and then from the stock exchange – of the market as a point (in time and space) where demand and supply meet. In this context, identification of the equilibrium calls for certain analytical assumptions – convexity of production sets and consumers' preference maps, rationality of economic agents – that are taken as given, without weighing them up against reality. The methodological choice of individualism – that is, of starting the analysis in any case from the behaviour of individual economic agents – brings with it insoluble aggregation problems, which are tacitly circumvented through recourse to partial equilibrium (and representative firm) analysis or analysis of 'one-commodity (and one representative agent) worlds'. On the other hand, if we stick to general economic equilibrium analysis, apart from the fact that in any case it entails the assumptions mentioned above, there can be no hope of arriving at sufficiently definite positive results, useful for an understanding of the real world.[6]

A process of abstraction – in the sense of a simplified representation of realities otherwise excessively complex and multifaceted – is unavoidable for any theory. But the kind of abstraction adopted should always be kept in mind, and repeatedly subjected to critical scrutiny, remembering that it is not the only possible one.

The systematic failures in satisfying this obvious requirement of scientific research activity are largely attributable to the subdivision into

less rigorous, simplified models (one-commodity, or in any case with aggregate capital) have the role of 'parable' as compared with the more rigorous theory, and are thus useful in empirical research and in teaching. This distinction, which has enjoyed enormous fortune, was however put forward before the erroneousness of the 'parable' was proved (cf. above, § 16.8). In any case, the idea of the 'two levels of truth', frequent in the history of religions, should not find room in the field of scientific research.

[6] Certainly this was not Walras's view; but the lengthy process of correcting and completing his original work at the analytic level has inevitably led to these outcomes (cf. above, chapter 12). Let us also recall Schumpeter's 1908 thesis: the theory of economic equilibrium is unable to determine the position of equilibrium, since inclusion of consumers' preferences among the parameters assumed as data for the problem at hand renders it in this respect a tautology devoid of heuristic value; its purpose, rather, is to determine the consequences of a variation in the parameters, through comparative static analyses (cf. above, § 15.3). Unfortunately, use of the theory to this end requires uniqueness and stability of equilibrium (apart from the stability of the parameters assumed as data for the problem, and in particular of the economic agents' preferences) and such requirements do not hold in general. (Obviously, the 'Bourbakian' axiomatic tradition is indifferent to this outcome, considering abstract theory as self-justifying; but this position, understandably born – and not always accepted – in the field of pure mathematics, cannot be extended to policy-oriented theorising.)

research fields increasingly cut off from one another. On the one hand, now that the history of economic thought has taken on the role of a distinct discipline, researchers working in other fields are losing sight of views alternative to the dominant one, losing the capacity for critical scrutiny of the assumptions – the 'representation of the world' – typical of the field in which they work, and indeed losing the motivation to invest time in such a critical scrutiny. On the other hand, as a consequence of the closure into separate specialised research fields, the confrontation with reality generally does not run to the basic assumptions derived from the subjective-marginalist approach, but stops at the level of the auxiliary assumptions (falling within what Lakatos calls the 'protective belt' of the research programmes: cf. above, § 1.3) utilised to apply the general theory to the chosen field of research.

Are we, then, to take it that confrontation with reality (or, in other words, the critical scrutiny of abstraction processes) has no role whatsoever in the evolution of economic thought? Such a bald statement is certainly wrong, especially if we consider sufficiently long intervals of time. The changes in ways of conceiving of the economic system and analysing its functioning illustrated in this volume have undoubtedly constituted, at least in part, an answer to changes coming about in the meantime in real world economies: suffice it to recall how the physiocratic theses on the centrality of agriculture have dissolved (while leaving a by no means insignificant heritage of concepts and analytical tools). However, to an appreciable extent – indeed, ever more importantly, especially since economics became a specific profession – the more or less sharp or gradual twists and turns in the path of theoretical thinking have been made in response to difficulties or opportunities arising at the analytical level. For instance, analytical difficulties undoubtedly played an important role, along with other factors, in abandonment of the classical approach based on the labour theory of value. In terms of responding to opportunities, we may mention developments in the mathematical field, such as calculus for the construction of the marginalist theoretical system, or topology for the axiomatic construction of general economic equilibrium theory. This phenomenon is certainly not limited to economics: Popper (1976) speaks of a 'world 3' precisely to indicate the relatively autonomous existence of a world of ideas alongside the physical-natural one ('world 1') and the world of human beings ('world 2').

The predominance, in research, of work on analytical refinements over critical appraisal of the theory's foundations also has another effect: as foreseen by evolutionary theories of technology (cf. above, § 17.8), phenomena of lock-in (or blockage) may also crop up in the theoretical debate. In other words, the gradual accumulation of results – theorems and models – within any specific approach, within any given system of abstraction-conceptualisation, that is, attributes that approach with a competitive advantage over its rivals, which – for a variety of causes often independent of the validity of the basic conception on which their theoretical construction is founded – have for some time seen rather less concentrated research activity. For instance, this may well be the case of the persistent dominance of today's mainstream approach (axiomatic equilibrium microeconomics, neoclassical synthesis macroeconomics, different forms of 'neoclassical syntheses' in other subfields of economics), despite the paucity of results endowed with heuristic power shown by the 'highbrow' theories, and the flimsy theoretical foundations of the 'lowbrow' analyses.[7]

3. Which of the various paths should we be betting on?

We thus arrive at the third of the issues considered in this chapter: among the different 'economic philosophies' – or general pictures of the functioning of the economy – emerging in the history of economic thought, which looks most promising? And how – along what lines – should we be trying to develop it?

As we have seen, these evaluations inevitably boil down to something of a personal bet: however, it should be a bet as well reasoned out as possible. In any case, it is surely better than uncritical acceptance of the fashion of the day: theoretical issues are not decided by a majority vote.

It is the historian who defines different research currents and schools of thought, and who draws lines between them. Artificial as they may be, these distinctions are not arbitrary, but the fruits of serious scientific work using the necessary philological tools. In the preceding pages, following a tradition established over tens of years that seems so far to have stood up to a fair amount of attack, we have recognised a substantial division between two approaches, classical and marginalist, while bearing in mind

---

[7] This situation may be compared to the case, frequently cited in the evolutionary theories of technological change, of the predominance of petrol-fuelled automobiles over electric ones, with a gap between the two 'technological paradigms' that has grown over time starting from an initial situation of approximate equivalence. Many today believe that it would have been better if the paradigm of the electric automobile had prevailed, due to the environmental fall-out of the petrol-fuelled automobile, the importance of which has become fully evident only recently. Another comparison may be that between nuclear energy and solar or wind energy: the relatively high costs of the latter compared to the former (if we leave aside the issue of nuclear waste, as nearly all cost-computation exercises do) stem at least in part from concentration of research efforts on nuclear energy (also, indeed above all, for military reasons). We can only wonder how widely solar or wind energy would have developed if comparable research efforts had gone into them.

that each appears extremely varied, and that there exists a 'no man's land' that both sides claim, inhabited by protagonists such as Keynes and Schumpeter.

Within this distinction, we have seen the limits that the subjective-marginalist approach came up against in its development. On the one hand (in the case of Marshall, but also in the case of the reflections of the Austrian school on competition as a learning process), we find ideas suggestive but vague, not incorporated in an analytical structure. On the other hand we have a formally rigorous axiomatic system, apparently capable of being extended to consider any and every economic issue but in reality compelled to leave the field to 'lowbrow' analyses whenever any attempt is made to apply it to real world issues. Furthermore, we saw that the kind of abstraction upon which this theorising relies displays very dubious features: from the assumptions of convexity in production sets and completeness of consumers' preferences to a 'strong', mono-dimensional notion of rationality and representation of the market as the point of encounter for supply and demand, rather than as a web of relations that embrace the agents active in a sector or field of economic activity (thus taking reference from the paradigm of the medieval fair or the stock exchange, rather than the flows of information in which competition resides). We also saw how more recent attempts at enriching the marginalist tradition by accommodating within it new ideas such as offered by Keynes had resulted in constructions that were neither rigorous nor realistic. The dominant tradition contains a rich set of tools clearly useful for the analysis of specific phenomena, and continues to generate attractive ideas (including asymmetric information, strategic interdependence, transaction costs); but it is hard to see why such instruments and ideas could not be utilised, *mutatis mutandis*, in the context of a different conceptual system taking the division of labour and the notion of the surplus as key concepts rather than rational economic agents' preferences and the scarcity of resources.

We thus arrive at the classical approach, based on the division of labour and the notion of the surplus. Its limits have also been illustrated, especially with regard to the labour theory of value and 'Say's law'. But we have also seen how the former limitation can be overcome through Sraffa's analysis, while for the latter integration with Keynesian ideas has been proposed as a solution. Obviously this course does not leave the original classical approach unchanged: the modifications required are by no means superficial.

One of the crucial aspects in the reconstruction of the classical approach has to do precisely with the way such diverse elements as Sraffian analysis of the relationship between relative prices and income distribution and Keynesian analysis of unemployment can be brought together, and indeed still others, like Minsky's theory of financial crises or Sylos Labini's oligopoly theory. This is an aspect we have already had occasion to mention (§ 16.9); here too we must limit ourselves to a few brief remarks.

Faced with the fragmentation of economic theory, which constitutes a dominant feature of the most recent period, we may specify three different attitudes, two of which are at opposite extremes while the third represents an intermediate position. The first, possibly most widespread and certainly simplest, consists in accepting the fragmentation without (at least explicitly) worrying about the connection between theories concerning different aspects of economic reality. The second, at the other extreme, lies in the attempt to trace all theoretical contributions back to a common foundation – the axiomatic treatment of general economic equilibrium – adding opportune specific assumptions (such as asymmetric information) to the basic axioms (*in primis*, rationality of economic agents) and representation of the functioning of the market as based on market clearing. We thus have a pure and very general theory, and a series of variants of the base model addressing different specific issues.

The third attitude stems from a critical evaluation of the first two. On the one hand, it is recognised that theories concerning specific aspects of economic reality must in any case be based on some general representation of the functioning of the economic system. Thus, the link between specific theory and general view is an aspect that we are bound to address if we wish to clarify the foundations upon which the specific theory rests. On the other hand, the idea of representing all aspects of economic reality with a single, general model is considered excessively far-fetched – an aspiration reminiscent of the ideas in early Wittgenstein and, significantly, abandoned in the face of Sraffa's criticisms (cf. above, § 16.8). What is left, then, is what we may call 'conceptual compatibility': the abstractions upon which the theoretical work inevitably relies should never – not even in such specific issues as the explanation of oil prices and their changes over time[8] – lead us into contradicting the basic representation of the functioning of the economy. In the case of the classical approach, this implies that analyses of specific issues should not contradict features such as the division of labour, and hence the multiplicity of commodities and economic agents, the movement of capital among sectors in search for the highest return, or the cumulative nature of many phenomena – in particular in the field of technology – and hence the dynamic-evolutionary nature of fundamental economic issues. Opening

---

[8] Cf. Roncaglia 1983a.

up to Keynesian analysis, moreover, also means adding uncertainty (not simply risk!) about the future to these characteristics.[9]

In tackling specific aspects of reality, economists will thus find themselves working in different 'analytic areas', producing theories in general not reducible to one general 'super-model', but with common features deriving from common reference to the real world societies in which we live and the basic representation of them characterising the chosen research approach. As we saw above, part of economic theory – that part which is commonly classified under the label of value theory – expresses (or seeks to express) in analytical terms a specific basic view of the functioning of the economy. Thus interpreted, the theory of value constitutes the 'heart' of economic science – the space where the main approaches come into close encounter with their respective cores of essential features that must be retained in the process of theorising on specific issues.

Following this path, reconstruction of the classical approach will not have to start from square one, but from a wealth of contributions regarding both the 'core' of economic theory and specific but nevertheless important aspects.[10] The different contributions will then have to be subjected to the verification of 'conceptual compatibility'; in many cases this may lead to reinterpretation and reformulation of the different theories.

Beyond this – admittedly vague – signposting we cannot go here. Of course, to see how good a recipe is, it must be tried out in the kitchen, but any attempt in this direction must be the subject of a separate work.

---

[9] Thus, for instance, from this point of view the assumption of a one-commodity world in mainstream macroeconomic models constitutes an erroneous abstraction, since it cannot be overcome in second approximation analyses (because of the need to drop the trade-off between wage and employment on which the results obtained in such models are based), while it concerns a crucial feature of the society in which we live.

[10] From this point of view, the fragmentation of economic research constitutes a most important positive element: lines in research on, for example, equitable and sustainable development, cumulative phenomena in technological change, the institutional pattern of different financial systems, globalisation and many others are largely external to the logic of the subjective approach.

References

[The year after the author's name indicates the original date of publication, except for pre-1500 writings. The original date of writing is occasionally indicated in square brakets. Page references in the text refer to the last of the editions quoted below not in brackets. When this is not an English edition, the translation of the passages quoted in the text is mine.]

Akerlof, G. 1970. 'The market for lemons', *Quarterly Journal of Economics* 84: 488–500.

Akhtar, M. A. 1979. 'An analytical outline of Sir James Steuart's macroeconomic model', *Oxford Economic Papers* 31: 283–302.

Allocati, A. (ed.) 1990. *Carteggio Loria-Graziani*. Roma: Ministero per i Beni Culturali e Ambientali, Pubblicazioni degli Archivi di Stato.

Alter, M. 1990. *Carl Menger and the origins of Austrian economics*. Boulder: Westview Press.

Althusser, L. 1965. *Pour Marx*. Paris: François Maspero.

Andrews, P. W. S. 1993. *The economics of competitive enterprise. Selected essays.* Ed. F. S. Lee and P. E. Earl. Aldershot: Edward Elgar.

Anonymous 1549. *A discourse of the common weal of this realm of England.* New edn. by E. Lamond, Cambridge: Cambridge University Press; repr. 1929.

Anonymous 1605. *Risposta sopra il discorso fatto per Marcantonio De Santis intorno agli effetti, che fa il cambio in Regno.* In De Santis, 1605b; repr. in Colapietra 1973, pp. 145–9.

Anonymous 1701. *Considerations on the East India trade.* London: J. Roberts; repr. in McCulloch 1856, pp. 541–629.

Anonymous 1821a. *An inquiry into those principles respecting the nature of demand and the necessity of consumption, lately advocated by Mr. Malthus, from which it is concluded, that taxation and the maintenance of unproductive consumers can be conducive to the progress of wealth.* London; repr. in S. Bailey, *A critical dissertation on the nature, measure and causes of value*, London: Frank Cass 1967.

Anonymous 1821b. *Observations on certain verbal disputes in political economy, particularly relating to value, and to demand and supply.* London: R. Hunter; repr. in S. Bailey, *A critical dissertation on the nature, measure and causes of value*, London: Frank Cass 1967.

Aquinas, Thomas. 1265–73. *Summa theologiae.* repr. in 5 vols., Roma 1962.

Aristotle 1926. *The Nicomachean ethics*. With an English trans. by H. Rackham, London: Heinemann and New York: Putnam's Sons.

—1977. *Politics*. With an English trans. by H. Rackham, Loeb Classic Library, vol. 21, Cambridge, Mass.: Harvard University Press.

(Pseudo) Aristotle 1935. *The Oeconomica*. With an English trans. by G. C. Armstrong, London: Heinemann and Cambridge, Mass.: Harvard University Press.

Arnon, A. 1991. *Thomas Tooke, pioneer of monetary theory*. Aldershot: Edward Elgar.

Arrow, K. J. 1951. *Social choice and individual values*. New York: Wiley.

—1962. 'The economic implications of learning by doing', *Review of Economic Studies* 26: 155–73.

Arrow, K. J. and Debreu, G. 1954. 'Existence of an equilibrium for a competitive economy', *Econometrica* 22: 265–90.

Arrow, K. J. and Hahn, F. H. 1971. *General competitive analysis*. San Francisco: Holden-Day.

Arthur, B. 1994. *Increasing returns and path dependence in the economy*. Ann Arbor: University of Michigan Press.

Asimakopulos, A. 1991. *Keynes's general theory and accumulation*. Cambridge: Cambridge University Press.

Aspromourgos, T. 1999. 'An early attempt at some mathematical economics: William Petty's 1687 algebra letter, together with a previously undisclosed fragment', *Journal of the History of Economic Thought* 21: 399–411.

—2001. 'The mind of the oeconomist: an overview of the "Petty Papers" archive', *History of Economic Ideas* 9: 39–101.

Augello, M. M. 1990. *Joseph Alois Schumpeter: a reference guide*. Berlin: Springer-Verlag.

Auspitz, R. and Lieben, R. 1889. *Untersuchungen über die Theorie des Preises*. Leipzig: Dunker & Humblot.

Axelrod, R. 1984. *The evolution of cooperation*. New York: Basic Books.

Babbage, C. 1832. *On the economy of machinery and manufactures*. London: Charles Knight; 4th edn. 1835; repr. New York: M. Kelley 1963.

Backhouse, R. E. 2003. 'The stabilization of price theory, 1920–1955', in Samuels, Biddle and Davis (eds.), pp. 308–24.

Bacon, F. 1620. *Novum organum*. London: Joannem Billium; repr. in *The works of Francis Bacon*, ed. J. Spedding, R. Lesline Ellis and D. Demon Heath, vol. 4, London: Longman and Co. 1858.

—1626. *New Atlantis*. London: J. H. for W. Lee; repr. in F. Bacon, '*The advancement of learning' and 'New Atlantis'*. Ed. T. Case, Oxford: Oxford University Press, 1974.

Bagehot, W. 1873. *Lombard Street*. London: H. S. King.

Bailey, S. 1825. *A critical dissertation on the nature, measure and causes of value*. London: R. Hunter; repr. London: Frank Cass 1967.

Bain, J. S. 1956. *Barriers to new competition*. Cambridge, Mass.: Harvard University Press.

Baran, P. A. 1957. *The political economy of growth*. New York: Monthly Review Press.

Baran, P. A. and Sweezy, P. M. 1966. *Monopoly capital. An essay on the American economic and social order*. New York: Monthly Review Press.

Barber, W. J. 2003. 'American economics to 1900', in Samuels, Biddle and Davis (eds.), pp. 231–45.

Barbon, N. 1690. *A discourse of trade*. London: Tho. Milbourn; repr. Baltimore: Johns Hopkins University Reprint 1905.

Barca, F. 1994. *Imprese in cerca di padrone*. Roma-Bari: Laterza.

Barkai, H. 1967. 'The empirical assumptions of Ricardo's 93 per cent labour theory of value', *Economica* 34: 418–23.

—1970. 'The labour theory of value as an operational proposition', *Economica* 37: 187–90.

Barnett, M. 1990. 'The papers of Carl Menger in the Special Collections Department, William R. Parkins Library, Duke University', in Caldwell (ed.), pp. 15–28.

Barone, E. 1908. 'Il ministro della produzione nello stato collettivista', *Giornale degli economisti* 2: 267–93 and 391–414. (English trans., 'The ministry of production in the collectivist state', in Hayek (ed.) 1935).

Barro, R. J. 1974. 'Are government bonds net wealth?', *Journal of Political Economy* 82: 1095–117.

Barro, R. J. and Grossman, H. I. 1971. 'A general disequilibrium model of income and employment', *American Economic Review* 61: 82–93.

Barton, J. 1817. *On the conditions of the labouring classes*. London: John and Arthur Arch.

Bastiat, C. F. 1850. *Harmonies économiques*. Paris: Guillaumin. English trans., *Economic harmonies*, Princeton: Van Nostrand 1964.

Baumol, W. J. 1959. *Business behaviour, value and growth*. New York: Harcourt & Co.

—1977. 'Say's (at least) eight laws, or what Say and James Mill may really have meant', *Economica* 44: 145–62.

Baumol, W. J., Panzar, J. C. and Willig, R. D. 1982. *Contestable markets and the theory of industry structure*. San Diego, Ca.: Harcourt Brace Jovanovich.

Beaugrand, P. 1981. *Henry Thornton: un précurseur de J. M. Keynes*. Paris: Presses Universitaires de France.

Becattini, G. 1975. 'Introduzione. Invito a una rilettura di Marshall', in A. and M. P. Marshall, *Economia della produzione*, Milano: Isedi, pp. ix–cxv.

—1989. 'Riflessioni sul distretto industriale marshalliano come concetto socio-economico', *Stato e mercato*, 25: 111–28.

—(ed.) 1990. *Il pensiero economico: temi, problemi e scuole*. Torino: Utet.

—2000. 'Anomalie marshalliane', *Rivista italiana degli economisti* 5: 3–56.

Beccaria, C. 1764. *Dei delitti e delle pene*. Livorno: Coltellini; repr. in F. Venturi (ed.), *Illuministi italiani*. *Tomo* III. Riformatori lombardi piemontesi e toscani, Milano-Napoli: Ricciardi 1958, pp. 27–105.

—1804. *Elementi di economia pubblica*, in P. Custodi (ed.), *Scrittori classici italiani di economia politica*, Milano: Destefanis, vol. 18, pp. 17–356 and vol. 19, pp. 391–543.

Bedeschi, G. 1990. *Storia del pensiero liberale*. Roma-Bari: Laterza.

Bellofiore, R. 1999. 'Introduzione, Nota biografica, Nota bibliografica', in L. von Mises, *Teoria della moneta e dei mezzi di circolazione*, Napoli: Edizioni scientifiche italiane, pp. xv–cxxvi.

Benini, R. 1907. 'Sull'uso delle formule empiriche nell'economia applicata', *Giornale degli economisti*, second series, 35: 1053–63.

Bentham, J. [1776]. 'Fragment on government', in *The works of Jeremy Bentham*, 9 vols., ed. J. Bowring, Edinburgh and London: William Tait-Simpkin and Marshall & Co., 1843–59, vol. 1, pp. 221–95; repr. in *'A comment on the commentaries' and 'A fragment on government'*, ed. J. H. Burns and H. L. A. Hart, London: Athlone Press 1977.

—[1787]. *Defence of usury*. Repr. in *Jeremy Bentham's economic writings*, 3 vols., W. Stark, London: Allen & Unwin with the Royal Economic Society, 1952, vol. 1, pp. 121–207.

—[1793–5]. *Manual of political economy*. Repr. in *Jeremy Bentham's economic writings*, 3 vols., ed. W. Stark, London: Allen & Unwin with the Royal Economic Society, 1952, vol. 1, pp. 219–73.

—[1801]. *The true alarm*. Repr. in *Jeremy Bentham's economic writings*, 3 vols., ed. W. Stark, London: Allen & Unwin with the Royal Economic Society, 1952, vol. 3, pp. 61–216.

Berg, M. 1980. *The machinery question and the making of political economy 1815– 1848*. Cambridge: Cambridge University Press.

Bergson, A. 1938. 'A reformulation of certain aspects of welfare economics', *Quarterly Journal of Economics* 52: 310–34.

Berle, A. A. and Means, G. 1932. *The modern corporation and private property*. New York: Commerce Clearing House.

Bernoulli, D. 1738. 'Specimen theoriae novae de mensura sortis', *Communicatio Academiae Scientiarum Imperialis*, Petersburg, 5: 175–92. English trans., 'Exposition of a new theory on the measurement of risk', *Econometrica* 1954, 22: 23–36.

Bernstein, E. 1899. *Die Voraussetzungen des Sozialismus und die Aufgaben der Sozialdemokratie*. Stuttgart: Dietz. English trans., *Evolutionary socialism*, New York: Huebsch 1909; repr. New York: Schocken 1961.

Bharadwaj, K. 1978. *Classical political economy and rise to dominance of supply and demand theories*. Calcutta: Orient Longman.

—1983. 'On a controversy over Ricardo's theory of distribution', *Cambridge Journal of Economics* 7: 11–36.

—1989. *Themes in value and distribution*. London: Unwin & Hyman.

Bharadwaj, K. and Schefold, B. (eds.) 1990. *Essays on Piero Sraffa. Critical perspectives on the revival of classical theory*. London: Routledge; repr. 1992.

Biagini, E. 1992. *Introduzione a Beccaria*. Roma-Bari: Laterza.

Bible. *The Jerusalem Bible*. London: Darton, Longman and Todd 1966.

Black, R. D. C. 1973. 'W. S. Jevons and the foundation of modern economics', in Black, Coats and Goodwin (eds.), pp. 98–112.

Black, R. D. C., Coats, A. W. and Goodwin, C. D. W. (eds.) 1973. *The marginal revolution in economics. Interpretation and evaluation*. Durham: Duke University Press.

Blaug, M. 1962. *Economic theory in retrospect*. Chicago: Richard D. Irwin; 5th edn. Cambridge: Cambridge University Press 1996.

—1973. 'Was there a marginal revolution?', in Black, Coats and Goodwin (eds.), pp. 3–14.

—2003. 'The formalist revolution of the 1950s', in Samuels, Biddle and Davis (eds.), pp. 395–410.

Bobbio, N. 1989. *Thomas Hobbes*. Torino: Einaudi.

Boettke, P. J. and Leeson, P. T. 2003. 'The Austrian school of economics, 1950–2000', in Samuels, Biddle and Davis (eds.), pp. 445–53.

Böhm-Bawerk, E. von 1884. *Kapital und Kapitalzins. I. Geschichte und Kritik der Kapitalzins-Theorien*. Innsbruck: Verlag der Wagner'schen Universitäts-Buchhandlung. English trans., *Capital and interest. A critical history of economical theory*, London: Macmillan 1890; repr. New York: Augustus M. Kelley.

—1889. *Kapital und Kapitalzins. Zweite Abteilung: Positive Theorie des Kapitales*. Innsbruck: Verlag der Wagner'schen Universitäts-Buchhandlung. English trans., *The positive theory of capital*, London: Macmillan 1891.

—1896. 'Zum Abschluss des Marxschen Systems', in O. von Boenigk (ed.), *Staatswissenschaftliche Arbeiten. Festgaben für Karl Knies*. Berlin: Haering. English trans., *Karl Marx and the close of his system*, London: Fisher Unwin 1898.

Boisguilbert, Pierre le Pesant de 1695. *Le détail de la France*. Rouen: no publisher; repr. in INED, 1966.

Bonar, J. 1931. *Theories of population from Raleigh to Arthur Young*. London: Allen & Unwin; repr. Bristol: Thoemmes Press 1992.

Bortkiewicz, L. von 1906–7. 'Wertrechnung und Preisrechnung im Marxschen System', *Archiv für Sozialwissenschaft und Sozialpolitik* 23 (1906) no. 1 and 25 (1907) nos. 1–2. English trans., 'Value and price in the Marxian system', *International Economic Papers* 1952, 52: 5–60.

—1907. 'Zur Berichtigung der grundlegenden theoretischen Konstruktion von Marx im dritten Band des "Kapital"', *Conrads Jahrbücher für Nationalökonomie und Statistik*, series 3, 34: 319–35. English trans., 'On the correction of Marx's fundamental theoretical construction in the third volume of *Capital*', in Sweezy (ed.) 1949.

Botero, G. 1588. *Delle cause della grandezza delle città*. 3 vols., Roma: Giovanni Martinelli; repr. Bologna: A. Forni 1990.

—1589. *Della ragion di Stato libri dieci*. Venezia: I. Gioliti; repr. Bologna: A. Forni 1990.

Bowles, M. 1972. 'The precursors of Jevons – the revolution that wasn't', *Manchester School* 40: 9–29.

Bowley, M. 1937. *Nassau Senior and classical economics*. London: Allen & Unwin; repr. 1967.

Box, G. E. P. and Jenkins, J. M. 1970. *Time series analysis: forecasting and control*. San Francisco: Holden-Day.

Boyer, G. 1990. *An economic history of English poor laws, 1750–1850*. Cambridge: Cambridge University Press.

Braverman, H. 1974. *Labor and monopoly capital. The degradation of work in the twentieth century*. New York: Monthly Review Press.

Bray, J. 1839. *Labour's wrongs and labour's remedy, or the age of might and the age of right*. Leeds: D. Green; repr. New York: A. M. Kelley 1968.

Brenner, R. 1978. 'Dobb on the transition from feudalism to capitalism', *Cambridge Journal of Economics* 2: 121–40.

Breton, Y. and Lutfalla, M. (eds.) 1991. *L'économie politique en France au XIX siècle*. Paris: Economica.

Brewer, A. 1988. 'Cantillon and the land theory of value', *History of Political Economy* 20: 1–14.

—1992. *Richard Cantillon pioneer of economic theory.* London: Routledge.

Bridel, P. 1997. *Money and general equilibrium theory. From Walras to Pareto (1870–1923).* Cheltenham: Edward Elgar.

Brock, W. A. and Dechart, W. D. 1991. 'Non-linear dynamical systems: instability and chaos in economics', in W. Hildenbrand and H. Sonnenschein (eds.), *Handbook of mathematical economics*, vol. 4, Amsterdam: North-Holland, pp. 2209–35.

Bronfenbrenner, M. 1966. 'Trends, cycles, and fads in economic writing', *American Economic Review* 56: 538–52.

Brundtland, G. H. (ed.) 1987. *Our common future* (Brundtland Report, World Commission on Environment and Development). Oxford: Oxford University Press.

Brusco, S. 1989. *Piccole imprese e distretti industriali.* Torino: Rosenberg & Sellier.

Bukharin, N. 1917. English trans., *Economic theory of the leisure class.* New York: Monthly Review Press 1972.

Bukharin, N. and Preobraženskij, E. 1919. English trans., *The ABC of communism.* Harmondsworth: Penguin Books 1969.

Buonarroti, F. 1828. *La conspiration pour l'égalité.* Bruxelles: n.p.

Burmeister, E. 1977. 'On the social significance of the reswitching controversy', *Revue d'économie politique* 87: 330–50.

—1979. 'Professor Pasinetti's "unobtrusive postulate", regular economies, and the existence of a well-behaved production function', *Revue d'économie politique* 89: 644–52.

Cairnes, J. E. 1874. *Some leading principles of political economy newly expounded.* London: Macmillan.

Caldwell, B. 1982. *Beyond positivism: economic methodology in the twentieth century.* London: Allen & Unwin.

Caldwell, B. J. (ed.) 1990. *Carl Menger and his legacy in economics.* Durham: Duke University Press.

Calzoni, G. and Rossi, E. 1980. *Credito, innovazioni e ciclo economico.* Milano: Franco Angeli.

Cammarota, L. 1981. *Storia della musica.* Roma-Bari: Laterza.

Campanella, T. [1602] 1964. *La città del sole.* Milano: Rizzoli.

Canard, N.-F. 1801. *Principes d'économie politique.* Paris: F. Buisson.

Candela, G. and Palazzi, M. (eds.) 1979. *Dibattito sulla fisiocrazia.* Firenze: La Nuova Italia.

Cannan, F. 1929. *A review of economic theory.* London: P. S. King & Son; repr., London: Frank Cass 1964.

Cantillon, R. 1755. *Essai sur la nature du commerce en général.* London: Fletcher Gyles. Repr. with English trans., *Essay on the nature of trade in general*, ed. H. Higgs, London: Macmillan 1931; repr., New York: M. Kelley 1964.

Caravale, G. (ed.) 1985. *The legacy of Ricardo.* Oxford: Blackwell.

Caravale, G. and Tosato, D. 1980. *Ricardo and the theory of value, distribution and growth.* London: Routledge & Kegan Paul.

Carey, H. C. 1837–40. *Principles of political economy*. 3 vols., Philadelphia: Carey, Lea & Blanchard.

Carlyle, T. 1888–9. *Works*. 37 vols., London: Chapman and Hall.

Casarosa, C. 1974. 'La teoria ricardiana della distribuzione e dello sviluppo economico', *Rivista di politica economica* 44: 959–1015.

—1978. 'A new formulation of the Ricardian system', *Oxford Economic Papers* 30: 38–63.

Cassel, G. 1918. *Theoretische Sozialökonomie*. Leipzig: C. F. Winter. English trans., *Theory of social economy*, London: T. F. Unwin 1923.

Cerroni, U. 1967. 'Prefazione', in P.-J. Proudhon, *Che cos'è la proprietà?*, Bari: Laterza, pp. vii–xxxvi.

Cesarano, F. 1983. 'On the role of the history of economic analysis', *History of Political Economy* 15: 63–82.

Chafuen, A. A. 1986. *Christians for freedom. Late-Scholastic economics*. San Francisco: Ignatius Press.

Chamberlin, E. 1933. *The theory of monopolistic competition*. Cambridge, Mass.: Harvard University Press.

Chaunu, P. 1982. *La civilisation de l'Europe des lumières*. Paris: Flammarion.

Child, J. 1668. *Brief observations concerning trade and interest of money*. London: E. Calvert and H. Mortlock; new edn. *A discourse about trade*, London: A. Sowle, 1690; repr. in appendix to Letwin 1959.

Chilosi, A. (ed.) 1979. *Kalecki*. Bologna: il Mulino.

Chiodi, G. 1983. *La teoria monetaria di Wicksell*. Roma: Nuova Italia Scientifica.

Ciocca, P. and Rinaldi, R. 1997. 'L'inflazione in Italia, 1914–20. Considerazioni a margine della tesi di laurea di Piero Sraffa', *Rivista di storia economica* 13: 3–40.

Cipolla, C. M. 1976. *Before the industrial revolution. European society and economy, 1000–1700*. London: Methuen; 3rd edn., London: Routledge 1993.

Clapham, J. A. 1922. 'Of empty economic boxes', *Economic Journal* 32: 305–14.

Clark, J. B. 1886. *The philosophy of wealth: economic principles newly formulated*. Boston: Ginn.

—1899. *The distribution of wealth: a theory of wages, interests and profits*. New York: Macmillan.

Clark, J. B. and Clark, J. M. 1912. *The control of trusts*. New York: Macmillan.

Clark, J. M. 1923. *Studies in the economics of overhead costs*, Chicago: University of Chicago Press.

—1926. *Social control of business*. Chicago: University of Chicago Press.

—1952. 'J. B. Clark', in H. W. Spiegel (ed.), *The development of economic thought*, New York: Wiley, pp. 592–612.

Clower, R. W. 1965. 'The Keynesian counter-revolution: a theoretical appraisal', in F. H. Hahn and F. P. R. Brechling (eds.), *The theory of interest rates*, London: Macmillan, pp. 103–25.

Coase, R. H. 1937. 'The nature of the firm', *Economica* 41: 386–405; repr. in R. H. Coase, *The firm, the market and the law*, Chicago: University of Chicago Press 1988, pp. 33–55.

Coats, A. W. 1973. 'The economic and social context of the marginal revolution of the 1980's', in Black, Coats and Goodwin (eds.), pp. 37–58.

Cobb, C. W. and Douglas, P. H. 1928. 'A theory of production', *American Economic Review* 18 (Supplement): 139–65.

Colapietra, R. (ed.) 1973. *Problemi monetari negli scrittori napoletani del Seicento*. Roma: Accademia Nazionale dei Lincei.

Cole, G. D. H. 1953. *Socialist thought: the forerunners (1789–1850)*. Vol. 1, London: Macmillan.

Colletti, L. 1969a. *Il marxismo e Hegel*. Bari: Laterza; 3rd edn. 1971.

—1969b. *Ideologia e società*. Bari: Laterza; 2nd edn. 1970.

Colquhoun, P. 1814. *Treatise on the wealth, power and resources of the British Empire*. London: J. Mawman.

Comte, A. 1830–42. *Cours de philosophie positive*. 6 vols., Paris: Bachelier.

Condillac, E. B. de 1776. *Le commerce et le gouvernement considérés relativement l'un à l'autre*. Amsterdam. English trans., *Commerce and government considered in their mutual relationship*, ed. S. and W. Eltis, Cheltenham: Edward Elgar 1997.

Condorcet, M. J. A. N. (Caritat, Marquis de) 1794. *Esquisse d'un tableau historique des progrès de l'esprit humain*. Paris: Agasse. English trans., *Sketch for a historical picture of the progress of the human mind*, ed. J. Barraclough, London: Weidenfeld & Nicolson 1955.

Corry, B. A. 1959. 'Malthus and Keynes: a reconsideration', *Economic Journal* 69: 717–24.

Corsi, M. 1984. 'Il sistema di fabbrica e la divisione del lavoro: il pensiero di Charles Babbage', *Quaderni di storia dell'economia politica* 3: 111–23.

—1991. *Division of labour, technical change and economic growth*. Aldershot: Avebury.

—1995. 'L'approccio stocastico nelle teorie della distribuzione del reddito', in M. Corsi (ed.), *Le diseguaglianze economiche*, Torino: Giappichelli, pp. 1–47.

Cournot, A.-A. 1838. *Recherches sur les principes mathématiques de la théorie de la richesse*. Paris: Hachette. English trans., *Mathematical principles of the theory of wealth*, London: Macmillan 1897; repr. San Diego: James and Gordon 1995.

Coyer, G.-F. 1768. *Chinki, histoire cochinchinoise qui peut servir à d'autres pays*. London: no publisher; Italian trans., *Chinki, storia cocincinese che può servire ad altri paesi*, ed. G. Gianelli, Genova: Università degli studi di Genova, Facoltà di scienze politiche, Pubblicazioni dell'Istituto di studi economici.

Croce, B. and Einaudi, L. 1957. *Liberismo e liberalismo*. Ed. P. Solari, Milano-Napoli: Riccardo Ricciardi editore.

Cross, R. 1982. 'The Duhem–Quine thesis, Lakatos and the appraisal of theories in macroeconomics', *Economic Journal* 92: 320–40.

Custodi, P. 1803. 'Notizie degli autori contenuti nel presente volume', in *Scrittori classici italiani di economia politica*, parte antica, tomo 1, Milano: Destefanis.

Cyert, R. M. and March, J. G. 1963. *A behavioural theory of the firm*. New York: Prentice-Hall.

D'Alembert, J. 1751. 'Discours préliminaire', in J. D'Alembert and D. Diderot (eds.), *Encyclopédie, ou dictionnaire raisonné des sciences, des arts et des métiers, par une societé de gens de lettres*. Livourne: Imprimerie des éditeurs, vol. 1, pp. i–xliv; repr. Paris: Éditions Gauthier, 1965.

Dahrendorf, R. 1979. *Lebenschancen. Anläufe zur sozialen und politischen Theorie.* Frankfurt am Main: Suhrkamp Verlag. Italian trans., *La libertà che cambia*, Roma-Bari: Laterza 1994.

—1995. *Economic opportunity, civil society and political liberty.* United Nations Research Institute for Social Development, Discussion paper no. 58.

Dardi, M. 1984. *Il giovane Marshall: accumulazione e mercato.* Bologna: Il Mulino.

Darwin, C. 1859. *On the origin of species by means of natural selection.* London: Murray; 6th edn., 1872.

—1871. *The descent of man, and selection in relation to sex.* London: Murray; 2nd edn., 1874.

—1958. *The autobiography of Charles Darwin (1809–1882) with original omissions restored.* Ed. N. Barlow, London: Collins. Repr. as vol. 29 of *The Works of Charles Darwin*, London: W. Pickering, 1989.

Dasgupta, A. 1993. *A history of Indian economic thought.* London: Routledge.

Davanzati, B. 1582. *Notizia dei cambi.* Repr. in *Scrittori classici italiani di economia politica*, ed. P. Custodi, parte antica, vol. 2, Milano: Destefanis 1804, pp. 51–69.

—1588. *Lezione delle monete.* Repr. in *Scrittori classici italiani di economia politica*, ed. P. Custodi, Parte antica, vol. 2, Milano: Destefanis 1804, pp. 15–50.

David, P. 1985. 'Clio and the economics of QWERTY', *American Economic Review, Papers and Proceedings* 75: 332–7.

Davidson, P. 1972. *Money and the real world.* London: Macmillan; 2nd edn. 1978.

—1994. *Post Keynesian macroeconomic theory.* Aldershot: Edward Elgar.

Deane, P. 1989. *The state and the economic system.* Oxford: Oxford University Press.

—2001. *The life and times of J. Neville Keynes.* Cheltenham: Edward Elgar.

Debreu, G. 1959. *Theory of value. An axiomatic analysis of economic equilibrium.* Cowles Foundation Monograph, no. 17, New Haven: Yale University Press.

de Cecco, M. 1993. 'Piero Sraffa's "Monetary inflation in Italy during and after the war"': an introduction', *Cambridge Journal of Economics* 17: 1–5.

De Finetti, B. 1930. 'Fondamenti logici del ragionamento probabilistico', *Bollettino dell'Unione matematica italiana* 9: 258–61.

—1931. *Probabilismo. Saggio critico sulla teoria delle probabilità e sul valore della scienza.* Napoli: Perrella.

—1937. 'La prévision, ses lois logiques, ses sources subjectives', *Annales de l'Institut Henri Poincaré* 7: 1–68.

Defoe, D. 1719. *The life and strange surprizing adventures of Robinson Crusoe, of York, mariner.* 3 vols., London: W. Taylor.

De Marchi, N. 1973. 'Mill and Cairnes and the emergence of marginalism in England', in Black, Coats and Goodwin (eds.), pp. 78–97.

—1988. *The Popperian legacy in economics.* Cambridge: Cambridge University Press.

De Marchi, N. and Blaug, M. (eds.) 1991. *Appraising economic theories. Studies in the methodology of research programs.* Aldershot: Edward Elgar.

Denis, H. 1965. *Histoire de la pensée économique.* Paris: Presses Universitaires de France. Italian trans., *Storia del pensiero economico*, 2 vols., Milano: Mondadori 1968, 2nd edn. 1973.

Denison, E. F. 1967. *Why growth rates differ: post-war experience in nine Western countries*. Washington: Brookings Institution.

d'épinay, L. and Galiani, F. [1769–82] 1996. *Epistolario*. Ed. S. Rapisarda, Palermo: Sellerio.

De Quincey, T. 1821–2. 'Confessions of an English opium eater', *London Magazine*, Sept. 1821–Oct. 1822; repr. in volume form, 1822; 2nd edn. 1856; repr. London: Grant Richards 1902.

—1824. 'Dialogues of three templars on political economy', *London Magazine*; repr. in T. De Quincey, *Collected writings*, ed. D. Masson, Edinburgh: A. and C. Black, vol. 9, repr. as *Political economy and politics*, New York: Augustus M. Kelley 1970, pp. 37–112.

—1844. *The logic of political economy*. Edinburgh: William Blackwood and Sons; repr. in T. De Quincey, *Collected writings*, ed. D. Masson, Edinburgh: A. and C. Black, vol. 9, pp. 118–294.

De Roover, R. 1958. 'The concept of the just price: theory and economic policy', *Journal of Economic History* 18: 418–34.

—1971. *La pensée économique des scholastiques. Doctrines et méthodes*. Montréal: Institut d'études médiévales.

De Santis, M. A. 1605a. *Intorno alli effetti, che fa il cambio in Regno*. Napoli: Costantino Vitale; repr. in Colapietra 1973, pp. 111–41.

—1605b. *Secondo discorso intorno agli effetti che fa il cambio in Regno. Sopra una risposta, che è stata fatta avverso del primo*. Napoli: Felice Stigliola; repr. in Colapietra 1973, pp. 143–62.

Descartes, R. 1637. *Discours de la méthode*. Leyda: I. Maire. English trans., *Discourse on the method for conducting one's reason well and for seeking truth in the sciences*, Indianapolis: Hackett 1988.

Dewey, D. 1987. 'Clark, John Bates', in Eatwell, Milgate and Newman (eds.), vol. 1, pp. 428–31.

Diggins, J. P. 1999. *Thornstein Veblen, theorist of the leisure class*. Princeton: Princeton University Press.

Dobb, M. 1928. *Russian economic development since the revolution*. London: Routledge.

—1946. *Studies in the development of capitalism*. London: Routledge.

—1955. *On economic theories and socialism*. London: Routledge.

—1973. *Theories of value and distribution since Adam Smith*. Cambridge: Cambridge University Press.

Dobb, M., Sweezy, P., Takabashi, H., Hulton, R. and Hill, C. 1954. *The transition from feudalism to capitalism. A symposium*. New York: Monthly Review Press.

Domar, E. D. 1946. 'Capital expansion, rate of growth and employment', *Econometrica* 14: 137–47.

Donzelli, F. 1986. *Il concetto di equilibrio nella teoria economica neoclassica*. Roma: NIS.

—1988. 'Introduzione', in F. A. von Hayek, *Conoscenza, mercato, pianificazione*, Bologna: Il Mulino, pp. 7–91.

—1997. *Pareto's mechanical dream*. Working Paper no. 97/07, Università degli Studi di Milano, Dipartimento di economia politica e aziendale.

Dorfman, R., Samuelson, P. and Solow, R. 1958. *Linear programming and economic analysis*. New York: McGraw-Hill.

Dosi, G. 1988. 'Sources, procedures, and microeconomic effects of innovations', *Journal of Economic Literature* 26: 1120–71.

Dougherty, C. R. S. 1972. 'On the rate of return and the rate of profit', *Economic Journal* 82: 1324–50.

Douglas, P. H. 1934. *Theory of wages*. New York: Macmillan.

Dunlop, J. T. 1938. 'The movement of real and money wage rates', *Economic Journal* 48: 413–34.

Du Pont de Nemours, P. (ed.) 1767–8. *Physiocratie, ou Constitution naturelle du gouvernement le plus avantageux au genre humain*. 2 vols., Paris: Merlin.

—(ed.) 1809–11. *Œuvres de M. Turgot*. 9 vols., Paris: Belin.

Eatwell, J. 1975a. 'The interpretation of Ricardo's "Essay on profits" ', *Economica* 42: 182–7.

—1975b. 'Mr. Sraffa's standard commodity and the rate of exploitation', *Quarterly Journal of Economics* 89: 543–55.

Eatwell, J., Milgate, M. and Newman, P. (eds.) 1987. *The new Palgrave. A dictionary of economics*. 4 vols., London: Macmillan.

Eden, F. 1797. *The state of the poor*. 3 vols., London: B. and J. White; repr. London: Cass 1966.

Edgeworth, F. Y. 1881. *Mathematical psychics. An essay on the application of mathematics to the moral sciences*. London: C. Kegan Paul; repr. San Diego: James and Gordon 1995.

—1894a. 'The pure theory of international values', *Economic Journal* 4; repr. in Edgeworth 1925, vol. 2, pp. 3–60.

—1894b. 'De Quincey, Thomas', in R. H. I. Palgrave (ed.), *Dictionary of economics*; repr. in Eatwell, Milgate and Newman (eds.) 1987, vol. 1, pp. 812–13.

—1925. *Papers relating to political economy*. 3 vols., London: Royal Economic Society; repr., New York: Burt Franklin 1970.

Eggertsson, T. 1990. *Economic behavior and institutions*. Cambridge: Cambridge University Press.

Egidi, M. 1975. 'Stabilità ed instabilità degli schemi sraffiani', *Economia internazionale* 28: 3–41.

Eichner, A. S. 1976. *The megacorp and oligopoly*. Cambridge: Cambridge University Press.

Einaudi, L. 1931. 'Per una nuova collana di economisti', *La riforma sociale* 42: 394–99.

—1932. 'Di un quesito intorno alla nascita della scienza economica', *La riforma sociale* 43: 219–25.

—1938. 'Una disputa a torto dimenticata fra autarcisti e liberisti', *Rivista di storia economica* 3: 132–63; repr. in L. Einaudi, *Saggi bibliografici e storici intorno alle dottrine economiche*, Roma: Edizioni di storia e letteratura 1953, pp. 117–51.

Elias, N. 1939. *Über den prozess der Zivilisation*. 2 vols., Basel: Hans zum Falken. English trans., *The civilizing process*, Oxford: Basil Blackwell 1994.

Ellman, M. 1987. 'Preobrazhensky, Evgenii Alexeyeich', in Eatwell, Milgate and Newman (eds.), vol. 3, pp. 945–7.

Eltis, W. 1984. *The classical theory of economic growth*. London: Macmillan.

Eshag, E. 1964. *From Marshall to Keynes*. Oxford: Basil Blackwell.

Fanno, M. 1912. *Le banche e il mercato monetario*. Roma: Athenaeum.

Faucci, R. 1986. *Einaudi*. Torino: Utet.

—1989. *Breve storia dell'economia politica*. Torino: Giappichelli; 2nd edn. 1991.

—1995. *L'economista scomodo. Vita e opere di Francesco Ferrara*. Palermo: Sellerio.

—2000. *L'economia politica in Italia. Dal Cinquecento ai nostri giorni*. Torino: Utet.

Fawcett, H. 1863. *Manual of political economy*. Cambridge; 4th edn., London: Macmillan 1874.

Ferguson, A. 1767. *An essay on the history of civil society*. Edinburgh: A. Kinkaid & J. Bell; repr. ed. D. Forbes, Edinburgh: Edinburgh University Press 1966.

Ferrara, F. 1852. 'Prefazione', in *Trattati italiani del secolo XVIII*, *Biblioteca dell'economista*, Prima serie, vol. 3, Torino: Pomba, pp. v–lxx.

Fetter, F. W. 1953. 'The authorship of economic articles in the "Edinburgh Review", 1802–1846', *Journal of Political Economy* 61: 232–59.

—1958. 'The economic articles in the "Quarterly Review" and their authors, 1809–1852', *Journal of Political Economy* 66: 47–64 and 154–70.

—1962a. 'Economic articles in the "Westminster Review" and their authors, 1824–51', *Journal of Political Economy* 70: 570–96.

—1962b. 'Robert Torrens: colonel of Marines and political economist', *Economica* 29: 152–65.

—1965. 'Economic controversy in the British reviews, 1802–1850', *Economica* 32: 424–37.

Feyerabend, P. 1975. *Against method. Outline of an anarchist theory of knowledge*. London: New Left Books.

Finley, M. I. 1970. 'Aristotle and economic analysis', *Past and Present* 47: 5–25.

—1973. *The ancient economy*. Berkeley–Los Angeles: University of California Press; repr. of the 2nd edn., Harmondsworth: Penguin Books, 1992.

Fisher, I 1892. *Mathematical investigations in the theory of value and prices*. New Haven: Transactions of the Connecticut Academy of Arts and Sciences; repr. New York: A. M. Kelley 1965.

Fitzmaurice, E. 1895. *The life of Sir William Petty, 1623–1687*. London: John Murray.

Flux, A. W. 1894. 'Review: K. Wicksell, *Über Wert, Kapital und Rente*; P. H. Wicksteed, *An essay on the coordination of the laws of distribution*', *Economic Journal* 4: 305–13.

Foner, P. S. (ed.) 1973. *When Karl Marx died*. New York: International Publishers.

Forges Davanzati, G. 1994. 'Introduzione', in T. Mun, *Il tesoro dell'Inghilterra*, Napoli: Edizioni scientifiche italiane, pp. 13–42.

Foxwell, H. S. 1899. 'Introduction', in A. Menger, *The right to the whole produce of labour*, London: Macmillan, pp. v–cx; repr. New York: Augustus M. Kelley 1970.

Friedman, M. 1953. 'The methodology of positive economics', in *Essays in positive economics*, Chicago: University of Chicago Press; repr. 1976, pp. 3–43.

—1956. 'The quantity theory of money. A restatement', in M. Friedman (ed.), *Studies in the quantity theory of money*, Chicago: University of Chicago Press, pp. 3–21.

—1968. 'The role of monetary policy', *American Economic Review* 58: 1–17.

Frish, R. 1933. 'Editorial', *Econometrica* 1: 1–4.

Fuà, G. (ed.) 1976. *Il 'Modellaccio': modello dell'economia italiana elaborato dal gruppo di Ancona*. 4 vols., Milano: Franco Angeli.

—1993. *Crescita economica. Le insidie delle cifre*. Bologna: il Mulino.

Fudenberg, D. and Tirole, J. 1991. *Game theory*. Cambridge, Mass.: MIT Press.

Fumagalli Beonio Brocchieri, M. T. and Parodi, M. 1989. *Storia della filosofia medievale*. Roma-Bari: Laterza.

Galbraith, J. K. 1955. *The affluent society*. Boston: Houghton Mifflin.

—1967. *The new industrial state*. Boston: Houghton Mifflin.

Galiani, F. 1751. *Della moneta*. Napoli: Giuseppe Raimondi; 2nd edn. Napoli: Stamperia simoniana 1780; repr. Milano: Feltrinelli 1963 (English trans., *On money*, ed. P. R. Toscano, Ann Arbor: University Microfilm International 1977).

—1770. *Dialogues sur le commerce des bléds*. Londres: no publisher; repr. ed. F. Nicolini, Milano-Napoli: Ricciardi 1959; Italian trans., *Dialoghi sul commercio dei grani*, Roma: Editori Riuniti 1978.

Galilei, G. 1623. *Il Saggiatore*. Roma: Giacomo Mascardi e Accademia dei Lincei; repr. in *Opere*, Milano-Napoli: Ricciardi 1953, pp. 89–352.

Gallaway, L. and Shukla, V. 1974. 'The neoclassical production function', *American Economic Review* 64: 348–58.

Gårdlund, T. 1956. *Knut Wicksell, rebell l det nya riket*. Stockholm: Bonniers; English trans., *The life of Knut Wicksell*, Stockholm: Almqvist & Wiksell 1958; new edition, Cheltenham: Elgar 1996.

Garegnani, P. 1960. *Il capitale nelle teorie della distribuzione*. Milano: Giuffrè.

—1970. 'Heterogeneous capital, the production function and the theory of distribution', *Review of Economic Studies* 37: 407–36.

—1976a. 'The neoclassical production function: comment', *American Economic Review* 66: 424–27.

—1976b. 'On a change in the notion of equilibrium in recent work on value and distribution: a comment on Samuelson', in M. Brown, K. Sato and P. Zarembka (eds.), *Essays in modern capital theory*, Amsterdam: North Holland, pp. 25–45.

—1981. *Marx e gli economisti classici*. Torino: Einaudi.

—1982. 'On Hollander's interpretation of Ricardo's early theory of profits', *Cambridge Journal of Economics* 6: 65–77.

—1984. 'Value and distribution in the classical economists and Marx', *Oxford Economic Papers* 36: 291–325.

—1988. 'Actual and normal magnitudes: a comment on Asimakopulos', *Political Economy* 4: 251–8.

—1990. 'Sraffa: classical versus marginalist analysis', in Bharadwaj and Schefold (eds.), pp. 112–41.

Genovesi, A. 1765–7. *Delle lezioni di commercio o sia d'economia civile*. 2 vols., Napoli: Fratelli Simone; repr. in *Scrittori classici italiani di economia politica*, ed. P. Custodi, vols. 14–16, Milano: Destefanis, 1803.

George, H. 1879. *Progress and poverty. An inquiry into the cause of industrial depressions and of increase of want with increase of wealth. The remedy.* Middleton: J. Bagot.

Georgescu-Roegen, N. 1983. 'Introduction', in H. H. Gossen, *The laws of human relations and the rules of human action derived therefrom,* Cambridge, Mass.: MIT Press.

—1985. 'The interplay between institutional and material factors: the problem and its status', in Kregel, Matzner and Roncaglia (eds.), pp. 297–326.

Gherity, J. A. 1994. 'The evolution of Adam Smith's theory of banking', *History of Political Economy* 26: 423–41.

Giacomin, A. 1996. *Il mercato e il potere. Le teorie della domanda effettiva di Boisguilbert, Cantillon, Quesnay.* Bologna: Clueb.

Gilibert, G. 1977. *Quesnay.* Milano: Etas libri.

—1990. 'La scuola russo-tedesca di economia matematica e la dottrina del flusso circolare', in Becattini (ed.), pp. 387–403.

—1998. 'Mani visibili, invisibili e nascoste', in SISSA-Laboratorio interdisciplinare, Laboratorio dell'immaginario scientifico, *Adam Smith e dintorni,* Napoli: Cuen, pp. 137–56.

Ginzburg, A. 1976. 'Introduzione', in A. Ginzburg (ed.), *I socialisti ricardiani,* Milano: Isedi, pp. ix–lxxx.

Giuliani, A. 1997. *Giustizia ed ordine economico.* Milano: Giuffrè.

Gleick, J. 1987. *Chaos: making a new science.* New York: Viking Press.

Godwin, W. 1793. *Enquiry concerning political justice, and its influence on morals and happiness.* London: G. G. and J. Robinson; repr. ed. I. Kramnick, Harmondsworth: Penguin Books 1976.

—1820. *Of population. An enquiry concerning the power of increase in the numbers of mankind, being an answer to Mr. Malthus's essay on that subject.* London: Longman, Hurst, Rees, Orme and Brown.

Goldman, L. (ed.) 1989. *The blind Victorian. Henry Fawcett and British liberalism.* Cambridge: Cambridge University Press.

Goodwin, R. M. 1967. 'A growth cycle', in C. H. Feinstein (ed.), *Socialism, capitalism and economic growth. Essays presented to Maurice Dobb,* Cambridge: Cambridge University Press, pp. 54–8.

—1970. *Elementary economics from the higher standpoint.* Cambridge: Cambridge University Press.

—1982. *Intervista a un economista.* Ed. M. Palazzi, Bologna: Biblioteca Walter Bigiavi, Facoltà di economia e commercio.

—1990. *Chaotic economic dynamics.* Oxford: Clarendon Press.

Gordon, D. 1965. 'The role of the history of economic thought in the understanding of modern economic theory', *American Economic Review* 55: 119–27.

Gossen, H. H. 1854. *Entwickelung der Gesetze des menschlichen Verkehrs, und der daraus fliessenden Regeln für menschliches Handeln.* Brunswick: Vieweg; 2nd edn. Berlin: Prager 1889. English trans., *The laws of human relations and the rules of human action derived therefrom,* ed. N. Georgescu-Roegen, Cambridge, Mass.: MIT Press 1983.

Gramsci, A. 1975. *Quaderni del carcere.* ed. V. Gerratana, Torino: Einaudi.

Gramsci, A. and Sraffa, P. 1924. 'Problemi di oggi e di domani', *Ordine nuovo,* 1–15 Apr., 1: 4.

Graunt, J. 1662. *Natural and political observations upon the bills of mortality*. London: John Martyn, James Allestry and Thomas Dicas; 5th edn. London: John Martyn 1676; repr. in Petty 1899, pp. 314–435.

Gray, J. 1825. *A lecture on human happiness*. Philadelphia: D. & S. Neall.

Gray, J. 1984. *Hayek on liberty*. Oxford: Blackwell; repr. 1986.

Graziani, A. (ed.) 1913. *Economisti del Cinque e Seicento*. Bari: Laterza.

Groenewegen, P. 1995. *A soaring eagle: Alfred Marshall, 1842–1924*. Aldershot: Edward Elgar.

Guger, A. and Walterskirchen, E. 1988. 'Fiscal and monetary policy in the Keynes–Kalecki tradition', in Kregel, Matzner and Roncaglia (eds.), pp. 103–32.

Haavelmo, T. 1944. 'The probability approach in econometrics', *Econometrica* 12 (Supplement): 1–118.

Haberler, G. 1950. 'Joseph Alois Schumpeter, 1883–1950', *Quarterly Journal of Economics* 64: 333–72.

Hacking, I. 1990. *The taming of chance*. Cambridge: Cambridge University Press.

Hahn, F. 1982a. 'The neo-Ricardians', *Cambridge Journal of Economics* 6: 353–74.

—1982b. 'Stability', in K. Arrow and M. Intriligator (eds.), *Handbook of mathematical economics*, Amsterdam: North Holland, vol. 2, ch. 16.

Hahn, F. and Matthews, R. C. O. 1964. 'The theory of economic growth: a survey', *Economic Journal* 74: 779–902.

Halévy, E. 1900. *La formation du radicalisme philosophique. La révolution et la doctrine de l'utilité (1789–1815)*. Paris: F. Alcan. English edn., *The growth of philosophic radicalism*, London: Faber and Gwyer 1928; repr. London: Faber and Faber 1972.

Hamowy, R. 1987. *The Scottish Enlightenment and the theory of spontaneous order*. Carbondale: Southern Illinois Press.

Hands, D. W. 2001. *Reflection without rules*. Cambridge: Cambridge University Press.

Hansen, A. 1938. *Full recovery or stagnation?* New York: Norton.

Harcourt, G. C. 1969. 'Some Cambridge controversies in the theory of capital', *Journal of Economic Literature* 7: 369–405.

—1972. *Some Cambridge controversies in the theory of capital*. Cambridge: Cambridge University Press.

Harrod, R. F. 1930. 'Notes on supply', *Economic Journal* 40: 232–41.

—1939. 'An essay in dynamic theory', *Economic Journal* 49: 14–33.

—1951. *The life of John Maynard Keynes*. London: Macmillan.

—1961. 'Review of P. Sraffa, *Production of commodities by means of commodities*', *Economic Journal* 71: 783–7.

Hart, N. 1996. 'Marshall's theory of value: the role of external economies', *Cambridge Journal of Economics* 20: 353–69.

Harvey, W. 1628. *Exercitatio anatomica de motu cordis et sanguinis*. Francoforti: G. Fitzeri. English trans., *The anatomical exercises*, ed. G. Keynes, New York: Dover Publications 1995.

Hausman, D. M. and McPherson, M. S. 1996. *Economic analysis and moral philosophy*. Cambridge: Cambridge University Press.

Hawtrey, R. G. 1919. *Currency and credit*. London: Longman.

Hayek, F. von 1931. *Prices and production*. London: Routledge (Italian trans., *Prezzi e produzione*, ed. M. Colonna, Napoli: Edizioni Scientifiche Italiane 1990).

—1931–2. 'Reflections on the pure theory of money of Mr. J. M. Keynes', *Economica* 11 (1931): 270–95 and 12 (1932): 22–44; repr. in F. von Hayek, *Contra Keynes and Cambridge*, ed. B. Caldwell, *The collected works of F. A. Hayek*, vol. 9, Chicago: University of Chicago Press 1995, pp. 121–46 and 174–97.

—1932a. 'Money and capital: a reply', *Economic Journal* 42: 237–49.

—1932b. 'A note on the development of the doctrine of "forced saving"', *Quarterly Journal of Economics* 47: 123–33.

—(ed.) 1935. *Collectivist economic planning*. London: Routledge.

—1941. *The pure theory of capital*. London: Routledge & Kegan Paul.

—1944. *The road to serfdom*. Chicago: Chicago University Press; repr. (with an introduction by M. Friedman) 1994.

—1988. *Conoscenza, mercato, pianificazione*. Ed. F. Donzelli, Bologna: il Mulino.

—1991. *The trend of economic thinking. Essays on political economists and economic history*. In W. W. Bartley III and S. Kresge (eds.), *The collected works of F. A. Hayek*, vol. 3, Chicago: University of Chicago Press.

—1994. *Hayek on Hayek*. Ed. S. Kresge and L. Wenar, Chicago: University of Chicago Press.

Heckscher, E. F. 1931. *Mercantilism*. 2 vols., London: Allen & Unwin; 2nd edn. 1955.

Heertje, A. (ed.) 1981. *Schumpeter's vision. Capitalism, socialism and democracy after 40 years*. Eastburne and New York: Praeger.

Helvetius, C. A. 1758. *De l'ésprit*. Paris: Durand.

Hennings, K. H. 1997. *The Austrian theory of value and capital*. Cheltenham: Edward Elgar.

Hey, J. D. and Winch, D. (eds.) 1990. *A century of economics. 100 years of the Royal Economic Society and the Economic Journal*. Oxford: Basil Blackwell.

Hicks, J. 1932. *The theory of wages*. London: Macmillan.

—1937. 'Mr. Keynes and the classics: a suggested interpretation', *Econometrica* 5: 147–59.

—1939. *Value and capital*. Oxford: Clarendon Press; 2nd edn. 1946.

—1969. *A theory of economic history*. Oxford: Oxford University Press.

—1973. *Capital and time. A neo-Austrian theory*. Oxford: Clarendon Press.

Hicks, J. and Allen, R. D. G. 1934. 'A reconsideration of the theory of value', *Economica* 1: 52–76 and 196–219.

Hicks, J. and Hollander, S. 1977. 'Mr Ricardo and the moderns', *Quarterly Journal of Economics* 91: 351–69.

Higgs, H. 1897. *The physiocrats*. London: Macmillan; repr. Bristol: Thoemmes Press 1993.

Hilferding, R. 1910. *Das Finanzkapital*. Wien: Wiener Volksbuchhandlung Ignaz Brand. English trans., *Finance capital: a study of the latest phase of capitalist development*, London: Routledge & Kegan Paul 1981.

Hirsch, F. 1976. *Social limits to growth*. Cambridge, Mass.: Harvard University Press.

Hirschman, A. 1977. *The passions and the interests*. Princeton: Princeton University Press.

—1982. 'Rival interpretations of market society: civilizing, destructive, or feeble?', *Journal of Economic Literature* 20: 1463–84.

Hobbes, T. 1651. *Leviathan*. Andrew Crooke, London; repr. ed. C. B. Macpherson, Harmondsworth: Penguin Books 1968, repr. 1987.

Hobson, J. 1902. *Imperialism: a study*. London: Nisbet.

—1914. *Work and wealth*. London: Macmillan.

Hodgskin, T. 1820. *Letter to Francis Place of May 28*. Manuscript kept at the British Museum, London; Italian trans. in A. Ginzburg (ed.), *Socialisti ricardiani*, Milano: Isedi 1976, pp. 295–308.

—1825. *Labour defended against the claims of capital or the unproductiveness of capital proved*. London: Knight and Lacey; repr. London: Hammersmith Bookshop 1964.

—1827. *Popular political economy*. London: C. Tait.

Hodgson, G. M. 2003. 'Institutional economics', in Samuels, Biddle and Davis (eds.), pp. 462–70.

Hollander, J. 1904. 'The development of Ricardo's theory of value', *Quarterly Journal of Economics* 18: 455–91.

—1910. *David Ricardo – a centenary estimate*. Baltimore; repr. New York: McKelley 1968.

Hollander, S. 1973a. 'Ricardo's analysis of the profit rate, 1813–15', *Economica* 40: 260–82.

—1973b. *The economics of Adam Smith*. Toronto: University of Toronto Press.

—1975. 'Ricardo and the corn profit model: reply to Eatwell', *Economica* 42: 188–202.

—1979. *The economics of David Ricardo*. Toronto: University of Toronto Press.

—1985. *The economics of John Stuart Mill*. 2 vols., Toronto: University of Toronto Press.

Horwitz, S. 2003. 'The Austrian marginalists: Menger, Böhm-Bawerk, and Wieser', in Samuels, Biddle and Davis (eds.), pp. 262–77.

Hosseini, H. 1998. 'Seeking the roots of Adam Smith's division of labour in medieval Persia', *History of Political Economy* 30: 653–81.

Howey, R. S. 1960. *The rise of the marginal utility school, 1870–1889*. Lawrence: University of Kansas Press; repr. New York: Columbia University Press 1989.

Hume, D. 1739–40. *A treatise of human nature*. 3 vols., London: John Noon; repr. Oxford: Clarendon Press 1978; repr. Bristol: Thoemmes 1990.

—[1740] 1938. *An abstract of a treatise on human nature*. With an introduction and ed. J. M. Keynes and P. Sraffa, Cambridge: Cambridge University Press.

—1752. *Political discourses*. Edinburgh: A. Kincaid and A. Donaldson; repr. in *Essays: moral, political, and literary*, ed. E. F. Miller, Indianapolis: Liberty Press 1987.

—1777. *The legacy of David Hume, Esq.: written by himself*. London: William Strahan; repr. in Hume, *Essays: moral, political and literary* cit., pp. xxviii–xlix.

Huntington, S. P. 1996. *The clash of civilization and the remaking of the world order*. New York: Simon & Schuster.

Hutcheson, F. 1755. *A system of moral philosophy*. 3 vols., London: A. Millar.

Hutchison, T. W. 1953. *A review of economic doctrines*. Oxford: Oxford University Press; repr. Bristol: Thoemmes Press 1993.

—1956. 'Bentham as an economist', *Economic Journal* 66: 288–306.

—1973. 'The "marginal revolution" and the decline and fall of English classical political economy', in Black, Coats and Goodwin (eds.), pp. 176–202.

—1988. *Before Adam Smith. The emergence of political economy 1662–1776*. Oxford: Basil Blackwell.

Im Hof, U. 1993. *Das Europa der Aufklärung*. München: C. H. Beck; Italian trans., *L'Europa dell'illuminismo*, Roma-Bari: Laterza 1993.

INED (Institut national d'études demographiques) 1958. *François Quesnay et la physiocratie*. 2 vols., Paris: Presses Universitaires de France.

—1966. *Pierre de Boisguilbert or la naissance de l'économie politique*. 2 vols., Paris: Presses Universitaires de France.

Ingram, J. K. 1888. *A history of political economy*. Edinburgh: A. & C. Black.

Ingrao, B. and Israel, G. 1987. *La mano invisibile. L'equilibrio economico nella storia della scienza*. Roma-Bari: Laterza. English trans., *The invisibile hand. Economic equilibrium in the history of science*. Cambridge, Mass.: MIT Press, 1990.

Ingrao, B. and Ranchetti, F. 1996. *Il mercato nel pensiero economico*. Milano: Ulrico Hoepli.

Institute of Statistics, Oxford University. 1944. *The economics of full employment*. Oxford: Basil Blackwell.

Isnard, A. N. 1781. *Traité des richesses*. 2 vols., London and Lausanne: F. Grasset.

Jaffé, W. 1983. *Essays on Walras*. Cambridge: Cambridge University Press.

James, P. 1979. *Population Malthus: his life and times*. London: Routledge.

Jennings, R. 1855. *Natural elements of political economy*. London: Longman, Brown, Green and Longmans.

Jevons, W. S. 1865. *The coal question*. London: Macmillan; repr. New York: Augustus M. Kelley 1965.

—1871. *The theory of political economy*. London: Macmillan; 2nd edn. 1879; repr. Harmondsworth: Penguin Books 1970.

—1874. *The principles of science: a treatise on logic and scientific method*. London: Macmillan; 2nd edn. 1877.

—1881. 'Richard Cantillon and the nationality of political economy', *Contemporary Review*, January; repr. in R. Cantillon, *Essai sur la nature du commerce en général*, ed. H. Higgs, London: Macmillan 1931 (repr. New York: Kelley 1964), pp. 333–60.

—1972–81. *Papers and correspondence*. 7 vols., ed. R. D. Collison Black and R. Könekamp, London: Macmillan.

Johnson, H. G. 1962. 'Review of *Production of commodities by means of commodities*', *Canadian Journal of Economics and Political Science* 28: 464–5.

Judges, A. V. 1939. 'The idea of a mercantile state', *Transactions of the Royal Historical Society*, 4th series 21: 41–69.

Kadish, A. and Freeman, R. D. 1990. 'Foundation and early years', in Hey and Winch (eds.), pp. 22–48.

Kahn, R. F. 1931. 'The relation of home investment to unemployment', *Economic Journal* 41: 173–98; repr. in Kahn, 1972, pp. 1–27.

—1954. 'Some notes on liquidity preference', *Manchester School* 22: 229–57; repr. in Kahn 1972, pp. 72–96.

—1972. *Selected essays on employment and growth*. Cambridge: Cambridge University Press.

—1973. 'SDR and aid', *Lloyd Bank Review*, October, 1–18.

—1974. *On re-reading Keynes*. Proceedings of the British Academy, vol. 60, pp. 361–92; repr. Oxford: Oxford University Press 1975.

—[1929] 1983. *L'economia del breve periodo*. Ed. M. Dardi, Torino: Boringhieri; English edn., *The economics of the short period*, New York: St. Martin's Press 1989.

—1984. *The making of Keynes's general theory*. Cambridge: Cambridge University Press.

Kaldor, N. 1942. 'Professor Hayek and the concertina effect', *Economica* 9: 359–82.

—1956. 'Alternative theories of distribution', *Review of Economic Studies* 23: 94–100.

—1957. 'A model of economic growth', *Economic Journal* 67: 591–624.

—1961. 'Capital accumulation and economic growth', in F. A. Lutz (ed.), *The theory of capital*, London: Macmillan, pp. 177–220.

—1966. 'Marginal productivity and the macro-economic theories of distribution', *Review of Economic Studies* 33: 309–19.

—1972. 'The irrelevance of equilibrium economics', *Economic Journal* 82: 1237–55.

Kaldor, N. and Mirrlees, J. 1962. 'A new model of economic growth', *Review of Economic Studies* 29: 174–92.

Kalecki, M. 1943. *Studies in economic dynamics*. London: Allen & Unwin.

—1954. *Theory of economic dynamics: an essay on cyclical and long-run changes in capitalist economy*. London: Allen & Unwin.

—1967. 'Zagadnienie realizacji u Tugana-Baranowskiego i Rózy Luksemburg', *Ekonomista* 2: 241–9. English trans., 'The problem of effective demand with Tugan-Baranowski and Rosa Luxemburg', in Kalecki 1971, pp. 146–55.

—1971. *Selected essays on the dynamics of the capitalist economy*. Cambridge: Cambridge University Press.

—1972, *Selected essays on the economic growth of the socialist and the mixed economy*. Cambridge: Cambridge University Press.

Kant, I. 1784. 'Idee zu einer allgemeinen Geschichte in Weltbürgerlicher Absicht', *Berlinische Monatsschrift* 4: 385–411. Italian trans., *Idea di una storia universale dal punto di vista cosmopolitico*, in I. Kant, *Scritti politici*, Torino: Utet 1956, 3rd edn. 1995, pp. 123–39 (English trans., *Perpetual peace*, ed. by M. Campbell Smith, New York: Garland 1972).

Kauder, E. 1965. *A history of marginal utility theory*. Princeton: Princeton University Press.

—1970. 'Austro-Marxism vs. Austro-Marginalism', *History of Political Economy* 2: 398–418.

Kautilya [fourth century BC] 1967. *Arthasastra*. Ed. R. Shamasastri, Mysore: Mysore Printing and Publishing House.

Kaye, F. B. 1924. 'Introduction', in B. Mandeville, *The fable of the bees*, ed. F. B. Kaye, Oxford: Clarendon Press, pp. xvii–cxlvi; repr. Indianapolis: Liberty Press 1988.

Keynes, J. M. 1913. *Indian currency and finance*. London: Macmillan; repr. in J. M. Keynes, *Collected writings*, vol. 1, London: Macmillan 1971.

—1919. *The economic consequences of the peace*. London: Macmillan; repr. in J. M. Keynes, *Collected writings*, vol. 2, London: Macmillan 1971.

—1921. *A treatise on probability*. London: Macmillan; repr. in J. M. Keynes, *Collected writings*, vol. 8, London: Macmillan 1973.

—1923. *A tract on monetary reform*. London: Macmillan; repr. in J. M. Keynes, *Collected writings*, vol. 4, London: Macmillan 1971 (Italian trans., ed. P. Sraffa, *La riforma monetaria*, Milano: Fratelli Treves 1925).

—1924. 'Alfred Marshall, 1842–1924', *Economic Journal* 34: 311–72 and 627–37. Repr. (first part only) in Keynes 1933, pp. 150–266 (pp. 161–231 of the 1972 edn.).

—1925. *The economic consequences of Mr. Churchill*. London: Hogarth Press; repr. in Keynes 1931, pp. 207–30 and in J. M. Keynes, *Collected writings*, vol. 9, pp. 272–94.

—1926. *The end of laissez-faire*. London: Hogarth Press; partly repr. in Keynes 1931.

—1930. *A treatise on money*. 2 vols., London: Macmillan; repr. in J. M. Keynes, *Collected writings*, vols. 5 and 6, London: Macmillan 1971.

—1931. *Essays in persuasion*. London: Macmillan; repr. in J. M. Keynes, *Collected writings*, vol. 9, London: Macmillan 1972.

—1933. *Essays in biography*. London: Macmillan; repr. in J. M. Keynes, *Collected writings*, vol. 10, London: Macmillan 1972.

—1936. *The general theory of employment, interest and money*. London: Macmillan; repr. in J. M. Keynes, *Collected writings*, vol. 7, London: Macmillan 1973.

—1937. 'The general theory of employment', *Quarterly Journal of Economics* 51: 200–23, repr. in Keynes 1973, vol. 14, pp. 109–23.

—1940. *How to pay for the war*. London: Macmillan; repr. in J. M. Keynes, *Collected writings*, vol. 9, London: Macmillan 1972, pp. 367–439.

—1973. *The general theory and after*. In *Collected writings*, vols. 13 (*Part I: preparation*) and 14 (*Part II: defense and development*), ed. D. Moggridge, London: Macmillan.

Keynes, J. N. 1891. *The scope and method of political economy*. London: Macmillan.

Kindleberger, C. P. 1978. *Manias, panics and crashes. A history of financial crisis*. New York: Basic Books.

—1989. *Economic laws and economic history*. Cambridge: Cambridge University Press.

—1996. *World economic primacy: 1500 to 1990*. Oxford: Oxford University Press.

Klein, L. R. 1991. 'Econometric contributions of the Cowles Commission, 1944–47. A retrospective view', *Banca Nazionale del Lavoro Quarterly Review* 44: 107–17.

Knight, F. H. 1921. *Risk, uncertainty and profit.* Boston: Houghton Mifflin.

Konus, A. A. 1970. 'The empirical assumptions of Ricardo's 93% labor theory of value', *Economica* 37: 185–6.

Kregel, J. A. 1976. 'Economic methodology in the face of uncertainty. The modelling methods of Keynes and the post-Keynesians', *Economic Journal* 86: 209–25.

—1983. 'Effective demand: origins and development of the notion', in J. A. Kregel (ed.), *Distribution, effective demand and international economic relations,* London: Macmillan, pp. 50–68.

—1992. 'Walras' auctionneer and Marshall's well informed dealers: time, market prices and normal supply prices', *Quaderni di storia dell'economia politica* 10: 531–51.

—1996. *Origini e sviluppo dei mercati finanziari.* Arezzo: Banca Popolare dell'Etruria e del Lazio.

Kregel, J. A., Matzner, E. and Roncaglia, A. (eds.) 1988. *Barriers to full employment.* London: Macmillan.

Krugman, P. R. 1990. *Rethinking international trade.* Cambridge, Mass.: MIT Press.

Kuhn, T. S. 1962. *The structure of scientific revolutions.* Princeton: Princeton University Press; 2nd edn. 1970.

Kula, W. 1958. *Rozwazania o historii.* Warszawa: Państwowe Wydawnictwo Naukowe. Italian trans., *Riflessioni sulla storia,* Venezia: Marsilio 1990 (English trans., *The problems and methods of economic history,* Aldershot: Ashgate 2001).

—1962. *Teoria ekonomiczna ustroju feudalnego.* Warszawa: Państwowe Wydawnictwo Naukowe. English trans., *An economic theory of the feudal system,* London: New Left Books 1976.

—1970. *Miary i ludzie.* Warszawa: Państwowe Wydawnictwo Naukowe. English trans. *Measures and men,* Princeton: Princeton University Press.

Kurz, H. and Salvadori, N. 1995. *Theory of production. A long period analysis.* Cambridge: Cambridge University Press.

Kydland, F. E. and Prescott, E. C. 1982. 'Time to build and aggregate fluctuations', *Economica* 50: 1345–70.

Lafargue, P. 1880. 'Le droit à la paresse', *L'égalité*; repr. Paris: Maspero 1969. English trans., *The right to be lazy,* Chicago: C. H. Kerr 1989.

Laidler, D. 1981. 'Adam Smith as a monetary economist', *Canadian Journal of Economics* 14: 185–200.

Lakatos, I. 1970. 'Falsification and the methodology of scientific research programmes', in I. Lakatos and A. Musgrave (eds.), *Criticism and the growth of knowledge,* Cambridge: Cambridge University Press, pp. 91–196.

—1978. *The methodology of scientific research programmes. Philosophical papers.* Cambridge: Cambridge University Press.

Lancaster, K. J. 1971. *Consumer demand: a new approach.* New York: Columbia University Press.

Landes, D. S. 1986. 'What do bosses really do?', *Journal of Economic History* 46: 585–623.

Lange, O. 1936–7. 'On the economic theory of socialism', *Review of Economic Studies* 4: 53–71 and 123–42.

Langholm, O. 1987. 'Scholastic economics', in Lowry (ed.) 1987b, pp. 115–35.

—1998. *The legacy of Scholasticism in economic thought.* Cambridge: Cambridge University Press.

Lansdowne. H. 1927. 'Introduction', in W. Petty, *Papers*, 2 vols., London: Constable, pp. xiii–xli.

Latsis, S. (ed.) 1976. *Method and appraisal in economics.* Cambridge: Cambridge University Press.

Lauerdale (James Maitland, count of) 1804. *Inquiry into the nature and origins of public wealth.* 2nd edn. 1819; repr., New York: Augustus M. Kelley 1962.

Leijonhufvud, A. 1968. *On Keynesian economics and the economics of Keynes.* London: Oxford University Press.

Lenin (Vladimir Ilyich Ulianov) 1898. English trans., *The development of capitalism in Russia*, Moscow: Foreign Languages Publishing House 1956.

—1916. English trans., *Imperialism, the highest stage of capitalism*, London: Junius 1996.

Leontief, W. 1941. *The structure of the American economy, 1919–1939.* New York: Oxford University Press; 2nd edn. 1951.

Leontief, W., Carter, A. P. and Petri, P. A. 1977. *The future of the world economy. A United Nations study.* New York: Oxford University Press.

Lerner, A. and Colander, D. 1980. *MAP, a market anti-inflation plan.* New York: Harcourt, Brace and Jovanovich.

Letwin, W. 1959. *Sir Josiah Child, merchant economist.* Boston: Harvard Graduate School of Business.

Levhari, D. 1965. 'A nonsubstitution theorem and switching of techniques', *Quarterly Journal of Economics* 79: 98–105.

Levhari, D. and Samuelson, P. 1966. 'The nonswitching theorem is false', *Quarterly Journal of Economics* 80: 518–19.

Levy, D. M. 2001. *How the dismal science got its name.* Ann Arbor: University of Michigan Press.

Lippi, M. 1976. *Marx. Il valore come costo sociale reale.* Milano: Etas libri. English trans., *Value and naturalism in Marx*, London: New Left Books, 1979.

—1979. *I prezzi di produzione.* Bologna: il Mulino.

Lipsey, R. G. and Lancaster, K. 1956. 'The general theory of second best', *Review of Economic Studies* 24: 11–32.

List, F. 1841. *Das nationale System der politischen Oekonomie.* Stuttgart: J. G. Cotta. English trans., *The national system of political economy*, ed. S. S. Lloyd, London: Longmans, Greene and Co. 1909.

Lloyd, W. F. 1837. *Lectures on population, value, poor laws and rent.* London; repr. New York: A. M. Kelley 1968.

Locke, J. 1689. *An essay concerning human understanding.* London: Thomas Basset; repr. ed. P. H. Nidditch, Oxford: Clarendon Press 1975.

—1690. *Two treatises of government.* London: Awnsham and John Churchill; critical edn., ed. P. Laslett, Cambridge: Cambridge University Press 1960; edn. quoted, London: J. M. Dent (Everyman's Library) 1975.

—1692. *Some considerations on the consequences of the lowering of interest, and raising the value of money*. London: A. and J. Churchill; repr. in *Locke on money*, 2 vols., ed. P. H. Kelly, Oxford: Clarendon Press 1991.

Longfield, M. 1834. *Lectures on political economy*. Dublin: R. Milliken & Son.

—1835. *Three lectures on commerce, and one on absenteeism*. Dublin: William Curry, Junior & Co.

Lowry, S. T. 1987a. 'The Greek heritage in economic thought', in Lowry 1987b, pp. 7–30.

—(ed.) 1987b. *Pre-classical economic thought*. Boston-Dordrecht-Lancaster: Kluwer Academic Publishers; repr. 1994.

—2003. 'Ancient and medieval economics', in Samuels, Biddle and Davis (eds.), pp. 11–27.

Lucas, R. E. 1972. 'Expectations and the neutrality of money', *Journal of Economic Theory* 4: 103–24.

—1976. 'Econometric policy evaluation: a critique', in K. Brenner and A. M. Meltzer (eds.), *The Phillips curve and labor markets*, Amsterdam: North Holland, pp. 19–46.

Luxemburg, R. 1913. *Die Akkumulation des Kapitals. Ein Beitrag zur ökonomischen Erklärung des Imperialismus*. Berlin: Paul Singer. Italian trans., *L'accumulazione del capitale*, Torino: Einaudi 1960; repr. 1968. English trans., *The accumulation of capital*, London: Routledge 2003.

Macfie, A. L. 1967. *The individual in society*. London: Allen & Unwin.

Machiavelli, N. [1513] 1960. *Il principe*. Milano: Feltrinelli. English transl., *The prince*, ed. R. M. Adams, New York: Norton 1992.

Maddison, A. 1984. 'Origins and impact of the welfare state, 1883–1983', *Banca Nazionale del Lavoro Quarterly Review* 37: 55–87.

Magnusson, L. (ed.) 1993. *Mercantilist economics*. Boston-Dordrecht-Lancaster: Kluwer Academic Publishers.

—2003. 'Mercantilism', in Samuels, Biddle and Davis (eds.), pp. 46–60.

Malcom, N. 1958. *Ludwig Wittgenstein: a memoir*. Oxford: Oxford University Press.

Malinvaud, E. 1977. *The theory of unemployment reconsidered*. Oxford: Basil Blackwell.

Maloney, J. 1985. *The professionalization of economics. Alfred Marshall and the dominance of orthodoxy*. Cambridge: Cambridge University Press; 2nd edn., New Brunswick, NJ: Transaction Publishers 1991.

Malthus, T. R. 1798. *An essay on the principle of population as it affects the future improvement of society*. London: J. Johnson; 2nd edn. 1803; critical edn., ed. P. James, Cambridge: Cambridge University Press 1989.

—1800. *An investigation of the cause of the present high price of provisions*. London: J. Johnson.

—1815. *An inquiry into the nature and progress of rent and the principles by which it is regulated*. London: John Murray.

—1820. *Principles of political economy*. London: John Murray; 2nd edn., London: William Pickering 1836; repr. New York: Augustus M. Kelley 1964.

—1823. *The measure of value stated and illustrated, with an application of it to the alterations in the value of the English currency since 1970*. London: John Murray; repr. in D. Ricardo, *Notes on Malthus's 'Measure of Value'*, ed. P. Porta, Cambridge: Cambridge University Press 1992.

Mandeville, B. 1705. *The grumbling hive: or, knaves turn'd honest*. London: Ballard; repr. in Mandeville 1714, pp. 17–37 of the 1924 edn.

—1714. *The fable of the bees, or private vices, public benefits*. London: J. Roberts; critical edn., ed. F. B. Haye, Oxford: Clarendon Press 1924; repr. Indianapolis: Liberty Press 1988.

—1720. *Free thoughts on religion*. London: Roberts.

—1732. *A letter to Dion*. London: Roberts; repr., ed. J. Viner, Augustan Reprint Society no. 41, 1953.

Mangoldt, K. E. von 1863. *Grundriss der Volkswirtschaftslehre*. Stuttgart: Maier.

Mann, T. 1901. *Buddenbrooks. Verfall einer Familie*. München: Fisher.

Mantoux, E. 1946. *The Carthaginian peace, or the economic consequences of Mr. Keynes*. London: Oxford University Press.

Marcet, J. 1806. *Conversations on chemistry*. London: Longman, Hurst, Rees & Orme.

—1816. *Conversations in political economy*. London: Longman, Hurst, Rees & Orme.

Marcuse, H. 1956. *One-dimensional man*. Boston: Beacon Press.

Marcuzzo, M. C. and Rosselli, A. 1986. *La teoria del gold standard*. Bologna: il Mulino. English trans., *Ricardo and the gold standard. The foundations of international monetary order*, London: Macmillan 1991.

—,— 1994. 'Ricardo's theory of money matters', *Revue économique* 45: 1251–67.

Marglin, S. A. 1974. 'What do bosses do?', *Review of Radical Political Economy* 6: 60–112.

Marris, R. 1964. *The economic theory of 'managerial' capitalism*. London: Macmillan.

Marshall, A. 1872. 'Mr. Jevons's *Theory of political economy*', *Academy*, 1 April; repr. in Marshall 1925, pp. 93–100.

—(and Mary Paley). 1879a. *The economics of industry*. London: Macmillan; Italian trans., *Economia della produzione*, Milano: Isedi 1975.

—1879b. *The pure theory of foreign trade. The pure theory of domestic values*. Cambridge: Privately printed; repr. in Marshall 1975, vol. 2, pp. 117–236.

—1890. *Principles of economics*. London: Macmillan; 8th edn. 1920; critical edn., ed. C. W. Guillebaud, 2 vols., London: Macmillan 1961.

—1892. *Elements of the economics of industry*. London: Macmillan.

—1919. *Industry and trade*. London: Macmillan.

—1923. *Money, credit and commerce*. London: Macmillan; repr., Fairfield: Augustus M. Kelley 1991.

—1925. *Memorials of Alfred Marshall*. Ed. A. C. Pigou, London: Macmillan.

—1926. *Official papers*. Ed. J. M. Keynes, London: Macmillan.

—1975. *The early economic writings of Alfred Marshall, 1867–1890*. Ed. J. K. Whitaker, 2 vols., London: Macmillan.

—1995. *Lectures to women*. Ed. T. Raffaelli, E. Biagini and R. McWilliams Tullberg, Aldershot: Edward Elgar.

—1996a. *The correspondence of Alfred Marshall, economist*. Ed. J. K. Whitaker, 3 vols., Cambridge: Cambridge University Press.

—1996b. *Official papers of Alfred Marshall. A supplement*. Ed. P. Groenewegen, Cambridge: Cambridge University Press.

Martineau, H. 1832–4. *Illustrations of political economy.* 9 vols., London: Charles Fox.

Marx, K. [1844] 1932. *Ökonomisch-philosophische Manuskripte aus dem Jahre 1844.* In *Karl Marx – Friedrich Engels Historisc-kritische Gesamtausgabe*, ed. V. Adoratskij, Berlin: Marx-Engels Gesamtausgabe (MEGA). English trans., 'Economic and philosophical manuscripts', in K. Marx, *Early writings*, ed. T. B. Bottomore, London: C. A. Watts & Co. 1963, pp. 61–219.

—[1845] 1888. 'Feuerbach', appendix to F. Engels, *Ludwig Feuerbach*, Stuttgart: Dietz. English trans., 'Theses on Feuerbach', in Marx and Engels 1959, pp. 283–6.

—1847. *Misère de la philosophie. Réponse à la philosophie de la misère de M. Proudhon.* Paris: A. Frank, and Bruxelles: C. G. Vogler. English trans., *The poverty of philosophy*, Moscow: Foreign Languages Publishing House 1962.

—1852. *Der achtzelinte Brumaire von Louis Bonaparte.* Die Revolution, no. 1. English trans., excerpts, 'The eighteenth brumaire of Louis Bonaparte', in Marx and Engels 1959, pp. 358–88.

—1857. *Zur Kritik der Politischen Ökonomie.* Berlin: Dietz. English trans., *Contributions to the critique of political economy*, London: Lawrence & Wishart 1970; passages quoted from Marx and Engels 1959, pp. 83–7.

—[1857–8] 1939–41. *Grundrisse der Kritik der politischen Ökonomie.* 2 vols., Moscow: Marx-Engels-Lenin Institute; repr. Berlin: Dietz Verlag 1953. English trans., *Foundations of a critique of political economy*, Harmondsworth: Penguin Books 1972.

—1867–94. *Das Kapital.* 3 vols., Hamburg: O. Meissner. English trans., *Capital*, London: Dent 1946 (for vols. 1 and 2) and Harmondsworth: Penguin Books 1976, repr. 1986 (for vol. 3).

—1905–10. *Theorien über den Mehrwert.* Ed. K. Kautsky, Stuttgart: Dietz. English trans., *Theories of surplus-value.* Moscow: Foreign Languages Publishing House and London: Lawrence and Wishart, Part 1, 1963; Part 2, 1969; Part 3, 1972.

Marx, K. and Engels, F. [1845–6] 1932. *Die Deutsche Ideologie.* Berlin: Marx-Engels Gesamtausgabe (MEGA). English trans., *The German ideology*, London: Lawrence and Wishart 1939; passages quoted from Marx and Engels 1959, pp. 287–302.

—,— 1848. *Manifest der Kommunistischen Partei.* London.: J. E. Burghard, Bildungs-Gesellschaft für Arbeiter; Italian trans., *Manifesto del partito comunista*, Torino: Einaudi, 4th edn. 1966. English trans., 'Manifesto of the Communist Party', in Marx and Engels 1959, pp. 43–82.

—,— 1878. 'Kritik des Gothaer Programms', Die Neue Zeit, no. 18. English trans., 'Critique of the Gotha programme', in Marx and Engels 1959, pp. 153–73.

—,— 1959. *Basic writings on politics and philosophy.* Ed. L. S. Feuer, New York: Anchor Books; new edn., London and New York: Fontana-Collins, 1969.

Mas-Colell, A., Whinston, M. D. and Green, J. R. 1995. *Microeconomic theory.* New York: Oxford University Press.

Massie, J. 1750. *An essay on the governing causes of the rate of interest.* London: T. Payne; repr. Baltimore: Johns Hopkins University Press 1912.

Mays, W. 1962. 'Jevons's conception of scientific method', *Manchester School* 30: 223–49.

McCloskey, D. 1985. *The rhetoric of economics.* Madison: University of Wisconsin Press.

—1994. *Knowledge and persuasion in economics.* Cambridge: Cambridge University Press.

McCord Wright, D. 1950. 'Schumpeter and Keynes', *Weltwirtschaftliches Archiv* 65: 185–96.

McCulloch, J. R. 1825. *The principles of political economy.* Edinburgh: William and Charles Tait, and London: Longmans and Co.

—1845. *The literature of political economy.* London: Longman, Brown, Green and Longmans; repr., Fairfield: Augustus M. Kelley 1991.

—(ed.) 1856. *A select collection of early English tracts on commerce.* London: Political Economy Club; repr. Cambridge: Economic History Society 1952; repr. McCulloch 1995, vol. 1.

—(ed.) 1995. *Classical writings in economics.* 6 vols., London: Pickering & Chatto.

McKenzie, L. W. 1954. 'On equilibrium in Graham's model of world trade and other competitive systems', *Econometrica* 2: 147–61.

McLean, I. and Hewitt, F. 1994. 'Introduction', in Condorcet, *Foundations of social choice and political theory*, Aldershot: Edward Elgar, pp. 1–90.

Meade, J. E. 1972. 'The theory of labour-managed firms and of profit sharing', *Economic Journal* 82: 402–28.

Meadows, D. H., Meadows D. L., Randers D. L. and Beherens W. W. III 1972. *The limits to growth.* New York: New American Library.

Medio, A. 1972. 'Profits and surplus value: appearance and reality in capitalist production', in E. K. Hunt and J. G. Schwartz (eds.), *A critique of economic theory*, Harmondsworth: Penguin, pp. 312–46.

Meek, R. L. 1950–1. 'Thomas Joplin and the theory of interest', *Review of Economic Studies* 18: 154–63.

—(ed.) 1953. *Marx and Engels on Malthus.* London: Lawrence and Wishart; repr. *Marx and Engels on the population bomb*, Berkeley: Ramparts Press Inc. 1971.

—1956. *Studies in the labour theory of value.* London: Lawrence and Wishart; 2nd edn. 1973.

—1961. 'Mr. Sraffa's rehabilitation of classical economics', *Scottish Journal of Political Economy* 8: 119–36; repr. in Meek 1967.

—1962. *The economics of physiocracy. Essays and translations.* London: Allen & Unwin.

—1967. *Economics and ideology and other essays.* London: Chapman and Hall.

—1976. *Social science and the ignoble savage.* Cambridge: Cambridge University Press.

—1977. *Smith, Marx and after.* London: Chapman and Hall.

Meenai, S. A. 1956. 'Robert Torrens – 1780–1864', *Economica* 22: 49–61.

Meikle, S. 1995. *Aristotle's economics.* Oxford: Oxford University Press.

Meldolesi, L. 1971. 'Il contributo di Bortkiewicz alla teoria del valore, della distribuzione e dell'origine del profitto', in L. von Bortkiewicz, *La teoria economica di Marx e altri saggi*, Torino: Einaudi, pp. ix–lxxxiii.

Menger, A. 1886. *Das Recht auf den vollen Arbeitsertrag.* Stuttgart: J. C. Cotta; 2nd edn. 1891. English trans., *The right to the whole produce of labour,* London: Macmillan 1899; repr. New York: Augustus M. Kelley 1970.

—1871. *Grundsätze der Volkswirtschaftslehre.* Wien: Braumuller; 2nd edn., ed. K. Menger, 1923. English trans., *Principles of economics,* New York: New York University Press 1981.

—1883. *Untersuchungen über die Methode der Sozialwissenschaften und der politischen Oekonomie insbesondere.* Berlin: Dunker & Humblot. English trans., *Problems of economics and sociology,* Urbana: University of Illinois Press 1963; repr. as *Investigations into the method of the social sciences with special reference to economics,* New York: New York University Press 1985.

—1884. *Die Irrthümer des Historismus in den deutschen Nationalökonomie.* Wien: Hölder; Italian trans., *Gli errori dello storicismo,* Milano: Rusconi 1991.

Mercier de la Rivière, P.-P. 1767. *L'ordre naturel et essentiel des sociétés politiques.* 2 vols., Londres: Jean Nourse.

Milgate, M. 1979. 'On the origin of the notion of intertemporal equilibrium', *Economica* 44: 1–10.

—1987. 'Carlyle, Thomas', in Eatwell, Milgate and Newman (eds.), vol. 1, p. 371.

Mill, J. 1807. *Commerce defended,* London: C. and R. Baldwin; repr. in J. Mill, *Selected economic writings,* ed. D. Winch, Edinburgh and London: Oliver & Boyd 1966, pp. 85–159.

—1818. 'Colonies', in *Supplement to the Encyclopaedia Britannica* (4th, 5th and 6th edns.), vol. 3, pp. 257–73.

—1821. *Elements of political economy.* London: Baldwin, Cradock and Joy; repr. in J. Mill, *Selected economic writings,* ed. D. Winch, Edinburgh and London: Oliver & Boyd 1966, pp. 203–366.

Mill, J. S. 1838. 'Bentham', *London and Westminster Review,* no. 29: 467–506; repr. in J. S. Mill and J. Bentham, *Utilitarianism and other essays,* ed. A. Ryan, London: Penguin Books 1987, pp. 132–75.

—1840. 'Coleridge', *London and Westminster Review,* no. 33: 257–302; repr. in J. S. Mill and J. Bentham, *Utilitarianism and other essays,* ed. A. Ryan, London: Penguin Books 1987, pp. 177–226.

—1843. *A system of logic.* 2 vols., London: John W. Parker.

—1844. *Essays on some unsettled questions of political economy.* London: John W. Parker; 2nd edn. 1874; repr. Clifton: Augustus M. Kelley, 1974; Italian trans., *Alcuni problemi insoluti dell'economia politica,* Milano: Isedi 1976.

—1848. *Principles of political economy.* London: John W. Parker.

—1859. *On liberty.* London: J. W. Parker. Repr. Northbrook, Ill.: AHM Publishing Co. 1947.

—1861. 'Utilitarianism', *Fraser's Magazine* 64: 383–4; repr. in J. S. Mill and J. Bentham, *Utilitarianism and other essays,* ed. A. Ryan, London: Penguin Books 1987, pp. 272–338.

—1869. 'Thornton on labour and its claims', *Fortnightly Review,* May–June, pp. 505–18 and 680–700.

—1873. *Autobiography.* London: Longmans, Green, Read and Dyer; repr., London: Oxford University Press 1971.

Minsky, H. P. 1975. *John Maynard Keynes.* New York: Columbia University Press.

—1982. *Can 'it' happen again? Essays on instability and finance.* Armonk, NY: M. E. Sharpe.

Mirabeau (Victor Riquetti, Marquis de) 1756. *L'ami des hommes.* Avignon: no publisher.

Mirowski, P. 1989. *More heat than light. Economics as social physics, physics as nature's economics.* Cambridge: Cambridge University Press.

—2002. *Machine dreams. Economics becomes a cyborg science.* Cambridge: Cambridge University Press.

Mises, L. von 1912. *Theorie des Geldes und der Umlaufsmittel.* Munich and Leipzig: Dunker & Humblot; 2nd edn. 1924; Italian trans., *Teoria della moneta e dei mezzi di circolazione.* Napoli: Edizioni scientifiche italiane, 1999.

—1920. 'Die Wirtschaftsrechnung im Sozialistischen Gemeinwesen', *Arkiv für Sozialwissenschaft und Sozialpolitik* 47: 86–121; English transl. in Hayek (ed.) 1935.

Mishan, E. J. 1967. *The costs of economic growth.* London: Staples Press.

Modigliani, F. 1944. 'Liquidity preference and the theory of interest and money', *Econometrica* 12: 45–88.

—1958. 'New developments on the oligopoly front', *Journal of Political Economy* 66: 215–32.

—1963. 'The monetary mechanism and its interaction with real phenomena', *Review of Economics and Statistics* 45 (Supplement): 79–107.

Modigliani, F. and Miller, M. 1958. 'The cost of capital, corporation finance and the theory of investment', *American Economic Review* 48: 161–97.

Moggridge, D. E. 1976. *Keynes.* Glasgow: Collins; 2nd edn. London: Macmillan 1980.

—1992. *Maynard Keynes. An economist's biography.* London: Routledge.

Montchrétien, A. de 1615. *Traicté de l'oeconomie politique.* Paris; critical edn., ed. F. Billacois, Genève: Droz 1999.

Montesquieu, C.-L. de Secondat de 1748. *De l'esprit des lois.* 2 vols., Genève: Barillot et Fils. English trans., *The spirit of the laws*, ed. A. M. Cohler, B. C. Miller and H. S. Stone, Cambridge: Cambridge University Press 1989.

More, T. 1516. *Utopia.* Louvain: T. Martens. English trans., *Utopia*, in *The complete works of St Thomas More*, vol. 4, ed. E. Surtz and J. H. Hexter, New Haven: Yale University Press 1965; repr. 1979.

Morelly, 1775. *Code de la nature.* Paris: Chez le vrai sage.

Morishima, M. 1973. *Marx's economics. A dual theory of value and growth.* Cambridge: Cambridge University Press.

—1977. *Walras' economics.* Cambridge: Cambridge University Press.

Moulin, H. and Young, H. P. 1987. 'Condorcet, Marie Jean Antoine Nicolas Caritat, Marquis de', in Eatwell, Milgate and Newman (eds.), vol. 1, pp. 566–7.

Mun, T. 1621. *A discourse of trade from England unto the East-Indies.* London: John Piper; repr. in McCulloch 1856, pp. 1–47.

—[c. 1630] 1664. *England's treasure by forraign trade.* London: Thomas Clark; repr. in McCulloch 1856, pp. 115–209; Italian trans., *Il tesoro dell'Inghilterra*, Napoli: Edizioni scientifiche italiane 1994.

Murphy, A. E. 1986. *Richard Cantillon: entrepreneur and economist*. Oxford: Clarendon Press.
—1997. *John Law. Economic theorist and policy-maker*. Oxford: Clarendon Press.
Muth, J. F. 1961. 'Rational expectations and the theory of price movements', *Econometrica* 29: 315–35.
Naldi, N. 1989. 'Petty's labour theory of prices', *Quaderni di storia dell'economia politica* 7: 3–36.
—1998a. 'Some notes on Piero Sraffa's biography, 1917–27', *Review of Political Economy* 10: 493–515.
—1998b. 'Sraffa a Perugia: novembre 1923–febbraio 1926', *History of Economic Ideas* 6: 105–32.
—1998c. 'Dicembre 1922: Piero Sraffa e Benito Mussolini', *Rivista italiana degli economisti* 3: 271–99.
Napoleoni, C. 1962. 'La posizione del consumo nella teoria economica', *La rivista trimestrale*, no. 1: 3–26.
—1965. *L'equilibrio economico generale. Studio introduttivo*. Torino: Boringhieri.
—1972. *Lezioni sul Capitolo sesto inedito di Marx*. Torino: Boringhieri.
—1976. *Il valore*. Milano: Isedi.
Nash, J. F. 1950. 'Equilibrium points in N-person games', *Proceedings of the National Academy of Sciences (USA)* 36: 48–9.
Neisser, H. 1932. 'Lohnhohe und beschäftigungsgrad in Marktgleichgewicht', *Weltwirtschaftliches Archiv* 36: 415–55.
Nelson, R. and Winter, S. 1982. *An evolutionary theory of economic change*. Cambridge, Mass.: Harvard University Press.
Neumann, J. von 1937. 'Über ein ökonomisches Gleichungssystem und eine Verallgemeinerung des Brouwerschen Fixpunktsatzes', in K. Menger (ed.), *Ergebrisse eines mathematischen Kolloquiums, 1935–36*, vol. 8, pp. 73–83, Wien: Deuticke. English trans., 'A model of general economic equilibrium', *Review of Economic Studies* 13 (1945): 1–9.
Neumann, J. von and Morgenstern, O. 1944. *Theory of games and economic behaviour*. Princeton: Princeton University Press; 2nd edn. 1947; 3rd edn. 1953.
Niehans, J. 1990. *A history of economic theory. Classic contributions, 1720–1980*. Baltimore: Johns Hopkins University Press.
Nikolaevskij, B. and Maenchen-Helfen, O. 1963, *Karl Marx. Eine Biographie*. Hannover: Dietz. English trans., *Karl Marx: man and fighter*, Harmondsworth: Penguin 1976.
North, D. 1691. *Discourses upon trade*. London: Basset; repr. in McCulloch 1856, pp. 509–40.
North, D. C. 1990. *Institutions, institutional change and economic performance*. Cambridge: Cambridge University Press.
Nove, A. 1970. 'M. I. Tugan-Baranowsky (1865–1919)', *History of Political Economy* 2: 246–62.
Nuccio, O. 1984–7. *Il pensiero economico italiano. I. Le fonti (1050–1450)*. 3 vols. (1984, 1985, 1987), Sassari: Edizioni Gallizzi.
O'Brien, D. P. 1970. *J. R. McCulloch. A study in classical economics*. London: Allen & Unwin.

—1975. *The classical economists.* Oxford: Clarendon Press.

—2003. 'Classical economics', in Samuels, Biddle and Davis (eds.), pp. 112–29.

O'Donnell, R. 1990. *Adam Smith's theory of value and distribution. A reappraisal.* New York: St. Martin's Press.

Ortes, G. 1790. *Riflessioni sulla popolazione delle nazioni in rapporto all'economia nazionale.* Firenze, s.e., repr. in P. Custodi (ed.), *Scrittori classici italiani di economia politica*, Parte moderna, vol. 24, Milano: Destefanis 1804, pp. 5–111.

Overstone (S. Jones Lloyd, Lord) 1971. *The correspondence of Lord Overstone*, ed. D. P. O'Brien, 3 vols., London: Cambridge University Press.

Owen, R. 1813. *A new view of society.* London: Cadell and Davies; repr. in R. Owen, *Report to the county of Lanark. A new view of society*, Harmondsworth: Penguin Books 1970, pp. 85–198.

—1820. *Report to the county of Lanark.* Lanark, 1 May; repr. in Owen 1857–8, vol. 2, pp. 261–310; repr. in R. Owen, *Report to the county of Lanark. A new view of society*, Harmondsworth: Penguin Books 1970, pp. 199–270.

—1857–8. *The life of Robert Owen, written by himself.* 2 vols., London: Effingham Wilson; repr. Fairfield: Augustus M. Kelley 1977.

Oxley, G. 1974. *Poor relief in England and Wales, 1601–1834.* London: David and Charles.

Pack, S. J. 1991. *Capitalism as a moral system.* Aldershot: Edward Elgar.

Paine, T. 1776. *Common sense.* London: J. Almon; repr. in *Common sense, rights of man and other essential writings*, New York: Signet Classic 2003.

—1791. *Rights of man.* London: J. S. Jordan; repr. in *Common sense, rights of man and other essential writings*, New York, Signet Classic 2003.

Pantaleoni, M. 1883. 'Contributo alla teoria del riparto delle spese pubbliche', *Rassegna italiana*, 15 ottobre; repr. in M. Pantaleoni, *Scritti vari di economia*, vol. 1, Milano-Palermo-Napoli: Remo Sandron 1904, pp. 49–110.

—1889. *Principii di economia pura.* Firenze: G. Barbera; 2nd edn. 1894. English trans., *Pure economics*, London: Macmillan 1898.

—1895. 'La caduta della Società Generale di Credito Mobiliare Italiano', *Giornale degli economisti*, aprile, pp. 357–417; maggio, pp. 517–64; novembre, pp. 437–503; repr. in M. Pantaleoni, *Scritti vari di economia*, vol. 3, Roma: Castellani 1910, pp. 323–615.

—1898. 'Dei criteri che devono informare la storia delle dottrine economiche', *Giornale degli economisti*, 4 novembre, repr. in Pantaleoni 1925, pp. 211–45.

—1925. *Erotemi di economia.* 2 vols., Bari: Laterza; repr. Padova: Cedam 1963.

Pareto, V. 1896. 'La courbe de la répartition de la richesse', in *Recueil publié par la Faculté de Droit de l'Université de Lausanne à l'occasion de l'Exposition nationale de 1896*, pp. 373–87. Italian trans., *La curva di ripartizione della ricchezza*, in M. Corsi (ed.), *Le diseguaglianze economiche*, Torino: Giappichelli 1995, pp. 51–70.

—1896–7. *Cours d'économie politique.* 2 vols., Lausanne: F. Rouge.

—1901–2. *Les systèmes socialistes.* 2 vols., Paris: Giard et Brière; 2nd edn. 1926.

—1906. *Manuale di economia politica.* Milano: Società editrice libraria; repr. Roma: Bizzarri 1965.

—1916. *Trattato di sociologia generale*. 2 vols., Firenze: Barbera; repr. Roma: Bizzarri 1964.

—1960. *Lettere a Pantaleoni*. 3 vols., Roma: Banca Nazionale del Lavoro.

—1964–89. *Oeuvres complètes*. 30 vols., ed. G. Busino, Genève: Droz.

—1973. *Epistolario, 1890–1923*. 2 vols., ed. G. Busino, Roma: Accademia Nazionale dei Lincei.

Parrinello, S. 1970. 'Introduzione a una teoria neoricardiana del commercio internazionale', *Studi economici* 25: 267–321.

Pasinetti, L. 1960. 'A mathematical formulation of the Ricardian system', *Review of Economic Studies* 27: 78–98 (repr. in Pasinetti 1974).

—1962. 'Rate of profit and income distribution in relation to the rate of economic growth', *Review of Economic Studies* 29: 267–79 (repr. in Pasinetti 1974).

—1965. 'A new theoretical approach to the problems of economic growth', *Academiae Pontificiae Scientiarum Scripta Varia*, no. 28: 571–696.

—1966. 'Changes in the rate of profits and switches of techniques', *Quarterly Journal of Economics* 80: 503–17.

—1969. 'Switches of technique and the "rate of return" in capital theory', *Economic Journal* 79: 508–31.

—1970. 'Again on capital theory and Solow's "rate of return"', *Economic Journal* 80: 428–31.

—1972. 'Reply to Mr. Dougherty', *Economic Journal* 82: 1351–2.

—1973. 'The notion of vertical integration in economic analysis', *Metroeconomica* 25: 1–29.

—1974. *Growth and income distribution. Essays in economic theory*. Cambridge Cambridge University Press.

—1975. *Lezioni di teoria della produzione*. Bologna: il Mulino. English trans., *Lectures on the theory of production*, London: Macmillan 1977.

—(ed.) 1977. *Contributi alla teoria della produzione congiunta*. Bologna: il Mulino.

—1979a. 'The unpalatability of the reswitching of techniques', *Revue d'économie politique* 89: 637–42.

—1979b. 'The "unobtrusive postulate" of neoclassical economic theory', *Revue d'économie politique* 89: 654–6.

—1981. *Structural change and economic growth*. Cambridge: Cambridge University Press.

—1984. 'The difficulty, and yet the necessity, of aiming at full employment: a comment on Nina Shapiro's Note', *Journal of Post Keynesian Economics* 7: 246–8.

—2000. 'Critique of the neoclassical theory of growth and distribution', *Banca Nazionale del Lavoro Quarterly Review* 53: 383–431.

Pasquinelli, A. and Marzetti Dall'Aste Brandolini, S. 1994. 'Introduzione', in J. M. Keynes, *Trattato sulla probabilità*, Bologna: Clueb, pp. ix–xxvi.

Patinkin, D. 1956. *Money, interest and prices. An interpretation of money and value theory*. Evanston, Ill.: Peterson; 2nd edn., abridged, Cambridge, Mass.: MIT Press 1989.

—1976. *Keynes's monetary thought: a study of its development*. Durham: Duke University Press.

—1987. 'Keynes, John Maynard', in Eatwell, Milgate and Newman (eds.), vol. 3, pp. 19–41.

Peach, T. 1993. *Interpreting Ricardo*. Cambridge: Cambridge University Press.

Peart, S. J. and Levy, D. M. 2003. 'Post-Ricardian British economics, 1830–1870', in Samuels, Biddle and Davis (eds.), pp. 130–47.

Pecchio, G. 1832. *Storia dell'economia pubblica in Italia*. Lugano: Ruggia; repr. Milano: Sugarco 1992.

Perrotta, C. 1988. *Produzione e lavoro produttivo nel mercantilismo e nell'illuminismo*. Galatina: Congedo.

—1991. 'Is the mercantilist theory of the favorable balance of trade really erroneous?', *History of Political Economy* 23: 301–36.

—1993. 'Early Spanish mercantilism: the first analysis of underdevelopment', in Magnusson (ed.) 1993, pp. 17–58.

—1997. 'The preclassical theory of development: increased consumption raises productivity', *History of Political Economy* 29: 295–326.

Pesciarelli, E. 1989. 'Introduzione', in A. Smith, *Lezioni di Glasgow*, Milano: Giuffrè, pp. ix–xvii.

Petty, W. 1662. *A treatise of taxes and contributions*. London: N. Brooke; repr. in Petty 1899, pp. 1–97.

—1674. *The discourse made before the Royal Society, the 26 November 1674 concerning the use of duplicate proportion in sundry important particulars*. London: John Martyn; partially repr. in Petty 1899, pp. 622–4.

—1690. *Political arithmetick*. London: Robert Clavel and Henry Mortlock; repr. in Petty 1899, pp. 233–313.

—1691a. *The political anatomy of Ireland*. London: D. Brown and W. Rogers; repr. in Petty 1899, pp. 121–231.

—1691b. *Verbum sapienti*. In appendix to W. Petty 1691a; repr. in Petty 1899, pp. 99–120.

—1695. *Quantulumcumque concerning money*. London: A. and J. Churchill; repr. in Petty 1899, pp. 437–48.

—1899. *Economic writings*. Ed. C. Hull, 2 vols., Cambridge: Cambridge University Press; repr. New York: Augustus M. Kelley 1963.

—1927. *Papers*. 2 vols., ed. H. Lansdowne, London: Constable.

—1928. *Petty–Southwell correspondence 1676–1687*. Ed. H. Lansdowne, London: Constable.

—1977. 'A dialogue on political arithmetic', in S. Matsukawa, 'Sir William Petty: an unpublished manuscript', *Hitostubashi Journal of Economics* 17: 33–50.

Phelps, E. S. 1967. 'Phillips curves, expectations of inflation and optimal unemployment over time', *Economica* 34: 254–81.

Phillips, A. W. 1958. 'The relationship between unemployment and the rate of change of money wage rates in the United Kingdom, 1861–1957', *Economica* 25: 283–99.

Pietranera, G. 1963. *La teoria del valore e dello sviluppo capitalistico in Adamo Smith*. Milano: Feltrinelli.

Pigou, A. C. 1912. *Wealth and welfare*. London: Macmillan; new edn., *The economics of welfare*, London: Macmillan 1920.

—1922. 'Empty economic boxes: a reply', *Economic Journal* 32: 458–65.

—1927a. *Industrial fluctuations*. London: Macmillan.

—1927b. 'The laws of diminishing and increasing cost', *Economic Journal* 37: 188–97.

—1928. 'An analysis of supply', *Economic Journal* 38: 238–57.

—1933. *The theory of unemployment*. London: Macmillan.

—1950. *Keynes's General Theory: a retrospective view*. London: Macmillan.

Place, F. 1822. *Illustrations and proofs of the principle of population*. London: Longman and Co.; repr. London: Allen & Unwin 1930.

Plato 1926. *Laws*. Ed. R. G. Burey, Loeb Classic Library, London: Heinemann and Cambridge, Mass.: Harvard University Press.

—1930. *The republic*. Books 1–5 (vol. 1), with an English trans. by P. Shorey, Loeb Classic Library, London: Heinemann and Cambridge, Mass.: Harvard University Press.

Poinsot, L. 1803. *Éléments de statique*. Paris; 8th edn. Paris: Bachelier 1842.

Political Economy Club 1882. *Minutes of proceedings*. vol. 4, London: Macmillan.

—1921. *Minutes of proceedings, 1899–1920, Roll of members and questions discussed, 1821–1920, with documents bearing on the history of the Club*. London: Macmillan.

Pollard, S. 1968. *The idea of progress*. London: C. A. Watts; repr. Harmondsworth: Penguin Books 1971.

Popper, K. R. 1934. *Logik der Forschnung*. Wien: Springer. Enlarged English edn., *The logic of scientific discovery*, London: Hutchinson 1959.

—1944–5. 'The poverty of historicism', *Economica* 11: 86–103 and 119–37; 12: 69–89; repr. in volume, London: Routledge & Kegan Paul 1957; 2nd edn. 1960; repr. 1972.

—1945. *The open society and its enemies*. 2 vols., London: Routledge & Kegan Paul; 5th edn. 1966.

—1969. *Conjectures and refutations*. London: Routledge & Kegan Paul.

—1976. *Unended quest. An intellectual autobiography*. Glasgow: Fontana-Collins.

Postlethwayt, M. 1751–5. *Universal dictionary of trade and commerce*. London: W. Strahan.

Pownall, T. 1776. *A letter from Governor Pownall to Adam Smith, L.L.D. F.R.S., being an examination of several points of doctrine, laid down in his 'Inquiry in to the nature and causes of the wealth of nations'*. London; repr. New York: Augustus M. Kelley 1967; repr. in Smith 1977, pp. 337–76.

Preobrazhensky, E. A. 1922. *Ot nepa k sotzializmu*. Moscow. English trans., *The new economics*, Oxford: Clarendon Press 1965.

Pribram, K. 1983. *A history of economic reasoning*. Baltimore: Johns Hopkins University Press.

Proudhon, P.-J. 1840. *Qu'est-ce que la propriété?* Paris: Brocard. English trans., *What is property?*, Cambridge: Cambridge University Press 1994.

Pufendorf, S. 1672. *De iure naturae et gentium libri octo*. Lund: A. Junghans. English trans. by C. and W. Oldfather, *The classics of international law*, vol. 2 no. 17, Oxford: Clarendon Press 1934.

Pyle, A. (ed.) 1994. *Population. Contemporary responses to Thomas Malthus*. Bristol: Thoemmes Press.

Quesnay, F. 1756. 'Fermiers', in *Encyclopédie*, vol. 6, pp. 528–40; repr. in INED, 1958, pp. 427–58.

—1757. 'Grains', in *Encyclopédie*, vol. 7, pp. 812–31; repr. in INED, 1958, pp. 793–812.

—1758–9. *Tableau économique*. Paris (1st edn. 1758; 2nd edn. 1759; 3rd edn. 1759). Repr. with an English trans. in M. Kuczynski and R. L. Meek, *Quesnay's tableau économique*, London: Macmillan and New York: Kelley 1972.

—1765. 'Observations sur le droit naturel des hommes réunis en société', *Journal de l'agriculture, du commerce et des finances* 2 (first part): 1–35; repr. in INED 1958, pp. 729–42.

Quine, W. V. O. 1951. 'Two dogmas of empiricism', *Philosophical Review* 60: 20–43.

Quinton, A. 1968. 'The later philosophy of Wittgenstein', in G. Pitcher (ed.), *Wittgenstein. A collection of critical essays*, London: Macmillan, pp. 1–21.

Radcliffe Report 1959. Committee on the working of the monetary system, London: HMSO.

Rae, J. 1834. *Statement of some new principles on the subject of political economy*. Boston: Hilliard Gray and Co.

Ramsey, F. P. 1928. 'A mathematical theory of saving', *Economic Journal* 38: 543–9.

—1931. *The foundations of mathematics*. London: Routledge & Kegan Paul.

Raphael, D. D. and Macfie, A. L. 1976. 'Introduction' to Smith 1759, critical edn., pp. 1–52.

Rau, K. H. 1826. *Grundsätze der Volkswirtschaftslehre*. Heidelberg: C. F. Winter; 4th edn. 1841; 7th edn. 1863.

Rauner, R. M. 1961. *Samuel Bailey and the classical theory of value*. London: G. Bell and Sons.

Ravenstone, P. 1821. *A few doubts as to the correctness of some opinions generally entertained on the subject of population and political economy*. London: J. Andrews; repr. New York: A. M. Kelley 1970.

Ravix, J. and Romani, P.-M. (eds.) 1997. *Turgot. Formation et distribution des richesses*. Paris: Flammarion.

Rawls, J. 1971. *A theory of justice*. Cambridge, Mass.: Harvard University Press.

Realfonzo, R. and Graziani, A. 1992. 'La *Teoria del credito e della circolazione* di Marco Fanno', in M. Fanno, *Teoria del credito e della circolazione*, Napoli: Edizioni scientifiche italiane, pp. xi–lxxiii.

Remak, R. 1929. 'Kann die Volkswirtschaftslehre eine exakte Wissenschaft werden?', *Jahrbucher für Nationalökonomie und Statistik* 131: 703–36.

Riazanov, D. 1927. *Karl Marx and Friedrich Engels*. London: Martin Lawrence.

Ricardo, D. 1951–5. *Works and correspondence*. 10 vols., ed. P. Sraffa, Cambridge: Cambridge University Press (vol. 11, *Indexes*, 1973).

Rickett, W. A. 1985–98. *Guanzi*. 2 vols., Princeton: Princeton University Press.

Ridolfi, M. 1972. 'Aspetti del sistema teorico di Alfred Marshall: una revisione critica di interpretazioni moderne', *Annali della Facoltà di scienze politiche, Università degli studi di Perugia* 2: 119–204.

—1973. 'Introduzione', in F. Quesnay, *Il 'tableau économique' e altri scritti di economia*, Milano: Isedi, pp. ix–lxxxi.

Robbins, L. 1928. 'The representative firm', *Economic Journal* 38: 387–404.

—1932. *An essay on the nature and significance of economic science*. London: Macmillan.

—1958. *Robert Torrens and the evolution of classical economics*. London: Macmillan.

—1971. *Autobiography of an economist*. London: Macmillan.

Robertson, D. 1915. *A study of industrial fluctuations*. London: P. S. King & Son; repr., London School of Economics and Political Science 1948.

—1924. 'Those empty boxes', *Economic Journal* 34: 16–30.

—1926. *Banking policy and the price level. An essay in the theory of trade cycle*. London: King and Son.

—1930. 'The trees of the forest', *Economic Journal* 40: 80–9.

Robinson, J. 1933. *The economics of imperfect competition*. London: Macmillan; 2nd edn. 1969.

—1953. 'The production function and the theory of capital', *Review of Economic Studies* 21: 81–106.

—1956. *The accumulation of capital*. London: Macmillan; 3rd edn. 1969.

—1961. 'Prelude to a critique of economic theory', *Oxford Economic Papers* 13: 53–8.

—1977. 'Michal Kalecki on the economics of capitalism', *Oxford Bulletin of Economics and Statistics* 39: 7–17.

Roll, E. 1945. *A history of economic thought*. London: Faber and Faber.

Romer, P. 1986. 'Increasing returns and long-run growth', *Journal of Political Economy* 94: 1002–37.

Roncaglia, A. 1972. 'Introduzione', in R. Torrens, *Saggio sulla produzione della ricchezza*, Milano: Isedi, pp. ix–xxxii.

—1973. 'La riduzione di lavoro complesso a lavoro semplice', *Note economiche* 6: 97–112.

—1974. 'Labour-power, subsistence wage and the rate of wages', *Australian Economic Papers* 13: 133–43.

—1975. *Sraffa e la teoria dei prezzi*. Roma-Bari: Laterza; 2nd edn. 1981. English trans. *Sraffa and the theory of prices*, Chichester: Wiley 1977.

—1977. *Petty: la nascita dell'economia politica*. Milano: Etas Libri. English trans. *Petty. The origins of political economy*, Armonk: M. E. Sharpe 1985.

—1982. 'Hollander's Ricardo', *Journal of Post Keynesian Economics* 4: 339–59.

—1983a. *L'economia del petrolio*. Roma-Bari: Laterza 1983. English trans. *The international oil market*, London: Macmillan 1985.

—1983b. 'Piero Sraffa: una bibliografia ragionata', *Studi economici* 38: 137–66.

—1987. *Schumpeter. È possibile una teoria dello sviluppo economico?* Arezzo: Banca Popolare dell'Etruria.

—1988. 'William Petty and the conceptual framework for the analysis of economic development', in K. Arrow (ed.), *The balance between industry and agriculture in economic development*, vol. 1. *Basic issues*, London: Macmillan, pp. 157–74.

—1989. 'Italian economic growth: a Smithian view', *Quaderni di storia dell'economia politica* 7: 227–34.

—1990a. 'Le scuole sraffiane', in Becattini (ed.), pp. 233–74. English trans., 'The Sraffian schools', *Review of Political Economy* 1991, 3: 187–219.

550   References

—1990b. 'Is the notion of long-period positions compatible with classical political economy?', *Political Economy* 6: 103–11.

—1993. 'Toward a post-Sraffian theory of income distribution', *Journal of Income Distribution* 3: 3–27.

—1994. 'Antonio Serras Theorie und ihre Rezeption', in A. Heertje et al., *Antonio Serra und sein 'Breve Trattato'*, Düsseldorf: Verlag Wirtschaft un Finanzen GmbH, pp. 41–64.

—1995a. 'Introduzione', in A. Smith, *La ricchezza delle nazioni*, Roma: Newton, pp. 1–11.

—1995b. 'On the compatibility between Keynes's and Sraffa's viewpoints on output levels', in G. Harcourt, A. Roncaglia and R. Rowley (eds.), *Income and employment in theory and practice*, London: Macmillan, pp. 111–25.

—1995c. 'Comment', *History of Political Economy* 27: 189–93.

—1999. *Sraffa: la biografia, l'opera, le scuole.* Roma-Bari: Laterza. English trans., *Piero Sraffa. His life, thought and cultural heritage*, London: Routledge 2001.

Roncaglia, A. and Tonveronachi, M. 1985. 'The pre-Keynesian roots of the neoclassical synthesis', *Cahiers d'économie politique* 10: 51–65.

Rorty, R. 1984. 'The historiography of philosophy', in R. Rorty, J. B. Schnewind and Q. Skinner (eds.), *Philosophy in History*, Cambridge: Cambridge University Press, pp. 49–75.

Roscher, W. 1854. *Die Grundlagen der Nationalökonomie.* Stuttgart: Gotta'schen Buchhandlung. English trans., *Principles of political economy*, Chicago: Callaghan 1878.

Rosdolsky, R. 1955. *Zur Entstehungsgeschichte des Marxschen 'Kapital'.* Frankfurt: Europäische Verlagsanstalt. English trans., *The making of Marx's 'Capital'*, ed. P. Burgess, London: Pluto Press 1977.

Rosenberg, N. 1965. 'Adam Smith on the division of labour: two views or one?', *Economica* 32: 127–39.

Ross, I. S. 1995. *The life of Adam Smith.* Oxford: Clarendon Press.

Ross, S. 1973. 'The economic theory of agency: the principal's problem', *American Economic Review* 63: 134–9.

Rosselli, A. 1985. 'The theory of the natural wage', in Caravale (ed.), pp. 239–54.

—1995. 'Antonio Serra e la teoria dei cambi', in A. Roncaglia (ed.), *Alle origini del pensiero economico in Italia. 1. Moneta e sviluppo negli economisti napoletani dei secoli XVII–XVIII*, Bologna: il Mulino, pp. 37–58.

Rossi, E. 1946. *Abolire la miseria.* La fiaccola; repr. ed. P. Sylos Labini, Roma-Bari: Laterza 1977.

Rossi, P. 1962. *I filosofi e le macchine, 1400–1700.* Milano: Feltrinelli.

—1997. *La nascita della scienza moderna in Europa.* Roma-Bari: Laterza.

Rostow, W. W. 1960. *The stages of economic growth.* Cambridge: Cambridge University Press.

Rotelli, C. 1982. *Le origini della controversia monetaria (1797–1844).* Bologna: Il Mulino.

Rothschild, E. 1992. 'Adam Smith and conservative economics', *Economic History Review* 45: 74–96.

—1994. 'Adam Smith and the invisible hand', *American Economic Review. Papers and Proceedings* 84: 319–22.

—1995. 'Social security and laissez faire in eigtheenth-century political economy', *Population and Development Review* 21: 711–44.

—2001. *Economic sentiments. Adam Smith, Condorcet and the Enlightenment.* Cambridge, Mass.: Harvard University Press.

Rousseau, J.-J. 1762. *Du contrat social.* Amsterdam: M. Rey. English trans., *The social contract*, London: J. M. Dent & Sons 1973.

Routh, G. 1975. *The origins of economic ideas.* London: Macmillan.

Russell, B. 1945. *A history of Western philosophy.* New York: Simon and Schuster; paperback edn., tenth repr. 1964.

Russell, B. and Whitehead, A. N. 1910–13. *Principia mathematica.* 3 vols., Cambridge: Cambridge University Press.

Rutheford, M. 2003. 'American institutional economics in the interwar period', in Samuels, Biddle and Davis (eds.), pp. 360–76.

Sabbatini, R. 1989. 'Il progetto di Keynes di stabilizzazione dei prezzi delle materie prime', *Quaderni di storia dell'economia politica* 7: 55–73.

Salvadori, M. L. 1976. *Kautsky e la rivoluzione socialista, 1880–1938.* Milano: Feltrinelli.

Samuels, W. J., Biddle, J. E. and Davis, J. B. (eds.) 2003. *A companion to the history of economic thought.* Oxford: Blackwell.

Samuelson, P. A. 1938. 'A note on the pure theory of consumers' behaviour', *Economica* 5: 632–56.

—1947. *Foundations of economic analysis.* Cambridge, Mass.: Harvard University Press.

—1948a. *Economics.* New York: McGraw-Hill.

—1948b. 'International trade and the equalization of factor prices', *Economic Journal* 58: 163–84.

—1962. 'Parable and realism in capital theory: the surrogate production function', *Review of Economic Studies* 29: 193–206.

—1966. 'A summing up', *Quarterly Journal of Economics* 80: 568–83.

—1987. 'Sraffian economics', in Eatwell, Milgate and Newman (eds.), vol. 4, pp. 452–61.

Sardoni, C. 1987. *Marx and Keynes on economic recession. The theory of unemployment and effective demand.* Brighton: Wheatsheaf.

Savage, L. J. 1954. *The foundation of statistics.* New York: Wiley.

Savary, J. 1675. *Le parfait negociant.* Paris: Louis Billaine; repr., Düsseldorf: Verlag Wirtschaft und Finanzen 1993.

Say, J. B. 1803. *Traité d'économie politique.* Paris: Deterville. English trans. *A treatise on political economy*, New Brunswick and London: Transaction Publishers 2000.

Scaruffi, G. 1582. *L'Alitinolfo.* Reggio: Hercoliano Bartoli; repr. as *Discorso sopra le monete e della vera proporzione tra l'oro e l'argento*, in P. Custodi (ed.), *Scrittori classici italiani di economia politica*, Parte antica, vol. 2, Milano: Destefanis 1804, pp. 71–322.

Schabas, M. 1990. *A world ruled by number.* Princeton: Princeton University Press.

Schefold, B. 1989. *Mr Sraffa on joint production and other essays*. London: Unwin & Hyman.

Schelle, G. 1913–23. *Œuvres de Turgot et documents le concernant*. 5 vols., Paris: Alcan.

Schultz, H. 1938. *Theory and measurement of demand*. Chicago: University of Chicago Press.

Schumpeter, J. 1906. 'Über die mathematische Methode der theoretischen Ökonomie', *Zeitschrift für Volkswirtschaft, Sozialpolitik und Verwaltung* 15: 30–49.

—1908. *Das Wesen und der Hauptinhalt der theoretischen Nationalökonomie*. München-Leipzig: Duncker & Humblot. Italian trans., *L'essenza e i principi dell'economia teorica*, Roma-Bari: Laterza 1982.

—1912. *Theorie der wirtschaftlichen Entwicklung*. München-Leipzig: Duncker & Humblot; 2nd edn. 1926; 3rd edn. 1931; 4th edn. 1935. English edn. *The theory of economic development*, Cambridge, Mass.: Harvard University Press 1934; repr. New York: Oxford University Press 1961; Italian trans. of the 2nd German edn., *Teoria dello sviluppo capitalistico*. Firenze: Sansoni 1971; repr. 1977.

—1914. 'Epochen der Dogmen- und Methodengeschichte', in *Grundriss der Sozialökonomie*, Tübingen: Mohr, first part, pp. 19–124. English trans., *Economic doctrine and method: an historical sketch*, London: Allen & Unwin and New York: Oxford University Press, 1954.

—1928. 'The instability of capitalism', *Economic Journal* 38: 361–86.

—1939. *Business cycles. A theoretical, historical and statistical analysis of the capitalist process*. 2 vols., New York and London: McGraw-Hill; repr., Philadelphia: Porcupine Press 1982; partial repr. ed. R. Fels, New York and London: McGraw-Hill 1964.

—1942. *Capitalism, socialism and democracy*. New York: Harper & Bros.; 2nd edn. 1947; 3rd edn. 1950; 4th edn. 1954; 5th edn. 1976; repr. London: Routledge 1994.

—1946. 'L'avenir de l'entreprise privée devant les tendences socialistes modernes', in *Comment sauvegarder l'entreprise privée*, Editions Association Professionelle des Industriels, Canada, pp. 103–8.

—1951a. *Ten great economists: from Marx to Keynes*. New York: Oxford University Press.

—1951b. *Imperialism and social classes*. New York: Kelley.

—1954. *History of economic analysis*. Ed. E. Boody Schumpeter, New York: Oxford University Press.

—1970. *Das Wesen des Geldes*. Ed. F. K. Mann, Göttingen: Vanderlöck und Ruprecht; Italian trans., *L'essenza della moneta*, Torino: Cassa di risparmio di Torino 1990.

Schwartz, P. 1968. *The new political economy of J. S. Mill*. London: Weidenfeld and Nicolson.

Screpanti, E. and Zenezini, M. (eds.) 1978. *Accumulazione del capitale e progresso tecnico*. Milano: Feltrinelli.

Scribano, M. E. 1974. 'Introduzione', in B. Mandeville, *Ricerca sulla natura della società*, Roma-Bari: Laterza, pp. vii–xxxii.

Scrope, G. P. 1833. *Principles of political economy*. London: Longman; repr. New York: Augustus M. Kelley 1969.

Sebastiani, M. (ed.) 1989. *Kalecki's relevance today*. London: Macmillan.

—1994. *Kalecki and unemployment equilibrium*. London: Macmillan.

Seligman, E. 1903. 'On some neglected British economists', *Economic Journal* 13: 335–63, 511–35.

Sen, A. 1984. *Resources, values and development*. Oxford: Basil Blackwell; Italian trans., *Risorse, valori e sviluppo*, Torino: Bollati-Boringhieri 1992.

—1987. 'Rational behaviour', in Eatwell, Milgate and Newman (eds.), vol. 4, pp. 68–76.

—1991. *Money and value: on the ethics and economics of finance*. Roma: Edizioni dell'Elefante.

Sen, A. and Williams, B. (eds.) 1982. *Utilitarianism and beyond*. Cambridge: Cambridge University Press.

Sen, S. R. 1957. *The economics of Sir James Steuart*. London: Bell.

Senior, W. N. 1827. *An introductory lecture on political economy*. London: J. Mawman.

—1836. *An outline of the science of political economy*. London: W. Cloves and Sons.

—1837. *Letters on the Factory Act*. London: B. Fellowes.

Serra, A. 1613. *Breve trattato delle cause che possono far abbondare li regni d'oro e d'argento dove non sono miniere con applicazione al Regno di Napoli*. Napoli: L. Scorriggio; repr., Düsseldorf: Verlag Wirtschaft und Finanzen GmbH 1994.

Seton, F. 1957. 'The "transformation problem"', *Review of Economic Studies* 23: 149–60.

Shaftesbury, Anthony Ashley Cooper, count of, 1711. *Characteristics of men, manners, opinions, times*. 3 vols., s.e., London; repr. Indianapolis: Liberty Fund 2001.

Shaw, G. B. (ed.) 1889. *Fabian essays in socialism*. London: Walter Scott; repr. Gloucester, Mass.: Peter Smith 1967.

Shove, G. F. 1928. 'Varying costs and marginal net products', *Economic Journal* 38: 258–66.

—1930. 'The representative firm and increasing returns', *Economic Journal* 40: 94–116.

Simon, H. A. 1957. *Models of man*. New York: Wiley.

—1979. *Models of thought*. New Haven: Yale University Press.

Sims, C. A. 1980. 'Macroeconomics and reality', *Econometrica* 48: 1–48.

—1982. 'Policy analysis with econometric models', *Brookings Papers on Economic Activity*, no. 1: 107–64.

Sismondi, S. de 1819. *Nouveaux principes d'économie politique, ou De la richesse dans ses rapports avec la population*. Paris: Delaunay; 2nd edn., Paris: Treuttel et Würst 1827. English trans., *New principles of political economy*, New Brunswick, NJ: Transaction Publishers 1991.

Skidelsky, R. 1983. *John Maynard Keynes. Hopes betrayed. 1883–1920*. London: Macmillan.

—1992. *John Maynard Keynes. The economist as saviour, 1920–1937*. London: Macmillan.

—2000. *John Maynard Keynes. Fighting for Britain, 1937–1946*. London: Macmillan.

Skinner, A. and Jones, P. (eds.) 1992. *Adam Smith reviewed*. Edinburgh: Edinburgh University Press.

Skinner, A. and Wilson, T. (eds.) 1975. *Essays on Adam Smith*. Oxford: Oxford University Press.

Slutsky, E. 1915. 'Sulla teoria del bilancio del consumatore', *Giornale degli economisti e rivista di statistica* 51: 1–26. English trans., 'On the theory of the budget of the consumer', in K. E. Boulding and G. J. Stigler (eds.), *Readings in price theory*, London: Allen & Unwin 1953, pp. 26–56.

Smith, A. 1759. *The theory of moral sentiments*. London: A. Millar; critical edn., ed. D. D. Raphael and A. L. Macfie, Oxford: Oxford University Press 1976.

—1776. *An inquiry into the nature and causes of the wealth of nations*. London: W. Strahan and T. Cadell; critical edn., ed. R. H. Campbell and A. S. Skinner, Oxford: Oxford University Press 1976.

—1795. *Essays on philosophical subjects*. London: T. Cadell and W. Davies; critical edn., ed. W. P. D. Wightman and J. C. Bryce, Oxford: Oxford University Press 1980.

—1977. *Correspondence*. Ed. E. C. Mossner and I. S. Ross, Oxford: Oxford University Press.

—1978. *Lectures on jurisprudence*. Ed. R. L. Meek, D. D. Raphael and P. G. Stein, Oxford: Oxford University Press.

—1983. *Lectures on rhetoric and belles lettres*. Ed. J. C. Bryce, Oxford: Oxford University Press.

Solow, R. M. 1956. 'A contribution to the theory of economic growth', *Quarterly Journal of Economics* 79: 65–94.

—1957. 'Technical change and the aggregate production function', *Review of Economics and Statistics* 39: 312–20.

—1963. *Capital theory and the rate of return*. Amsterdam: North Holland.

—1967. 'The interest rate and transition between techniques', in C. H. Feinstein (ed.), *Socialism, capitalism and economic growth. Essays presented to Maurice Dobb*, Cambridge: Cambridge University Press, pp. 30–9.

—1970. 'On the rate of return: reply to Pasinetti', *Economic Journal* 80: 423–8.

—2000. 'The neoclassical theory of growth and distribution', *Banca Nazionale del Lavoro Quarterly Review* 53: 349–81.

Sowell, T. 1960. 'Marx's "increasing misery" doctrine', *American Economic Review* 50: 111–20.

—1972. *Say's law: an historical analysis*. Princeton: Princeton University Press.

Spaventa, L. 1968. 'Realism without parables in capital theory', in *Recherches récentes sur la fonction de production*, Centre d'études et de recherches universitaire de Namur, pp. 15–45.

Spence, W. 1807. *Britain independent of commerce*. London: T. Cadell and W. Davies.

Spiegel, H. W. 1971. *The growth of economic thought*. Englewood Cliffs: Prentice-Hall; 3rd edn. 1991, Durham: Duke University Press.

—1987. 'Scholastic economic thought', in Eatwell, Milgate and Newman (eds.), vol. 4, pp. 259–61.

Spini, G. 1992. *Le origini del socialismo. Da Utopia alla bandiera rossa*. Torino: Einaudi.

Sraffa, P. 1920. *L'inflazione monetaria in Italia durante e dopo la guerra*. Milano: Scuola tipografica salesiana. English trans., 'Monetary inflation in Italy during and after the war', *Cambridge Journal of Economics* 1993, 17: 7–26.

—1922a. 'The bank crisis in Italy', *Economic Journal* 32: 178–97.

—1922b. 'Italian banking today', *Manchester Guardian Commercial. The reconstruction of Europe*, 7 December, no. 11: 675–6.

—1923. 'Opinioni', *La rivoluzione liberale* 2: 128.

—1924. 'Obituary. Maffeo Pantaleoni', *Economic Journal* 34: 648–53.

—1925. 'Sulle relazioni fra costo e quantità prodotta', *Annali di economia* 2: 277–328. English trans., 'On the relations between cost and quantity produced', *Italian Economic Papers*, 1998, 3: 323–63.

—1926. 'The laws of returns under competitive conditions', *Economic Journal* 36: 535–50.

—1927. 'Due lettere a Tasca', *Stato operaio* 1: 1089–95; repr. as *Il vero significato della 'quota 90'*, in L. Villari (ed.), *Il capitalismo italiano del Novecento*, Bari: Laterza 1972, pp. 180–91.

—1930a. 'A criticism' and 'A Rejoinder', in 'Symposium on increasing returns and the representative firm', *Economic Journal* 40: 89–93.

—1930b. 'An alleged correction of Ricardo', *Quarterly Journal of Economics* 44: 539–44.

—1932. 'Dr. Hayek on money and capital' and 'A rejoinder', *Economic Journal* 42: 42–53, 249–51.

—1951. 'Introduction', in Ricardo 1951–5, vol. 1, pp. xiii–lxii.

—1960. *Production of commodities by means of commodities*. Cambridge: Cambridge University Press.

—1962. 'Production of commodities: a comment', *Economic Journal* 72: 477–9.

—1991. *Lettere a Tania per Gramsci*. Ed. V. Gerratana, Roma: Editori Riuniti.

Stackelberg, H. von 1933. 'Zwei kritische Bemerkungen zur Preistheorie Gustav Cassel', *Zeitschrift für Nationalökonomie* 4: 456–72.

Steedman, I. 1972. 'Jevons's theory of capital and interest', *Manchester School* 40: 31–52; repr. in Steedman 1989, pp. 145–67.

—1977. *Marx after Sraffa*. London: New Left Books.

—1979. *Trade amongst growing economies*. Cambridge: Cambridge University Press.

—1984. 'Natural prices, differential profit rates and the classical competitive process', *Manchester School* 52: 123–39; repr. in Steedman 1989, pp. 98–116.

—1987. 'Wicksteed, Philip Henry', in Eatwell, Milgate and Newman (eds.), vol. 4, pp. 915–19.

—1989. *From exploitation to altruism*. Cambridge: Polity Press.

—1991. 'Research programmes: a Sraffian view', in De Marchi and Blaug (eds.), pp. 435–50.

—1992. 'Introduction', in P. H. Wicksteed, *The co-ordination of the laws of distribution*, Aldershot: Edward Elgar, pp. 3–45.

—(ed.) 1995. *Socialism and marginalism in economics, 1870–1930*. London: Routledge.

Steindl, J. 1945. *Small and big business. Economic problems of the size of firms*. Oxford: Basil Blackwell; new Italian edn., *Piccola e grande impresa. Problemi economici della dimensione dell'impresa*, Milano: Franco Angeli 1991.

—1952. *Maturity and stagnation in American capitalism*. Oxford: Basil Blackwell; repr. New York: Monthly Review Press 1976.

—1965. *Random processes and the growth of firms*. London: Griffin.

—1990. *Economic papers, 1941–88*. London: Macmillan.

Steuart, J. 1767. *An inquiry into the principles of political oeconomy*. 2 vols., London: A. Millar and T. Cadell; critical edn., ed. A. S. Skinner, Edinburgh and London: Oliver and Boyd 1966.

Stewart, D. 1794. 'Account of the life and writings of Adam Smith LL. D.', *Transactions of the Royal Society of Edinburgh* 3: 55–137; repr. in Smith 1795 (1980), pp. 269–332.

Stigler, G. J. 1941. *Production and distribution theories. The formative period*. New York: Macmillan.

—1950. 'The development of utility theory', *Journal of Political Economy* 58: 307–27 and 373–96; repr. in Stigler 1965, pp. 66–155.

—1951. 'The division of labor is limited by the extent of the market', *Journal of Political Economy* 59: 185–93.

—1952. 'The Ricardian theory of value and distribution', *Journal of Political Economy* 60: 187–207; repr. in Stigler 1965, pp. 156–97.

—1958. 'Ricardo and the 93% labour theory of value', *American Economic Review* 48: 357–67; repr. in Stigler 1965, pp. 326–42.

—1965. *Essays in the history of economics*. Chicago: University of Chicago Press.

—1973. 'The adoption of the marginal utility theory', in Black, Coats and Goodwin (eds.), pp. 305–20.

Stolper, W. F. 1951. 'Reflection on Schumpeter's writings' in S. E. Harris (ed.), *Schumpeter social scientist*, Cambridge, Mass.: Harvard University Press, pp. 102–9; repr. in *Review of Economics and Statistics* 33, 1951: 170–7.

Stone, R. 1997. *Some British empiricists in the social sciences, 1650–1900*. Cambridge: Cambridge University Press.

Strachey, L. 1931. *Portraits in miniature and other essays*. London: Chatto and Windus.

Streissler, E. W. 1973. 'To what extent was the Austrian school marginalist?', in Black, Coats and Goodwin (eds.), pp. 160–75.

—1990a. 'The influence of German economics on the work of Menger and Marshall', in Caldwell (ed.), pp. 31–68.

—1990b. 'Carl Menger on economic policy: the lectures to Crown Prince Rudolf', in Caldwell (ed.), pp. 107–30.

Streissler, E. W. and Streissler, M. (eds.) 1994. *Carl Menger on economic policy: the lectures to Crown Prince Rudolf of Austria*. Aldershot: Edward Elgar.

Swan, T. W. 1956. 'Economic growth and capital accumulation', *Economic Record* 32: 334–61.

Swedberg, R. 1991. *Schumpeter. A biography*. Princeton: Princeton University Press.

Sweezy, P. 1942. *The theory of capitalist development*. New York: Monthly Review Press; repr. 1968.

—(ed.) 1949. *Karl Marx and the close of his system*. New York: Augustus M. Kelley.

—1951. 'Introduction', in Schumpeter 1951b; repr. in S. E. Harris (ed.), *Schumpeter social scientist*, Cambridge, Mass.: Harvard University Press 1951, pp. 119–24.

Sylos Labini, P. 1950. 'Le problème des cycles économiques de longue durée', *Economie Appliquée* 3 : 481–95.

—1954. 'Il problema dello sviluppo economico in Marx ed in Schumpeter', in G. U. Papi (ed.), *Teoria dello sviluppo economico*, Milano: Giuffrè. English trans., 'The problem of economic growth in Marx and Schumpeter', in Sylos Labini 1984, pp. 37–78.

—1956. *Oligopolio e progresso tecnico*. Milano: Giuffrè; 4th edn. Torino: Einaudi 1967. English trans., *Oligopoly and technical progress*, Cambridge, Mass.: Harvard University Press 1962; 2nd edn. 1969.

—1967. 'Prices, distribution and investment in Italy 1951–1966: an interpretation', *Banca Nazionale del Lavoro Quarterly Review* 20: 316–75.

—1972. *Sindacati, inflazione e produttività*. Roma-Bari: Laterza. English trans., *Trade unions, inflation and productivity*, Westmead: Saxon House 1974.

—(ed.) 1973. *Prezzi relativi e distribuzione del reddito*. Torino: Boringhieri.

—1974. *Saggio sulle classi sociali*. Roma-Bari: Laterza.

—1976. 'Competition: the product markets', in Wilson and Skinner (eds.), pp. 200–32.

—1983. *Il sottosviluppo e l'economia contemporanea*. Roma-Bari: Laterza.

—1984. *The forces of economic growth and decline*. Cambridge, Mass.: MIT Press.

—2000. *Sottosviluppo. Una strategia di riforme*. Roma-Bari: Laterza. English trans., *Underdevelopment. A strategy for reform*, Cambridge: Cambridge University Press 2001.

Tagliacozzo, G. (ed.) 1937. *Economisti napoletani dei sec. XVII e XVIII*. Bologna: Cappelli.

Tarantelli, E. 1978. *Il ruolo economico del sindacato*. Roma-Bari: Laterza.

—1986. *Economia politica del lavoro*. Torino: Utet.

Tarascio, V. 1971. 'Some recent developments in the history of economic thought in the United States', *History of Political Economy* 3: 419–31.

—1973. 'Vilfredo Pareto and marginalism', in Black, Coats and Goodwin (eds.), pp. 140–59.

Targetti, F. 1988. *Nicholas Kaldor*. Bologna: il Mulino.

Tarshis, L. 1939. 'Changes in real and money wages', *Economic Journal* 49: 150–4.

Tawney, R. H. 1926. *Religion and the rise of capitalism*. London: Murray; repr. Harmondsworth: Penguin Books 1975.

Taylor, F. W. 1947. *Scientific management*. New York: Harper & Bros.

Thompson, W. 1824. *An inquiry into the principles of the distribution of wealth most conducive to human happiness*. London: Longman, Hurst, Rees, Orme, Brown and Green-Wheatley and Adlard.

Thornton, H. 1802. *Enquiry into the nature and effects of the paper credit of Great Britain*. London: Hatchard; repr. ed. F. Hayek, London School of Economics, 1939.

Thornton, W. T. 1869. *On labour: its wrongful claims and rightful dues, its actual present and possible future*. London: Macmillan; 2nd edn. 1870.

Thünen, J. H. von 1826–50. *Der isolierte Staat in Beziehung auf Landwirtschaft und Nationalökonomie*. Part one, Hamburg: Perthes 1826; Part two, Rostock: Leopold 1850; Part three, Rostock: Leopold 1850 and 1863. English trans. of Part one, *Isolated state*, ed. P. Hall, Oxford: Pergamon Press 1966.

Thweatt, W. O. 1976. 'James Mill and the early development of comparative advantage', *History of Political Economy* 8: 207–34.

Tiberi, M. 1969. *La distribuzione del reddito nei modelli di sviluppo e di equilibrio economico generale*. Milano: Giuffrè.

Tirole, J. 1988. *The theory of industrial organization*. Cambridge, Mass.: MIT Press.

Tobin, J. 1958. 'Liquidity preference as behavior towards risk', *Review of Economic Studies* 25: 65–86.

Togliatti, P. (ed.) 1962. *La formazione del gruppo dirigente del Partito comunista italiano*. Roma: Editori Riuniti.

Tonveronachi, M. 1982. 'Monetarism and fixed rules in H. C. Simons', *Banca Nazionale del Lavoro Quarterly Review* 35: 181–203.

—1983. *J. M. Keynes. Dall'instabilità ciclica all'equilibrio di sottoccupazione*. Roma: NIS.

—1988. *Struttura ed evoluzione dei sistemi finanziari*. Arezzo: Banca Popolare dell'Etruria e del Lazio.

—1990. 'Teorie monetarie a Chicago', in Becattini (ed.), pp. 349–85.

—1991. 'Alcune considerazioni in tema di teorie finanziarie e processi di valorizzazione', in J. A. Kregel (ed.), *Nuove interpretazioni dell'analisi monetaria di Keynes*, Bologna: il Mulino, pp. 59–66.

Tooke, T. 1838–57. *History of prices, 1793–1856*. 6 vols., London: Longman, Orme, Brown, Green & Longmans.

—1844. *An inquiry into the currency principle*. London: Longman, Brown, Green & Longmans; repr., Series of reprints of scarce works in political economy, no. 15, London School of Economics and Political Sciences 1959.

Torrens, R. 1808. *The economists refuted*. London: S. A. Oddy, and Dublin: C. LaGrange.

—1812. *An essay on money and paper currency*. London: J. Johnson & Co.

—1815. *An essay on the external corn trade*. London: J. Hatchard.

—1817. 'A paper on the means of reducing the poors rates and of affording effectual and permanent relief to the labouring classes', *The Pamphleteer* no. 20: 509–28.

—1818. 'Strictures on Mr. Ricardo's doctrine respecting exchangeable value', *Edinburgh Magazine*, Oct., pp. 335–8.

—1821. *An essay on the production of wealth*. London: Longman, Rees, Orme, Brown & Longmans.

—1835. *Colonization of South Australia*. London: Longman, Rees, Orme, Brown & Green.

—1837. *A letter to the Right Honourable Lord Viscount Melbourne on the causes of the recent derangement in the money market and on bank reform*. London: Longman, Rees, Orme, Brown & Green.

—2000. *Collected works*. Ed. G. De Vivo, 8 vols., Bristol: Thoemmes Press.

Triffin, R. 1940. *Monopolistic competition and general equilibrium theory*. Cambridge, Mass.: Harvard University Press.

Tsuru, S. 1942. 'On reproduction schemes', in appendix to Sweezy, pp. 365–74.

Tucker, G. 1960. *Progress and profits in British economic thought 1650–1850*. Cambridge: Cambridge University Press.

Tugan-Baranovsky, M. J. 1905. *Theoretische Grundlagen des Marxismus*. Leipzig: Duncker & Humblot.

Turgot, A.-R.-J. [1759]. *Éloge de Vincent de Gournai*. Original text in Schelle 1913–23; repr. in Ravix and Romani 1997, pp. 123–53.

—[1766]. *Réflexions sur la formation et la distribution des richesses*. Publ. in 1769–70 in *Éphémérides du citoyen* with changes introduced by Du Pont de Nemours; original text in Schelle, 1913–23, vol. 2, pp. 533–601; repr. in Ravix and Romani 1997, pp. 157–226.

Urbinati, N. 2002. *Mill on democracy. From the Athenian polis to representative government*. Chicago: University of Chicago Press.

Ure, A. 1835. *The philosophy of manufacture*. London: Knight.

Vaggi, G. 1987. *The economics of François Quesnay*. London: Macmillan.

—1993. 'Teorie della ricchezza dal mercantilismo a Smith', in G. Lunghini (ed.), *Valori e prezzi*, Torino: Utet, pp. 21–62.

Valeriani, L. M. 1806. *Del prezzo delle cose tutte mercatabili*. Bologna: Ulisse Ramponi.

Vanek, J. 1970. *The general theory of labor managed market economies*. Ithaca: Cornell University Press.

Veblen, T. 1899. *The theory of the leisure class*. New York: Macmillan.

—1904. *The theory of business enterprise*. New York: Charles Scribner's Sons.

—1919. *The place of science in modern civilization*. New York: Huebsch.

Venturi, F. (ed.) 1958. *Illuministi italiani. Tomo III. Riformatori lombardi, piemontesi e toscani*. Milano-Napoli: Ricciardi.

Venturi, F. (ed.) 1962. *Illuministi italiani. Tomo V. Riformatori napoletani*. Milano-Napoli: Ricciardi.

—1969–90. *Settecento riformatore*. 5 vols., Torino: Einaudi.

Verdoorn, P. 1949. 'Fattori che regolano lo sviluppo della produttività del lavoro', *L'industria* 1: 3–10.

Verri, P. 1781. *Discorsi sull'indole del piacere e del dolore; sulla felicità; e sulla economia politica*. Milano: Giuseppe Marelli; repr. Roma: Archivi Edizioni 1974.

Vianello, F. 1973. 'Pluslavoro e profitto nell'analisi di Marx', in Sylos Labini (ed.), pp. 75–117.

Vicarelli, F. 1977. *Keynes. L'instabilità del capitalismo*. Milano: Etas libri. English trans., *Keynes: the instability of capitalism*, Philadelphia: University of Pennsylvania Press 1984.

Vicarelli, S. 1975. 'Il "problema della trasformazione": fine di una controversia', *Note economiche* 8: 91–138.

Vilar, P. 1960. *Oro y moneda en la historia (1450–1920)*. Barcelona: Ediciones Ariel; English trans., *A history of gold and money*, London: Verso 1991.

Villetti, R. 1978. 'Lavoro diviso e lavoro costrittivo', in R. Villetti (ed.), *Socialismo e divisione del lavoro*, Quaderni di Mondoperaio, no. 8, Roma: Mondo Operaio-Edizioni Avanti!, pp. ix–lxxii.

Viner, J. 1927. 'Adam Smith and laissez-faire', *Journal of Political Economy* 35: 198–232; repr. in Viner 1991, pp. 85–113.

—1931. 'Cost curves and supply curves', *Zeitschrift für Nationalökonomie* 3: 23–46.

—1937. *Studies in the theory of international trade*. New York: Harper.

—1949. 'Bentham and J. S. Mill: the utilitarian background', *American Economic Review* 39: 360–82; repr. in Viner 1991, pp. 154–75.

—1953. 'Introduction', in B. de Mandedville, *A letter to Dion* [1732], Augustan Reprint Society, no. 41, Berkeley: University of California, pp. 1–15; repr. in Viner 1991, pp. 176–88.

—1978. 'Religious thought and economic society: four chapters of an unfinished work', ed. and with an introduction by J. Melitz and D. Winch, *History of Political Economy* 10: 1–192.

—1991. *Essays on the intellectual history of economics*. Ed. D. A. Irwin, Princeton: Princeton University Press.

Vint, J. 1994. *Capital and wages. A Lakatosian history of the wages fund doctrine*. Aldershot: Edward Elgar.

Wakefield, E. G. 1829. *A letter from Sidney, the principal town of Australasia*. London: Joseph Cross.

—1833. *England and America*. 2 vols., London: R. Bentley.

Wald, A. 1936. 'Über einige Gleichungssysteme der Mathematischen Ökonomie', *Zeitschrift für Nationalökonomie* 7: 637–70. English trans., 'On some systems of equations of mathematical economics', *Econometrica* 19 (1951): 368–403.

Walker, D. A. 1987. 'Bibliography of the writings of Léon Walras', *History of Political Economy* 19: 667–702.

—1996. *Walras's market models*. Cambridge: Cambridge University Press.

—2003. 'Early general equilibrium economics', in Samuels, Biddle and Davis (eds.), pp. 278–93.

Wallace, R. 1761 *Various prospects of mankind, nature and providence*. London: A. Millar.

Walras, A. A. 1831. *De la nature de la richesse et de l'origine de la valeur*. Paris: Alexandre Johanneau.

—1849. *Théorie de la richesse sociale ou résumé des principes fondamentaux de l'économie politique*. Paris: Guillaumin.

Walras, L. 1858. *Francis Sauveur*. Paris: E. Dentu.

—1867. 'La Bourse et le credit', in *Paris guide, par les principaux écrivains et artistes de la France, deuxième partie*, Paris: Librairie Internationale, pp. 1731–51; repr. in Auguste et Leon Walras, *Oeuvres économiques complètes*. Vol. 7, *Mélanges d'économie politique et sociale*, Paris: Economica 1987, pp. 180–200.

—1874. *Éléments d'économie politique pure*. Lausanne: Corbaz; second part, 1877; 2nd edn. 1889, 3rd edn. 1896, 4th edn. 1900, 'definitive' edn. 1926. English trans. of the 1926 edn., ed. W. Jaffé, *Elements of pure economics*, London: Irwin Inc. 1954; repr. London: Allen & Unwin 1965.

—1880. 'La Bourse, la spéculation et l'agiotage', *Bibliothèque Universelle et Revue Suisse* no. 5 (March): 452–76 and no. 6 (April): 66–94.

—1896. *Études d'économie sociale. Théorie de la répartition de la richesse sociale*. Lausanne: Corbaz; repr. Paris: Economica 1990.

—1898. *Études d'économie politique appliquée. Théorie de la production de la richesse sociale*. Ed. definitive ed. by G. Leduc, Lausanne 1936; repr. Paris: Economica 1992.

—1965a. *Correspondence and related papers*. Ed. W. Jaffé, 3 vols., Amsterdam: North Holland.

—[1909] 1965b. 'Notice autobiographique', in Walras 1965a, vol. 1, pp. 1–15. Italian trans., *Nota autobiografica*, in Ingrao and Ranchetti 1996, pp. 258–71.

Weber, M. 1904–5. 'Die protestantische Ethik und der Geist des Kapitalismus', *Archiv für Sozialwissenschaft und Sozialpolitik* 20–1; 2nd edn. in *Gesammelte Aufsätze zur Religionssoziologie*, Tübingen: Mohr 1922. English trans., *The Protestant ethic and the spirit of capitalism*, London: Allen & Unwin 1930.

—1922. *Wirtschaft und Gesellschaft*. 2 vols., Tübingen: Mohr. English trans., *Economy and society*, New York: Bedminster Press 1968.

Weintraub, E. R. 1991. *Stabilizing dynamics*. Cambridge: Cambridge University Press.

West, E. 1815. *Essay on the application of capital to land*. London: T. Underwood.

West, E. G. 1976. *Adam Smith. The man and his works*. Indianapolis: Liberty Press.

Whately, R. 1831. *Introductory lectures on political economy*. London: B. Fellowes; 2nd edn. 1832.

Whitaker, J. K. 1990. 'What happened to the second volume of the *Principles*? The thorny path to Marshall's last books', in J. K. Whitaker (ed.), *Centenary essays on Alfred Marshall*, Cambridge: Cambridge University Press, pp. 193–222.

Wicksell, K. 1893. *Über Wert, Kapital, und Rente*. Jena: G. Fischer. English trans., *Value, capital and rent*, London: Allen & Unwin 1954.

—1898. *Geldzins und Güterpreise bestimmenden Ursachen*. Jena: G. Fischer. English trans., *Interest and prices*, London: Macmillan.

—1900. 'Om gränsproduktivitaten såsom grundval för den nationalekonomiska fördelningen', *Ekonomisk Tidskrift* 2: 305–37. English trans., 'Marginal productivity as the basis for distribution in economics', in K. Wicksell, *Selected papers on economic theory*, London: Allen & Unwin 1958, pp. 93–121.

—1901–6. *Forelasningar i nationalekonomi*. 2 vols., Stockholm-Lund: Fritzes-Berlingska. English trans., *Lectures on political economy*, 2 vols., London: Routledge & Kegan Paul 1934–5.

—1919. 'Professor Cassels ekonomiska system', *Ekonomisk Tidskrift* 21: 195–226. English trans., 'Professor Cassel's system of economics', in K. Wicksell,

Lectures on political economy, 2 vols., London: Routledge & Kegan Paul 1934–5, pp. 93–121.

—1923. 'Realkapital och kapitalränta', *Ekonomisk Tidskrift* 25: 145–80. English trans., 'Real capital and interest', in K. Wicksell, *Lectures on political economy*, 2 vols., London: Routledge & Kegan Paul 1934–5, vol. 1, pp. 258–99.

Wicksteed, P. H. 1884. '*Das Kapital*: a criticism', *To-Day* 2: 388–409; repr. in P. H. Wicksteed, *The common sense of political economy and selected papers and reviews on economic theory*, ed. L. Robbins, London: Routledge 1934, vol. 2, pp. 705–24.

—1888. *The alphabet of economic science. Part I, Elements of the theory of value or worth*. London: Macmillan.

—1894. *An essay on the co-ordination of the laws of distribution*. London: Macmillan; repr. ed. I. Steedman, Aldershot: Edward Elgar 1992.

—1910. *The common sense of political economy*. London: Macmillan; repr. ed. L. Robbins, 2 vols., London: Routledge 1933.

Wieser, F. von 1884. *Über den Ursprung und die Hauptgesetze des wirtschaftlichen Wertes*. Wien: Hölder.

—1889. *Der Natürliche Werth*. Wien: Hölder. English trans., *Natural value*, London: Macmillan 1893.

—1914. *Theorie der gesellschaftlichen Wirtschaft*. In *Grundriss der Sozialökonomik*, vols. 1 and 2, Tübingen: Mohr-Siebeck. English trans., *Social economics*, New York: Greenberg 1927.

—1926. *Das Gesetz der Macht*. Wien: Springer.

Wiles, R. C. 1986. 'The development of mercantilist economic thought'. In Lowry (ed.), pp. 147–73.

Williams, K. 1981. *From pauperism to poverty*. London: Routledge.

Williamson, O. 1975. *Markets and hierarchies: analysis and antitrust implications*. New York: Free Press.

—1986. *Economic organization*. Brighton: Wheatsheaf Books.

Wilson, T. 1572. *A discourse uppon usurye*. Londini: Rychardi Tottelli; repr. ed. R. H. Tawney, London: Bell 1926; repr. London: Frank Cass 1963.

Wilson, T. and Skinner, A. S. (eds.) 1976. *The market and the state*. Oxford: Clarendon Press.

Winch, D. 1962. 'What price the history of economic thought?', *Scottish Journal of Political Economy* 9: 193–204.

—1965. *Classical political economy and colonies*. London: Bell & Sons.

—1978. *Adam Smith's politics*. Cambridge: Cambridge University Press.

—1987. *Malthus*. Oxford: Oxford University Press.

Winternitz, J. 1948. 'Values and prices: a solution of the so-called transformation problem', *Economic Journal* 58: 276–80.

Wittgenstein, L. 1921. 'Logisch-philosophische Abhandlung', *Annalen der Naturphilosophie*, 14: 185–262. English edn. with revisions and the German text, *Tractatus logico-philosophicus*. London: Kegan Paul, 1922.

—1953. *Philosophische Untersuchungen* (with English trans., *Philosophical investigations*). Ed. G. E. M. Anscombe and R. Rhees, Oxford: Blackwell; repr. 1972.

Wood, A. 1975. *A theory of profits*. Cambridge: Cambridge University Press.

Wood, D. 2002. *Medieval economic thought*. Cambridge: Cambridge University Press.

Wright, G. H. von 1955. 'Ludwig Wittgenstein: a biographical sketch', *Philosophical Review* 64; repr. in Malcom 1958, pp. 5–28.

Xenophon 1914. *Cyropaedia*. English trans. by W. Miller, Loeb Classic Library, London: Heinemann and New York: Putnam's Sons.

—1923. *Memorabilia and Oeconomicus*. Ed. E. Capps, T. E. Page and W. H. D. Rouse, Loeb Classic Library, London: Heinemann and New York: Putnam's Sons.

Young, A. 1928. 'Increasing returns and economic progress', *Economic Journal* 38: 527–42.

Zeuthen, F. 1933. 'Das Prinzip der Knappheit, technische Kombination und ökonomische Qualität', *Zeitschrift für Nationalökonomie* 4: 1–24.

Index of names

Abélard, P., 33–4
Accursius, 40
Adams, H. C., 372
Akerlof, G., 473–4
Akermann, G., 313
Akhtar, M. A., 113
Albert the Great, 38
Allen, R. D. G., 339
Allocati, A., 370
Alter, M., 297, 298, 299, 305
Althusser, L., 270
Ambrose, St, Bishop of Milan, 29, 38
Amodio, L., 275
Anderson, J., 184
Andreatta, B., 495
Andrews, P., 412
Antoninus, Bishop of Florence, 40, 135
Aristarchus of Samos, 7
Aristotle, 18, 19, 22, 25–8, 30, 32, 35, 36, 38, 39, 72, 84, 116, 124–5, 126, 294, 316, 433
Arnon, A., 199
Arrow, K. J., 12, 145, 280, 340, 341, 346–8, 471, 490
Arthur, B., 498
Asimakopulos, A., 391, 415
Aspromourgos, T., 55
Augello, M. M., 416
Augustine, St, Bishop of Hippo, 29, 30, 38, 39
Aupetit, A., 337
Auspitz, R., 298
Axelrod, R., 497

Babbage, C., xi, 230–2, 240
Babeuf, F.-N., 226, 244, 246
Bach, J. S., 290
Backhouse, R. E., 339, 374
Bacon, F., 24, 55–6, 57–8, 128
Bagehot, W., 370
Bagiotti, A., 328

Bailey, S., xi, 192, 208, 215–18, 219, 226–7, 243, 284, 289
Bain, J. S., 470, 477
Bakunin, M., 247
Baran, P., 276–7
Barber, W. J., 376
Barbon, N., 58–61, 80, 81
Barca, F., 504
Barkai, H., 192
Barnett, M., 297
Barone, E., 318, 337
Barro, R. J., 201, 483
Bartley, W. W. III, 316
Barton, J., 204
Bastiat, C. F., 5, 208
Bauer, B., 244–5
Bauer, O., 274, 417
Baumol, W. J., 166, 444, 470, 476, 478
Beaugrand, P., 199
Becattini, G., xiii, 352, 356, 357, 383
Beccaria, C., 18, 50, 84, 90, 110, 156, 175, 282
Bedeschi, G., 82
Bell, V., 385
Bellarmino, R., Cardinal, 57
Bellofiore, R., 309
Benedict XIV (Prospero Lambertini), Pope, 36
Benini, R., 494
Bentham, J., 20, 37, 38, 84, 110, 160, 165, 174–8, 208, 233–7, 254, 279, 285, 288–90, 292, 319, 331
Berg, M., 205
Bergson, A., 378
Berle, A., 375, 476
Bernardine from Siena, St, 40, 135, 300, 362
Bernoulli, D., 278, 345
Bernstein, E., 272–3
Besicovitch, A. S., 449
Bhaduri, A., 415

Bharadwaj, K., 9, 185, 187, 218, 360, 364, 377, 415, 461
Biagini, E., 110, 351
Bismarck, O. von, 273, 304
Black, R. D. C., 279, 287, 288
Blanc, L., 226
Blanqui, A., 209
Blanqui, L., 209
Blaug, M., 9, 15, 143, 165, 279, 282, 283, 355, 481
Bobbio, N., 83–4
Bodin, J., 47
Boethius, 28
Boettke, P. J., 321
Böhm-Bawerk, E. von, 167, 229, 266, 281, 294, 297, 300, 301, 308–19, 373, 417, 423, 435, 458
Boisguilbert, P. le Pesant de, 79–80, 94
Bonar, J., 161
Boniface VIII (Benedetto Caetani), Pope, 32
Boninsegni, P., 337
Boody, E., 419
Boole, G., 287–8
Bordiga, A., 439
Bortkiewicz, L. von, 266–7, 269, 335
Botero, G., 50, 51, 160–1, 443
Bourbaki, N., 348
Bowles, M., 282
Bowley, M., 172, 228, 230, 235
Box, G. E. P., 495
Boyer, G., 171
Brandolin, S., xiii
Braverman, H., 232
Bray, J., 221
Brenner, R., 94, 308
Brentano, L., 307, 312
Breton, Y., 208
Brewer, A., 93
Bridel, P., 336
Brock, W. A., 499
Bronfenbrenner, M., 4
Brouwer, L. E., 343, 344, 446
Brown, F., 384
Brugge, A., 312
Brundtland, G. H., 503
Brus, W., 276
Brusco, S., 383
Brutus, M. I., 428
Bryce, J. C., 121
Buccleuch, H. S., Duke of, 117
Buchanan, J., 370
Bukharin, N., 274–5, 290
Buonarroti, F., 244, 246
Buridan, G., 39–40

Burke, E., 303
Burlamaqui, J. J., 326
Burmeister, E., 459
Busino, G., 337

Caesar, I., 21, 29, 428
Cairnes, J. E., 239
Caldwell, B. J., 3, 297
Calvin, J., 37
Calzoni, G., 426
Cammarota, L., 54
Campanella, T., 24, 226
Campbell, R. H., 121
Canard, N.-F., 326
Candela, G., 100
Cannan, F., 55, 191
Cantillon, R., 12, 50, 59, 77, 79, 80, 90–6, 103, 105, 113, 131, 136, 138, 149, 161, 164, 165, 173, 283, 286, 323, 367, 368
Caravale, G., 184
Carey, H. C., 185
Carlyle, T., 163, 207, 233, 235
Carmichael, G., 78
Casarosa, C., 184
Cassel, G., 313, 342–3, 344, 347
Cattaneo, C., 209
Cerroni, U., 255
Cesarano, F., 3, 4
Chafuen, A. A., 30, 37, 38, 39, 40, 47, 107, 308
Chamberlin, E., 381, 427, 430, 441
Chaunu, P., 104
Cherbuliez, A. E., 230
Chevalier, M., 230, 233
Child, J., 81, 170
Chilosi, A., 412
Chiodi, G., 314
Churchill, W., 386
Cicero, M. T., 28
Ciocca, P., 437
Cipolla, C. M., 23, 47
Clapham, J. A., 377, 380, 427, 440–1
Clark, C., 493
Clark, J. B., 295, 329, 372
Clark, J. M., 372, 373, 376
Clower, R., 483
Coase, R. H., 469, 475, 479
Coats, A. W., 279, 280
Cobb, C., 494
Cobden, R., 186
Colander, R., 407
Colbert, J.-B., 44, 79, 97
Cole, G. D. H., 221, 224, 226
Coleridge, S. T., 233, 235
Colletti, L., 153, 270

Colquhoun, P., 223
Commons, J., 376
Comte, A., 240, 307, 338, 358
Condillac, E. B., 104, 120, 226, 234, 282, 326
Condorcet, M. J. A. N. Caritat, marquis of, 86, 150, 156–8, 160, 161, 163, 287–8
Constantine, 29
Copernicus, N., 7, 47, 57, 119
Corry, B. A., 168
Corsi, M., xiii, 129, 230, 338
Cosmo, U., 438
Cournot, A.-A., 143, 208, 283, 323–4, 326, 364
Coyer, G. F., 105
Croce, B., 338, 436
Cromwell, O., 54
Cross, R., 496
Custodi, P., 48, 50, 51, 110, 161
Cyert, R. M., 501
Cyprian, St, Bishop of Carthage, 30, 160

Dahrendorf, R., 480, 504
D'Alembert, J., 97, 98, 117, 128
D'Annunzio, G., 371
Dante Alighieri, 294
Dardi, M., 351, 357
Darwin, C., 160, 304, 356, 361, 382
Dasgupta, A., 23
Davanzati, B., 42, 47, 109, 282
Davenant, C., 57, 77–8, 81, 92, 129
David, P., 498
Davidson, P., 480, 499
Deane, P., 77, 82, 143, 377, 384
Debreu, G., 12, 104, 145, 280, 340, 341, 346–8, 471
De Cecco, M., 437
Dechert, W. D., 499
De Finetti, B., 345, 390
Defoe, D., 79, 80, 171
Deleyre, A., 128
De Marchi, N., 6, 9, 236
Democritus, 245
De Morgan, A., 287–8
Denis, H., 71, 169
Denison, E. F., 490
De Quincey, T., xi, 143, 208, 217, 218–20, 243, 507
De Roover, R., 27, 34, 37, 38, 39–40
De Rosa, G., 337
De Santis, M. A., 48, 49, 51
Descartes, R., 54, 57, 96, 104, 108, 111, 115, 143, 156–77, 237, 331
de Viti de Marco, A., 370

De Vivo, G., 209
Dewey, D., 372
Diderot, D., 97, 104, 128
Diggins, J. P., 375, 376
Di Nardi, G., 370, 371
Diodorus Siculus, 18, 126
Dobb, M., 5, 9, 138, 243, 253, 308, 318, 413, 450, 461
Domar, E., 462, 488
Donzelli, F., xiii, 291, 317, 321, 339
Dorfman, R., 492
Dosi, G., 382
Dougherty, C. R. S., 459
Douglas, P., 373, 494
Duhem, P., 6
Dumoulin, C., 37
Dunlop, J. T., 402
Duns Scotus, J., 30, 33, 38, 39
Du Pont de Nemours, P., 97, 105
Dupuit, A., 282–3, 323–4

Eatwell, J., 187, 267, 463
Eden, F., 171
Edgeworth, F. Y., 219, 239, 294–6, 334, 335, 339, 417, 443, 448
Eggertsson, T., 479
Egidi, M., 144
Eichner, A., 477
Einaudi, L., 50, 62, 341, 435, 451
Elias, N., 85
Ellman, M., 275
Eltis, W., 168
Ely, R., 372, 376
Engel, E., 304, 462, 491, 494
Engels, F., 86, 154, 162, 245–9, 263, 271, 272, 323
Epicurus, 28, 245
Épinay, L.-P. Tardieu d'Esclavelles, Madame d', 108
Eshag, E., 369
Euclid, 115
Euler, 373

Fabius Maximus Cunctator, 273
Fanno, M., 315
Faucci, R., 110, 151, 209, 282, 287, 289, 304, 436
Fawcett, H., 239, 351
Ferguson, A., 112, 152, 250, 368
Ferrara, F., 50, 151, 228, 304
Fetter, F. W., 208, 209
Feuerbach, L., 244–6
Feyerabend, P., 6, 8, 9, 10, 120, 420
Filangieri, G., 50, 110, 156
Finley, M. I., 24, 28

Fisher, I., 325, 339, 340, 369, 372, 393, 436
Fitzmaurice, E., 53, 173
Flux, A. W., 373
Foner, P. S., 249
Forges Davanzati, G., 42
Fourier, C., 226
Foxwell, H. S., 221, 222
Francis of Assisi, St, 29
Franklin, B., 118
Freeman, R. D., 367
Friedman, M., 415, 421, 470, 484–5
Frish, R., 419, 494
Fuà, G., 495, 502
Fudenberg, D., 497
Fullarton, J., 199, 215
Fumagalli Beonio Brocchieri, M. T., 33
Fuoco, F., 209

Galbraith, K., 268, 375, 480
Galiani, F., 48, 51, 104, 107–10, 113, 135, 142, 148, 156–7, 178, 226–7, 282, 284, 289, 323, 506
Galilei, G., 57–8, 119
Gallaway, L., 459
Ganilh, C., 209, 230
Gårdlund, T., 312
Garegnani, P., 187, 270, 314, 335, 415, 454, 458, 459, 462
Garnier, J., 209, 230
Gauss, C. F., 356, 491
Genovesi, A., 18, 50, 109–10, 156
George, H., 225, 294
Georgescu-Roegen, N., 11, 283, 360
Gerson, J., 38
Ghazali, A. H., 128
Gherity, J. A., 151
Giacomin, A., 94
Gilibert, G., 100, 145, 492
Ginzburg, A., 168, 222, 225
Gioja, M., 209
Giuliani, A., 9, 120
Gleick, J., 499
Gobetti, P., 436, 438
Gödel, K., 349
Godwin, W., 158–9, 161, 163, 247
Goethe, J. W., 235
Goldman, L., 239, 351
Goodwin, C. D. W., 279
Goodwin, R., 259, 413, 419, 499
Gordon, D., 3
Gossen, H. H., 230, 283
Gournay, V. de, 79, 106
Gramsci, A., 59, 179, 435, 436, 438–40, 445, 448

Graunt, J., 54, 368
Gray, J. (1799–1883), 221–3, 226
Gray, J., 316
Graziani, A. (1865–1944), 305, 370
Graziani, A. (b. 1933), 315, 335
Gresham, T., 41
Groenewegen, P., 18, 350, 353, 360, 366, 367
Grosseteste, Robert, 28
Grossman, H. I., 483
Grotius (H. de Groot), 78, 81
Grouchy (S. Condorcet) Madame de, 150
Guger, A., 410
Guillebaud, C. W., 352, 359
Gutenberg, J., 23

Haavelmo, T., 494–5
Haberler, G., 418
Hacking, I., 357, 491
Hahn, F. H., 347, 454, 472, 489
Hales, J., 41, 42
Halévy, E., 175
Hall, C., 223
Hammurabi, 23
Hamowy, R., 112
Hands, W., 3, 5, 6, 234
Hansen, A., 412, 429
Haq, M. ul, 503
Harcourt, G. C., xiii, 415, 459
Harrod, R., 275, 384, 398, 441, 458, 459, 460, 462, 470, 488–91
Harsanyi, J., 178
Hart, N., 361
Harvey, W., 20, 61
Hausman, D. M., 502
Hawtrey, R. G., 369, 392
Hayek, F. von, 33, 199, 306, 309–12, 314–15, 321, 335, 341, 369, 383, 391, 407, 408, 413, 425, 435, 436, 438, 441, 449, 450, 458, 460
Heckscher, E. F., 42, 43, 202
Heertje, A., 428
Hegel, G. W. F., 221, 244, 249–50, 273, 303
Héloïse, wife of Abélard, 33
Helvetius, C.-A., 175
Hennings, K. H., 310
Hermann, F. B. W., 298
Hewitt, F., 157
Hey, J. D., 367
Hicks, J., 4, 184, 205, 314, 320, 329, 339, 345, 350, 373, 396–8, 406, 407, 408, 481–2, 487
Higgs, H., 96, 100
Hilbert, D., 343, 348–9

Hildebrand, B., 303, 309
Hilferding, R., 268, 274, 417, 429, 480
Hill, C., 253
Hirsch, F., 86
Hirschman, A. O., 85, 86
Hobbes, T., 54, 55, 57–8, 60, 62, 82, 120, 124, 125
Hobson, J., 169, 274, 278
Hodgskin, T., 221–5
Hodgson, G. M., 479
Hollander, J., 191, 211, 451
Hollander, S., 121, 184, 187, 238, 324
Holt, A., 118
Horwitz, S., 300
Hosseini, H., 128
Howey, R. S., 279, 327, 330
Huberman, L., 277
Hùfeland, G., 230
Hull, C., 54, 55, 63
Hulton, R., 253
Hume, D., 86, 91, 94, 104, 111–14, 116–18, 119, 122, 150, 153, 197, 234, 235, 449
Huntington, S. P., 248
Hutcheson, F., 78, 88, 111–14, 115, 118, 123, 125, 126, 175
Hutchison, T. W., 76, 80, 81, 113, 178, 279

Im Hof, U., 104
Ingram, J. K., 304, 358
Ingrao, B., 324, 326, 330, 332, 344, 345, 346, 347
Innocent III, Pope, 30
Isnard, A. N., 326
Israel, G., 324, 326, 330, 344, 345, 346, 347

Jaffé, W., 313, 326, 328, 330
James I, King of England, 53
James, P., 159, 161
Jenkins, J. M., 495
Jennings, R., 288
Jerome, St, 29, 30
Jevons, L., 286
Jevons, T., 286
Jevons, W. S., xii, 57, 72, 90, 91, 181, 208, 222, 229, 234, 236, 278–9, 281, 282–3, 285, 297–9, 301, 324, 350, 351, 353–4, 362, 368, 371, 379, 422, 435, 451, 491, 500, 503
John Chrysostom, 29
Johnson, E., 384
Jones, P., 121
Jones, R., 163, 304

Judges, A. V., 43
Juglar, C., 427
Justinian, 40

Kadish, A., 367
Kahn, R., 380–1, 398, 403, 411, 413–14, 487
Kahnemann, D., 502
Kaldor, N., 62, 318, 411, 413–15, 487, 489, 490
Kalecki, M., 276, 412, 462
Kames (Henry Home), Lord, 116
Kant, I., 111, 125, 439
Kauder, E., 274, 279
Kautilya, 23
Kautsky, K., 249, 272, 418
Kaye, F. B., 87, 88
Kennedy, J., 480
Kent, Duke of, 222
Keynes, J. M., xii, 4, 5, 34, 37, 42, 91, 120, 167, 168, 203, 249, 296, 314, 319–20, 341, 350, 352, 353, 369, 376–7, 378–9, 380, 383, 384–415, 419, 420, 428, 429, 431, 437, 441, 443, 444, 445–6, 448–51, 460–1, 462, 466, 470, 477, 480–4, 487–9, 491, 493, 495, 512
Keynes, J. N., 384, 388
Kindleberger, C. P., 173, 488, 494
King, G., 57, 77–8, 129
Kitchin, J., 427
Klein, L., 494–5
Knapp, G. F., 312
Knies, K., 121, 303, 309, 372
Knight, F. H., 391, 441, 484, 501
Kondratieff, N. D., 337, 427–8
Könekamp, R., 287
Konus, A. A., 192
Koopmans, T., 494
Kregel, J. A., 9, 391, 397, 408, 415, 480, 487
Krugman, P. R., 203, 498
Kuhn, T. S., 1, 5, 6–7, 8, 9, 420
Kula, W., 1, 14, 21, 22, 192
Kurz, H., 459, 461
Kuznetz, S., 491
Kydland, F. E., 486

Lactantius, 29, 30
Lafargue, P., 225–6
La Fontaine, J. de, 87
Laidler, D., 151
Lakatos, I., 1, 5, 6, 8, 9, 243, 420, 510
Lamarck, J.-B. de, 360–1, 382
Lancaster, K. J., 300, 378
Landes, D., 475

Lange, O., 276, 318
Langenstein, H. von, 39
Langholm, O., 38, 39, 40, 41
Lansdowne (H. E. W. Fitzmaurice) sixth
  marquis of, 55
Lassalle, F., 247
Latsis, S., 7
Lauerdale (James Maitland, count of), 57,
  167–8, 226
Lavoisier, A.-L., 20
Law, J., 81, 90, 173
Leeson, P. T., 321
Leibnitz, G. W. von, 41, 57, 346
Leijonhufvud, A., 483
Lenin (Vladimir Il'ič Ul'janov), 254, 271,
  274
Leo XIII (Vincenzo Gioacchino Pecci),
  Pope, 31, 36
Leontief, W., 323, 419, 462, 493
Lerner, A., 398, 407
Leslie, T. E. C., 304, 358
Lessius (L. de Lays), 37
Letwin, W., 81
Levhari, D., 459
Levy, D. M., 233
Lieben, R., 298
Lindhal, E., 314, 321, 407
Linnaeus (von Linné) C., 357
Lippi, M., xiii, 270, 461, 506
Lipsey, R. G., 378
List, F., 51, 203, 303
Lloyd, W. F., 208, 217, 229, 284
Locke, J., 61, 76–7, 78, 80–3, 88, 92, 95,
  96, 115, 176, 197, 225
Longfield, M., 199, 217, 229, 284
Lopokova, L., 386
Lorenz, K., 316
Loria, A., 370
Lotka, A. J., 361
Louis XIV (Le Roi Soleil), King of France,
  44
Louis XV, King of France, 77, 96
Lovett, A., xiii
Lowry, S. T., 24, 25, 27
Lucas, R. E., 470, 485, 495
Lutfalla, M., 208
Luxemburg, R., 169, 254, 275–6, 411

Mably, G. B. de, 226
Macfie, A. L., 121
Machiavelli, N., 20, 22, 58, 60, 84–5
Maddison, A., 305
Maenchen-Helfen, O., 245
Magnusson, L., 41, 43
Malcom, N., 447

Malebranche, N., 96
Malinvaud, E., 483
Maloney, J., 18, 367
Malthus, D., 159
Malthus, T., 30, 65, 113, 157, 158–69,
  172, 181, 183, 184, 187–9, 191, 193,
  194–5, 199, 208, 210–11, 214, 217,
  225, 226, 241, 259, 290, 291, 302, 319,
  390, 451, 502
Malynes, G., 43
Mandeville, B. de, 28, 77, 84, 87–9, 124,
  125, 171, 367
Mangoldt, H. K. E. von, 302
Mann, T., 365
Mantoux, É., 386
Marcet, J., 209
March, J. G., 501
Marchesi, C., 445
Marcuse, H., 277
Marcuzzo, C., 192, 197, 198
Marglin, S., 475
Mark Antony, 428
Markowitz, H., 484
Marris, R., 476–7
Marshak, J., 494
Marshall, A., xii, 18, 24, 53, 65, 72, 77,
  143, 148, 159, 186, 202, 217, 219, 220,
  227, 239, 241–3, 278, 281, 286, 287,
  294–6, 298, 299, 306, 310, 324, 329,
  335, 340, 342, 347, 349, 350–83,
  384–5, 388, 390, 392–5, 397, 402,
  413–14, 417, 435, 440–4, 445, 451,
  478, 491, 512
Martineau, H., 209
Marx, K., xi, 5, 24, 31, 39, 55, 67, 71, 86,
  90, 93, 131, 132, 152–4, 158, 162, 167,
  168, 179, 195–6, 214, 217, 220, 221,
  222, 224, 225–6, 228, 231–2, 240,
  244–77, 294–6, 299, 301, 307–8, 316,
  323, 324, 367, 411, 416, 427, 428, 429,
  431, 433, 435, 455, 456, 460, 463–4,
  465, 486, 492, 506
Marzetti Dall'Aste Brandolini, S., 390
Mas-Colell, A., 473
Massie, J., 81
Matthews, R. C. O., 489
Matteotti, G., 371
Mattioli, R., 449
Maurice, P., xiii
Maurice Robinson, J. V.: see Robinson, J.
Mays, W., 288
Mazarino, G., Cardinal, 44
Mazzini, G., 336
McCloskey, D., 8, 10, 120
McCord Wright, D., 428

McCulloch, J. R., xi, 42, 50, 165, 172,
  200, 204, 208, 217, 218, 219–21, 230
McKenzie, L., 347
McLean, I., 157
McPherson, M. S., 502
McWilliams Tullberg, R., 351
Meade, J. E., 396, 397, 415, 504
Meadows, D. H., 503
Means, G., 375, 476
Medina, J. de, 39
Medio, A., 267, 463
Meek, R. L., 9, 71, 83, 100, 121, 126,
  159, 162, 168, 262, 263, 270, 463
Meenai, S. A., 209
Meikle, S., 27, 28
Meldolesi, L., 267
Menenius Agrippa, 31
Menger, A., 221, 223
Menger, C., xii, 221, 229, 278–9, 281,
  285, 290, 297–306, 308, 324, 339,
  341–435
Menger, K., 297, 343–4
Mercado, T. de, 30, 47
Mercier de la Rivière, P.-P., 97
Merton, R., 484
Milgate, M., 163, 321
Mill, J., xi, 160, 165–6, 172, 181, 189, 199,
  201, 208–10, 216, 218, 233, 239, 450
Mill, J. S., xi, 34, 84, 125, 143, 158, 160,
  165–7, 168, 172, 174, 176, 178, 186,
  199, 202, 208, 214, 217, 218–20, 223,
  230, 233–43, 280, 284, 286, 288–91,
  324, 329, 351, 353, 354, 358, 362, 367,
  388–9, 433, 503, 507
Millar, J., 112
Miller, M., 477, 484
Minsky, H. P., 375, 391, 419, 480, 487,
  488, 513
Mirabeau (Victor Riqueti, marquis of), 41,
  90, 96, 97, 161, 368
Mirowski, P., 324, 348, 473, 502
Mises, L. von, 309, 315, 318, 319, 321,
  335, 417, 425
Mishan, E. J., 502
Misselden, E., 43
Mitchell, W. C., 376
Modigliani, F., 398, 415, 477, 482, 484,
  495
Moggridge, D. E., 384, 391, 396
Mohr, J. C. B. (Paul Siebeck), 307
Montchrétien, A. de, 18, 45
Montesquieu, C.-L. de Secondat, baron of
  La Brède and of, 84, 86, 106, 126, 324
Moore, G. E., 384
Moore, H., 494

Morandi, R., 451
More, T., 24, 38, 42, 170, 226
Morellet, A., 104
Morelly, 226
Morgenstern, O., 284, 345, 347, 473
Morishima, M., 267, 324, 330
Mossner, E. C., 121
Moulin, H., 157
Müller, A., 303
Mun, T., 42–3, 45, 47, 201
Murphy, A. E., 81, 90, 173
Mussolini, B., 337, 371, 437
Muth, J. F., 485
Myrdal, G., 314, 407, 451

Naldi, N., xiii, 71, 437, 445
Napoleon Bonaparte, 180, 210
Napoleoni, C., 270, 330
Nash, J. F., 345, 347, 348
Navarro (M. de Azpilcueta), 47
Necker, J., 156–8, 160–1, 163, 503
Neisser, H., 343
Nelson, R., 382, 478
Neumann, J. von, 214, 256, 284, 343–8,
  461, 473, 493
Newton, I., 57, 77, 81, 107, 115, 143,
  230, 324, 346
Niehans, J., 283, 296, 329, 337, 339, 341
Nikolaevskij, B., 245
North, D., 79, 80
North, D. C., 479
North, J., xiii
Nove, A., 275
Nuccio, O., 35, 40
Nuti, M., 415

O'Brien, D. P., 200, 215, 219, 220, 221
O'Donnell, R., 138
Ohlin, B., 202, 229, 314, 407
Opie, R., 424, 427
Oresme, N., 41
Ortes, G., 50, 160–1
Overstone (S. Jones Lloyd) Lord, 199,
  215
Owen, R., 158, 222–3
Oxley, G., 171

Pacioli, L., 22
Pack, S. J., 121
Paine, T., 86, 150, 158
Palazzi, M., 100
Paley, M., 351–2, 356
Palmieri, G., 110, 156
Pantaleoni, M., 2, 337, 370–2, 423, 440
Papi, G. U., 371

Pareto, V., 280, 325, 328, 330, 334, 336–40, 341, 342, 345, 370, 423, 428, 445, 491, 494
Parodi, M., 33
Parrinello, S., 461
Pasinetti, L., 187, 391, 415, 459, 463, 470, 487, 490
Pasquinelli, A., 390
Patinkin, D., 396, 482, 494
Paul (Saul of Tarsus), St, 24, 30
Peach, T., 184, 187, 188, 191, 192, 193
Pearson, K., 491
Peart, S. J., 233
Pecchio, G., 50, 51
Peel, R., 199
Peirce, C., 374
Penn, W., 173
Pericles, 21
Perrotta, C., xiii, 43, 45, 46, 51, 80
Pesciarelli, E., 78
Peter of Johann Olivi, 39, 40
Petty, W., x, xiii, 12, 23, 45, 50, 53–75, 76, 77–8, 80, 81, 83, 90–3, 95, 105, 119–20, 126, 128, 131, 136, 138, 149, 173, 195, 197, 216, 224, 282, 284, 285–94, 341, 361, 367, 368, 491, 493, 506–7
Phelps, E. S., 485
Phillips, A. W., 260, 483
Piccard, A. P., 330
Pietranera, G., 71
Pigou, A. C., 5, 352–3, 364, 371, 372, 376, 380, 385, 392, 395, 397, 405, 413–14, 435, 441, 444–61
Pius XI (Achille Ratti), Pope, 428
Place, F., 160, 161, 223
Plato, 18, 22, 25–7, 30, 32, 120, 126, 316
Pliny the younger, 47
Poincaré, J.-H., 331
Poinsot, L., 327
Pollard, S., 104
Pompadour, J.-A. Poisson, marquess of, 96
Popper, K. R., 6, 32–3, 316, 510
Postlethwayt, M., 79, 90, 368
Pownall, T., 145–9
Preobrazhensky, E., 275
Prescott, E. C., 486, 490
Pribram, K., 30, 31, 32, 33, 36, 51, 104
Privitera, G., xiii
Proudhon, P.-J., 224, 244, 247, 255
Ptolemy, 7, 119
Pufendorf, S., 57, 78, 81, 111, 178
Pyle, A., 159
Pythagoras, 54

Quesnay, F., 12, 59, 61, 77, 80, 90, 91, 96–103, 104, 106, 107, 117, 131, 138, 149, 167, 286, 323
Quetelet, A., 356
Quine, W. V. O., 6
Quinton, A., 448

Rae, J., 229–30
Raffaelli, T., 351
Ramsey, F. P., 345, 390, 446, 449
Ranchetti, F., 330, 332
Raphael, D. D., 121
Rau, K. H., 143, 283, 298, 360
Rauner, R. M., 215, 216
Ravenstone, P. (pseudonym of Pullen, R.), 225
Ravix, J., 105, 106
Rawls, J., 378, 502
Rayleigh, Lord (J. W. Strutt), 351
Realfonzo, R., 315
Reddaway, W. B., 398
Régis, J., 337
Remak, R., 343
Renner, K., 418, 429
Riazanov, D., 245
Ricardo, D., xi, 5, 9, 17, 20, 31, 40, 57, 65, 139, 159, 161, 162, 164, 165, 168, 169, 172, 178, 179–205, 207–26, 239, 243, 244, 253, 256, 257, 263, 280, 282, 284, 286, 294, 298, 308, 324, 329, 350, 354, 358, 361, 363, 367, 389, 413, 433–4, 435, 445, 449, 450–2, 455–6, 460–1, 463–5, 506
Rickett, W. A., 23
Ridolfi, M., 100, 360, 361, 364
Rinaldi, R., 437
Robbins, L., 168, 174, 209, 211, 215, 273, 313, 316, 441
Robertson, D., 4, 366, 369, 377, 391–2, 413, 441, 444, 450
Robespierre, M. de, 157
Robinson, A., 397, 413, 451
Robinson, J., 380–1, 384, 411, 413–14, 427, 459, 487
Rodbertus, J. K., 221, 259
Romani, P.-M., 105, 106
Romer, P., 470, 490
Roncaglia, A., xiii, 12, 16, 46, 53, 59, 67, 154, 162, 184, 196, 209, 213, 264, 267, 280, 287, 291, 405, 416, 423, 435–513
Roncaglia, G., xiii
Roosevelt, F. D., 315, 318, 420
Rorty, R., 15
Roscelin (Roscellinus) of Compiègne, 33
Roscher, W., 298, 303–4, 305, 309, 360

Rosdolsky, R., 270
Rosenberg, N., 152
Ross, I. S., 112, 115, 116–18, 121, 122, 125, 153
Ross, S., 473
Rosselli, A., 49, 184, 192, 197, 198
Rosselli, C., 436
Rosselli, N., 436
Rossi, Enzo, 426
Rossi, Ernesto, 226, 271, 504
Rossi, Paolo, 21, 57
Rossi, Pellegrino, 209
Rostow, W., 491
Rotelli, C., 200
Rothschild, E., 150, 156, 157, 163
Rothschild, N., 180
Rousseau, J.-J., 104, 153, 234
Routh, G., 74
Rudolph of Austria, 297, 300
Ruskin, J., 163, 233
Russell, B., 32, 384, 389, 446
Rutheford, M., 376

Sabbatini, R., 411
Saint-Simon, Cl.-H. de Rouvroy, count of, 226
Salvadori, M. L., 272
Salvadori, N., 459
Samuelson, P. A., 202, 229, 339, 345, 350, 361, 374, 398, 415, 419, 433, 459, 481, 492, 508
Sardoni, C., 259
Savage, L. J., 345, 390–1
Savary, J., 78
Say, J. B., 5, 50, 132, 164–7, 180, 183, 197, 203, 208, 219, 230, 239, 259, 282, 304, 324, 327
Say, L., 107, 327
Scaruffi, G., 47, 51
Schabas, M., 285, 288
Schefold, B., 415, 461
Schelle, G., 105
Schlesinger, K., 343–4
Schlick, M., 446
Schmoller, G. von, 259, 303–5, 358, 421
Schrödinger, E., 316
Schucht, T. (Tatiana), 179, 440
Schultz, H., 339, 494
Schumpeter, J., ix, xii, 1, 3, 4, 5, 7, 11, 13, 31, 33, 39, 42, 43, 50, 55, 80, 86, 94, 107, 108, 110, 112, 119, 126, 148, 159, 161–4, 165, 169, 174, 175, 180, 184, 200, 203, 208, 209, 220, 230, 231, 235, 241, 243, 249, 261, 268, 277, 282, 283, 284, 286, 299, 304, 305, 308, 309, 311,

316, 319, 330, 335, 337, 342, 373, 382, 392, 416–34, 441, 451, 486, 509
Schwartz, P., 233, 243
Screpanti, E., 463
Scribano, M. E., 88, 89
Scrope, G. P., 208, 229
Sebastiani, M., 412
Seligman, E., 211
Sells, G., xiii
Sen, A., 175, 178, 415, 501, 502
Sen, S. R., 113
Seneca, L. A., 25–8
Senior, W. N., 72, 172, 173, 208, 217, 226–9, 240, 284, 310, 326, 360
Serra, A., 42, 45, 46–52, 201
Seton, F., 267
Shaftesbury, A. A. Cooper, count of, 88–9, 125
Sharpe, W., 484
Shaw, G. B., 273
Shove, G. F., 377, 381, 441–61
Shukla, V., 459
Sidgwick, H., 351, 354, 356, 367
Simmel, G., 306
Simon, H., 501
Simons, H., 484
Sims, C. A., 495–6
Singh, A., 415
Sismondi, J.-Ch.-L. Simonde de, 167–9, 208, 259
Skidelsky, R., 34, 384, 386
Skinner, A. S., 113, 121
Slutsky, E., 339
Smith, A., xi, 4, 5, 7, 9, 12, 20, 25, 27, 28, 32, 34, 37, 38, 40, 41, 43, 44, 45, 46, 50, 51, 60, 67, 71, 72, 76–7, 78, 83, 84–5, 86, 88, 90, 91–2, 96, 97–9, 104, 106–7, 110, 111–13, 115–54, 156–7, 162, 163, 164–7, 168, 173, 174, 176, 178, 179, 181–3, 187, 189–90, 192, 194–5, 196, 197, 203–4, 209, 210, 219, 223, 224, 225–6, 230, 232, 233, 235, 237, 240–3, 250, 256, 260, 263, 271–2, 282, 284, 286, 291, 292, 294, 298, 302, 303–4, 324–5, 358, 368, 389, 433–4, 435, 449, 461, 465, 470, 475–6, 491, 499, 500, 506
Smith, M., 115, 118
Smith, T., 42
Smith, V., 502
Socrates, 120
Solow, R. M., 459, 470, 489–91, 492
Sombart, W., 306
Southwell, R., 55
Sowell, T., 166, 262

Spaventa, L., 415, 459
Spence, W., 165, 210
Spencer, H., 304, 338, 360, 374, 382
Spiegel, H. W., 23, 27, 28, 30, 36, 37, 38, 41, 47, 208, 284, 291, 299, 337
Spiethoff, A., 306
Spini, G., 24, 226
Sraffa, A., 435
Sraffa, P., xii, xiii, 9, 11, 16, 65, 70, 139, 159, 179, 181, 187, 189, 191, 211–14, 216, 225, 228, 267, 269–70, 279, 280, 294, 312, 318, 320, 341, 349, 360, 363, 364, 365, 366, 370, 372, 373, 380–1, 386, 397–8, 413, 415, 427, 435, 489, 491, 492–3, 506, 512, 513
Stackelberg, H. von, 343
Stalin (J. V. Džugašvili), 271, 275–6
Steedman, I., 9, 144, 270, 273, 294, 295–6, 312, 321, 507
Stein, P. G., 121
Steindl, J., 412, 477, 498
Steuart, J., 112–13, 184
Stewart, D., 112, 115, 150
Stigler, G. J., 125, 128, 192, 279, 339, 350, 373
Stiglitz, J., 483
Stirner, M., 244–5
Stone, R., 77, 415, 491–3
Stolper, W. F., 433
Strachey, L., 104, 384–5
Strahan, W., 118
Streissler, E. W., 283, 297, 298, 300, 302, 303, 312, 360
Streissler, M., 300
Sumner, W. G., 374, 376
Süssmilch, J. P., 161
Swan, T., 490
Swedberg, R., 416, 418
Sweezy, P., 245, 253, 263, 270, 275, 276–7, 419
Sylos Labini, P., xiii, 139, 141, 182, 261, 262, 268, 337, 412, 419, 428, 444, 465–7, 470, 477, 495, 513

Tagliacozzo, G., 52
Takabashi, H., 253
Tarantelli, E., 504
Tarascio, V. J., 4, 339
Targetti, F., 415
Tarshis, L., 398, 402
Tasca, A., 438
Tawney, R. H., 36, 39, 308
Taylor, F. W., 231
Taylor, H., 232, 233
Terentius, 77

Theodoretus of Cyr, 29
Thomas Aquinas, St, 27, 31, 34–6, 38–40, 294
Thompson, T. P., 291
Thompson, W., 163, 221–3
Thornton, H., 198, 199, 319
Thornton, W., 242
Thünen, J. H. von, 283
Thweatt, W. O., 189
Tiberi, M., 335, 459
Tinbergen, J., 494, 495
Tirole, J., 497, 499
Tobin, J., 484
Tocqueville, A. de, 234
Togliatti, P., 439
Tonveronachi, M., xiii, 369, 391, 396, 397, 405, 480, 484
Tooke, T., 57, 199, 210, 241
Torrens, R., xi, xiii, 162, 165–7, 168, 172, 173–4, 183, 189, 191, 199, 201, 208–16, 218, 259
Tosato, D., 184, 335
Townshend, C., 117
Toynbee, A., 352
Triffin, R., 381
Trotsky, L., 247, 271
Tsuru, S., 100, 419
Tucker, G., 81, 95, 168
Tugan-Baranovsky, M. J., 275, 411
Turgot, A.-R.-J., 37, 79, 80, 96, 97, 99, 103–7, 117, 126, 130, 142, 156, 160, 165, 184, 226, 283, 326, 506
Twerski, A., 502

Urbinati, N., 234
Ure, A., 232–3

Vaggi, G., 42, 100
Valente, L., xiii
Valeriani, L. M., 282
Vanek, J., 504
Veblen, T., 304, 374–6, 479
Venturi, F., 110, 111
Verdoorn, P., 490
Verri, P., 50, 84, 110, 156, 175, 282, 289
Vianello, F., 267
Vicarelli, F., 391
Vicarelli, S., 267, 464
Vico, G., 108
Vilar, P., 47
Villetti, R., xiii, 271
Viner, J., 4, 28, 29, 30, 35, 36, 39, 88, 89, 125, 151, 211, 237, 308, 364, 372–4, 377, 380, 397, 484

Vint, J., 243
Vitoria, F. de, 30
Voltaire (pseud. of F.-M. Arouet), 104,
    108, 117
Volterra, V., 259, 413

Wagner, A., 259, 312
Wakefield, E. G., 173–4
Wald, A., 343, 347
Walker, D. A., 283, 327, 328, 329, 330,
    331, 332, 333, 334, 335, 336, 337
Wallace, R., 161
Waller, E., 54
Walpole, R., 86
Walras, A. A., 283, 326–7, 328
Walras, L., xii, 12, 104, 107, 164, 165,
    206, 229, 278–9, 280, 283, 285, 290,
    297, 298–9, 301, 312, 313, 322–37,
    340, 342–3, 345, 350, 368, 379, 423,
    433, 435, 445, 472, 491–2, 506,
    509
Walters, M., xiii
Walterskirchen, E., 410
Warville, B. de, 255
Watson, A., 449
Webb, B., 273
Webb, S., 273
Weber, M., 36, 85, 306–8, 422, 429
Weintraub, E. R., 472
Weintraub, S., 487
Weitling, W., 224
West, E. G., 115, 184, 211
Westphalen, J. von, 245
Whately, R., 217, 229, 284
Whitaker, J. K., 351, 353, 358

Whitehead, A. N., 384, 389
Wicksell, K., 160, 161, 199, 206, 311–15,
    319–20, 373, 383, 407, 458, 494
Wicksteed, P. H., 273, 278, 294, 309, 332,
    373, 507
Wieser, F. von, 278, 281, 301, 308–9, 312,
    315
Wightman, W. P. D., 121
Wiles, R. C., 43, 46
William of Champeaux, 33
William of Occam, 33
Williams, B., 178, 502
Williams, K., 171
Williamson, O., 479
Wilson, T. (1525–81), 34, 36–7
Wilson, T. (b. 1916), 121
Winch, D., 14, 121, 159, 173, 367
Winter, S., 382, 478
Winternitz, J., 267
Wittgenstein, L., 11, 316, 344, 348–9,
    435, 445, 446–8, 513
Wollstonecraft, M., 150, 158
Wood, A., 477
Wood, D., 30, 34, 36, 38
Woolf, V., 385
Wright, G. H. von, 447

Xenophon 18, 25, 26, 126

Young, A. 444
Young, H. P., 157

Zaghini, E., 335
Zenezini, M., 463
Zeuthen, F., 343

Subject index

Absolute value: 72, 135, 192, 195–6, 216–18, 270, 327, 450, 456
Abstinence: 227, 240, 310, 360
Accumulation: 46, 126, 131, 133, 166, 182–5, 205, 258, 275–6, 302, 310, 329, 334–5, 452
Aggregate demand: 165–6, 276, 400–2, 481
Agriculture: 21, 45, 79, 94, 96–103, 105, 111, 126, 159–60, 162, 185, 209, 240, 242, 275, 510
Alienation: 152–3, 249–50
Allocation of resources: 291, 323–4
American Economic Association: 372, 419, 479
Analytic statements: 3, 6
Anarchism: 158, 222, 247, 255
Anarchist theory of knowledge: 8, 10
Anatomy: 55
Anti-trust policy: 373
Arc view: xi, 279–80, 452
Arthasastra: 23
Artisans: 22, 99–103, 130
Astronomy: 7, 15, 117, 119
Asymmetric information: 473–4, 513
Asymmetries in economic policy: 410
Austrian Institute for Economic Research: 315
Austrian school: xii, 2, 32, 297–321, 335, 371, 391, 425, 512
Avances annuelles, foncières, primitives: 99, 100
Axiomatic analysis: 10, 66, 288, 306, 325, 329, 332, 340, 343–9, 390, 469, 471–2, 508, 509, 511, 512

Balance of payments: 49–50, 386
Balance of trade: 43, 45, 49, 61, 79, 91, 114
Banking: 45, 151, 197–200, 416, 425, 437, 473
Banking School: 199–200, 215

Bank of England: 179, 180–1, 199, 215, 386
Barriers to entry: 141, 444, 466–7, 477–8
Barter: 28, 147–8, 320
Beggar-my-neighbour policies: 408, 409, 410
Benevolence: 111–12, 113, 123
Bible: 23–4, 29, 30, 35, 57, 160, 308
Bilateral monopoly: 296, 297, 301
Biology: 354–5, 382, 478
Birth control: 160, 163, 233
Blood, circulation of the: 20, 61, 91
Bourgeoisie: 44, 430
Bourbakism: 348, 509
British Economic Association: 352, 367
Budget constraint: 290, 331, 332, 341
Buffer stocks: 411
Bullionists: 41–3, 198–200
Bureaucracy: 307–8, 429
Business cycles: 259–61, 307, 314–15, 319–20, 335, 391–2, 394–7, 402, 411–12, 413, 426–8, 486, 489

Calculus: 236, 280, 289, 290, 345, 510
Cambridge equation: 342, 369, 393
Cambridge school: 315, 368–9, 380–1, 413–15, 487
Cameralists: 40, 41, 127
Capital: 167, 183, 212–14, 229, 253, 293–4, 310–11, 313–14, 317, 327, 332–5, 372–3, 458–9, 489, 507
  circulating and fixed capital: 191, 213–14, 265
  constant and variable capital: 258, 262, 264–7
Capitalism: 16, 36, 44, 58, 60, 85, 130, 244–5, 248, 251–6, 261–3, 270–6, 306, 307–8, 375, 387, 416, 428–31, 453, 499
Capitalists: 129–32, 182–6, 222, 251–68, 327
Cardinal utility: 331, 338–9, 341, 345

Central banking: 198, 199
Chaos theory: 499–500
Characteristics, demand for: 300
Chemistry: 20
Chicago school: 125, 151, 484
Church, as *corpus mysticum*: 32
Church Fathers: *see* Patristic thought
Circular flow: xi, 61, 91, 100–3, 105, 131, 167, 244, 250, 279, 403, 424, 452, 466
Civilisation: 83–4, 86–7, 127, 302
Classes: 5, 26–7, 91–2, 99–103, 129–32, 138, 181, 189, 268–9
Colbertism: 41, 44, 98
Colonies: 46, 118, 149, 170, 172–4, 185, 214
Commerce: 30, 35, 110, 126, 127, 152, 214
Commodity fetishism: 250–1
Communism: 25, 29, 31, 153, 224, 226, 240, 246, 248, 249, 256, 261, 270, 271, 316, 438–9, 445
Comparative costs, Comparative advantage: 185–6, 189, 201–3, 211, 354, 451
Comparative statics: 332, 336, 337, 342, 423, 509
Compensation, theory of: 170, 204–5
Competition: 11, 38, 66, 67, 95, 129, 131, 140, 142, 186, 239, 265, 321, 324, 331, 340, 360–4, 374, 427, 430, 436–42, 443–52
  competition of capitals: 130, 140, 166, 238, 263, 306, 325
  free competition: 140–1, 329–30, 466
  imperfect competition: 379–81, 414, 443
  monopolistic competition: 239, 381
  perfect competition: 145, 283, 379–80
Competitive view: 5–11, 14, 16
Complacibilitas: 40, 41, 135, 288–9, 300, 362
Consequentialist ethics: xii, 20, 174–5, 234–6, 286, 290, 502
Consumer behaviour: 238, 290, 300, 374
Consumer's surplus: 283, 378–80
Consumption: 80, 168, 393, 401–11, 494
Contestable markets: 444, 478
Contingent markets: 65, 347, 472
Contract curve: 296
Cooperativism: 158, 222–5, 240, 242, 330
Corn Laws: 186, 189–211, 214, 287
Corn model: 69–70, 187–9, 213, 456
Corn standard: 139, 182
Costs: 184

cost curves: 128, 364–5, 373–4, 377
  opportunity costs: 292–5, 309
  physical costs: 73, 136, 216
  real costs: 220, 227, 292–5, 507
  transaction costs: 302, 469, 475
Councils, of the Catholic Church: 36
Cowles Commission: 334, 344, 347, 473, 494–5
Credit, 199, 329, 334–5, 425; *see also* Banking
Crises: 168, 259, 275, 416, 488, 507, 513
Cumulative processes: 314, 498
Cumulative view: 2–5, 14
Currency School: 199–200, 215
Customs and habits: 133, 143, 177, 235, 238, 252, 362, 375, 406, 423, 449

Damnum emergens: 35
Demand: 91, 164, 167, 186, 192–3, 239, 280, 281–5, 322–6, 329–48, 354–5
  demand curves: 22, 110, 143–5, 281–5, 295, 302, 329, 330–2, 337, 355, 360, 361–2, 380, 436–42, 443
  effectual demand: 93–4, 112, 142–4
Democracy: 233–4, 438, 503
Demography: 54, 368
Deontological ethics: 19, 174–5, 234, 502
Development: 424, 425–6, 465, 503
Diamonds: 63–8
Dictatorship of the proletariat: 154, 270–6
Disequilibrium: 314, 319–21, 332, 483
Dismal science: 163–4
Distribution: 62, 69, 130, 145, 148, 183–90, 193–4, 225, 227, 240, 261, 280, 295, 313–14, 328, 338, 341, 372, 403, 412, 415, 452, 453, 455, 461, 465, 489, 494; *see also* Profits, Rents, Wages
Disutility: 177, 281, 293
Division of labour: 13, 18, 19, 26, 71, 88, 112, 123, 126–33, 137, 139, 145–9, 152–4, 167, 196, 197, 210–11, 231–3, 250–1, 261–3, 270–2, 279, 294, 302, 363, 452, 468, 476, 508, 513
Double-entry bookkeeping: 22, 493
Doux commerce: 86–7, 104
Duties: 182, 185–6, 214, 216
Dynamics: 181–6, 302, 306, 373, 416, 463

East India Company: 42, 79, 81, 152, 165, 233, 239
Econometrics: 64, 493–6
Econometric Society: 341–2, 419, 494
Economic agent: *see Homo oeconomicus*

Economic Journal: 352, 357, 367, 385, 437, 440, 448
Economies of scale: 365–9; *see also* Returns to scale
Edinburgh Review: 208
Education: 133, 149, 152, 153, 157, 162, 221, 223, 228, 235, 375, 441
Effective demand, point of: 400–2, 460
Efficiency wages: 483
Egalitarianism: 236, 295
Elasticity: 366
Employment: 61, 113, 145, 183, 203–5, 261, 393–5, 399, 401–2, 409, 411–12, 459, 482
Enclosures: 203
Encyclicals: 36, 416
Encyclopédie: 104, 108, 117, 128, 157
Engel's law: 304, 462, 494
Energy: 286–7, 511
Enlightenment, 83, 86–7, 96, 103–11, 126, 154, 155–6, 175, 176, 303; *see also* Scottish Enlightenment:
Entrepreneurs: 38, 50, 94, 148, 150, 165, 226, 306, 308, 327, 333, 365–6, 382, 397, 401, 403, 416, 424–6, 431
Environment: 239, 341, 502–3
Equilibrium: 22, 111, 129, 130, 145, 165, 279–80, 281–96, 300, 301, 302, 306, 315–17, 319–21, 324, 329–35, 348, 354–6, 360–5, 383, 393, 397, 402, 403, 408, 422–3, 449, 454, 462, 481, 500, 509
Esprit de système: 104, 108, 156
Ethology: 240, 291, 362
Euler's theorem: 373
Evolutionary economics: 83, 111, 272–3, 306, 345, 351, 356–7, 360–1, 371–4, 376, 382–3, 444, 478–9, 498, 500, 510–11
Ex ante and *ex post*: 408
Exchange: 22, 38, 328, 329–39
Exchange rate: 354–5, 395, 412, 438
Expectations: 390, 399, 404–5, 407, 408–9, 487
Experimental economics: 501–2
Exploitation: 251–6, 264, 270
Externalities: 377–8

Fabians: 273, 312
Factors of production: 74, 145, 165, 167, 183, 184, 202, 220, 227, 279–80, 295, 333, 372–3, 458–9
Family: 83–4
Farmers: 97–103, 130
Fear: 160–3

Felicific calculus: 175–8, 234–6, 288–90
Feudalism: 19, 21, 44, 59, 124, 130, 248, 253, 255, 261, 413
Financial capital: 95, 253, 269, 274, 477, 480
Financial markets: 21, 35, 47, 81, 144, 151, 399, 404–5, 460, 514
Firm: 128–9, 323, 361–6, 373–4, 377, 379–81, 382, 397, 440–4, 469–70, 474–9, 496–7
Fiscal policies: 44, 45, 396, 406
Forced saving: 309, 319–20, 425, 436, 449
Foreign exchange, 43, 91; *see also* Exchange rate, Foreign trade
Foreign investment: 49, 61
Foreign trade: 43, 44, 45–6, 61–2, 79, 114, 185–6, 201–3, 214, 229, 239, 354–5, 461
Forward contracts: 35
Free goods: 343–4
French Revolution: xi, 106, 150, 155–8
Full cost principle: 412

Game theory: 284, 345, 470, 472–3, 496–8
Gaussian (normal) curve: 356
Gender issues: 26–7, 233, 375
General equilibrium: 65, 318, 322–48, 359, 368, 371, 381, 406, 407, 454, 457, 469, 471–4, 481, 492–3, 506, 509, 513
Globalisation: 60, 123, 504, 514
Gold: 41, 42, 45, 49, 61, 114, 183, 197–8, 286
Gold standard: 41, 114, 200, 392, 414
Gravitation metaphor: 107, 142–3, 144, 175, 219, 324, 423, 464
Gresham's law: 41, 473
Growth: 414, 415, 461, 462, 470, 488–91
Guanzi: 23
Guilds: 38, 105, 106, 156

Habits: *see* Customs and habits
Historical materialism: 106, 245–6, 247–8
Historical reconstructions: x, 5, 15
Historical school: 2, 42, 163, 182, 237, 259, 298, 303–6, 358, 376, 421, 479
History of economic thought, role of: ix, 1, 2, 3–5, 9–17, 431
Holism: 316
Homo oeconomicus: xi, xii, 12, 52, 122, 124–5, 145, 148, 174, 209, 236–8, 289–92, 299, 300, 301, 305, 318, 323, 339, 357, 375–6, 422, 425, 434, 506
Hours of work: 228, 252–4, 264, 407

Household economics: 25
Hunting: 106, 126

Imperialism: 254, 274
Impossibility theorem: 346
Imputation theory: 281, 300, 309
Income: 341, 393–4, 403, 485
Increasing risk principle: 412
Index numbers of prices: 137, 229, 341,
    393, 436
Indifference curves: 296, 338–9, 341
Industrial concentration: 169, 240, 262,
    268–9, 429, 430
Industrial democracy: 504
Industrial district: 383
Industrial reserve army: 259–60
Industry: 51, 361–6, 373–4, 377, 380–1,
    440–4
Infant industry: 202, 303
Inflation: 314, 319, 392, 407, 409, 425,
    435–67, 483
Information: 321; see also Asymmetric
    information
Innovations: 426, 427; see also Technical
    progress
Input–output analysis: 323, 491–3
Insider–outsider models: 483
Institution, Institutionalism: 126, 157,
    196, 304, 341, 374–6, 470, 479–80
Insurance: 157
Interest, Interest rate: 35–8, 80–1, 95, 100,
    110, 114, 151, 199, 229, 253–67,
    294, 310–11, 314, 319–20, 334–5,
    341, 344, 372–3, 392, 394, 398,
    403–6, 423–4, 460
Interests and passions: 84–9, 120, 122,
    130, 174, 176, 500
International Economic Association:
    420
International institutions: 387, 395,
    409–11
International trade: see Foreign trade
International Working Men's Association:
    224, 247–3
Interpersonal comparisons of utility: 177,
    290, 295, 340
Intertemporal analysis: 65, 136–7, 139,
    321, 341, 347, 472
Investment: 166, 168, 184, 259, 318, 319,
    390, 393–4, 401–4, 407, 462, 477,
    481, 487
Invisible hand: 89, 144–5, 148, 322–6
Iron law of wages: 130, 158, 161–2, 247,
    260
IS-LM model: 406, 407, 481–2, 487

Journal of Economic Issues: 479
Jurisprudence: 116
Justice: 28, 39, 123, 124–6, 223, 235,
    253–5, 378
Just price: 16, 28, 34, 38–40, 78, 107

King's law: 57, 77

Labour: 30, 81–3, 93, 109, 129–32,
    136–8, 146, 148, 167, 192, 195–6,
    217, 242, 249–55, 264, 268–9, 281,
    293–5, 310–11, 362–3, 482
  compulsory labour: 23–4, 153–4, 272
  necessary and surplus labour: 224,
    253–62
  productive and unproductive labour: 46,
    71, 92, 99–103, 127–33, 165, 167,
    223, 257
Labour power: 251–5
Labour theory of value: 39, 70–3, 81,
    136–8, 189–90, 191–2, 197, 212–13,
    216, 218, 220, 221, 239, 253, 256,
    258, 263–7, 269–70, 293, 295–6, 451,
    464, 506, 510
Laissez-faire: 44, 51, 88, 176
Land: 59, 72–4, 83, 93, 95, 97–103, 105,
    133, 173–4, 184–5, 225, 456
Land banks: 61
Landlords: 129–32, 164, 168, 182–6,
    222
Land registry: 45, 60, 83
Language, birth of: 146
Language games: 447–8
Lausanne school: 302, 321, 322, 325
Law of increasing misery: 169, 256, 261–2,
    269, 465
Law of one price: 16, 140, 141, 361, 430
Law of proletarianisation: 231–2, 261–2,
    465
Law of the falling rate of profits: 262–3,
    463, 465
Laws of movement of capitalism: 231–3,
    256, 261–3, 268–9
League of the communists: 246
Learning by doing: 490
Liberalism, economic and political, 79, 84,
    106, 123, 124–5, 133, 149–54, 156,
    157, 208–9, 233, 234, 242, 300, 315,
    318, 387–8, 392, 399, 422, 436, 465,
    484; see also Laissez-faire
Libertinism: 88–9
Linear programming: 492–3
Liquidity preference: 404–5
Logic: 239, 286–8
Logical positivism: 446

London School of Economics: 273, 407, 413, 437
Lucrum cessans: 35
Luxury consumption: 21, 30, 61, 93–4, 98, 113, 131, 182, 184, 253, 257–8

Machinery: 183, 203–5, 231–3, 260, 262–3
Macroeconomics: 459, 470, 480–8, 495, 496–7, 508, 514
Managerial capitalism: 375, 415, 476
Marginalist approach: xi, xii, 16, 22, 141, 149, 174, 177–8, 186, 206, 229, 241, 278–96, 297, 312, 393, 450, 457–9, 481, 512
Marginal product: 74, 283, 303, 311, 313, 451
Marginal utility: 178, 219, 227–9, 230, 278–96, 302, 309, 326, 332, 363, 422
Market, notion of: 11, 21–2, 38, 41, 63–8, 86–7, 110, 122, 140, 251, 281, 301, 317, 322, 362, 374, 408, 509, 512
Medieval economics: 19
Menu costs: 483
Mercantilism: 5, 43–6, 51, 79, 84, 98, 112, 114, 124, 126, 127, 151, 254–5
Merchants: 78–9, 132
Metaphysical statements: 3
Methodenstreit: 303–6, 421
Methodological individualism: 32–4, 285, 291, 299, 302, 315–16, 361, 421–2, 509
Methodological liberalism: 119, 420–2
Microeconomics: 474
Mint: 49, 81, 286
Mississippi Company: 90, 173
Monetarism: 426, 484–5; *see also* Quantity theory of money
Monetary policy: 406, 491, 497
Money: 21, 35–6, 42–3, 47, 49–50, 60–1, 79–81, 83, 95–6, 114, 126, 151, 166, 180–5, 192, 196–200, 215, 255, 282, 302, 314–15, 319, 321, 329, 336, 341–2, 362, 368–9, 383, 391–4, 404–6, 414, 415, 419, 437–8, 481–2, 484, 485, 487–8
Monopoly: 38, 46, 143, 152, 216, 234, 240, 274, 329
Multiplier: 80, 397, 403, 413
Music: 53–4

Nash equilibrium: 345, 473
National Bureau of Economic Research: 316, 376

National income accounting: 77, 131, 139, 415, 493
Nationalisation: 259, 330, 418
Natural law: 16, 19, 20, 21, 78, 83–4, 97, 119–20, 124, 143, 221, 224, 240, 338, 356
Needs: 299–300, 362, 422
Neoclassical synthesis: xii, 379, 383, 397–8, 407, 477, 479, 481–4, 511
New School for Social Research: 479
Nobel prize: 315, 346, 347, 351, 370, 374, 415, 451, 473, 475, 479, 481, 482, 483, 484, 485, 490, 491, 493–4, 501, 502
Nominalism: 32–3, 38
Non-competing groups: 239
Normal price: 356
Normal science: 7

Oligopoly: 375, 412, 444, 477–8, 513
Ophelimity: 339
Ordinal utility: 338–9, 341
Organic composition of capital: 262–3, 265, 267

Pain: 27, 111, 175–7, 234–6, 293
Par, between labour and land: 72–5, 92–3
Paradigm, in science: 7–10
Pareto optimality: 296, 338–40, 378
Pareto's law: 338
Partial equilibrium analysis: 295, 324, 359, 362, 365, 378, 440–2, 474, 509
Passions: *see* Interests and passions
Path dependency: 332, 498
Patristic thought: 25, 28–31, 38
Period, long and short; long and short run: 143, 219, 355, 458–63
Period analysis: 169, 317, 320–1, 393–4, 408
Period of production: 195, 294, 310–11, 313, 319–20, 458
Phillips curve: 260, 483, 485, 486
Philosophical radicalism: 175, 231, 502
Physics: 55, 57, 324, 327, 328, 338, 358
Physiocrats: 5, 45, 96–103, 104, 117, 126, 132, 151, 164–5, 210, 216, 433, 510
Pigou effect: 379, 482
Plagiarism: 368
Planning: 140, 223, 225, 272, 274–6, 317–18, 412, 503
Pleasure: 27, 111, 175–7, 234–6, 288–93
Political anatomy: 31, 58–61
Political arithmetic: 54, 55–8, 77–8, 90–1, 119–20, 129, 223, 434, 491
Political Economy Club: 199, 207–10, 215

Poor laws: 169–72, 228
Population: 30, 113, 130, 157, 159–64,
    169, 172–4, 183–4, 240–1, 312, 361,
    489
Portfolio choice: 484
Positivism: 2–3, 6, 240
Post-Keynesians: 487–8
Poverty: 30, 81, 105, 156–7, 161–3,
    170–2, 203, 225; see also Poor laws
Preferences: 177, 291–2, 302, 330, 362,
    390, 471, 509
Prey–predator cycle: 259, 413
Price
    bon prix and prix fondamental: 98
    current and political prices: 64, 66–9
    general price level: 342, 393, 397,
        398–406
    market and natural prices: 22, 38, 63–9,
        78, 91, 138, 139–45, 192–3, 194, 219,
        223, 224, 242, 243, 324, 327, 499,
        507
    price theory: 79, 111, 138–9, 178,
        279–80, 354–5, 358, 422, 478
    prices of production: 69, 71–5, 212–14,
        256, 263–7, 269–70, 454, 455, 456,
        461, 464
    short and long period prices: 143,
        219
Primitive (or primary) accumulation:
    253
Principal-agent problem: 473
Printing, invention of: 23
Private property: 21, 25–6, 28, 29–30, 45,
    59, 81–3, 95, 96, 132, 157, 224, 226,
    240, 302, 431, 479
Probability theory: 388–91
Production function: 373, 451–9, 472,
    490, 494
Productivity: 71, 80, 127–8, 367–73, 395
Professionalisation of economics: 18, 280,
    284–5, 366–8, 510
Profit, rate of: 75, 99, 130, 144, 168, 186,
    191, 213, 227, 254, 262–7, 269–70,
    295, 398, 453, 458–9, 460, 462, 464,
    466–7
Profits: 11, 72, 94–5, 114, 130, 138–9,
    182–5, 200, 205, 223–4, 228, 253,
    255, 260, 270, 333, 393–4
Profit-sharing schemes: 169, 240, 504
Profit upon alienation: 46, 254–5
Progress: 10, 12, 87, 88–9, 104, 105, 113,
    117, 123, 154, 155–7, 163–4, 172,
    174, 209, 242, 271–2, 302, 356, 503,
    506
Property rights: see Private property

Protectionism: 79, 202; see also Infant
    industry
Protestantism: 24, 36, 85, 112, 116, 226,
    306, 308
Public choice theory: 370
Public debt: 180, 201, 418, 485
Public finance: 152, 309, 371
Public works: 152, 229, 283
Purchasing power parity: 313

Quantity theory of money: 47, 114, 168,
    183, 196–8, 341–2, 393, 436–7,
    484
Quarterly Review: 208

Rand Corporation: 473
Raritas: 39–40, 109
Rational expectations: 201, 485–6, 496
Rationality: 292, 339, 361, 374, 497,
    500–1, 508, 512, 513
Rational reconstructions: x, 15, 27
Real-bills doctrine: 151, 199
Realism: 32–3
Reformist thought: 110, 154, 158, 271,
    461–5
Rent: 11, 69–70, 94, 100, 107, 130,
    138–9, 182, 189–90, 200, 211, 217,
    221–3, 225, 253, 283, 295, 363,
    451
Representative firm: 365–6, 380, 444
Reproduction schemes: 275, 323, 492
Reswitching of techniques: 458
Returns to scale: 364
    constant: 109, 295, 333, 347, 373, 449,
        454, 457, 492, 493
    decreasing: 183, 347, 441–2
    increasing: 107–8, 128, 129, 203, 228,
        240, 340, 355, 442, 470, 490, 499
Revealed preferences: 339
Rhetorical method: 8, 10, 120
Ricardian equivalence theorem: 199,
    200–1
Ricardian socialism: xi, 158, 208, 220,
    221–6, 255, 270
Riches: 190
Risk: 281, 348, 390, 391
Royal Economic Society: 357, 359, 384,
    385, 449, 450
Royal Society: 54

St Petersburg's paradox: 284–5, 345
Salamanca school: 30, 37, 40, 47
Savage: 83
Saving: 167, 168, 334, 393–4, 403, 405–6,
    481

Say's law: 164–7, 180, 183–9, 197, 203, 239, 259
Scarcity, 64, 135, 226–30, 279–80, 281–5, 300, 323, 326, 441; *see also Raritas*
Scholasticism: 28, 31–6, 56, 72, 107, 142, 148, 178, 189, 281, 289, 298–9, 300, 307, 362, 433
Scientific research programmes: 5, 8, 10
Scientific revolutions: 5, 7, 10
Scottish Enlightenment: 32, 84, 111–14, 120, 124–5, 143, 148, 152, 156, 237, 250, 292
Second-best theory: 378
Sectors of the economy: 59, 78, 91–2, 99–103, 119, 129, 133
Self-interest: 84–9, 112, 113, 121–5, 147, 176–7, 237, 255, 331, 498
Sensism: 120, 176, 234, 287–8, 291, 506
Sequential analysis: *see* Period analysis
Short causal chains: 324, 359, 393, 406
Skills: 21, 75, 128, 147–8, 231–3, 264
Slavery: 19, 25, 26–7, 30, 118, 163, 233
Social contract: 82, 124, 146, 234
Socialism: 169, 220, 221, 226, 240, 242, 248, 249, 255, 256, 259, 262, 271–6, 304, 306, 308, 314, 324, 428
Sociology: 240, 307, 337, 365–6, 382
South Sea Company: 152
Spontaneous order: 111, 113, 317–18
Stability of equilibrium: 332, 336, 342, 347, 355, 472, 488, 499, 509
Stages theory: 60, 106, 110, 126, 490
Stagnation: 167, 412
Standard commodity: 193–4, 195–6, 213, 267, 449–56, 463
Standards of measure: 22, 192, 326–7
State: 22, 26, 32, 40, 41, 43, 44, 58–63, 125, 126, 151, 259, 316, 330
Static analysis: 327, 373
Stationary state: 184, 242, 361
Statistics: 55–6, 63, 303–4, 357, 493
Stochastic processes: 498–9
Stock exchange: 9, 329–30
Stocks and flows: 341, 404
Subjective value: xi, xii, 81, 105, 108–9, 110, 132, 135, 142, 165, 167, 168, 177, 216–17, 219, 230, 275, 278–96, 298–302, 323, 353, 371, 506
Subsidies: 378
Subsistence: 72, 93, 130, 131, 159–63, 181–4, 210, 252, 256–8
Substitution: 283, 299, 302, 323
Supply: 91, 164, 192–3, 227, 281–3, 322–6, 401

Supply curve: 22, 143–5, 283, 295, 302, 361–4, 373–4, 440–3
Supply-side economics: 486
Surplus: 21, 51, 69–71, 91, 97–103, 105, 131–2, 182–4, 189–90, 210, 244, 252–4, 257–8, 270, 276, 329–48, 451–64, 466
Sustainable development: 239, 502–3, 514
Sympathy: 112, 121–5
Synthetic statements: 3, 6
Swedish school: 312–14, 317, 407–8

Tableau économique: 97–103, 323
Tâtonnement: 330, 331–2, 333–4
Taxes: 62–3, 105, 118, 152, 180, 200–1, 329, 378, 485–6
Technical change, Technical progress: 170, 183, 203–5, 232, 257, 260–1, 287, 382, 410, 470, 478, 490–1, 498, 511, 514
Technological lock-in: 498, 510–11
Temporary equilibrium: 321
Tobin's *q*: 484
Trade cycle: *see* Business cycle
Trade unions: 130, 224, 243, 252, 482
Transformation problem: 256, 263, 269–70, 299, 464

Uncertainty: 157, 301, 315, 321, 331, 335, 388–91, 399, 407, 487, 502, 514
Under-consumption: 167–9, 259, 276, 319
Unemployment: 5, 70–1, 257, 260, 379, 395–6, 410, 481, 483, 489
Universities: 18, 115–16, 273, 305, 366–8
Usury: 34–8, 151
Utilitarianism: xii, 19, 111, 122, 123, 174–8, 222, 234–7, 255, 284, 285, 289, 331, 422, 500
Utility: 39–40, 80, 106, 109, 135, 177–8, 219, 226–30, 235–6, 281, 289–95, 301, 323, 330, 347
Utopias: 24, 155–7, 226

Valeur appréciative, valeurs estimatives: 106–7
Value in exchange: 16–17, 27, 92–3, 106, 109, 113, 134–9, 141, 178, 193–6, 202, 212, 216, 242, 282, 284, 301, 453
Value in use: 27, 134–5, 282, 284–5, 288
Velocity of circulation: 47, 61, 80, 95, 197, 341–2, 369, 485
Vertical integration: 461
Virtuositas: 40, 41, 135, 289, 300, 362

Wages: 72, 74, 105, 130, 138–9, 149, 163, 168, 169, 172, 181–4, 221, 241, 252–3, 260, 263, 295, 311–14, 319, 360, 372–3, 379, 395, 398–402, 409, 464, 481, 483
Wages fund doctrine: 170, 241, 242–3
Waiting: 310, 360
Walras's law: 332–42, 481
Warranted rate of growth: 488–9

Water–diamond (or Water–gold) paradox: 39, 109, 135, 178, 284
Wealth: 45–6, 95, 238, 326, 328
Wealth of nations, notion of: 18, 45, 48–52, 114, 127–34, 190, 227, 452, 453–66
Welfare economics: 145, 339–40, 377–8
Welfare state: 163, 273, 305–20, 480
Westminster Review: 208, 216, 291
Work, Workers: *see* Labour